Dictionary of British History

The Wordsworth
Dictionary of British History

Editorial Consultant
J.P. Kenyon
Professor of Modern History, University of St. Andrews

—

Foreword by Norman Stone,
Professor of Modern History, University of Oxford

Wordsworth Reference

This edition published 1994 by Wordsworth Editions Ltd.
Cumberland House, Crib Street, Ware, Hertfordshire SG12 9ET.

ISBN 1-85326-322-2

Printed and bound in Great Britain by Mackays of Chatham PLC.

Editors
John Grace BA, PhD
Judith Ravenscroft BA, MPhil
Jackie Smith BA

Jennifer Speake MA, BPhil
Keith Walker MA

Contributors
J. E. Abbott BA
H. H. R. Bailes BA, PhD
Barbara Barrett BA
M. G. Burns BA
Kathleen Clarke BA
P. B. Clarke MA, MPhil
S. R. Elliot CD, BComm, psc
D. J. Ferraro BA, MA
Jane A. Freeman BA
B. J. Golding BA, PhD
C. A. R. Hills MA
Jonathan Hunt BA
J. Gwynfor Jones MA, PhD
Michael MacCarthy-Morrogh BA

D. Huw Owen BA, PhD
I. G. Pears
Christopher Rice BA
Michael Roulstone
Michael Scherk BA
Jennifer Drake-Brockman MA, BPhil
David Stevenson BA, PhD
John Tyler MA
Maurice Waite BA
Margaret A. Wallis MA
P. O. G. White MA
Rosalind Williams BA
C. S. P. Wolstenholme MA

Contents

Preface

THIS BOOK covers the history of the British Isles and its overseas possessions from the Roman conquest until 1970. The three thousand or so articles encompass domestic political and social events, foreign affairs, and major cultural and scientific developments, together with the men or women who have influenced or been influenced by the multifarious events that make up a country's history. The alphabetical arrangement of the main body of the book is complemented by a Chronology – a year-by-year survey of events in British history and, shown in italic type, of major developments on the Continent and in America.

J. P. Kenyon

Foreword

Norman Stone, Professor of Modern History,
University of Oxford

THE PRESENT Director of the National Gallery in London, a Scot, remarked upon appointment that when he was young he had thought of England as a place you had to go through to reach France. Another immigrant to England remarked in the 1940s that when you came to England you loved the first six months, hated the next ten years and then began to love the country once more. As a Scot myself I can see what these people mean. In fact I only began to see the great interest of English history when I started to write a book about continental Europe in 1900: England fitted into my European pattern, but in a very odd way. For instance, England had a Conservative party that managed, quite early on, to do what continental equivalents – the ancestors of today's Christian Democrats – disastrously failed to do. Throne, Altar, Nobility got votes, maintained stable government that was nevertheless creative and was even on occasion susceptible to argument. Therefore England never vacillated between Communism and Fascism as was the case in other European countries and, from roughly the middle of the eighteenth century, the English model had a hold on the European mind.

In other words, something serious happened in the British Isles about which every historian must be interested. The trouble is that it is quite complicated and all kinds of oddities abound. For instance, when would you guess that serfdom was abolished in England? Everyone else in the Western World, including the Scots, got round to it in the later part of the eighteenth century. However, I learn from John Kenyon's magnificently efficient book, that serfdom was only formally abolished in England this century. 'Copyhold', if you look it up, meant doing feudal services (doubtless the handing over of a mangelwurzel on Boxing Day) in return for land and, though partially abolished in 1922, these final relics of feudal services were not finally abolished in England until 1935. Therefore a fascinating question about English history is: why was England the first country to abolish slavery and the last to consign serfdom to history?

These peculiarities of English – and to a much lesser extent Scottish – history go on and on. The German historian, Otto Hintze, noted that in England you encountered institutions alive and functioning which had become fossilized elsewhere sometime during the eighteenth century. Europe modernized through the State and much time and not a little blood was expended in fighting about institutions. The English just took institutions and made them do something else. Sometimes the very words mean their opposite. For instance, 'Public' schools used to be charitable institutions to assist the poor and are now private, while the 'Trust Law' invented, with some antecedents, in the early seventeenth century, really means 'Mistrust Law', because you need straw figures to keep the State from devouring your property. I fault John Kenyon for not including either of these pieces of 'Old English Humbug' in this dictionary, but this is the only fault I can find. Otherwise, if there is a matter of important historical record – date of battle, contents of an Act, even pieces of early agricultural progress – it is included in this book. The British Empire too is included in its essentials although, since this eventually occupied a quarter of the world's land area, there are inevitable limits to the depth of the coverage.

The British, and now I am including the Scots, have done some astonishingly good historical work, and in John Kenyon we have a distinguished historian who has used it all to make within the pages of this dictionary, a book that will be a key building-block in the architecture of further historical enquiries. We do not nowadays go weak at the knees over 'our island story', but it is a story just the same which in modern times has done more to shape the world we know today than any other. This dictionary will provide the answer for anyone pondering why the predominant language in the world today is English.

Norman Stone
Oxford, March 1994

A

Abbeville, treaty of. See Paris, treaty of (1259).

Abercromby, Sir Ralph (1734-1801). General. His promotion was delayed by his opposition to the war against the American colonies (1775-83). He first distinguished himself during the French Revolutionary War in the organization of the retreat of his demoralized brigade from Flanders (1794-95). He then led a successful expedition to the French West Indies (1795-96), capturing Trinidad and St Lucia. He assumed command in the Mediterranean (1800) and executed the amphibious landing of an Anglo-Turkish force in Egypt (1801). He was killed fighting against French forces at Alexandria.

Aberdeen, George Hamilton-Gordon, 4th earl of (1784-1860). Prime minister (1852-55). He joined Wellington's cabinet as chancellor of the duchy of Lancaster (1828) and was then foreign secretary (1828-30). He served *Peel as secretary for war and the colonies (1834-35) and as foreign secretary (1841-46), improving Anglo-French and Anglo-American relations. He resigned with Peel over the *Corn Laws (1846) and succeeded him as leader of the Peelites. He formed a Peelite-Whig coalition government (1852) but was forced to resign (1855) over his mismanagement of the. *Crimean War. Aberdeen was also a scholar, presiding over the Society of Antiquaries (1812-46). He demonstrated his religious concerns by his unsuccessful attempts to prevent the *disruption (1843).

Abernethy, treaty of (1072). The agreement by which Malcolm III of Scots paid homage to William I of England, who had invaded Scotland. The precise terms of the treaty are not known.

abjuration of the realm. An oath to leave the realm for ever. It was an alternative to *outlawry for a criminal who had claimed *sanctuary. The abjuror was obliged to confess his crime before promising to renounce England and could only return following a royal pardon.

abolition movement. See slavery.

Aboukir Bay, battle of (1 Aug 1798). A naval engagement during the French Revolutionary War, also known as the battle of the Nile. Nelson attacked the French in harbour at dusk, destroying 11 of their 13 ships of the line; French casualties and prisoners numbered some 6200. The victory nullified the value of Napoleon's successes on land during his Egyptian campaign.

Acadia. The name France gave to its possessions on the Atlantic seaboard of North America, comprising modern Nova Scotia, Prince Edward Island, New Brunswick, and parts of Quebec and Maine. The French first settled here in 1604, but Acadia changed hands several times between Britain and France in the 17th and 18th centuries. In 1713, by the treaty of Utrecht, Britain acquired most of modern Nova Scotia and in 1755 deported many Acadians for refusing to take the oath of loyalty. By the peace of Paris (1763) all Acadia was ceded to Britain.

Aclea, battle of (851). A battle, probably fought at modern Oakley, in which the forces of Wessex under *Aethelwulf defeated the Danes. One of the few English victories against the *Danish invasions in this period, it increased the power of Wessex.

Acre. The site (modern Akka, near Haifa in Israel) of three engagements important in British history. **1.** (June-July 1191) The recovery of Acre, taken by Saladin in 1187, was the chief aim of the third *crusade. Richard the Lionheart arrived before Acre in June 1191 and under his leadership the city was retaken in July. **2.** (March-May 1799) Acre, held by the Turks, was bombarded for 61 days by Napoleon I during the French Revolutionary War. British ships aided the Turks and Napoleon was forced to raise the siege and return to Egypt. **3.** (3 Nov 1840) Acre, held by Mehemet Ali, ruler of Egypt who was in revolt against his Turkish overlords and in control of Syria, was bombarded by a combined British and Turkish fleet. The city was taken and Syria was restored to Turkey by the convention of London (1841).

act of Grace (1717). The general pardon issued to rebellious *Jacobites. The act released several hundred rebels either under sentence of death or serving terms of imprisonment for their involvement in the 1715 rebellion.

act of parliament. A legislative enactment of *parliament; a statute. Draft statutes, or bills, developed out of petitions to the king seeking redress of grievances, which originated in the reign (1272-1307) of Edward I. Those seeking redress of private grievances were the forerunners of private bills, which are originated chiefly by local authorities desiring a particular power; those seeking redress of grievances affecting the whole country were the forerunners of public bills, which are generally introduced by a minister or by a private member. The first recorded petition by the *House of Commons was presented in 1327. During the 15th century, following complaints that laws frequently differed from the petitions that gave rise to them, parliament came to present draft statutes rather than petitions.

Bills may be presented in either the House of Commons or the *House of Lords, with the exception, since the *Parliament Act (1911), of money bills. In its first reading a bill is merely announced, and the order given for its printing; in its second reading it is debated and, if passed, enters the committee stage, in which it is examined by a *standing committee or a committee of the whole House. An amended bill then enters the report stage before receiving its third reading. It is then referred to the other House, in which the same procedure takes place. When a bill has passed both Houses it receives the royal assent and becomes an act of parliament.

Acton, John Emerich Dalberg Acton, 1st Baron (1834-1902). Historian. He led the liberal English Catholics, remaining in the Roman Catholic Church despite his strong opposition to the doctrine of papal infallibility. An MP (1859-65), his political ideology of Christian liberalism greatly influenced Gladstone. Lord Acton helped found the *English Historical Review* (1886) and planned the multivolume *Cambridge Modern History* (1899-1912). His lectures given while Regius Professor of Modern History at Cambridge (1895-1902) were published posthumously.

Acton Burnel, Statute of. See Merchants, Statute of.

Adam brothers. Four Scottish-born architects, of whom the best known are Robert (1728-92) and James (1732-94). Influenced by his travels in Italy (1755-57), Robert's work reflected the carefully planned exteriors and interiors of classicism, which he interpreted with a simplicity that produced a light and airy effect. Together, the brothers designed Kenwood House (1768) in Hampstead, London, and Osterley Park (1780), near Brentford, Middlesex. Robert's work in London included Apsley House (1775) and in Edinburgh, Charlotte Square (1791). The other brothers were William (c. 1738-1822), Robert's business manager, and John.

Addington, Henry, 1st Viscount Sidmouth (1757-1844). Prime minister (1801-04), after serving as speaker of the House of Commons (1789-1801). He initially achieved his policy of peace and retrenchment, concluding the treaty of *Amiens (1802) and abolishing income tax. His half-hearted* attitude to the Napoleonic threat lost him the support of *Pitt the younger, forcing his resignation. He was created Viscount Sidmouth in 1805. As home secretary (1812-22) he treated the *Luddites harshly, and his attempts to suppress radical newspapers and political movements were partly responsible for the *Peterloo massacre (1819).

Addison, Joseph (1672-1719). Essayist and Whig MP (1708-19), who held several minor government posts. He contributed essays to Richard *Steele's *The Tatler* (1709-11), and the two men founded the *Spectator* in 1711. He defended the Whig government's handling of the War of the Spanish Succession and later supported the Hanoverian succession.

Addled Parliament (5 April-7 June 1614). The second parliament of the reign of James I, so called because it was dissolved without passing any bills. Summoned to vote supplies, the parliament attacked impositions and James dismissed it.

Adelaide (1792-1849). Queen consort of William IV (1830-37). Daughter of the Duke of Saxe-Coburg Meiningen, she married William in 1818. She died childless.

Aden. A former British crown colony. Aden formed part of the Ottoman (Turkish) Empire from the 16th century until 1802, when Britain annexed it, establishing a refuelling station on the route to India. Strategically of great importance, in 1937 Aden became a crown colony and in 1962 was given partial self-government. It was part of Saudi Arabia from 1963 until 1967, when it became the capital of South Yemen.

Admiralty, Board of. A former government department responsible for administering the *navy (1832-1964). It replaced the Navy Board, established in 1546, which in turn grew out of the office, dating from the 13th century, of the keeper of the king's ships. The board comprised six lords commissioners, who divided the former office of lord high admiral; the first was always a member of the government, four were naval officers (the sea lords), and the sixth a civil lord. In 1964 the board was absorbed into the Ministry of *Defence.

Adrian, Edgar Douglas Adrian, 1st Baron (1889-1977). Physiologist, author of *The Basis of Sensation* (1928). He was cowinner of the Nobel prize for medicine and physiology (1932) with Sir Charles Sherrington (1861-1952) for discoveries concerning the function of the nerve cells. Adrian was awarded the OM (1942) and served as president of the Royal Society (1950-55). He was master of Trinity College, Cambridge, from 1951 and chancellor of the university from 1968.

Adrian IV. Pope (1154-59). Born Nicholas Breakspear, he is the only English pope. He was a vigorous defender of papal supremacy in the conflict with the emperor Frederick I. His bull *Laudabiliter* authorized Henry II to conquer and to rule Ireland; it was later refuted.

adulterine castles. Unlicensed private *castles built by barons during the troubles of Stephen's reign (1135-54). These strongholds enabled their owners to prey on the surrounding countryside and to defy both Stephen and Matilda. As order was restored after 1153, Stephen and later Henry II were able to destroy these castles systematically.

Adventurers. Those Englishmen who in 1642 helped finance the forces raised to suppress the Irish Rebellion. In return for their contribution of £1,000,000 they were awarded 2 500 000 acres of land confiscated from Irish rebels. Their possession of these lands was confirmed by the Acts of *Settlement, after the Cromwellian reconquest of Ireland (1652) and after the Restoration (1662). (*See also* Merchants Adventurers.)

advowson. The right of presentation to a benefice by a bishop or layman. Lay patronage dates from the 8th century, when laymen began to build churches on their land. Advowsons still exist as property rights tenable by British citizens who are not Roman Catholics.

Adwalton (or Atherton) Moor, battle of (30 June 1643). A battle of the Civil War, fought near Bradford in Yorkshire. Royalist forces defeated the parliamentary army, commanded by Lord *Fairfax and his son Sir Thomas Fairfax, and drove it back upon Hull. The royalists went on to occupy the West Riding of Yorkshire.

Aelfric (c. 955-c. 1010). Writer and ecclesiastic, called Grammaticus. A monk at Winchester and later abbot of Cerne and then Eynsham, Aelfric was the finest prose stylist of late Anglo-Saxon England. His works include the *Catholic Homilies* (two sets of sermons), *Lives of the Saints*, and a Latin grammar.

Aethelbald (d. 757). King of Mercia (716–57). By 731 Aethelbald had established himself as *bretwalda, overlord of all kingdoms south of the Humber. His reign was marked by internal peace but he was murdered, for obscure reasons, by his bodyguard.

Aethelbert (c. 552–616). King of Kent (c. 560–616) who became the first English king to be converted to Christianity. His marriage to a Frankish princess, Bertha, a Christian, was an important factor in *Augustine's introduction of Christianity into Kent, Aethelbert's conversion (597), and the establishment of the church in southeast England. His legal code is the earliest to survive from Anglo-Saxon England.

Aethelfleda (died c. 918). Daughter of Alfred the Great and wife of Aethelred, ealdorman of Mercia, with whom she led Mercian resistance to the Danes. On Aethelred's death Aethelfleda ruled as "lady of the Mercians", achieving notable successes against both the Danes and Welsh and constructing *burhs (fortresses) to establish Anglo-Saxon positions in the Midlands.

Aethelred I (d. 871). King of Wessex (866–71), who, together with his brother and successor *Alfred, led resistance to the Danish invasion of England. After ousting the Danes from Mercia (870) Aethelred was defeated by them near Reading but immediately afterwards won a crushing victory at *Ashdown (871). Defeated shortly afterwards at Merton, Aethelred died of wounds received in battle.

Aethelred (II) the Unready (c. 968–1016). King of England (978–1013, 1014–16). Aethelred was crowned after his mother, Aelfthryth (or Elfrida), murdered his half-brother *Edward the Martyr. Aethelred's blunders earned him the nickname Unready (deriving from the Old English Redeless, devoid of counsel) and the weakness of England during his reign encouraged a renewal of the *Danish invasions. At least five times he bought off the Danes with tributes of silver (*danegeld), and on *St Brice's day 1002 he ordered the massacre of all Danes in his realms. In 1013 *Sweyn I Forkbeard of Denmark seized the English throne, but Aethelred was restored after Sweyn's death (1014).

Aethelred. *See* Ailred of Rievaulx.

Aethelwulf (d. 858). King of Wessex (839–56), whose reign saw the first *Danish invasions of England. After sustaining a defeat at sea in 842 Aethelwulf routed the invaders at the battle of *Aclea (851). Noted for his piety, Aethelwulf resigned the kingdom in 856 to his rebellious son Aethelbald (d. 860) in order to avoid civil war.

Afghanistan. A country in south central Asia, control of which was contested in the 19th and 20th centuries by Russia and British India. The first Afghan War (1838–42) followed the restoration by the British of an unpopular emir (ruler) in the capital Kabul. They remained in occupation until rebellion forced their withdrawal; the former emir was restored. In the second Afghan War (1878–80) the British, after the assassination of the British resident, again occupied Kabul and subsidized an emir of their choice. The conflict culminated in the marathon 23-day march of British troops, led by Maj. Gen. *Roberts, from Kabul to Kandahar—a distance of 504 km (313 mi), where he defeated a rival emir. In 1907 an Anglo-Russian agreement guaranteed the independence of Afghanistan and gave Britain influence over the country's foreign affairs. The third Afghan War (1919) broke out following an Afghan invasion of India. The conflict was concluded by the treaty of Rawalpindi, and Afghanistan obtained full independence.

Africa, exploration of. The discovery of the interior of the continent of Africa by European travellers and explorers, which took place between about 1788 and 1880.

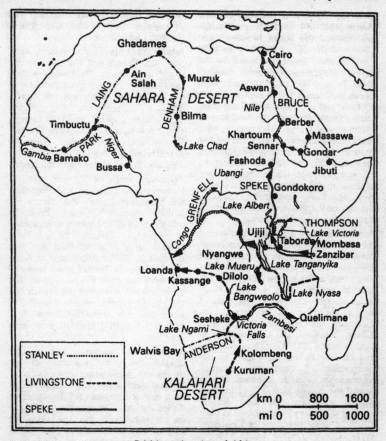

British exploration of Africa

In 1795 Mungo *Park was sent by the African Association to explore the course of the *Niger river in West Africa and established that it flowed eastwards. He again went to Africa in 1805 but was killed in the Bussa Rapids on the Niger. In 1822 Dixon *Denham and Hugh *Clapperton crossed the Sahara from Tripoli and explored Bornu and Hausaland. In 1830 John and Richard *Lander travelled along the Niger to its delta and charted its lower course. The French were also active in West Africa.

Gaspard Mollien discovered the sources of the Senegal and Gambia rivers, and René Caillié travelled from Senegal to Timbuctu and across the Sahara to Tangier. One of the greatest explorers was the German, Heinrich Barth, who travelled an immense distance through Bornu, Hausaland, and as far as Timbuctu. His *Travels* (1857-58) are still a valuable source of information on West Africa.

In East Africa the Germans J. L. Krapf and J. Rebmann were the first Europeans to see Mounts Kilimanjaro and Kenya (1847-49), while Gustav Nachtigal explored the Sudan between Lake Chad and the Nile (1870-74). In 1858 *Burton and *Speke, sponsored by the Royal Geographical Society, reached Lake Tanganyika, and four years later Speke and James Grant explored Lake Victoria and the Nile, also discovering Lake Nyasa. Perhaps the best-known explorer was David *Livingstone, who spent most of his life charting the map of central Africa. In three major journeys between 1853 and 1873 he discovered the Victoria Falls, traced long stretches of the Zambesi, and explored the Congo river and Lake Tanganyika. *Stanley, the last of the explorers of this period, traced the course of the Congo.

Africa, partition of. The division of Africa among the colonizing European nations, which took place between about 1885 (see Berlin conference) and 1900. The scramble for territory in Africa was sparked off by King Leopold II of Belgium, who claimed a vast tract of land in the region of the Congo river. Germany then claimed South West Africa, Togoland, the Cameroons, and East Africa (1881-85). This prompted France and Britain to obtain formal recognition of their own, already considerable, interests in Africa. France gained the largest area of land in West Africa; generally the less densely populated territory from Senegal to Lake Chad, touching the coast at Dahomey, Ivory Coast, Guinea, and Senegal. French Equatorial Africa included part of the Congo, Chad, the Central African Republic, and the Sudan and joined Algeria. Britain consolidated its position in the more densely populated areas—in The Gambia, Sierra Leone (1898), Ghana (1902), and Nigeria (1900). In East Africa Britain obtained British East Africa (now Kenya and Uganda) and further south Cecil *Rhodes and his *British South Africa Company had claimed Southern Rhodesia (present-day Zimbabwe), Northern Rhodesia (Zambia), Nyasaland (Malawi), and Bechuanaland (Botswana). Portugal

obtained Angola, Mozambique, and Portuguese Guinea. See also British Empire; imperialism.

Agadir crisis (1911). An incident resulting from French and German imperial rivalry in Morocco. The French military expedition to Fez prompted Germany to send a gunboat to the port of Agadir. Britain's support for France was expressed in a speech by Lloyd George, and following negotiations the German navy withdrew from Morocco. The crisis strengthened the Anglo-French *entente cordiale. See also Algeciras conference.

Agincourt, battle of (25 Oct 1415). A battle between England and France in the *Hundred Years' War. Henry V's striking victory revived England's military prestige and greatly strengthened his claims in France. The exhausted English army of about 9000 men was engaged by 20 000 Frenchmen at Agincourt, where the limited space favoured the more compact English forces. The undisciplined charges of the French and the skilled English archers contributed to the outcome. About 6000 French lives and perhaps 1600 English may have been lost.

agitators (or **agents**). The soldiers elected—two by each regiment—in 1647 to resist parliament's proposals to disband most of the army without either back pay or indemnity for damage done during the war. The agitators had *Charles I imprisoned by the army at Newmarket and featured prominently in the *Putney debates. By 1648 their influence declined and officers resumed control.

agrarian revolution. The widespread changes in agriculture during the 18th century, involving the large-scale introduction of enclosed fields, of new farming techniques and crops, and the substitution of commercial for subsistence farming. Some authorities now dispute the term, believing that there was gradual change over several centuries; most, however, accept that the 18th century saw the intensification and wider application, especially on light soils, of innovations first introduced in the 17th century or earlier.

An important element in the revolution was *enclosure, as formerly farming had been based upon the medieval system of large open fields in which individual farmers cultivated strips; innovation on a large scale was thus impossible. Although enclosure was widespread during the 16th and 17th centuries, some counties becoming fully enclosed, between 1730 and 1820 there were 3500 separate Enclosure Acts, which resulted in the almost total enclosure of the Midlands and north. Enclosure made possible improvements in scientific stock breeding, land use, and rotation and increased the cultivated area, but it also led to dispossession of poorer farmers and to agrarian discontent among labourers, who were now landless.

Higher yields at this time were largely dependent on animal manure, and the problem of keeping stock over winter was largely solved by the introduction of fodder crops, especially turnips and clover; these, which became widely accepted in the 18th century, were usually planted in three-year rotations. New agricultural implements were also introduced. Especially important were the wheeled seed drill to replace scattering of seed by hand, pioneered by Jethro *Tull in 1701, and the horse hoe to eliminate weeds from between the rows of plants produced by the seed drill. Wooden ploughs gave way to iron ones, drawn now by horses rather than oxen (but not until the 19th century on heavy soils).

There was a strong spirit of innovation. Scientific stock breeding, for sheep and cattle, was pioneered by Robert *Bakewell, who practised intensive in-breeding of animals possessing the points he wanted to encourage. Aristocratic landowners, such as *Coke of Holkham and Charles, Viscount *Townshend, were quick to introduce new methods on their estates. Coke, who introduced long leases for tenants under condition that they would improve, became a much quoted model

to gentleman farmers. George III was an enthusiastic patron of agricultural improvement, such agricultural writers as Arthur *Young were influential, and in 1793 a Board of *Agriculture was set up to produce agricultural reports on a county basis. Scientific research stations, such as that at Roehampton, mostly date from the 19th century.

The process of agrarian improvement was speeded up during the Napoleonic Wars in conditions of blockade, and resulted in a great expansion of the cultivated area—a process that continued throughout the 19th century. The agrarian revolution was intimately connected with the *industrial revolution, in that it increased domestic demand and prosperity, allowed trade to expand, and enabled a rapidly growing population to be fed.

Agricola, Gnaeus Julius (39–93 AD). Governor of Roman Britain. Agricola intensified the Roman occupation of northern Britain and his fleet was the first to circumnavigate the island. He was recalled to Rome in 87 by Domitian, who was jealous of Agricola's successes.

Agriculture, Board of. The name by which the government department dealing with agriculture was originally known. The first Board of Agriculture was set up in 1793, with Arthur *Young as secretary and Sir John Sinclair (1754–1835) as president. Its initial aim was to make a county-by-county agricultural report. Until 1822, when it was disbanded, the Board did much to stimulate agricultural improvement. A modern government department under this name was formed in 1893 from various administrative bodies. Fisheries became the responsibility of the Board in 1903, but it lost forestry affairs to the Forestry Commission in 1919, when it was renamed the Ministry of Agriculture and Fisheries. In 1955 it absorbed the Ministry of Food to become known as the Ministry of Agriculture, Fisheries and Food.

Aidan, St (d. 651). Irish monk at Iona. Consecrated bishop of Lindisfarne at the request of King *Oswald, he founded a monastery there (635) and went on to establish the Celtic church in Northumbria. He was noted as a preacher and ascetic. After Oswald's death (642) his successor Oswin continued royal patronage of Aidan, who died only a few days after Oswin's murder. Feast day: 31 Aug.

aids, feudal (or **auxilia**). A source of royal revenue under *feudalism. They were paid by all those who held land of the king. Feudal aids were taken when a king's son was knighted, when his daughter was married, and, in the event of the king's capture (e.g. Richard I's), to pay for his ransom.

Ailred (or **Aethelred**) **of Rievaulx, St** (c. 1109–1167). Writer and abbot. He spent much of his early life in the service of David I of Scotland and became a monk in about 1134. He was finally abbot of Rievaulx, Yorkshire (1147–67). His works on history include a life of Edward the Confessor.

Aix-la-Chapelle, treaty of (18 Oct 1748). The treaty that concluded the War of *Austrian Succession. Maria Theresa's succession to Habsburg territories was confirmed, except for Silesia and Glatz, which Prussia retained. France repudiated Charles Edward Stuart, the young pretender, recognized the Hanoverian Succession, and restored Madras to Britain. Britain restored Louisburg to France. The treaty left many issues unsolved and war broke out again eight years later (see Seven Years' War).

Alabama. A warship launched in Liverpool in May 1862 for use by the Confederate states of America, then at war with the US government. Before its capture by the Federal government in June 1864 the *Alabama* inflicted considerable damage on Federal shipping. The USA claimed compensation from Britain, which paid $15,500,000 in 1872, after international arbitration.

Alamein, battle of El (23 Oct–4 Nov 1942). A battle during the North African campaign of World War II, a decisive British victory. Planned by Wavell, prepared by Auchinleck, and launched by Montgomery's Eighth Army, the attack pushed back Rommel's forces from the strategic El Alamein position guarding the approaches to Alexandria, 96 km (60 mi) to the east, and initiated the continuing Axis retreat from North Africa. During the 12 days of fighting the Eighth Army sustained 8000 casualties against German and Italian losses of 60 000, half of them prisoners.

Alban, St (died c. 305). British protomartyr, executed during the Diocletianic persecution at *Verulamium, which subsequently took his name. A fugitive priest whom he was sheltering converted Alban to Christianity. According to Bede's account he gave himself up in the priest's place and was martyred. The priest was apparently arrested and martyred some days later. Feast day: 22 June.

Albany, Alexander Stewart, 3rd duke of (and **earl of March**) (c. 1454–?1485). Second son of James II of Scotland. In 1479 Albany was imprisoned by his brother James III, but he escaped to France and won recognition from the English as king of Scots. He took part in invasions of Scotland in 1482 (see Fotheringhay, treaty of) and 1484 but then fled finally to France.

Albany, John Stewart, 4th duke of (?1484–1536). Son of Alexander Stewart, duke of Albany (James III's brother). He was brought up in France, but returned to Scotland in 1515 and became governor for the infant James V. In 1517 he returned to France to negotiate for help against the English, but the French made peace with England and detained Albany until 1521. In 1524 his regency was ended and he spent the rest of his life on the Continent.

Albany, Robert Stewart, 1st duke of (c. 1340–1420). Third son of Robert II of Scotland. Through the increasing infirmity of his brother Robert III he came to be virtual ruler of Scotland. After Robert's death (1406) Albany ruled as governor, making little attempt to secure the release of Robert's successor James I from captivity in England.

Albert (1819-61). Prince consort of Queen Victoria. Albert Francis Charles Augustus Emmanuel was the younger son of Ernest I, duke of Saxe-Coburg-Gotha. He married Victoria, his first cousin, in 1840. Acting as her political adviser and mentor, Prince Albert persuaded her to shed her anti-Tory bias. Because he was a foreigner, with stiff and awkward manners, Albert was unpopular at first. His devotion to duty and his valuable advice on foreign policy, however, won him the respect of political leaders. He earned public esteem as an enthusiastic patron of the arts, sciences, and industry, especially for his organization of the *Great Exhibition of 1851. He died prematurely, of typhoid.

Albuera, battle of (16 May 1811). A battle during the Peninsular War between some 24 000 French troops under Soult and 35 000 allied troops (9000 of them British) under Sir William (later Viscount) Beresford (1768-1854). The British retained Badajoz and inflicted 9000 casualties on the French for the loss of 4000 of their own troops.

Alcuin (735-804). Scholar. Born at York, where he became (778) master of the cathedral school, Alcuin moved to the court of Charlemagne at the latter's request and became the leading figure in the first stage of the Carolingian renaissance. Renowned as a theologian, Alcuin produced the standard medieval version of the Bible and later became abbot of Tours. He was prominent in arranging Charlemagne's coronation as emperor of the West in 800 AD.

alderman. A senior member of a municipal corporation or county council. The word derives from the Anglo-Saxon *ealdorman. The office was abolished, except in the *City of London, in 1972.

Aldermaston marches. *See* Campaign for Nuclear Disarmament.

Alexander I (c. 1077-1124). King of Scots (1107-24), fifth son of Malcolm III by his second wife Margaret. He succeeded his brother Edgar and married Sybilla, an illegitimate daughter of Henry I of England; he had no legitimate children. For most of his reign he was forced to cede control of much of southern Scotland to his brother, who was to succeed him as David I. Alexander was called "the Strong", but too little is known of the events of his reign to judge whether the epithet was justified. Noted for his piety, he promoted monastic institutions and encouraged religious reforms. He opposed the attempts of the English archbishops to establish their authority over the Scottish church.

Alexander II (1198-1249). King of Scots (1214-49), son of William (I) the Lion. He intervened in the Barons' War in England in 1215 in pursuance of Scottish claims to the three northern counties, but eventually (by the treaty of *York of 1237) abandoned the claims in return for lands in England. Alexander successfully asserted royal authority in the remoter northern and western areas of his kingdom and attempted to wrest control of the Western Isles from the Norwegian crown. He died during a military expedition to the Isles. He was succeeded by Alexander III, his son by his second wife, Marie, the daughter of a French baron. His first wife Joan, daughter of King John of England, died childless.

Alexander III (1241-86). King of Scots (1249-86), succeeding his father Alexander II. He successfully resisted pressure to do homage to the kings of England for his kingdom, but the main achievement of his reign was the annexation of the Western Isles by the treaty of *Perth (1266). Because of the troubles that befell Scotland after Alexander's accidental death his reign, by contrast, has sometimes been called a golden age. While this claim may be exaggerated the latter part of his reign does seem to have been a time of stability. Alexander's children by his first wife Margaret (daughter of Henry III of England) all predeceased him and he had no children by his second wife, Yolande, daughter of the comte de Dreux. He was succeeded by his only grandchild, *Margaret, the maid of Norway.

Alexander, Sir William, 1st earl of Stirling (c. 1576-1640). Scottish poet, courtier, and statesman. In the 1620s Alexander led unsuccessful attempts to establish
a Scottish colony in Nova Scotia. He
served Charles I as his Scottish secretary
from 1626 to 1640 and was created an
earl in 1633. His poetry includes the
sonnets collected in Aurora (1604).

Alexander of Tunis, Harold Alexander,
1st Earl (1891-1969). Field marshal. He
commanded at *Dunkirk, where he was
the last officer to leave French shores,
and in Burma (1942). He was appointed
commander in chief in the Middle East
and his forces defeated those of the Axis
in Egypt, Libya, and Tunis (1943) and
then in Italy (1944). At the end of the
war he was allied supreme commander
in the Mediterranean and was subsequently governor general of Canada
(1946-52).

Alexandra (1844-1925). Queen consort
of Edward VII (1901-10). Daughter of
Christian IX of Denmark, she married
Edward in 1863. She tolerated her
husband's infidelities and was much
loved and respected by the British
people. She founded Queen Alexandra's
Imperial (now Royal) Army Nursing
Corps (1902) and instituted the Alexandra Rose Day (1912) in aid of hospitals.

Alfred the Great (849-99). King of
Wessex (871-99), renowned for his
defence of England against the Danes
and for his encouragement of learning.
The *Danish invasion of Wessex in 871
ended in inconclusive peace, and in 876
the Danes struck again. Based at Athelney, Alfred harassed the enemy until
winning, in 878, the great victory at
*Edington. It is to this period that the
probably apocryphal story (told in the
12th-century Chronicle of St Neot's) of
Alfred burning the cakes relates. The
subsequent peace with the Danish leader
*Guthrum gave the Danes control over
much of eastern England (see Danelaw),
but by 890 Alfred's authority was
acknowledged over all of the remainder
of England.

In the years that followed Edington,
Alfred reorganized the *fyrd, streng-

thened the system of *burhs (fortresses),
and developed a fleet, which enabled
him to repel further Danish invasions in
the 890s. His remarkable patronage of
learning brought many scholars to the
Wessex court, including his biographer
*Asser, and he himself translated a
number of Latin texts, including
Boethius, Bede, Orosius, and the Pastoral
Care of Pope Gregory the Great. He
may have initiated the compilation of
the Anglo-Saxon Chronicle. Alfred is
also noted for his laws, the Dooms of
Alfred, which were inspired by the codes
of Aethelbert of Kent, Ine of Wessex,
and Offa of Mercia.

Algeciras conference (16 Jan-7 April
1906). An international meeting in
Algeciras, Spain, held at Germany's
insistence, which regulated intervention
by France and Spain in the internal
affairs of Morocco. It confirmed the
Anglo-French *entente cordiale and
marked a stage in the division of Europe
before World War I into opposing
camps. See also Agadir crisis.

allegiance. The bond linking a man to
his lord and a subject to the monarch.
Formal declarations of allegiance were
important during the middle ages, when
they most commonly took the form of
*homage. Payments were also made by
medieval monarchs to secure the informal allegiance of foreign rulers.

Allen, William, Cardinal (1532-94).
Scholar and polemicist, in exile from
1565. In 1568 he founded a seminary at
Douai to train Englishmen as priests.
There he directed the translation of the
Reim-Douai *Bible. He arranged the
first *Jesuit mission to England in 1580.
A champion of the cause of Philip II of
Spain, he hoped, if Philip's *armada
succeeded, to become archbishop of
Canterbury. He was created a cardinal
in 1587.

Allenby, Edmund Allenby, 1st Viscount
(1861-1936). Field marshal. He served
in south Africa, taking part in the second
Boer War (1899-1902). In World War I
he commanded the cavalry on the
western front and in 1917 was given
command of the Egyptian Expeditionary

force. In his campaign against the Turks in Palestine he captured Jerusalem in Dec 1917 and, after defeating the enemy on the plain of Megiddo, took Damascus and Aleppo (Oct). In 1919 he was created a field marshal and ennobled.

Alleyn, Edward (1566-1626). Tragic actor, who founded Dulwich College. Alleyn had interests in a London bear-baiting house and the Fortune Theatre, Cripplegate. In 1605 he purchased the manor of Dulwich, where he later endowed a college modelled on the public schools Charterhouse, Winchester, and Eton.

allied powers (or **allies**). The states that were allied against Germany, and its allies, in *World War I (compare central powers) and *World War II (compare Axis). The allied powers included the UK, Russia, and the USA.

All the Talents, Ministry of (Feb 1806-March 1807). The administration under Lord *Grenville that principally comprised followers of Charles James *Fox (who was foreign secretary until his death in Sept 1806). The ministry's conduct of the Napoleonic War, following abortive peace negotiations, was generally unsuccessful. Its lasting achievement was the abolition of the slave trade (March 1807; see slavery).

Alma, battle of the (20 Sept 1854). The first battle of the Crimean War, a major victory of the French and British over the Russians. The allies cleared the way to Sebastopol and inflicted some 6000 casualties upon the Russians.

Alnwick, battles of. 1. (13 Nov 1093) The battle, fought near Alnwick, Northumberland, that followed the invasion of England by Malcolm III Canmore, king of Scots, after William II of England had extended royal control over Cumbria and fortified Carlisle. Both Malcolm and his son Edward were killed. **2.** (13 June 1174) The battle that followed the invasion by William the Lion, king of Scots, who was supporting the baronial rebellion against *Henry II. William was captured by the royal army, thereby ending the rebellion.

Amboina, massacre of (1623). The torture and murder of ten English merchants by the Dutch on the island of Amboina in the Moluccas. It was the culmination of a conflict of commercial interests between the English and Dutch in the Spice Islands, from which the British *East India Company now removed itself.

Ambrosius Aurelianus (5th century). British military leader. Member of a prominent Romano-British family, Ambrosius Aurelianus, known as Emrys in the Welsh tradition, led the resistance of the British against the Saxons and achieved a significant military victory.

amercement. In the Anglo-Saxon and Norman periods, a money penalty imposed on an offender in the court of his lord. The word comes from the Norman French à merci, at the mercy of the count or king, for the amount of an amercement was originally arbitrary and a fruitful source of income for a lord. It came gradually to be fixed in many cases, and in others Magna Carta (1215) stipulated that a free man should be amerced according to his means. Amercements gradually gave way to fines.

American Revolution (1775-83). The war of American independence. In the mid-18th century the 13 American colonies (Connecticut, Delaware, Georgia, Massachusetts, Maryland, New Hampshire, New Jersey, New York, North Carolina, Pennsylvania, Rhode Island, South Carolina, Virginia) were antagonized by the assertion by the British parliament of its right to tax the colonists (see Stamp Act; Townshend, Charles). Their resentment was expressed in such incidents as the *Boston massacre (1770) and the *Boston tea party (1773), to which Britain responded with the *Intolerable Acts (1774). In April 1775 war broke out at Lexington and Concord. The Americans invaded Canada in the autumn but were forced to retreat in early 1776. On 4 July the continental congress issued the Declaration of Independence, and shortly afterwards Gen. Howe landed on Long Island, defeating Washington at White Plains. In 1777

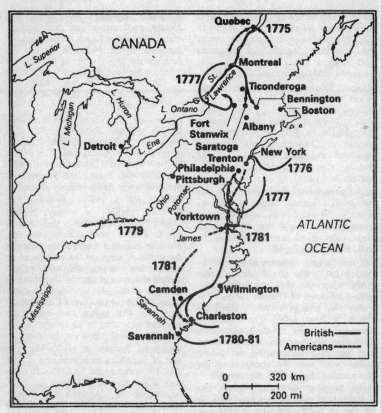

Major British and American offensives in the American Revolution

Britain suffered a serious setback with the surrender of Burgoyne at *Saratoga, which brought France into the war on the American side. In 1778–80 the British did well in the south, but in 1781 American victory was assured by the British surrender at *Yorktown. At sea, Rodney's successes in the West Indies, notably in the battle of the Saints, were insufficient to mitigate the failure on land, and in 1783 Britain recognized American independence in the treaty of Versailles.

The American Revolution aroused great passions in British politics: George III and Lord *North, intent on suppres- sing the colonists, came under violent attack from men such as Burke, Rock- ingham, Shelburne, and Fox.

Amherst, Jeffrey Amherst, 1st Baron (1717–97). General. He entered the army at the age of 14 and, after a distinguished career in Germany and the Netherlands, commanded an expedi- tionary force against the French in North America. He captured Louisburg (1758), Ticonderoga, and Crown Point (1759), opening the approaches to the St Lawrence and Montreal. He was sub- sequently made commander in chief and, after the French surrender, became governor general of British North America.

amicable grant (1524). The *forced loan from all men owning property in land or goods that Wolsey attempted to collect to pay for the war against France. It led to riots and was withdrawn by the king, Henry VIII.

Amiens, mise of (23 Jan 1264). The judgment (mise) given by Louis IX of France on the issues dividing Henry III and the barons. Louis declared for Henry and annulled the *Provisions of Oxford, which had already been condemned by the pope. The mise resulted in increased unrest in the English counties and the outbreak of the second *Barons' War.

Amiens, treaty of (27 March 1802). A treaty between France, Britain, Spain, and Holland, ending the first phase of the *French Revolutionary and Napoleonic Wars. The treaty was no more than a truce, although Britain and France relinquished many of their conquests. Hostilities were resumed in May 1803.

Amritsar, massacre of (13 April 1919). An incident in Amritsar, Punjab, when British troops under Gen. Reginald Dyer (1864-1927) fired on Indians who were protesting against the extension of the British government's emergency powers to combat subversive activity. Some 379 Indians were killed and 1200 injured.

Anabaptists. Believers in adult rebaptism. The radical Anabaptist sect originated in Zurich in about 1524 and was at its most prominent in England in the 1530s. They seem to have influenced the late-16th-century Brownists (see Browne, Robert).

Anderson, Elizabeth Garrett (1836-1917). Doctor and feminist. Unable to obtain formal medical training because she was a woman, she studied privately and in 1865 became the first woman to qualify as a doctor in England. Her dispensary for women and children developed into the Elizabeth Garrett Anderson Hospital. Her persistent campaigning helped women obtain equal status in the medical profession, and she supported her sister, Millicent Garrett *Fawcett, in the campaign for women's suffrage.

Andrew, St. Patron saint of Scotland, apostle, and brother of Simon Peter. His relics were brought to Scotland, probably in the 8th century, and the diagonal cross associated with him, the Saltire, became a national symbol and later the national flag. St Andrew's day is celebrated on 30 Nov.

Andrewes, Lancelot (1555-1626). Bishop of Winchester from 1619, a leading preacher and scholar of his day. He attended the *Hampton Court conference (1603-04) and worked on the *Authorized Version of the Bible.

Aneirin (late 6th century). Welsh poet. His *Y Gododdin* presents individual portraits of British warriors who marched from Manaw Gododdin (near modern Edinburgh) and were overwhelmed by a Saxon force at Catraeth (Catterick, Yorkshire). The surviving text appears in the *Book of Aneirin* (c. 1250).

Angevins. A royal dynasty descended from the counts of *Anjou. The comital dynasty originated in the 10th century, and in 1128 Geoffrey Plantagenet, count of Anjou, married Matilda, daughter of Henry I of England. In 1154, on the death of Stephen, their son succeeded to the English throne as Henry II. Although the dynasty survived till the death of *Richard III (1485) only Henry and his sons *Richard (I) and *John are styled Angevin kings (see Plantagenet, house of). Under Henry II the Angevin empire stretched from Scotland to the Pyrenees, taking in England, much of Wales and Ireland, Normandy, Anjou, and Aquitaine. Most of the French possessions (including Anjou) were lost by John. The Angevins were noted for their ruthless exercise of royal power, which they greatly extended and which aroused considerable baronial and ecclesiastical hostility that culminated in the Magna Carta crisis (1215).

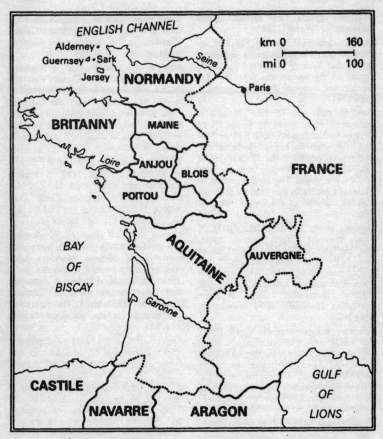

The continental inheritance of the first Angevin king Henry II

Angles. A Germanic people who, together with the *Saxons and *Jutes, invaded and settled in Britain in the 5th century. They probably came originally from Angeln, a region in Schleswig, north Germany, and were first settled in Britain as *foederati (auxiliary soldiers) in the 4th century. Their invasions and settlements were predominantly in northern and eastern England, and two early Anglo-Saxon kingdoms, *East Anglia and *Middle Anglia, were named after them. England also takes its name from the Angles.

Anglesey. An island off the coast of north Wales. At the time of the Roman conquest Anglesey was an important centre of the *Druids, who were massacred here in 61 AD. The main residence of the dynasty of *Gwynedd was at Aberffraw and the island, known as the Mother of Wales, supplied grain for the remainder of Gwynedd. Following the conquest by Edward I

Anglesey formed one of the three shires of northwest Wales (1284).

Anglo-American War (1812-15). A conflict between Britain and the USA, often called the War of 1812. It arose from the seizure of US shipping attempting to run the British blockade of France during the Napoleonic War. The continued British presence in Canada was an underlying cause of American hostility. At sea, the war soon swung decisively in favour of the British. On land, American attempts to invade Canada were repulsed, although in 1813 American forces captured and burned York (Toronto). British invasions of American territory proved equally ineffective. Ross' victory at Bladensburg (1814) was followed by his capture of Washington and the burning of public buildings (including the White House), but US successes at Plattsburgh and Fort McHenry restored the balance. The conflict continued into early 1815, when news of the concluding treaty of *Ghent (24 Dec 1814) reached the USA.

Anglo-Catholicism A movement based on the Catholic tradition within Anglicanism. Developing from the *Oxford movement, Anglo-Catholicism's High Church emphasis on the Christian sacraments and the apostolic succession from early Christianity brought new life and forcefulness into the Church of England from the mid-19th century.

Anglo-French entente. *See* entente cordiale.

Anglo-Japanese alliance. A defensive treaty concluded between Great Britain and Japan in 1902 and renewed twice thereafter (1905, 1911). The treaty aimed to prevent Russian expansion in the Far East and ensured Japan's participation in World War I on the allied side. The alliance was terminated in 1921 at the *Washington conference.

Anglo-Russian entente (1907). An agreement between Britain and Russia, by which tension was lessened over Afghanistan, Tibet, and Persia. It followed the Anglo-French *entente cordiale of 1904 and marked a signi-ficant stage in the evolution of the European system of alliances prior to World War I.

Anglo-Saxon Chronicle. A history in ánnalistic form of Anglo-Saxon England. It exists in seven contemporary manuscripts, one of which (the *Peterborough Chronicle*) continues until 1154. It originated in the reign (871-99) of Alfred the Great, who may have directed its compilation.

Anglo-Scottish wars. A series of conflicts between England and Scotland, precipitated in 1293, when the reigning Scots king, *John Balliol, renounced his allegiance to Edward I of England. In 1296 Edward defeated the Scots at *Dunbar and assumed personal sovereignty over Scotland. Rebellion erupted in 1297 under the leadership of Sir William *Wallace but was crushed by 1303. The struggle for independence was revived by *Robert the Bruce. In 1314 his forces inflicted a shattering defeat at *Bannockburn upon Edward I's successor, Edward II, who thereafter abandoned his attempt to reconquer Scotland. Edward III, on his accession in 1328, recognized the independence of Scotland by the treaty of *Edinburgh. He resumed hostilities in the 1340s, but after 1346 he was absorbed by his French wars and ceased to prosecute the Scottish war seriously. Strife on the border, however, remained endemic.

Anguilla. *See* St Kitts.

Angus, earls of. *See* Douglas.

Anjou. A historic province of west central France, an English possession from 1154, when Henry II became the first *Angevin king of England, until 1204, when it was lost to Philip II Augustus of France.

annates. Payments of the *first fruits, made towards the support of the papacy by bishops on their appointment, which amounted to about a third of their first year's income. In an attempt to force the pope to grant him a divorce Henry VIII secured the passage of the Act of Annates (1532), which suspended payment of annates. The act, which was confirmed in 1533, further enabled bishops to be consecrated by the archbishop of his province and an archbishop by two bishops appointed by the king. A further act (1534), passed after Henry's breach with Rome, confirmed the ban and laid down procedures for the election of bishops.

Anne (1665-1714). Queen of England and Scotland (Great Britain from 1707) and of Ireland (1702-14), the last Stuart sovereign. In 1683 she married Prince George of Denmark. A devout Anglican, she supported the Glorious Revolution (1688), which deposed her father James II and brought her brother in law and sister, William III and Mary II, to the throne. In 1701, after the death of the last of the five of her children who had survived birth (she was pregnant 18 times), she agreed to the Act of *Settlement, providing for the Hanoverian succession. Anne initially backed the war policy of John Churchill, duke of *Marlborough, whose wife Sarah had long exerted a strong influence on her, and unwillingly accepted the government of the Whig *junto. In 1710, however, with the War of the Spanish Succession in stalemate and the Whig leadership unpopular, Anne returned to her earlier Tory principles. Mrs *Masham (née Abigail Hill) supplanted Sarah Churchill, and the Tories under Harley and Bolingbroke replaced the junto. Anne's Anglican sympathies led her to set up *Queen Anne's Bounty in 1704, but the most significant event of her reign was *union with Scotland.

Anne Boleyn (1507-36). Queen consort of Henry VIII (1533-36). Daughter of Sir Thomas Boleyn (1477-1539), later earl of Wiltshire, she became the king's mistress while he was planning to divorce his first wife, *Catherine of Aragon. She was pregnant when Henry married her but greatly disappointed the king by giving birth to a daughter, the future Queen Elizabeth. The couple's failure to have the son Henry longed for caused him to have her executed for several alleged offences of adultery, including incest with her brother. *See also* Reformation.

Anne of Bohemia (1366-94). Queen consort of England as the first wife of Richard II from 1382; daughter of Emperor Charles IV. Her extravagance aggravated Richard's poor relations with parliament. She died, childless, of the plague.

Anne of Cleves (1515-57). Queen consort of Henry VIII. Daughter of a powerful Protestant prince, John of Cleves, she became Henry's fourth wife in Jan 1540. The marriage was arranged by Thomas *Cromwell to strengthen English links with Protestant Europe. Henry, however, came to favour a Catholic alliance and (having been encouraged beforehand by Holbein's portrait of her) found Anne, in person, unattractive. In July 1540 he divorced her, alleging that the marriage was unconsummated. Anne remained in England until her death.

Anne of Denmark (1574-1619). Queen consort of Scotland (1589-1619) and of England (1603-19) as the wife from 1589 of James VI of Scotland (James I of England and Ireland); daughter of Frederick II of Denmark. She died in debt because of her heavy expenditure on buildings and court entertainments (appearing herself in Ben Jonson's masques). She was suspected of being a Roman Catholic.

Anselm, St (?1033-1109). Benedictine monk and scholar. He became abbot at Bec, Normandy (1078), and succeeded Lanfranc as archbishop of Canterbury (1093-1109). Following conflict with William Rufus he was exiled, recalled on the accession of Henry I (1100), but again exiled over the *investiture contest. Reconciliation with Henry enabled him to return in 1107. Feast day: 21 Aug.

Anson, George Anson, Baron (1697-1752). Admiral. Promoted rear admiral after his successful voyage around the world (1740-44) and vice admiral in 1746, Anson defeated the French fleet off Cape Finisterre (1747). As first lord of the admiralty (1751-56, 1757-62) he carried out valuable naval reforms and deserves some of the credit for British successes in the *Seven Years' War.

Anti-Corn-Law League. See corn laws.

Antigua. An island in the West Indies and a state in association with the UK within the Commonwealth. It was discovered by Christopher Columbus (1493) and settled by English colonists in 1632. Part of the colony of the *Leeward Islands (1871-1956), it became a *West Indies Associated State in 1967.

Antonine wall. A turf wall, 59 km (37 mi) long, built from the Forth to the Clyde in 140-42, during the reign of Antoninus Pius. A ditch, 19 km (12 ft) deep, in front of the wall was guarded by small forts separated by short distances. The construction of this wall was technically more advanced than that of *Hadrian's wall, further south. The Antonine wall was finally abandoned at the end of the 2nd century.

appeasement. British foreign policy (1937-39) that aimed at halting German and Italian expansion by concession rather than force. Appeasement was particularly associated with the British prime minister Neville Chamberlain, who believed that the aims of Hitler and Mussolini were limited and that once these were achieved European stability would be assured. Appeasement also entailed rejection of the principle of collective security as embodied in the League of Nations. The *Munich agreement (Sept 1938) witnessed appeasement at its height, but the policy was discredited when Hitler invaded independent Czechoslovakia (March 1939) in defiance of the agreement.

appellant, lords. The five magnates —*Thomas of Woodstock, duke of Gloucester, Richard Fitzalan, earl of Arundel (1346-97), Thomas de Beauchamp, earl of Warwick (d. 1401), Henry Bolingbroke, earl of Derby (later *Henry IV), and Thomas *Mowbray, 3rd earl of Nottingham (1386-1405) —who brought an "appeal" of treason against five of Richard II's courtiers in the *Merciless Parliament (1388). The appellants, whose action asserted the judicial supremacy of parliament, controlled government policy until 1397,

when a royalist reaction swept them from power.

Appin murder (1752). The murder of Colin Campbell of Glenure, factor of the forefeited Jacobite estates of the Stewarts of Appin and the Camerons, while on his way to evict some Stewart tenants. James Stewart "of the Glens" was hanged for the crime but was probably innocent. The murder inspired Robert Louis Stevenson's *Kidnapped* (1886).

Apprentices, Statute of (1563). An act that attempted to counter social unrest by encouraging employment and regulating the contracts of apprentices. It dealt with choices of occupation, length and terms of training, hours, and wages. Enforcement of the act appears to have been neglected by central and local government.

Aquitaine. A region of southwest France, extending from the Pyrenees to the river Loire. The duchy of Aquitaine was acquired by England in 1154 as a result of the marriage of Henry II to Eleanor of Aquitaine. The French kings gradually regained parts of Aquitaine, which was finally lost by the English at the end of the *Hundred Years' War (1453).

Arbroath, declaration of (1320). A letter sent by the barons of Scotland to Pope John XXII asserting their country's freedom. Its stirring rhetoric—"For so long as there shall remain but one hundred of us alive, we will never consent to subject ourselves to the dominion of the English"—has made it the classic statement of Scotland's independance.

Arbuthnot, John. See John Bull.

Arches, Court of. The court of appeal of the archbishop of Canterbury, so called because it used to sit in the London church of St Mary-le-Bow over a row of arches. Of medieval origin, it still exists and is presided over by the dean of Arches, who hears appeals from bishops, deans, and archdeacons. See ecclesiastical courts.

archives, British national. The official historical records of Britain, dating in many branches of government from the 12th century. By an act of 1838 the *Public Record Office was established as a repository for government documents, most of which are now available for public inspection after the lapse of 30 years. In 1959 a comprehensive Public Record Office Act repealed previous acts and transferred control of the national archives from the master of the rolls to the lord chancellor.

Argyll, Archibald Campbell, 5th earl of (1530–73). Scottish nobleman, who, after initially supporting John *Knox and the Scottish Reformation, became an adherent of Mary Queen of Scots. Argyll was implicated in Darnley's murder and commanded Mary's army at the battle of *Langside (1568). After Mary's flight Argyll submitted to Moray and later became lord high chancellor of Scotland (1572).

Argyll, Archibald Campbell, 1st marquess and 8th earl of (1598–1661). A prominent *covenanter, who opposed Charles I in Scotland in the 1630s. During the Civil War Argyll fought the royalists, suffering heavy losses against Montrose's Highlanders (1644–45). However, after Charles I's execution (1649) Argyll broke with the English parliamentarians and assisted at Charles II's Scottish coronation at Scone (1650). Besieged at Inverary, he submitted to parliamentary forces (1652) and later sat as an MP (1658) in the Commonwealth parliament. At the Restoration he was beheaded for high treason.

Argyll, Archibald Campbell, 9th earl of (1629–85). A prominent member of the royalist cause in Scotland during the 1650s, who was imprisoned (1661–63) following his father's conviction for treason at the Restoration. Appointed (1667) to pacify the Highlands, his opposition to extreme measures, and in particular to the Scottish Test Act (1681), incurred the enmity of the duke of York (later James II). As high commissioner of Scotland, York sentenced Argyll to death, on dubious charges (1681). After escaping to Holland, Argyll became involved with the opposi-

tion to James II and in 1685 invaded Scotland on behalf of the duke of *Monmouth. The rebellion failed, and Argyll was executed.

Argyll, Archibald Campbell, 10th earl and 1st duke of (d. 1703). Scottish nobleman, who was associated with the massacre of *Glencoe (1692). Son of the 9th earl of Argyll, he failed to win James II's favour, or to regain the family estates forfeited after the *Monmouth rebellion, and gave his support to William III. He was one of the commissioners to offer William the Scottish crown and in 1689 his estates were returned. He subsequently gained many honours, notably a dukedom (1701).

Argyll, Archibald Campbell, 3rd duke of (1682–1761). Lord high treasurer of Scotland from 1705, when he was created earl of Islay, who promoted the union of Scotland with England (1707). He fought against the Jacobites at *Sheriffmuir (1715) and was subsequently Walpole's chief adviser on Scottish affairs. He became duke of Argyll in 1743.

Argyll, Colin Campbell, 6th earl of (d. 1584). Scottish nobleman, who succeeded his half-brother Archibald Campbell in 1573. He conspired with Atholl to overthrow the regent Morton (1578) but, after raising an army, submitted in the following year. He may have been involved in the *Ruthven raid.

Argyll, John Campbell, 2nd duke of (1678–1743). Scottish soldier. He played a leading part in bringing about English-Scottish union (1707). After serving with distinction in Flanders (1706–09), he became (1712) commander in chief in Scotland and at the battle of *Sheriffmuir (1715) suppressed the earl of Mar's Jacobite rebellion.

Arkwright, Sir Richard (1732–92). Industrialist, who in 1769 patented the water frame, a spinning frame powered by water. The invention made textile spinning a factory industry. Although he was probably not the inventor of the water frame, Arkwright—a self-educated man who had begun his career as a barber and wigmaker—opened many cotton mills to exploit it and by 1782 employed 5000 workers. At his death he left £500,000.

Arlington, Henry Bennet, 1st earl of (1618-85). Secretary of state (1662-74). Exiled during the Civil War, Arlington served as Charles II's agent in Spain (1658-61) before being recalled to serve as secretary of state. Following the dismissal of *Clarendon (1667), Arlington, a member of the *cabal, was entrusted with the conduct of foreign affairs. He concluded (with the aid of Sir William *Temple) the anti-Catholic *triple alliance (1668) and was later reluctantly involved in negotiating the secret treaty of *Dover (1670) with Louix XIV. An attempt by the Commons (1674) to impeach Arlington as an agent of Charles II's policies failed, but he resigned shortly afterwards. For the remainder of his life he held the court appointment of lord chamberlain.

armada, Spanish (1588). A Spanish fleet designed to carry a crusading army to invade England, to rally Roman Catholic support, and to overthrow the "heretical" Queen Elizabeth I. Some 130 Spanish ships reached the Channel carrying 24 000 soldiers and sailors. They were met by 197 English ships, which, although much smaller, were more manoeuvrable and had superior weaponry. The armada was defeated in the battle of *Gravelines (9 Aug 1588) and was forced to circumnavigate the British Isles in order to escape. Only 86 Spanish ships survived.

Armagh. The county town of a county of the same name in Northern Ireland. It grew up around the ancient fortress of Ard Macha, from · which the name derives. In the 5th century St Patrick made it the ecclesiastical centre of Ireland, and it is now the seat of both a Church of Ireland and a Roman Catholic archbishop, both primates of all Ireland.

armed neutrality. In international law, the principle that neutral states may resort to action to force those engaged in war to respect their rights, in particular that of the protection of merchant ships

by accompanying warships. The assertion that "free states make free goods" was asserted by the league of armed neutrality (1780) of Denmark, Russia, and Sweden, which also maintained that *blockades must, in international law, be effective. In 1799, during the French Revolutionary War, Britain denied the principle, and in 1800 Denmark, Prussia, Russia, and Sweden formed a second league of armed neutrality. The principle was stated in the Declaration of *Paris (1856).

Arminians. Supporters of the anti-Calvinist doctrines of the Dutch theologian, Jacobus Arminius (1560-1609). In England, Archbishop *Laud was one of the leading advocates of Arminianism, which with its rejection of predestination and emphasis on episcopacy provoked suspicions that Arminians were sympathetic to Roman Catholicism.

Arms, Assize of (1181). A legislative enactment requiring that all freemen (and, from 1225, villeins) supply themselves with weapons and military equipment according to their wealth. It remained in force until the Militia Act (1662). See also militia.

army, standing. An army permanently maintained by the state (compare militia). Until the 17th century, monarchs relied on the feudal levy and then *mercenaries to man their armies for foreign campaigns. The first standing army was the *New Model Army, formed (1645) by the parliamentarians in the Civil War. It was disbanded at the Restoration (1660), after which the *Coldstream Guards was maintained by Charles II, who also raised two regiments of. life guards. James II maintained a standing army, which was condemned in the Bill of Rights (1689), and the subsequent *Mutiny Act gave control of the army to parliament.

Arne, Thomas (Augustine) (1710-1778). Composer. He was the conductor first of the Drury Lane theatre (1744-60), moving then to Covent Garden. He is remembered chiefly for his composition "Rule Britannia" (1740).

Arnhem, battle of (Sept 1944). A battle during the final stages of World War II. A British airborne assault, it aimed at capturing the key Neder Rijn bridge at the Dutch town of Arnhem ahead of Montgomery's advancing armies. The attack, the most northerly of a number of similar operations, was a costly failure. Unexpectedly fierce German opposition and the inability of ground forces to break through according to schedule led to the evacuation of the depleted airborne troops (some 2200) after the bridge had been held for three days. About 7000 dead or captured men were left behind.

Arnold, Matthew (1822-88). Writer, son of Thomas *Arnold. He was best known as a poet, publishing three volumes of poetry (1885) and holding the professorship of poetry at Oxford (1857-67). Also a literary critic, Arnold fiercely criticized English cultural life in *Culture and Anarchy* (1869). As an inspector of schools (1851-83) he made substantial contributions to the development of English education.

Arnold, Thomas (1795-1842). Headmaster of Rugby School (1828-42), an influential educational reformer. He greatly improved public-school standards by emphasizing that teaching should stimulate further learning and by including French and mathematics in the curriculum. He made the chapel the centre of school life and encouraged games: hence the term muscular Christianity, which was applied to his ideas.

Arran, James Hamilton, 2nd earl of (c. 1516-75). Governor of Scotland for the infant Mary Queen of Scots (1542-54). At first he favoured reform in religion and pro-English policies but was soon won back to Roman Catholicism and alliance with France. In 1554 he resigned his governorship in favour of Mary of Guise and was created duke of Châtelherault by the French. In 1559-60 he supported the lords of the *Congregation against her.

Arran, James Stewart, earl of (c. 1545-1596). Scottish magnate. Stewart spent most of his life on the Continent, but on returning to Scotland in 1577 or 1578 he won the favour of James VI, being created earl in 1581. After James escaped from the *Ruthven raiders in 1583 Arran became his most trusted adviser. On the return of extreme Protestant leaders from exile in 1585, however, his power collapsed and James deserted him.

array, commission of. A *commission authorizing a person—often a soldier —to muster and array those liable for military service (*see* Arms, Assize of) in order to raise a force for royal service. Such commissions were issued from the late 12th century until superseded in the appointment of *lieutenants in the 16th century. Edward III (reigned 1327-77) stipulated that a force so raised should not serve outside its county except to meet a foreign invasion. However, the system was used to levy troops for the French and Scottish wars.

Arrow War (1856-60). A war between China and the allies France and Britain, which sought to further their trading rights in China. It was provoked by the forced boarding of an English ship, the *Arrow*, by Chinese officials and the murder of a French missionary in China. The Chinese were soon overpowered but refused to ratify the treaty of Tientsin (1858). The allies proceeded to take Peking, and in 1860, by the Peking convention, agreed to open further ports to western traders and to allow foreigners to reside in Peking. *See also* Opium War.

Arthur. A legendary British military leader, who may be based on a historical figure. According to the 9th-century *Nennius, Arthur commanded a combined British force against the Saxons, defeated them at Mount Badon (518), and was mortally wounded at Camlan (537). The contemporary *Gildas refers to Badon (which he dates around 500) but does not connect Arthur with the battle. The legends associated with Arthur appear in Welsh literature in the 10th century. Among later writers who contributed to the tales, centring on Arthur's court, the Company of the Round Table, and the search for the

Holy Grail, was the 12th-century *Geoffrey of Monmouth.

Arthur of Brittany. Nephew of Richard I. He was named as heir apparent by Richard in 1190, but the king subsequently recognized his own brother John as his heir. After John's accession, Arthur, supported by the French king Philip II Augustus, claimed English territories in France and in the ensuing conflict was captured, and perhaps murdered, by John.

Articles, lords of the. A committee of the Scottish parliament, which emerged in the 15th century to prepare legislation to be passed by the full parliament. The articles became an instrument of royal control over parliament and were therefore abolished by the covenanters in 1640. Revived in 1661, they were finally abolished in 1690.

articles of religion. A customary way of defining points of religious faith and ceremony during the *Reformation. Henry VIII's government issued ten articles in 1536, but more significant were the six articles issued in 1539. These reflect the king's essential conservatism in religion, reasserting a number of traditional Catholic doctrines, such as transubstantiation (see Eucharist). During Edward VI's reign, England adopted a form of religion much closer to the Calvinist pattern, which is reflected by the 42 articles (1553). Transubstantiation was now rejected and only two sacraments—baptism and the Eucharist—were accepted. The 42 articles provided most of the substance of the 39 articles (1563), a cornerstone of Elizabeth I's religious settlement and still valid.

Arundel, Thomas (1353-1414). Chancellor and archbishop of Canterbury. He was twice chancellor under Richard II (1386-89, 1391-96), who made him archbishop of Canterbury in 1396. In the following year he was impeached and banished, implicated with his brother (one of the lords *appellant). He returned to England with the deposer Henry Bolingbroke, whom he crowned as Henry IV. Again appointed chancellor

in 1407, he was overthrown by the Beauforts in 1410 but was restored in 1412. He was an implacable opponent of the *Lollards.

Arundel castle. A house in West Sussex belonging to the dukes of Norfolk. A *castle occupied the site before the Norman conquest, but the earliest remaining parts of the structure date from the Norman period. Once the necessity for defence had abated the castle was gradually converted into a house, being remodelled in the 18th century and again in the 1890s.

Ascham, Roger (1515-68). Scholar. He gained a fellowship at Cambridge (1534), was secretary to the English ambassador at the court of Charles V (1550-53), and served as tutor to the princess Elizabeth (1548-50). He was later Latin secretary to Edward VI and then, when she became queen, to Elizabeth. His most famous works are *Toxophilius* (1545) and *The Scholemaster* (1570).

Ashantiland. An area, corresponding to most of modern Ghana, that was a powerful empire in the 18th and 19th centuries. Late in the 17th century Osei Tutu united the Akan-speaking peoples of the Oyoko clan into the Ashanti nation. By military conquest he and his successors established the Ashanti empire. At the height of its power under Osei Bonsu (1801-24), it defeated a British force in 1824. In 1873-74, however, Sir Garnet *Wolseley gained a series of victories against the Ashanti, acquiring the southern provinces, which became part of the *Gold Coast Colony. After the arrest and exile of Asantehene Prempe I in 1896 and the Ashanti rebellion (1900-01) Ashantiland was annexed by Britain (1901).

Ashby versus White (1702-05). A legal action arising from the refusal by William White, the Tory mayor of Aylesbury, to accept the votes of certain Whig electors. One among them, Matthew Ashby, brought a successful action against White. The decision was reversed by the Queen's Bench (1704) and then again reversed by the Lords. Five other Aylesbury electors then brought similar actions and were imprisoned by the Commons for contempt. The crisis was only resolved by the dissolution of parliament, after which the electors were released and won their actions.

Ashdown, battle of (c. 8 Jan 871). A battle on the Berkshire Downs ("Ashdown"), in which Alfred the Great led the West Saxons to victory over the Danes. Contemporary chroniclers exaggerated the importance of this battle, since the West Saxons subsequently suffered heavy defeats.

Ashingdon, battle of (18 Oct 1016). A battle in which *Edmund Ironside of England was decisively defeated by *Cnut and the Danes. Edmund was forced to partition England, giving the north to Cnut and keeping the south for himself. Edmund died before the agreement could be implemented and Cnut became king of England in the following month.

Ashley Cooper. *See* Shaftesbury, earls of.

Ashmole, Elias (1617-92). Scholar and one of the first English Freemasons. The Ashmolean Museum (opened 1683) was formed from a collection of curiosities that Ashmole inherited, developed, and donated to Oxford University.

asiento de negros. A contract made with the Spanish crown for the supply and sale of slaves from Africa to the Spanish American colonies. The supplier was granted a monopoly and therefore paid a fee for the contract. It was held by England's African Company from 1713 to 1750.

Aske, Robert (d. 1537). The leader of the *Pilgrimage of Grace in Yorkshire. After taking part in the insurrection of 1536 he was apparently reconciled to Henry VIII but was executed in York after a second outbreak of the revolt.

Askew, Anne (c. 1521-46). Protestant martyr, who, after refusing to recant her repudiation of transubstantiation (*see* Eucharist), was burned at the stake at Smithfield. Bishop *Gardiner tried unsuccessfully to implicate Catherine

Parr and Archbishop Cranmer with Anne Askew, whose death inspired a Protestant reaction.

Asquith, Herbert Henry Asquith, 1st earl of Oxford and (1852-1928). Prime minister (1908-16) and leader of the Liberal Party (1908-26). Born in Yorkshire and educated at Balliol College, Oxford, he qualified as a barrister and became an MP in 1886. He was home secretary from 1892 to 1895 and became chancellor of the exchequer after the landslide Liberal election victory of 1906. In April 1908 he succeeded Campbell-Bannerman as Liberal leader and prime minister. From then until 1914, he faced a number of major problems: the crisis over the powers of the House of Lords, which followed Lloyd George's people's budget (1909) and was resolved by the *Parliament Act (1911); the challenge from the suffragettes (*see* women's movement); severe industrial troubles; and the danger of civil war over the question of home rule for Ireland (granted in 1914). Other notable legislation introduced by his government included the National Insurance Act (1911; *see* national insurance). From the outbreak of World War I in 1914 he led a coalition government but was considered insufficiently vigorous and was ousted by Lloyd George with Conservative backing in Dec 1916. Despite being offered the post of lord chancellor in 1918 Asquith never became reconciled to Lloyd George, and the consequent division in the Liberal Party was a factor in its decline during the interwar period. Asquith, who was created earl in 1925, remained party leader until 1926.

Asquith, Margot (1864-1945). Famous political hostess, second wife (1894-1928) of the Liberal leader H. H. Asquith. She wrote several autobiographical volumes.

Asser (died c. 909). Welsh monk, who was tutor to *Alfred the Great. He wrote a chronicle of English history from 849 to 887, which included a life of Alfred. He was richly rewarded by his patron, who appointed him bishop of Sherborne.

assizes. Legislative enactments, such as the Assize of *Clarendon (1166), judicial proceedings, or the writs giving rise to such proceedings. Henry II, in response to the anarchy of Stephen's reign, instituted the Assizes of *Novel Disseisin and *Mort d'Ancestor, to reinstate persons wrongfully dispossessed of land, and the *Grand Assize to determine titles to disputed lands. Magna Carta stipulated that Assizes of Novel Disseisin and Mort d'Ancestor (both possessory, or petty, assizes; see also Darrein Presentment, Assize of) might only be taken in the shires in which the disputed land lay. The consequent system of sending justices on circuit to take these assizes was extended by the Statute of Westminster (1285). The justices had four commissions: of *oyer and terminer, of gaol delivery, of *nisi prius, and of peace (see peace, commission of the). By 1972 all assize courts had been abolished; their criminal jurisdiction is exercised by the Crown Court and their civil jurisdiction by the High Court. See also Utrum Assize.

Astor, Nancy Astor, Viscountess (1879-1964). Conservative politician, the first woman to sit in the House of Commons (1919-45). Witty and outspoken, Lady Astor, who was American-born, campaigned for women's causes and temperance; she also supported *appeasement.

Athelney, Isle of. A former island at the junction of the rivers Tone and Parrett in Somerset. In 878 King Alfred retreated to Athelney from the invading Danes and launched from here the counterattack that ended in victory at Edington. He later founded a monastery on Athelney, since excavated, and the famous Alfred jewel was found here in 1693.

Athelstan (895-939). King of England. Crowned king of Wessex and Mercia in 925, in the following year Athelstan was acknowledged king of all the English. His reign was marked by successful raids against the Welsh in the west and southwest, the invasion of Scotland, and the defeat of an alliance between Danish

forces and rebellious minor kings at the battle of *Brunanburh (937).

Atherton Moor, battle of. See Adwalton Moor, battle of.

Atholl, John Murray, 2nd earl and 1st marquess of (?1635-1703). Justice general of Scotland (1670-78). A supporter of Lauderdale (Charles II's secretary for Scottish affairs), he withdrew his allegiance after the defeat of the *covenanters at Bothwell Brig (1679) and pleaded with the king to modify his savage policy towards the covenanters. In 1685 he was responsible for the capture of Archibald Campbell, 9th earl of Argyll. He professed loyalty to William III (1688) but did conspicuously little to further his cause and was later involved in intrigues against him.

Atholl, John Stewart, 4th earl of (d. 1579). An opponent of the Reformation, active in Scottish politics from the 1540s. He was one of the closest advisers of *Mary Queen of Scots (1565-67). After the murder of Darnley he supported those who forced her to abdicate but subsequently worked for her restoration. After helping to persuade James VI (later James I of England) to dismiss the regent *Morton (1578), he became chancellor.

Atlantic Charter. A programme of peace aims announced in Aug 1941 by Britain and the USA, shortly before US entry into World War II. The charter supported the general principles of national self-determination and nonaggression, but scrupulously avoided binding its signatories to any specific commitments.

Atlantic triangle. The trade between Britain, West Africa, and the West Indies. Britain shipped cloth and ironware to West Africa, where they were exchanged for slaves. The slaves were taken across the Atlantic and sold as labour for the sugar plantations of the West Indies. The slaves were sold for sugar, which was brought back to Britain, where it was refined and sold to the Continent. This profitable trade, at its height in the 18th century, was monopolized by British merchants.

Atrebates. A British tribe whose territories included parts of Hampshire and Berkshire. Their tribal badge was the triple-tailed House, which appears on their coins. Their main town was *Silchester (Calleva Atrebatum). They seem to have accepted the Roman invasion with little resistance.

attainder (from Anglo-Norman *attaindre*, to convict). The extinction of the rights of a person convicted of a felony and sentenced to death or outlawry. The blood of the attainted person was regarded as being corrupted (the word was thought incorrectly to derive from the Latin *tingere*, to dye), and he could neither inherit land nor pass it on to an heir. Attainder was also the outcome of legislation. Bills of attainder (or of pains and penalties) were introduced from about 1459 and were intensively and arbitrarily used by Henry VIII, especially against opponents of the *Reformation. The procedure was last adopted against Lord Edward *Fitzgerald in 1697. It was abolished in 1870, except in sentences of outlawry, in which it lasted until 1938.

Atterbury's plot (April 1722). An abortive *Jacobite conspiracy, named after Francis Atterbury (1663-1732), Tory bishop of Rochester. Conspirators included the duke of Norfolk; one, Layer, was executed. Atterbury, exiled for life by parliament, joined James Edward Stuart in France. Walpole's firm action in the affair, which helped discredit all Tories as Jacobites, strengthened his position as prime minister.

attorney at law. From the 13th century, a person appointed by a suitor to appear in court on the suitor's behalf. A distinction came to be made between an attorney, who prepared a legal case, and a *serjeant at law, who presented it in court. In 1873 attorneys were designated solicitors.

Attlee, C(lement) R(ichard) Attlee, 1st Earl (1883-1967). Prime minister (1945-51). A barrister, Attlee became a Labour MP in 1922. A junior minister under MacDonald (1924, 1929-31), he refused to serve in the *national government and

became leader of the Labour Party and of the opposition in 1935 (succeeding Lansbury). Between 1935 and 1939, he advocated collective security against Germany and Italy but opposed such defence measures as conscription. Attlee took Labour into Winston Churchill's wartime coalition, serving in the war cabinet as lord privy seal (1940-42), secretary for the dominions (1942-43), and lord president of the council (1943-45); he also acted as deputy prime minister (1942-45). After winning the 1945 election, Attlee became prime minister, the first Labour premier to command an overall Commons majority. At home, Attlee's two administrations (1945-50, 1950-51) saw enormous social and economic changes, with the introduction of the so-called welfare state and major *nationalization schemes. Britain's serious economic difficulties, however, forced the government to introduce austerity measures and, ultimately, *devaluation. Britain participated in the *Marshall plan. Abroad, the *Potsdam agreement and the ending of hostilities with Japan were followed by resistance to the Soviet Union in the Cold War (including the *Berlin airlift and the establishment of the *North Atlantic Treaty Organization), recognition of communist China, and war in Korea (1950-53). India (partitioned into India and Pakistan), Burma, and Ceylon received their independence, and the British mandate in Palestine was ended. After losing the 1951 election Attlee was leader of the opposition until Dec 1955, being succeeded by *Gaitskell.

attorney general. The senior counsel of the crown, who represents the crown in the courts and acts as legal adviser to the government. The office dates from the 14th century. The attorney general has, since the late 17th century, usually been an MP and is appointed on the advice of the government in power. Thus the office has a political as well as legal function.

Attwood, Thomas (1783-1856). Economist and leader, through his Birmingham Political Union, of popular agitation

(1830–32) for the first reform bill. Subsequently, although MP for Birmingham (1832–39), Attwood had negligible influence. In 1839 he presented the first Chartist petition (see Chartism).

Aubrey, John (1626–97). Antiquary and writer. *Miscellanies* (1696), a collection of ghost stories and folklore, was published during his lifetime, but most of his work was edited after his death, including the lively biographies of his contemporaries, such as Bacon, Milton, and Hobbes, published in 1813 as *Lives of Eminent Men* and in 1898 as *Brief Lives.*

Auchinleck, Sir Claude (1884–1981). Field marshal. As commander in the Middle East (1941–43), he halted the German advance into Egypt (1942) but was subsequently forced back to El Alamein (July 1943) and was succeeded by Montgomery. From 1943 to 1947 he was commander in chief in India.

Aughrim, battle of (12 July 1691). An engagement during the pacification of Ireland following the battle of the *Boyne. The army of William III commanded by Godert de *Ginkel (later 1st earl of Athlone) encountered and scattered a Jacobite army, composed of Irish and French troops, near Aughrim in Galway.

Augmentations, Court of. A financial institution set up by Thomas Cromwell in 1536 to administer the revenues from newly acquired *crown lands, especially the estates of dissolved monasteries. It was reformed in 1547 and thereafter administered all crown lands until its abolition in 1554, when its business was transferred to the *Exchequer.

Augsburg, League of. See grand alliance.

Augustine of Canterbury, St (d. 604). The first archbishop of Canterbury. Sent by Pope Gregory on a mission to the kingdom of Kent, Augustine and his party landed at Thanet in 597. King Ethelbert welcomed the missionaries cautiously but allowed them freedom to preach and was himself baptized some months later. In Nov 597 Augustine, in Gaul, was consecrated archbishop and on his return to Kent initiated the construction of a church at Canterbury. In 598 he consulted the pope on the organization of the church in England and on papal advice created 12 dioceses. In 603 Augustine met the British bishops representing the Celtic church and tried to settle the differences between the Roman and the Celtic churches, particularly over the method of calculating the date of Easter. The negotiations failed and the differences were only finally settled at the synod of *Whitby (664). Despite his somewhat narrow and inflexible character Augustine laid the foundations for the establishment of Christianity in England.

auld alliance. The alliance of Scotland with France, beginning at the end of the 13th century and frequently renewed. It was finally broken by the establishment of Protestantism in Scotland (1560).

Auldearn, battle of (9 May 1645). A battle, fought east of Nairn, in which the royalist marquess of *Montrose defeated a numerically superior covenanting army. Montrose was taken by surprise, and only the remarkable fighting qualities of his Highland and Irish troops turned near disaster into victory.

Austin, Herbert Austin, 1st Baron (1866–1941). Motor-car manufacturer and philanthropist. He founded the Austin company (1905), produced the "Baby" Austin Seven car from 1922, and greatly helped popularize motoring in Britain.

Australia. A federated commonwealth in the south Pacific. East Australia was claimed by Capt. Cook in 1770, and *New South Wales was founded in 1788 as a British penal settlement. Initially administered as a huge prison, the colony suffered much disruption in its first years and failed to become self-supporting. In the early 19th century, however, both immigration of free settlers and exploration were encouraged. Discovery of rich pastures behind the Blue Mountains prompted cultivation of the hinterland. By mid-century, most of the grazing land in eastern Australia had also been occupied. Tasmania was settled in 1803, and new settlements were made in what was to be Queensland (1824), in Western Australia (1829), and in South Australia (1836).

During the 1840s demands for self-government arose. These were reinforced after 1851 by the gold rushes, which rapidly trebled Australia's population and promoted the swift advance of its economy. By 1860 all the Australian colonies, except Western Australia, had been granted responsible government. The disadvantages of having five governments within what was in effect one economy was aggravated by the errection of tarrif barriers by the colonial governments against each other. Accordingly, federation was proposed, much debated, and finally implemented in 1901, when Australia became an independent dominion of the British Empire. The state governments within the Commonwealth of Australia retained many powers, but, in principle, control of matters affecting the whole continent was vested in the federal government, sited from 1911 in the Australian Capital Territory, in Canberra (founded 1913). Its subsequent attempts to amend the constitution and extend its powers were largely resisted. Both state and central governments closely follow the British model. Australia is a member of the (British) Commonwealth.

Austrian Succession, War of the (1740-48). A European conflict in which Britain and its allies campaigned to enforce the *pragmatic sanction, which guaranteed the succession of Maria Theresa to the personal dominions of her father, the emperor Charles VI, and that of her husband Francis to the imperial title. Francis' claim was challenged by Charles Albert of Bavaria, supported by the French and Frederick II of Prussia, who precipitated the war by seizing the Austrian province of Silesia in 1740. An allied army led by George II was formed in 1742 and, although war was not declared until 1744, defeated the French at *Dettingen in 1743. Meanwhile, fighting had broken out between England and France in

India and North America, and the issue was further confused by the War of *Jenkin's Ear between England and Spain, which began in 1739. Charles Albert was elected emperor, but on his death in 1745 he was succeeded by Francis, and Maria Theresa ceded Silesia. The French general de Saxe now defeated the British at Fontenoy (1745) and occupied the Austrian Netherlands, and the French encouraged the *Jacobite rebellion in Scotland (1745-46). The war then declined into a stalemate and was concluded by the treaty of *Aix-la-Chapelle (1748).

Authorized (or King James) Version of the Bible (1611). The translation of the *Bible ordered by James I following the *Hampton Court conference (1604). About 50 scholars were employed between 1607 and 1611 to produce a translation based on Tyndale's Bishops' Bible (1568) but referring to all pre-existing English versions. An outstanding example of English prose, the Authorized Version held the field unchallenged for almost three centuries.

Avice (or Isabel) of Gloucester (d. 1217). Queen consort of King John (1199-1200). They married in 1189 but were childless, and John was absolved from the marriage to marry *Isabel of Angoulême. Retiring to estates in Berkhamsted, Avice married the justiciar Geoffrey fitz Peter and after his death (1213) the justiciar Hubert de *Burgh.

Avranches, compromise of (21 May 1172). An agreement between Henry II and the church after the murder of Thomas *Becket, archbishop of Canterbury. Henry was absolved of blame for Becket's murder and did penance before the cathedral at Avranches in Normandy. He also agreed to revoke all new customs detrimental to the church and, although the constitutions of *Clarendon were not cited, to allow appeals to Rome.

Axis. The pact of friendship formed between Germany and Italy in 1936 and confirmed by a military alliance in 1939. The term "Axis powers" is commonly applied to the alliance of Germany, Italy, and Japan during World War II.

B

Babington plot (1586). A conspiracy, organized by Anthony Babington (1561-86), to assassinate Elizabeth I, to liberate Mary Stuart from captivity, and to rally support among English Roman Catholics for a Spanish invasion force. Babington's letter to Mary giving details of the plot was intercepted by *Walsingham. Babington and his five associates were arrested, confessed to the conspiracy, and were executed. Mary's implication in the plot led ultimately to her trial and execution.

bachelor. Originally, a *knight too young to have his own banner and therefore attached to the company of another. From the mid-13th century bachelors included independent knights, who were loyal to a lord but did not hold land of him. These groupings of men around tenants in chief degenerated in the 13th century into the abuse of *livery and maintenance. *See also* bastard feudalism.

Bacon, Francis, 1st Baron Verulam, Viscount St Albans (1561-1626). Lawyer, statesman, and philosopher. He qualified as a lawyer in 1582 and entered parliament two years later. In 1600 he was prosecuting counsel in the trial of his former patron, the 2nd earl of Essex. During the reign of James I, Bacon championed the cause of the royal prerogative against that of the common law in a number of legal conflicts with Sir Edward *Coke. He was appointed attorney general in 1613, a privy councillor in 1616, and lord chancellor in 1618, but he fell from power three years later when he was impeached on charges of corruption. His *Essays* (1597, 1625) are classics of literature, and in *The Advancement of Learning* (1605) and *Novum Organum* (1620) he propounded a radical system of philosophy, which held the field for nearly a hundred years.

Bacon, Roger (?1214-1294). Franciscan monk and scholar, who taught at Oxford and Paris and was named *doctor mirabilis.* He studied alchemy and languages but is best known for his scientific work—especially in optics. His order condemned and imprisoned him for heretical teachings.

Baden-Powell, Robert Baden-Powell, 1st Baron (1857-1941). Soldier, who specialized in scouting and reconnaissance. He became a popular hero during the siege of *Mafeking (1899-1900), when the garrison under his command successfully held out against the Boers for 217 days. He founded the Boy Scouts in 1907 and the Girl Guides in 1909. His ideas were published in *Scouting for Boys* (1908).

Baffin, William (1584-1622). Navigator and explorer. While piloting several expeditions in search of the northwest passage (1612-16) he discovered and explored Baffin Bay (1616) and reached as far north as 77° 45'.

Bagehot, Walter (1826-77). Economist, journalist, and political theorist. He was called to the Bar but turned to a literary career and was editor of *The Economist* (1860-1877). His books include *The English Constitution* (1867), in which he defined the rights of the monarch as "to be consulted, to encourage, and to warn".

bail. The practice of freeing an arrested person on condition that other persons, called sureties, guarantee his or her future appearance in court to face the charge against him or her. Bail derives from the Anglo-Saxon practice of *mainprize.

Baird, John Logie (1888-1946). Inventor of television, which he first demonstrated in 1926 at the Royal Institution.

Bakewell, Robert (1725-1795). Noted agriculturalist. He radically improved livestock breeding, especially of cattle and sheep, to produce quality meat and introduced the new breeds of long-wool Leicester sheep and longhorn cattle.

Balaclava, battle of (25 Oct 1854). A battle during the Crimean War. A Russian attack on the British-held port of Balaclava, aimed at weakening the Anglo-French siege of *Sebastopol, was initially repulsed by Highland infantry and a charge by the 4th Dragoon Guards (the Heavy Brigade). Their success was then dissipated by confused orders, leading to the *charge of the Light Brigade and an inconclusive end to the battle.

Baldwin of Bewdley, Stanley Baldwin, 1st Earl (1867-1947). Prime minister (1923-24, 1924-29, 1935-37). A Conservative MP from 1908 to 1937, when he was created an earl, in 1917 he was parliamentary private secretary to Lloyd George's chancellor of the exchequer, Bonar Law, and then (1917-21) financial secretary to the Treasury. His opposition, while president of the board of trade (1921-22), to Lloyd George's coalition government was supported by the majority of Conservative MPs and helped bring about its downfall. Baldwin served as chancellor of the exchequer (1922-23) in Bonar Law's government, succeeding him as prime minister in May 1923. In the subsequent election (Dec 1923) the Conservatives lost their majority and resigned in Jan 1924. Returned in Dec 1924, Baldwin in his second ministry was faced by the *general strike (1926); he announced a state of emergency and passed the retaliatory Trade Disputes Act (1927). Defeated in the election of 1929, he served as lord president of the council (1931-35) in the *national government and became prime minister for the third time, in succession to *MacDonald, in 1935. His government negotiated the *Hoare-Laval pact (1935), widely condemned for its proposal to permit Italy to annex Ethiopia, and negotiated the abdication of *Edward VIII (1936). He retired in 1937. He was also a writer, his books including *England.*

Balfour, Arthur James Balfour, 1st Earl (1848-1930). Prime minister (1902-05). He was elected an MP in 1874 and in 1886 joined his uncle Lord Salisbury's cabinet as chief secretary for Scotland. In the following year he was appointed chief secretary for Ireland, in which post

he opposed home rule, firmly repressing rebellion, while making concessions to demands for land reform (in his phrase "killing home rule by kindness"). He succeeded Salisbury as prime minister, and his ministry was responsible for the Education Act (1902), the Irish Land Purchase Act (1903), and the Anglo-French *entente cordiale and for the creation of the Committee of *Imperial Defence (1904). In 1905 the government resigned following the split in the party over tariffs, and the Conservatives lost the subsequent general election, and Balfour his seat. He was soon returned to parliament and continued in the party leadership until 1911. In World War I he served as first lord of the admiralty (1915-16) and then, under Lloyd George, as foreign secretary (1916-19). He exerted little influence on war policy and is best known for the Balfour declaration (1917), which favoured "the establishment in Palestine of a national home for the Jewish people". Subsequently twice lord president of the council (1919-22, 1925-29), he represented Britain in the League of Nations (1920-22) and played an important role in the drafting of the Statute of Westminster (1931). Also a philosopher, he published *Defence of Philosophical Doubt* (1879) and *Theism and Humanism* (1914).

Baliol. *See* Balliol.

Ball, John (d. 1381). A leader of the *peasants' revolt (1381). A wandering priest who preached social equality, he was released from a Kentish prison by Wat Tyler's rebels, whom Ball then accompanied on their march to London. He was hanged at St Albans.

Balliol (or Baliol). An Anglo-Norman family, two of whose members, *John de Balliol and *Edward de Balliol, became kings of Scotland.

Ballot Act (1872). The statute that introduced secret voting at local and general elections. Proposed intermittently since the 1830s (and one of the demands made by the *Chartists), the secret ballot attracted little popular interest. Its opponents argued that open voting was more honest, but continuing cases of bribery and intimidation led to the eventual passage of the Ballot Act. Its main political effect was in Ireland, where, freeing the voter from intimidation, it enabled *Parnell to create a nationalist party.

Baltimore, George Calvert, 1st Baron (?1580-1632). Founder of Maryland, in America. He was secretary of state from 1619 until 1625, when he declared himself a Roman Catholic and resigned, being granted an Irish barony. After an abortive attempt to found a settlement in Newfoundland he obtained a patent (1632) to settle land north of Virginia, naming it Maryland in honour of Charles I's consort Henrietta Maria. Following Baltimore's death his sons implemented his plan, making Maryland notable for religious toleration.

Bamburgh. The capital of the Northumbrian kings from the 6th century, when King *Ida of Bernicia fortified the rock of Bamburgh overlooking the North Sea. It later became the chief stronghold of English resistance against Scottish invasion, controlled by a high reeve directly subordinate to the English king. Bamburgh castle was rebuilt in the 12th and 13th centuries. During the Wars of the *Roses it was one of the last castles to hold out for the Lancastrians, serving as their base in the north from 1462 to 1464.

Banda, Dr Hastings (born ?1906). Life president of Malawi. Trained as a physician in the USA, Banda returned home to head the Malawi Congress Party and lead his country (formerly Nyasaland) to independence in 1964.

Bangorian controversy. A religious dispute caused by a sermon preached by Benjamin Hoadly (1676-1761), bishop of Bangor and a *Latitudinarian, on 31 March 1717. The sermon, delivered before George I, questioned the temporal authority of the church. It was widely attacked, and the Convocations of Canterbury and York were prorogued by the king in order to prevent their expected condemnation of Hoadly. Canterbury did not meet again, except

formally, until 1852, and York, until 1861.

bank holidays. The days on which, since 1871, the banks are closed and which have also become public holidays. The Bank Holidays Act (1871) and subsequent acts and proclamations designated six bank holidays common to England, Scotland, and Ireland (New Year, Good Friday, May Day, Spring, Late Summer, and Christmas Day); Easter Monday and Boxing Day are also bank holidays in England and Northern Ireland, and in the latter 12 July (the anniversary of the *Boyne) is too.

Bank of England. The central bank of the United Kingdom. The bank was incorporated by an act of parliament in 1694 under a royal charter for 12 years with the title "the Governor and Company of the Bank of England". Its purpose was to provide finance for William III's French wars. Its original 1268 shareholders subscribed £1,200,000 which was loaned to the government at a rate of interest of 8% per annum plus £100,000 per annum for expenses. It was forbidden to lend money to the crown without the consent of parliament so as to prevent the crown using the bank as an alternative source of revenue. It was given the right to issue notes against the security of its loan to the government. An act of 1708 confirmed the bank's privileged position, limiting banks that issued notes to six partners, in effect preventing the establishment of other joint-stock banks in England until 1826. It became banker to the exchequer and the principal government departments, as well as doing ordinary banking business. In 1750 the administration of the *national debt was entrusted to the bank. By 1770 most private banks in London had stopped issuing their own notes and used Bank of England notes, but its notes did not circulate widely in the provinces, where the bank had no branches till 1826. In 1833 its notes were made legal tender (i.e. must be taken in payment of a debt), confirming what had been customary for some years. The Bank Charter Act (1844) led ultimately to the bank's monopoly in the issue of English bank notes, although Scottish banks retained the right. It also introduced the principle of the fixed fiduciary issue, which remained basically unchanged till 1928; it allowed the bank to issue notes up to £14 million, backed by government securities, which was the fiduciary issue, and all notes issued in excess had to be covered pound for pound by gold. By the late 19th century all commercial banks kept a substantial balance with the Bank of England, which could be withdrawn in gold at will; it thus became the keeper of the central gold reserve and therefore responsible for the control of credit. At the outbreak of World War I in 1914, in order to concentrate the country's gold reserve at the Bank of England, and safeguard it, arrangements were made to issue £1 and 10 shillings treasury notes, which circulated with bank notes as legal tender; gold disappeared from circulation. In 1928 the Bank of England assumed control of the treasury note issue but was not obliged to redeem bank notes in gold coin; the note issue became wholly fiduciary, and the amount was ratified from time to time by parliament. The bank's gold was handed over to the exchange equalization account at the outbreak of World War II. The Bank of England was nationalized in 1946 and today acts as the agent and adviser for governmental financial policies, enforcing exchange control and using the bank rate and directives to commercial banks to control inflation and the supply of credit.

Bank of Ireland. The first joint-stock bank in Ireland, founded in Dublin in 1783. In 1845 all restrictions on other joint-stock banks in Ireland were removed, with the result that the Bank of Ireland did not become a true central bank. In 1943 the Irish government instituted the Central Bank, which was granted the sole right to issue Irish bank notes.

Bank of Scotland. The first joint-stock bank in Scotland, established in Edinburgh in 1695. Its 21-year monopoly on

banking ended in 1716, after which a number of other joint-stock banks were founded. It retains the right of note issue, as do all five Scottish banks, which are not restricted by the Bank of England's monopoly.

Banks, Sir Joseph (1743-1820). Naturalist. He took part in Cook's voyage round the world (1768-71), recording it in his *Journal,* and subsequently pressed for the colonization of New South Wales. His scientific collections are in the British Museum. He was president of the Royal Society (1778-1820).

banks and banking. A financial service principally concerned with safeguarding deposits, making loans, and providing a means of payment. In Britain a system of banking developed during the 17th century through London goldsmiths, who issued promises to pay for coin deposited with them. These promises to pay became the first bank notes, passing from hand to hand. As experience showed that demand for the return of all deposits would not normally be made at the same moment notes came to be issued as loans unrelated to money held. The °Bank of England was formed in 1694 to meet the financial requirements of the government and the demand for a better regulated banking system. In 1760 there were about 25 banks in London and by 1800 there were about 70. Banks outside London grew rapidly and by the early years of the 19th century there were over 700. The Bank Charter Act (1844) eventually gave the Bank of England a monopoly of the issue of notes in England. The increasing scale of industry and the need for greater resources led to a steady amalgamation of the numerous small banks into larger organizations with a network of branches. This facilitated greater cooperation on policy between banks and the Bank of England, and the emergence after World War I of the Big Five clearing banks—Barclays, Midland, Lloyds, National Provincial, and Westminster, the last two being amalgamated in 1968 to form the National Westminster Bank.

Bannockburn, battle of (24 June 1314). The battle in which Robert I of Scotland decisively defeated Edward II's English force, which was trying to relieve Stirling castle. Robert was able as a result of his victory not only to keep the English out of Scotland, except for Berwick-upon-Tweed, but also to raid deep into northern England. Although the battle temporarily gave the Scots ascendancy, it failed to persuade the English to abandon their attempt to subdue Scotland (see Anglo-Scottish wars). Nevertheless, Bannockburn, coming after so many Scottish defeats, provided an important boost to the morale of the Scots in their many later defeats.

Baptists. A nonconformist communion believing in spiritual regeneration through adult baptism. In 1609 the exiled John Smyth (1554-1612) founded the first Baptist church, in Amsterdam, and by 1612 the sect was established in England; in 1639 the first Baptist settlement in New England was founded. In contrast to the *Arminianism of the so-called General Baptists, many of whom were influenced by *Unitarianism in the 18th century, the Strict (or Particular) Baptists held Calvinist beliefs. The merging of the two Baptist groups was begun by the Baptist General Union (1813) and was largely completed by 1891.

Barbados. An independent island in the West Indies, formerly a British possession. It was settled in the early 17th century by the British, and slaves were brought here from West Africa to work the sugar plantations. Becoming a member of the federation of the West Indies in 1958, it obtained self-government in 1961 and full independence within the Commonwealth in 1966.

Barbour, John (c. 1320-1395). Scottish poet and cleric. His epic poem *The Brus* is based on the exploits of Robert (I) the Bruce.

bard. A Celtic poet who recited verses about the exploits of his tribe. Medieval Welsh bardic tradition is essentially oral and is traced to *Taliesin in the 6th century. The laws of *Hywel Dda assig-ned to the household bard an honourable position in the royal courts of Wales. Bardic schools were established, which taught the rudiments of alliterative poetry, story-telling, heraldry, and grammar. Competitive meetings (see *eisteddfod*) were held and itinerant bards composed grandiloquent odes in the courts of princes and, after 1282, in the mansion houses of the Welsh gentry, who continued the traditional patronage. The period 1450-1550 represented the golden age of the bardic system, which afterwards declined.

Barebones Parliament (4 July-12 Dec 1653). An assembly composed of 140 "godly men" chosen by Oliver Cromwell and the Council of Officers. Also called the Nominated Parliament, it was nicknamed after Praisegod Barbon, or Barebones (?1596-1679), a sectarian preacher and one of its members. The gulf between the various ideologies represented proved unbridgeable and the conservatives, alarmed by the proposed radical reforms, voted to end the assembly. The dissolution of Barebones heralded the *Instrument of Government and the proclamation of Oliver Cromwell as lord protector.

Barham Down. The site near Canterbury of two military camps in the 13th century. 1. In 1213 King John mobilized an army here against the threat of a French invasion. The defeat of the French fleet off Damme (Flanders) removed the threat, but John had demonstrated his continuing capacity to retain the confidence of a powerful following. 2. In 1264, during the second *Barons' War, the Montfortians, displaying a similar strength, maintained a large camp for several months against a threatened invasion led by exiled supporters of Henry III.

Baring, Alexander, 1st Baron Ashburton (1774-1848). Financier and politician. He was a partner in the Baring banking house and an MP from 1806 to 1835. He negotiated with the USA the treaty (1842) that settled the long-disputed boundary between Canada and Maine.

Baring, Evelyn, 1st earl of Cromer (1841-1917). Administrator and diplomat. After serving (1872-76) as secretary to the viceroy of India he went to Egypt, where, in 1883, he became agent and consul general. He was the virtual ruler of Egypt until 1907, and the period of his administration has thus been called the Veiled Protectorate. A financial expert, he introduced wide-ranging reforms that brought Egypt solvency and then prosperity. His administration also saw the solution of the Sudan crisis, with Kitchener's reconquest. He was created Baron Cromer in 1892, viscount in 1898, and earl in 1901.

Barnardo, Thomas John (1845-1905). Philanthropist, noted as the founder of the children's homes that bear his name. Converted to evangelical Christianity, Barnardo planned to become a medical missionary but instead founded a mission for destitute children in London (1867). He opened his first children's home in 1870 and his organization has since helped hundreds of thousands of children.

Barnet, battle of (14 April 1471). A battle of the Wars of the Roses. The Yorkist Edward IV, returned from exile in the Netherlands, marched on London, where he was joined by his brother *Clarence, and captured Henry VI. At Barnet, in a thick fog and with only 2000 men, he defeated the Lancastrians led by Warwick, who was killed. Edward's army marched on to the decisive victory at *Tewkesbury.

baron. The fifth and lowest rank of the *peerage. Until the 13th century the term was applied to all tenants in chief —those who held land directly from the king. A distinction came to be made between those summoned to court by personal writ (the greater barons) and those summoned by general writ (the lesser barons), which Magna Carta (1215) confirmed. A new criterion of definition was introduced in the 14th century, when baronies were created by personal summons to parliament and had no basis in land tenure.

The law life peers (created since 1876) and other life peers (since 1958) are ranked as barons and baronesses.

baronet. A hereditary honour ranked above a knight and below a baron. The dignity was introduced by James I in 1611 to raise money to suppress rebellion in Ulster, for baronets were required to pay £1,080 for the honour. They were also obliged to possess an annual income of £1,000. Baronets, who were permitted to adopt the prefix "Sir", were introduced into Scotland in 1625.

Barons' Wars. 1. (1215-17) The civil war between King *John and the barons. John's failure to honour the terms of *Magna Carta provoked the barons to offer the crown to Louis, son of Philip II Augustus of France. Following Louis' landing in Kent (May 1216), John, who had campaigned successfully in the Midlands and the north, lost most of southeast England. In Oct the king died, and with the crowning of his son as Henry III and the reissue of Magna Carta the tide turned for the royalists. The defeat of the barons at *Lincoln and the capture of French supply ships off Sandwich forced Louis to accept the treaty of *Kingston-upon-Thames (12 Sept 1217). **2.** (1264-67) The civil war between Henry III and the barons led by Simon de *Montfort. The barons' cause —to limit royal power—was aided by Henry's financial problems in the 1250s: not only did the king have to raise extra revenue for a papal crusade, but he needed money from the barons for his campaigns in Wales and France. When Henry made further financial demands to pay for the expeditionary force in support of the claim of his brother Edmund, earl of Lancaster, to the Sicilian throne the barons insisted on political reforms as the price of their cooperation. In 1258 they issued the *Provisions of Oxford—limitations on royal power, which the king reluctantly accepted. Finding these irksome he referred them for arbitration to the French king, whose decision that the provisions were not binding made war inevitable (see Amiens, mise of). Henry declared that the barons opposing him were rebels and on 13 May 1264 Simon de Montfort repudiated his feudal oath. The war began with the battle of *Lewes, in which de Montfort defeated and captured the king. The barons then quarrelled among themselves and Gilbert, earl of Gloucester, and Roger *Mortimer joined the king's side. The war continued with the siege of *Kenilworth and the battle of *Evesham (1265), when the royal forces, led by Henry's eldest son, Edward, defeated the barons and killed de Montfort. Fighting ended with the proclamation of peace on 16 Sept 1265, but baronial resistance continued, notably at Kenilworth and the Cinque Ports, until 1267, when Edward overcame the last pocket of opposition on the Isle of Ely. Despite the barons' defeat the war marked an important stage in English constitutional development, and many of the reforms demanded by the barons were subsequently granted by Edward I. See also Kenilworth, dictum of.

Barotseland. The home of the Lozi people in western Zambia (formerly *Northern Rhodesia). The Lozi granted mining rights to the *British South Africa Company in 1890. They maintained their unity under colonial rule and tried unsuccessfully to secede from independent Zambia (1964).

barrier treaties. Three treaties (1709, 1713, 1715) drawn up by Britain during the War of the Spanish Succession (1701–14). They restored to the United Provinces the right to garrison certain towns along the southern border of the Netherlands as a line of defence against France. The first treaty offered the Dutch generous territorial and commercial terms but was greatly modified by the subsequent two treaties.

Barrow, Henry (c. 1550–1593). Church reformer, who advocated the separation of church from state and the establishment of independent congregations. He was imprisoned (1586–93) for sedition and executed at Tyburn. Many of his followers, called Barrowists, fled to Holland and then to America following

the Conventicle Act 1593 (see also Browne, Robert).

Barton, Elizabeth (c. 1506–1534). Servant, known as "the holy maid of Kent". After an illness in 1525 she experienced trances and uttered prophecies, the authenticity of which was confirmed by some ecclesiastics. However, her prophecies began to involve Henry VIII, condemning his proposed divorce from Catherine of Aragon and marriage to Anne Boleyn. A bill of attainder found her and her alleged supporters (including Sir Thomas *More, whose name, however, was subsequently removed) guilty of treason, and she was executed at Tyburn.

bastard feudalism. A term applied to the ties between lords and their followers whose service, whether military or administrative, was retained in the late middle ages in return for fees, rather than land. It bore only superficial resemblances to territorial *feudalism. Bastard feudalism derived originally from the military needs of English kings in the French, Scottish, and Welsh wars, for indentured retainers formed the equivalent of standing armies, which were available for service not only to their lords but also to the king. Abuses of the system (see livery and maintenance) have often been blamed for the civil disturbances of the 15th century (see Roses, Wars of the).

Basutoland. A former British protectorate in southern Africa. In the 1830s the Basuti nation was consolidated under Mosheshwe. Conflict with the Boers soon arose over frontiers with the Orange Free State (1858, 1865), and in 1868 Britain annexed Basutoland. From 1871 the Cape government administered it, but after the War of the Guns (1880) it was returned to the British government (1884). Basutoland, as the kingdom of Lesotho, became independent in 1966 and is a member of the Commonwealth.

Bate's case (1606). A legal case arising from the refusal of John Bate, a merchant, to pay an *imposition on currants levied by James I. Bate's case came before the court of the *Exchequer, which found in the crown's favour. The decision of Chief Baron (Thomas) Fleming (1544-1613) stated that the king might, by virtue of his *prerogative, levy customs duties at the ports for the control of foreign trade, but he might not impose levies for purposes of taxation without parliamentary consent.

Bath. A town in the county of Avon. Built on the River Avon, Bath (as Aquae Sulis) first rose to prominence under the Romans because of the presence there of natural springs. Remains of the Roman town are still to be seen. The importance of Bath collapsed with the Roman Empire, and it remained an obscure provincial town until the 18th century, when the springs again brought it into prominence. It became a fashionable watering place, initially for medicinal purposes, but later as an out-of-season social centre. Under the direction of the architects John Wood and his son, Bath expanded according to a plan remarkable for its coherence and elegance. Central to the development was the crescent, a curved range of individual houses integrated by a unified façade, the most notable being the Royal Crescent. The other single most impressive construction is The Circus, a circular piazza designed as a Roman amphitheatre turned inside out. Other notable buildings include Pulteney Bridge and the Pump Room, at which the celebrated Beau *Nash officiated. Social change and the development of transport brought the decline of the watering place, however, at the beginning of the 19th century.

Battle abbey. A religious foundation established in 1067 by William the Conqueror to commemorate his victory at the battle of *Hastings. The abbey is located near the site of the battle.

Bayeux tapestry. A linen strip 48 cm (19 in) wide and over 70 m (231 ft) long, with needlework designs depicting events in the life of *Harold, the last Anglo-Saxon king. The tapestry was intended to demonstrate the legitimacy of the Norman claim to the English throne. Although its manufacture is traditionally

associated with Queen Matilda, the wife of William the Conqueror, the tapestry may have been commissioned by Odo, bishop of Bayeux (in Normandy), where it is preserved today. The date of its manufacture is much disputed.

Baylis, Lilian (1874-1937). London theatre manager. She transformed the Old Vic from a temperance hall into a centre for Shakespearean drama and made the formerly derelict Sadler's Wells Theatre internationally famous for opera and ballet.

Beachy Head, battle of (10 July 1690). A naval battle of the War of the Grand Alliance, in which the English and Dutch were defeated by the French off Beachy Head.

Beaconsfield, Benjamin Disraeli, 1st earl of. See Disraeli, Benjamin.

Beaton, Cardinal David (?1494-1546). Archbishop of St Andrews from 1539, succeeding his uncle, Cardinal James Beaton. In 1543 Beaton became chancellor and restored pro-French and pro-Catholic policies in Scotland. Personal enemies and supporters of George *Wishart, who was burned by Beaton for heresy, combined to murder him.

Beatty of the North Sea and of Brooksby, David Beatty, 1st Earl (1871-1936). Admiral. In World War I he commanded at *Dogger Bank (1915). At *Jutland (1916), commanding British battle cruisers, he decoyed the German fleet northwards, permitting *Jellicoe to engage. Subsequently he attempted unsuccessfully to block its retreat. He believed that the lack of clear information was partly responsible for the inconclusive result of the battle and, as first sea lord (1919-27), tried to make fleet battle instructions clearer.

Beauchamp, Guy de, earl of Warwick (1272-1315). A lord *ordainer in 1310. He was primarily responsible for the seizure and murder (1312) of Piers *Gaveston, Edward II's unpopular favourite.

Beauchamp, Richard de, earl of Warwick (1382-1439). Soldier. He fought the Percys at the battle of *Shrewsbury in

1403, helped suppress the Lollards (1414), and from 1415 to 1421 had a distinguished military career in the war against France. In 1422 he was appointed a member of the council of regency for Henry VI and in 1437 became lieutenant of France and Normandy.

Beaufort. A family descended from *John of Gaunt, duke of Lancaster (fourth son of Edward III), and his mistress (later his wife) Catherine *Swinford. Their children were legitimized in 1397, and their descendants, notably Edmund Beaufort, 2nd duke of Somerset (d. 1455), and his son Henry Beaufort, 3rd duke of Somerset (1436-64), were prominent supporters of the Lancastrians in the Wars of the *Roses. Margaret *Beaufort was the mother of Henry VII.

Beaufort, Henry, Cardinal (d. 1447). Bishop of Winchester. Second son of *John of Gaunt and Catherine Swinford, he was appointed bishop of Lincoln in 1398 and of Winchester in 1404. He served three times as chancellor (1403-04, 1413-17, 1424-26). A cardinal from 1426, he acted as a papal legate in Germany, Hungary, and Bohemia. He came into conflict with Humphrey, duke of Gloucester, in the 1430s and 1440s but retained his political influence until his death.

Beaufort, Margaret (1443-1509). Countess of Richmond and Derby, heiress of John Beaufort, 1st duke of Somerset. In 1455 she married Edmund *Tudor, earl of Richmond (d. 1456). Their son, Henry VII, claimed the English throne by virtue of his mother's descent from *John of Gaunt. The defection of her third husband, Thomas *Stanley, from the Yorkist to the Lancastrian cause was a crucial factor in Henry's victory at Bosworth. After her son's accession she devoted herself to learning and translating devotional works from French to English. She supported *Caxton and patronized foundations at Oxford and Cambridge.

Beaumont, Robert de, earl of Leicester (1104-68). A powerful supporter, with his twin brother Waleran of Meulan (1104-66), of King Stephen against

Matilda. He nevertheless became (1155, 1156) justiciar under Henry II and ruled the kingdom in his absence (1158-63, 1165).

Beaverbrook, William Maxwell Aitken, 1st Baron (1879-1964). Canadian-born politician and newspaper proprietor, who made his fortune in business before coming to Britain and becoming a Conservative MP (1910). He became minister of information in 1918. After the war he devoted himself to his newspaper empire. He obtained a majority interest in the *Daily Express* (1919), founded the *Sunday Express* (1921), and acquired the London *Evening Standard* (1929). In 1929 he began his campaign for "Empire Free Trade". He joined the war cabinet in 1940 and was minister of aircraft production (1940-41).

Bechuanaland. A former British protectorate, north of South Africa between the Orange and Zambesi rivers. Home of the Bamangwato, it was annexed by Britain in 1885. As Botswana, it became independent in 1966 under Seretse *Khama and is a member of the Commonwealth.

Becket, Thomas (?1118-1170). Archbishop of Canterbury. Of Norman origin, he was educated in London, Paris, and Bologna. Henry II appointed him chancellor in 1155 and archbishop, despite Becket's unwillingness, in 1162. Becket opposed Henry's attempts to bring the church within the jurisdiction of the king's courts and insisted on the right of ecclesiastical courts to try clergy (see Clarendon, constitutions of). After a bitter quarrel the archbishop went into exile (1164) in France, returning in 1170, when a reconciliation with Henry was patched up. Hostility remained, however, and Henry's ill-considered remarks moved four of his knights to murder the archbishop in Canterbury cathedral on 29 Dec 1170. Becket was canonized in 1173 and his tomb attracted pilgrims from all over Europe. Henry was forced to make a number of concessions to the church as part of his penance (see Avranches, compromise of).

bedchamber crisis (7-13 May 1839). A constitutional dispute that followed the resignation, in anticipation of parliamentary defeat, of Melbourne, Queen Victoria's trusted Whig prime minister. The Tory leader Peel proceeded to form a government and asked the queen to dismiss those of her ladies of the bedchamber whose husbands were Whigs. Victoria, who found Peel unsympathetic, refused and appealed, unconstitutionally, to Melbourne to continue in office. He did so, and the dispute was only finally resolved in Aug 1841, when Melbourne's government fell and, under the moderating influence of Prince Albert, Victoria dismissed three of her ladies.

Bede (673-735). Anglo-Saxon historian and scholar, born in Northumbria, who spent most of his life in the monastery at *Jarrow. A student of Latin, Greek, and Hebrew, he was renowned for his scholarship and was known after his death as the Venerable Bede. *The Ecclesiastical History of the English People*, which Bede completed in 731, is the most important history written in England before the 16th century. King *Alfred supervised its translation into Old English. Bede popularized the method of dating *anno domini* and wrote on a variety of subjects, including physical science, rhetoric, and astronomy.

Bedford, duke of. *See* John of Lancaster.

Bedlam. Originally, the abbreviated name of the Bethlem Royal Hospital. Founded in 1247, the hospital was the first asylum for the insane in England. It moved to Moorfields in 1676 and from 1815 to 1931 was located at what is now the Imperial War Museum, in Lambeth, south London. In 1931 it moved to Beckenham in Kent, becoming part of the Kings College Hospital Group. From its notoriety during the 15th and 16th centuries Bedlam came to signify uncontrolled uproar.

Beefeaters. *See* Yeomen of the Guard.

Belgae. A Gallic tribe that invaded Britain in the 1st century BC. There they occupied a territory that stretched from the Isle of Wight to the Bristol Channel, including parts of Hampshire, Wiltshire, and Avon. They also extended their influence over other southern British tribes. The Belgae, who offered strong opposition to the Roman invasion in 43 AD, introduced *coinage to Britain.

Belgian neutrality. The status of Belgium that was embodied in the treaty of London (1839) and recognized as binding by all the great powers of Europe from 1822 until 1914. Apart from the 1815 agreement to defend Swiss neutrality, it was the only generally agreed principle of European diplomacy during most of the 19th century. The German invasion of Belgium was the immediate cause of the British declaration of war in 1914 (*see* World War I).

Belize, Colony of. A British crown colony on the Caribbean coast of Central America. A British colony from 1862 and named British Honduras, it was granted internal self-government in 1964. Guatemalan claims to it delayed its independence until 1981.

Bell, Gertrude (1868-1926). Traveller in Asia and the Middle East. As adviser to the British government on Arabia she played an important role in the establishment of the new state of Iraq after World War I. She founded the national museum in Baghdad. Her books include *The Desert and the Sown* (1907) and *Amurath to Amurath* (1911); her letters have also been published (1947).

Benbow, John (1653-1702). Naval commander, whose exploits in the wars of William III's reign against the French made him a popular hero. While commanding in the West Indies (1701-02), he died from wounds received during an engagement with a French squadron.

benefit of clergy. A concession granted to the church by Henry II in the constitutions of *Clarendon (1164). If a man accused of a crime could prove he was a cleric he was tried in an ecclesiastical court, the penalties of which did not include the death sentence. The ability to recite a verse from the Latin Bible (the so-called neck verse) was often accepted as proof. The scope of benefit was gradually restricted, being finally abolished in 1825.

benefit societies. See friendly societies.

benevolence. A sum of money extorted as a "gift" by the monarch. The term was first used in 1473, during the reign of Edward IV, to describe a request for financial aid that the government did not intend to repay (compare forced loan). In 1484, under Richard III, parliament declared benevolences illegal. However, they continued to be raised, and the Tudor Henry VII argued that the 1484 act was unlawful because Richard III had been a usurper. Benevolences were again condemned in the Petition of Right (1628), and Charles I made the last, abortive, attempt to raise the tax in 1633.

Bengal. A former province of British India, in the northeast. Bengal was under Mogul rule from 1576 until 1765, when, following Clive's victory at *Plassey (1757), the Moguls ceded Bengal, Bihar, and Orissa to the *East India Company. The company, which had been established in Bengal since 1633, placed its own nominee upon the throne and ruled through a governor. The last governor, Warren *Hastings, was named governor general of Bengal in 1774, when he was given responsibility for other company possessions in the subcontinent. The crown took direct control of the administration in 1858 (see India Acts), and in 1877 Bengal, together with Bihar and Orissa, became a province. The partition of Bengal (1905) by Lord *Curzon provoked considerable unrest, and in 1912 was revoked. At the same time Bihar and Orissa were detached from Bengal to form a separate province. In 1947 Bengal was divided between India and Pakistan.

Benin. The capital of Bendel state in Nigeria and from the 14th to 17th centuries an important kingdom in West Africa. Benin had contacts with Portuguese traders and missionaries in the 16th century and at its height ruled an area stretching from Lagos to the Niger delta. Its power declined in the 19th century and, following defeat by the

British in 1896, it was incorporated into the Southern Nigerian colony.

Bentham,   Jeremy   (1748-1832). Exponent of *utilitarianism, which he applied to various social institutions. Bentham refuted (Fragment on Government, 1776) *Blackstone's idealization of the English legal system and, in his greatest work, An Introduction to the Principles of Morals and Legislation (1789), argued that legislation must achieve the "greatest happiness of the greatest number". He also became a leading theoretician of parliamentary reform.

Bentinck, Lord George (1802-48). A leading opponent of *corn law repeal. On Peel's conversion to repeal, Bentinck, a backbench MP since 1828 but best known as a racehorse owner, accepted leadership of the protectionist group (encouraged by its ablest member, Disraeli). After repeal (1846), Bentinck helped defeat Peel's government and continued advocating protectionist measures, although he resigned the group leadership in 1847.

Bentley, Richard (1662-1742). Scholar. A clergyman, and master of Trinity College, Cambridge, Bentley was the foremost classical scholar of his age. He became involved in famous public controversies, over both literary criticism (notably with Charles Boyle) and his authoritarian management of his college.

Beowulf. An Anglo-Saxon epic poem written between about 672 and 782. Beowulf, the protagonist, is nephew of the king of the Gaetas, a southern Swedish people. He slays Grendel, a monster who has been ravaging the neighbouring Danish kingdom, and also Grendel's mother. Later, when he is king of the Gaetas, Beowulf's kingdom is attacked by a dragon, which he kills, but he is fatally injured in the struggle. The poem sheds light on Anglo-Saxon aristocratic traditions, and some of its characters (but not Beowulf) and events are historical.

Berengaria of Navarre (d. ?1230). Queen consort of Richard I. She married Richard in Cyprus in 1191, while he was on the third crusade. They had no children. While Richard was imprisoned in Germany (1192-94) she lived in Poitou. She retired to Le Mans in Maine after his death.

Berkeley, George, Bishop (1685-1753). Philosopher. Born in Ireland, he was bishop of Cloyne (1734-52). In his philosophical work, which carried on from *Locke, Berkeley argued that what is not perceived does not exist. Berkeley's original and influential theory was explained in three major works, all written before he had reached the age of 30: *An Essay towards a New Theory of Vision* (1709), *Principles of Human Knowledge* (1710), and *Dialogues between Hylas and Philonous* (1713).

Berlin, congress of (13 June-13 July 1878). A conference attended by representatives of Russia, Great Britain, France, Germany, Austria, Italy, and Turkey to settle the *eastern question following the Russo-Turkish War (1877-78). Bulgarian autonomy was recognized, and Montenegro, Romania, and Serbia were acknowledged as independent principalities. Britain gained Cyprus, and Lord Beaconsfield, the British delegate, returned home announcing his achievement of "peace with honour" (a phrase later adopted by Neville Chamberlain to describe the *Munich agreement).

Berlin airlift (1948-49). An operation by Britain, France, and the USA to counter a Russian blockade of West Berlin by supplying the city by air. Moves by the western powers to create a West German federal government in their occupation zones, coupled with currency reform (the introduction of a new German *Mark), led the Soviet Union (June 1948) to cut road and rail links between western Germany and the allied zones of Berlin. The allies responded by flying in 1.6 million tonnes of supplies in the 11 months until the blockade was lifted (May 1949) and by counterembargoing strategic goods for the eastern bloc.

Berlin conference (1884-85). A meeting of the representatives of all the European nations, the USA, and Turkey, called by the German chancellor Bismarck to decide the status of the Congo and Niger river basins. Agreements reached formed an important stage in the partition of *Africa. Britain recognized Germany's claims to the Cameroons (and to New Guinea) and in return won the support of Bismarck against the competition of the French in Nigeria.

Bermuda. A British crown colony in the western north Atlantic. Named after its Spanish discoverer, Juan Bermudez, Bermuda was settled by English people in the 17th century and soon had a large Black slave population. Internal self-government was granted by a new constitution in 1968, but demands for independence subsequently increased, and in 1977 the British governor Sir Richard Sharples was assassinated.

Bernard (d. 1148). Bishop of St David's from 1115. A Norman, he reformed the organization of the diocese but, despite swearing an oath of obedience to the archbishop of Canterbury, sought unsuccessfully to establish St David's as a metropolitan see independent of Canterbury.

Bernicia. One of the two divisions of the Anglo-Saxon kingdom of Northumbria. Its northern boundary was the Firth of Forth, its southern either the rivers Tyne or Tees. The kingdom was established by *Ida, who settled at *Bamburgh in 547 and founded a dynasty that reigned, either in Bernicia or in a united Northumbria, for most of the 6th century.

Berwick, treaty of. 1. (3 Oct 1357) The treaty by which Edward III of England released David II of Scotland from captivity, which lasted 11 years, in return for a ransom of 100,000 marks, which was never fully paid. **2.** (27 Feb 1560) A treaty between the English and the Scottish lords of the *Congregation, by which the English agreed to send the Scots military aid to help them preserve their "old freedom and liberty"; the

English were intervening to help the Protestant lords overthrow the Roman Catholic regent Mary of Guise. 3. (18 June 1639) The treaty that ended the first *Bishops' War between Charles I and the covenanters. It failed to provide the basis for a permanent settlement as it satisfied neither party and there was disagreement as to the exact nature of some verbal promises the king had made in addition to the written agreement.

Bessemer, Sir Henry (1813-98). Inventor and engineer, who introduced the Bessemer process of steelmaking in 1855. The process converted pig iron into steel by using a blast of air to remove impurities. It inaugurated the era of cheap steel. Bessemer founded (1859) his own steelworks at Sheffield and was knighted in 1879. His many other inventions include a pioneer typesetting machine.

Bess of Hardwick. See Shrewsbury, Elizabeth Talbot, countess of.

Bevan, Aneurin (1897-1960). An MP from 1929 to 1960, who as health minister under *Attlee (1945-51) established the *National Health Service. Leader of the Labour Left and a noted orator, he resigned from office in 1951 in protest against cuts in spending on social services. He ultimately cooperated with Gaitskell, after being defeated by him in the contest for the party leadership (1955).

Beveridge, William Henry Beveridge, 1st Baron (1879-1963). Economist and social reformer; director of the London School of Economics (1919-37). An expert on unemployment problems, he was chairman of a committee appointed by the World War II coalition government to review social insurance schemes (1941-42). Its report (1942), generally known as the Beveridge report, proposed a comprehensive *national insurance scheme that formed the basis of postwar legislation. Beveridge, a Liberal MP (1944-45), was created a baron in 1946.

Bevin, Ernest (1881-1951). Trade unionist and Labour MP. General secretary of the Transport and General Workers'

Union (1921-40), which he helped form, Bevin then became an MP and was the wartime minister of labour (1940-45). As foreign secretary under *Attlee (1945-51), he helped implement the *Marshall plan and create the *North Atlantic Treaty Organization.

Bible. The earliest surviving renderings in English of passages of the Bible are by the Anglo-Saxon homilist *Aelfric (c. 955-c. 1010). Two complete Middle English versions from the Vulgate were originated (c. 1375-96) by the *Lollards. At the Reformation the revival of scholarship and the Protestant emphasis on individual religious exercises stimulated vernacular translations. William *Tyndale translated the New Testament (published 1525) from Greek and the Pentateuch (the first five books of the Old Testament) from Hebrew. Miles *Coverdale's Bible (1535), based chiefly on the Vulgate and Tyndale, was the first complete English Bible. The Bible that appeared in 1537 under the name of Thomas Matthew (the pseudonym probably of John Rogers) was licensed for general reading by Henry VIII and formed the basis for Coverdale's Great Bible (1539), also called the Treacle Bible (from its rendering of Jeremiah 8.22). The 1540 edition of the Great Bible contained a preface by *Cranmer, after whom it is sometimes named. In 1560 English refugees from the Marian persecutions produced the Geneva Bible (so called from its place of publication), or Breeches Bible (from its translation of Genesis 3.7), which had marginal glosses that recommended it to the Puritans. From 1571 to 1611 the Bishops' Bible (1568), a translation instigated by the anti-Puritan Archbishop *Parker, was the official version. Meanwhile, Cardinal *Allen initiated, for Roman Catholics, the translation known as the Reim-Douai Bible. The *Hampton Court conference (1604) commissioned the *Authorized (or King James) Version of the Bible (1611), which quickly became the standard English Bible. The Revised Version (New Testament, 1881; Old Testament,

1885) incorporated numerous textual improvements, but its departures from the familiar prose of the Authorized Version earned it a hostile reception. The New English Bible (completed 1970) attempts to combine the best modern international scholarship with a contemporary idiom.

Parts of the Bible were translated into Welsh in the middle ages. In 1563 an act ordered that the translation of the Bible and Book of Common Prayer was to be completed by 1567, the work being entrusted to the bishops of Wales and the bishop of Hereford. Only the New Testament appeared in that year, translated principally by William *Salesbury and Bishop Richard *Davies, and it was William Morgan (d. 1604) who completed the task (1588). A revised edition by John *Davies appeared in 1620, followed by the five-shilling edition in 1630. Of many subsequent editions, Peter Williams' (1770) is outstanding, its excellence of style making the Bible the most valued achievement of the Welsh language.

billeting, forced. The compulsory quartering of military or naval personnel on private households. The abuse of the practice under Charles I led to its specific condemnation in the *Petition of Right (1628). It was again declared illegal in 1679 but was practised under both Charles II and James II. Condemned again in the *Bill of Rights (1689), billeting on innkeepers was subsequently allowed by successive *Mutiny Acts.

Bill of Rights (Oct 1689). The constitutional outcome of the Glorious Revolution of 1688-89. Incorporating the *Declaration of Rights, it condemned the reign of James II and justified the offer of the throne to William of Orange and Mary. The bill attacked James for attempting to subvert the Protestant religion and the fundamental laws of the realm. It denounced him for using *suspending and *dispensing powers, levying money without parliamentary consent, and maintaining a standing army in peacetime. The Bill of Rights placed few restrictions on the

new monarchs' powers and prerogatives. It laid down the principles of parliamentary supremacy, requesting free elections, frequent parliaments, and freedom of speech within parliament. The bill declared William and Mary king and queen and excluded any Roman Catholic from the succession.

Birkbeck, George (1776-1841). Pioneer of adult education. Birkbeck instituted science lectures at low fees for "mechanics"—the industrial revolution's new skilled workmen—in Glasgow (1800). He founded the London Mechanics' Institution (now Birkbeck College in the University of London) in 1824. "Mechanics' institutes" were subsequently established throughout industrial Britain.

Birkenhead, 1st earl of. See Smith, F(rederick) E(dwin).

birth control. The prevention of conception. Birth control, or family planning, has been practised since antiquity but only formally discussed since the late 18th century, when *Malthus expressed fears for the effects of increases in population. Bentham and Place were among the earliest advocates of contraception techniques, rather than sexual abstinence, as a means of controlling the number of births, but the subject remained generally taboo for most of the 19th century. In 1877 Charles *Bradlaugh and Annie Besant (1847-1933) were prosecuted for republishing The Fruits of Philosophy (1832), an account of methods of birth control, by an American Charles Knowlton. However, the wider practise of contraception is thought partly to account for the marked fall in birth rates towards 1900. In 1921 Marie *Stopes opened the first family-planning clinic, and birth control subsequently became widespread. Contraception relied chiefly on the condom and diaphragm until the introduction of oral contraception (the Pill) in 1960.

Bishops' Wars (1639-40). Hostilities between the English and Scots, provoked by the attempts of Charles I to impose Anglicanism on Scotland. The immediate cause of hostilities was the attempted introduction of the English prayer book to Scotland, to which the National Assembly responded by abolishing · episcopacy. The so-called first Bishops' War went no further than a meeting outside Berwick of the opposing forces, after which peace was made (*see* Berwick, treaty of). Charles refused, however, to accept the abolition of episcopacy in Scotland and summoned the *Short Parliament to obtain supplies for a resumption of war. Refused assistance, he secured aid from the Irish parliament, and war was resumed (1640) at the initiative of *Strafford. The Scots invaded England, routing the royal army near Newcastle. The treaty of *Ripon ended the conflict, and Charles was forced to summon parliament again (*see* Long Parliament).

Black Book of the Household. A record of the management of the *royal household. Commissioned by Edward IV as part of his reorganization of the household, the Black Book was compiled in 1471-72. Modelling their system on Edward III's methods, the authors detail expenditure appropriate to the various ranks of the peerage. For the royal household they advocated outward splendour combined with efficient economy behind the scenes.

black death. An outbreak of bubonic *plague, originating in China, that affected the whole of Europe, reaching England in 1348. Further outbreaks in successive decades reduced the overall population by an estimated one-third, resulting in severe labour shortages. Government attempts to reverse the consequent rise in wages (*see* Labourers, Statute of) provoked resentment that was one of the causes of the *peasants' revolt. *See also* great plague.

black hole of Calcutta. A guard room, 5.5 m (18 ft) by 4.5 m (15 ft), in which 146 British soldiers were said to have been confined over the night of 20-21 June 1756. Their commander John Holwell (1711-98) alleged that only 25 men survived. The atrocity was perpetrated by Siraj-ud-Dawlah, nawab of Bengal, who had attacked the British

garrison in protest against the fortification of Calcutta by the East India Company.

Black Rod, Gentleman Usher of the. An officer of the House of Lords. Instituted in 1350, the Black Rod's duties include summoning the Commons to the Lords to hear a speech from the throne. He is required to knock three times at the door of the Commons with his staff of office, an ebony stick—the Black Rod, to gain admittance. This ceremony symbolizes the right of the Commons to freedom from interference.

Blackstone, Sir William (1723-80). Jurist. Blackstone published the immensely influential *Commentaries on the Laws of England* (four vols, 1765-69), the first clear overall description of English law. It was attacked by Jeremy *Bentham, who accused Blackstone of being opposed to legal reform. He was an MP (1761-70) and then a judge of the Court of Common Pleas.

black week (10-15 Dec 1899). A period during the second Boer War when the Afrikaners inflicted three major defeats on the British. These were at Stormberg (10 Dec), at Magersfontein (11 Dec), and at Colenso (15 Dec), where *Botha defeated *Buller. Nearly 3000 British troops were killed. Black week aroused alarm in Britain and forced the government to send more troops to South Africa.

Blake, Robert (1599-1657). Admiral. He was appointed general at sea in 1649 and led the English fleet against the Dutch (1652-54) and against the Spanish (1656-57). His articles of war and fighting instructions represented fundamental reforms, which helped to lay the foundations of England's maritime supremacy.

Blake, William (1757-1827). Poet, painter, engraver, and mystic. He produced a series of his own poems, hand engraved and illustrated, including *Songs of Innocence* (1789) and *Songs of Experience* (1794). His later works, which possess a strong visionary quality include *The Book of Job* (1820-26).

Blanketeers, march of the (March 1817). An attempt by Manchester spinners and weavers—called blanketeers because many carried blankets—to march to London to petition the prince regent over economic and political grievances. The march was halted by troops and the leaders imprisoned.

Blenheim, battle of (13 Aug 1704). A battle of the War of the Spanish Succession, a major victory for the duke of Marlborough and Eugene of Savoy. The battle took place at Blenheim (German name: Blindheim), Bavaria, on the Danube. Over 50 000 combined English and Austrian troops and, under Camille, comte de Tallard, 60 000 French and Bavarian troops were involved. The French were unprepared for the allied attack, which broke through Tallard's centre. Over half the Franco-Bavarian troops were captured, wounded, or killed, and Tallard was taken prisoner. Vienna was saved from the French and Bavaria withdrew from the war. *Blenheim palace in Oxfordshire was built after the battle as a national gift to the duke of Marlborough.

Blenheim palace. A palace at Woodstock, Oxfordshire. Blenheim was built at the expense partly of the nation to commemorate the victories of the duke of Marlborough against Louis XIV. It was designed by John *Vanbrugh and Nicholas *Hawksmoor and begun in 1705. Its size, the sumptuousness of the decoration, and complexity of design make it one of the masterpieces of baroque architecture. Capability *Brown redesigned the gardens later in the century, on the lines of the arrangement of forces at the battle of Blenheim.

Blitz. *See* Britain, battle of.

blockade. The positioning of land, sea, or air forces to prevent access to an enemy's city, coastline, etc. Prior to World War I a blockade was legal in international law only if it was declared in advance and effectively maintained. Blockades were regularly employed by the Royal Navy from 1747, especially against France in the *French

Revolutionary and Napoleonic Wars (1792-1815). Since World War I legislation has been adapted to legalize the long-range blockades that are maintained by submarines and aircraft.

Bloemfontein convention (23 Feb 1854). A treaty revoking British sovereignty over the Orange River Territory in south Africa. The Territory then became the *Orange Free State.

Blood, Colonel Thomas (?1618-1680). Irish adventurer. In 1663 he attempted to capture Dublin castle and seize the lord lieutenant. The plot was betrayed and Blood fled in disguise to Holland. On his return he conspired unsuccessfully to assassinate James Butler, duke of *Ormonde (1670), and in the following year attempted to steal the crown jewels from the Tower. He was subsequently pardoned by Charles II and his Irish estates were restored to him.

bloody assizes (Sept 1685). The circuit of the west country after the duke of *Monmouth's rebellion in 1685. The assizes were led by the lord chief justice *Jeffreys, who dealt mercilessly with anyone implicated in the abortive rebellion. Some 320 alleged rebels were sentenced to death. In most cases the victims were hung, drawn, and quartered. A further 800 prisoners were transported. In recognition of his "many eminent and faithful services" James II made Jeffreys lord chancellor.

Bloody Sunday (13 Nov 1887). The day on which a radical meeting in Trafalgar Square was dispersed by the police, with over a hundred casualties. The meeting was organized by the Social Democratic Federation to demand the release of the Irish MP William *O'Brien. Its outcome greatly embittered relations between the authorities and the labour movement.

Boadicea. *See* Boudicca.

Bodley, Sir Thomas (1545-1613). Diplomat and scholar, who refounded the university library at Oxford. Named the Bodleian in his honour, the library was opened in 1602. Bodley served as ambassador to the Netherlands (1589-96).

Boer Wars. The wars between Britain and the Afrikaners (or Boers) of South Africa. In the first Boer War (1880–81) the Transvaal under Kruger rebelled against the British government and won a convincing victory at *Majuba Hill (1881). By the *Pretoria convention Britain recognized the Transvaal's independence.

The second war (1899–1902) was sparked off by the *Jameson raid. Tension was high on the Witwatersrand in the Transvaal, where the predominantly British uitlanders (foreigners) who mined the gold were denied political rights. In 1899 the Boers moved against the British in Natal and the Northern Cape. They besieged *Ladysmith, *Kimberley, and *Mafeking, and *black week in Dec saw major British defeats. After the Boer victory at Spion Kop (Jan 1900), the British moved more troops in under Lords *Roberts and *Kitchener. The besieged towns were relieved and the British took Bloemfontein, Johannesburg, and Pretoria by June. However, the war was not yet over. Using guerrilla tactics on the terrain they knew so well the Boers inflicted further losses on the British. Kitchener's response was a scorched-earth policy and the Boer women and children were rounded up and put into concentration camps, where many died. The Boers were finally forced to seek peace in 1902 (see Vereeniging, peace of).

Bolingbroke, Henry St John, 1st Viscount (1678–1751). Brilliant orator and Tory politician, who served as secretary of state (1710–14). He took a leading part in the negotiation (1711–13) of the treaties of *Utrecht. His Jacobite links made him unacceptable to George I, and after the new king dismissed him from office he went into exile and was attainted. He was pardoned in 1725 and returned to Britain, where he was prominent in the opposition to Walpole's government. He expounded the Tory political philosophy in his writings, and his *Idea of a Patriot King* (1749) was once thought to have influenced George III (see patriot king).

Boniface, St (680–755). The apostle to the Saxons in Germany. Born in Crediton, his original name was Winfrith. At Rome in 718 he gained the support of Pope Gregory II, who gave him the name Boniface and sent him to convert the Saxons. He built monasteries and organized the church, winning many converts. He suffered martyrdom at Dokkum in 755.

Book of Common Prayer. The liturgy of the Church of England. Both the first prayer book (1549) and the second (1552) of Edward VI are substantially the work of *Cranmer. The first replaced Latin services with English, and in doctrine and ritual constituted a compromise between reformers and traditionalists, pleasing neither. The second more Protestant prayer book revised the Holy Communion office, ordered that the surplice rather than other vestments be worn, and removed all references to the Mass and altar. In 1559 Elizabeth I's Act of *Uniformity enforced use of the 1552 prayer book, with minor modifications.

Book of Kells (8th century). A manuscript copy of the Gospels in Latin, written at the monastery of Kells in Meath, Ireland. It is regarded as one of the five greatest illuminated manuscripts of its time and is now in Trinity College Library, Dublin.

Booth, William (1829–1912). Founder of the *Salvation Army. A Methodist minister, Booth, with his wife Catherine (1829–90), founded a "Christian Mission" in Whitechapel, London, in 1865. Spreading to other cities, the movement was reorganized (1878) as the Salvation Army, Booth becoming its "general".

Booth's rising (Aug 1659). A royalist revolt, led by Sir George Booth (later 1st Baron Delamere; 1622–84), against the Protectorate government. In May 1659 Booth joined Presbyterian royalists, who were planning a number of uprisings throughout England. He took Chester on 19 Aug but was defeated at Nantwich

Bridge by Gen. Lambert and imprisoned in the Tower. Booth's rising and the other revolts of 1659, although unsuccessful, heralded the Restoration in 1660.

Border, the. The dividing line between England and Scotland. By the 11th century the Scots had succeeded in extending their authority over what is now Scotland south of the Forth, but their further claims to Cumberland, Westmorland, and Northumberland led to frequent disputes with England until 1237. Then, by the treaty of *York, Alexander II abandoned claims to these areas and the Border was settled on roughly the present line from Berwick-upon-Tweed to the Solway Firth. Berwick-upon-Tweed, however, did not finally pass into English hands until 1482. The frequent warfare between the kingdoms, political sensitivity even in peacetime, and isolation caused by bad communications combined to make the Border region turbulent and lawless until after the union of the crowns in 1603. *See also* Anglo-Scottish wars; Wardens of the Marches.

Borneo. The third largest island in the world, southeast of the Malay peninsula. The British occupied the north of Borneo in the 1840s and acquired the states of *Sarawak, *Brunei, and *North Borneo. The remaining two-thirds of Borneo is Indonesian.

borough. A town granted legal liberties and privileges by charter and, subsequently, represented in parliament. Boroughs derive from the Anglo-Saxon *burhs (settlements designated by the Wessex kings as defensive centres against the Vikings), many of which later developed as markets. By the 12th century the sovereign and tenants in chief were granting (for a price) charters of liberties to towns under their control that conceded varying rights of self-government, legal autonomy, and tenurial privileges. In the late middle ages boroughs came to be those towns that were represented in parliament and incorporated (i.e. given corporate status to issue by-laws, possess a common seal, and hold lands communally). They were governed by municipal corporations, the membership of which was regulated by the *Municipal Corporations Act. (1835). Boroughs outside Greater London were abolished by the Local Government Act (1972), but the status may still be conferred by royal charter on a district. The Scottish equivalent of a borough is termed a burgh.

Boroughbridge, battle of (16 March 1322). An engagement during the reign of Edward II. The defeat (and subsequent execution) of Thomas, earl of Lancaster, leader of the rebellious barons (*see* ordainers, lords) inaugurated a brief period of royal freedom from baronial control.

Boston massacre (1770). A confrontation between British troops and a crowd in Boston, Massachusetts. The troops were provoked into opening fire and five colonists died. *See also* American Revolution.

Boston tea party (16 Dec 1773). The destruction of imported tea in the harbour at Boston, Massachusetts, in protest against the Tea Act, which enforced the import of cheap tea to relieve the East India Company of surplus stocks. Disguised as Indians, a gang of about 50 men boarded East India Company ships, emptying some 300 chests of tea into the water. The incident provoked the retaliatory *Intolerable Acts.

Boswell, James (1740-95). Scottish lawyer, diarist, and biographer of Samuel *Johnson. Boswell met Johnson in London in 1763 and began his *Life of Johnson* (1791) after Johnson's death in 1784. Boswell's richly detailed diaries and papers were not discovered until the 1920s.

Bosworth Field, battle of (22 Aug 1485). The battle that ended the Wars of the Roses. Henry Tudor landed at Milford Haven in Wales and advanced to meet Richard III at Bosworth Field in Leicestershire. The treason of the Stanley family after the battle had begun hastened the defeat of Richard, who was killed by the Stanleys' men. He was the first English king to die in battle since

1066. Following his victory, Henry was crowned King Henry VII—the first Tudor monarch.

Botany Bay. An inlet of the coast of New South Wales, Australia, south of Sydney Harbour. It was discovered by Capt. Cook in 1770. The British government planned to establish a convict colony here, but Arthur Phillip (1738–1814), commanding the first fleet of convict ships, realized the potentialities of the magnificent harbour just to the north (which Cook missed), and there founded Sydney, the first British settlement in Australia (1788). See also transportation.

Botha, Louis (1862–1919). South African soldier and statesman. Commander in chief (1900–02) during the second *Boer War, he represented the Boers at the peace negotiations at Vereeniging. In 1907, when the Transvaal became self-governing, he formed its government, and in 1910 he became the first prime minister of the Union of *South Africa. He organized the capture of German southwest Africa in World War I and attended the Paris peace conference (1919).

Bothwell, Francis Stewart, 5th earl of (?1563–1611). One of the most active and inconsistent of the nobles whose turbulence troubled James VI; nephew of the 4th earl. His career of treason and conspiracy, mainly in cooperation with extreme Protestant interests but sometimes allied to Roman Catholics, culminated after 1590 in a series of violent attempts to seize the king. His title was forfeited in 1592, and he was forced to flee abroad in 1595. He died in Italy.

Bothwell, James Hepburn, 4th earl of (c. 1535–1578). Third husband of *Mary Queen of Scots. A Protestant, Bothwell nevertheless opposed alliance with England in 1559–60 and suffered imprisonment and exile in 1561–65. By 1565 he had won the favour of the queen and in 1567 was involved in the murder of her second husband, Lord Darnley, evidently hoping to marry her. Very soon after the murder Bothwell divorced his wife and married Mary. He was

created duke of Orkney. After the encounter at *Carberry Hill he fled first to Orkney, then to Denmark, where he was imprisoned until his death. See also casket letters.

Bothwell Bridge, battle of (22 June 1679). The battle in which the rebel covenanters of southwest Scotland were defeated by 10 000 men under the duke of Monmouth. Of about 4000 rebels perhaps 200 to 400 were killed and 1200 captured.

Botswana. See Bechuanaland.

Boudicca (or Boadicea) (d. 62). Queen of the *Iceni, who led a revolt against the Romans (61). Prasutagas, her husband, left his kingdom jointly to his daughters and the emperor, but this did not prevent Roman agents from seizing the kingdom, assaulting Boudicca, and raping her daughters after the death of Prasutagas. Boudicca then led the Iceni in rebellion against Roman rule, while the governor Paulinus was campaigning in Wales. The Iceni sacked Colchester, St Albans, and London, causing heavy Roman casualties. Paulinus returned from Wales and defeated Boudicca, who then committed suicide.

Boulton, Matthew (1728–1809). Birmingham coin and hardware manufacturer, who greatly stimulated industrial innovation. Moving to the Soho works outside Birmingham in 1762, he worked with James *Watt on the development of the steam engine. His employee William *Murdock pioneered gas lighting, and his firm supplied the Royal Mint with improved coin-making machinery.

Bounty, mutiny on the (1789). A mutiny aboard HMS *Bounty*, sailing from Tahiti and commanded by Lieut. William Bligh (1754–1817). Bligh was cast off with 18 men in a small boat, which he navigated some 5760 km (3600 mi) to Timor. The mutineers returned to Tahiti and some settled on the tiny island of *Pitcairn. Ten mutineers were eventually court-martialled (1792) and three hanged.

Bouvines, battle of (27 July 1214). A battle in which the French king Philip II Augustus decisively defeated the combined forces of the emperor Otto IV, the count of Flanders, and King John of England, near Bouvines in North France. It confirmed Philip's acquisition of England's Angevin possessions.

Bow Street Runners. The first organized *police force in London. It was established by the writer Henry Fielding, who was chief magistrate at Bow Street (1748). In 1757 the Bow Street Runners were empowered to serve outside the City. The foot patrols became part of the newly formed Metropolitan Police in 1829; the horse patrols were abolished in 1839.

Boxer rising (1899). A nationalist reaction in China against the intrusion of European powers. Attacks by the Boxers (members of the secret Society of Harmonious Fists) upon churches and Chinese Christians were followed by the siege of foreign legations in Peking. The European powers, with the assistance of Japan and the USA, suppressed the rebellion and strengthened their hold upon the Chinese government.

boycott. Social and commercial ostracism. The term originated in 1880, during the Irish land agitation, when tenants protesting against evictions ostracized Lord Erne's estate manager in Mayo, Capt. Charles Boycott (1832-97). Parnell immediately advocated the same tactics against others who evicted tenants or who took over their land. Boycott, unable to buy or sell any goods, was eventually forced to leave Ireland.

Boyle, Richard, 1st earl of Cork (1566-1643). Anglo-Irish magnate. Born in England, he arrived in Dublin in 1588. By a judicious marriage and by a combination of daring, efficiency, and dishonesty he made himself the wealthiest landowner in southwest Ireland. He was created earl of Cork in 1620 and became lord high treasurer in 1631. During the 1630s he lost royal favour because of his intrigues against Wentworth (later earl of *Strafford), but took his revenge by giving evidence against Wentworth at his impeachment. In 1642 he successfully suppressed the rebellion in his territories.

Boyle, Robert (1627-91). Physicist, who formulated Boyle's law, that the volume of a gas varies inversely with the pressure of its unit mass. His book, *The Skeptical Chymist* (1661), proposed a theory of matter as composed of irreducible elements and demolished the traditional Aristotelian view of the four elements.

Boyne, battle of the (1 July 1690). The battle that established William III's control over Ireland. In 1690 William invaded Ireland, where the former King James II had gathered support, and defeated James at the river Boyne, north of Dublin. It was not an overwhelming victory because the Jacobite army, although forced to retreat southwards, escaped almost intact. However, James fled to France and William was able to take Dublin. The Boyne and the subsequent battle of *Aughrim are still celebrated by *Ulster Unionists on 12 July, the old style date of the Boyne and the new style date of Aughrim (*see* calendar).

Bracton (or **Bratton**, or **Bretton**), **Henry de** (d. 1268). Judge. His greatest work was *On the Laws and Customs of England* (written 1235-59), the first systematic discussion of the subject. He also compiled a collection of over 2000 legal cases, which he annotated.

Braddock, Edward (1695-1755). Soldier. In 1754 Braddock was appointed commander in chief in North America, charged with driving the French from their recently acquired American territories. His forces were ambushed and defeated at Fort Duquesne (1755), and Braddock himself was mortally wounded.

Bradlaugh, Charles (1833-91). Radical political and social propagandist. A republican and atheist, Bradlaugh possessed a flair for publicity that ultimately advanced several of his causes. Notable among his achievements was the right to affirm instead of swear religious oaths in parliament and the law courts, obtained through his struggle (1880-86) to take his seat as an MP without swearing the parliamentary oath. He was also an advocate of *birth control.

Bramham Moor, battle of (19 Feb 1408). The battle, near Tadcaster in Yorkshire, in which the rebellions of the *Percys against Henry IV were finally defeated. Henry Percy, 1st earl of Northumberland, was killed.

Brandon, Charles, 1st duke of Suffolk (1484-1545). Soldier. He was made duke of Suffolk (1514) following his bravery in the 1513 French campaign. Sent to Paris (1515) to arrange the marriage of Henry VIII's sister Mary to Francis I of France, he secretly married her himself, incurring Henry's temporary anger. Brandon was the grandfather of Lady Jane *Grey.

Braose, William de (d. 1211). A supporter of King John, who rewarded him with great estates in Wales. De Braose failed to pay his dues despite frequent demands from the king. He was outlawed in 1210 and died in France.

Bray, Vicar of. The vicar of the village of Bray in Berkshire who is the subject of an anonymous English ballad. He is supposed to have maintained his living during the period of religious changes from 1660 to 1714 by changing his principles to accord with those of the government. Other sources suggest that he lived in the 16th century, during the period of the Reformation and the Marian reaction.

Breda, Declaration of (4 Apr 1660). The declaration in which Charles II made the concessions that smoothed the way for his restoration. Charles offered a free and general pardon (with certain exceptions) to those who had acted against the crown during the Civil War and Interregnum. He confirmed all sales of royalist lands made in the same period. Furthermore, he promised swift payment of the army's arrears, and a measure of religious liberty to tender consciences. All the clauses were subject to ratification by parliament.

Brétigny, treaty of (1360). A treaty between England and France, which brought peace for nine years during the *Hundred Years' War. Edward III received full sovereignty over Gascony,

Calais, and Ponthieu. King John of France was to be ransomed for £500,000, and was released after payment of a first instalment, and Edward was to give up his claim to the French throne, a renunciation he never formally made.

bretwalda. The title of the ruler who achieved military predominance over the *heptarchy between the 5th and 9th centuries. It derived from *Bretenanwealda*, meaning lord of Britain. Subject kings owed him tribute, suit of court, and military service. They were also required to seek his permission to grant land.

Brian Boru (?926-1014). High king of Ireland (1002-1014); younger son of Cennedig, ruler of Dal Cais in Munster. After defeating the Danes of Limerick and the Eoganachta of Munster he gradually extended his authority over southern Ireland (Munster and Leinster). As high king he exercised effective jurisdiction over nearly all Ireland, the last to do so. After his forces had decisively defeated the Danes at *Clontarf, the ailing king was murdered in his tent by fleeing Danes.

Bridgewater canal. The first entirely man-made *canal in Britain, constructed by James *Brindley for Francis Egerton, 3rd duke of Bridgewater (1736-1803) to link his coalmine at Worsley with Manchester, 16 km (10 mi) away. Opened in 1761, the canal cut the price of coal in Manchester by half. It was extended from Manchester to Liverpool in 1776.

Brigantes. The largest British tribe at the Roman conquest, which took its name from the Celtic goddess Brigantia. The Brigantes' chief town was Aldbrough and their coins have been found throughout Yorkshire. Their early contacts with the Romans were friendly but after internal dissension *Agricola annexed their territory (79-81).

Bright, John (1811-89). Liberal politician, orator, free trader, and franchise reformer. A Quaker and Lancashire cotton-mill owner, and an MP from 1843, he was Cobden's lieutenant in the

*Anti-Corn Law League, and generally opposed factory legislation on *laissez-faire* grounds. Bright's campaign to extend the franchise, culminating (1866) in vast public meetings, helped bring about Disraeli's 1867 Reform Act. As a cabinet minister under Gladstone (1868-70, 1873-74, 1880-82), Bright, although opposing home rule, helped formulate Irish land reform.

Brindley, James (1716-72). Pioneer *canal builder, who was one of the outstanding innovators of the industrial revolution. Brindley, who began his career as a millwright and was a self-taught engineer, was chosen by the duke of Bridgewater to build the *Bridgewater canal, completed in 1761. An eccentric, who retired to bed to consider engineering problems and made no written calculations or drawings, Brindley built or designed 575 km (360 mi) of canal. His relatively primitive methods included following the contours of the land.

Bristol. A city and the county town of Avon. A cathedral and university city, Bristol has derived its prosperity chiefly from its port. It is first known to have been inhabited in the 10th century, and it received its first charter in 1155. In 1353, by virtue of its trade in wine and wool, it was made a *staple town, and in 1373 it became a county, a status that it lost in 1974 following local government reorganization. In 1497 John Cabot sailed from Bristol on his voyage of discovery to North America, in the colonization of which many natives of Bristol subsequently took part. In the Civil War it was taken by royalists under Prince Rupert in 1643 and by parliamentary forces in 1645, after a siege directed by Fairfax. In the 17th and 18th centuries the maritime trade through Bristol was mainly in slaves from West Africa bound for the West Indies and in cocoa, tobacco, and sugar. Brunel's ships, the *Great Western* and the *Great Britain*, were launched here in 1838 and 1843.

Britain. The country was so named by Julius Caesar, who mistakenly believed that his predecessors, the Belgic invaders of Britain, were Britanni. Earlier Greek travellers had called it the Pretanic Islands, perhaps because its inhabitants were named Pretani. *See also* Lower Britain; Upper Britain.

Britain, battle of (10 July-31 Oct 1940). A prolonged engagement between British and German air forces that effectively frustrated the planned German invasion of Britain. Hitler's invasion plans demanded, as a preliminary, elimination of British air superiority and massive air bombardment of cities. German bombers attacked RAF fighter-command air bases in southeast England but, when close to success, switched their assault (7 Sept) to London (the so-called Blitz). The tactical superiority of RAF fighter command, under *Dowding, resulted in heavy German losses (1733 German aircraft as against 915 British). On 17 Sept, the invasion was postponed, and on 12 Oct abandoned for the winter.

British Academy. An institution, formed in 1901 and incorporated in 1902, to promote "historical, philosophical, and philological studies". Its membership is limited to 350 Fellows, elected for their distinction in one of the fields of study encouraged by the Academy. Its counterpart for the sciences is the *Royal Society.

British Broadcasting Corporation (BBC). A public service organization, established under royal charter in 1927. The BBC succeeded the British Broadcasting Company, founded by radio manufacturers in 1922. It received a broadcasting monopoly, financed by the licence fees of set owners, overseas broadcasting being government-financed, and opened the world's first television service in 1936. Its first director general was John (later Lord) *Reith. The BBC's monopoly ended in the early 1950s with the introduction of commercial television (and subsequently radio), now under the Independent Broadcasting Authority.

British Columbia. A province of western Canada. The region was claimed for Britain by Capt. Cook in 1778, explored by George *Vancouver in the 1790s, and was subsequently contested by the Northwest Company and *Hudson's Bay Company, which were united in 1821. In 1858 it became a crown colony and in 1871 part of the Canadian Confederation.

British Council. An organization, established in 1934 and incorporated in 1940, to promote abroad a wider knowledge of Britain and its culture and language. Financed by government grants, its main activities are the teaching of English abroad, the development of science teaching and new educational methods, and the maintenance of libraries and information centres.

British Empire. British possessions overseas, acquired for commercial, territorial, or strategic reasons (see imperialism), which ultimately covered a quarter of the world. Colonization began in the early 17th century in North America, in Virginia, Maryland, and New England. In *Canada rivalry with France was resolved in Britain's favour in the Seven Years' War (1756-63), but the 13 American colonies were lost with their attainment of independence as a result of the *American Revolution (1775-83). In India the *East India Company flourished from the 17th century, and here also Britain emerged victorious over its French rivals during the Seven Years' War. Britain's territorial gains in the Napoleonic Wars (1803-15) included *Trinidad, *Tobago, and *St Lucia in the West Indies, *Mauritius, *Ceylon, and the *Cape of Good Hope. The 19th century witnessed the European scramble for *Africa, in which Britain's first settlement had been on James Island in the Gambia river (1661). Following American independence newly discovered *Australia provided a location for transported convicts. *New Zealand came under British control in 1840. *Hong Kong was acquired in 1841 and *Burma in 1886. The *Colonial Office was responsible for the colonies, most of which became self-governing. In the mid-19th century responsible government was granted to Canada, Australia, New Zealand, and South Africa, which

subsequently became *dominions (compare crown colony). Regular *imperial conferences were held from 1907, and in 1931 the British Empire gave way to the association of equal partners called the *Commonwealth.

British Expeditionary Force (BEF). Initially, the one cavalry and six infantry regiments of regular soldiers (with supporting troops) who were sent to France at the beginning of World War I (1914). They were known as the "Old Contemptibles", and suffered very heavy casualties. The BEF later totalled six armies. It again served in France and Belgium at the beginning of World War II (1939-40) and was compelled to withdraw from the Belgian border by the victorious Germans. Ten of its divisions and one tank brigade were successfully evacuated from *Dunkirk, two divisions were evacuated from Brittany; the 51st Highland Division was captured near Le Havre.

British Guiana. A British colony in South America. Settled by the Dutch West India Company (1616-21), it was taken by Britain in 1814. Renamed Guyana, it gained independence within the *Commonwealth in 1966.

British Honduras. See Belize, Colony of.

British Museum. The principal national museum. It dates from 1753, when parliament voted funds to buy and house the scientific collections of Sir Hans Sloane (1660-1753), a former president of the Royal Society, and the Harleian manuscript collection (originated by Robert Harley, earl of Oxford). The museum's vast collections have been built up by purchases with public money, gifts, and as a result of its right (under the Copyright Acts) to receive a copy of every publication issued in Britain. Two historic sections of the British Museum are now no longer part of it. The British Museum (Natural History) became a separate institution in 1963 and the British Museum library became part of the new British Library in 1973.

British South Africa Company. The trading company founded by Cecil

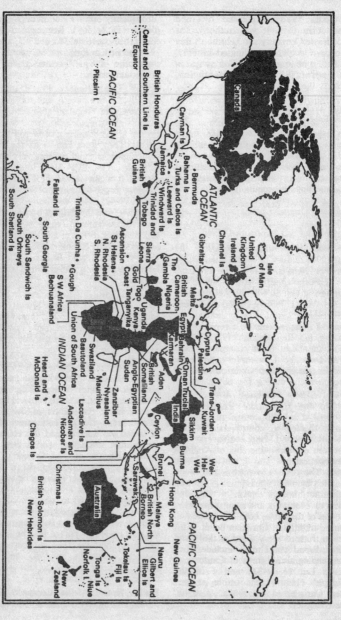

The British Empire in 1920

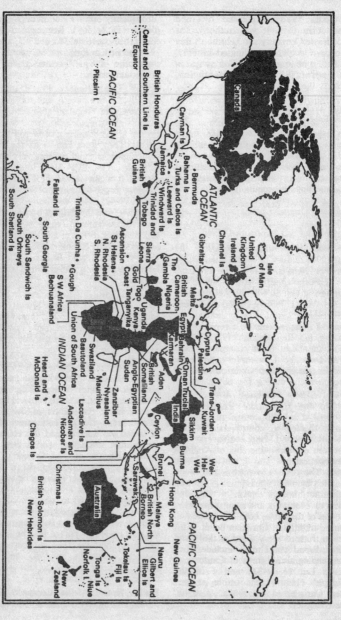

50

Canada

United Kingdom
Ireland

Isle of Man

ATLANTIC OCEAN

Channel Is

Central and Southern Line Is

Equator

PACIFIC OCEAN

Pitcairn I.

British Honduras

Cayman Is

Bahama Is

Bermuda

Turks and Caicos Is

Jamaica

Leeward Is

Windward Is

Trinidad and Tobago

British Guiana

Falkland Is

Tristan Da Cunha

South Georgia

South Sandwich Is

South Orkneys
South Shetland Is

Gibraltar

Malta

Cyprus

Sierra Leone

Gold Coast

Ascension

St Helena

N. Rhodesia

S. Rhodesia

Gough

S W Africa

Bechuanaland

Togo

Nigeria

The Gambia

British Cameroon

Uganda

Kenya

Tanganyika

Basutoland

Union of South Africa

Swaziland

Heard and McDonald Is

Egypt

Bahrain

Palestine

Trans-Jordan

Kuwait

Oman
Trucial

Aden

British Somaliland

Anglo-Egyptian Sudan

Nyasaland

Zanzibar

Mauritius

INDIAN OCEAN

Chagos Is

Sikkim

India

Ceylon

Karmaran

Lacadive Is

Andaman and Nicobar Is

Burma

Wei-Hai-Wei

Sarawak

Malaya

British North Borneo

Brunei

Hong Kong

New Guinea

Nauru

Gilbert and Ellice Is

Christmas I.

British Solomon Is

New Hebrides

Australia

Tokelau Is

Tonga Is

Norfolk I.

Niue

Fiji Is

New Zealand

PACIFIC OCEAN

*Rhodes and incorporated by royal charter in 1889. It was authorized to administer territory in central Africa, where it acquired trading and mining rights from local chiefs. Company rule in Northern Rhodesia lasted until 1924, when the Colonial Office assumed control; in Southern Rhodesia it lasted until 1923, when the White settlers were granted responsible government.

British Union of Fascists (BUF). A political organization founded in Oct 1932 by Sir Oswald *Mosley. The BUF's declared fascism and antisemitism aroused violence at street demonstrations and meetings, especially in the East End of London, but was checked by the Public Order Act (1936). It was banned, under wartime regulations, in May 1940, and Mosley was imprisoned (1940-43).

Britten, Benjamin, Baron (1913-76). Composer and pianist. His works include the operas Peter Grimes (1945) and Death in Venice (1973), the Spring Symphony (1949), and the War Requiem (1962). He founded the Aldeburgh Festival (1948).

broad-bottom administration (Nov 1744-March 1754). The ministry of Henry *Pelham and his brother Thomas, duke of *Newcastle. It was so termed because of the range of political factions it comprised.

broad church movement. A movement within the Church of England that adopted a middle course in the two major theological controversies of the Victorian period. One controversy was between extreme adherents of Anglican *evangelicalism and *Anglo-Catholicism. The other arose from the revulsion felt by many Christians against new scientific thinking, especially *Darwin's ideas on evolution, and against historical studies of the Bible, both of which challenged traditional Christian belief in the literal truth of every word of the Scriptures. Broad churchmen included two outstanding archbishops of Canterbury, A. C. Tait (1869-82) and Frederick Temple (1896-1902). Among others were Christian socialists, such as Charles *Kingsley.

Brougham, Henry Peter Brougham, 1st Baron (1778-1868). Lawyer and Whig MP (1810-12, 1816-30), for his defence of Queen Caroline in 1820. As lord chancellor (1830-33) he played an important part in the debates over the parliamentary reform bill. He contributed to law reform and advocated working-class education and the abolition of slavery. He helped to found University College, London, in 1828. The brougham, a four-wheeled horse-drawn closed carriage, was named after him.

Brown, Lancelot (1715-83). Landscape gardener and architect, the leading designer of the typical 18th-century naturalistic country-house garden (following William *Kent). He acquired the nickname "Capability" Brown from his habit of saying, when asked for advice on redesigning a garden, "I see great capability of improvement here". Among his most notable achievements are the grounds at *Blenheim palace, Oxfordshire.

Browne, Robert (c. 1550-1633). Puritan separatist, whose Brownist movement was a forerunner of the *Congregationalists. His attacks on the established church began in 1580, when he established an independent congregation in Norwich, and in the following year he fled with his followers to Middelburg in Holland. On his return to England (1584) he reconciled himself with the established church and was later ordained (1591). He died in gaol, after being imprisoned for assault. See also Barrow, Henry.

Bruce, Edward (c. 1276-1318). The brother of Robert (I) the Bruce of Scotland, in many of whose campaigns he fought. Edward went to Ireland in 1315 to lead resistance to the English and was crowned high king the following year. He was killed in battle at Dundalk.

Bruce, James (1730-94). Explorer, who, after reaching Ethiopia (1769), became the first European to discover (1770) the source of the Blue Nile (Lake Tana). Earlier, he had travelled widely in North Africa and the Near East, and served as consul in Algiers. His *Travels to Discover the Source of the Nile* (1790) is a classic of exploration.

Bruce, Robert (1210–95). The descendant of a younger brother of William the Lion, who was regarded as heir presumptive to the Scottish throne from 1237 to 1241, while Alexander II was childless. After the death of Alexander III (1286) Bruce took up arms in support of his claim to the throne, and was one of the *competitors in 1290–92. He transferred his claim to his son Robert *Bruce, earl of Carrick, when John de Balliol became king of Scots (1292).

Bruce, Robert, earl of Carrick (1253–1304). Son of Robert *Bruce. Because of his great age the elder Bruce transferred his claim to the Scottish throne to his son in 1292. Carrick's son, also called Robert Bruce, later became King *Robert I of Scotland.

Brummell, George (1778–1840). Dandy, known as "Beau" Brummell. His elegance and style, and friendship with the Prince of Wales (later George IV), enabled him to become virtual dictator of Regency fashion from about 1800. By 1813, however, he had quarrelled with the prince. He fled to France in 1816 to escape from his creditors, dying in an asylum for the insane.

Brunanburgh, battle of (937). A battle at an unknown site in northern England between the forces of Wessex and Mercia under *Athelstan and an allied force of Picts, Scots, Irish Norsemen, and Britons under the kings of Scots and of Strathclyde. Athelstan's victory is celebrated in an Old English poem.

Brunei. An Islamic state in northwest *Borneo. It became a British protectorate in 1888, acquired self-government in 1971 and became independent in 1983.

Brunel, Isambard Kingdom (1806–1859). Engineer, son of Sir Marc *Brunel. He is most famous for three ships—the *Great Western* (1837), the first regularly to cross the Atlantic, the *Great Britain* (1843), and the *Great Eastern* (1858). He also designed the Clifton suspension bridge (completed 1864) and, as chief

engineer to the Great Western Railway (1833–46), pioneered the broad gauge (7 ft) and built more than 1609 km (1000 mi) of railway.

Brunel, Sir Marc Isambard (1769–1849). Engineer, born in France, best known for his invention of a tunnelling shield (patented 1818) used to construct the Thames tunnel from Rotherhithe to Wapping (1843). His son was Isambard Kingdom *Brunel.

Brut (or **Brutus**). The legendary great-grandson of Aeneas, ancestor of the Romans. According to tradition he was banished from Rome and sailed with Trojan companions to Britain, where he founded New Troy (later London). His story was recounted in the chronicle of *Geoffrey of Monmouth and subsequently embroidered in such works as the 12th century *Roman de Brut* by Wace. The legend derives from "Bryt", the early name for a Briton.

Buchan, John, 1st Baron Tweedsmuir (1875–1940). Scottish writer and statesman. He served on the staff of the British Army during World War I and was governor general of Canada (1935–40). His popular novels include the adventure story *Prester John* (1910) and the secret-service thrillers *The Thirty-Nine Steps* (1915) and *Greenmantle* (1916).

Buchanan, George (1506–82). Scottish historian, political theorist, and Latin poet. Buchanan studied and taught in France for many years, returning home in 1561. Although favoured by Mary Queen of Scots he became the most influential propagandist of her deposition, and his tract *De jure regni apud Scotos* (1579) achieved widespread notoriety for its opposition to royal absolutism. He acted for a time as James VI's tutor.

Buckingham, George Villiers, 1st duke of (1592–1628). Royal favourite, who wielded enormous power during the reigns of James I and Charles I. He entered James' service in 1614, rose rapidly, and was created earl (1617), marquess (1618), and then duke (1623) of Buckingham. He acquired great wealth through his marriage (1620) to the earl of Rutland's heiress, Lady Katherine Manners. He accompanied the future Charles I to Madrid in 1623 to assist in abortive negotiations for a marriage between Charles and the king of Spain's daughter. In 1625 an attack on *Cádiz ordered by him failed for lack of organization, and in the following year his force of 8000 was unable to relieve the Huguenots (French Protestants) at *La Rochelle. He himself attempted its relief in 1627, but this expedition also failed. Charles dissolved one parliament in 1626 and prorogued another in 1628 because of their attempts to impeach Buckingham. He was assassinated at Portsmouth while en route once more for La Rochelle.

Buckingham, George Villiers, 2nd duke of (1628-87). Son of the 1st duke of Buckingham, he was brought up together with the children of Charles I, whom he served in the Civil War. In 1648 he fled to the Netherlands, returning briefly in 1651 to fight with Charles II at Worcester. He remained in exile until 1657, being imprisoned (1658-59). After the Restoration he became a privy councillor (1662) and, after helping to bring about the fall of the earl of Clarendon in 1667, joined the *cabal. He was displaced as the king's confidant by Arlington and was not privy to the secret clauses in the treaty of *Dover (1670). He nevertheless became a focus of parliamentary dissatisfaction and was dismissed in 1674. Also a playwright, he wrote The Rehearsal (1671), a parody of Restoration drama.

Buckingham palace. The London residence of the monarch. Built for John Sheffield, duke of Buckingham (1648-1721), at the beginning of the 18th century on the site of an earlier house, Buckingham palace became the property of the crown in 1762, when it and its contents were bought by George III. It was extended and largely rebuilt for George IV by John *Nash but was not permanently occupied by the monarch until the reign of Queen Victoria. The

main façade, facing the Mall, was added at the beginning of the 20th century.

Buckinghamshire election case. See Ashby versus White; Goodwin's case.

budget. The review for the past financial year and forecast for the coming financial year of government expenditure and revenues. The term was first applied to the government's accounts in 1733, but the parliamentary review of both expenditure and revenues was introduced by Pitt the younger during the Napoleonic War. During the 19th century the budget became the responsibility of the *chancellor of the exchequer, and successive holders of the office, especially since Gladstone in the mid-19th century, have developed the budget into a cornerstone of government economic policy. It is presented annually (more frequently in times of crisis), usually in April, when the chancellor is described as opening his budget (from the French bougette, little bag)—the case in which he carries his papers.

Buller, Sir Redvers (Henry) (1839-1908). British general. He was awarded the Victoria Cross in 1879 for bravery in the Cape Frontier Wars and was knighted in 1882. He initiated important reforms as quartermaster general from 1887 and adjutant general from 1890, but his conduct of the second *Boer War was unsuccessful.

Bunker Hill, battle of (17 June 1775). A battle during the American Revolution. Bunker Hill (properly Breed's Hill) on the outskirts of Boston, held by New England militiamen, was assaulted and eventually taken by some 2300 British troops under Maj. Gen. William *Howe. Although outnumbering their opponents by two to one, the British needed three assaults to capture the position, losing about a thousand men to the colonists' 450. The severe casualties inflicted on British regular troops greatly strengthened the colonists' morale.

Bunyan, John (1628-88). Puritan writer. He served in the parliamentary army during the Civil War and subsequently became a Baptist preacher. After the

Restoration he was imprisoned for 12 years (1660-72) for holding Baptist religious services. While in prison he wrote *Grace Abounding* (1666), the story of his spiritual conversion, and *Pilgrim's Progress* (1678), a religious allegory. The latter's eloquence and vivid characterization has made it one of the most widely read books in English.

Burbage, James (c. 1530-1597). Actor and joiner, who built the first English theatre at Shoreditch, London (1576). The theatre was later moved to Bankside and renamed the Globe. Burbage also built Blackfriars theatre in 1596. Shakespeare, and Burbage's son Richard, acted in both theatres.

Burbage, Richard (c. 1567-1619). Actor. A contemporary and associate of Shakespeare, Burbage was the first player of a number of Shakespearean roles, including Henry V, Hamlet, and Lear. He also acted in plays by Ben Johnson and John Webster, and was noted for his performances in tragedy. He held shares in the Globe and Blackfriars theatres, which were built by his father James *Burbage.

Burdett, Sir Francis (1770-1844). Politician and leader of radical causes, including parliamentary reform and Catholic emancipation. He became an MP in 1796 and bitterly opposed the war with France. An attempt to arrest him for a published attack on the House of Commons led to riots and eventually his imprisonment (1810). He was again imprisoned (1820) for condemning the *Peterloo massacre. Burdett was a Conservative MP from 1837 to 1844. He married Sophia Coutts, daughter of a banker, and their daughter was Angela, Baroness Burdett-Coutts, noted as a philanthropist.

burgh. See borough.

Burgh, Hubert de (d. 1243). Chief justiciar of England. He supported King John in the negotiations that led to the signing of Magna Carta and was appointed justiciar in 1215. His most notable achievement in the subsequent first *Barons' War was to prevent an invasion

by defeating a French fleet in the Channel, although greatly outnumbered by the French (1217). After the death (1219) of the regent, William Marshal, 1st earl of Pembroke, de Burgh was the most powerful man in the state until his fall from power in 1232.

Burgh, Richard de, 2nd earl of Ulster (?1259-1326). Anglo-Irish magnate. He was a loyal supporter of royal interests and led royalist forces against Edward *Bruce in 1315. However, his daughter Elizabeth was married to Robert Bruce (Edward's brother), and he was imprisoned in 1317 as a safeguard when Robert joined Edward in Ireland.

Burghley, 1st Baron. See Cecil, William.

Burgoyne, John (1722-92). General and playwright. In the American Revolution he led British troops from Canada against the American colonies. In 1777 he captured Ticonderoga and Fort Edward, but expected support did not arrive and he was forced to surrender to superior American forces at *Saratoga. His plays include *The Heiress* (1786).

burh. In Anglo-Saxon England, a fortified dwelling or town. The burhs of Wessex were strengthened by Alfred the Great (reigned 871-99) as defences against the Danish invasions.

Burke, Edmund (1729-97). Philosopher, politician, and orator. An Irishman, he became an MP in 1765 and joined the *Rockingham Whigs. In the pamphlet *Thoughts on the Cause of the Present Discontents* (1770) he argued that George III was upsetting the balance between crown and parliament in the British constitution by seeking to rule without due acknowledgement of the party political system. His opposition to government policies towards the American colonists was expressed, notably, in two famous speeches, "On American Taxation" (1774) and "On Moving His Resolutions for Conciliation with the Colonies" (1777). He also campaigned for "economical" reform, which would reduce administrative waste and abolish sinecures (see place acts), for the abolition of the slave trade, and for the Irish cause. He served as paymaster of the forces in Rockingham's ministry of 1782 and again in the Fox-North coalition of 1783. He subsequently played a leading part in the impeachment of Warren *Hastings. His commitment to responsible aristocratic government led him to condemn the French Revolution, both in parliament and in his *Reflections on the French Revolution* (1790), which led to his final break with the Whigs and their leader Charles James Fox. Burke's emphasis on freedom within the limits imposed by constitutional continuity became a major element in Conservative philosophy. He also wrote an influential book on aesthetics, *A Philosophical Enquiry into the Origin of Our Ideas of the Sublime and Beautiful* (1757).

burking. Murdering in the manner used by William Burke (1792-1829) and his partner in Edinburgh William Hare, who suffocated or strangled their victims and sold the corpses for dissection. Hare escaped trial by giving evidence against Burke, who was hanged.

Burma. A country in southeast Asia and a former British colony. Strategically situated between India and China, Burma was engaged in three wars against Britain during the 19th century: in the first (1824-26) Britain acquired Rangoon, in the second (1852), Lower Burma, and in the third (1885), Upper Burma. A province of India from 1862, in 1937 it became a separate crown colony. In 1948 it left the Commonwealth and became an independent republic.

Burns, Robert (1759-96). Scottish poet, who wrote in his native dialect and is regarded as Scotland's national poet. Son of an Ayrshire tenant farmer, Burns thought of emigrating but the popularity of his first published collection of poems (1786) encouraged him to remain in Scotland. From 1791 he worked as an excise official. He died of rheumatic fever after falling asleep by the roadside following a heavy drinking session.

Burton, Sir Richard (1821-90). Explorer, orientalist, and diplomat. In 1853, while travelling in Arabia, he visited Mecca, disguised as a Muslim pilgrim. In 1857-

58 he was sent by the Royal Geographical Society to explore East Africa with *Speke and discovered Lake Tanganyika. The author of several books, he also made a remarkable literal translation of *The Arabian Nights* (16 vols, 1885-88).

Bushell's case (1670). The legal case in which Lord Chief Justice Vaughan ruled that members of a jury could not be punished for their verdict. When members of a jury were fined for finding William Penn and another Quaker not guilty of unlawful assembly, one of the jurymen, Edward Bushell refused to pay and was imprisoned. Following a writ of *habeas corpus he was discharged by Vaughan.

Bute, John Stuart, 3rd earl of (1713-92). Prime minister. Before the accession of George III, Bute was his tutor and "dearest friend", encouraging his determination fully to exercise royal powers. Entering the cabinet on George's accession (1760), he was prime minister (1762-63), replacing Newcastle. Bute ended British participation in the *Seven Years' War but attracted intense public hostility and resigned in April 1763. His influence with the king ended after 1765. *See also* North Briton.

Butler. *See* Ormonde, earls and dukes of.

Butler, Josephine (Elizabeth) (1828-1906). Social reformer, notable for her successful campaign to abolish state regulation of prostitutes in seaports and garrison towns. The controls, which, under successive Contagious Diseases Acts (1864, 1866, 1869), required prostitutes to be registered, licensed, and medically examined, were finally repealed in 1886. Mrs Butler also fought the "white-slave traffic", which supplied women for brothels abroad.

Butler, Richard Austen Butler, Baron (1902-82). Statesman. A Conservative MP (1929-65; life peer, 1965), Butler was *education minister (1941-45), giving his name to the 1944 Education Act. In successive cabinets (1951-64) he held the highest offices, but the premiership eluded him.

Butler, Thomas, earl of Ossory (1634-80). Rear admiral. Eldest son of the first duke of *Ormonde, he was an insignificant politician in England. He distinguished himself in the navy and was an admiral in the third *Dutch War (1672-74). A truculent individual, he fought a number of duels.

Butt, Isaac (1813-79). Irish nationalist and founder of the Home Rule Association (1870). A lawyer, he defended many *Fenians in court, and as a result he was converted to the cause of Irish *home rule. He led the home rule party at Westminster from 1871 until he was displaced by *Parnell in 1878.

Button, Sir Thomas (d. 1634). Welsh admiral and explorer. He commanded an expedition to find a northwest passage to Asia (1612-13), searched for Henry Hudson, and explored Hudson Bay. He later became admiral of the Irish coast.

bye plot (1603). A Roman Catholic plot to kidnap James I and compel him to grant toleration. Organized by a priest William Watson, with the support of a number of Puritans, the plot was betrayed by a Jesuit. The conspirators were tried together with those in the *main (or principal) plot, of which the "bye" plot was not, in fact, an offshoot. Watson was executed and the fining of *recusants was severely enforced.

Byng, George, 1st Viscount Torrington (1663-1733). Naval commander and statesman. Byng held a succession of high-ranking commands (1704-20), becoming admiral of the fleet in 1718. As commander in the Mediterranean (1718-20) he destroyed a Spanish fleet off Cape Passaro (1718). He served as first lord of the admiralty (1727-33).

Byng, John (1704-57). Admiral, fourth son of George *Byng, Lord Torrington. In 1756 he was sent to relieve the garrison in Minorca but retired without doing so, after fighting an indecisive engagement with the French. Court-martialled for neglect of duty, Byng was found guilty and shot in 1757.

Byrd, William (?1540-1623). Organist and composer, who was the founder of a school of English madrigalists. He composed much polyphonic church music and is regarded as the leading musician of the Elizabethan and early Stuart periods.

Byron, George Gordon, 6th Baron (1788-1824). Romantic poet. His semiautobiographical poem *Childe Harold's Pilgrimage* (1812) won him immediate acclaim. After the breakdown of his marriage in 1816 Byron left England for Europe, where he wrote *Don Juan* (1819-24). In 1823 he travelled to Greece to join in the struggle for Greek independence. He died in the following year.

C

cabal. A group of advisers to Charles II in the early 1670s; its name is derived from the initials of its members: *Clifford, *Arlington, *Buckingham, Ashley (later 1st earl of *Shaftesbury), and *Lauderdale. The cabal has been regarded as a precursor of the modern *cabinet, but it had no official status and was discarded by the king when political expediency demanded.

cabinet. The committee, comprising the leading members of the party or coalition in power under the chairmanship of the *prime minister, that decides government policies. The cabinet originated in Charles II's practice of consulting a few important ministers (rather than the entire, unwieldy, Privy Council) in his private apartment (cabinet). The checks on monarchical power introduced by the Glorious Revolution (1688-89) made increasingly necessary a relatively homogeneous body of ministers to manage parliament and ensure majorities for money supplies and the maintenance of the armed forces. Under Anne, this body became known as the cabinet. From George I's reign, the sovereign ceased regularly to attend cabinet meetings, and the first lord of the treasury (*see* Treasury), henceforward presiding over the cabinet, began to take on the role of

a prime minister. The sovereign,
however, retained extensive powers to
choose ministers and influence policy;
there was little idea of collective responsibility and the prime minister remained
generally dependent on royal confidence,
as well as on his colleagues and
parliament. After George III's early
attempt to exercise his powers more
fully, administrations from that (1783)
of William Pitt the younger onwards
marked steady advances in defined
cabinet membership, collective responsibility to parliament (see ministerial
responsibility), and the prime minister's
executive authority. These characteristics, combined in Victoria's and subsequent reigns with the progressive
restriction of royal powers, universal
suffrage, and the modern party system,
have produced the cabinet's present
dominant position in the country's
government.

Cabot, John (c. 1450–c. 1499). Explorer
and navigator. Born in Genoa, he settled
in England in 1484. Under Henry VII's
patronage he sailed from Bristol in 1497,
with his son Sebastian Cabot (c. 1476–
1557). They landed at a place that may
have been in southern Labrador,
Newfoundland, or Cape Breton Island
(the coasts of which Sebastian mapped);
the Cabots, however, believed themselves
to be in Asia. John died at sea during a
second expedition. Sebastian became
(1512) cartographer to Henry VIII and,
later, governor of the Merchants Adventurers.

Cade's rebellion (1450). A rebellion of
Kentish gentry, led by Jack Cade, in
protest against high taxes and alleged
corruption in Henry VI's council. At
the beginning of July, after defeating a
royal army at Sevenoaks (18 June), Cade
entered London and received considerable popular support. Following a
number of executions, including that of
the lord treasurer Saye and Sele, and
attacks on property, the rebels were
forced to flee. Cade was mortally wounded while attempting to evade arrest at
Heathfield, Sussex.

Cádiz. A city on the Atlantic coast of
Spain. In 1587 Sir Francis Drake burned
and sank ships in the harbour here
("singeing the king of Spain's beard"),
thus delaying the sailing of the *armada.
In 1596 Cádiz was sacked by a fleet
under the earl of Essex and Lord Howard
of Effingham, who obtained considerable
loot. Cádiz was also the object of an
expedition, badly organized by the duke
of Buckingham, which failed to capture
either the city or the Spanish treasure
fleet (1625).

Cadog, St (c. 450). Celtic saint and
monastic founder. Son of Gwynllyw,
ruler in southeast Wales. Cadog
travelled extensively along the western
seaways. His monastery at Llancarfan,
in the Vale of Glamorgan, was renowned
as a centre of learning. The *Life of
Cadog* was written in the 12th century.
Feast day: 24 Jan.

Cadwaladr ap Cadwallon (d. 664). Son
of *Cadwallon and ruler of Gwynedd,
who appears prominently in the Welsh
medieval prophetic tradition. *Geoffrey
of Monmouth narrated Merlin's prophecy that Cadwaladr would lead the
British to victory over the Saxons, and
Henry VII in 1485 unfurled the red
dragon of Cadwaladr.

Cadwaladr ap Gruffudd (d. 1172). Lord
of Merionydd and Ceredigion. Son of
*Gruffudd ap Cynan, he conquered
Merionydd in 1121 and Ceredigion in
1135 in alliance with his brother *Owain
ap Gruffudd. When, in 1137, Owain
succeeded his father Cadwaladr became
lord of these territories until 1143, when
he quarrelled with Owain and was
expelled. He then allied with Henry II
of England, who restored his possessions
in 1157, but he aided his brother against
Henry's invasion in 1165.

Cadwallon (d. 633). Ruler of Gwynedd
who, in alliance with Penda, ruler of
Mercia, defeated Edwin, the Northumbrian leader, at Hatfield Chase (?632).
Cadwallon's army subsequently ravaged
Northumbria but he was killed by
Oswald, Edwin's successor, near Hexham (633). His defeat signified the
failure of surviving British kingdoms to

limit the extension of English authority in northern Britain.

Cadwgan (d. 1111). A prince of Gwynedd, who became lord of Powys. He was one of the leaders of the Welsh revolt against William II (1094) and resisted William's invasion in 1097. In 1100 he was granted part of Powys as a fief by the earl of Shrewsbury and in 1110 received it all from Henry I. He was murdered by his nephew in a family feud.

Caedmon, St (7th century). Author of the earliest surviving poem in Old English. This work, a nine-line fragment, is known from its transcription by Bede in his *Ecclesiastical History*. Caedmon (according to Bede) was an oxherd on the estates of Whitby abbey who, after miraculously receiving the gift of song, was received as a monk and wrote many poems on religious themes. None of these has, however, been positively identified. Feast day: 11 or 12 Feb.

Caedwalla (?659-689). King of Wessex. Of obscure origin, Caedwalla seized the throne of Wessex in 686. Conquests of the Isle of Wight, Sussex, Surrey, and Kent followed, although Caedwalla succeeded in gaining permanent control only of the first of these. He died in Rome shortly after being baptized in the presence of the pope.

Caernarfon (English name: Caernarvon). The administrative headquarters of Gwynedd in northwest Wales. Although near a prehistoric settlement, modern Caernarfon was founded in 1098 by Hugh Lupus, who built a fortress here. The present *castle, one of the most complex in Britain, was begun in 1284 by Edward I. The investiture of Charles, prince of Wales, took place here in 1969. The town itself exists because of the castle; it has little industry and is now primarily a tourist centre.

Caesar, Julius (102-44 BC). Roman general and statesman. In 55 BC, in the course of his conquest of Gaul, Caesar made his first expedition to Britain but was forced to leave after a few weeks when bad weather damaged his exposed

fleet on the Kent coast. The following year he invaded with more troops and, after heavy fighting, defeated the British leader *Cassivellaunus, who agreed to pay tribute. A storm once more wrecked most of Caesar's fleet and he returned to Gaul with great difficulty.

Calais. A French port on the Strait of Dover. Following the battle of Crécy (1346) in the Hundred Years' War, it was captured by Edward III after a siege lasting nearly a year. Rodin's statue commemorates the six burghers who surrendered themselves to Edward to save the town. Calais remained English until retaken by France in 1558.

Caledonia. The Roman name for that part of Scotland lying north of the Firths of Forth and Clyde. Roman attempts to conquer the region were unsuccessful and even Severus' victory in 209 AD only temporarily coerced Caledonia's independent tribes.

Caledonian canal. The canal opened in 1823 to link the east and west coasts of Scotland through the Great Glen, from Inverness to Fort William. Over half of its 100-km (60-mi) length consists of lochs. Although a triumph of engineering it was a commercial failure.

calendar. A system for reckoning the beginning, length, and divisions of years. England used the Julian calendar, introduced by Julius Caesar in 46 BC, until 1752, when it adopted the Gregorian calendar, sponsored by Pope Gregory XIII and accepted in Roman Catholic countries in 1582. In England, in 1752, 2 Sept was followed immediately by 14 Sept, and 1 Jan was designated New year's day (as it had been in Scotland since 1600), in place of 25 March (which replaced 25 Dec in the 14th century). Dates during the period in which both calendars were in use are termed old style dates if determined by the Julian calendar and new style if determined by the Gregorian. New style dates are given in this book.

Cambridge (or Southampton) plot (1415). A conspiracy planned by Richard, earl of Cambridge, Sir Thomas

Grey, and Henry, 3rd Baron Scrope. They intended to kill Henry V and his three brothers at Southampton prior to the king's departure for France and to proclaim Edmund de *Mortimer, 5th earl of March, king. The latter revealed the plot and the three conspirators were executed.

Cambridge, George William Frederick Charles, 2nd duke of (1819-1904). Soldier, a cousin of Queen Victoria. He commanded a division during the Crimean War and was field marshal commanding in chief (1856-87) and then commander in chief (1887-95) of the British army. Despite his early advocacy of army reform the duke became notorious for military conservatism, opposing the reforms of Edward *Cardwell.

Camden, William (1551-1623). Antiquary and historian. His greatest work was *Britannia*, first published in Latin in 1586 and dedicated to his patron, Lord Burghley. It combines a history with a topographical survey, county by county. The standard edition (in English) was published in 1600 and dedicated to Queen Elizabeth.

Cameroon. A country on the coast of West Africa formerly called the Cameroons. The Cameroons became a German colony in 1884 and in 1919, after World War I, was divided between Britain and France, which from 1922 administered their zones under League of Nations *mandate. In 1947 Cameroon became a UN trust territory and in 1960 the French Cameroons became independent as the United Republic of Cameroon. Following a plebiscite in 1961 the north of the British Cameroons joined independent Nigeria and the south became part of Cameroon.

Campaign for Nuclear Disarmament (CND). An organization, founded in 1958, to campaign for British, and ultimately international, abandonment of nuclear weapons. In its early years the CND held annual Aldermaston marches, a form of peaceful protest in which thousands marched at Easter from the Atomic Weapons Research Establishment at Aldermaston, Berkshire, to Trafalgar Square, London. After the signing of the international *nuclear test-ban treaty (1963), which partially banned nuclear tests, it declined but revived in the 1980s.

Campbell. *See* Argyll, earls and dukes of.

Campbell, Colin, Baron Clyde (1792-1863). Soldier. Campbell was commissioned in 1808 and served throughout the Peninsular War. Posted to China (1842-46), he later commanded the Highland brigade in the Crimea. As commander in chief in India (1857-60) he played a leading role in suppressing the *Indian mutiny, receiving a peerage for his services (1858). As a general Campbell was notable for his ability to inspire intense personal devotion.

Campbell-Bannerman, Sir Henry (1846-1908). Prime minister. After being elected a Liberal MP in 1868 Campbell-Bannerman held junior posts at the Admiralty and War Office in Gladstone's first two administrations and then served as chief secretary for Ireland (1884-85). He entered the cabinet as secretary for war (1886, 1892-95), an office in which he speeded army reform by successfully pressing for the retirement of the conservative commander in chief, the duke of *Cambridge, cousin of Queen Victoria. Succeeding Sir William Harcourt in 1899 as Liberal leader in the Commons (and thus, effectively, of the party), Campbell-Bannerman aroused opposition from Liberal imperialists by condemning the concentration camps established in the Boer War as "the methods of barbarism". However, by 1905, when, following Balfour's resignation, he was called upon to form a government, Campbell-Bannerman had restored party unity and led the Liberals to a landslide victory in the 1906 general election. He constructed a brilliant cabinet, which included *Asquith, *Lloyd George, and Winston *Churchill, but much of its proposed legislation failed to pass the Lords. Measures to reach the statute book included the Trade Disputes Act (1906), Merchant Shipping Act (1907), and Patents Act

(1907), while abroad self-government was granted to the Transvaal (1906) and the Orange River Colony (1907). Advancing ill-health forced Campbell-Bannerman to hand over the government to Asquith, and he died 17 days later (22 April).

Camperdown, battle of (11 Oct 1797). A naval battle between the British under Admiral Duncan and a Dutch invasion fleet under Admiral de Winter, fought off the Dutch coast. The British captured nine of the 16 Dutch ships, effectively eliminating the risk of a Dutch invasion in Ireland during the Irish rebellion (1798).

Campion, Edmund (1540–81). Jesuit martyr. Campion spent several years in Jesuit seminaries on the Continent before returning to England on the first Jesuit mission. He was eventually arrested, falsely implicated in a plot against Elizabeth I, and hanged at Tyburn.

Canada. A country in north North America and a member of the Commonwealth. It was first explored by the French, in the early 16th century. By the early 17th century the English were competing for a stake in the valuable fur trade, and in 1670 the *Hudson's Bay Company was formed. By 1763 Britain was supreme in Canada, securing the Hudson's Bay territories, *Newfoundland, and *Nova Scotia by the treaty of *Utrecht (1713) and *Quebec, *Prince Edward Island, and *Cape Breton Island by the treaty of *Paris (1763). In 1791, by the Constitutional Act, the province of Quebec was divided into Upper and Lower Canada; rebellions there, led by *Papineau and *Mackenzie, brought about the crucial appointment of Lord *Durham as governor. His "Report on the Affairs of British North America" (1839) led to the union of Upper and Lower Canada (1840) and the creation of the first Canadian parliament (1841). The attainment of responsible self-government was completed by the British North America Act (1867). It established the *dominion of Canada, comprising a federation of the former Upper and Lower Canada, *New Brunswick, and Nova Scotia; the territories of the Hudson's Bay Company were purchased in 1869 (becoming the provinces of Manitoba, Saskatchewan, and the Yukon Territory); *British Columbia, Prince Edward Island, and Newfoundland joined the federation in 1871, 1873, and 1949 respectively.

canals. Navigable inland artificial waterways linking rivers or seas. The first modern British canal was the *Bridgewater canal (1761), which inspired a boom in canal building to exploit the developing markets of the industrial and agrarian revolutions. Canals were built and administered by companies authorized by act of parliament. They charged tolls for passage and ran barge fleets, charging for carriage. The French Revolutionary and Napoleonic Wars (1793–1815) further boosted traffic, canals facilitating military transport. In subsequent decades, however, canals declined as military traffic dwindled, trade recovered slowly from the wars, and *roads offered severe competition. After 1830 *railway competition was ruinous to canals, traffic on which was impeded by the geographical need for many locks and the lack of a standard gauge. In the 20th century road haulage further eroded canal traffic, and in 1947, after successive government investigations, most canals were nationalized. *See also* Caledonian canal; Ellesmere canal.

Canning, George (1770–1827). Prime minister. An MP from 1794, Canning held junior posts under Pitt the younger (1796–1801, 1804–06). While foreign secretary (1807–09) Canning quarrelled with his colleague *Castlereagh over British military reverses in Spain and the failed *Walcheren expedition, and fought a duel with him (1809) on Putney Heath. Jealousy of Castlereagh kept Canning out of office until 1816, when, as secretary of the India Board, he became responsible for government policy in India. Resigning (1821) over the government's treatment of Queen Caroline, he subsequently re-entered the cabinet, following Castlereagh's suicide, as foreign secretary and leader of the House of Commons (1822-27). As leader of the progressive Tories, he promoted liberal policies at home and abroad, replacing Castlereagh's support of European autocracies through the congress system by policies that opposed international intervention against liberal and revolutionary movements, notably in South America and Greece. His short term of office as prime minister (1827), was troubled by the attacks of former colleagues, many of whom refused to serve under him.

Canning, Stratford, 1st Viscount Stratford de Redcliffe (1786-1880). Diplomat. Canning (viscount, 1852) was *chargé d'affaires* in Turkey (1810-12), envoy in Switzerland (1814-20), and envoy in the USA (1820-24), returning to Turkey as ambassador from 1825 to 1828. An MP from 1828 to 1841, he was then again ambassador to Turkey (1842, 1848-58). A key figure in events leading up to the *Crimean War, he exercised a unique influence as the unrivalled British authority on the *eastern question.

Canons, Book of. The collection of 151 canon laws of the Church of England, passed, at the instigation of Archbishop Bancroft, in 1604 by the convocation of Canterbury and in 1606 by that of York. They are still in force, although with some modifications.

Canterbury. The administrative centre of Kent and seat of the primate of all England, the archbishop of Canterbury. Canterbury (Roman Durovernum) has never been of any great economic importance in the history of England and, although briefly, during the Anglo-Saxon period, the capital of the kingdom of Kent, has also had little political significance. Its ecclesiastical importance derives from the fact that St *Augustine, who came to England to convert the population to Christianity, landed in Kent (597) and was given protection by King *Aethelbert. Canterbury consequently became the centre of English Christianity, and, despite challenges for that position from York in the 10th century, remained so. Notable arch-

bishops, who have sometimes wielded considerable political power, have included *Lanfranc, *Anselm, Thomas *Becket, and Thomas *Cranmer. The city is now primarily of importance as a tourist centre, the main attraction being *Canterbury cathedral.

Canterbury, quitclaim of (5 Dec 1189). The surrender by Richard I of the English claim to feudal superiority over William I of Scotland contained in the treaty of *Falaise (1174).

Canterbury cathedral. The cathedral church of the primate of all England, properly called the Cathedral of Christchurch. It is one of the most beautiful buildings in England. A church has been on this site since the 7th century, but the present building is largely composed of one section built in the romanesque style between 1070 and 1089, and another, consisting of the nave and towers, in 14th-century gothic. The choir, one of the earliest examples of gothic in England, was designed by the Frenchman William of Sens as the shrine to St Thomas Becket, who was murdered here in 1170. *See also* Canterbury.

Canute. *See* Cnut.

Cape Breton Island. An island northeast of *Nova Scotia, Canada, and part of that province. Discovered by John Cabot in 1497, it became a French possession in 1632. It was captured by the British in 1745, restored to France in 1748, and seized again in 1758; it was formally ceded to Britian by the treaty of Paris (1763). It formed part of Nova Scotia, except during the years 1784-1819, when it constituted a separate colony.

Cape of Good Hope. A headland 305 m (1000 ft) high, south of Cape Town in *South Africa. First reached by the Portuguese explorer Bartolomeu Dias (1487), it was rounded by Vasco da Gama (1497). Cape Province, the largest of the four South African provinces, was formerly known as Cape of Good Hope Colony. Settled by the Dutch in 1652, it was captured in 1806 by the British, to whom it was formally ceded in 1814.

Representative government was introduced in 1853 and responsible government in 1872. In 1910 it became part of the Union of South Africa.

Cape St Vincent, battle of (14 Feb 1797). The naval engagement in which Admiral Sir John *Jervis defeated, with 15 ships, a Spanish fleet of 27. This striking victory, which gave a much needed boost to British naval morale, was attributable to the careful strategy of Jervis and to the intrepidity of Nelson, who engaged six enemy vessels single-handed.

capital punishment. Punishment for a crime by death. It is named from the Latin *caput* head, because decapitation or, in Britain, hanging came to be the most common method of capital punishment. It was for many centuries the penalty not only for murder and *treason but for any felony. Hanging involved slow strangulation until 1783, when *Tyburn was replaced by *Newgate for London executions and the drop began to be used. Hanging was the penalty for an increasing number of offences in the 18th century, although there were many more condemnations than executions. The death sentence for most of these offences was removed in Peel's *criminal law reform, and after 1838 no one was hanged except for murder or attempted murder, treason, piracy with violence, and arson. Public executions ended in 1868. Hanging for murder was abolished in 1965 and for arson in 1971; it remains available for treason and piracy with violence.

Caractacus (or Caratacus) (1st century AD). Chief of the *Catuvellauni, who, together with his brother Togodumnus, led British resistance to the Roman invasion of 43 AD.

Caradon, Hugh Foot, Baron (1907-). Public servant (life peer, 1964). The last British governor of Cyprus (1957-60), he helped negotiate Cypriot independence. He was minister of state for foreign affairs and UK representative at the UN (1964-70).

Caratacus. *See* Caractacus.

Carberry Hill, "battle" of (15 June 1567). A bloodless confrontation between the forces of *Mary Queen of Scots and the earl of *Bothwell and those of the rebel *confederate lords. While the two sides were negotiating the queen's forces began to disperse and she surrendered to the rebels.

Carbisdale, battle of (27 April 1650). The battle in which a royalist force, invading mainland Scotland from the Orkneys under the leadership of Montrose, was surprised and routed by three troops of horse from the covenanters' army. Montrose was subsequently captured and executed.

Cardigan, James Thomas Brudenell, 7th earl of (1797-1868). Cavalry commander, who in 1854 led the *charge of the Light Brigade at the battle of *Balaclava. The charge, although heroic, was futile and resulted from a misinterpreted order. However, it made Cardigan a popular hero in Britain. The knitted woollen jacket, the cardigan, is named after him.

Cardwell, Edward Cardwell, Viscount (1813-86). Secretary for war (1868-74), who introduced wide-ranging military reforms. An MP from 1842 until 1874, when he was created a viscount, Cardwell was secretary for war under Gladstone. His chief reforms, achieved in spite of considerable opposition from the army establishment, included the abolition of flogging in peacetime (1868); a shorter enlistment term of six years' active duty and six years' reserve duty and the subordination of the commander in chief to the war secretary (1870); and the abolition of the purchase of commissions (1871). He also reduced the number of overseas garrisons, created the system of county infantry regiments, and introduced an efficient breech-loading rifle.

Carlyle, Thomas (1795-1881). Essayist and historian. His works include the philosophical and partly autobiographical *Sartor Resartus* (1833-34), *The French Revolution* (1837), and studies of Oliver Cromwell (1845) and Frederick the Great (1858-65).

Carnarvon, Henry Howard Molyneux
Herbert, 4th earl of (1831-90). Conservative colonial secretary (1866-67, 1874-
78). In his first term he achieved passage
of the British North America Act (1867),
which created Canada's federal system.
In his second term he failed in his attempt
to achieve a confederation of British and
Afrikaner South Africa. As lord
lieutenant of Ireland (1885-86) he
favoured conciliation towards Irish
nationalism and a degree of devolved
self-government, negotiating privately,
and abortively, with *Parnell for this
purpose.

Carnatic Wars (1780-92). A series of
wars between the British East India
company and a coalition of Hyderabad,
Mysore, and the Maratha tribes. In 1780
the armies of the coalition swept over
the Carnatic (or Karnatik, the area
occupied by the Kananese-speaking
people—roughly modern Mysore) but
were defeated in the following year by
the commander of the company's armies,
Warren Hastings. War was renewed in
1789 with Tipu, ruler of Mysore, who,
after being finally defeated by Cornwallis, governor general of India, was
forced to cede about half of his territories.

Caroline of Ansbach (1683-1737). Queen
consort of George II (whom she married
in 1705). Intelligent and good-looking,
she exercised a strong and generally
beneficial influence over George, helping
maintain *Walpole in office.

Caroline of Brunswick (1768-1821).
Queen consort (1820-21) of George IV.
Their marriage (from 1795) was unhappy
and they separated soon after the birth
of their child, Charlotte, in 1796.
Caroline travelled widely in Europe,
where her eccentric behaviour caused
considerable scandal (see delicate
investigation). Popular support for
Caroline thwarted the government's
efforts to dissolve the marriage (1820),
but she was excluded from George's
coronation in Westminster Abbey
(1821).

Carr, Robert, earl of Somerset (1586-
1645). A favourite of James I from 1607.

Created Viscount Rochester in 1611 and
earl of Somerset in 1613, by 1614 he was
replaced in the king's affections by
George Villiers. Somerset and his wife
(formerly the countess of Essex) were
imprisoned in 1616 for the murder of Sir
Thomas *Overbury, who had opposed
their marriage. Subsequently pardoned
by James, they lived out their lives in
obscurity.

Carron ironworks. An ironworks in Stir-
lingshire, opened in 1760. It became a
prototype of the large new factories of
the *industrial revolution and a symbol
of industrial power to writers and
thinkers. From 1776 the carronade, a
short light naval gun, which proved
enormously successful, was produced at
Carron. By 1800 it was the largest
munitions works in Europe.

Carson, Edward Carson, Baron (1854-
1935). Lawyer and Ulster Unionist.
Born in southern Ireland, Carson practised law in Dublin and was a Conservative MP (1892-1921) and solicitor-
general (1900-06). In 1910 he became
leader of the Unionists. He organized
the Ulster Volunteers and threatened
rebellion in the province if the Liberal
government's *home rule bill became
law; he was responsible for gun running
to Ulster in 1914. For most of the war
he served in the cabinet and was afterwards lord of appeal (1921-29).

Carteret, Sir George (?1609-1680).
Royalist, naval commander, and colonial
proprietor. During the Civil War Carteret held his native Jersey as the royalist
governor (1643-51) and at the Restoration served as treasurer of the navy
(1660-67). He became one of the
original proprietors of Carolina (1663)
and of a region between the Hudson and
Delaware rivers that he named New
Jersey (1664).

Carteret, John Carteret, Baron (and
Earl Granville) (1690-1763). Secretary
of state (1721-24, 1742-44). Walpole
and Townshend, fearing his rivalry,
succeeded in removing him to Ireland as
lord lieutenant (1724-30). Again
secretary of state following Walpole's
resignation, he organized Britain's allia: .

ces in the War of the *Austrian Succession. His highhandedness alienated allies and colleagues, and he was accused, notably by Pitt the elder, of favouring Hanover at Britain's expense. He resigned in 1744 and was created Earl Granville. After an unsuccessful attempt to form an administration (1746) he played no further major role.

Cartwright, Thomas (1535-1603). Puritan divine. He lost his professorship of divinity at Cambridge (1570) for criticizing the Church of England's constitution. After a period in Geneva he returned to England and published the *Admonition to Parliament* (1572), a manifesto that attacked Anglican liturgical practices and demanded Presbyterian government. Fleeing to the Continent to avoid arrest, he returned in 1585 and was imprisoned (1590-92) for his continued support of Presbyterianism. He was the author of the *millenary petition, presented to James I in 1603, shortly before Cartwright's death.

Casement, Sir Roger (David) (1864-1916). Irish nationalist. He joined the consular service in 1892 and gained a reputation for revealing the exploitation of native workers in the Belgian Congo and Peru, for which he was knighted (1912). Retiring in 1912, he became an ardent Irish nationalist and in 1914, after the outbreak of World War I, went to Germany to seek aid for the movement against British rule. Returning to Ireland on the eve of the *Easter rising (1916), he was captured and executed for high treason. The authenticity of his diaries, which describe homosexual practices, was long disputed.

casket letters. A collection of letters contained in a casket that had belonged to *Bothwell. They were produced in 1568 by the opponents of *Mary Queen of Scots to provide evidence that she and Bothwell had plotted the death of her husband *Darnley. The letters were probably forgeries, but they may have included passages from genuine letters by Mary.

Cassivellaunus (1st century BC). Chief of the *Catuvellauni and leader of the forces opposing Julius Caesar during the Roman invasion of Britain in 54 BC. Defeated in battle, Cassivéllaunus adopted guerrilla tactics against the invaders until forced to surrender after the capture of his stronghold at present-day Wheathampstead, Hertfordshire. He agreed to pay an annual tribute to Rome and to limit the territorial expansion of his tribe.

Castillon, battle of (17 July 1453). The final battle of the Hundred Years' War. After an expedition, commanded by John Talbot, 1st earl of *Shrewsbury, had reoccupied part of Gascony, it attempted to lift the siege of Castillon by an attack on the French encampment. French artillery helped break up the assault, during which Shrewsbury was killed. The English force disintegrated, leaving Gascony to be reoccupied by the French.

castle. A fortified building designed to facilitate the defence of a route, town, or territory. Much of the technique of castle building depended on siting the fortress at the most useful and defensible spot. Castles are thus frequently to be found either at the fordable parts of rivers (e.g. Oxford castle, of which only the motte, or mound, remains) or at the narrower parts of valleys (e.g. Corfe castle, Dorset). The style of castle built depended on the resources available to the builders and the degree of strength required to be able to withstand siege. The earliest forms in England, hillforts built by the Celts, consisted of little more than ditches and ramparts built on a piece of tactically advantageous land and were easily overcome by the superior military ability of the Romans. The Anglo-Saxons built forts and *burhs, but the castle as a fortified private residence was a Norman innovation. The earliest Norman castles, the motte and bailey (the inner courtyard), were also simple earth and wood defences but rapidly gave way to the more secure stone keep (e.g. Rochester and Dover castles, both 12th century). As methods of waging war developed, so the castle had to become more sophisticated. Mining techniques made the 90° angles of a keep vulnerable, so polygonal towers, often with round angle towers, were developed. More advanced siege equipment (such as catapults) necessitated the building of outer walls, again with towers with angled slits and battlements to give the maximum angles of fire for the defenders. Similarly, moats became wider and deeper. The most complex castles in Britain were those built by Edward I in the 13th century (e.g. Harlech and *Caernarfon castles) to secure Wales. The introduction of gunpowder (since it became impossible to build walls strong enough to withstand sustained cannon fire) and the establishment of strong monarchical authority in the 16th century rendered such strong defences ineffective. *See also* adulterine castles.

Castle Howard. A country house built after 1700 for the earl of Carlisle. It was the first design of John *Vanbrugh. Built on a vast scale, and in a highly individual baroque style, Castle Howard owes much in plan to the work of Sir Christopher Wren and to Versailles, the palace built for Louis XIV of France.

Castlereagh, Robert Stewart, Viscount (1769-1822). Foreign secretary (1812-22). He was chief secretary for Ireland (1798-1801) and helped bring about its union with Great Britain; he resigned when George III refused to consent to Catholic emancipation. As war secretary (1805-06, 1807-09) he secured Wellington's appointment as commander in Portugal but resigned following a duel (after the *Walcheren expedition) with his fellow-minister George *Canning. His greatest work was as foreign secretary (1812-22). In the post-Napoleonic congress of *Vienna he secured British trading and strategic interests and sought lasting peace through the congress system of diplomacy. At home, however, he was savagely attacked as spokesman for the repressive policies of Liverpool's administration. He committed suicide.

Catesby, Robert (1573-1605). The chief conspirator in the *gunpowder plot. A fanatical Roman Catholic, he took part in the uprising of the 2nd earl of *Essex

in 1601, for which he was imprisoned. On the discovery of the gunpowder plot (1605) he fled to Holbeche House, Staffordshire, and was shot while resisting arrest.

Catherine Howard (d. 1542). Queen consort of Henry VIII, his fifth wife. A granddaughter of Thomas Howard, 2nd duke of Norfolk, Catherine, before her marriage to Henry in 1540, had been betrothed to a cousin, Thomas Culpepper, and later confessed to having been the mistress of Thomas Dereham and of Henry Mannock, her music teacher. Her confession of these affairs, together with subsequent indiscretions, led to her execution for high treason, but there is no evidence that she was ever unfaithful to Henry.

Catherine of Aragon (1485-1536). Queen consort of Henry VIII (1509-33), his first wife, and daughter of Ferdinand and Isabella of Spain. Previously married to Henry's elder brother Prince Arthur (d. 1502), Catherine obtained papal dispensation to marry Henry in 1509. Of her six children, who included two sons, only Princess Mary—later Mary I —survived. Her failure to produce a male heir to the throne led Henry, in 1527, unsuccessfully to seek an annulment of the marriage from Pope Clement VII. In 1531 he separated from Catherine and in 1533 he married *Anne Boleyn. Catherine, designated "princess dowager", spent her remaining years in enforced seclusion.

Catherine of Braganza (1638-1705). Queen consort (1662-85) of Charles II. She was a Portuguese princess, whose marriage to Charles brought England, as part of a diplomatic alliance with Portugal, the ports of Bombay and Tangier. Despite Charles' numerous infidelities, Catherine remained fond of him but bore him no children. Attempts to implicate her in the *popish plot (1678-80) failed. A staunch Roman Catholic, Catherine succeeded in reconciling Charles to Roman Catholicism on his deathbed. She returned to Portugal in 1692.

Catherine of Valois (1401-37). Queen consort of Henry V. Daughter of Charles VI of France, she married Henry as part of the Anglo-French treaty of *Troyes (1420). After Henry's death she married Owen *Tudor and by him bore Edmund, father of Henry VII.

Catherine Parr (1512-48). Queen consort of Henry VIII (1543-47), his sixth wife. A daughter of Sir Thomas Parr (d. 1517) of Kendal, Catherine had already been twice married—to Edward Borough (d. 1529) and John Neville, Lord Latimer (d. 1542)—before reluctantly agreeing to marry the king. A well-educated and religious woman, apparently sympathetic to Protestantism, Catherine proved a sympathetic stepmother to Henry's three children and attempted to restrain religious persecution.

Catholic Apostolic Church. A religious sect established in 1832 under the leadership of Edward Irving (1792-1834), a Scottish minister, and Henry Drummond (1786-1860), an MP. Revivalist in origin, the sect, whose members were also called Irvingites, believed in the imminence of Christ's second coming. It sought to re-establish the early church's apostolic organization but gradually adopted Catholic practices. Its influence was slight by the end of the 19th century.

Catholic Association. An Irish organization, founded by Daniel *O'Connell in 1823, to work for *Catholic emancipation. The association was founded by a levy on its supporters of a penny a month—the so-called catholic rent, which amounted to £1,000 a week by 1825. Although suppressed (1825), it changed its name and continued its efforts. With the passing of the Catholic Emancipation Act (1829) its aim was achieved and the association was dissolved.

Catholic emancipation. The achievement of full civil and political rights for *Roman Catholics. Catholics were subjected to the *penal laws from 1571 and, in Ireland, also to the *Penal Code (1695-1727). Relief began to be granted to both Irish and English Catholics in the late 18th century, but the right to sit in parliament was still denied them. Although *Pitt the younger and some of his cabinet colleagues supported full Catholic emancipation early in the 19th century the opposition of George III and Tory politicians delayed emancipation until 1828, when *O'Connell was elected to represent Co. Clare. The strength of O'Connell's support in Ireland and the fear of severe disturbances persuaded the duke of Wellington and George IV to concede Catholic emancipation in 1829.

Cato Street conspiracy (1820). A revolutionary plot involving some 20 radical extremists, under Arthur Thistlewood (1770-1820), a veteran of *Spa Fields, who planned to assassinate the members of the cabinet and seize power. Police and troops arrested the conspirators in a hayloft in Cato Street, in Marylebone, London. Thistlewood and four others were hanged.

Catuvellauni. A powerful Belgic tribe, based in the south Midlands. The capital of the Catuvellauni was at first near present-day Wheathampstead, Hertfordshire. After their defeat by Julius Caesar in 54 BC they built, under their leader *Cassivellaunus, a new capital at *Verulamium. The Catuvellauni were not finally subdued until after Boudicca's rebellion in 60 AD.

cavaliers. *See* royalists.

Cavell, Edith (1865-1915). A nurse whose execution by the Germans in World War I made her a national heroine. As matron of a Brussels hospital, she helped organize an escape network for allied soldiers after Germany occupied Belgium. Arrested (Aug 1915), she was court-martialled and shot (Oct 1915). Her last words were: "Patriotism is not enough; I must have no hatred or bitterness towards anyone".

Cavendish, Lord Frederick Charles (1836-82). An MP from 1865 and brother of the 8th duke of Devonshire, Cavendish was appointed chief secretary for Ireland in 1882 to assist Gladstone's efforts to conciliate Irish nationalism under the *Kilmainham treaty. Within hours of reaching Dublin he was murdered (with his undersecretary, T. H. Burke) by terrorists in Phoenix Park (6 May 1882).

Caxton, William (?1422–1491). The first English printer. Born in Kent, he served as a mercer's apprentice before establishing himself in business at Bruges in about 1446. In 1465 he was appointed a governor of the Merchants Adventurers, negotiating commercial treaties on their behalf. He learnt the art of *printing at Cologne in the early 1470s and in 1476 returned to England. In 1477 the first book was issued from his press at Westminster, Earl *Rivers' *Dictes and Sayenges of the Phylosophers*. Between then and his death Caxton produced about 80 complete volumes, including Chaucer's *The Canterbury Tales*, and also found time to work on translations. On his death the press was taken over by his chief assistant, Wynkyn de Worde.

Cecil, Robert, 1st earl of Salisbury and 1st Viscount Cranborne (1563–1612). Statesman, second son of William *Cecil, Lord Burghley, whom he succeeded as Elizabeth I's chief minister in 1598. The ease of the Stuart succession owed much to Cecil's management, and in 1605 James I made him earl of Salisbury. An able administrator, he served James as chief secretary and, from 1608, as lord treasurer. Towards the end of his life he lost James' favour because of his failure to obtain additional revenues from parliament and also because of the rise of Robert Carr in the king's affections.

Cecil, William, 1st Baron Burghley (1520–98). Statesman. Cecil proved himself an astute politician during the troubled decade before the accession (1558) of Elizabeth I. In 1558 he became Elizabeth I's principal secretary of state administering foreign policy. In religious matters he was more sympathetic than the queen to the Puritans and persuaded her to aid the French Huguenots (1567) and the Dutch Calvinists (1585). In 1571 he was created Baron Burghley and in the following year became lord treasurer. He presided over the Court of

*Exchequer, introducing many important financial reforms. It was almost certainly Burghley who persuaded Elizabeth to sign Mary Stuart's death warrant (1587). He believed it was crucial for England that Elizabeth should marry, but this was the one major point on which Elizabeth refused his advice. He was succeeded as the queen's chief minister by his son Robert *Cecil.

Celtic church. The church in the British Isles from the introduction of Christianity in the 2nd or 3rd centuries until St *Augustine's mission from Rome in 597. The Celtic church had close ties with Rome until the Anglo-Saxon invasions in the 5th and 6th centuries cut off communications with the Continent. Thus by the time of Augustine's mission the Celtic Christians were unwilling to submit to Roman authority. Although differences were largely settled at the synod of *Whitby (664) Celtic Christian influences continued for centuries in Wales and Ireland.

Celtic fields. The system of land cultivation, introduced by the Celts, who divided land into small rectangular enclosed fields individually cultivated. After the Roman conquest Celtic fields coexisted with *villas, but the Saxons' system of open fields came to supersede both.

Celts. A prehistoric people of Britain. The Celts, who used iron instruments and weapons, occupied extensive areas of central and western Europe, including the British Isles, in the prehistoric era, and between about 500 and 250 BC were the most powerful people north of the Alps. Reputed to be tall, fair, and well built, they were renowned for their artistic skills and craftsmanship. The *Druids played a prominent role in their religion. Two of the principal dialects spoken evolved into distinctive languages: Goidelic into Irish and Scottish Gaelic and Manx and Brythonic into Cornish, Welsh, and Breton. The Celts were organized into tribal groupings, and in Wales in the 1st century AD, on the eve of the Roman conquest, the main tribes were the

*Deceangli, *Demetae, *Ordovices, and *Silures. Their settlements were based on hill forts, which often constituted tribal capitals.

The Celts, except in Ireland, were forced to submit to the victorious Roman armies, but following the departure of the Roman legions in the late 4th century Celtic kingdoms emerged in Wales.

censorship. See Licensing Act; lord chamberlain of the household; Stationers' Company.

Census Act (1800). The statute that established the taking of population censuses. The introduction of censuses (an early example of the influence of *utilitarianism), together with the *registration of births, marriages, and deaths, and marked the start of the data collection essential for modern administration. Censuses have been taken at ten-year intervals since 1801 (except in 1941).

Central African Federation. A federation of the British protectorates of Northern Rhodesia (now Zambia) and Nyasaland (Malawi), and the colony of Southern Rhodesia (Zimbabwe), established in 1953. Sir Godfrey Huggins (1953–56) and then Sir Roy *Welensky (1956–63) were its prime ministers. The federation, also called the Federation of Rhodesia and Nyasaland, was not supported by the African population and was dissolved in 1963.

Central Bank. See Bank of Ireland.

Central Criminal Court. See Old Bailey.

central powers. See World War I.

Central Treaty Organization (CENTO). A military and economic alliance between Britain, Iran, Pakistan, and Turkey; the USA is an associate member. CENTO was formed in 1959 in succession to the Baghdad pact, signed (1955) by Iraq, Turkey, and Pakistan.

Cenwulf (d. 821). King of Mercia. After seizing the throne from *Offa's son (796), Cenwulf maintained Mercian supremacy over southern England (except Wessex) and continued Mercian expansion into Wales with frequent raids and invasions. His reign was marked by ecclesiastical quarrels, including an abortive attempt

to substitute London for Canterbury as the principal English see.

Ceolwulph (died c. 875). Mercian *thegn appointed king of Mercia by the Danes in about 873. Although recognized by the church, he effectively controlled only half of Mercia, the remainder being divided among the Danes.

ceorl. An Anglo-Saxon peasant farmer ranking between serf and noble. He either owned his own land or received it from a lord to whom he was therefore tied by labour services. He was liable for military service (in the *fyrd) and taxes. In court he was entitled to have three of his peers to support his oath. By the 11th century wealthy ceorls could become *thegns, but most ceorls lost their personal freedom after the Norman conquest, and "churl" came to mean an ill-bred person. See also gebur; geneat; kotsetla.

Cerdic (d. 534). King of Wessex. Reputedly the first king of the West Saxons, Cerdic is said to have landed with five ships near Southampton and to have defeated the British in a number of campaigns in Hampshire. By tradition the landing took place in 495 but is more likely to have been in 514, five years before Cerdic ascended the throne. After establishing his power to the south and west of the middle Thames, Cerdic was halted by the British victory at Mons Badonicus, although he later conquered the Isle of Wight (530).

Ceylon. A former British colony in southeast Asia. Marco Polo visited Ceylon in 1294. Portuguese settlers arrived in the 16th century but were overrun by the Dutch a century later. The British captured Ceylon during the Napoleonic War and under the treaty of Amiens (1802) it became a British crown colony. Extensive reforms following riots in 1848 included the encouragement of coffee cultivation, later superseded in importance by the growing of tea and rubber. Ceylon attained dominion status in 1948, prior to becoming the republic of Sri Lanka (1972).

Chadwick, Sir Edwin (1800-90). Social reformer. A disciple of Bentham, Chadwick was secretary of the Poor Law Commission (1834-46). His famous Report...on an Inquiry into the Sanitary Condition of the Labouring Population of Great Britain (1842) helped secure passage of the Public Health Act (1848). The act's provisions included the establishment of a Board of Health, of which Chadwick was a commissioner until 1854, when it was abolished partly because of his failure to deal tactfully with colleagues.

chamber. In the middle ages, the place in which a great lord, especially the monarch, lived. A distinction came to be made between the great chamber (the hall) and the private apartments of the king, and under the Tudors a further division of the bedchamber, or household above stairs, into the guard chamber, the presence chamber (where the king gave audience), and the privy (private) chamber. These arrangements were reproduced wherever a peripatetic court went. Also a financial department of the royal household, under the Yorkists and Henry VII the chamber was the central financial institution of government; revenues were paid there rather than to the *Exchequer. The privy chamber was of political importance under Henry VIII.

chamberlain. A servant in the king's *chamber. Originally, several chamberlains were appointed but from the reign of Edward II (1307-27) only one held the office at a time, having responsibility for the management of the king's finances. See also lord chamberlain of the household; lord great chamberlain.

Chamberlain, Sir Austen (1863-1937). Statesman, son of Joseph Chamberlain and half-brother of Neville Chamberlain. An MP (1892-1937), he was chancellor of the exchequer (1903-05, 1919-21) and Conservative leader (1921-22). As foreign secretary (1924-29) he negotiated the Locarno pact (1925) with the major European powers, winning the Nobel peace prize.

Chamberlain, Joseph (1836-1914). Statesman; father of Neville and Austen

Chamberlain. A Unitarian and an industrialist, Chamberlain was mayor of Birmingham from 1873 to 1875, transforming the city into a model of municipal development. Entering national politics as a Liberal MP (1876), he became, with Sir Charles *Dilke, a leader of the party's radical wing. While president of the Board of Trade (1880-85) in Gladstone's second ministry, he presented an "unauthorized programme", which included the call for smallholdings ("three acres and a cow") for agricultural labourers. In 1886 he became president of the Local Government Board but, committed to imperial-unity, resigned when Gladstone was converted to the cause of Irish *home rule and led the Liberal *Unionists into alliance with the Conservatives. As secretary for the colonies (1895-1903) under Salisbury, he was engaged chiefly with the conduct of the second Boer War. He resigned in 1903 to campaign for the abandonment of free trade in favour of tariffs, an issue that split the Conservative Party and caused the government's resignation in 1905. Chamberlain's active career was ended by a crippling stroke in 1906.

Chamberlain, Neville (1869-1940). Prime minister at the outbreak of *World War II. Son of Joseph Chamberlain, he was a Conservative MP from 1918 to 1940. As minister of health (1923, 1924-29), he promoted council-house building and reformed poor-relief administration. Chancellor of the exchequer (1931-37) in the *national government, he succeeded *Baldwin as prime minister in May 1937 and rapidly developed personal direction of foreign policy, aimed at establishing peaceful relations with Hitler and Mussolini. This *appeasement policy had wide public support, although provoking Eden's resignation and bitter opposition from, notably, Winston Churchill. The *Munich pact, ceding Czechoslovak territory to Germany, followed in Sept 1938. After Germany occupied the rest of Czechoslovakia (March 1939), however, Chamberlain's government "guaranteed" Poland against German attack. Thus, when Germany invaded Poland Britain declared war (3 Sept). In May 1940, following allied disasters in Norway, many Conservatives rebelled against Chamberlain's leadership. He resigned, and Churchill became prime minister. Chamberlain joined Churchill's cabinet, but resigned, a dying man, in Oct 1940.

chancellor. The king's chief secretary, an office that originated in the reign of Edward the Confessor. The name derives from the Latin, *cancellarius*, a clerk of a law court in the Roman Empire who sat *ad cancellos*, at the railing separating the judges from the public. The chancellor kept the great seal and presided over *Chancery, becoming in the late 13th century judge of its developing equity court (*see* lord (high) chancellor). He also sat in the Exchequer, his deputy in which was to become *chancellor of the exchequer.

Chancellor, Richard (d. 1556). Navigator. He was a pilot on an expedition (1553) led by Sir Hugh Willoughby in search of a northeast passage to China. His was the only ship to reach the White Sea, from which he travelled overland to Moscow. He negotiated with the tsar a trade agreement that led to the formation (1555) of the *Muscovy Company with a monopoly of Russian trade.

chancellor of the exchequer. The cabinet minister responsible for economic policy and national finance. He is responsible for government revenue, presents budgets and the finance acts consequent on them, and determines the overall strategy of government spending. The office dates from the 13th century, when the clerk who assisted the *chancellor in the *Exchequer acquired the title. From being merely deputy to the treasurer in the Upper Exchequer, it grew in importance as a result of the Exchequer reforms of 1554 and the tenure (1566-89) of Sir Walter Mildmay. In the 18th century the chancellor of the exchequer became the second lord commissioner of the treasury and, as the first lord of the treasury took on the role of *prime

minister, the chancellor assumed complete responsibility for national finances. The judicial functions of the office were abolished in the 19th century.

Chancery. From Anglo-Saxon times, the writing office that developed from the royal chapel. The chief clerk (cleric) was called the *chancellor from the time of Edward the Confessor. Grants and acts made under the *great seal were recorded from the reign of King John. In the 13th century Chancery moved out of the court to permanent offices and declined in political importance. It acquired new prominence, however, as the *lord chancellor's court administering *equity jurisdiction to supplement the common law. The court was abolished by the *Judicature Act (1873), by which time Chancery's former administrative responsibilities had been taken over by modern government departments.

Channel Islands. An archipelago in the English Channel. *Jersey, *Guernsey, Alderney, Brechou, Great Sark, Little Sark, Herm, Jethou, and Lihou are UK crown dependencies. Formerly part of Normandy, they have been attached to England since the Norman invasion of 1066. They are divided into the bailiwicks of Guernsey and Jersey, each of which is self-governing with significantly different tax laws from the UK. In World War II, the Islands were left undefended by Britain and were the only British territory to be occupied by Germany. They were not liberated until May 1945, almost a year after the allied invasion of Normandy. The Islands include the French possessions Roches Douvres and the Îles Chansey.

Channel tunnel. A projected tunnel under the straits of Dover. The idea of a tunnel was first proposed in 1802, but only in the 1860s were plans drawn up and French and English companies formed. In 1882 work began on a pilot tunnel from Folkestone but in the following year, following a press outcry, was halted by the British government for reasons of national security. The proposal was revived in the 1960s and again in the 1970s.

chantry. A chapel built or endowed by an individual to ensure the singing therein in perpetuity of masses for his or her soul. Some chantries were independent buildings, but many formed parts of churches; the chantry priest was often the local schoolmaster. At the time of their suppression (1545-47) there were more than 2300 chantries in existence.

chapter. The clergy of a cathedral presided over by the dean and subordinate to the bishop. The chapter administers the diocese in the absence of the bishop, and by the 11th century it had assumed responsibility for his election.

charge of the Light Brigade (25 Oct 1854). A British cavalry action during the battle of *Balaclava. Misunderstanding between the commander in chief Lord *Raglan and the cavalry commander Lord *Lucan led the Light Brigade under Lord *Cardigan to attack wrongly identified Russian artillery positions up a heavily defended valley. The charge, although demonstrating great discipline and heroism, proved futile and resulted in the loss of a third of the 673 cavalrymen involved. The action inspired Tennyson's poem "Charge of the Light Brigade" (1854).

Charles I (1600-49). King of England, Scotland, and Ireland (1625-49), second son of James I and Anne of Denmark. A sickly child, Charles became heir to the throne at the death of his brother, Henry, in 1612. Shortly after his accession he married *Henrietta Maria of France.

Charles' reign was dominated by his struggle with parliament, culminating in the *Civil War. The causes of this conflict were complex but the basic issues were constitutional and religious. The constitutional dispute centred on the extent of the royal *prerogative; parliament used its right to vote new taxes as a weapon in its fight against royal power. The religious issue was equally important; the king opposed the attempts of the Puritans, strongly represented in parliament, to purge the Anglican Church of what they considered were its

Roman Catholic tendencies. Tension was heightened still more by the king's marriage to a Roman Catholic and his devotion to the duke of *Buckingham, who embroiled England in costly and futile foreign adventures.

Charles dissolved his first parliament (1625) after it had voted him only one-seventh of the revenue he needed and had attacked both Buckingham and the king's Roman Catholic leanings. The second parliament (1626) was also dissolved after it had tried to impeach Buckingham and refused to grant money to the king. During its first session (1628) the third parliament won the king's reluctant consent to the *Petition of Right. Its second session was so stormy that Charles dissolved it and attempted to rule without parliament for the next eleven years (1629-40).

In the capable hands of Thomas Wentworth (later 1st earl of *Strafford) and Archbishop *Laud the so-called *eleven years' tyranny achieved some successes. Revenue was raised by various expedients and some administrative reforms were introduced; however, the religious policy of Charles and Laud caused the government's downfall. The Scots' defiance of royal attempts to impose an Anglican church settlement in Scotland, in particular their resistance to the new Prayer Book and the episcopacy, led to the two *Bishops' Wars (1639-40) between Charles and the Scottish Presbyterians. The Scottish successes and his financial embarrassment compelled the king to summon the so-called *Short Parliament (April-May 1640), which was soon dissolved because it insisted on discussing its grievances before voting the king any money.

Further defeats in Scotland forced Charles to summon the *Long Parliament in Nov 1640. This proved even more uncooperative than its predecessors and successfully impeached Strafford (executed 1641) and Laud (executed 1645) for treason despite the king's efforts to save them. In Nov 1641 the House of Commons stated its demands in the *Grand Remonstrance. The open breach between king and parliament came early in 1642, when Charles unsuccessfully tried to arrest one member of the Lords and *five members of the Commons for treason. The king left London, and for the next seven months both sides built up their military strengths. In Aug 1642 Charles raised the royal standard at Nottingham and the Civil War began.

Charles was captured at Newark (1646) by the Scots, who handed him over to the English parliamentarians (1647). He escaped and, after secret negotiations with the Scots, agreed to accept the Presbyterian religion in Scotland and to establish Presbyterianism in England within three years. The Scots in return agreed to support the king against the English parliamentarians.

After the defeat of the king's Scottish supporters at Preston (1648) the English army demanded his death. He was taken to London and tried by a special parliamentary court. Sentenced to death, he was beheaded in Whitehall on 30 Jan 1649.

Charles II (1630-85). King of England, Scotland, and Ireland (1660-85). After the execution of his father Charles I in 1649 he was crowned at Scone by the Scots. In 1651 he invaded England at the head of a Scottish army but was defeated by Oliver Cromwell at *Worcester. Charles fled to the Continent, where he lived for nine years in exile. The political instability that followed Cromwell's death inspired Monck to engineer the restoration of the monarchy, and after issuing the conciliatory Declaration of *Breda Charles was proclaimed king. In May 1660 he entered London in triumph. Two years later he married the Portuguese princess Catherine of Braganza; there were no children of the marriage but Charles had many illegitimate offspring, including the duke of *Monmouth.

His early reign was plagued by his indebtedness, which led him to sell Dunkirk to the French in 1662. However, the *Navigation Acts (1660, 1663) contributed to the development of British commerce, and Charles' reign

also saw the introduction of important administrative reforms, notably at the Treasury. Until 1667 Charles' government was in the hands of Edward Hyde, earl of *Clarendon, but following the disastrous second *Dutch War the king dismissed his chief minister, replacing him with a group of advisers known as the *cabal. In 1668 he negotiated the *triple alliance with Sweden and the Dutch Republic against France, but he then entered into a secret agreement with the French king Louis XIV. By the treaty of *Dover (1670), negotiated through Charles' sister Henrietta Anne, duchesse d'Orléans, the king agreed to support Louis against the Dutch, in return for territorial gains and annual subsidies, and (in a secret clause) to announce his conversion to Catholicism.

The queen's childlessness and the marriage in 1673 of Charles' brother James, duke of York, to the Catholic Mary of Modena intensified fears of a Catholic succession. Following the *popish plot (1678) Charles faced three intractable parliaments, which attempted to exclude York from the succession. Thereafter he ruled without parliament and in his last years enjoyed some of his former popularity. He died a Catholic.

Charles, prince of Wales (1948-   ). The eldest son of *Elizabeth II and heir-apparent to the British throne. Created Prince of Wales in 1958 (invested at Caernarfon, 1969), he graduated from Cambridge University (1970), having also studied Welsh at Aberystwyth. After learning to fly in the RAF, he joined the Royal Navy (1971), but gave up active service in 1976 for full-time royal duties. In 1981 he married Lady Diana Spencer.

Charles Edward Stuart, the young pretender (1720-88). Son of *James Edward Stuart, the old pretender. In the last Stuart attempt to regain the Scottish and English thrones, Charles landed in Scotland in July 1745 and raised his standard at Glenfinnan. With an army of Highlanders and other *Jacobites, he took Edinburgh, won the battle of *Prestonpans (Sept 1745), and reached

Derby before retreating (Dec 1745). After a last victory at Falkirk (Jan 1746) his army was destroyed at *Culloden (April 1746). Sheltered by faithful followers, including Flora *MacDonald, he escaped to France. Charles ended his days in Italy, a drunkard, but is more kindly remembered as the gallant young "Bonnie Prince Charlie".

charter. Formal evidence in writing of a contract. Charters date from the 7th century, when they were largely concerned with grants of land and written in Latin. There are monastic records of title deeds for St Augustine's abbey at Canterbury from the time of Aethelbert of Kent (reigned 560-616), for Abingdon monastery from 687, and for Hyde monastery from Alfred's reign (871-99). Charters were issued by the king, the church, and the great magnates and often concluded legal action. Although their language was technical, they were susceptible to forgery because they were not sealed and the names of witnesses often had to be written by the clerks who drafted them.

Borough charters date from the reign of William I, and over 300 had been granted by 1216, notably by Richard and John. The privileges granted included the right of paying *firma burgi*, a fixed rent independent of the exactions of sheriffs, exemption from legal actions outside the borough, self-government through the election of magistrates, and the right of returning writs direct to the king.

Chartism. A movement for political reform (1838-48), so called from *The People's Charter* (1838), drafted largely by William *Lovett. The *Charter* made six demands: annual parliaments, universal male suffrage, equal electoral districts, an end to property qualification for MPs, voting by ballot, and payment of MPs. The movement became, under such demagogic leaders as Feargus *O'Connor and James Bronterre *O'Brien, an expression of working-class resentment against economic distress, the poor law, and the failure of the attempt to develop trades unionism. In July 1839 parliament

refused to consider a Chartist petition (presented by *Attwood), carrying 1 200 000 signatures. The Chartists, increasingly disunited, abandoned a proposed retaliatory general strike, although violent outbreaks, such as the *Newport rising, occurred. In May 1842 parliament rejected a new petition, for which O'Connor collected 3 000 000 signatures, and Chartism began to decline. O'Connor made a final attempt to revive the movement in April 1848, when he threatened a mass procession to take a third petition to parliament. When, however, the government prepared military resistance, he called off the demonstration. Chartism was of little significance thereafter, although it did not die out until 1858.

Chatham, 1st earl of. *See* Pitt the elder, William, 1st earl of Chatham.

Chatsworth house. A house in Derbyshire, the seat of the dukes of Devonshire. The original house was completed by Bess of Hardwick (*see* Shrewsbury, Elizabeth Talbot, countess of) in the 16th century. Damaged during the Civil War, it was demolished. The present house was built in the years 1687-1706 by the 4th earl (later 1st duke) of Devonshire and contains a valuable art collection and library.

Chaucer, Geoffrey (?1340-1400). Poet. Son of a London vintner, he entered royal service in 1357. His familiarity with French and Italian literature was acquired on travels abroad on royal business, and while visiting Genoa and Florence (1372-73) he may have met Boccaccio and Petrarch. In 1374 he became comptroller of customs, a post he held until 1386, and from 1389 to 1391 he was clerk of the king's works. He received a pension from Henry IV in 1399. *The Canterbury Tales* (begun about 1387), his best-known work, is a collection of 23 stories related by members of a group of pilgrims on their way to Becket's shrine at Canterbury.

Chequers. The prime minister's official country residence since 1921. A Tudor mansion in the Chilterns, about 50 km (30 mi) from London, Chequers was given to the nation in 1917 by Viscount Lee of Fareham.

Chester. The administrative centre of Cheshire. On the site of a Roman town of some size (named Deva), Chester's main importance has been strategic, in that its position made its possession vital for the control of north Wales. Under the Normans it became a *palatinate and its earl was given considerable independence in return for securing the Anglo-Welsh border. The powers of the earl of Chester proved, however, to be sufficient to cause disruption within England itself, and in 1241 Henry III acquired the area for the crown. The earldom has since been one of the titles of the prince of Wales. Chester's importance subsequently diminished. It is notable for its success in preserving such a large number of old buildings within its extensive town walls.

Chesterfield, Philip Dormer Stanhope, 4th earl of (1694-1773). Writer and politician. Chesterfield—lord lieutenant of Ireland (1745-46) and secretary of state (1746-48)—is best remembered for his *Letters* to his illegitimate son and his godson, giving guidance for life in fashionable society.

Chevy Chase, battle of. *See* Otterburn, battle of.

Chichele, Henry (?1362-1443). Archbishop of Canterbury from 1414. An able administrator, he was envoy to France (1410, 1413) and helped govern the kingdom during Henry V's absence in France (1415). He was active against the Lollards, but earned the displeasure of Pope Martin V for his failure to have the Statutes of *Provisors and *Praemunire repealed. He founded All Souls' College, Oxford, in 1438, and several professorships are named after him.

Chiltern Hundreds. Three hundreds (Stoke, Desborough, and Burnham) in south central England. An MP cannot resign his seat, but if he wishes to retire he may apply for one of two stewardships, the holder of which, since he becomes a paid officer of the crown,

may not (since 1707) sit in parliament. There were formerly several such stewardships, but since 1957 there have been only two—the Chiltern Hundreds and the Manor of Northstead in Yorkshire.

Chimney Sweepers Act (1875). An act of parliament banning anyone under the age of 21 from ascending a chimney-flue for the purpose of cleaning it. Earlier acts (1840, 1864), introduced by *Shaftesbury, had failed to curb the scandal of the child chimney sweep. Employers were now required to have an annual licence and not to take on apprentices under the age of 16.

Chindits. *See* Wingate, Orde.

Chippendale, Thomas (?1718-1779). Furniture designer, whose *Gentleman and Cabinet-Maker's Director* (1754) established him as the leading influence on English furniture design during the period 1750-80. Chippendale worked mainly in mahogany—at that time relatively unknown in Britain—and became particularly associated with the English rococo style, although he also produced gothic and Chinese designs.

Chippenham, treaty of. *See* Wedmore, treaty of.

chivalry. The knightly class (*see* knight) of medieval Europe, or its ideology and behaviour. Chivalric values of honour and courtesy developed under the impetus of the crusades in 12th-century France. They found their clearest English expression in tourneys (*see* tournament) and in the development, stimulated by the Hundred Years' War, of such orders of *knighthood as those of the Garter and the Bath.

Chivalry, Court of (or Court Military). A court, held before the lord high constable and earl marshal, having jurisdiction in such matters as the bearing of arms. Dating from the 14th century, it was not summoned between 1757 and 1955, when it was revived to deal with a complaint by Manchester Corporation that its arms were being used unlawfully.

cholera. A highly infectious and often fatal intestinal disease. During the 19th century the first outbreak of cholera occurred in 1831-33. Introduced into the northeast ports from Russia, it first appeared in Sunderland. Further outbreaks occurred in 1848-49, 1854, and 1866. On each occasion the disease spread with alarming rapidity, largely because of the lack of sanitation in the new industrial towns. The outbreaks provided a spur to public health legislation, which led to the eradication of the disease.

Christian Socialism. A mid-19th-century movement that emphasized the social principles of Christianity. Led by John Malcolm Forbes Ludlow (1821-1911), F. D. Maurice (1805-72), Charles *Kingsley, and Thomas Hughes (1822-96), the author of Tom Brown's Schooldays, it was active after the failure of Chartism in 1848. The Christian Socialists opposed *laissez-faire, attempted to develop industrial cooperatives, and founded the Working Men's College (1854).

church, pre-Reformation. The date of the introduction of Christianity to Britain is not known but an organized *Celtic church was in existence by the early 4th century. The Anglo-Saxon invasions (mid-5th to early 6th centuries) drove the Celts into Wales and the southwest. Missionaries from Scotland and Ireland and St *Augustine's mission from Rome (597) gradually converted the pagan invaders. Differences (e.g. over the date of Easter) between the Celtic and Roman churches were resolved in favour of Rome at the synod of *Whitby (664), allowing the centralized organization of the English church under *Theodore of Tarsus, consecrated archbishop of Canterbury by the pope in 668. The Anglo-Saxon church subsequently flourished, fostering missionary activity (see Boniface, St), and learning (see Bede) until the Danish raids and invasions in the 9th and 10th centuries brought chaos. The rule of Alfred the Great and his successors in Wessex ensured continuity, and under Edgar (957-75) St *Dunstan reformed many church abuses.

The *Norman conquest brought the English church back into the orbit of continental Christianity. The religious revival under Archbishop *Lanfranc was characterized by extensive building of churches and cathedrals. The establishment of separate *ecclesiastical courts, enforcing Roman canon law, allowed greater papal control of the church and gave rise to conflict between church and crown in the 12th and 13th centuries. Following the *investiture controversy between St *Anselm and Henry I and the bitter conflict between Thomas *Becket and Henry II in the 12th century, substantial gains in power were made by the church in the reigns of John and of Henry III. During the 14th and 15th centuries, however, the church fell into disrepute, and the crown was consequently able to strengthen its position. The papal exile at Avignon (1309-77) and the Great Schism (1378-1417) in the church greatly weakened the papacy, and limitations on its power in England were introduced under *Edward III. Meanwhile, resentment of ecclesiastical privilege and taxation, spiritual frustrations, and objections to the ostentatious wealth and laxity of the monasteries gave rise to successive waves of anticlericalism (see Lollards). Such dissatisfactions paved the way for the *Reformation and the establishment of the *Church of England.

Church Commissioners. The body that manages the temporal affairs of the Church of England. Created in 1948 by the amalgamation of the former Ecclesiastical Commissioners (first appointed in 1836) and the commissioners of *Queen Anne's Bounty, the Church Commissioners are responsible for the administration of church properties and finances and for the reorganization, when necessary, of parishes.

Churchill, Lord Randolph (Henry Spencer) (1849-95). Conservative politician; father of Sir Winston Churchill. An MP from 1874, Churchill became a prominent advocate of Tory Democracy as leader of the *Fourth Party. He established a power base in the National Union of Conservative Associations, becoming its president in 1884. He was secretary for India (1885-86) under Salisbury and chancellor of the exchequer from Aug to Dec 1886. He then resigned in the face of opposition, especially from the secretary for war W. H. Smith (1825-91), to defence cuts in his proposed budget. A progressive illness brought his premature death.

Churchill, Sir Winston (Leonard Spencer) (1874-1965). Statesman. Elder son of Lord Randolph *Churchill, after training at Sandhurst he served in India (1897) and the Sudan (1898). He was a war correspondent in south Africa during the second Boer War (1899-1902) and was briefly captured. He was elected a Conservative MP in 1901 but, committed to *free trade and laissez-faire, joined the Liberals in 1904, when the Conservatives were divided by Joseph Chamberlain's advocacy of tariffs. He was successively president of the Board of Trade (1908-10), home secretary (1910-11), and first lord of the Admiralty (1911-15). Criticized for the failure of the naval expedition to the Dardanelles (1915), he was demoted to the chancellorship of the duchy of Lancaster and resigned shortly afterwards. He then rejoined the army and served as a colonel in France. Appointed minister of munitions in 1917, he encouraged the development of the *tank. He was out of parliament from 1922 to 1924, when, re-elected as a constitutionalist, he became chancellor of the exchequer under Baldwin. He failed to deal effectively with the deflation and unemployment that followed the adoption in 1925 of the gold bullion standard. The government fell in 1929, and Churchill did not again hold office until the outbreak of *World War II. During the 1930s he consistently advocated prevention of German expansion, developing at his house at Chartwell, with the help of the physicist F. A. Lindemann (1886-1951; later 1st Viscount Cherwell), a sophisticated intelligence centre. In 1939, after war was declared, he was appointed first lord of the Admiralty and in May 1940 replaced Chamberlain. As wartime

prime minister, Churchill came into his own, displaying outstanding ability as a leader and as an inspirational orator. He negotiated the victorious alliance with the Soviet Union and the USA and, travelling widely throughout the war, met Stalin and Roosevelt (or Truman) at three major conferences, in *Tehran (1943), *Yalta, and *Potsdam (both 1945). Half-way through the last his caretaker government was defeated at the polls and Labour came to power. In opposition, he advocated Anglo-American alliance against the Soviet Union, which, he said (in a speech in the USA in 1946), had pulled an "iron curtain" between west and east Europe, and campaigned for European unity. He pursued both these aims while once more prime minister, from 1951 until his resignation, at the age of 80, in 1955.

Churchill, also a writer, published several histories and biographies, including *The Second World War* (6 vols, 1948-54), *A History of the English-Speaking Peoples* (4 vols, 1956-58), and *Marlborough: His Life and Times* (1933-38).

Church in Wales. The church created in 1920 following the disestablishment (see disestablishmentarianism) of the Welsh church. The Anglican church in Wales commanded the support of most Welsh until the rise of *nonconformity—itself partly a response to the decline in the spiritual standards and effectiveness of the Anglican ministry—in the 18th century. By the end of the 19th century some three-quarters of Welsh Protestant churchgoers were nonconformists, but demands for the disestablishment of the Anglican church were not met until passage of the Welsh Church Act (1914) and the Welsh Church (Temporalities) Act (1919). The church in Wales has its own archbishop and is divided into six dioceses (St David's, Llandaff, Bangor, St Asaph, Monmouth, and Swansea and Brecon).

Church of England. The national church in England, established in the 16th century during the *Reformation (see also church, pre-Reformation). The doctrines of the Church of England are contained in the 39 articles (see articles of religion), drawn up in 1563 and comprising the basis of Elizabeth I's religious settlement. A compromise between Catholicism and Calvinism, the Elizabethan settlement not only antagonized *Roman Catholics but failed to satisfy the increasing number of Puritans who wanted far-reaching reform of Church doctrine and practice (see vestiarian controversy). Uniformity was imposed by the Court of High Commission and *recusants were severely penalized. Demands for *Presbyterianism increased under James I, whose reign saw the preparation of the *Authorized Version of the Bible. The rise of the *High Church party under Charles I increased anti-episcopal feeling and contributed to the breakdown in relations between king and parliament. During the Civil War parliament introduced Presbyterian reforms (see Westminster Assembly) but, following its purge by the *Independents of the New Model Army, they were abandoned. The Restoration (1660) re-established the Church of England. The *Savoy conference (1661) made minor revisions to the *Book of Common Prayer and the Clarendon code and Test Acts penalized *nonconformists (or dissenters) and Catholics. Charles II's attempts to obtain toleration through *Declarations of Indulgence (1662, 1672) were thwarted by parliament, and James II's openly pro-Catholic policies were a major cause of the Glorious Revolution (1688). Limited toleration for nonconformists was secured by the *Toleration Act (1689), but the *nonjurors were excluded from the Church. The 18th century saw the emergence of a Whig Low Church party, known as *Latitudinarians, whose conflict with the Tory High Church party gave rise to the *Bangorian controversy (1717). Decline in the religious efficacy of the Church was countered by the *Methodists and *evangelicals, as well as by the growth of *missionary societies and *Sunday schools. Reform of major abuses, such as *pluralism and *nonresidence, was

not finally accomplished until the early 19th century. The *Oxford movement emphasized the Catholic traditions of Anglicanism and caused much general debate over Church ceremonial. At the same time the Church was forced to respond to the challenge to biblical authority posed by advances in science (see Darwin, Charles) and to the changing patterns of urban and rural life caused by the *industrial revolution. An attempt to resolve the problem of the relationship between church and state was made in 1919, when an act of parliament set up the Church Assembly empowered to prepare ecclesiastical legislation for parliamentary approval. However, the Assembly's revised prayer books (1927, 1928) were both rejected by parliament. The 20th century has seen the rise of the ecumenical movement, a drastic decline in the numbers of members, and efforts towards unity with nonconformist churches. The breadth of doctrinal belief prevailing in the modern Church has been emphasized by the controversy over the "demythologization" of Christianity. Modern translations of the *Bible and revised liturgies have also provoked debate.

Church of Ireland. The Protestant episcopal church of Ireland. The key statutes of the Henrician *Reformation were passed by the Dublin parliament in 1536 and Roman Catholics were subsequently penalized (see Penal Code). After *Catholic emancipation had been secured (1829) resentment against the minority Protestant church intensified, focusing on the hated payment of *tithes. Tithes were commuted in 1838, and in 1869 Gladstone carried an act for the disestablishment (see disestablishmentarianism) of the Protestant church, which was also partly disendowed.

Church of Scotland. The reformed Calvinist church that was given official approval by the Scottish Reformation of 1560. The church gradually split into *Presbyterian and *Episcopalian factions in the late 16th century through controversies over the structure of church government, state control, and (by the early 17th century) forms of worship. At first both factions remained within a single church. During the 17th century there were many upheavals in the Church of Scotland, notably the restoration of episcopacy by James VI, its abolition by the *covenanters in 1638, its restoration in 1661, and its final abolition in favour of Presbyterianism in 1689-90. When Presbyterianism was re-established in 1690, the dissentients formed their own episcopal Church of Scotland. The moderate nature of the 1690 settlement, with its tacit acceptance of state control, and the Church's later acceptance of lay patronage (abolished in 1690 but restored in 1712), led some of the more extreme conventiclers (see conventicle) to defy its authority. The Church was further weakened by the secessions of 1733 and 1761, and by the *disruption of 1843. In 1929 union with the United Free Church drew back into the establishment the heirs of many of those who had seceded.

cinque ports. A group of southeast Channel ports, which from the 11th to 16th centuries provided the crown with its permanent fleet in return for certain privileges, including exemption from payment of tallage. The original five —Hastings, Romney, Hythe, Sandwich, and Dover (the so-called "head" ports) —were joined by neighbouring "member" ports, which numbered more than 30 by the 13th century. Winchelsea and Rye, at first members of Hastings, were accepted by the 14th century as head ports. A warden of the cinque ports, first appointed in 1268, presided over a court exercising a local civil jurisdiction until 1855. The cinque ports declined with the development of the *navy, but an honorary lord warden continues to be appointed.

Cirencester. A town in Gloucestershire. As Roman Corinium it was the capital of the *Dobuni. Cirencester's medieval importance derived primarily from its role as a market town, dealing particularly in wool. It never became a centre of industry and is now an agricultural and tourist centre.

City of London, Corporation of the. The governing body of the City of London. The City's charter, first granted in 1079, was confirmed in 1215. It comprises three courts: the Court of Common Council, composed of the lord *mayor, the 25 other *aldermen, and 155 councillors, which is responsible for the government of the City from the Guildhall; the Court of Aldermen, which elects the lord *mayor; and the Court of Common Hall, composed of the lord mayor, the 25 other aldermen, and the freemen and liverymen (see livery companies), which elects the *sheriffs.

civil list. An allowance granted from the *Consolidated Fund by parliament to the sovereign to meet the expenses of the royal household. The first Civil List Act was passed in 1697, when the list covered the expenses of civil government and gave the crown considerable powers of *patronage. In 1761 George III surrendered the revenues of the *crown lands in return for an annual payment. Since 1831 it has covered no government expenses and since 1901 grants have been made to other members of the royal family.

civil service. The public body responsible for the administration of government. There is no statutory definition of the civil service, and the phrase was not used before the 19th century. The Royal Commission of 1921 defined civil servants as "servants of the crown...employed in a civil capacity and...paid wholly and directly out of moneys voted by Parliament", and in that sense the civil service developed only in the late 19th century. But its antecedents can be found early in the middle ages, when clerics and then laymen were employed to fulfil administrative functions in the *royal household. By the 13th century permanent administrative departments had settled at Westminster. The bureaucratic reforms of Thomas Cromwell in the 1530s and others in the 1550s were further important developments as the scope of government expanded. It was in this period that *Whitehall became the centre of administration.

There was further expansion in the 17th and 18th centuries, and by about 1800 there were some 75 offices employing 16 000 officials. Appointments were by *patronage, posts were a source of private profit, public funds were often in private accounts, and there was no coordination between departments. The scope of government increased extensively in the early 19th century, with reforms in the *poor law, public health, and later the development of state *education, requiring administrative reforms. The Northcote-Trevelyan Report (1854), prepared by Sir Stafford Northcote (1818-87) and Sir Charles Trevelyan (1807-86), is usually regarded as the foundation of the modern civil service, recommending recruitment by competitive examination, promotion by merit, the grading of employment, and a single integrated service. The Civil Service Commission was set up in 1855 to supervise recruitment. Competitive examination was introduced in 1870, and the *Treasury was given the power to approve the rules for testing candidates. A major reorganization in 1921 divided the service into four main classes. Following the Fulton Report (1968) a Civil Service Department was created under the prime minister to manage all aspects of the service.

Civil War (1642-49). An armed conflict between royalist and parliamentary forces, arising from the constitutional, economic, and religious differences between *Charles I and the *Long Parliament. Following the *Grand Remonstrance and the failure of the attempt to arrest the *five members, Charles raised his standard at Nottingham (22 Aug 1642). Royalist strength lay mainly in the north and west, while parliament drew its support principally from the south and east, especially in London. Charles' aim was to take London, but, following an indecisive engagement at *Edgehill, he was confronted by a parliamentary force at *Turnham Green, on the outskirts of London, and fell back on Oxford, which became the royalist capital for the

duration of the war. During 1643 the three royalist armies—that of Charles, based in Oxford, of William Cavendish, duke of *Newcastle, in Yorkshire, and of Ralph *Hopton in the southwest —pursued the strategic aim of effecting a junction and then marching on London. The plan, despite royalist victories at *Adwalton Moor and *Roundway Down, remained unfulfilled at the end of the year.

The adherence of the Scots to the parliamentary cause (Sept 1643) by the *Solemn League and Covenant tilted the balance of strength against Charles and opened the way to the royalist defeat at *Marston Moor (July 1644) and the loss of the north. In the southwest Hopton's advance into Hampshire was checked. During the remaining months of 1644 the royalist cause recovered some ground with the surrender of a parliamentary force at *Lostwithiel, in Cornwall, but Charles was baulked in his attempt to march on London at the second battle of *Newbury. The formation of the *New Model Army in Feb 1645, commanded by *Fairfax and *Cromwell, together with the king's rejection of the terms offered at the Uxbridge negotiations (Jan-Feb 1645), intensified the struggle, culminating in a decisive royalist defeat at *Naseby (June 1645). Parliamentary command of the southwest followed the victory at *Langport in July. Hostilities dragged on until, in June 1646, Oxford fell to parliament. Charles, placing himself in the hands of the Scots under *Leslie at Newark, was given up to parliament (Jan 1647) after refusing to take the Covenant.

This first phase of the Civil War was followed throughout 1647 by fruitless attempts by the army and parliament to arrive at a settlement with the king. Dissensions among the victors encouraged Charles to play off one faction against the other, and, after rejecting the army's *Heads of the Proposals, he escaped to the Isle of Wight. Here, he turned once more to the Scots and by the *Engagement (Dec 1647) secured their support in return for an undertaking to introduce Presbyterianism into England. Royalist risings in Wales, Kent, and Essex (March 1648) initiated the second phase of the Civil War, but were suppressed by Cromwell and Fairfax. In July a Scots army under the duke of Hamilton invaded England but in Aug was defeated by Cromwell after a three-day battle at *Preston. Charles was captured, brought to trial, and executed (Jan 1649). In May England became the *Commonwealth of England. Cromwell's subsequent campaigns in Ireland (1649-50), notorious for the massacres at *Drogheda and Wexford, and against the Scottish royalists, whom he defeated at *Dunbar (1650) and at *Worcester (1651), brought hostilities to an end.

Claim of Right (11 April 1689). The list, drawn up by the Scottish convention of estates, of the unconstitutional and illegal actions of James VII (James II of England), which had led to him forfeiting the throne. The Claim was based on the English *Declaration of Rights but, in declaring that James was deposed rather than that he had abdicated, was more radical.

clans (Gaelic for: children or offspring). Semiautonomous political, military, and social units in the Scottish Highlands, which emerged at the end of the 14th century. Clans were formed partly to counteract the growing lawlessness that resulted from the decline of the monarchy, although the clans themselves were also partly to blame for this lawlessness. In theory a clan consisted of all the descendants of a common ancestor, who was regarded as the founder of the clan and who gave his name to it (e.g. MacDonald, son of Donald). In practice many clansmen were tenants, dependants, or followers who had no blood relationship with the chief's family. In the west many chiefs were descendants of prefeudal local leaders, either Celtic or Norse, who had accepted feudal tenure but now reasserted more traditional kinship claims to authority. In the east the founders of many clans were alien feudal landlords whose descendants adopted local customs, accepting the

Gaelic language, culture, and form of chieftancy. Thus feudalism could be at least as important as kinship in creating a clan, while naked aggression and conquest could be as important as either in extending a chief's power. In the 18th century the social and economic influences of the Lowlands combined with political and military pressure to destroy clanship, especially after the failure of the 1745 *Jacobite rising.

Clapham Sect. A group of wealthy and influential adherents of Anglican *evangelicalism, active about 1785-1830, notable for humanitarian activities. The group acquired its name (originally semihumorous) because several of them lived in Clapham (then an outer London village). Of the members the best known was William *Wilberforce, but others included the banker Henry Thornton (1760-1815), James Stephen (1758-1832), and Granville Sharp (1735-1813). The sect campaigned for the abolition of *slavery, promoted missionary societies and education of the poor, but opposed radical changes in British society.

Clapperton, Hugh (1788-1827). Scottish explorer. With *Denham and Walter Oudney, he crossed the Sahara to Lake Chad (1823) and travelled through Bornu and Hausaland. In 1825 he returned to Africa, with Richard *Lander, to trace the course of the Niger. Clapperton died near Sokoto, weakened by the hardships of the expedition.

Clare, Gilbert de, 9th earl of Clare and 7th earl of Hertford (and 8th earl of Gloucester) (1243-95). Magnate, prominent in the second *Barons' War. A member of the baronial party at the Oxford Parliament in 1258, he refused to take the oath of allegiance to Prince Edward in 1263. However, after quarrelling with the barons' leader Simon de *Montfort he became (1266) a royalist supporter. He acted as mediator between Henry III and the rebels in 1267 and secured the accession of Edward I in 1272, cementing their friendship by taking Joan, Edward's daughter, as his second wife.

The territories of the chief clans and families of Scotland

Clare, Richard de, 2nd earl of Pembroke and Striguil (d. 1176). Conqueror in Ireland, called Richard Strongbow. He supported the dethroned king of Leinster, *Dermot MacMurrough, whose daughter Eva he married, and captured Waterford and Dublin (1170). He suppressed a rising that followed Dermot's death (1171) but was forced to surrender his conquests to Henry II. However, after assisting Henry in Normandy (1173), Wexford, Waterford, and Dublin were granted to him. He was said to have killed his son for being a coward.

Clarence, George, duke of (1449-78). Brother of Edward IV. He was lord lieutenant of Ireland from 1462 to 1469, when he married Isabel, eldest daughter of Warwick the kingmaker. Clarence and Warwick twice (1469, 1470) invaded England, but after the restoration of Henry VI Clarence gave his support to Edward, whom he helped to regain the throne (1471). Quarrels between the brothers culminated in Clarence's attainder for plotting by necromancy Edward's death. Clarence was executed, by drowning according to rumour.

Clarence, Thomas, duke of (c. 1388-1421). Second son of Henry IV. He was appointed lieutenant of Ireland in 1401 and led several raids on the French coast. He played an important part in Henry V's French campaign, dying in action at Beaugé.

Clarence (and Avondale), Albert Victor, duke of (1864-92). The elder son of Edward, prince of Wales (later Edward VII). By his death, the succession to the throne passed to his brother, the future George V.

Clarendon, Assize of (1166). A legislative enactment, comprising a code of 22 articles for the administration of justice, issued by Henry II. Its most significant provision instituted the *jury. It was amplified by the Assize of Northampton (1176).

Clarendon, constitutions of (30 Jan 1164). A written statement made by Henry II at Clarendon, near Salisbury, of the relationship between church and state that had been established under his predecessors. The most controversial clause related to *benefit of clergy and laid down that, if a clerk in holy orders was convicted of a crime in a church court, he should then be available for punishment by the lay authorities. *Becket's objection to this clause brought him into open conflict with the king.

Clarendon, Edward Hyde, 1st earl of (1609-74). Statesman. A lawyer, Hyde first became involved in politics in 1640, when he became a member of the *Short Parliament. Critical of Charles I's fiscal policies, he nevertheless resisted attempts to abolish royal prerogatives. Following publication of the *Grand Remonstrance (1641) he tried unsuccessfully to reconcile king and parliament and served as one of Charles' chief advisers during the first stage of the Civil War. He went into exile in 1646 and during the Interregnum drafted his famous *The True Historical Narrative of the Rebellion* (first published 1702-04). In exile in

France he became Charles II's closest adviser and after Richard Cromwell's fall negotiated the *Restoration. He became Baron Hyde in 1660, when his daughter Anne married Charles' brother James, and earl of Clarendon in 1661. As lord chancellor he urged moderation in the treatment of the king's former opponents and took a more tolerant attitude to nonconformity than that of the *Clarendon code, named after him. The disasters of the second *Dutch War brought his fall from power in 1667, and although an attempt to impeach him failed he was forced into exile and died in France.

Clarendon code (1661-65). A series of parliamentary measures aimed at re-establishing the position of the Anglican church following the Restoration. The code was named after the king's chief minister, Edward Hyde, 1st earl of *Clarendon, who, however, supported the measures with reluctance. As a result of the legislation (the *Corporation Act, 1661; the Act of *Uniformity, 1662; the *Conventicle Act, 1664; and the *Five Mile Act, 1665), 2000 Anglican clergy were forced to resign their livings, and the permanent religious and social breach between Anglicanism and non-conformity effectively came into being.

Clarkson, Thomas (1760-1846). Leader, with *Wilberforce, of the movement for the abolition of *slavery. Clarkson wrote a two-volume history of the slave trade (1808) and in 1823 became vice president of the Anti-Slavery Society.

Claudius (10 BC-54 AD). Roman emperor (41-54 AD). In 43 AD, encouraged by internal discord among the British tribes, he began the invasion of Britain that led to its incorporation in the Roman Empire. He took a personal part in the campaign and was present at the capture of Camulodunum (Colchester), the capital of *Caractacus.

Clerk's Act. *See* Place Acts.

Clifford, Rosamond (died c. 1176). Mistress of Henry II, called Fair Rosamond. There is no evidence for contemporary stories of *Eleanor of

Aquitaine's jealousy and consequent murder of Rosamond, who was buried in Godstow abbey.

Clifford, Thomas, 1st Baron Clifford of Chudleigh (1630-73). Statesman. A member of Charles II's *cabal, he was party to the secret treaty of *Dover (1670) and as secretary of state recommended (1672) a 12-month "stop of the exchequer", ruining commercial credit. A Roman Catholic, he was forced to resign by the *Test Act (1673).

Clinton, Sir Henry (c. 1738-1795). Soldier, born in Newfoundland, who joined the British army in 1751. He was appointed commander in chief in North America in 1778, succeeding Howe. He resigned (1781) after quarrelling with Cornwallis. He later sat in parliament (1772-84, 1790) and was appointed governor of Gibraltar in 1794.

Clive, Robert, Baron (1725-74). One of the founders of British *India. Son of a Shropshire lawyer, Clive arrived in Madras as a clerk in the East India Company (1744). Suffering from depression, he attempted suicide and, when his pistol failed, concluded "I am destined for something". The struggle between the French and English to dominate India provided his opportunity. Transferring to the Company's army, he established his fame by his capture and defence, for 53 days against a French-Indian force, of Arcot (1751) and his share in other victories of the *Carnatic Wars. He became governor of Madras in 1756 and, summoned to Bengal after the tragedy of the *black hole of Calcutta, defeated Siraj-ud-Dawlah at *Plassey (1757), becoming effective ruler of Bengal. In 1760 he returned to England, planning a political career, and became an MP (1761). In the following year he was created Baron Clive in the Irish peerage. Returning to Bengal in 1765, as governor and commander in chief, he reorganized the Company's administration. Back in England in 1767, he was attacked for his vast *nabob fortune and was obliged to submit to a parliamentary inquiry (1772-73). He

was cleared but, ill and depressed, committed suicide shortly afterwards.

Clontarf, battle of (23 April 1014). A battle in which a large force of Scandinavians, led by the Danish king of Dublin, fought *Brian Boru, high king of Ireland. Brian was killed but the Scandinavians were defeated, and their power was thereafter limited to their sea ports.

Cnut (or Canute) (c. 994-1035). King of Denmark and England. He accompanied his father Sweyn Forkbeard on his invasion of England (1013) and was chosen king of Denmark (1014) on Sweyn's death. A protracted struggle with *Edmund Ironside, king of Wessex, for control of England ended with Edmund's murder in 1016, and Cnut was crowned in 1017. In the same year he married Emma, the widow of Aethelred II, and by the early 1020s was depending on English more than Danish advisers. His reign was marked by legal and military reforms and, apart from an expedition to Scotland in 1027, internal peace. The famous story of how Cnut demonstrated to flatterers the limitation of his powers, by failing to make the waves recede, was told by *Henry of Huntingdon.

Coalbrookdale (or Ironbridge). A town in Shropshire, which was the centre of the British iron industry in the 18th century. Abraham *Darby developed his iron-smelting process here in about 1713, and the Coalbrookdale Works became important in the production of cylinders for *Newcomen's steam engine. The first iron bridge, designed by Darby's grandson and cast in 1778, crosses the river Severn here.

Cobbett, William (1762-1835). Journalist and radical campaigner. Cobbett founded the *Political Register* in 1802 and *Parliamentary Debates* (later *Hansard) in 1803. An anti-establishment radical from 1805, Cobbett remained at heart a Tory democrat and idealized preindustrial England. He was imprisoned (1810-12) for opposing the flogging of militiamen. A leader of the post-1815 reform movement, he fled to America in 1817, returning to England in 1819. His

Rural Rides (1830) vividly describes England in the 1820s.

Cobden, Richard (1804–65). Politician and leader of the movement to repeal the *corn laws. A Sussex farmer's son, Cobden became a textile manufacturer in Manchester. A prominent advocate of free trade and internationalism, Cobden, with John *Bright, was the foremost figure in the successful campaign (1839–46) of the Anti-Corn Law League. An MP from 1841, he lost his seat (1857) as a result of his opposition to the Crimean War but returned to parliament in 1859. Although Cobden refused government office, he negotiated a commercial treaty with France (1860) that helped end a period of extreme Anglo-French tension.

Cochrane, Thomas, 10th earl of Dundonald (1775–1860). Naval commander, called Lord Cochrane. He served as lieutenant and captain during the Napoleonic War but was imprisoned on a charge of fraud in 1814 and expelled from the navy and parliament. On his release he went abroad and commanded the Chilean navy (1817–22) and the Brazilian navy (1823–25) during the two countries' wars of independence. In 1832 he was reinstated in the Royal Navy as a rear admiral and later served as commander in chief in North America and the West Indies.

Cockayne project. A patent granted by James I, at the expense of the *Merchants Adventurers company, to Sir William Cockayne (d. 1626) to dye and finish cloth before export, buttressed by a ban (1614) on the export of undyed cloth. The scheme severely damaged the cloth trade and by 1617 had foundered because foreign buyers preferred undressed cloth, especially in view of the inferiority of English dyers.

coercion acts. Laws passed in the 1880s to give the Irish administration special powers to combat agrarian unrest. The first act (1881) was aimed at the suppression of the agrarian violence that followed the campaign of the *Irish Land League; it suspended *habeas corpus, giving the authorities special powers of arbitrary arrest. A second act (1882) followed the *Phoenix Park murders; these and further acts in the 1880s failed to subdue Irish discontent.

coffee houses. Centres of political, literary, business, and social life, which grew up after coffee was introduced to Europe in the 17th century. Charles II tried to suppress them as possible centres of sedition. They flourished in the 18th century, when London's 2000 coffee houses included Wills and Buttons, patronized by Johnson, Dryden, Addison, and Pope, and Whites, whose fashionable clients are shown in Hogarth's *The Rake's Progress.* The roles of the coffee houses were later taken over by newspapers, public houses, and private clubs.

coinage. Metal currency. Coinage was introduced to Britain by the *Belgae in the 1st century BC, and the earliest British coins were struck in gold. The Romans, whose coins were in use from the 1st to 5th centuries AD, divided the *libra* (pound) into 20 *solidi* (shillings) and the *solidus* into 12 *denarii* (pennies). From about 600 silver coins (sceats) were minted, and the silver penny, introduced by Offa of Mercia (reigned 757–96), was the main coin in circulation until the reintroduction of gold coins in the 14th century. The mark, a monetary unit introduced in the Danelaw, represented 128, and later 160, silver pennies. Halfpennies were introduced in the 9th century (and not withdrawn until 1969) and farthings in 1279 (minted until 1961). Following the Norman conquest the quality of coins began to deteriorate through poor craftsmanship and clipping (removing small pieces of metal while passing the coin on at face value). They reached a low point in the mid-12th century.

The gold noble (worth 6 shillings and 8 pence) was introduced by Edward III and, with Henry VI's angel (worth 6 shillings and 8 pence, the noble being revalued at 8 shillings and 4 pence), was the chief currency until the 17th century. Edward also introduced the groat (4 pennies), which survived until 1856. The pound, worth 240 silver pennies, was first minted in 1489, while the gold crown (5 shillings) and half-crown were introduced in 1526, and their silver counterparts in 1551. Henry VIII first minted the shilling. The guinea, introduced in 1662 and with a value fixed in 1717 at 21 shillings, remained the basis of the currency until 1816, when it was replaced by what came to be called the sovereign (with a value of 20 shillings). Gold coins were last struck in 1917, and silver, debased in 1921, gave way to cupro-nickel in 1947.

Coke, Sir Edward (1552-1634). Lawyer and politician, who championed the common law against the royal *prerogative. Elected to parliament in 1589 he became speaker of the House of Commons in 1593 and attorney general in 1594, being responsible for the prosecutions for treason of Essex (1601), Raleigh (1603), and the conspirators in the gunpowder plot (1605). In 1606 he was appointed chief justice of the Court of Common Pleas. His opposition to the Court of *High Commission and to royal *proclamations, which he maintained could not change the common law or create new offences, brought him into conflict with James I. In an attempt to silence Coke, the king appointed him chief justice of the King's Bench, the first to be called lord chief justice. He continued, however, to defend the common law and in 1616 was dismissed. Re-entering parliament in 1621, he was prominent in the opposition to the crown and was largely responsible for the drafting of the *Petition of Right (1628).

Coke of Holkham, Thomas William, 1st earl of Leicester (1752-1842). Agriculturalist. He inherited the Holkham estate in Norfolk (with its magnificent Palladian mansion) in 1776. He was an MP (1776-1806, 1807-32) but devoted his life to the improvement of farming. Many of Coke's techniques were not original, but he developed them to an advanced stage and publicized them, with hundreds of visitors attending his "Holkham meetings". Using marl and manure as fertilizers, he transformed the sandy soil, introduced wheat in place of rye, rotated crops, and bred improved sheep, cattle, and pigs. A model landlord, he encouraged good husbandry by granting tenants long leases. He was created earl of Leicester in 1837.

Colchester. The administrative centre of Essex. A medieval market town of some importance, Colchester was founded by *Cunobelinus, and named Camulodunum, shortly after the Roman invasion. It was the site of a notable engagement in the rebellion of *Boudicca, who slaughtered most of the inhabitants. From then on Colchester has scarcely figured in English history and is now primarily notable for the quality of its architectural remains. It is the site of some of the finest Roman ruins in the country, as well as of one of the most impressive Norman keeps.

Coldstream Guards. The second regiment of footguards, part of the Household Division of the British army. Raised by Cromwell in 1650 for service in Scotland under *Monck, the regiment acquired its present name following an overnight halt at the Border village of Coldstream during Monck's decisive march to London in 1660. Units of the Coldstreams have participated in many historic actions, among them *Oudenarde (1708), *Malplaquet (1709), and *Dettingen (1743), as well as fighting under Wellington in the Peninsular campaign and at Waterloo. The regiment won seven Victoria Crosses during World War I, and between 1939 and 1945 took part with distinction in the North African, Italian, and Normandy campaigns.

Colenso, John William (1814-83). Anglican bishop of Natal (1853-69). Questions asked by his Zulu converts caused him to doubt the accuracy of the Pentateuch (the first five books of the Old Testament), and in 1863 he was charged with heresy. Despite his acquittal Colenso was dismissed in 1869, but he nevertheless continued his episcopate. His writings include a Zulu grammar and dictionary and a Zulu translation of the New Testament.

Colet, John (?1467-1519). Humanist and theologian. He was dean of St Paul's (1504-19) and in 1509 founded St Paul's School.

Collingwood, Cuthbert Collingwood, 1st Baron (1750-1810). Naval commander. Collingwood served his friend Nelson as a lieutenant (1778), fought at the battle of Cape St Vincent (1797), and was promoted vice admiral in 1804. Following Nelson's death, he took command at Trafalgar. Thereafter, Collingwood had a somewhat undistinguished career commanding fleets off Spain and Sicily. He died at sea.

Collins, Michael (1890-1922). Irish nationalist from Cork, who fought in the *Easter rising. Elected MP in 1918, he was a minister in the *Sinn Féin government (1919-21) and a leader of the struggle against the British authorities, who offered £10,000 for his arrest. In Dec 1921 he signed the Anglo-Irish treaty, which was repudiated by many Republicans and led to civil war in Ireland. Ten days after taking over the leadership of the transitional government he was killed by Republicans in an ambush.

Colman, St (d. 679). Ionan monk, born in Mayo, who became bishop of Lindisfarne in 661. His defence of Celtic practices at the synod of Whitby (664) was defeated by Wilfrid, and Colman subsequently retired to Iona and then Mayo. Feast day: 18 Feb or 8 Aug.

Colombo plan. A plan for the cooperative economic development of south and southeast Asia after World War II, initiated by Commonwealth foreign ministers meeting at Colombo, Ceylon, in 1951. It has 21 members in the region and six (Australia, Canada, Japan, New Zealand, UK, and USA) elsewhere. Donor countries provide financial aid, technical assistance, and training facilities for developing countries of the region.

colonia (Latin: colony). Under the Roman Empire, a settlement established to provide land for soldiers on the completion of their service. *Colonia*

developed into centres of Roman civilization, such as those at Camulodunum (*see* Colchester), Glevum (*see* Gloucester), Lindum (*see* Lincoln), and Eboracum (*see* York).

colonial conferences. *See* imperial conferences.

Colonial Office. A government department established in 1854. Its forerunners were the Council for the Colonies (1670-72), Council for Trade and Plantations (1672-75), and Board of Trade and Plantations (1696-1782). A secretary of state for the colonies existed from 1768 to 1782, when the newly created Home Department took charge of them. From 1794 to 1854 colonies were administered by the secretary of state for war. The granting of self-government to most colonies led to the merger in 1966 of the Colonial Office with the Commonwealth Relations Office (*see* Foreign and Commonwealth Office).

Columba, St (521-97). Irish missionary in Scotland. Expelled from Ireland in 563, Columba founded the monastery of *Iona, spreading Irish monastic ideals in the kingdom of Dalriada and seeking to convert the Picts. Feast day: 9 June.

Combination Acts (1799, 1800). Two acts that forbade the "combining" of two or more people for the purpose of obtaining a wage increase, better working conditions, etc. (*see* trade union). That of 1800 was repealed in 1824.

commissions. Warrants, especially those under the *great seal, empowering certain persons to act in a particular capacity; or the bodies of persons thus empowered to act. From the 13th century justices of the *assize held commissions of the *peace, *oyer and terminer, gaol delivery, and *nisi prius. Commissions of array or muster were issued in times of war. Parliamentary taxes were collected by commissions. Thomas Cromwell exercised his vicegerency by commission, and used commissions to dissolve the monasteries. The Court of *High Commission enforced the Elizabethan church settlement. In the 19th and 20th centuries, commissions of inquiry have often preceded major legislation.

common law. The body of legal principles evolved by judges from custom and precedent. Common law developed in the 12th century, as local courts administering local law declined, and the law administered by the king's justices, common to the whole kingdom, gained ground. The most important common law courts were *Common Pleas, dealing with disputes between subject and subject, *King's Bench, dealing with matters affecting the king, and the Court of *Exchequer, dealing with financial matters. Common law is contrasted with statute law, the written law of parliament to which it is complementary; with *equity jurisdiction in Chancery; and with canon law, the law of the church.

Common Pleas, Court of. The oldest of the *common law courts, founded in the 12th century. It dealt originally with all civil disputes between subjects. Expense and longwindedness made it vulnerable to encroachment by other courts, e.g. the Court of *Requests, in Elizabeth I's reign. In 1873 its jurisdiction passed to the High Court of Justice.

Commonwealth. A loose association of independent countries, and their dependencies, and associated states, which were formerly part of the *British Empire; their populations comprise a quarter of mankind. The term British Commonwealth came to be used during World War I to describe the relationship between Britain and the self-governing *dominions, and at the Paris Peace Conference (1919) the dominions and India were separately represented and individually became signatories of the Covenant, and members, of the League of Nations. At the 1926 *imperial conference A. J. *Balfour defined the relationship between Britain and the dominions, a statement that became the doctrine of the Commonwealth of Nations established by the Statute of *Westminster (1931). Dominion governments might freely pass legislation that was incompatible with British laws, and no British law was enforceable in a dominion without its consent. Voluntary allegiance to the British crown was the bond between the members of the Commohwealth.

After World War II India (1947), Ceylon (1948), and Burma (1948) gained their independence, India and Ceylon remaining within the Commonwealth (which was no longer defined as "British") while Burma left it. In 1949, following India's announcement of its intention to become a republic, the meeting of Commonwealth Heads of Government agreed that republics might remain within the Commonwealth so long as they acknowledged the reigning British sovereign as "the symbol of the free association of its independent member nations and as such the head of the Commonwealth". In the period since 1957 independence has been granted to almost all Britain's former colonies, and most have chosen to remain within the Commonwealth. In 1949 Ireland, in 1961 South Africa, and in 1972 Pakistan resigned from the Commonwealth.

The Dominions Office, which had been established in 1925 to deal with Britain's relations with the members of the Commonwealth, was replaced in 1947 by the Commonwealth Relations Office. This was merged with the *Colonial Office in 1966 to form the Commonwealth Office, which was amalgamated with the Foreign Office in 1968 to form the *Foreign and Commonwealth Office. The Commonwealth Secretariat was established (1965) in London to promote relations between Commonwealth members, and their heads of government meet periodically to discuss matters of mutual interest. Commonwealth countries formerly enjoyed special trading arrangements with Britain and other member states (see imperial preference).

Commonwealth of England. The term commonly used to describe the period of republican government in Britain during the *Interregnum (1649-60), but applied more specifically to the years (1649-53, 1659-60) that preceded and followed Oliver Cromwell's experiment in personal government under the *Protectorate. Following the execution of Charles I (Jan 1649) and the abolition of the monarchy and the House of Lords (March 1649) a "Commonwealth or Free-State" was declared by the *Rump of the Long Parliament (19 May 1649). Supreme authority was vested in the House of Commons, while the executive powers of the monarchy were taken up by a Council of State of 40 members, 31 of whom were MPs. Under the new government military operations continued against the Scots, leading to Commonwealth victories at *Dunbar (1650) and *Worcester (1651) and de facto incorporation of Scotland in the republic. Rebellion in Ireland was ruthlessly suppressed (1649-50), while at sea the navy defeated the royalist fleet of Prince Rupert, established control over the America colonies, and fought a maritime war against the Dutch (see Dutch Wars). Finances were secured by taxation and the confiscation of royalist properties, censorship was imposed, and strict control of public morality was attempted by such measures as the Blasphemy Act (1650). The Rump's dilatoriness, however, in pressing forward with the radical social reforms demanded by the army, together with its attempt to turn itself into a nonelected oligarchy, led to its dismissal (April 1653) by Cromwell. After three months of army rule, Cromwell sought constitutional backing by calling the nominated *Barebones Parliament, but with the failure (Dec 1653) of the experiment accepted the *Instrument of Government establishing the Protectorate and bringing the first phase of the Commonwealth to an end.

Following Cromwell's death and the failure of Richard *Cromwell to provide strong government, the Commonwealth was effectively revived with the recall of the Rump (May 1659) by the army. Continued friction between the two, however, as well as between parliamentary factions, condemned the second phase of republican government to failure, and an expanded House of Commons negotiated for the restoration

of Charles II (8 May 1660) on the basis of the Declaration of *Breda.

competitors. The 13 men who put forward claims to the throne of Scotland after the death of *Margaret, the maid of Norway. See great cause.

composition fine. In Anglo-Saxon law, a fine paid by an offender to the plaintiff in compensation for an injury. The amount paid depended on the plaintiff's wer (see wergild).

compounding. The payment of a fine by royalists after the Civil War to avoid prosecution or confiscation of their properties. These fines ranged in severity from between a tenth to a third of an estate's total value.

Compton, Henry (1632-1713). Bishop of London. Younger son of the 2nd earl of Northampton, he was ordained in 1662 and made bishop of London in 1675. An opponent of James II's pro-Catholic policies, he was the only ecclesiastic to sign the invitation (1688) to William of Orange to occupy the English throne. He was embittered by his failure to become archbishop of Canterbury despite having acted as such during *Sancroft's suspension and ended his career as a High Tory.

compurgation. See wager of law.

Comyn, John, lord of Badenoch (died c. 1303). One of the *guardians of Scotland appointed in 1286. Called John the Black, he was one of the *competitors for the throne in 1290 but supported the claims of John Balliol, whose sister he married.

Comyn, John, lord of Badenoch (d. 1306). Called John the Red, he was the son of John the Black and supported John *Balliol. He was murdered at Dumfries by Robert Bruce shortly before the latter declared himself king, perhaps because Robert wanted to remove a rival claimant to the throne.

condominium. The joint exercise of sovereignty over a territory by two or more states, such as that of France and Britain over the New Hebrides (1906-80).

confederate lords. Opponents of the marriage in 1567, soon after *Darnley's murder, between *Mary Queen of Scots and the earl of *Bothwell. They secured Mary's defeat at Langside, imprisoned her, and forced her to abdicate the Scottish throne in favour of her infant son, James VI, the future *James I of England.

Congregation, lords of the. Scottish signatories of a pact, or covenant (1557), to support the Protestant "Congregation of God". Their demands included public exposition of the Scriptures and the use of the new English Book of Common Prayer. See Reformation.

Congregationalists. Members of a nonconformist association of local autonomous churches. Congregationalists hold Calvinist doctrines and acknowledge the priesthood of all believers. Robert *Browne established (1580) the first independent congregation in Norwich, for which he was imprisoned, and his contemporaries Henry *Barrow and John *Penry were both hanged for their separatist beliefs. The *Independents, as they came to be known, came to the fore of the parliamentary cause during the Civil War and enjoyed freedom of worship under the Protectorate. Their right to worship was suspended by the Act of Uniformity (1662) but renewed by the Toleration Act (1689). The Congregational Union was formed in 1832 and reasserted the independence of its member churches. In 1972 the Congregationalists merged with the English Presbyterians to form the United Reformed Church.

congress system. An attempt to maintain peace in Europe after the Napoleonic Wars by regular diplomatic meetings of the representatives of the four major powers. The system was established in 1815 by the *quadruple alliance of Britain, Austria, Russia, and Prussia. Congresses were held at Aix-la-Chapelle (1818), Troppau (1820), Laibach (1821), and Verona (1822), but Britain was increasingly unsympathetic to the readiness of its allies to interfere in the internal affairs of other countries and did not attend the final congress, at St Petersburg (1825).

Congreve, William (1670-1729). Dramatist, a master of the comedy of manners. In his early career he enjoyed the patronage of the poet Dryden. Congreve's plays, which satirized the fashionable society of his day, include Love for Love (1695) and The Way of the World (1700). A supporter of the Whig party, he benefited in later life from a number of sinecure offices.

Connaught (or Connacht). A province of northwest Ireland and one of the five ancient kingdoms (see also Leinster; Meath; Munster; Ulster). Little is known of the ancient line of Connaught kings, displaced in the 4th century AD by members of the Tara dynasty, who ruled until the Anglo-Norman conquest. In the 12th century *Rory O'Connor of Connaught was recognized as high king of Ireland. Cathal Crobderg, brother and successor of Rory O'Connor, was the last Tara king of Connaught. In 1227, shortly after Cathal Crobderg's death, Henry III granted Connaught to Richard de Burgh, who conquered it by 1235. De Burgh's many descendants now bear the name of Burke. In 1576 Connaught was shired, and in the middle of the 17th century the area was set aside for Irishmen displaced by the Cromwellian settlers in Ireland. Connaught is still regarded as the most typically Irish part of Ireland.

conscription. The compulsory enlistment of civilians to serve in the armed forces. Until World War I Britain had been defended by the Royal Navy and a comparatively small standing *army of volunteers, but the heavy casualties of 1914-15 and the unprecedented demand for soldiers led to the introduction of conscription of unmarried, and then married, men aged 18-41 early in 1916. During World War II the conscription of men (and of women from Dec 1941) was organized to take into account economic as well as military needs. Conscription continued until 1962.

Conservative Party. One of the two major political parties, which emerged in the 1830s from the *Tory grouping; the name Tory is still commonly used to designate Conservative. Under *Peel the Tory party adapted to the effects of the *Reform Act (1832), stating its belief —notably in Peel's *Tamworth manifesto (1834)—in moderate reform together with acknowledgement of landed and industrial interests. Peel's second ministry (1841-46) introduced several notable reforms, including the repeal of the *corn laws (1846), which, however, split the party. Many Peelites subsequently joined the emerging *Liberal Party, while the Conservative Party took coherent form under the leadership of *Disraeli (later Lord Beaconsfield). Its programme was based on a commitment to traditional institutions, the defence of the British Empire, and social reform. In 1886 many Liberal opponents of Irish home rule allied with the Conservative Party, which was led after Beaconsfield's death by *Salisbury (1881-1902) and then Balfour (1902-11). In 1912 the so-called Liberal *Unionists and the Conservatives merged into the Conservative and Unionist Party, which remains the party's official name. The Conservatives, having been out of office since 1905, when Joseph Chamberlain's proposals for tariff reform divided the party, joined the coalition government (1915-22) led by Asquith and then by Lloyd George. In 1922 the party was again returned to power under Bonar *Law. It lost to Labour, now replacing the Liberals as the other major party, in 1923, but again formed a government in 1924, remaining in power under *Baldwin until 1929. Conservatives dominated the *national government (1931-35), and Baldwin was again prime minister from 1935 to 1937, when he was succeeded as Conservative leader by Neville *Chamberlain. After the outbreak of World War II Chamberlain was replaced by *Churchill, who led the wartime coalition government. The party was defeated in the election of 1945, but returned to power in 1951, remaining in office until 1964 under, successively, Churchill, Anthony *Eden, Harold *Macmillan, and Sir Alec

Douglas-Home (see Home of the Hirsel, Alexander Douglas-Home, Baron). In this period the party presided over the decolonization of much of Britain's former empire and made a first, unsuccessful, attempt to obtain membership of the EEC. This was finally achieved in 1973 under Douglas-Home's successor, Edward *Heath, who took the Conservatives back into power in 1970. After losing both the elections of 1974, Heath was replaced by Margaret Thatcher (1925-), who in 1979 became the first woman prime minister in British history.

The party has, in the postwar period, adapted its policies to meet the Labour challenge, but remains committed to free enterprise and opposed to nationalization. Based on individual membership through constituency associations, the party gives great powers to its leader, who has been elected since 1965 by MPs rather than, as formerly, by "the necessary processes of consultation". It is financed by individual subscriptions and gifts and also by contributions from business interests.

Consolidated Fund. The revenues held in the Exchequer account at the Bank of England. Established in 1787 by Pitt the younger, it originally "consolidated" separate customs and excise revenues into a single fund. The main expenditure from it is now the interest on and management of the *national debt. It also provides for payments on the *Civil List.

constable. An officer of local government. The word was applied to the high constables of the hundreds (abolished in 1869); to the petty constables of parishes (abolished in 1872); but especially to the paid *police forces established in the 19th century.

Constable, John (1776-1837). Landscape painter. Constable, a Suffolk miller's son, painted with great naturalism, recording the preindustrial English countryside in such works as *Flatford Mill* (1817) and *The Hay Wain* (1821). Although he was much respected in France, he was not generally recognized in England in his lifetime.

Constantine (d. 820). King of the Picts (c. 789-820). He probably succeeded in asserting his authority over *Dalriada after 811, a task made easier by the weakening of that kingdom by Viking raids.

Constantine I (died c. 877). King (c. 862-c. 877) of Scotia (Scotland north of the Forth), son of Kenneth MacAlpin, and successor of his uncle Donald I. He was killed in battle against the Vikings, who invaded his kingdom several times.

Constantine II (d. 952). King of Scotia (900-43). He was the first king of Scotia known to have exercised authority south of the Forth, Strathclyde being dependent on him. Under Constantine Scotia suffered much from Viking incursions. In 934 Athelstan of England, who was challenging Constantine's claim to Northumbria, invaded Scotia; Constantine's attempt at retaliation in 937 in alliance with the Norse of Dublin and possibly the king of Strathclyde was defeated at *Brunanburh in Yorkshire. Constantine abdicated to become a monk.

Constantine III (d. 997). King (995-97) of Scotia (Scotland north of the Forth), the son of Culen, king of Scotia. He may have been responsible for the killing of his predecessor Kenneth II, and he himself was soon murdered, perhaps by Kenneth III.

continental system. The economic warfare practised (1806-13) by Napoleon against Britain, aimed at ruining British trade by excluding it from continental Europe. Retaliation by Britain against neutral ships trading with France helped spark off the *Anglo-American War of 1812. British naval supremacy eventually led to the breakdown of the system.

conventicle. A meeting for unauthorized worship. The Conventicle Act (1593) imposed penalties on those who declined to attend Church of England services and attended conventicles. That of 1664, forming part of the *Clarendon code, only forbade conventicles of more than five people who were not members of

the same household. Expiring in 1668, it was renewed in 1670.

convention parliament. An extraordinary meeting of parliament without the summons of the sovereign. Two parliaments in particular have been so called. Both passed acts establishing their legality and the legislation of each was confirmed by subsequent parliaments. 1. (14 April-29 Dec 1660) The parliament that recalled Charles II to the English throne. It was also empowered to settle problems arising from the Interregnum. There were three principal areas of business: procuring indemnity for all those involved in the rebellion or Interregnum government, with the exception of certain named individuals (see Indemnity and Oblivion, Act of); settling conflicting claims to confiscated properties; and granting Charles, in return for his surrender of the crown's remaining feudal dues, a fixed annual income for life of £1,200,000. 2. (1-23 Feb 1689) The parliament that met after the overthrow of James II. It declared the throne vacant and offered it to William and Mary on condition of their acceptance of the *Declaration of Rights.

convoy. A group of vessels escorted by warships. The system was introduced (1917) in World War I by Lloyd George, in the face of opposition from the Admiralty, to protect British merchant shipping from the attacks of German submarines. It successfully reduced shipping losses.

Cook, Captain James (1728-79). Navigator and explorer of the Pacific and Antarctic. Cook served with the Royal Navy and in 1768 was appointed commander of the *Endeavour*, taking members of the Royal Society on an expedition to Tahiti. On the return journey he mapped the coasts of New Zealand, explored the southeast coast of Australia, and navigated the Great Barrier Reef (1770-71). On his second voyage (1772-75) he explored the Antarctic. Cook devised a diet high in vitamin C to maintain the health of his crew, none of whom died of scurvy on either voyage. On his third voyage

(1776-80), in search of the northwest passage, he failed to discover a navigable waterway connecting the North Pacific and North Atlantic. He was killed by Hawaiian islanders during the course of the voyage.

Cooper, Samuel (1609-72). Miniaturist. He painted portraits of Cromwell as lord protector and, after the Restoration, of the royal family. Cooper is mentioned in Samuel Pepys' diary, Mrs Pepys having sat for him.

cooperative movement. A movement to prevent consumer exploitation by means of societies that manufacture, buy, or sell produce either without profit or with profits distributed among members. Robert *Owen is generally regarded as the founder of the movement. The first cooperative store was opened by the Rochdale Pioneers in 1844, and the movement grew rapidly after the legalization of cooperatives in 1852. The Cooperative Wholesale Society (CWS), the national trading and banking organization in which cooperatives are federated, was established in 1863, and the Scottish CWS in 1868. The Cooperative Union, founded in 1869, is the movement's advisory and educational body, and the Cooperative Party (1917), which is closely allied with the Labour Party, represents cooperative interests in politics.

Coote, Sir Eyre (1726-83). British general in India. He fought under Clive at *Plassey (1757) and won the victory of Wandiwash (1760), taking Pondicherry (1761). He was then appointed commander of the East India Company forces in Bengal. As commander in chief in India (1778) he defeated Hyder Ali of Mysore, an ally of the French, at Porto Novo (1781).

Copenhagen, battle of (2 April 1801). A naval action during the Napoleonic War in which a British fleet under Admiral Sir Hyde Parker (1714-82) and Nelson, under heavy fire from shore batteries, destroyed or captured 17 Danish warships. The attack effectively prevented the renewal of the league of armed neutrality of Denmark, Sweden, Russia, and Prussia. The engagement saw the famous incident in which Nelson, by putting his telescope to his blind eye, circumvented Parker's orders for withdrawal.

copyhold. A form of land tenure, so called because the holder had a copy of the record of his holding in the manorial role. By the 15th century most *villeins had become copyholders as most of the services they owed to their lord were commuted to money payments. "£10 copyholders"—those with land worth £10 annually—were given the vote in 1832 and "£5 copyholders" in 1867 (see Reform Acts). The last feudal obligations attached to copyhold were abolished in 1935.

copyright. The right to produce copies of an original literary, musical, or artistic work and a recording, film, or broadcast. The first legislation was enacted in 1709, when authors of books were given copyright for 14 years, renewable, if they were then still living, for a further 14 years. In 1814 it was extended to 28 years, in 1842 to 42 years. Other acts had meanwhile covered engravings, sculpture, plays, and lectures; the 1842 act included music; in 1862 copyright was extended to paintings, drawings, and photographs. The Copyright Act (1911) was a major reform of over 20 statutes. The present law dates from 1956, when films and television and sound broadcasting were covered by the law; the term of copyright is 50 years from the author's death or, if later, from the publication of the work in question. All works protected by copyright bear the symbol ©.

Cork, 1st earl of. See Boyle, Richard.

corn laws. Legislation aimed at protecting British agriculture by charging duties on imported grain. Corn laws had been applied since the middle ages but only became a major political issue after 1815. A law of that year, banning the import of foreign grain until the home price had reached 80 shillings a quarter, proved unworkable, and was replaced in 1828 by a sliding scale. The Anti-Corn-Law League, founded in 1839 and promoted by factory owners under the leadership of *Cobden and *Bright, denounced the system as benefiting landowners at everyone else's expense; landowners replied that industrialists wanted cheap bread to keep wages down. The Conservative prime minister *Peel finally secured the repeal of the corn laws (June 1846) with a bill that retained only a nominal duty (which was abolished in 1869). The issue split the Conservative Party and ended Peel's career.

Cornwallis, Charles Cornwallis, 1st Marquess (1738-1805) Soldier, politician, and administrator. During the American Revolution Cornwallis, although probably the most competent British general, was compelled to surrender at *Yorktown. As governor general in India (1786-93), he initiated major reforms of the legal and police systems, of land ownership and taxation in Bengal, and of the British official service. As lord lieutenant of Ireland (1798-1801), he suppressed the 1798 rebellion and helped effect union with Great Britain.

coronation. The hallowing, investing, and crowning of the sovereign by the archbishop of Canterbury as head of the lords spiritual. Essentially a religious rite, coronation has always consisted of (a) the recognition and oath, which form the contract between the sovereign and the people; (b) the consecration of the sovereign by anointing; (c) the investiture and crowning; and (d) the enthronement and homage. The rite was originally based on that used for the coronation of the popes. The present one is directly descended from that used at King Edgar's coronation in 973 AD. For the coronation of James I it was for the first time translated from Latin into English.

Before the Norman conquest, coronations took place sometimes at Kingston-upon-Thames, but also at Bath (Edgar) and Winchester (Edward the Confessor). Since the conquest they have been held in Westminster abbey. The coronation chair was commissioned by Edward I in 1297 to house the stone of *Scone,

captured from the Scots in 1296. *See also* regalia.

corporation. A succession or association of individuals regarded in law as having an identity separate from that of the individuals themselves. Corporations sole are individual persons successively holding the same office (e.g. a bishopric); corporations aggregate are many persons acting together, such as the municipal corporations that formerly governed *boroughs. The concept derives from Roman law: a *collegium* was a body that had the right of perpetual succession—hence the maxim "a corporation can never die". A corporation uses a common seal, can sue and be sued, can acquire and hold land, and can make by-laws. Corporations can be created only by the sovereign or by statute. *See also* municipal corporation.

Corporation Act (1661). An act, forming part of the *Clarendon code, that excluded from municipal office those who refused to take communion in the Church of England, to swear the oaths of allegiance, supremacy, and nonresistance, and to reject the *Solemn League and Covenant. It was repealed in 1828 (*see* Toleration Acts).

Corresponding Society. A radical organization, founded in London in Jan 1792 by a shoemaker, Thomas Hardy (1752-1832). The society, which soon had provincial branches, advocated universal adult male suffrage and annual parliaments, becoming a target for government repression of *Jacobinism. At a radical convention in Edinburgh in 1793 plans were made for operating underground, and several of the society's leaders were condemned to transportation. Hardy and other radicals, including *Tooke, were charged with treason in 1794 but acquitted. The society was banned in 1799.

Corrupt Practices Acts. Legislation against bribing or intimidating voters in elections. An act of 1854 defined corrupt practices and provided for the appointment of auditors. It was followed by the first really effective act in 1883, which forms the basis for modern procedures.

It defined corrupt practices more precisely, fixed a maximum figure to be spent by candidates during an election, strengthened measures of control, and introduced severe penalties for offences.

Cort, Henry (1740-1800). An ironmaster at Fareham, in Hampshire, who in 1784 devised the puddling process for making wrought iron. Puddling removed carbon and other impurities from pig iron, thus rendering it less brittle, and stimulated development of the iron industry.

Coruña, battle of (16-18 Jan 1809). A battle during the Peninsular War. A British force of 29 000 men under Sir John *Moore, following a disastrous midwinter retreat, attempted to embark at La Coruña. Here, Moore's infantry stood and defeated the pursuing French forces of Marshal Soult, but Moore himself was mortally wounded during the action.

Cosgrave, William Thomas (1880-1965). Irish nationalist, who was the first president of the Irish Free State. He fought in the *Easter rising (1916) and became a *Sinn Féin MP in 1918. Cosgrave accepted the terms of the Anglo-Irish treaty (1921) and after the death of *Griffith and then *Collins was president of the Executive Council of the Irish Free State (1922-32). His son Liam Cosgrave (1920-) was Fine Gael prime minister (1973-77) of Ireland.

Council in the Marches. The council created by Edward IV in 1471 to administer the lands of the *prince of Wales in the Principality and the Marches. It subsequently obtained commissions to supervise law and order. By 1536 it sat continually at Ludlow and in 1543 was given statutory powers in Wales, Herefordshire, Worcestershire, Gloucestershire, and Shropshire. It was finally abolished in 1689.

Council of Salisbury (1 Aug 1086). A meeting, summoned by William I, at which, according to the *Anglo-Saxon Chronicle*, all his tenants in chief and subtenants swore fealty to him. Although the council was large it is unlikely that all landholders were present, but rather only the tenants in chief and their most important vassals. The oath served to strengthen the king's control over, and relationship with, his more prominent subjects.

Council of State. The executive body during the Interregnum (1649-60). It was elected by the Rump of the Long Parliament after the execution of Charles I and the abolition of the House of Lords (1649). It had 41 members, 31 being MPs, and was elected annually. During the *Protectorate (1653-59) the executive consisted of the protector and the Council of State comprising 22 members elected for life. It was abolished in 1660.

Council of the North. A council established by Richard III to administer the north of England. The council was dissolved in 1509 but was revived by Wolsey in 1525 and became a permanent body in 1537. Administering the law in Yorkshire, Northumberland, Cumberland, Westmorland, and Durham, it became identified with often unpopular government policy, especially under the presidency (1628-32) of Wentworth (later earl of *Strafford). It was abolished by the Long Parliament in 1641.

Council of the West. A council established in 1539 to administer Devon and Cornwall and to forestall a possible western rebellion following the *Pilgrimage of Grace (1536). Little is known of its operations and it was abolished by 1547.

Country Party. The parliamentary opposition to royal policies and the *Court Party during the late 17th and early 18th centuries. Under Charles II the party, whose leaders included Anthony Ashley Cooper, 1st earl of *Shaftesbury, consisted largely of landed MPs, free from dependence on royal patronage, and committed to anti-Catholicism and individual liberty. Following the anti-Catholic *Test Act and *exclusion bills, members of the Country Party came to be labelled *Whigs. However, the inherent distrust for court and crown, which strongly motivated the party's adherents, was transferred during the Whig administrations of William III to the Country Party of Robert Harley, 1st earl of *Oxford, who disliked the factional label Tory.

county. The name the Normans gave to the Anglo-Saxon *shire. The counties were administered by *sheriffs until the 16th century, when the *justices of the peace became the most important local officials. Responsibility for local government passed to the newly established county councils by the *Local Government Act (1888). The 40 English, 12 Welsh, and 30 Scottish counties were reorganized by the Local Government Act 1972 in England and Wales and the Local Government (Scotland) Act 1973, when 45 English counties, 8 Welsh counties, and, in Scotland, 9 regions and 3 island areas were created; Northern Ireland has six counties.

county councils. Elected authorities established by the *Local Government Act (1888). The councils, including a London County Council, with steadily increasing responsibilities, replaced county administration by justices of the peace and other traditional authorities. In 1963 the London Government Act created a new Greater London Council, while the Local Government Act (1972) redrew metropolitan and nonmetropolitan county boundaries in England and Wales. Comparable Scottish reorganization was introduced in 1973.

county court. A civil court, established in its modern form in 1846. The county court of Anglo-Saxon England was the shiremoot, a civil court presided over by the ealdorman and later the sheriff. Following the introduction of *assizes in the 13th century the county court declined in importance, being used only for such matters as the election of sheriffs. It was re-established in 1846 as a court for the settlement of small financial claims, especially the recovery of debts.

coupon election (14 Dec 1918). A general election called by *Lloyd George, leader of the Liberal-Conservative coalition government. Coalition candidates received a letter of endorsement from Lloyd George and the Conservative leader Bonar *Law. Their opponents —chiefly Liberals who opposed Lloyd George and supported *Asquith and Labour candidates—contemptuously called this "the coupon". The coalition, mostly Conservatives, won overwhelmingly.

Courcy, John de (d. ?1219). Norman conqueror of Ulster. The facts of his life are obscure, but it is known that he landed in Ulster with about 300 men in 1176 and conquered Antrim and Down. In 1185 he was appointed justiciar of Ireland but later he refused to submit to King John. In 1204 John de Courcy was defeated by Hugh de Lacy, who became 1st earl of Ulster in 1205.

court baron. A court held before the freemen of a *manor to deal with such matters as services owed by tenants to the lord and personal actions by tenants for the recovery of debts or damages worth less than 40 shillings. Neither the lord nor his steward were permitted to imprison or fine. Although obsolete, courts baron have not been abolished. *Compare* court leet.

Courtenay, Peter (d. 1492). Bishop of Winchester. He was made bishop of Exeter in 1478 but, after attempting to raise an army against Richard III, was attainted. Restored by Henry VII, he was made bishop of Winchester in 1487.

court leet. A court of record that the lord of a hundred or manor might be authorized by royal charter to summon annually. Its chief functions were to inspect the members of the hundred, etc. (see frankpledge), and to punish misdemeanours. The steward of the leet was the judge and he might fine or imprison.

court martial. A court summoned by the crown or under its authority to try offences committed against military or nonmilitary law by members of the armed services. Courts martial date from the reign (1625-49) of Charles I but were formally established by the *Mutiny Act (1689). Those appearing before a court martial are not exempt from the jurisdiction of the ordinary courts. Appeals have been allowed since 1951.

Court Party. Parliamentary supporters of Charles II and his successors. Formed originally round Thomas Osborne, earl of *Danby, following the breakup (1672–73) of the *cabal, the party was composed of royalist and Anglican sympathizers who, from interest and principle, sought to maintain the orderly functioning of government. Although the *Tory party, which emerged following the crisis over the *exclusion bills (1679–80), drew its strength largely from court supporters, the fluid state of party allegiance, allied with the magnet of government patronage, ensured the support of many moderates for government policies irrespective of the new party labels. *Compare* Country Party.

Covenant, National (1638). A manifesto and bond of alliance signed by those opposed to Charles I's religious policies in Scotland. It was accepted enthusiastically in much of the Lowlands. The Covenant repeats an anti-Catholic "Negative Confession" of 1581, lists acts of parliament condemning Catholicism, and binds its adherents to remain united to each other and to God in upholding true religion. *See also* Solemn League and Covenant.

covenanters. The supporters of the National *Covenant and the *Solemn League and Covenant. They ruled Scotland from 1638 to 1651. The early unity of the movement had given way to warring factions by the late 1640s (*see* Kirk Party). In the Restoration period those who resisted episcopacy and other aspects of the Church of Scotland, and as a result suffered persecution, are generally called covenanters, although not all were committed to maintaining the covenants.

Coverdale, Miles (?1488–1569). Translator of the *Bible. A zealous Protestant, Coverdale was briefly bishop of Exeter (1551–53). His translation of the Bible, published in Zurich in 1535, was the first complete printed English Bible.

Cranmer, Thomas (1489–1556). Archbishop of Canterbury (1533–56). In 1529, at the request of Henry VIII, he prepared a treatise justifying the invalidity of the king's marriage to Catherine of Aragon. After becoming archbishop he declared it void and then pronounced that the marriage of Henry and Anne Boleyn was valid. He exerted an enormous influence on the English *Reformation. After the accession of Edward VI he was largely responsible for the two *Books of Common Prayer (1549, 1552) and the 42 *articles (1553). After the succession of Mary he was burned at the stake (*see* Marian reaction).

Crécy, battle of (26 Aug 1346). A decisive battle between England and France in the Hundred Years' War. Edward III and the Black Prince were leading their forces into Ponthieu when they were attacked by a larger French army. The English were nevertheless victorious, largely because of their skilled archers and superior tactical skill. Edward proceeded to conquer Calais.

Crewe's Act. *See* Place Acts.

Crimean War (1854–56). A conflict between Russia on the one side and France, Britain, Turkey, and Piedmont on the other. Russia, as self-proclaimed protector of Slav Christians living under Turkish rule, occupied (July 1853) the Danubian principalities of Moldavia and Wallachia (present-day Romania), which then formed part of the Ottoman (Turkish) Empire. Turkey retaliated by declaring war (Oct 1853) and was followed by Britain and France (March 1854). British and French fears of Russian expansion into Europe at Turkish expense were an underlying cause of the conflict.

Campaigning (apart from two ineffective Baltic expeditions) was confined to the Crimea, where much of the allied effort was directed towards reducing the Russian fortress of Sebastopol. The early allied success at the battle of the *Alma (Sept 1854) was confirmed by the failure of Russian attacks at the battles of *Balaclava (Oct 1854) and *Inkerman

(Nov 1854). Winter put an end to further campaigning and it was not until Sept 1855 that the Russians withdrew from Sebastopol, effectively signalling the end of hostilities, which were formally concluded by the treaty of *Paris (March 1856).

Most of the massive death toll of the war (some 45 000 British, 180 000 French, and 450 000 Russians were killed) was attributable to disease and deprivation. Revelation of these appalling conditions (mitigated by the work of Florence *Nightingale) led to the fall of the *Aberdeen government, while the ineffective generalship of *Raglan provided an abiding impulse to army reform. Internationally, the war confirmed Turkey's traditional subservience to Britain but destroyed the illusion that the concert of Europe, established in 1815 by the treaties of Vienna, still persisted.

criminal law reform. The rationalization and humanization of the criminal law, especially by Sir Robert Peel. It was inspired largely by Sir Samuel Romilly (1757-1818) and Jeremy Bentham. In 1819 a parliamentary committee of inquiry under the chairmanship of Sir James Mackintosh (1765-1832) laid the foundations of acts passed in 1823, 1826-27, and 1828-30. They abolished *capital punishment for most of the 200 offences that then carried it and constituted the first ever revision of a mass of legislation dating from the reign of Henry III; for example, 90 acts dealing with theft were reduced to one. Procedure was also greatly simplified. See also prison reform.

Cripps, Sir (Richard) Stafford (1889-1952). Chancellor of the exchequer in the Labour government after World War II. A barrister, Cripps became a Labour MP in 1931. He was expelled from the party in Jan 1939 for demanding a Popular Front that included communists but was readmitted in 1945. Ambassador to Moscow (1940-42), he served in Winston Churchill's wartime coalition government (1942-45), visiting India (1942) in an unsuccessful attempt to negotiate self-government. Cripps was president of the board of trade (1945-47) and as chancellor of the exchequer (1947-50) introduced stringent austerity measures and devaluation.

Cromer, 1st earl of. See Baring, Evelyn, 1st earl of Cromer.

Crompton, Samuel (1753-1827). Inventor. Born in Bolton, Crompton, in 1779, invented the *mule, a spinning machine that, combining the merits of previous inventions, spun fine strong thread. Cromptom could not afford to patent his invention and earned little from its success. In 1812, however, the House of Commons made him a grant of £5,000, which he used to enter business, unsuccessfully, as a bleacher and then as a cotton merchant.

Cromwell, Oliver (1599-1658). Statesman and soldier. Born in Huntingdon of a distinguished but comparatively impoverished squirearchal family. He came under Puritan influence at Sidney Sussex College, Cambridge, which was intensified during the 1630s, although his precise religious orientation is still in dispute. Elected to the Long Parliament for Cambridge City, he made something of a name as a radical, and profited by his kinship with John Pym, Oliver St John, and the Huntingdonshire magnate, the 2nd earl of Manchester. When war broke out he soon revealed a natural aptitude for cavalry organization and tactics in the Army of the Eastern Association, under Manchester's command, and played a decisive part in the victory of Marston Moor (1644). Dissatisfied with the conduct of the war, he pushed through the *Self-Denying Ordinance in the winter of 1644-45, removing the existing generals, including Manchester, and the ordinance creating a *New Model Army, of which he was appointed general of horse and second in command (to Sir Thomas Fairfax). He played a major role in the decisive royalist defeat at Naseby (1645) and the negotiations for a settlement that followed. His role in these negotiations is ambiguous, and he was accused by parliament and the king of complicity in the army revolt of 1647 and by the *Levellers of working for a royalist restoration. His victory at Preston (Aug 1648) in the second Civil War, the first battle in which he held independent command, confirmed his stature. However, he left his son in law Henry *Ireton to eliminate dissidents from the Long Parliament (see Pride's purge) and to establish a court to try the king, attracting further accusations of hypocrisy then and since. After the execution of the king he embarked on the subjugation of Ireland, during which he ordered the controversial massacres of civilians at *Drogheda and Wexford (1649). On Fairfax's resignation (1650) he succeeded him as commander in chief and invaded Scotland, defeating the Scots army at Dunbar, near Edinburgh (3 Sept 1650). When Charles II led another Scots army into England the following year he comprehensively defeated him at Worcester (3 Sept 1651). As the most powerful living Englishman, he then became the focus for general discontent with the *Rump of the Long Parliament: its repressive religious policy, its war with Holland (1652–54), and its failure to proceed to a final constitutional settlement. He forcibly dissolved the Rump (April 1653) and assembled *Barebones Parliament, nominated by the religious congregations. A disastrous failure, it dissolved itself in Dec 1653 and Cromwell promulgated the *Instrument of Government, which created for him the office of lord protector, assisted by a single-chamber parliament elected on new lines. This was only a modified success; he failed to reach agreement with his first parliament in 1654 and ruled increasingly by decree, but his benevolent despotism was generally acceptable to a weary nation, particularly his imposition of religious toleration and his efforts to demilitarize the government. His second parliament, in 1657, after the radicals had been excluded, offered him the kingship in the *Humble Petition and Advice. He refused the kingship, but the modified Humble Petition strengthened his authority, especially against the discon-

tented army generals. His death (3 Sept 1658) revealed the fact that the regime depended entirely on him; his son and successor Richard was deposed after six months, and central authority virtually collapsed. A chain of events was set in motion that led directly to Charles II's restoration in April 1660. Controversy still surrounds many episodes in Cromwell's career, and his character and motives in general, but he is acknowledged to be the greatest English general who ever lived, rivalled only by Marlborough and Wellington.

Cromwell, Richard (1626–1712). Lord protector of England (1658–59), eldest son of Oliver Cromwell. Under his father's protectorship he served in parliament and was proclaimed successor on his death (1658). He displayed little aptitude for the office and following conflict with the army was dismissed by the recalled *Rump of the Long Parliament. In 1660 he escaped to France, returning in 1680 and spending the rest of his life in seclusion.

Cromwell, Thomas, earl of Essex (c. 1485–1540). Statesman. Of humble origins, Cromwell began his career as a dependant of Cardinal Wolsey, becoming his collector of revenues in 1514. After the fall of Wolsey, Cromwell rapidly rose in power during the 1530s to become Henry VIII's closest adviser; he became a member of the Privy Council in 1531, was subsequently the king's principal secretary, master of the rolls, lord privy seal, and finally, in 1539, was appointed lord great chamberlain of England. He was created earl of Essex in 1540. He arranged the king's divorce from Catherine of Aragon in 1533 and presided over the separation of the English church from Rome (see Reformation). As vicegerent he dissolved the monasteries and transferred their wealth to the crown (1536–39). He is now particularly remembered for his administrative reforms, which some historians have described as a "revolution". He fell from favour after persuading the king to marry Anne of Cleves, whom the king found unattractive, and he was executed on a trumped-up charge of treason.

crossbow. A bow, made of wood or, later, steel, that was fixed to a stock, the string being released by a trigger mechanism. Crossbows were widely used by foot soldiers in Europe from the late 10th century. They were heavier and more cumbersome than *longbows but had greater powers of penetration.

crown colony. A territory acquired by settlement, or by conquest or cession, that is without responsible government and governed by a *governor responsible to the crown through the Foreign and Commonwealth Office (formerly through the *Colonial Office). In most colonies the powers of the governor were gradually devolved to legislative and executive councils. *Compare* dominion.

Crown Estate Commissioners. The body that administers the *crown lands. Following the crown's surrender of the revenues from its estates in 1761 advocates of the sale of crown lands became increasingly vociferous. In 1810 commissioners of woods, forests, and land revenues were appointed to supervise sales, purchases, and management of the royal estates. These were replaced (1923-27) by the Commissioners of Crown Lands, which were renamed the Crown Estate Commissioners in 1956.

crown jewels. *See* regalia.

crown lands. The personal estates of the medieval kings of England. At the time of the Domesday Book (1087) they comprised 1400 manors not granted to feudal tenants in chief. Henry IV added the estates of the duchy of Lancaster, Edward IV the earldom of Warwick, Henry VII the earldom of Richmond, and Henry VIII the monastic lands. From time to time land reverted to the crown by *escheat or *attainder. The wars of the 1540s and subsequent inflation led to the sale of much crown land in the late 16th and 17th centuries. Since 1761 the revenues of the crown lands have been surrendered by the monarch for the reign in return for an

annual payment (*see* civil list). They are administered by the *Crown Estate Commissioners.

crusades. The holy wars fought by the Christian powers of western Europe with the purpose of delivering the Holy Land from Islam and restoring it to Christian rule. The first crusade (1095-99), in which Robert, duke of Normandy took part, captured Jerusalem in 1099 and established four crusader states. The second Crusade (1147-48) achieved nothing, and the fall of Jerusalem (1187) to the sultan Saladin inspired the third crusade (1189-92), led by Richard I of England, Philip II Augustus of France, and the emperor Frederick I Barbarossa. After the capture of *Acre, Richard took Jaffa and was within 12 miles of Jerusalem when his supplies ran out and he was forced to make peace with Saladin. On his way home Richard was given into the hands of the emperor Henry VI and ransomed. English participants in subsequent crusades included Prince Edward, later Edward I, who in 1271 joined the crusade of Louis IX of France, gaining a reputation as a gifted soldier.

Crystal Palace. An exhibition hall built for the *Great Exhibition. Designed by Joseph *Paxton, it was a huge iron construction with nearly 300 000 panes of glass in the walls and roof. It was dismantled and rebuilt at Sydenham in 1854 and was accidentally burned down in 1936.

Culloden, battle of (16 April 1746). The last battle of the Jacobite rebellion, in which Prince Charles Edward Stuart was defeated by an English army under William Augustus, duke of Cumberland. The battle, at Culloden Moor near Inverness, was short but decisive: in just 40 minutes a fifth of the 5000-strong Highland army was killed and the rebellion firmly crushed. The duke of Cumberland lost only 50 of his 9000 men. Culloden was the last land battle to be fought in Britain.

Cumberland, Ernest Augustus, duke of (1771-1851). King of Hanover (1837-51), fifth son of George III. Ernest was notorious for his savagely reactionary political views, especially his opposition to parliamentary reform, and an attempt was made on his life in 1810. He succeeded William IV in Hanover, where the Salic Law, permitting only male heirs, prevented the succession of the British queen Victoria.

Cumberland, William Augustus, duke of (1721-65). Soldier, third son of George II. He fought in both the War of the Austrian Succession and the Seven Years' War but is best known for his defeat of the Jacobites at *Culloden in 1746.

Cunedda (early 5th century). British warrior. Cunedda, together with his sons and armed followers, moved from Manaw Gododdin, near modern Edinburgh, to northwest Wales to defend Britain against barbarian invaders from Ireland. *Maelgwn Gwynedd and the rulers of several Welsh kingdoms, including Ceredigion and Meirionnydd, claimed descent from Cunedda.

Cunobelinus (1st century AD). British ruler, who, from his capital at Camulodunum (Colchester), held sway over most of southeast Britain between about 10 AD and 42 AD. His relations with the Romans were friendly, and he allowed traders to operate in his kingdom. He died sometime before 43 AD. He is the original of Shakespeare's Cymbeline.

curia regis. The royal court of the Norman and Angevin kings. Initially it fulfilled all the functions of royal government. It served as a judicial court for all matters concerning the king's person, rights, and lands and for tenurial cases involving his tenants in chief. It was also the foremost executive and legislative body, in which the king and his magnates declared new laws and customs. In its social and ceremonial function, meeting three times a year at Easter, Pentecost, and Christmas, it served to demonstrate the royal dignity. Its officials, for example the *dispenser, *steward, and *chamberlain, were powerful officers of state, as well as being magnates in their own right. The curia declined in importance during the

12th and 13th centuries as royal government became more bureaucratic and sedentary and as new specialized government offices, such as the *Chancery, *Exchequer, and *Wardrobe, developed.

Curragh mutiny (March 1914). An incident in which the commanding officer and 56 other officers of the 3rd Cavalry Brigade, stationed at the Curragh, near Dublin, opted for dismissal rather than "coerce" the Ulster Protestants to accept Irish home rule. The incident may partially explain why the government was not prepared to force Ulster to accept home rule. The secretary for war, J. E. B. Seely (later 1st Baron Mottistone; 1868-1947), and the chief of the imperial general staff, Sir John French, indicated that the officers should not be required to serve against the north; the cabinet disagreed and Seely and French resigned their offices.

cursitors. Twenty-four clerks of the Court of Chancery, each of whom made out writs *de cursu* (i.e. on routine matters) in the shire to which he was appointed. The office was abolished in 1835.

Curzon, George Nathaniel Curzon, 1st Marquess (1859-1925). Statesman. A Conservative MP from 1886 to 1898, when he became Baron Curzon, he was undersecretary for foreign affairs (1895-98). In 1898 he was appointed viceroy of India, where his administration was noted for the formation of the North West Frontier Province (1901), the partition of *Bengal (1905), and the introduction of administrative reforms. His viceroyalty, which is also remembered for its splendour, ended with Curzon's resignation (1905) following disagreements with Kitchener, the commander in chief in India. Curzon subsequently served as lord privy seal (1915-16) in Asquith's coalition government and as foreign secretary (1919-24) under three consecutive prime ministers, Lloyd George (whose personal handling of major foreign-policy issues brought the two men into conflict), Bonar Law, and Baldwin. Curzon was intellectually brilliant, but his arrogance made many enemies and his strong claim to succeed Law as prime minister in 1923 was passed over.

Curzon line. The line proposed by the foreign secretary Lord Curzon in 1919, during the Russo-Polish War, as the boundary between Poland and the Soviet Union. It was finally accepted by the two states in 1945.

custom duty. A duty charged on imported or exported goods. The main features of British customs date from the reign (1272-1307) of Edward I, during which they were first raised on wool, woolfells, and leather. *Tunnage and poundage date from the reign (1307-27) of Edward II. *Impositions were additional customs raised by royal *prerogative; they were greatly increased after the favourable judgment in *Bate's case (1606). In 1787 Pitt the younger simplified the network of custom duties, which were administered together with *excise duties from 1909.

Cuthbert, St (d. 687). Bishop of Lindisfarne. Originally a shepherd, Cuthbert entered the Celtic monastery of Melrose in 651 and in 664 became prior of Lindisfarne. From 676 to 684 (when he became bishop) he was a hermit on the Farne Islands, to which he returned in 686. His life symbolizes the ascetic tradition of the Celtic church, and he had a high reputation as a preacher and bishop. His relics were moved to Durham in 1104.

Cymbeline. *See* Cunobelinus.

Cyprus. An island state in the Mediterranean, with a mixed Greek and Turkish population. Britain became directly involved in Cyprus during the 1875-78 eastern crisis (*see* eastern question), when the island was under Ottoman (Turkish) rule. In 1878, at the congress of *Berlin, Disraeli, the British prime minister, persuaded the sultan to cede the administration of Cyprus to Britain, in return for which Disraeli promised to maintain Britain's traditional support of the Turkish empire. In 1914, following Turkey's entry into World War I in support of Germany, the island was formally annexed by Britain. In 1925 it was declared a crown colony. After 1930 the *enosis* movement for union with Greece gathered strength among Greek Cypriots. Archbishop Makarios (1913-77) became the movement's leader in 1950. When his peaceful methods failed to secure union, right-wing extremists launched a guerrilla war, which forced Britain to declare a state of emergency in 1955. In 1957 a constitution, granting Cyprus independence but protecting the rights of its Turkish minority (20% of the population), was drafted. The new republic, based upon this constitution, was declared in 1960; and in 1961 Cyprus became a member of the Commonwealth.

D

Dafydd ap Gruffudd (d. 1283). Prince of Gwynedd, third son of *Gruffudd ap Llywelyn and younger brother of *Llywelyn ap Gruffudd. He attacked Hawarden castle (1282), thus drawing his brother Llywelyn with him into a second war of independence against Edward I. He was captured and put to death at Shrewsbury.

Dafydd ap Llywelyn (d. 1246). Prince of Gwynedd, younger and legitimate son of *Llywelyn ap Iorwerth. His mother was Joan, illegitimate daughter of King John of England. He succeeded his father in 1240 but, before his accession, was fiercely opposed by his elder illegitimate brother, Gruffudd ap Llywelyn (d. 1244). Relations became strained between him and Henry III concerning lands in Gwynedd and matters were not resolved on his sudden death, which left Gwynedd in a critical situation. He was buried in Aberconwy abbey.

Dáil Éireann (Irish: Assembly of Ireland). The lower chamber of the two-tier Oireachtas, or National Parliament, in Ireland, the upper chamber being the Seanad Éireann. It was first proclaimed by the *Sinn Féin in 1919, rivalling the

Westminster government until the Anglo-Irish treaty (1921). Its powers are similar to those of the British House of Commons, but its members, called deputies, are elected by proportional representation.

Dalhousie, James Ramsay, 1st marquess of (1812-60). Governor general of India (1847-56). Dalhousie's achievements included introducing railways and telegraphs to India and promoting women's rights. He annexed extensive former protectorates, notably the Punjab (1849) and Oudh (1856), and lower Burma (1852). Dalhousie's confident belief (like most British administrators) in westernization contributed to social and religious strains, which underlay the *Indian mutiny.

Dalriada (or Dal Riata). A kingdom in present-day Co. Antrim, Ireland, inhabited by *Scots. They colonized the southwest Highlands of Scotland, where, in about 500, they established a kingdom also called Dalriada.

Dalrymple, James, 1st Viscount Stair (1619-95). Lawyer. In 1681 he was forced to resign as president of the Court of Session, and fled to Holland because of his opposition to the Test Act oath designed to ensure the succession of James, Charles II's Roman Catholic brother, to the throne. Stair was restored to office and raised to the peerage by William III in 1690. His *Institutions of the Law of Scotland* (1681) was a major contribution to the codification of Scottish law.

Dalrymple, John, 1st earl of Stair (1648-1707). Son of James *Dalrymple, 1st Viscount Stair. He was fined and imprisoned in 1682-83 after his father fled to Holland, but subsequently served James II in Scotland as lord advocate and justice clerk. Winning the favour of William III, he was again appointed lord advocate (1689-92) and joint secretary of state (1691-95). He was widely hated for his part in instigating the massacre of *Glencoe, but was created an earl in 1703.

Dalton, Hugh, Baron (1887-1962). Labour MP (1924-31, 1935-59; life peer, 1960). He served in the wartime cabinet (1940-45). He was *Attlee's chancellor of the exchequer (1945-47), resigning after leaking budget secrets, and, later, minister of planning (1950-51).

Dampier, William (c. 1652-1715). Explorer. After an adventurous early life as a buccaneer, in 1699 Dampier was given command of an expedition, which explored the coasts of west Australia and New Guinea. He subsequently made two more voyages and published *A New Voyage Round the World* (1697). The Dampier Archipelago is named after him.

Danby, Thomas Osborne, 1st earl of (and 1st duke of Leeds) (1631-1712). Statesman. He entered parliament in 1665 and by 1673, after becoming lord treasurer, he was Charles II's chief minister. Created earl of Danby in 1674 (and duke of Leeds in 1694), he used bribes and patronage in an attempt to build up a court party in parliament. He was hostile to France, negotiating the marriage of the anti-French William of Orange to Charles' niece Mary (1677), but nevertheless negotiated the secret subsidies made by Louis XIV of France to Charles in return for English neutrality. When his involvement was revealed he was impeached and imprisoned in the Tower (1679-84). He subsequently joined the Whig opposition to James II and was William III's chief minister from 1690 to 1695, when he was once more impeached for corruption. The charge was not pursued, but he never regained his influence.

Danegeld. A tribute paid by the English to buy peace from the Danes during the reign (978-1016) of Aethelred II. Raised by taxation, the first payment (991) was 20 000 pounds of silver. Later kings continued to impose such levies for military purposes. That raised by Cnut after 1013 for the upkeep of his *housecarles was called heregeld. See also geld.

Danelaw. The parts of north, central, and eastern England in which Danish, rather than Saxon, laws and customs prevailed. These areas were settled by Danes in the late 9th and the 10th centuries. King Edgar (reigned 959-75) granted autonomy to the inhabitants of the Danelaw. In the 11th and 12th centuries it designated eastern England between the rivers Tees and Thames, where Danish customary law prevailed.

Danish invasions. The incursions of Danish raiders into Anglo-Saxon England. These began with isolated raids in the late 8th century but had become a campaign of conquest and settlement by 865, when a large force of Danes conquered East Anglia. The Danes then captured York and attacked Northumbria and Mercia. King Alfred (reigned 871-99) and his successors succeeded in preserving Wessex, but both Danes and Norwegians continued to settle in northern England. Their numbers have almost certainly been exaggerated but they had a considerable impact on the northern and eastern shires, influencing place names, customs, and laws (see Danelaw). Further raiding (980-1016) ended with the accession to the English throne of the Danish king *Cnut (1016). See map on p. 104.

Darby, Abraham (?1678-1717). Ironfounder whose pioneer method of smelting iron ore with coke, thereby removing the sulphur content, facilitated the manufacture of thin castings for hollow objects. He established his famous works at *Coalbrookdale in 1709.

Dardanelles. See Gallipoli expedition.

Darién scheme. The attempt by the Company of Scotland Trading to Africa and the Indies (founded 1695) to establish a Scottish colony on the Darién coast of the Isthmus of Panama (1698-1700). The scheme failed through Scottish incompetence, English opposition on the ground that the scheme threatened the monopoly of the East India Company, and Spanish hostility. The failure embittered Scotland's relations with England for some years and deepened its economic problems.

Darnley, Henry Stewart, Lord (1545-67). Son of Matthew Stewart, 4th earl of Lennox (1516-71), and Lady Margaret Douglas (1515-78), daughter of Margaret Tudor, Darnley married *Mary Queen of Scots in 1565 and was granted the title of king. Mary quickly concluded that he was too unreliable to be allowed any real power and, jealous of the influence of Rizzio, Mary's secretary, Darnley took part in his murder (1566). He was himself murdered in the following year.

Darrein Presentment, Assize of. A judicial proceeding, or the writ giving rise to it, which investigated who had last presented a priest to a benefice and therefore had the right of presentment (*advowson). Since the right fell automatically to the bishop after three months the speed with which *assizes were able to be brought was of particular importance in those of Darrein Presentment. Instituted by the constitutions of *Clarendon (1164), it was abolished in 1833.

Dartmouth, George Legge, 1st Baron (1648-91). Soldier and naval commander. He served in the second Dutch War (1665-67), Flanders (1678), and, after being created Baron Dartmouth (1682), the Tangier expedition (1683-84). He died in the Tower after being accused of plotting to surrender Portsmouth to the French.

Darwin, Charles (Robert) (1809-82). Scientist. Darwin's early enthusiasm for natural history was developed by his voyage with Captain Robert Fitzroy on board the *Beagle* (1831-36). From his geological discoveries and observations of natural life on the islands off the coast of South America he formulated his theory of evolution by natural selection, or evolution as a result of the survival only of those whose characteristics are best suited to the environment. His book *The Origin of Species* (1859) aroused considerable opposition, mainly from the church, and led to the historic debate at Oxford in 1860, between Thomas Huxley, Darwin's supporter, and Bishop

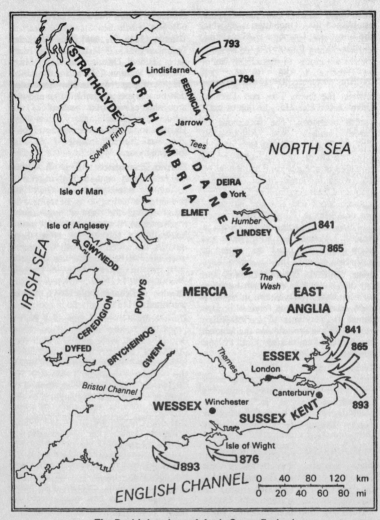

The Danish invasions of Anglo-Saxon England

Samuel Wilberforce, on whether man was descended from "apes or angels".

Dashwood, Sir Francis, 15th Baron le Despenser (1708-81). Politician best known as the founder of the dissolute *Hell-Fire Club. He became an MP in 1741 and was chancellor of the exchequer (1762-63) and joint postmaster general (1770-81).

David (or Dewi), St (6th century). The patron saint of Wales. Son of Sant, ruler of Ceredigion, David was educated at

Llanilltud Fawr. An ascete, he established many monasteries of which the most important was St David's (Tyddewi). He emerged as the leader of the church in Wales at a synod held at Llanddewi Brefi. His *Life* was written by Rhigyfarch (c. 1090). Feast day: 1 March.

David I (c. 1084-1153). King of Scots (1124-53), sixth son of Malcolm III and Margaret. David ruled southern Scotland under his brother, Alexander I, whom he succeeded. During his reign Norman influences prevailed in both church and state. He was outstanding in his generosity to the church, founding several monasteries. He also founded the burghs of Edinburgh, Berwick, Roxburgh, and Stirling. David encouraged the spread of feudal tenure through the settlement of Normans, English, and Flemings and favoured Anglo-Norman institutions in government. Celtic resentment at these policies led to rebellions in the north but these were crushed. Intervention on behalf of the empress Matilda in England brought defeat at the battle of the *Standard (1138), but David eventually won recognition of his claims to the northern counties of England from the future Henry II. David married Maud (or Matilda), daughter and heiress of the earl of Huntingdon, and was succeeded by his grandson Malcolm IV.

David II (1324-71). King of Scots (1329-71), succeeding his father Robert I. After the victories of *Edward Balliol and his English allies at Dupplin Muir (1332) and Halidon Hill (1333), he was sent to France for safety (1334). David returned to Scotland in 1341, but when he invaded England he was defeated and captured at Neville's Cross (1346). He was freed in 1357, after promising a huge ransom—which was never paid in full. Although he had difficulty in asserting his authority over his nobles and he has been described as a weak and rash king, he did in fact show both energy and ability as a ruler. At the age of four he was married to Joan, a sister of Edward III. After Joan's death he married

Margaret Drummond (1363). He died childless.

Davies, John (d. 1644). Welsh scholar, grammarian, and lexicographer, rector of Mallwyd, Merioneth. He assisted William Morgan to translate the *Bible into Welsh and was largely responsible for the revised edition (1620). He also published a *Welsh Grammar* (1621) and a *Welsh-Latin* and *Latin-Welsh Dictionary* (1632). He was one of a renowned group of scholars who laid the basis of modern Welsh linguistic studies.

Davies, Richard (c. 1501-1581). Bishop of St Asaph and St David's. With William *Salesbury he translated the New Testament into Welsh (1567). He was a leading Protestant humanist, whose residence at Abergwili became a centre of scholarly activity. He was largely responsible for the legislation that provided for the translation of the *Bible into Welsh (1563) and contributed to the Bishops' Bible (1568).

Davitt, Michael (1846-1906). Irish nationalist. He initially favoured armed rebellion against the English and was imprisoned (1870-77) for *Fenian activities. He later joined *Parnell in founding the *Irish Land League (1879) and served two further prison sentences (1881-82, 1883). He was elected an MP in 1882, while in gaol (and was unable to take his seat), and again in 1892 and 1895. In 1889 he was summoned before the Parnell commission and spoke for five days for the defence.

Davy, Sir Humphry (1778-1829). Scientist and president (1820-29) of the Royal Society. Most of his achievements were in chemistry—he discovered such elements as sodium, calcium, and potassium—but he is best remembered for developing the miners' safety lamp.

D-day (6 June 1944). The date of the allied landing in Normandy, signalling the start of the long-awaited invasion of Europe in *World War II. Planning for the invasion—called Operation Overlord —began in March 1941. Lessons learned in the Mediterranean were combined with meticulous intelligence reports on

the German defences and troop disposi-
tions. After a one-day delay, ordered by
Gen. *Eisenhower to take advantage of
clearer weather, two British, one
Canadian, and two US divisions landed
in the Baie de la Seine, Normandy; one
British and two American airborne
divisions protected their flanks, while
naval and air support bombarded enemy
positions ashore. By nightfall nearly
160 000 troops had landed, and within
five days the beachhead was secure. The
Germans, outnumbered and under air
attack, could not reinforce their defences.

death duties. A tax paid on the capital
value of assets owned by a person at his
or her death. Introduced by Sir William
Harcourt, Liberal chancellor of the exchequer, in the Finance Act (1894), they
superseded *Goschen's estate duty
(1889). Their scope was extended by
successive governments, but the many
loopholes led to their replacement in
1975 with the capital transfer tax, levied
on gifts made in a person's lifetime as
well as on death. This was replaced by
an inheritance tax in 1986.

debenture. A voucher given in the royal
household or government department
(especially, in the 17th and 18th
centuries, the Ordnance Office) certify-
ing a payment due (Latin debentur, they
are due) for goods supplied, services
rendered, or for arrears of pay. More
recently the term has been applied to
loans secured on fixed assets.

Deceangli. A Celtic tribe in northeast
Wales. Defeated by the Romans in either
48 or 49 AD, they subsequently offered
no further resistance.

Declaration of Rights (Feb 1689). A
statement, drawn up by the *convention
parliament, of the unconstitutional acts
of James II. William and Mary were
proclaimed sovereigns after their
acceptance of the Declaration, which
was embodied in the subsequent *Bill of
Rights (Oct 1689). See also Claim of
Right.

Declarations of Indulgence. Statements
issued by Charles II and James II

committing themselves to a relaxation of
the *penal laws against dissenters and
Roman Catholics. In Dec 1662 Charles
promised, pending parliamentary approval, which was not forthcoming, to use
the royal *dispensing power to relieve
recusants. In 1672, on the eve of the
third *Dutch War, he suspended (see
suspending power) the penal laws, an
act that was condemned by parliament,
which passed the *Test Act (1673) in
retaliation. James also twice declared a
suspension of the penal laws (1687,
1688), the second declaration leading to
the trial of the *seven bishops.

Declaratory Act. See Stamp Act.

Dee, John (1527-1608). Astrologer,
mathematician, and alchemist. He was
appointed to a living under Edward VI
but under Mary I was persecuted and
imprisoned until 1555. He gained the
favour of Elizabeth I, for whom he
practised astrology and horoscopy.

deed poll. The signed and sealed declaration of one person binding that person to
a particular course of action (such as a
change of name). A deed poll is cut
evenly at the edges (polled) and not
indented, as was an *indenture.

De Facto Act (1495). The popular name
for a statute that protected from the law
of treason those who had supported
Richard III, who was acknowledged to
have been king "for the time being" (i.e.
in fact). It was a gesture of conciliation
to erstwhile Yorkists by Henry VII and
offered protection to his own followers
in the event of a counter-revolution.

Defence, Ministry of. The government
department responsible for the armed
forces and the implementation of
national defence policies. Coordination
between the three services developed
after the appointment in 1936 of a
minister for the coordination of defence.
The process of unifying the defence
administration was accelerated by World
War II, and in 1947 a ministry of defence
was established with responsibility for
harmonizing the activities of the
*Admiralty, *War Office, and Air Minis-
try. These bodies were finally merged to

form the present Ministry of Defence in 1964.

Defence of the Realm Act (DORA). An act passed in Aug 1914, investing the British government with emergency powers. The act, which was repeatedly revised and strengthened during World War I, armed the government with sweeping powers to requisition raw materials, to control labour, and to censor all cables and foreign correspondence. It was superseded by the Emergency Powers Act (1920), which allowed the sovereign to declare by proclamation a state of emergency.

Defender of the Faith (Latin: *Fidei Defensor*). The title conferred on Henry VIII by Pope Leo X in 1521, in recognition of the king's book against Martin Luther, *Assertio septem sacramentorum*. The title was recognized by parliament in 1544 and has since that date been borne by all British monarchs. F. D. or Fid. Def. is still stamped on UK coins.

Defoe, Daniel (1660-1731). Writer. Defoe's early pamphlets of the 1680s and 1690s supported the Protestant religion and the Glorious Revolution of 1688-89. His services were later employed by the government to win support for the War of the Spanish Succession and union with Scotland. He edited (1704-13) his own newspaper, *The Review*, and later turned to novels, publishing his most famous work, *Robinson Crusoe*, in 1719.

de heretico comburendo (1401). An act directed originally against the *Lollards. Persons convicted of heresy by the ecclesiastical courts were to be handed over to the secular courts, which would sentence them to death by burning. The act was repealed (1547) by Edward VI but revived (1554) by Mary. It was finally repealed (1559) by Elizabeth.

Deheubarth. A kingdom constituted in southwest Wales in the 10th century, comprising Ystrad Tywi (approximating to what was later (until 1974) Carmarthenshire), Ceredigion (Cardiganshire), the early rulers of which claimed descent from *Cunedda, and the kingdom of *Dyfed. Prominent rulers included *Hywel Dda, *Maredudd ab Owain, and *Rhys ap Tewdwr. Territory was lost to the Normans in the late 11th and early 12th centuries with the creation of marcher lordships in southwest Wales, but *Rhys ap Gruffudd exercised immense authority in the second half of the 12th century.

Deira. An Anglo-Saxon kingdom, corresponding to modern Yorkshire with its capital at York. Its first king was Aelle (d. 588), and its greatest ruler was Edwin (617-33), whose reign was notable for the preaching of *Paulinus, first bishop of York. After the mid-7th century it formed, with *Bernicia, the kingdom of *Northumbria.

delicate investigation (1806). An inquiry into the private life of *Caroline of Brunswick. Caroline's indiscreet lifestyle, after her husband, the future George IV, deserted her, caused rumours that she had an illegitimate child. The Ministry of All the Talents initiated an investigation by a committee of the Privy Council, which cleared her of the main accusations.

delinquents. *See* malignants.

Delius, Frederick (1862-1934). British composer of German descent. Largely self-taught, he settled at Grez-sur-Loing near Paris in 1897. Blind and paralysed in old age, Delius dictated his last works to his amanuensis Eric Fenby (1906-). His works include the opera *A Village Romeo and Juliet* (1900-01), *A Mass of Life* (1904-05), and *On Hearing the First Cuckoo in Spring* (1912).

demesne. That part of a manor kept by the lord for himself as distinct from land held of him by tenants. It was exploited directly for the lord by his villeins, the amount of work owed to him varying according to region and season. Ancient demesne was the land that was recorded in Domesday as having been in the possession of the crown in 1066; it included the boroughs. Towards the end of the 14th century the combined effects of depopulation caused by the *black death, the flight of villeins, and the low price of grain led many lords to lease the demesne.

Demetae. A Celtic tribe in southwest Wales, with its capital possibly at Carmarthen. The Demetae do not seem to have offered any resistance to the Romans. The names of the medieval kingdom and modern county of *Dyfed are derived from "Demetia".

Denham, Dixon (1786-1828). Soldier and explorer in Africa. Denham served in the Peninsular War and fought at Waterloo. During the 1820s he travelled extensively throughout North and West Africa, crossing the Tebu desert in 1823 and exploring Lake Chad in 1824. Appointed governor of Sierra Leone in 1828, Denham died of fever shortly after arriving in the colony.

Denham, Sir John (1615-69). Poet. His most successful works were the blank-verse drama *The Sophy* (1641) and the poem *Cooper's Hill* (1642). During the Civil War he was involved in secret service for Charles I and his son, and after the Restoration he was made a knight of the Bath and became a member of the Royal Society.

Deorham (or **Dyrham**), **battle of** (577). A battle between Ceawlin of Wessex, *bretwalda of southern England, and the Britons at Deorham, north of Bath. Ceawlin's victory divided the western Britons from those of the southwest and ensured the capture of Gloucester, Cirencester, and Bath.

Derby, Edward George Stanley, 14th earl of (1799-1869). Prime minister. A Whig MP from 1820, Derby, however, served as undersecretary for war and the colonies (1827-28) in the progressive Tory ministries of Canning and Goderich. As secretary for Ireland (1830-33) in Grey's Whig ministry, he carried an Irish Education Act (1831) and proved an outstanding parliamentary orator. Secretary for war and the colonies (1833-34), he promoted the abolition of slavery but then resigned over Russell's proposal to use Irish church revenues for secular purposes. In 1835 he allied himself with Peel and was

again secretary for war and the colonies (1841-45) in Peel's second ministry, resigning over Peel's repeal of the corn laws. During the 1850s and 1860s Derby was leader of the main body of protectionist Conservatives and supported Disraeli in the task of rebuilding the party. As head of two short-lived minority governments (Feb-June 1852, 1858-59) Derby unsuccessfully proposed further franchise reform, but his third minority administration (1866-68) succeeded in carrying the second Reform Act (1867).

Derby, Edward Henry Stanley, 15th earl of (1826-93). Son of the 14th earl of Derby and a Conservative MP (1848-69), he served his father as secretary for India (1858-59) and as foreign secretary (1866-68), a post he held once more (1874-78) under Disraeli. He resigned in 1878 in protest against Disraeli's support of Turkey against Russia (*see* eastern question). Changing party allegiance, he joined Gladstone's second administration as colonial secretary (1882-85) but broke with Gladstone over Irish home rule in 1886. He led the Liberal *Unionists in the House of Lords (1886-91).

Derby, James Stanley, 7th earl of (1607-51). Royalist commander in the Civil War, who played a prominent role in Prince Rupert's campaign (1644). His wife Charlotte de la Trémoille (1599-1664) is remembered for her heroic defence of Latham House, where in 1644 she held out for four months against parliamentarian attack. Stanley subsequently withdrew with his wife to the Isle of Man and in 1651 was captured at Worcester and beheaded.

Derby, Thomas Stanley, 2nd Baron Stanley and 1st earl of (c.1435-1504). The magnate who, at the battle of *Bosworth (1485), betrayed Richard III and placed the crown on the head of Henry VII, his own stepson.

Dermot MacMurrough (or **Diarmid MacMurchada**) (?1110-1171). King of Leinster (1126-71). A fierce and cruel ruler, who laid claim to all southern Ireland, Dermot was driven out of

Ireland by the high king, *Rory O'Connor, in 1166. With the approval of Henry II, Dermot recruited the help of Richard de *Clare (Strongbow) in exchange for the hand of his daughter and the succession to Leinster. With de Clare's help Dermot regained his kindom in 1170. Strongbow succeeded to the throne when Dermot died in 1171 and Leinster became an English fief, the beginning of the subjection of *Ireland to English rule.

dervish. A member of a Muslim order of ascetics, some of whom perform an ecstatic whirling dance. The fanatical followers of the *Mahdi in the Sudan and of *Mad Mullah in Somaliland were dervishes.

Desmond revolt (1579-83). The rebellion of Gerald Fitzgerald, 15th (and last) earl of Desmond, an Anglo-Irish magnate who resisted the extension of English authority over his territories in southwest Ireland. In this rebellion some leaders tried to rouse Roman Catholic opinion against the power of English Protestants in Ireland. After Desmond was killed (1583) his estates of half a million acres went to English settlers.

Despard plot (1802). A plot by E. M. Despard (1751-1803), a colonial officer who had been unfairly dismissed, to seize key points in London and to assassinate George III. Despard was arrested in Nov 1802 and executed in 1803, but the affair contributed to a widespread fear of revolutionary conspiracy.

Despenser, Henry le (d. 1406). Bishop of Norwich from 1370. He helped suppress the *peasants' revolt in 1381. In 1383 he led an unsuccessful crusade to Flanders against the supporters of the Avignon pope Clement VII (see Norwich crusade). He was one of the few prominent men to remain loyal to the cause of Richard II in 1399, for which he was imprisoned.

Despenser (the elder), Hugh le, earl of Winchester (1262-1326). Favourite of *Edward II. He was banished with his son and namesake in 1321, and on his recall by the king was made earl of

Winchester (1322). He was executed by Queen Isabel and Roger de Mortimer.

Despenser (the younger), Hugh le (d. 1326). Favourite of *Edward II. A confederacy of marcher lords was formed against him in 1321, and he was banished. Recalled by the king (1322), he reached the summit of his career after the defeat of Thomas, earl of Lancaster, at Boroughbridge (1322). When Queen Isabel and Roger de Mortimer usurped the kingdom Despenser tried to flee but was captured and beheaded at Hereford.

Dettingen, battle of (27 June 1743). A battle of the War of the Austrian Succession, remembered as the last time a British sovereign commanded an army in battle. British, Hanoverian, and Austrian troops, under George II, defeated a French and Bavarian army. A projected subsequent offensive against France itself was, however, frustrated, largely because Prussia re-entered the war against Austria.

De Valera, Eamon (1882-1975). Irish statesman. Born in New York of a Spanish father and an Irish mother, De Valera was a commandant in the *Easter rising (1916). He was condemned to death, but the sentence was commuted and he was released in 1917. Elected as a *Sinn Féin MP, he led the movement from 1917 to 1926 and was president of Sinn Féin's provisional government from 1919 to 1922. After rejecting the terms of the Anglo-Irish treaty (1921) he withdrew from active politics until 1926 when he founded *Fianna Fáil. His party won the 1932 election and he was president of the Executive Council of the Irish Free State (1932-37). He served the new republic as prime minister (1937-48, 1951-54, 1957-59) and was president (1959-73).

devaluation. The reduction of the value of a national currency in terms of foreign currencies, usually a deliberate act of government to offset economic difficulties. The pound sterling was officially devalued in 1949 (as against the US dollar, from $4.03 to $2.80) and 1967 ($2.40). Devaluation has the effect of reducing the price of a nation's exports, while increasing the price of imports, and should thus correct a balance of payments deficit. Since 1972, the value of the pound has floated freely against other currencies.

devolution. The transfer of specified administrative and legislative powers from the central to regional governments and legislatures. The system of government in *Northern Ireland from 1921 to 1972 was a form of devolution. Limited devolution was proposed for Scotland and Wales in 1978 but failed to obtain approval in referendums in March 1979.

Devonshire, Spencer Compton Cavendish, 8th duke of (1833-1908). Statesman. He was known by the courtesy title marquess of Hartington from 1858 to 1891, when he succeeded as 8th duke, and was an MP (1857-68, 1869-91). A Liberal, he was secretary for war (1866) under Russell and postmaster general (1868-74) in Gladstone's first cabinet. During Gladstone's semiretirement (1875-80) he was party leader. Subsequently secretary for India (1880-82) and secretary for war (1882-85), he opposed Irish home rule (1886) and joined Joseph Chamberlain in forming the Liberal Unionists. He served as lord president of the council in Salisbury's and Balfour's Conservative-Unionist cabinets (1895-1903).

Devonshire, William Cavendish, 1st duke of (1641-1707). A leading member of the *Country Party. He advocated the deposition of James II and was lord high steward at the coronation in 1689 of William III. He rebuilt *Chatsworth house (1687-1706).

Diamond Jubilee (1897). A national celebration marking 60 years of Victoria's reign. Intended as an even greater national and imperial event than the *Golden Jubilee (1887), the Diamond Jubilee is often regarded as symbolizing the summit of British power. Its most splendid public events were an immense military procession, including 30 000 troops from all parts of the Empire, escorting the queen to a service at St Paul's Cathedral in London, and a review of the fleet at Spithead.

Dickens, Charles (1812-70). Victorian novelist and social critic. His insecure childhood, family poverty, and early work as a child labourer in a blacking factory gave Dickens the substance of his novels. He subsequently worked as a reporter in the law courts and in parliament. In his enormously successful novels, which include Oliver Twist (1837-39), The Old Curiosity Shop (1840-41), David Copperfield (1849-50), and Great Expectations (1860-61), he protested against the cruelty, hypocrisy, and selfishness of industrial England and the evils of the poor laws and the education system.

Diggers. A small extreme group that attempted to practise a form of agrarian communism during the *Commonwealth. Seeing the Civil War as a defeat for the landowning class, 20 Diggers, under the leadership of Gerrard *Winstanley, assembled at St George's Hill, Surrey, in April 1649, to set up a colony in which land was cultivated communally. Believers in passive resistance, the Diggers were harassed by legal action and mob violence, and by 1650 had been dispersed.

Digges, Sir Dudley (1583-1639). Diplomat and judge. A founder shareholder in the East India Company, he negotiated commercial agreements abroad. He opened the attempted impeachment of the duke of Buckingham in 1626.

Dilke, Sir Charles Wentworth (1843-1911). Radical politician. Dilke's widely read Greater Britain (1868) expounded a philosophy of imperial expansion, which, as an MP (1868-86), he combined with advocacy of radical domestic reforms and republicanism. Under Gladstone he was undersecretary at the Foreign Office (1880-82) and president of the Local Government Board (1882-85) but then lost his parliamentary seat after being cited as co-respondent in a divorce case. He was once more an MP from 1892 to 1911 but did not again hold office.

Dillon, John (1851-1927). Irish nationalist and MP (1880-83, 1885-1918). In 1890, for sincere political reasons, he turned against *Parnell and led the majority of the Irish party until 1900, when he accepted the leadership of *Redmond. More radical than Redmond, he strongly supported *home rule, but in 1918 lost his seat to a member of *Sinn Féin.

diplomatic revolution (1756). The reversal of European alliances, between Britain and Austria and between France and Prussia, that had been established during the War of the *Austrian Succession (1740-48). Britain, by the convention of Westminster (Jan 1756), now became allied with Prussia; France joined with Austria by the first treaty of Versailles (May 1756). Concern to safeguard George II's Hanoverian possessions underlay the British change of position, while Austria now saw Prussia rather than its traditional enemy, France, as the main threat. This *renversement des alliances* (as it was also known) was to involve Britain during the ensuing *Seven Years' War (1756-63), as a result of its colonial rivalry with France, in the continental conflict between Austria and Prussia.

disarmament. A policy, adopted by Baldwin's Conservative government in 1925, to reduce the level of Britain's defences. Disarmament was desirable for reasons of economy, and it was defended on the grounds that, with the USA and France friendly and Germany defeated, massive armaments were no longer needed. Until the early 1930s, all three major political parties supported disarmament, and it was relinquished as a policy only in 1935, following the failure of the international disarmament conference held at Geneva (1932-34).

Discipline, Books of. 1. (1560-61) The programme of the Scottish Protestant reformers, led by John Knox. It regulated the use of church revenues to finance the ministry, the structure of the church, and education. 2. (1578) The more radical programme of Andrew *Melville, demanding a Presbyterian

system of church government and insisting that the church must be free from state control.

disestablishmentarianism. The belief that formal links between church and state are unjustifiable and should be terminated. Disestablishment was carried into effect in the Anglican church in Ireland (see Church of Ireland) in 1871 (under an act passed in 1869) and in Wales (see Church in Wales) in 1920 (under legislation in 1914 and 1919).

disinherited. 1. Those supporters of Simon de Montfort whose estates were forfeited by the crown following the barons' defeat at Evesham (1265). The dictum of *Kenilworth enabled the disinherited to redeem their property. 2. Men whose estates were forfeited for supporting the English against Robert I of Scotland. Many of the disinherited supported the claims of *Edward Balliol to the throne in 1332.

dispenser. An official in the royal and baronial households who distributed (dispensed) food and wine. The family named le *Despenser was probably descended from the dispensers in the household of the earls of Chester.

dispensing power. A royal *prerogative right to exempt individuals from a particular law, utilized by monarchs from Henry III (reigned 1216-72) onwards. Its use by James II was upheld by the decision in *Godden versus Hales (1685), but the Bill of Rights (1689) declared it illegal. See also suspending power.

Disraeli, Benjamin, 1st earl of Beaconsfield (1804-81). Prime minister and novelist. The son of a Spanish Jew, Disraeli was baptized a Christian in 1817. An MP from 1837, Disraeli expressed his romantic Toryism through his leadership of the *Young England group and through his successful political novels Coningsby (1844) and Sybil (1845). Seen as an outsider by many Conservatives, Disraeli was not given office in Peel's second ministry. He attacked Peel for repealing the corn laws (1846) and as leader of the protectionist

Conservatives in the Commons helped rebuild the party's fortunes (1848-52). Disraeli's first experience of office came as chancellor of the exchequer in *Derby's three short-lived minority governments (1852, 1858, 1866-68), when he was largely responsible for the second *Reform Act (1867), which, by enfranchising ratepayers, nearly doubled the electorate. Succeeding Derby as party leader in 1868, Disraeli was briefly prime minister (Feb-Dec 1868). In opposition (1868-74), he successfully attacked Gladstone's foreign and Irish policies.

Disraeli's second ministry (1874-80) was the first majority Conservative government since 1846. At home, it made useful social reforms, including a major Public Health Act (1875) and a Merchant Shipping Act (1876). However, Disraeli's main interests were abroad. Anticipating parliamentary approval, he borrowed £4 million to purchase a near half-share in the Suez Canal Company (1875) and made Queen Victoria empress of India (1876). On close terms with the sovereign, he was created earl of Beaconsfield in the same year. He sought to limit Russian expansion in eastern Europe and achieved decisive success at the congress of *Berlin (1878), which allowed Britain to occupy Cyprus. Disraeli retired after losing the election of 1880 and died in 1881.

Besides *Sybil* and *Coningsby*, Disraeli wrote six other novels, notably *Lothair* (1870).

disruption (1843). The withdrawal of over 470 ministers (out of about 1200) and almost 40% of communicants from the Church of Scotland to form the Free Church. This was the culmination of ten years of conflict within the church over lay patronage in the appointment of ministers and, more generally, state interference in church affairs, both of which were denounced by those who seceded from the established church.

dissolution of parliament. The termination of a parliament. A general election must follow. Originally at the sole discretion of the sovereign, the right of dissolution has been limited by statute since 1694 and parliament is now dissolved by the sovereign on ministerial advice. The *Parliament Act (1911) limits the life of a parliament to five years, although the prime minister may request a dissolution at any time. *See also* prorogation of parliament.

dissolution of the monasteries. The suppression of the monastic houses of England and Wales and the transfer of their property to the crown in an effort to boost royal income. It was organized by Thomas Cromwell between 1536 and 1540. A visitation of all monastic houses conducted from 1535 to 1536 revealed the hoped for examples of misconduct that provided some moral justification for the policy. Approximately 800 institutions were affected, and although their 9000 inmates received some compensation the dissolution provoked resentment that contributed to the *Pilgrimage of Grace. For Henry VIII the policy meant an additional income well in excess of £90,000 a year. Most of the property was sold off to the English gentry through the Court of Augmentations.

distraint. 1. *See* distress. **2.** The obligation of persons owning land of a certain value (originally £20) or holding a knight's *fee to accept knighthood. It was introduced by Henry III to increase revenues from feudal incidents. Charles I's insistence that all owners of land with an annual value of £40 assume knighthood provoked the Long Parliament to abolish compulsory knighthood (1641).

distress (or distraint). The seizure of a wrongdoer's movable property by the person wronged. In feudal law, a lord possessed the right to seize the property, also called distress and generally comprising livestock, of a tenant who had failed to perform services owing to him. The Statute of *Marlborough (1267) and subsequent legislation attempted to regulate abuses in distress.

divine right of kings. The doctrine that a monarch in the direct line of succession has a divine right to his throne and that rebellion against him is a sin. It was first argued in England in the *Homily against Wilful Rebellion* (1569). Where active obedience to an evil ruler was impossible, it was held that *nonresistance was required. The doctrine was held by many 17th-century clergy and was asserted in the canons ecclesiastical of 1640, which every parish priest had to read out to his congregation four times a year. It was partly in obedience to this principle that many of the *nonjurors were unable to take the oath of allegiance to William III.

Dobuni (or **Dobunni**). A British tribe the territory of which embraced present-day Gloucestershire and Somerset, with its capital at Cirencester. They offered little resistance to the Roman invasion of 43 AD and quickly adopted Roman culture.

Dodington, George Bubb, Baron Melcombe (1691–1762). Politician and archetypal representative of the 18th-century "place-hunter". An MP (1722–61; ennobled 1761), Dodington controlled several pocket boroughs but, although shifting from patron to patron, achieved only minor office. His published diary remains a valuable historical source.

Dogger Bank. A sandbank in the central North Sea about 100 km (60 mi) off the northwest coast of England, the scene of several battles and international incidents, including: 1. (5 Aug 1781) A battle during the American Revolution between the English and Dutch. It ended inconclusively. 2. (21 Oct 1904) An incident, during the Russo-Japanese War (1904–05), in which the Russian Baltic fleet, coming upon the Hull fishing fleet at night and assuming that the vessels were Japanese torpedo boats, opened fire, sinking trawlers and killing fishermen. Russia apologized and paid compensation to Britain. 3. (24 Jan 1915) A battle, during World War I, between a British squadron under Admiral Beatty and a German squadron under Vice Admiral Franz von Hipper. The British sunk one of Hipper's three ships.

Domesday Book. The most comprehensive and detailed record of property compiled anywhere in Europe during the middle ages. Conceived by William the Conqueror at Christmas 1085 in Gloucester, the survey's primary purpose was to provide maximum yield from the land tax. It received its name in the 12th century to signify that, like the Day of Judgment, there could be no appeal from its verdict. The survey was carried out during 1086. Each shire was visited by groups of royal commissioners, who conducted their investigations from the shire courts. Every village was expected to reply to a variable list of questions, including the identity of landholders, the size and use of land, the number and status of its cultivators, and its value, "all threefold, before 1066, when King William gave it and now". The truth of the replies was attested by juries consisting of an equal number of Englishmen and Normans. The information was then condensed and tabulated, shire by shire, on the basis of feudal ownership: the king's estates were listed followed by those belonging to the ecclesiastical and lay tenants in chief, women, English thegns, etc. The survey was eventually recorded in two volumes, one dealing with the counties of Norfolk, Suffolk, and Essex (Little Domesday) and the other with the remainder, which were held at the Treasury in Winchester. The four northernmost counties, London, and Winchester were not included. The survey caused considerable resentment and, in some places, riots. Domesday Book is now in the Public Record Office.

Dominica. The largest of the *Windward Islands. French settlers arrived in 1632, meeting fierce resistance from the indigenous Caribs. Captured by the British in 1759, during the Seven Years' War, it was ceded to Britain by the treaty of Paris (1763), when it became part of the federation of the Windward Islands. The French regained possession in 1778 but again lost it to Britain in 1782. In 1871 Dominica was federated with the Leeward Islands and in 1940 again became part of the Windward Islands. A West Indies Associated State from 1967, it gained independence as a member of the Commonwealth in 1978.

dominion. A country of the British Empire and, later, the Commonwealth of Nations that had autonomy in domestic and foreign affairs. *Canada received dominion status in 1867, and in the Statute of Westminster (1931) the term was also applied to *Australia, *New Zealand, *South Africa, *Newfoundland, and the *Irish Free State. It fell into disuse after World War II.

Domus Conversorum (Latin: house of the converted). A building erected by Henry III to house Jews converted to Christianity. When, in 1290, the Jews were expelled from England Chancery stored their rolls and records in the building, which was demolished in 1717. The Public Record Office later occupied the site in Chancery Lane.

Donald III Bane (c. 1031–1100). King of Scots (1093–94, 1094–97), after seizing the throne on the death of his brother Malcolm III. His sobriquet Bane means "fair". He was dethroned by Malcolm's son, Duncan II, in 1094. He soon regained power but was defeated and captured by another of Malcolm's sons, Edgar, who had him blinded and imprisoned until his death. Both Duncan and Edgar were supported by the English against Donald.

Donne, John (1572–1631). Metaphysical poet and preacher. Educated at Oxford, Cambridge, and Lincoln's Inn, he then inherited and squandered a huge fortune. Donne gradually turned to religion, writing a number of anti-Catholic pamphlets before taking holy orders (1615). He became a fashionable preacher and, in 1621, dean of St Paul's. His verse ranged from the love poetry of his youth to poetry on satirical and religious themes.

Don Pacifico affair (1850). An incident arising from the claim by David Pacifico (1784–1854), a Gibraltarian living in Athens, for compensation from the Greek government after a mob destroyed his house (1847). Greece finally accepted compromise terms on this and other British claims after Palmerston (then foreign secretary) had sent a fleet to blockade Piraeus (Jan–April 1850). France then accused Britain of breaking an agreement to protect Greek independence. Palmerston defended his nationalist policies in a famous House of Commons speech (June) comparing a British subject's rights anywhere in the world to the claim of an ancient Roman that *Civis Romanus sum* ("I am a Roman citizen").

doom. In the Anglo-Saxon period, a judicial judgment. Anglo-Saxon laws, such as those issued by King Alfred, were called dooms.

Dorset, 1st earl of. *See* Sackville, Thomas.

Douglas, Sir Archibald (?1296–1333). Regent of Scotland. In 1332 Douglas defeated Edward Balliol, the newly crowned king of Scotland, and was appointed regent in 1333. He died in the same year, at the battle of *Halidon Hill, defeated by Edward III on behalf of Balliol.

Douglas, Archibald, 5th earl of Angus (c. 1449–1513). Scottish magnate, who was responsible for the hanging of the favourites of James III of Scotland at Lauder Bridge in 1482. The episode, which brought Angus the sobriquet Bell-the-Cat, may well have been largely invented by later historians. Angus's record under both James III and James IV suggests that his outstanding quality was unreliability.

Douglas, Archibald, 6th earl of Angus (?1489–1557). Grandson and namesake of the 5th earl of Angus. In 1514 he married *Margaret Tudor, mother of the young James V of Scots. Appointed to the council of regency when the regent John Stewart, 1st duke of *Albany, went to France, Angus quarrelled with the president of the council James Hamilton, earl of *Arran, and was sent into exile (1520). He returned in 1524 but after quarrelling with his wife obtained, with the support of Henry VIII of England, charge of James V. In 1528 he was attainted and lived in England until the king's death in 1542. He held command at Pinkie (1547).

Douglas, Archibald Douglas, 3rd earl of (c. 1328–c. 1400). Illegitimate son of Sir James Douglas, he became constable of Edinburgh (1361) and served as royal ambassador to France in 1369, being largely responsible for the renewed Franco-Scottish alliance in 1371. He became earl in 1385 and continued to play an important part in Scottish politics. He led the invasion of England in 1388 (see Otterburn, battle of).

Douglas, Archibald Douglas, 4th earl of (c. 1369–1424). Soldier. He was captured at *Homildon Hill (1402) by the Percys, whom he supported at the battle of *Shrewsbury (1403), when he was again captured—by Henry IV. He subsequently supported Charles VIII of France in the Hundred Years' War, receiving the duchy of Touraine, and was killed by the English at *Verneuil.

Douglas, Sir James (c. 1286–1330). Soldier and close friend of Robert I of Scotland. After Robert's death Douglas, "The Good Sir James", took the king's heart and carried it in battle against the Moors in Spain, where he was killed.

Douglas, Janet, Lady Glamis (d. 1537). Granddaughter of Archibald *Douglas, 5th earl of Angus ("Bell-the-Cat"). She was falsely accused of poisoning her husband John, 6th Lord Glamis, and then of conspiring to murder James V. In 1537 she was burned alive on the Castle hill at Edinburgh.

Douglas-Home, Sir Alec. See Home of the Hirsel, Alexander Frederick Douglas-Home, Baron.

Dover, treaty of (1 June 1670). A treaty negotiated between Charles II and Louis XIV of France, for which Charles' sister *Henrietta Anne acted as intermediary. Charles agreed to help Louis' plan to annex Holland, in return for territorial gains. In a secret clause he undertook to announce his conversion to Roman Catholicism in return for a subsidy. The treaty was followed by the third *Dutch War.

Dowding, Hugh Dowding, 1st Baron (1882–1970). Air chief marshal, who headed the RAF Fighter Command during the battle of *Britain. He served as a squadron commander in World War I and subsequently in various positions at home and abroad. In 1930, as a member of the Air Council for Research and Development, he encouraged the development of advanced fighters, such as the Spitfire and Hurricane. In the early part of World War II he organized the air defence of Britain, and his tactical skill was chiefly responsible for the defeat of the Luftwaffe.

Dowland, John (?1563–1626). Composer and lutenist. He was court lutenist at Brunswick, Hesse, and Denmark, returning to England to enter James I's service in 1606. His works include lute songs and *Lachrymae*, a collection of instrumental pavanes. His son Robert Dowland (c. 1586–1641) was lutenist to Charles I.

Downing Street. A street in Westminster, London, the name of which is synonymous with British government. It comprises a block of buildings (reconstructed 1960–63) that includes "Number 10", the official residence of prime ministers since Walpole, "Number 11", the chancellor of the exchequer's residence, and the Foreign and Commonwealth Office. It is named after Sir George Downing (1623–84), secretary to the Treasury.

Drake, Sir Francis (c. 1540–1596). Admiral and explorer. With Sir John *Hawkins, a relative, Drake abandoned the cross-Channel trade for more adventurous and lucrative buccaneering expeditions to the Spanish Main (1567–68). In 1572 he was granted a privateering commission and, during a raid on the Isthmus of Panama, sighted the Pacific. In Dec 1577 he embarked in the *Pelican* to explore the Pacific and, reaching the Strait of Magellan in Aug 1578, renamed his ship the *Golden Hind*. Rounding Cape Horn, Drake plundered the Pacific coast of South America and claimed New Albion—now California—for England. He returned to England (Sept 1580) via the East Indies and Cape of

Good Hope, thus becoming the first Englishman to circumnavigate the world. For this achievement he was knighted by Queen Elizabeth on board the *Hind* at Deptford in 1581. Drake renewed his raids on Spanish ships and possessions in the West Indies and in 1587 ventured into Cádiz harbour. There, in an exploit described by Drake as "singeing the king of Spain's beard", he sank or crippled more than 30 Spanish ships, thus delaying the planned invasion of England. In 1588 he played an important part in the defeat of the Spanish *armada. His continued harassment of the Spaniards ended only with his death at sea in 1596.

dreadnoughts. A class of British battleship named after its prototype, the *Dreadnought*, launched in 1906. Unlike earlier classes, dreadnoughts carried no secondary armament, being equipped solely with ten 300 mm (12 in) guns mounted in five turrets. Laden, they displaced about 21 650 tonnes and had a speed of 21 knots (39 km per hour). Their combination of firepower revolutionized naval warfare and gave Britain a strategic advantage in the World Wars that not even the submarine and mine entirely overcame.

Drogheda massacre (11 Sept 1649). The killing of the defenders of Drogheda by the parliamentarians under Cromwell. Drogheda, a port north of Dublin, was occupied by English and Irish royalists who defied *Cromwell's call to surrender. Cromwell then stormed the town and ordered the killing of the 2500 members of the garrison.

Druids. The priesthood in the religion of the *Celts; they were also concerned with education and the law. They emphasized the immortality and transmigration of the soul and participated in the sacrifice of animal and even human victims to the numerous deities of their religion. *Anglesey was a centre of the Druids, whose practices, especially those involving human sacrifices, horrified the Romans, who massacred the Anglesey Druids in 61 AD and destroyed their sacred groves of oak. Thereafter, organized Druidism

disappeared until revived in a modified form in the 19th century. Its connection with *Stonehenge has not been proven.

Dryden, John (1631–1700). Poet. The most celebrated literary figure of the Restoration, in 1667 he was appointed poet laureate. In the 1680s he turned to political satire with *Absalom and Achitophel* (1681), an attack on the 1st earl of *Shaftesbury and the Whigs. After James II succeeded to the throne Dryden became a Roman Catholic (1686) but, with the accession in 1689 of the Protestant William III, fell from royal favour and lost the laureateship.

Dublin. A city on the east coast of Ireland and, since 1922, capital of the Republic of Ireland. Recent excavations prove it was founded by the Vikings in the 9th century. After being captured by the Normans (1170), it became the major town of Ireland. Until the 17th century Dublin was a medieval walled town with a population of about 5000. After the 1660s it grew rapidly and by 1680 numbered 60 000 inhabitants, the second largest city in the British Isles. During the 18th century many of the beautiful Georgian houses and streets, which distinguish Dublin today, were laid out. In the 19th and 20th centuries the city has grown steadily but has not been heavily industrialized.

Dudley, Lord Guildford (d. 1554). Fourth son of the duke of *Northumberland. He was married by his father to Lady Jane *Grey (1553), in an attempt to thwart the succession of Mary to the throne. The plot failed, and Dudley was executed.

duke. The highest rank of the *peerage, originating in 1337 with the creation as duke of Cornwall of *Edward, the Black Prince. The first nonroyal duke was Robert de Vere, 9th earl of *Oxford, created duke of Ireland in 1386.

Dumnonii. A British tribe whose territory covered present-day Cornwall and part of Devon, with its capital at Exeter (Isca Dumnoniorum). The Dumnonii were overrun in the early years of the Roman invasion of 43 AD.

Dunaverty, massacre of (1647). The killing of 250-300 Highlanders, who had been holding Dunaverty castle against the *covenanters, after they had surrendered unconditionally.

Dunbar, battle of. 1. (27 April 1296) The battle in which Edward I of England defeated John Balliol of Scotland, who had renounced his allegiance to Edward. John subsequently resigned his kingdom to the English king. 2. (3 Sept 1650) The battle in which the English under Cromwell defeated a superior Scottish army under Lieut. Gen. David Leslie. The *Kirk Party's purging of the Scottish army of all considered ungodly, and the interference of its ministers in military affairs, contributed to the Scottish defeat.

Dunbar, William (c. 1465-c. 1530). Scots poet. He was a Franciscan novice before becoming (c. 1500) court poet to *James IV, receiving a royal pension. He wrote a number of lyrical and courtly poems but is chiefly noted as a satirist.

Duncan I (c. 1010-1040). King of Scots (1034-40), succeeding his grandfather Malcolm II. At his accession Duncan was already king of Strathclyde, which thus became united to Scotia. In 1040 Duncan unsuccessfully besieged Durham and was twice defeated by Thorfinn, earl of Orkney, before being killed by Macbeth.

Duncan II (c. 1060-1094). King of Scots (1094), eldest son of Malcolm III. Duncan, with English help, defeated his uncle Donald Bane to become king but was soon murdered and Donald regained the throne.

Duncan of Camperdown, Adam Duncan, Viscount (1731-1804). Naval commander. As a lieutenant, Duncan was present at the blockade of Brest (1755). He became an admiral in 1795 and was commander in chief in the North Sea from 1795 to 1801. His defeat of the Dutch admiral De Winter off *Camperdown in 1797, when 9 out of 16 Dutch vessels were captured, effectively deprived the Irish rebellion of foreign assistance.

Dundalk, battle of (14 Oct 1318). A battle between English and Scottish forces in Ireland. Edward *Bruce, sent to Ireland by his brother *Robert, king of Scots, had been proclaimed king of Ireland by the people of Ulster in 1315. Edward Bruce failed to establish his authority over Ireland and was defeated and killed by the English at Dundalk.

Dundas, Henry, 1st Viscount Melville (1742-1811). MP from 1774 (viscount, 1802), who became Pitt the younger's closest colleague as treasurer of the navy (1784-1800), home secretary (1791-94), secretary of war (1794-1801), president of the India Board (1793-1801), and first lord of the admiralty (1804-05). Accused of misappropriating Admiralty funds (1805), Melville was ultimately acquitted but the scandal ended his career. He was a remarkable election and patronage manager.

Dundee, 1st Viscount. *See* Graham of Claverhouse, John.

dunes, battle of the (14 June 1658). A battle in which Cromwell's English troops and their French allies defeated the Spanish near Dunkirk, then in the Spanish Netherlands. The English troops, under Sir William Lockhart (1621-76), had been sent to support Marshal de Turenne of France in his siege of Dunkirk. The Spanish forces, backed by English royalists under James, duke of York, came to relieve the besieged town. They were attacked on the dunes by the Anglo-French army and forced to retreat.

Dunkirk, evacuation from (27 May-4 June 1940). The mass evacuation of allied troops from continental Europe during World War II. German advances down the Somme and in Belgium trapped the *British Expeditionary Force and French forces between Ostend and Dunkirk and a British-led counter attack (21 May), although abortive, led to the temporary halt of the German advance, on Hitler's instructions. British and allied troops retreated to the beaches of Dunkirk, where they were evacuated by an 850-strong flotilla of naval and civilian craft under RAF protection. The so-called Operation Dynamo resulted in the rescue of 233 000 British and 113 000 allied troops, but with the loss of all their heavy weapons and transport, and of 235 vessels and 106 aircraft involved in the evacuation.

Dunning's resolution (April 1780). A proposal, passed by the House of Commons, that "the influence of the crown has increased, is increasing, and ought to be diminished". It was proposed by John Dunning (1731-83), an opponent of George III and Lord North, in particular of their policies towards the American Revolution.

Dunsinane. A hill in the Sidlaw Hills, in Tayside Region. On its summit is a ruined fort said to be *Macbeth's castle. In Shakespeare's play Macbeth was killed here by Malcolm (III) Canmore.

Dunstable, John (c. 1385-1453). Composer, who was also noted as a mathematician. He probably travelled to France in the service of the duke of Bedford and influenced European music with the sonorous harmonies of the English tradition.

Dunstan, St (c. 925-988). Archbishop of Canterbury, who exercised a powerful influence on successive kings of England. Of noble birth, Dunstan was appointed abbot of Glastonbury (c. 943), in which position he helped revive English monastic life while also acting as treasurer to King Edred. Banished (c. 956) by Edwy, he was restored by Edgar, who made him bishop of Worcester and London (957) and subsequently (c. 960) archbishop of Canterbury. He reinvigorated English religious life and also became noted as a craftsman and musician. Feast day: 19 May.

duoviri (Latin: two men). The joint administration by two men of branches of the Roman imperial civil service. In the *colonia* one pair of *duoviri* were elected to administer law and a second pair to oversee finance and building.

Dupplin Muir, battle of (11 Aug 1332). The battle, fought near Perth, in which *Edward Balliol and the *disinherited, aided by the English, defeated a Scottish

army led by the earl of Mar, guardian of the realm during David II's minority. In the following month Balliol was crowned Edward I of Scotland.

durbar. A ceremonial audience held by an Indian ruler or the court in which it is held. Durbars were adopted by British governors in India, the most famous being George V's coronation durbar in Delhi (Dec 1911).

Durham, John George Lambton, 1st earl of (1792-1840). Statesman, who originated the Durham report on Canada (1839). A leading radical, who believed in colonial development, Durham was an MP from 1813 to 1828 (created Baron Durham, 1828; earl, 1833) and served in Grey's cabinet (1830-33). He was appointed governor general in Canada in 1838, after the revolts of *Papineau and *Mackenzie highlighted discontent in Lower and Upper Canada. Advised by Edward Gibbon *Wakefield, he recommended the union of Lower and Upper Canada and that colonial governments should be responsible to their parliaments, rather than the British government, for local affairs—in effect, internal self-government. His report—the "Report on the Affairs of British North America" (1839)—is now seen as providing the basis for subsequent British policy in its colonies, in anticipation of their independence.

Durham cathedral. A cathedral that is one of the best examples of the romanesque style in Europe. It owes much of its beauty externally to its site, on an outcrop of rock immediately above the river Wear. Internally it is notable particularly for the high quality of the carvings on the pillars, which are cut in a variety of geometric patterns, and on the capitals, which indicate considerable Scandinavian influence. Unlike most romanesque buildings, Durham was not subsequently rebuilt, the only significant addition being the Galilee chapel added in the 12th century.

Dutch Wars. 1. (1652-54) The war between England and the Dutch Republic that followed the anti-Dutch *Navigation Act (1651). The Dutch under Tromp defeated the English off Dungeness (Dec 1652), but following his defeat and death off Texel (1653) the war was concluded by the treaty of Westminster (1654). The peace settlement included Dutch compensation for the massacre of *Amboina (1623). 2. (1665-67) A war, caused by continuing commercial rivalry, that was formally declared after the Dutch capture of England's Gold Coast forts and the English capture of New Amsterdam (New York, named after James, duke of York, later James II) in 1664. Defeated off Lowestoft in June 1665, the Dutch then secured a series of victories aided, from Jan 1666, by the French. England was weakened by the great plague and the Fire of London, and the war culminated in the destruction of ships docked at Chatham. The treaty of Breda (July 1667) concluded the war. 3. (1672-74) A war that followed Charles II's commitment in the treaty of *Dover (1670) to support the invasion by Louis XIV of France of the Dutch Republic. The Anglo-Dutch aspect of the war was entirely indecisive and was concluded by the treaty of Westminster (1674).

Dyfed. A Welsh kingdom in southwest Wales; its name is derived from the tribal Demetae. The ruling dynasty claimed to be of Irish descent. In the time of *Hywel Dda, Dyfed was incorporated into the kingdom of *Deheubarth. The conquest of Dyfed in the late 11th century led to the establishment of the lordship of Pembroke.

Dyrham, battle of. See Deorham, battle of.

E

Eadwig. See Edwy.

ealdorman. A noble of the highest social rank in Anglo-Saxon England, appointed by the king to govern a *shire. Ealdormen were responsible for the shire military levy and secular law in the shire moot. From the 10th or 11th century ealdormen became powerful local magnates, with control over more than one shire, and became known as *earls.

earl. The chief royal representative in the shires, replacing the Anglo-Saxon *ealdorman in the Danish areas of England in the 10th century and throughout the country under Cnut (reigned 1016-35). Although the office was nominally in the gift of the king, the earls had such political and landed power that the tendency was towards hereditability. In the shire the earl commanded the *fyrd, presided over the court, and received a third of the profits of justice. During the 11th century earls ruled over provinces, such as Wessex and Northumbria, and were replaced in shire administration by the *sheriffs. In the 12th century the title of earl became one of nobility (see peerage).

East Anglia. An Anglo-Saxon kingdom corresponding approximately to modern Norfolk, Suffolk, and some of Cambridgeshire. It was founded by the East *Angles in about 500 AD and came under the control of Mercia in the 7th century and of the Danish invaders in the 9th century. It was conquered by Wessex in 917 and in the 11th century constituted an earldom. Its wealth is evidenced by the treasure found at *Sutton Hoo.

eastern question. A leading issue in European diplomacy during the 19th century. The problem arose from the weakness and incipient disintegration of the Ottoman (Turkish) Empire. For several centuries the Turks had ruled much of the Near East and southeastern Europe, but in the 19th century the empire was threatened by the tide of nationalism, which caused many of the Christian peoples of the Balkans to rise in revolt. The problem was intensified by the interests and rivalries in the area of the Great Powers. Russia, notably, aimed at unrestricted access from the Black Sea to the Mediterranean, and the century saw three Russo-Turkish wars, as well as two other wars in which France and Britain, as well as Russia, were involved. Britain's policy throughout was consistent. Fearing that the disintegration of Turkey might leave the Mediterranean trading routes and the route to India open to Russian threat, it supported Turkey against Russia. The tradition began in 1791, when *Pitt the younger denounced Russian threats to Turkey. From the 1830s to the 1850s British policy was to prevent Russia seizing the Bosporus, and after the *Crimean War (1854-56) the strait was closed to foreign warships. In 1878, at the Congress of *Berlin, Britain was able to strip Russia of many of the gains it had made by the treaty of San Stefano (March, 1878)—at the same time acquiring Cyprus for itself. There was, however, a radical tradition in British foreign policy that despised the backward, sometimes barbaric, Ottoman Empire, and sympathized with struggling emergent nations. This led to British support for the Greeks during the Greek War of Independence (1821-27), as well as opposition (led by *Gladstone) to pro-Turkish policies after the Bulgarian massacres of 1876 and the Armenian atrocities of 1894-96.

The problem continued important to World War I, and in 1914 Turkey entered the war on the side of the Central Powers.

Easter rising (24-29 April 1916). An armed insurrection in Dublin. Five battalions of the Irish Republican Brotherhood (*see* Fenian Society) under Patrick Pearse and 200 men of the Citizen Army under James Connolly, a total of 2000 armed men, took up central positions in the city on Easter Monday. Pearse proclaimed the establishment of the Irish Republic, styling himself president of the Provisional Government. Vigorous street fighting commenced but within a week the insurgents surrendered unconditionally; their hopes that the rising would spread throughout the country were not fulfilled. Fifteen of the leaders were executed; 3000 others were interned but soon released.

East India Company. A trading company incorporated by royal charter in 1600. The company intended to take advantage of the decline in Portugal's commercial power in the Far East, but the Dutch forced the British to withdraw from the Dutch East Indies following the massacre of *Amboina (1623), and the company subsequently established itself in *Bengal. Rivalry with France broke into open warfare in the 18th century, but English supremacy in *India was secured by the victories of *Clive, in the company's employ, in the Seven Years' War (1756-63). Criticism of the company's administration of the subcontinent led to a series of restrictive Government of *India Acts, culminating in the crown's assumption of full responsibility for India in 1858, following the *Indian mutiny. The company survived until 1873.

Eastland Company. A trading company incorporated in 1579 to trade with the Baltic area. Cloth was exported in return for timber, tar, hemp, and cordage—vital naval stores. The company was threatened by increasing competition from the Dutch, whose merchant ships were better fitted for the trade, and the company's monopoly was ended in 1673.

ecclesiastical courts. Courts that administer canon law. They had jurisdiction not only over all legal matters to do with the clergy (which caused conflict with the lay courts; *see* benefit of clergy) and the maintenance of orthodoxy, but over a wide range of cases affecting the laity, especially the enforcement of *tithes and *mortuaries, sexual offences, matrimonial and testamentary affairs, and perjury. They fell into disrepute in the later 16th century but retained important jurisdictions, especially over probate and matrimonial cases, until 1857. Their scope is now limited almost entirely to matters affecting the clergy. Appeal from the archdeacons' courts lay with the bishop's consistory, or diocesan, court, and the archbishops' consistory courts (the Court of *Arches for Canterbury and Chancery for York). Appeals to Rome were restricted during the 14th century (*see* praemunire) and abolished during the *Reformation. Since 1833 appeals have lain with the Judicial Committee of the Privy Council.

economical reform. *See* Burke, Edmund; place acts.

Eden, Sir Anthony, 1st earl of Avon
(1897-1977). Prime minister. A Conservative MP (1923-57; earl, 1961), he
became foreign secretary (following
*Hoare) in Dec 1935 but resigned in
Feb 1938 over policy and personal
disagreements with Neville *Chamberlain. Returning to the cabinet as
dominions secretary at the beginning of
World War II, he became war secretary
(May 1940) under Churchill. Foreign
secretary again from Dec 1940 to July
1945, he was intimately involved in allied
policy making. He returned as Churchill's foreign secretary in Oct 1951, now
dealing especially with problems posed
by Soviet and Chinese communism and
rising Arab nationalism. Long
recognized as Churchill's heir, he finally
became prime minister in April 1955,
but his premiership was soon terminated
by the *Suez crisis (1956). His health
gave way and he resigned in Jan 1957,
being succeeded by Macmillan.

Edgar (c. 944-975). King of Northumbria and Mercia (957-75) and of England
(959-75). Younger son of Edmund I, he
succeeded his elder brother Edwy.
According to legend, at his coronation at
Bath in 973 Edgar was rowed on the
river Dee by seven Welsh and Scottish
kings, a story that is probably apocryphal but that testifies to his dominance
over England. An efficient administrator, he was advised by Archbishops
*Dunstan (of Canterbury) and Oswald
(of York) and fostered the 10th-century
revival of *monasticism.

Edgar (c. 1074-1107). King of Scots
(1097-1107), fourth son of Malcolm III.
On his father's death in 1093 Edgar fled
to England. Having gained English help
by agreeing to hold Scotland as a vassal
of William II, he overthrew his uncle
Donald III Bane. He died unmarried
and was succeeded by his brother
Alexander I.

Edgar the Aetheling (d. 1125). Anglo-
Saxon prince (aetheling). The great-
nephew of Edward the Confessor and
strongest hereditary claimant to the
throne on Edward's death, Edgar was
passed over in favour of *Harold II in

1066. After the Norman conquest he
submitted to William I, but revolts were
raised in Edgar's name and he was forced
to flee to Scotland and then to Flanders
before again making peace with William
(1074). He fought for *Robert Curthose
against Henry I and was captured at
*Tinchebrai (1106), but soon released.

Edgehill, battle of (23 Oct 1642). The first
major battle of the Civil War, fought between the parliamentarians under the
earl of Essex and the royalists led by
Charles I and Prince Rupert. It ended
indecisively, with both sides claiming
victory, but Charles subsequently felt
confident enough to reject parliament's
overtures for peace.

Edinburgh. The capital city of Scotland,
on the south side of the Firth of Forth.
The Old Town was crowded on the
spine of land running down from the
castle rock (see Edinburgh castle)
through Canongate to the abbey of
Holyrood. The earliest references to the
town occur in the early 12th century,
when it was already a royal burgh; but
the city was slow to emerge as the
acknowledged capital of Scotland,
probably because its location made it
vulnerable to attacks by the English.
During the 12th century Edinburgh
became the administrative centre of
Scotland and during the reign of James
III (1460-88) parliament normally met
here. However, not until James IV
(reigned 1488-1513) built the palace of
*Holyroodhouse and established the
Court of Sessions in Edinburgh was the
city finally established as the Scottish
capital. The burgh gained control over
South Leith in 1329 and over North
Leith and the burgh of Canongate in the
early 17th century. In the late 18th
century Edinburgh was renowned for the
architecture of the New Town, built to
the north of the Old Town, and for the
distinction of its intellectual life, which
brought the burgh the somewhat exaggerated title of "The Athens of the
North".

Edinburgh, treaty of. 1. (17 March 1328)
The treaty by which the English, having
renounced any superiority over Scotland,

recognized the latter as an independent kingdom under Robert I. The English ratified the treaty at Northampton on 4 May. 2. (6 July 1560) The treaty by which England and France agreed that their forces should withdraw from Scotland. The French had refused to negotiate with the lords of the *Congregation as they were in rebellion against Mary Queen of Scots, but concessions to the Scots appended to the treaty authorized the summoning of the Scottish parliament in her name.

Edinburgh castle. References to a fort on the castle rock in Edinburgh occur from the late 6th century, but the earliest surviving building is St Margaret's Chapel (c. 1100). The palace block was built in the 15th century and the Great Hall in the 16th. The castle has been frequently besieged and captured. Why it was often called "the maidens' castle" is unknown.

Edington, battle of (May 878). A battle, fought south of Chippenham in Wiltshire, between a force commanded by King *Alfred of Wessex and the invading Danes under Guthrum. Edington was a decisive victory for Alfred and forced the Danes to withdraw from Wessex and retire into East Anglia.

Edith (d. 1075). Queen consort of Edward the Confessor. The daughter of Earl *Godwine, Edith married Edward in 1045, thereby strengthening her family's influence over the king. Briefly repudiated by Edward in 1051 at the time of the anti-Godwine reaction, she submitted to William I after the conquest and played no further part in public life.

Edmund I (921-46). King of England (939-46). Edmund succeeded his half-brother Athelstan as king and reconquered Danish Mercia in 944. In 945 he ravaged and conquered the kingdom of Strathclyde. A friend of *Dunstan, Edmund was the first king to support the 10th-century monastic reform in England (see monasticism).

Edmund II Ironside (c. 993-1016). King of Wessex. Son of Aethelred II, Edmund led expeditions against the Danes in

1015 and was chosen king of England by the Londoners in 1016. After inconclusive battles he was heavily defeated by his rival *Cnut at *Ashingdon. In the ensuing treaty he was granted Wessex, while Cnut held the rest of England. Edmund died shortly afterwards.

Edmund, earl of Lancaster (1245-96). Second son of Henry III. In 1254 Henry accepted for Edmund, but failed to claim, the pope's offer of the kingdom of Sicily. Edmund accompanied his brother Edward on crusade (1271), took part in the campaign against Llywelyn ap Gruffudd (1277-82), and as regent (1286-89) suppressed the revolt of Rhys ap Maredudd. His marriage (1275) to Blanche of Artois brought him Champagne.

Edmund . Rich, St (?1175-1240). Archbishop of Canterbury (1234-40). He criticized Henry III for relying on foreign favourites and, with baronial support, forced the king to expel them. A Roman legate, Cardinal Otto, requested by Henry, countered Edmund's every direction and he was forced to retire. Feast day: 16 Nov.

Edred (d. 955). King of England (946-55), succeeding his brother Edmund I. Edred invaded Northumbria in 947 to expel their new Viking king, Eric Bloodaxe. Eric was finally expelled in 954, and Northumbria was brought permanently under English control.

education. During the early Anglo-Saxon period the control of education in England became the responsibility of the Christian *church. The monastic and cathedral schools originally established for the clergy and those intending to enter the monasteries gradually admitted lay pupils and broadened the curriculum to include the classics, grammar, logic, rhetoric, geometry, and arithmetic. The church continued to dominate education until the end of the middle ages; the universities at Oxford and Cambridge developed around centres of learning established by the clergy in the 12th and 13th centuries and the number of cathedral grammar schools rose to approximately 400. A basic education was provided in some areas for the children of the poor, usually by the local parish priest. In the 15th-16th centuries English humanists, such as John *Colet, who founded St Paul's School, and Sir Thomas *More, helped to establish a revival of classical learning and liberal studies. During the 16th and 17th centuries the spread of Calvinist reforms by the Puritans in England and the Presbyterians in Scotland led to an emphasis on the study of English, science, modern languages, and sport. The rapid industrialization of Britain from the mid-18th century onwards, combined with the state's reluctance to intervene in the educational sphere, prompted the Church of England and other religious bodies to establish a system of voluntary elementary education. It was not until W. E. *Forster's Education Act (1870) that universal elementary education was introduced in England and Wales, and school boards were set up to establish schools in districts in which no voluntary school existed. In 1880 A. J. Mundella's act made elementary education compulsory, and in 1891 the payment of fees in elementary schools was virtually abolished. Secondary education, however, remained the province of voluntary and private enterprise. The reforms of Frederick Temple (1821-1902), Henry Montagu Butler (1833-1918), and Thomas *Arnold led to an increased demand for public school places, and during the latter half of the 19th century several girls' high schools and boarding schools were established. Several new universities were also set up during the 19th century. The Balfour Act (1902) replaced the school boards by local education authorities, which were responsible for both elementary and secondary education. H. A. L. *Fisher's Education Act (1918) increased the powers of the local authorities and raised the school-leaving age to 14. The R. A. Butler Act (1944) inaugurated a system of universal secondary education, while maintaining the dual system of grant-assisted independent schools and local authority schools. Postwar developments include the widespread introduction of comprehensive education, which was initiated in 1965, and the incorporation of many of the ideas of the progressive educationalists (e.g. Froebel, Montessori, A. S. Neill) into the state schools, especially at the primary level.

Scotland's educational system has remained quite separate from that of England and Wales, the secretary of state for Scotland being responsible for the administration of the country's education. Most of the main features of the Education Act (1944) in England and Wales were contained in the Education Act (1945) in Scotland, and by the 1970s approximately 40% of the Scottish schools had become comprehensive.

Edward I (1239-1307). King of England (1272-1307). Eldest son of Henry III, Edward was twice married: first (1254) to Eleanor of Castile and second (1299) to Margaret of France. His formidable military talents were revealed against the rebellious barons at *Evesham (1265), and his reign was much troubled by war. In Wales he faced the opposition of *Llywelyn ap Gruffudd from 1277 to 1282, when Llywelyn's death enabled Edward to extend English administration and law to the Principality (see Rhuddlan, Statute of); a subsequent (1294-95) Welsh rebellion was effectively, if ruthlessly, subdued. In Scotland he suffered three major rebellions. The first, led by *John Balliol, was defeated at *Dunbar in 1296 but the second, under William *Wallace, continued after Edward's victory at *Falkirk (1298) until 1305; Edward died on his way to subdue the third—that of *Robert the Bruce (see also Anglo-Scottish wars). The king's French possessions also involved him in conflict. Philip the Fair of France invaded Gascony in 1294, and peace was not made until 1299, following which Edward married Philip's sister. The strain on the royal finances was enormous, and Edward faced serious opposition from Archbishop Winchelsea, who resisted the king's attempts to tax the church, and from the barons, who compelled him to promise not to levy further arbitrary taxes. Trouble came also from Winchelsea's predecessor, *Peckham, who had reasserted the rights of the ecclesiastical courts.

Edward's reign witnessed important legal and administrative reforms. The Statutes of *Gloucester (1278) and *Winchester (1285) and the statutes *quo warranto and *quia emptores (both 1290) were enacted; and the constitutional importance of parliament grew (see Model Parliament). However, a resurgence of antisemitism led to the expulsion in 1290 of the *Jews, partly for the financial benefits accruing to the crown from forfeitures. He was succeeded by his son Edward II.

Edward II (1284-1327), King of England (1307-27), son of Edward I and Eleanor of Castile. Born in Caernarfon, he was the first English *prince of Wales (1301-07). In 1308 he married Isabel of France. Initially England rejoiced at the accession of the handsome young king, but his extravagance and foolishness made his reign a troubled one. His infatuation with Piers *Gaveston angered the barons, who in 1308 forced the king to banish his favourite to Ireland. Gaveston's return in 1309 was one of the provocations that led to the appointment of the lords *ordainers, who forced the king to accept the limitations on royal power contained in the *Ordinances (1311). Gaveston was again banished, and his return together with Edward's attempts to evade the Ordinances led to civil war (1312). Gaveston was executed and the disastrous Scottish campaign, notably the defeat at *Bannockburn (1314), so weakened Edward's position that he yielded his authority to his chief opponent and cousin, *Thomas, earl of Lancaster. By 1316, however, the king had regained much of his power from the incompetent Thomas and in 1318 found a new favourite, the younger Hugh le *Despenser. Renewed baronial complaints led to the banishment of Despenser and his father (1321). In 1322 the king recalled them and successfully

renewed the war against the barons, capturing and beheading Thomas of Lancaster. Edward was now able to revoke the Ordinances, only to encounter opposition from his wife. In 1325 Queen Isabel, furious at the loss of her estates and humiliated by the king's love for the young Despenser, went to France. There she fell in love with Roger de *Mortimer, a bitter enemy of the Despensers. In 1326 Isabel and Mortimer invaded England and in 1327 deposed Edward, who died, probably murdered, in Berkeley castle in Gloucestershire. He was succeeded by his son Edward III.

Edward III (1312-77). King of England (1327-77), son of Edward II and Isabel of France; he married Philippa of Hainault in 1328. He became king after his mother and her lover, Roger de *Mortimer, forced his father to abdicate, but he assumed personal control of the administration only in 1330, when he had Mortimer executed.

Edward did much to revive the prestige of the English monarchy after his father's disastrous reign. He conciliated the barons, pursued an enlightened commercial policy, and reorganized the navy. His reign, however, was dominated by his wars with Scotland and France. He sought to undermine Scottish independence (see Anglo-Scottish wars), supporting the coronation of Edward Balliol in 1332 and twice defeating Edward's rival David II—at Halidon Hill (1333) and at Neville's Cross (1346), when David was taken prisoner.

In 1337 Edward led England into the *Hundred Years' War against France, claiming not only full sovereignty over Aquitaine but also the French throne, taking (1340) the title king of France. He was initially successful, winning notable victories at *Sluys, at sea (1340), and *Crécy (1346) and conquering Calais (1347). In 1355 he resumed hostilities against France to protect his French domains, and at the great victory at *Poitiers (1356) King John II of France was captured. His next campaign

(1359-60) failed and by the treaty of *Brétigny (1360) he renounced his claim to the French throne in exchange for recognition of his full sovereignty over his French domains. In the last years of his reign he became increasingly senile and fell under the influence of his mistress Alice Perrers, while government was largely in the hands of his fourth son, *John of Gaunt.

Edward IV (1442-83). King of England (1461-70, 1471-83) during the Wars of the *Roses. Son of Richard, duke of York, and Cecily, daughter of Ralph Neville, earl of Westmorland, Edward was crowned after defeating the Lancastrians at *Mortimer's Cross and *Towton. His marriage (1464) to Elizabeth, daughter of the powerful Richard Woodville, Earl Rivers, alienated Edward's ally Warwick the kingmaker, and following the king's negotiation (1467) of an alliance with France, while Warwick was coming to an agreement with France's enemy, Burgundy, Warwick briefly imprisoned (1469) the king. Forced to flee abroad, in 1470 Warwick invaded England with Edward's brother, the duke of Clarence, forcing Edward's own retreat to Flanders. He returned in March 1471, and in April defeated and killed Warwick at *Barnet and captured Margaret, Henry VI's queen, at *Tewkesbury. His throne secure, in 1475 Edward invaded France with Charles the Bold (1433-77), duke of Burgundy, but allowed himself to be bought off for a large downpayment and an annual pension (see Picquigny, treaty of). Financially untroubled for the rest of his reign, Edward instituted administrative reforms and more effective enforcement of law and order, notably in the Marches. He was also a book collector (his collection is now in the British Library) and a patron of William Caxton.

Edward V (1470-?1483). King of England (April-June 1483). Eldest surviving son of Edward IV and Elizabeth Woodville, he was created prince of Wales in 1471. On the death of Edward IV (1483) his brother Richard, duke of

Gloucester, became protector for the 12-year-old Edward V, whom he imprisoned together with the king's younger brother Richard, duke of York, in the Tower of London. Gloucester's claim that Edward and Richard were illegitimate and that he himself was the rightful heir to the throne was acknowledged by parliament, and on the same day (25 June) the leaders of Edward's Woodville supporters were executed. On the 26th Gloucester became King Richard III. The fate of the two princes remains unknown. Contemporaries rumoured that Richard had ordered their murder, and in the 16th century his culpability was asserted in histories written by Sir Thomas More and Polydore Vergil. Some historians, however, have held Henry VII responsible, suggesting that the first Tudor king had the princes murdered as possible rivals after his victory over Richard III at Bosworth. Skeletons found near the White Tower in 1674 were shown in 1933 to be those of two children of about the age of Edward and Richard in 1483. It seems likely that they were murdered, but the identity of their murderer has still to be proven.

Edward VI (1537-53). King of England and Ireland (1547-53). Son of Henry VIII and Jane Seymour, Edward was intelligent, with scholarly tastes. The extreme Protestantism he displayed on his accession served the purposes of the council of regency that governed in his name. Led initially by the king's uncle Edward Seymour (later duke of *Somerset), the council came to be dominated by a faction led by the earl of Warwick (later duke of *Northumberland), which overthrew Somerset in 1549. Protestantism was consolidated by measures that included the 1552 Book of Common Prayer (see Reformation). Edward's health, never robust, began to fail in 1552, and a month before his death he was persuaded by Northumberland to exclude his half-sisters Mary and Elizabeth from the succession in favour of Northumberland's daughter in law Lady Jane *Grey.

Edward VII (1841-1910). King of the United Kingdom (1901-10). Eldest son of Victoria, he was created prince of Wales in the year of his birth. He was strictly brought up but became leader of a sophisticated section of society (named, with reference to his London home, the "Marlborough House set") and pursued a life devoted largely to pleasure. Partly in consequence, he was virtually excluded from royal political responsibilities by Victoria, being denied access to reports of cabinet meetings until 1892. His charm and worldliness, however, endeared him to large sections of the public. As king, Edward strengthened the position of the monarchy by reviving royal public ceremonial. Politically, he had less influence than Victoria, lacking both experience and detailed application. His practice of making visits abroad encouraged an exaggerated belief in his influence on foreign policy. His Paris visit in May 1903 undoubtedly promoted French public acceptance of the Anglo-French *entente cordiale, but this was counterbalanced by German suspicions that such contacts were aimed at the encirclement of Germany. During the crisis over the parliament bill (1910), Edward refused to agree to the creation of new peers to force the passage of the bill until a general election had been held. In 1863 Edward married Alexandra, princess of Denmark, and he was succeeded by his second son, who had become heir apparent on the death (1892) of his elder brother, the duke of Clarence, and who reigned as George V.

Edward VIII (1894-1972). King of the United Kingdom (20 Jan-11 Dec 1936). Eldest son of George V, Edward was created prince of Wales in 1911 and served as an army staff officer throughout World War I. As prince of Wales he achieved great popularity by his charm and informal manners, as well as for his concern for the plight of the unemployed during the Depression. His brief reign, however, was unhappy. He wished to marry Mrs Wallis Simpson (an American, who was divorced for the second time in Oct 1936), but the prime minister,

Baldwin, supported by church and Commonwealth leaders, maintained that he could not also remain king. Edward therefore abdicated, before he had been crowned, in George VI's favour. Created duke of Windsor, he married Mrs Simpson in June 1937. He served as governor of the Bahamas from 1940 to 1945, subsequently settling in France.

Edward, prince of Wales (1453-71). Only son of Henry VI. While his ailing father struggled to hold his throne against the Yorkists in the Wars of the Roses, Edward was looked after by his mother Margaret of Anjou, first in Scotland (1461) and then in France (1462). In 1470 he joined Warwick's invasion of England but in 1471 he was killed at the battle of *Tewkesbury.

Edward, the Black Prince (1330-76). Eldest son of Edward III and Philippa of Hainault, famous for his campaigns in the *Hundred Years' War. Created duke of Cornwall in 1337, the first English duke, he married Joan of Kent in 1361. His sobriquet is probably not contemporary and is said to refer to his habit of wearing black armour. He fought at Crécy (1346) and won the great victory at *Poitiers (1356). In 1367 he intervened in the Castilian war and was victorious at Najera. However, his misrule as prince of Aquitaine (1362-72) provoked the nobles to appeal to the French king, and in the ensuing revolt Edward ordered the notorious massacre at Limoges (1370). In 1371, his health broken, he returned to England.

Edward Balliol (?1283-1364). Eldest son of *John Balliol, king of Scots. He claimed the Scottish throne during the minority of David II and after his victory at *Dupplin Muir (1332) was crowned king of Scots. Three months later he was forced by a Scottish alliance to abandon the throne. In 1333 he was restored to the throne by Edward III of England but ceded most of southern Scotland in return. He failed to establish his authority over the Scots and in 1356 gave up his lands to Edward. *See also* Anglo-Scottish wars.

Edward of Norwich, 2nd duke of York
(?1373-1415). Son of Edmund de
*Langley and grandson of Edward III.
He was created earl of Rutland in 1390
and duke of Albemarle in 1397. He
accompanied Richard II to Ireland in
1399 but then deserted him in support of
Henry Bolinbroke. In 1404 he became a
member of the royal council and in 1415
joined Henry V in France, where he died
on the field of Agincourt.

Edward the Aetheling (d. 1054). Son of
Edmund II, his title *aetheling* means
prince. On the accession of *Cnut,
Edward fled to Hungary and married
into the imperial dynasty. As the closest
in line to Edward the Confessor, he
returned to England in 1054 but died
before he could reach court.

Edward the Confessor, St (c. 1003-66).
King of England (1042-66). Son of
Aethelred the Unready and Emma,
daughter of Richard II, duke of
Normandy, during *Cnut's reign Edward
lived in exile in Normandy. He was
crowned in 1043 and in 1045 married
Edith, daughter of Earl *Godwine.
Thereafter Godwine's family dominated
royal policy. Edward lost popularity by
placing Normans in high offices in an
attempt to counterbalance Godwine's
influence. Tension between the two
parties led to Godwine's brief exile
(1051), but he quickly re-established
supremacy. In his last years Edward
increasingly turned from secular affairs,
control of the country being left to the
great earls, such as Godwine's son
*Harold. Famed for his asceticism and
piety, Edward was buried in *Westminster abbey (which he founded). He was
canonized in 1161. Feast day: 13 Oct.

Edward the Elder (d. 924). King of
Wessex (899-924). After succeeding his
father Alfred, Edward brought all the
Danish territories south of the Humber
under his authority and gained control
over much of Wales. He was, however,
frequently faced with unrest in Mercia,
which he annexed in 918. He was
acknowledged as overlord by Scotia,
Strathclyde, and York.

Edward the Martyr, St (c. 963-78 AD).
King of England. After succeeding his
father Edgar in 975, Edward found his
claim to the throne disputed by supporters of his younger half-brother
Aethelred. Edward's assassination while
visiting Aethelred at Corfe brought the
latter to the throne as Aethelred II.

Edwin (d. 632). King of Northumbria
(617-632). Son of Aelle, king of Deira,
he defeated Aethelric, king of neighbouring Bernicia to become king of a
united Northumbria. He was ultimately
acknowledged as *bretwalda* (overlord)
of all England except Kent. In 625 he
married Aethelburh, Christian daughter
of Aethelbert of Kent, and was converted to Christianity (627) by *Paulinus,
whom he appointed archbishop of York.
He died in battle against Penda of
Mercia.

Edwy (or Eadwig) (d. 959). King of
England from 955, succeeding his uncle
Edred. Edwy's reign was marked by
personal animosity to *Dunstan, whom
he exiled. In 957 the Northumbrians
and Mercians renounced their allegiance
to Edwy in favour of his brother *Edgar,
and until his death Edwy ruled only over
the area south of the Thames.

Egbert (or Ecgbert) (d. 839). King of
Wessex (802-39). Son of a vassal king
of Kent, Egbert was forced into exile
(789) by *Offa and lived at the court of
Charlemagne until 802, when he was
elected king of Wessex. In 825 he
defeated Beornwulf of Mercia at the
battle of Ellendun, and in 828 he
temporarily annexed Mercia. Northumbria recognized his lordship and he was
styled *bretwalda in 829. However,
*Wiglaf re-established Mercian indepen-
dence in 830, and thereafter Egbert was
effective ruler only of Wessex and its
dependent kingdoms of Surrey, Sussex,
Kent, and Essex.

Egypt. A country in NE Africa and a
former British protectorate. From the
late 18th century Britain and France
were rivals for the control of Egypt,
which was nominally under Ottoman
(Turkish) suzerainty, and in 1876
established joint control over Egyptian

finances. In 1882, after suppressing a nationalist revolt, Britain acquired sole control and *Baring became virtual ruler of the country. In 1915, after Ottoman suzerainty had been rejected following its entry into World War I, Egypt became a British protectorate. In 1922 its independence under Fuad I was recognized and in 1936, following the conclusion of the 20-year Anglo-Egyptian alliance, the protectorate formally ended.

Éire (Irish: Ireland). The official name from 1937 to 1949 for what was previously (1921-37) called the *Irish Free State and subsequently (since 1949) the Republic of Ireland.

eisteddfod (Welsh: session). In the middle ages, literary and musical competitions. *Eisteddfodau* were revived in Elizabeth's reign as examinations in the bardic craft (see bard). They degenerated into convivial sessions in taverns until, under the patronage of Y *Gwyneddigion*, a London-Welsh society, they were revived in 1789 and became the major Welsh cultural event.

Eldon, John Scott, 1st earl of (1751-1838). Lawyer and politician. An MP (1783-1801), Eldon served as solicitor general (1788-93) and attorney general (1793-99), before being ennobled as Baron Eldon and appointed lord chief justice in 1801. As lord chancellor (1801-06, 1807-27) Eldon became noted as a leader of the most extreme Tories and a rigid opponent of all forms of political liberalism, including the abolition of the slave trade and Roman Catholic emancipation. As a judge his painstaking methods led to scandalous delays in the Court of Chancery.

Eleanor of Aquitaine (?1122-1204). Heiress of Aquitaine and queen of France (1137-52) as Louis VII's wife and of England (1152-89) as Henry II's wife. A lively and beautiful woman, Eleanor was unhappy with Louis, whom she described as more monk than king, and the marriage ended in divorce. To avoid importunate suitors she almost immediately married Henry of Anjou, later Henry II of England (reigned 1154-89), and with the acquisition of Aquitaine Henry's French domains outstripped those of Louis. Eleanor and Henry had seven surviving children, but their marriage was stormy and Eleanor lived mostly with her son Richard (the Lionheart) in Aquitaine, where she was a notable patron of poets. In 1173 Eleanor aided her sons' rebellion against Henry and was imprisoned until after Henry's death. She acted decisively to support the accession of her sons Richard I (1189) and John (1199).

Eleanor of Castile (1246-90). Queen of England (1272-90) as the wife of Edward I, whom she married in 1254. She accompanied her husband on crusade (1270-73) and succeeded to the county of Ponthieu in 1272, which remained in English possession until 1336. She died at Hadby in Nottinghamshire, and Edward built the Eleanor Crosses wherever her body rested on its way to her funeral in London—at Lincoln, Grantham, Stamford, Geddington, Northampton, Stony Stratford, Woburn, Dunstable, St Albans, Waltham, and (in London) West Cheap and Charing Cross.

Eleanor of Provence (1223-91). Queen of England (1236-72), as the wife of Henry III. She was active and forceful but insensitive to the feelings of the English, who bitterly resented the favour she showed to her relatives from Savoy. During the second *Barons' War (1264-67) she became leader of the royal exiles in France and ran heavily into debt raising troops and ships for her husband. When Henry died she retired to a convent at Amesbury in Wiltshire.

eleven years' tyranny (1629-40). The period of Charles I's reign during which no parliament was summoned. It is associated with the government of *thorough implemented by Strafford and Laud. The king's determination to avoid calling a parliament stemmed from the Commons' defiance of him in 1629 over his fiscal and High Church policies, culminating in an attack on the royal prerogative of adjourning parliament. Without a parliament to vote him funds lack of money was a decisive factor in the king's vacillating foreign policy during the next 11 years. His failure to support European Protestant leaders, and the peace concluded with Spain (1630), exacerbated English suspicions of his leanings towards Roman Catholicism. Ingenious revivals and extensions of old forms of taxation, most notoriously *ship money, caused increasing resentment. In ecclesiastical matters Charles intended to maintain established Anglicanism, and Laud and the Court of the *Star Chamber acted vigorously against Puritanism. Their insistence upon uniformity led in 1637 to the ill-advised attempt to impose a liturgy close to that of the English *Book of Common Prayer upon Scotland. Armed resistance ensued (see Bishops' Wars), and after an abortive attempt to reassert his authority with inadequate military resources, Charles was eventually forced to summon a parliament (1640) in order to obtain money (see Short Parliament).

Elgar, Sir Edward (William) (1857–1934). Composer. His most famous works include the *Enigma Variations* (1899) and *Pomp and Circumstance* marches (1901–30) for orchestra and his setting of Cardinal Newman's *Dream of Gerontius* (1900) for solo voices, chorus, and orchestra. Elgar was master of the king's music from 1924.

Elgin marbles. Parts of the Parthenon frieze, and other sculptures from the Acropolis in Athens, now in the British Museum. The museum bought the sculptures (1816) from Thomas Bruce, 7th earl of Elgin (1766–1841), who had acquired them (1801–03) in Athens (then under Turkish rule) and brought them to England. Elgin's action has been defended on the ground that he saved the sculptures from probable destruction. The museum has rejected requests for their return to Greece.

Eliot, Sir John (1592–1632). Parliamentarian. He entered parliament in 1624 and was imprisoned in 1626 for his part in the impeachment of *Buckingham. In 1627 he was returned to the Tower for refusing to pay a *forced loan, and in 1629 he began his third and last term of imprisonment for helping to draft inflammatory Commons' resolutions against unparliamentary taxation and Arminianism. He died of consumption in the Tower.

Elizabeth I (1533–1603). Queen of England and Ireland (1558–1603). Daughter of Henry VIII and Anne Boleyn, Elizabeth, following her mother's execution, was declared illegitimate by parliament (1536), and suffered a lonely childhood, much of it spent in the company of her young brother Edward. She was rigorously educated, studying Latin and Greek under Roger *Ascham. The accession of her sister as *Mary I in 1553 increased the insecurity of Elizabeth's position for, although herself an opponent of religious extremism, she was seen as the natural focus for the Protestant faction. Accused of involvement in Sir Thomas *Wyatt's rebellion, she was imprisoned briefly in the Tower before being placed under house arrest at Woodstock (1554).

At her accession in 1558 Elizabeth inherited a nation deeply divided by religious strife. She set about restoring the moderate Anglicanism of her father: Mary's grants to the Roman Catholic orders were reclaimed; the Anglican service was reintroduced (1559) and the 39 articles, formulating the established doctrine of the church, were adopted (1563); an Act of *Supremacy defined Elizabeth as supreme governor of the church (1559); and new bishops, including Matthew *Parker as archbishop of Canterbury, were appointed. Abroad, the war with France was ended by the treaty of Cateau-Cambrésis (1559). Economic reforms included the calling in of the debased coinage of the previous three reigns. Elizabeth appointed as her chief secretary William *Cecil, who remained her trusted adviser and friend until his death in 1598. Parliament, anxious to secure the Protestant succession, urged her to marry but she refused, although throughout her reign she used marriage as a diplomatic counter in her relations with France and the Habsburgs. She conducted romantic relationships with a number of men, notably with Robert Dudley, earl of *Leicester, and, later in life, with Robert Devereux, earl of *Essex.

Ten years of restored stability came under threat when, in 1568, Elizabeth's cousin *Mary Queen of Scots sought refuge in England. As a potential Catholic claimant to the English throne Mary became the focus of Catholic conspiracies, such as the *northern rebellion (1569). The danger increased in 1570, when the pope excommunicated Elizabeth, absolving her subjects from their allegiance to her. Further conspiracies, such as the *Ridolfi plot (1571), developed, but it was not until the discovery of *Babington's conspiracy (1586) that Elizabeth was finally persuaded to authorize Mary's trial and subsequent execution for treason, a move she later claimed to regret bitterly.

Fully conscious of the threat to English independence from the two great Roman Catholic powers, France and Spain, Elizabeth fought shy of European involvements. She gave aid reluctantly to the French Huguenots and the Dutch Protestants and gave only secret consent to Drake's attacks on the Spanish treasure fleets. When Spain at last turned to quell England, the defeat of the *armada made her a legend throughout Europe. However, she would still not be drawn into open war, continuing to endorse the campaign of privateering and raiés on Spanish bases, such as that of Essex on *Cádiz in 1596.

As prudent financially as she was cautious diplomatically, Elizabeth financed government from her own revenues and called parliament to vote supplies only 13 times during her reign. Her management of parliament was marked by a willingness to compromise and demonstrated a political skill notably lacking in her Stuart successors. By her cultivation of the image of "Gloriana" and by her evident devotion to the welfare of her subjects, she helped create a national self-confidence that bore fruit in the last 15 years of her reign, notably in literature in the works of such writers as Marlowe, Spenser, and Shakespeare.

Elizabeth II (1926–   ). Queen of the United Kingdom from 1952, elder daughter of George VI. She married *Philip, duke of Edinburgh, in Nov 1947, and they have four children, *Charles (prince of Wales), Andrew (duke of York; 1960–   ), Edward (1964–   ), and Anne (Princess Royal; 1950–   ). See also Windsor, house of.

Elizabeth, Electress Palatine (1596–1662). Eldest daughter of James I. In 1613 she married Frederick, the elector Palatine, whose acceptance of the Bohemian crown in 1619 gave rise to the Thirty Years' War. Following Frederick's defeat he and Elizabeth fled to The Hague, where she remained until able to return to England (1661) after the Restoration. The Act of *Settlement (1701) vested the succession to the English throne in Elizabeth's descendants.

Elizabeth, the Queen Mother (1900–   ) Queen consort of the United Kingdom (1936-52) as the wife of George VI, whom she married in 1923. Formerly Lady Elizabeth Bowes-Lyon, daughter of the 14th earl of Strathmore, she had two children, Elizabeth II and Princess Margaret.

Elizabeth Woodville (c. 1437-1492). Queen consort of Edward IV, the daughter of Richard Woodville, Earl Rivers. She secretly married Edward IV in 1464 and was crowned the following year. The influence she used in securing favours for her family connections made her enemies and following Edward's death she sought sanctuary at Westminster. She died in Bermondsey abbey.

Ellesmere canal. An inland waterway forming an important link in the Shropshire Union network. Authorized by statute (1793) and engineered by Thomas *Telford and William Baker, the canal ran from the Dee at Llangollen, via Frankton (where it met the Montgomeryshire canal), to the Mersey-Trent canal at Middlewich. Sections were closed after 1850, but it remained important until 1921.

Elyot, Sir Thomas (?1490-1546). Author of *The Boke Called the Governour* (1531), on the education of princes, which he dedicated to Henry VIII. He subsequently served Henry as an ambassador.

Emma of Normandy (d. 1052). Daughter of Richard I of Normandy and the wife of Aethelred the Unready (1002-16) and then of Cnut (1017-35). On Cnut's death she attempted unsuccessfully to seize the throne for her son *Harthacnut and fled into exile. Returning when Harthacnut became king (1040), she later came into conflict with her son by Aethelred —Edward the Confessor.

Emrys. *See* Ambrosius Aurelianus.

enclosure. The conversion of the open-field system of farming into that of enclosed fields, completed by the early 19th century. The enclosure by landlords of open fields, commons, and waste lands occurred in the middle ages. Extensive enclosure, especially for sheep farming, took place in the 16th century, causing considerable social unrest (*see* Pilgrimage of Grace; Kett's rebellion). In spite of legislation against enclosure, by 1700 about half the arable land in England and Wales was enclosed. The farming improvements of the *agrarian revolution were inoperable in open fields and, together with the food demands of an increasing population, brought about a relentless movement towards enclosure in the second half of the 18th century. Implemented mostly by enclosure acts (private acts of parliament), by 1815 almost all usable farming land was enclosed. These enclosures, while essential for revolutionizing farming and food supply, had unfavourable social effects. Although land reallocation under an enclosure act theoretically compensated those losing their rights to common land, in practice most lacked the capital to utilize the land, and many smallholders could not live adequately from their new plots; further, landless labourers received no compensation.

Engagement. 1. (Dec 1647) A treaty between Charles I and the Scots. The former agreed to confirm the *Solemn League and Covenant, to establish Presbyterian church government in England for three years, and to unite England and Scotland more closely. In return the "Engagers", an alliance of moderate *covenanters and royalists, undertook to restore the king to power. Cromwell destroyed the Engagers' army at Preston in Aug 1648, and the *Kirk Party then seized power in Scotland. 2. (Sept 1650) An oath of allegiance to a government without king or House of Lords imposed by the English Commonwealth on all men over 18. It aroused a furious debate —the Engagement Controversy.

Englishry. In the middle ages, the proof that a murdered man was English, by which the hundred in which he was killed escaped payment of a *murder fine. Dating from the reign of Henry I, the law of Englishry distinguished between English and Normans and, in the Marches of Wales, between Anglo-Normans and Welsh, but it may have derived from a law passed by Cnut to protect his Danish followers from the hazard of being murdered by hostile Englishmen. It was abolished in 1340.

entente cordiale. The diplomatic rapprochement between France and Britain in 1904, which culminated in their formal alliance in World War I against the central powers. The prewar friendship between the French and British governments encouraged their military planners to draft common contingency plans for operation against Germany, which formed the basis for allied strategy in 1914. *See also* Anglo-Russian entente.

Episcopal Church of Scotland. The church formed by those who refused to accept the victory of Presbyterianism in the Church of Scotland in 1690. The first bishops were secretly consecrated in 1705. The *Toleration Act (1712) allowed Episcopalian worship to those who would abjure the Jacobite cause but the majority, the *nonjurors, refused. Episcopalian involvement in the 1715 and 1745 Jacobite risings led to renewed persecution. It is in full communion with the Church of England.

equity. The body of law, established by judicial precedents in the Court of *Chancery, concerned with providing remedies for wrongs not covered by the *common law.

Ermine Street. The Anglo-Saxon name for the Roman road from London to Lincoln, which like other Roman roads, probably followed the line of earlier prehistoric tracks. It was constructed by legionary troops in the years immediately following the Roman occupation of 43 AD. The name is also applied to the road from Silchester to Cirencester and Gloucester.

Erskine, Thomas Erskine, 1st Baron (1750-1823). Lawyer and politician. A brilliant court-room barrister, Erskine won fame as an advocate of personal liberties, notably in defending radicals (including *Paine and *Tooke) prosecuted for sedition and treason in the 1790s. He was ineffective as a parliamentary speaker and as lord chancellor in the Ministry of *All the Talents (1806-07) was undistinguished.

escheat. One of the feudal incidents. If the holder of land ceased to be able to perform the services owed to his lord in return for it, either because he had been outlawed or imprisoned for a felony, or because the line of succession had failed, then the land returned to the lord. It was abolished in 1925. *See also* relief.

esquire. *See* squire.

Essex. The kingdom of the East *Saxons. Its chief town was London. It fell under Mercian control in 664 and was subjected to Wessex in 825. Alfred the Great granted it to the Danish king *Guthrum in 878. It became a shire in the 10th century.

Essex, Robert Devereux, 2nd earl of (1567-1601). Courtier and soldier, whose celebrated relationship with Elizabeth I led eventually to his downfall. Elder son of Walter Devereux, 1st earl of Essex, and stepson of Robert Dudley, earl of *Leicester, Essex fought with distinction in the Netherlands (1585) and in 1593

was appointed to the Privy Council. Following the death of Leicester, Essex became and remained Elizabeth's favourite despite his marriage (1590) to Sir Philip Sidney's widow, Frances (née Walsingham). In 1596 he attacked and captured Cádiz, but the failure of an expedition to the Azores (1597), together with his increasing arrogance and the opposition of the Cecil faction, led to a decline in his position at court. Appointed (1599) to put down *O'Neill's revolt in Ireland, he conducted a dilatory campaign and, after concluding a truce, returned to England in defiance of Elizabeth's instructions. After a brief imprisonment, he attempted without success to raise a rebellion in London against the government and was condemned and executed for high treason. The author of numerous sonnets, Essex was also a patron of literature, in particular of Francis *Bacon, who, however, acted as a prosecutor at his trial.

Essex, Robert Devereux, 3rd earl of (1591-1646). Commander of the parliamentary forces in the first years of the Civil War. Son of the 2nd earl, Essex, after serving Charles I at Cádiz (1625) and during the first *Bishops' War (1639), declared against the king at the outset of the Civil War and was appointed to command the parliamentary army. He fought at *Edgehill, captured Reading, relieved Gloucester, and won the first battle of *Newbury. His defeat at *Lostwithiel (1644), together with the overall lack of success of his campaigns, led to pressure for the formation of the *New Model Army. He resigned his command (April 1645) shortly before the passing of the *Self-Denying Ordinance.

Essex, Walter Devereux, 1st earl of (1541-76). Soldier. Essex (then Viscount Hereford) raised a force to quell the *northern rebellion (1569) and in 1573 led an expedition to subdue and occupy Ulster. Despite ruthless massacres and the execution (accomplished by treachery) of the rebel leader Sir Brian MacPhelim, the campaign was unsuccessful, and in 1575 Essex was recalled by Elizabeth I, acting on the advice of *Leicester. Appointed earl marshal, Essex returned to Ireland the following year but died in Dublin shortly after his arrival.

Etaples, treaty of (Nov 1492). A treaty between Henry VII of England and Charles VIII of France, which ended the Anglo-French war of 1489-92. Henry renounced England's historic claims to French territory (apart from Calais) in return for the costs of his campaign in Britanny and arrears of payments due under the treaty of *Picquigny (1475) —a total of 745,000 gold crowns, payable in annual instalments of 50,000 crowns.

Eucharist. The central act of Christian worship, the consecration of bread and wine in commemoration of Christ's Last Supper. Transubstantiation (the Roman Catholic doctrine of the conversion in the Eucharist of the bread and wine into Christ's body and blood) was condemned in the 39 articles (1563; see articles of religion). These adopted a flexible doctrinal position influenced by Luther's consubstantiation (the coexistence after the Eucharist of the bread and wine and Christ's body and blood) and Calvin's virtualism (the receiving by communicants of the "virtue" of Christ's body and blood). Nonconformist churches were influenced by Zwingli's emphasis on the purely memorial function of the Eucharist.

European Economic Community (EEC). A grouping of western European countries for the purpose of economic and political cooperation. It was established by the treaty of Rome (25 March 1957) and its founding members were France, West Germany, Italy, Belgium, and Luxembourg. In Aug 1961 the UK, with Denmark, Norway, and the Republic of Ireland, applied for EEC membership. Negotiations dragged on until 1963, when France vetoed the applications. It did so again in 1967, but in 1970, following Gen. de Gaulle's resignation as president of France, negotiations were resumed, and on 1 Jan 1973 Britain, Denmark, and Ireland became members of the EEC. British membership was endorsed by the first-ever national referendum (5 June 1975), held by the Labour government, which renegotiated the terms of British membership. The European Commission, with headquarters in Brussels, Belgium, implements EEC policies, which are decided upon by the Council of Ministers (representing the member governments). The legislative proposals of the Commission are commented upon by the European parliament, which is based in Strasbourg, France, and has been directly elected since 1979. The Court of Justice administers European law in Luxembourg.

European Free Trade Association (EFTA). A grouping of European countries not belonging to the EEC; Britain was a member from 1960 to 1972. Established largely at Britain's suggestion, EFTA became operative, with seven members, in May 1960, after the failure of negotiations for a wider free trade area that included EEC members. Britain and Denmark left EFTA at the end of 1972, on joining the EEC (1 Jan 1973).

European Recovery Programme. See Marshall plan.

Eustace (d. 1153). Son of King *Stephen. Eustace took a prominent part in the civil war of Stephen's reign during which he gained notoriety as a brutal soldier. His early death helped pave the way for Henry II's succession.

evangelicalism. A Christian belief that emphasizes personal salvation and reliance on the Bible. It was powerfully influential in Britain (inheriting the *Puritan tradition) in Protestant churches and society from the late 18th century. The term refers to those evangelicals who remained Anglican after the *Methodists separated from the Church of England, i.e. from about 1785. Evangelical Anglicans, such as *Wilberforce, other *Clapham Sect members, Hannah *More, and, later, the 7th earl of *Shaftesbury, were active in humanitarian causes. By the 1840s, evangelical principles of individual and (increasingly) social responsibility permeated most levels of society but within the Anglican Church itself evangelicalism was being challenged, as a religious force, by *Anglo-Catholicism.

Evelyn, John (1620–1706). Royalist and diarist, a founder member of the Royal Society (1662). He served in a number of public offices after the Restoration, but his fame rests chiefly on his *Diary* (published in 1818), which covered the period from the early 1640s until his death.

Evesham, battle of (4 Aug 1265). The battle of the second Barons' War in which Simon de Montfort was killed. Henry III's son Edward met the advancing baronial army at Evesham, Worcestershire, having already surprised de Montfort's son Simon at Kenilworth. The battle, which was brief but bloody, permitted the release of Henry III from imprisonment by the barons.

Exchequer. The financial and accounting office of medieval England. At first part of the royal household of the Norman kings, it settled at Westminster in 1172. As described in the *Dialogus de Scaccário*, written (1176–79) by Henry II's treasurer Richard Fitznigel, it consisted of the Lower Exchequer, or Exchequer of Receipt, and the Upper Exchequer, or Exchequer of Account. Reckoning was by means of counters on a chequered table (*scaccarium*) based on the abacus. It gradually gave way to the *Treasury, and the Exchequer now denotes the Bank of England account into which public monies are paid to form the *Consolidated Fund. The use of *tallies as receipts continued until the 19th century; the fire in which they were burned destroyed the Houses of Parliament in 1834. The common-law court of Exchequer grew out of the department of state, from which it separated in 1312, and is now a division of the *High Court. *See also* chancellor of the exchequer.

excise. A tax imposed on the sale of commodities, such as alcoholic drinks and tobacco, and licences, such as those payable on motor cars. Excise was first levied in England in 1643, on ale, beer, cider, and perry, to finance the par-

liamentary army but was foreshadowed in the granting of *monopolies. The Restoration parliament granted Charles II the existing excise duties for life, and an additional hereditary excise in lieu of the abolished feudal revenues. The unpopularity of the duties was reflected in the furore created by Walpole's excise bill (1733), which proposed to extend his excise scheme. The administration of excise was united with that of *custom duties in 1909, under the newly established Board of Customs and Excise.

exclusion bills. Three bills, introduced by the *Country Party, that were designed to exclude James, duke of York, from the succession. Parliament was dissolved after the second reading of the first (1679), and the second (1680) was rejected by the Lords. The third (1681) was introduced in the *Oxford Parliament, which the king hastily dissolved.

eyre. The circuit of courts visited by itinerant justices (justices in eyre). Tours of the country for this purpose date from before 1130 but were regularized in 1176 by Henry II. In the 13th century, with the development of *assizes, the general eyre fell into disuse and the last mention of such a commission occurs in 1374; it was retained for the administration of the Forest Law until 1641.

F

Fabian Society. An organization, founded in 1884, to achieve socialism through gradual and democratic means. It is named after the Roman general Quintus Fabius Maximus (nicknamed Cunctator, or Delayer), whose military successes were the result of patient cautious tactics. Among its early members were Sidney and Beatrice *Webb, G. B. *Shaw, H. G. *Wells, and Clement *Attlee. It helped establish the *Labour Party, on the policies of which it exerted an enormous influence. It has published many research papers (including *Fabian*

Essays (1889), edited by Shaw) and sponsors lectures and summer schools.

factory acts. Legislation to protect factory workers. The Health and Morals of Apprentices Act (1802) limited working hours of "parish apprentices" (pauper children hired by factory owners) and provided for their basic schooling. The Factory Act (1819) aimed at protecting "free" children hired out by their parents and banned the employment in cotton mills of those under nine and those between nine and 16 for more than 12 hours. The Factory Act (1833) was the outcome of the campaign for a ten-hour day—the ten-hour movement—led by Richard *Oastler and, in parliament, by Lord Ashley (later 7th earl of *Shaftesbury). This was the first really effective factory act since it provided proper enforcement inspectors. It fixed a maximum 48-hour week for children aged nine to 13 and a 68-hour week for those under 18. It also banned those under nine from most textile mills and required the part-time education of factory children. The 1844 act limited the working day of women to 12 hours and of children aged eight to 13 to 6½ hours. The 1847 act obtained a ten-hour day for women and children under 18. Legislation in 1850 and 1853 allowed textile factories to remain open for only 12 hours, thus effectively limiting the working day of all textile workers. Factory legislation was gradually extended to other industries, to be consolidated in acts of 1878, 1895, 1901, and 1937. Present-day regulations for the safety, health, and welfare of factory workers are based on the Factories Act (1961) and the Health and Safety at Work Act (1974). *See also* mines acts.

fair. A local gathering for trading and entertainment. Fairs were probably a postconquest development. Itinerant traders (merchants, pedlars, hawkers), travelling the country, established a regular circuit of fairs to coincide with local holidays or saints' days. Fairs were usually held in the grounds of churches, and the consequent damage to church property was legislated against in the reign (1272–1307) of Edward I. Courts of summary jurisdiction (*see* piepowder court) were set up to try offenders. Some fairs specialized in, for example, horse trading (Horncastle, Lincolnshire), wool (Stourbridge, Cambridgeshire), and sheep (Weyhill, Hampshire). The most famous English fair was Bartholomew Fair, held at West Smithfield, London, from 1133 to 1855. The Puck Fair and Pattern, at which a puck goat is enthroned, is still held annually at Killorglin, Co. Kerry.

Fairfax, Ferdinando, 2nd Baron (1584–1648). Member of the Long Parliament who commanded parliamentary forces in Yorkshire in the Civil War. He was defeated at *Adwalton Moor (1643) and was subsequently governor of Hull (1643–44) and York (1644–45). His son was Thomas *Fairfax.

Fairfax, Thomas, 3rd Baron Fairfax (1612–71). Parliamentarian general during the Civil War. Fairfax fought in the Netherlands (1629–31) and during the first Bishops' War (1639). During the Civil War he was active in Yorkshire, Lincolnshire, and Cheshire, notably at the battle of *Marston Moor (1644). In 1645 he was appointed commander of the *New Model Army, which he led that same year to its decisive victory over the royalists at the battle of *Naseby. Primarily a military man, Fairfax was not actively concerned with the army's growing political role and played little part in Charles I's trial and execution. Although a member of the Council of State he remained in the background during the Commonwealth and resigned his command in 1650. In 1658 he emerged in support of the restoration of a constitutional monarchy and led the party sent to The Hague to treat with Charles II. He spent his final years writing two autobiographical works.

Falaise, treaty of (1174). A treaty between the kings of Scotland and England. William I of Scots, who had been captured while invading England, agreed to Henry II's terms for his release. He became Henry's vassal, doing homage to him for Scotland, swearing fealty, and agreeing to surrender certain castles (*see* Canterbury, quitclaim of).

Falkirk, battle of. 1. (22 July 1298) A battle in which Edward I of England was victorious over the Scots. Sir William *Wallace unwisely decided to face the English forces in open battle, but his cavalry fled and his spearmen proved no match for the English archers. This English victory led to Wallace's fall from power. **2.** (17 Jan 1746) A battle in which the Jacobite army of *Charles Edward Stuart, the young pretender, was victorious over royalist forces under the command of Henry Hawley (d. 1759). Despite this victory the Jacobites continued their retreat northwards.

Falkland, Lucius Cary, 2nd Viscount (1610-43). Politician and soldier. After fighting for Charles I in the first Bishops' War (1639), Falkland emerged during the Short and Long Parliaments as a moderate opponent of royalist policies. He opposed clerical involvement in secular affairs and vigorously attacked Archbishop Laud (1641). As relations between king and parliament worsened, however, he gradually moved back to the royalist camp, voting against the *Root and Branch Petition and the *Grand Remonstrance. He became Charles I's secretary of state in 1642 and died fighting for the king at the battle of Newbury. He figures prominently in the history of the Civil War written by his friend Edward Hyde (earl of *Clarendon).

Falkland Islands. A British crown colony (since 1892) in the South Atlantic Ocean, comprising two main islands of East and West Falkland and about a hundred smaller islands; South Georgia and the South Sandwich Group constitute the Falkland Islands Dependencies. From 1764 France, Spain, Britain, and Argentina founded settlements and laid competing claims to the Islands. In 1982 they were invaded by Argentina; to protect the 1200 inhabitants (mostly of British origin) a British task force ousted the invaders.

Falstaff, Sir John. *See* Fastolf, Sir John.

Fashoda incident (1898). A confrontation between Britain and France, rivals in the Egyptian Sudan, following the French occupation of the fort at Fashoda. Diplomatic negotiations eventually induced France to withdraw.

Fastolf, Sir John (c. 1378-1459). Soldier, who fought at Agincourt (1415) and other battles (including the *Herrings) of the Hundred Years' War. His name, in the form Falstaff, was immortalized by Shakespeare, in *Henry IV*, Parts I and II, and *The Merry Wives of Windsor*, in which he appears as a cowardly dissolute clown. He was in fact a brave soldier and ruthless businessman.

Fawcett, Dame Millicent Garrett (1847-1929). Suffragette; president (1897-1919) of the National Union of Women's Suffrage Societies. She was opposed to the militant tactics of the Pankhursts, believing that the enfranchisement of women could be achieved by peaceful means. She described her campaign for women's suffrage (obtained in 1918 and 1928; *see* women's movement) in *What I Remember* (1924). Sister of Elizabeth Garrett *Anderson, she married (1867) Henry Fawcett (1833-84), an MP (1865-84), who was blind.

Fawkes, Guy (1570-1606). Conspirator in the *gunpowder plot. He was arrested in the cellars of the Houses of Parliament and executed after betraying, under torture, his fellow conspirators. His effigy is customarily burned on Guy Fawkes' day (5 Nov).

fealty. The loyalty sworn by a vassal to his lord. It followed the act of *homage. While making the oath the vassal placed his hand on the Scriptures or on a casket containing relics. The oath survives in the *coronation service.

fee (or **fief**). Land granted to a *knight by his lord in return for military service. By the 12th century such land was regarded as heritable. Its size varied and it could be subdivided by *subinfeudation or inheritance. The word was later extended to offices of profit similarly held, and thence to the sums that those who held such offices were authorized to demand as payment for the exercise of their official functions. It was later extended to denote the remuneration due to lawyers and physicians, and in modern times to the sum due to any professional man for services provided.

Fenian Society. An Irish revolutionary society committed to the establishment of an independent republic of Ireland. Formed in New York in 1858 by James Stephens (1825-1901), one of the survivors of Young Ireland's abortive rising in 1848, its members were known as the Fenians or the Brotherhood and later as the Irish Republican Brotherhood (IRB). The Fenians soon penetrated the security forces in Ireland, but their rising in 1867 was a failure, although it served to alert Gladstone to the Irish problem. The IRB continued to exist into the 20th century but after 1916 was eclipsed by the *Irish Republican Army.

Fens. A low-lying area of east England in Lincolnshire, Cambridgeshire, Norfolk, and Suffolk. It was once a bay of the North Sea that, except for the Wash, became silted up and turned into peat marsh. Francis Russell, 4th earl of Bedford (1593-1641), began the draining of the southern region, now known as the Bedford Level, employing the Dutch engineer Sir Cornelius Vermuyden (1595-?1683). Drainage has had the effect of lowering the peat by about 3 m, resulting in such severe floods from overflowing rivers as those of March 1947.

Festival of Britain (May-Sept 1951). A festival celebrated throughout Britain to commemorate the centenary of the *Great Exhibition and to offset the austerity of the 1940s. The central feature was the South Bank Exhibition, London, for which the Royal Festival Hall was built.

feudalism. A system of land tenure, characteristic of medieval Europe, in which property is held by a vassal (the feudal inferior) of his lord (the feudal superior) in return for a pledge of *homage and services, principally military, and certain other incidents. In England, land was granted by the king to his tenants in chief, who might pass on part of their service, in return for grants of land, to tenants, and these tenants might do likewise. All land was held directly or indirectly (see mesne tenure) of the king, who was the feudal superior of all tenants.

The question whether feudalism was introduced into England by the Normans has been much disputed. There are almost no cases of land held for specific military service in Anglo-Saxon England and the *knight, often regarded as an essential component of feudal society, was unknown in England before 1066; his home, the *castle, was also a Norman innovation. Although the feudal host provided the nucleus of the Anglo-Norman army kings also relied heavily upon mercenaries and specialist soldiers. Soon after the conquest money payment (*scutage) was being exacted from the holders of *fees (lands held in return for the service of one knight) in place of military service and the money was used to hire mercenaries. This process was hastened by increasingly sophisticated warfare and the needs of English kings in the 12th and 13th centuries for almost permanent armies to serve in France, Wales, and Scotland. The military justification for feudal tenure therefore declined at the same time as the development of royal justice contributed to the decline of the private jurisdictions of feudal lords. See also bastard feudalism.

Fianna Fáil (Irish: soldiers of destiny). An Irish political party founded in 1926 by *De Valera from moderate Sinn Fein members prepared to take the oath of allegiance to the crown in order to enter the Irish parliament. Traditionally more sympathetic to republicanism than its rival Fine Gael, it has been in power in 1932-48, 1951-54, 1957-73, 1977-81, 1982, and since 1987; its leaders have been De Valera, Sean Lemass, Jack Lynch, and Charles J. Haughey.

field of the cloth of gold (June 1520). A meeting near Calais between Henry VIII of England and Francis I of France. Surrounded by prodigious extravagance, including fountains running with wine, the display of friendship was a shallow one. In Aug 1521 Wolsey concluded a treaty against France with the emperor Charles V.

Fifteen Rebellion. See Jacobites.

fifth monarchy men. An extreme Puritan sect active during the Commonwealth and Protectorate. Its members took their name from their belief that the fifth monarchy (the rule of Christ and the saints, succeeding that of the Assyrian, Persian, Greek, and Roman monarchies, which was foretold in Daniel 2) was at hand. They welcomed the calling of *Barebones Parliament (the "parliament of saints"), but its failure and the establishment of the Protectorate turned them into opponents of Cromwell, and their leaders were imprisoned. Two abortive risings (1657, 1661) led by Thomas Venner were put down, and Venner was executed.

Fiji. An island group in the South Pacific and a former British colony. It was discovered by Tasman in 1643 and visited by Capt. Cook in 1774 and Capt. Bligh in 1789 but did not attract European settlement until the search for sandalwood in the 19th century. Following internal intertribal disputes, Fiji became a British protectorate (1874). It attained independence within the Commonwealth in 1970.

Filmer, Sir Robert (d. 1653). Royalist and political theorist. In his chief work *Patriarcha, or the Natural Power of Kings Asserted* (1680) Filmer defended a patriarchal theory of monarchy against the social contract—the theory of government expounded by *Hobbes, *Locke, and others.

Finch. See Nottingham, earls of.

Finch, Sir John, Baron Finch of Fordwich (1584-1660). Chief justice of the Court of Common Pleas (1635-40). While speaker of the House of Commons he was held down in his chair by MPs to

prevent his adjourning the recalcitrant house (1629). As chief justice he gained notoriety for his judgment on *ship money (1637). In 1640 he was impeached by the Long Parliament and forced to flee to Holland. He returned to England at the Restoration.

Finn MacCool (2nd or 3rd century AD). A mythical Irish leader celebrated in Celtic sagas. His followers, known as the Fianna (Irish: warriors), were selected as an image by Irish nationalists —the Fenians—in the 19th century.

Fire of London (2-5 Sept 1666). The fire that broke out in the early hours of 2 Sept in a baker's shop in Pudding Lane and destroyed four-fifths of the City of London. It spread as far west as the Temple, destroying 87 parish churches and 13 200 houses, as well as St Paul's, the Guildhall, and other public buildings, but claimed fewer than 20 lives. Wren's plans for reconstructing the 430 devastated acres, on both sides of the City walls, were not adopted, but he was responsible for 51 new churches.

first fruits and tenths. The first year's income from a benefice and a tenth of the incumbent's income in subsequent years. Until the Act of *Annates (1532) they were paid to the pope, but, with Henry VIII's *Reformation legislation, they were acquired by the crown. The Court of First Fruits and Tenths was established in 1540 to administer them; it was joined to the Exchequer in 1554. The income from first fruits and tenths funded *Queen Anne's Bounty (1703).

Fisher, H(erbert) A(lbert) L(aurens) (1865-1940). Politician and historian. As president of the Board of Education (1916-26) he introduced the Education Act (1918), which made *education compulsory up to the age of 14. His publications include *A History of Europe* (3 vols, 1935).

Fisher, John, 1st Baron Fisher of Kilverstone (1841-1920). First sea lord (1904-10, 1914-15), who was largely responsible for the naval reforms that gave Britain naval supremacy at the start of World War I. He modernized the administration and did much to introduce such modern ships as destroyers (1893), dreadnoughts (1906), and battle cruisers (1909). Unhappy with the lukewarm attitude of Asquith's government to naval rearmament he resigned in 1910, but returned to serve as first sea lord under Churchill (1914). He resigned again in 1915 in protest against the *Gallipoli expedition.

Fisher, St John (1469-1535). Bishop of Rochester from 1504. A leading scholar and theologian, he resisted the spread of Protestant doctrines in England. Fisher vigorously opposed Henry VIII's intention to divorce Catherine of Aragon and was executed for treason after refusing to swear the oath imposed by the Act of Succession (1534). He was canonized in 1935.

Fitzgerald, Lord Edward (1763-98). Irish nationalist. A member of the Anglo-Irish aristocracy, he served in the British army and in the 1780s was an MP in the Irish parliament. Inspired by the French Revolution, he joined the *United Irishmen in 1796 but was captured and mortally wounded before the Irish rebellion of 1798.

Fitzgerald, Gerald, 15th earl of Desmond. See Desmond revolt.

Fitzgerald, Gerald, 8th earl of Kildare (d. 1513). Lord deputy of Ireland (1481-94, 1496-1513), member of a powerful Anglo-Norman family in Ireland that regarded the office of deputy almost as a prerogative of its house. A supporter of the Yorkist cause in England, he was deprived of the deputyship (1494-96) for backing the pretender Perkin Warbeck against Henry VII.

Fitzgerald, Gerald, 9th earl of Kildare (1487-1534). Lord deputy of Ireland (1513-20, 1524-26, 1532-33), during a period of increasing English control of Irish affairs. He was twice (1526-29, 1533-34) imprisoned, on charges of treason, in the Tower of London, where he died.

Fitzgerald, James (1570-1601). Heir to the rebel 15th earl of Desmond (see Desmond revolt). He was brought up a

Protestant in England but was confined to the Tower of London (1584-1600) following his father's final rebellion, thus acquiring his sobriquet, the Tower Earl. In 1600 he was sent by the English to Ireland to win the allegiance of the Geraldine rebels, but failed in his mission and returned to London.

Fitzgerald, James (Fitzmaurice) (d. 1579). A cousin of Gerald Fitzgerald, 15th earl of Desmond, whose earldom he tried to usurp. He also rebelled against the crown (1569-73). Pardoned, but unrepentant, he withdrew to the Continent to gain support for another rebellion. He returned in 1579 but was killed by hostile Irish.

Fitzgerald, Raymond (d. 1182). One of the Norman conquerors of Ireland. He invaded Ireland in 1170 and was instrumental in the capture of Waterford and Dublin (1170) and Limerick (1175). Physically vast (and nicknamed Le Gros), he was the personification of Norman fighting qualities.

Fitzgerald, Thomas, Baron Offaly and 10th earl of Kildare (1513-37). Son of Gerald Fitzgerald, 9th earl of Kildare. On his father's imprisonment in England in 1533, he rebelled against the crown. He was defeated, captured, and executed. His death ended the power of the house of Kildare.

Fitzosbern, William, earl of Hereford (d. 1071). Norman lord. Closely associated, as lord of Breteuil, with William I in Normandy, he was granted the earldom of Hereford (1067) after the Norman conquest. He extended Norman influence westwards and built strong castles at Wigmore, Clifford, Ewyas Harold, Monmouth, and Chepstow. The Hereford charter, the model for numerous charters granted to Welsh boroughs, was based on that of Breteuil.

Fitzroy, Henry, duke of Richmond (1519-36). Lord admiral from 1525 and lord lieutenant of Ireland from 1529. The illegitimate son of *Henry VIII by Elizabeth Blount, he was widely regarded as Henry's heir.

five articles of Perth. Liturgical reforms forced on Scotland by James VI (I of England) through a general assembly at Perth (1618). They were confirmed by parliament (1621) despite bitter opposition from those with Presbyterian sympathies and others who thought the articles were Catholic in tendency. The most controversial article ordered kneeling at communion to receive the species of the bread and wine.

Five Boroughs. The east midland towns of Leicester, Lincoln, Derby, Stamford, and Nottingham. Originally fortified bases of Danish armies, they were settled by Danish soldiers and had an independent legal identity within the *Danelaw. Their laws contain the first provision in England for a sworn jury to determine guilt by a majority verdict.

five knights' case (1627). A legal action arising from the imprisonment in March 1627 of five men for their refusal to pay the *forced loan demanded by Charles I. The knights (Sir John Corbet, Sir Thomas Darnel, Sir Walter Erle, Sir Edmund Hampden, and Sir John Heveningham) demanded to be brought to trial or to be released on bail. The Court of King's Bench refused bail but failed to give judgment on the crucial question whether or not the crown had the power, as it pleaded, to commit without showing cause. The knights were released in 1628. See also Petition of Right.

five members. Five MPs—*Pym, *Hampden, *Hesilrige, *Holles, and William Strode—whom Charles I attempted to arrest on 4 Jan 1642. The king tried to obtain the impeachment of the members (together with Lord Mandeville) and ordered the Lords to arrest them. When they refused, Charles, accompanied by a force of swordsmen, entered the Commons to arrest them himself. He discovered, however, that "all the birds are flown". They had taken refuge in the City, which refused to surrender them, and a week later they returned triumphantly to the House. This incident united Lords and Commons against the king and led ultimately to the Civil War.

Five Mile Act (1665). The final act of the *Clarendon code. Unless nonconformist ministers took an oath of *nonresistance, they were forbidden to go within five miles of their former places of ministry and of corporate towns. They were also barred from teaching in schools. The act was repealed in 1812.

five-power treaty. See Washington conference.

Flambard, Ranulf (d. 1128). Bishop of Durham (1099-1128), who was a leading adviser to William II Rufus.

Fleet prison. A gaol in London, formerly standing beside the Fleet river. Probably established as a royal prison in the 12th century, from the 17th century the Fleet housed chiefly debtors. It became notorious for scandalous conditions and for the runaway marriages in its vicinity (banned by the *Marriage Act 1753). It was closed in 1842 and demolished in 1844.

Fleming, Sir Alexander (1881-1955). Scottish bacteriologist. Professor of bacteriology (1928-48) at London University and on the staff of St Mary's Hospital, London, Fleming is best known for his discovery of penicillin. He was awarded the Nobel prize for medicine (with H. W. Florey and E. B. Chain) in 1945.

flight of the earls. The departure of Hugh *O'Neill, earl of Tyrone, and Rory *O'Donnell, earl of Tyrconnell, to the Continent in 1607. Both men were Ulster chiefs who fought against Elizabeth until their final submission in 1603. Although pardoned, they found the increasing English intervention an intolerable challenge to their traditional jurisdiction. Their flight left Ulster open to settlement by the Scots and English.

Flinders, Matthew (1774-1814). Naval officer and navigator, who surveyed the coast of Australia. Between 1795 and 1800 Flinders helped George Bass (1771-1803) chart the southeast coast of the continent, an expedition that established that Tasmania was an island (1798). Commanding his own expedition (1801-03), Flinders sailed round Australia, mapping a large part of the southern, eastern, and northern coasts.

Flodden, battle of (9 Sept 1513). The battle fought at Flodden Edge, Northumberland, in which the English defeated an invading Scottish army. While Henry VIII was campaigning against France, the Scots crossed the border but were soundly beaten by the English under the able 70-year-old Thomas Howard, earl of Surrey. Each side had between 20 000 and 30 000 men. The English lost 1500; the Scots 10 000, including their king, James IV.

Floyd's case (1621). The attempt by the House of Commons to punish an elderly Roman Catholic, Edward Floyd, for speaking disparagingly of *James I's son in law, Frederick V, Elector Palatine. The king objected that the Commons had no judicial power unless their own privileges were involved, an argument that the Commons conceded. However, the House of Lords sentenced Floyd to be whipped, branded, and pilloried.

Foedera. A collection of treaties (*foedera*), letters, and other documents related to contacts between England and the Continent down to 1654. Its full title is *Foedera, Conventiones, et cujuscunque generis Acta Publica*. Published in 20 volumes betweeen 1704 and 1735, volumes 1-15 were edited by Thomas Rymer (1641-1713) and volumes 16-20 by Robert Sanderson (1660-1741). The *Foedera* provide an important primary source for the study of English history.

foederati. The name given by the Romans to those barbarian tribes settled within the empire who, in return for subsidies and grants of land, defended the imperial frontiers. The practice began in the 3rd century AD, and evidence suggests that *foederati* were stationed in England during the following century.

Foliot, Gilbert (d. 1187). Bishop of Hereford (1147-63) and of London (1163-87). An enemy of *Becket, he was excommunicated by him in 1167 and 1169 and again in 1170 for officiating at the crowning (unauthorized by

the church) of Henry II's son. Foliot continued to be an important adviser to Henry after Becket's death.

Fontenoy, battle of (11 May 1745). A battle during the War of the Austrian Succession. A combined force of English, Hanoverian, Austrian, and Dutch troops, 50 000 strong, advancing under the command of the duke of Cumberland to relieve Tournai, was confronted by a French army of 52 000 under Marshal Saxe. After initial successes, heavy casualties forced the allied troops to retreat, leaving the way open for the French to take Tournai and occupy most of Flanders over the ensuing four months.

food rent (or **feorm**). In Anglo-Saxon England, a food payment to the king to provide for the royal court on journeys. The duty, which was fixed at the amount necessary to support the royal household for 24 hours, was mainly—although not exclusively—imposed upon royal estates.

forced loan. A means whereby the crown raised money without parliamentary consent. Both Henry VII and Henry VIII raised forced loans, but resistance to them grew, notably in the reigns of the first two Stuarts (*see* five knights' case). Condemned in the Petition of Right (1628), they were declared illegal by the Bill of Rights (1689).

Foreign and Commonwealth Office (FCO). The government department that deals with Britain's relations with foreign and *Commonwealth countries. It was formed in 1968 from the amalgamation of the Commonwealth Office (established by the merger in 1966 of the Commonwealth Relations Office and the *Colonial Office) and the Foreign Office. The Foreign Office developed from the office of the secretary of state for foreign affairs, which was established in 1782 to replace the Northern Department (*compare* Home Office). The FCO, which includes the Diplomatic Service and the Overseas Development Administration, is headed by the secretary of state for foreign and commonwealth affairs (the foreign secretary).

forest. The right of keeping wild beasts and fowls in a specific area, not necessarily wooded, for the purpose of hunting. The royal forests were protected by forest laws, enacted mainly between 1066 and 1189. Penalties for infringement of the laws were severe and included capital punishment and mutilation, both abolished by the Forest Charter (1217). The abolition of the forest laws, little enforced after 1688, was completed by 1817.

Forfeited Estates, Commission of. The board appointed after the *Jacobite rebellion of 1715 to assess and sell lands confiscated from the rebels. The commission sold the forfeited estates with difficulty, making little profit. Forfeitures made after the 1745 rebellion were not sold but administered by the revived commission; they were restored to their owners in 1784.

forfeiture. The loss of property, right, or privilege by law, as a consequence of a crime. It was usual in cases of *attainder for treason, the property in question reverting to the crown. It was virtually abolished by the Forfeiture Act (1870).

forma regiminis (28 June 1264). A "form of government" drawn up by parliament after the capture of Henry III at Lewes during the second *Barons' War. It established a council of nine men to advise the king. The nine were to be chosen by Simon de *Montfort, Stephen Bersted, bishop of Chichester, and Gilbert de Clare, 8th earl of Gloucester, who retained effective control of government. The *forma regiminis* was expected to remain effective until a permanent settlement had been negotiated between the two sides, but it lasted only until the royalist victory at Evesham in Aug 1265.

Formigny, battle of (15 April 1450). A battle between England and France in the *Hundred Years' War. It was a decisive defeat for the English force on its way to relieve the English garrison in Caen, which was being besieged by the French. Nearly 4000 English troops were killed and in the next four months the French were able to expel the English from Normandy.

Form of Apology and Satisfaction (1604). A declaration by the House of Commons outlining its view of parliamentary rights and privileges following its clash with James I over *Goodwin's case. Besides restating basic principles of freedom of speech and election, the Apology sought changes in royal feudal dues, notably *wardship and marriage. Although later seen as a milestone in the constitutional struggle between crown and parliament, the Apology was, in fact, never delivered to James.

Forster, William Edward (1818-86). Liberal MP (1861-86), who, as vice president of the council (1868-74), introduced the Elementary Education Act (1870), making elementary *education available in England and Wales to all children between the ages of 5 and 13. As chief secretary for Ireland (1880-82), Forster unsuccessfully attempted coercion against Irish agrarian terrorism, resigning after the conciliatory *Kilmainham treaty. His successor was Lord Frederick *Cavendish.

Forty-Five Rebellion. See Jacobites.

Foss (or Fosse) **Way.** The Anglo-Saxon name for the Roman road running from the Devonshire coast at Axmouth to Lincoln via Bath and Cirencester. Constructed in the years following the Roman occupation in 43 AD, the route crossed the tribal territories of the Dobuni and Coritani and was defended by a number of forts. It was a major link in the Roman communications network in England.

Fotheringhay, treaty of (10-11 June 1482). An agreement between Edward IV and Alexander, duke of Albany, styling himself king of Scots, by which Albany undertook to dethrone his brother James III of Scots. In return for English help he agreed to become Edward's vassal and to cede parts of southern Scotland to him. Albany made peace with his brother soon afterwards.

Fotheringhay castle. The castle in Northamptonshire to which Mary Queen of Scots was moved after the failure of the Babington plot in 1586; she was executed here in the following year. Richard III was born here.

four-power treaty. *See* Washington conference.

Fourth Party. The nickname for a radical Conservative group (1800-85) led by Lord Randolph *Churchill. Other leading members included Sir Henry Drummond Wolff (1830-1908) and (Sir) J. E. Gorst (1835-1916); A. J. Balfour was also associated with the group, which was noted for its advocacy of Tory Democracy—reforms in the organization of the Conservative Party that would give greater power to the rank and file. The *Primrose League was founded by members of the Fourth Party.

Fox, Charles James (1749-1806). MP from 1768 and champion of liberal causes. Of immense personal charm, Fox (Henry Fox's son) was a friend of Edmund Burke and became a leader of the Whigs. An opponent of the policies towards the American colonies of George III and Lord North, he became, after North's fall, secretary of state for foreign affairs (the first) in Rockingham's ministry (1782). He declined to serve under Shelburne (1782) and in 1783, in alliance with North, secured the downfall of Shelburne's government. However, the Fox-North coalition (described by George III as "unprincipled") under Portland was short-lived, falling with the defeat of a bill for the reform of the East India Company (1783). He subsequently became the principal opponent of Pitt the younger. He welcomed the French Revolution, was initially sympathetic towards Napoleon, but as foreign secretary (1806) in the Ministry of All the Talents (1806) recognized peace was impossible on Napoleon's terms. Shortly before his death he secured a resolution to abolish the slave trade. He was buried in Westminster abbey, beside Pitt.

Fox, George (1624-91). Founder of the *Quakers. He began to preach in his native Leicestershire in 1647 and later in Scotland, Ireland, and abroad. He soon attracted a considerable following and suffered frequent imprisonments for his nonconformist views. His *Journal* was published in 1694.

Fox, Henry, 1st Baron Holland (1705-74). Politician, notorious for self-enrichment and his skill in parliamentary manipulation. An MP from 1738 (ennobled 1763), Fox was secretary at war (1746-54) and secretary of state (1755-56). As paymaster general (1757-65), he used the office to acquire an immense fortune. His expertise in controlling patronage was used most notably in helping to carry the treaty of *Paris (1763) through parliament. His son was Charles James *Fox and his grandson, 3rd Baron *Holland.

Foxe, John (1516-87). Protestant writer. A strict Calvinist, Foxe took refuge (1554-59) in Europe during the *Marian reaction. His so-called "Book of Martyrs" (*Rerum in ecclesia gestarum...commentarii*, 1559; English version, *Acts and Monuments*, 1563) vividly describes the martyrdoms of persecuted Christians, especially of contemporary English Protestants.

Foxe, Richard (c. 1448-1528). Bishop of Durham (1494) and then Winchester (1501), who served Henry VII as a diplomat and councillor. In Henry VIII's reign he gradually lost his political pre-eminence to Thomas *Wolsey.

franchise. The right to elect members of the *House of Commons. The term originates in the setting free (French *franchir*, to set free) of the unfree by *manumission. The franchise denoted first the body of freemen in a manor, borough, etc., and then their rights, including the right to vote. This depended largely on property qualifications. Between 1430 and 1832 the English county franchise was limited to residents possessing a *freehold worth 40 shillings a year. Borough members were elected on a variety of franchises. The *Reform Act of 1832 unified the borough franchises, that of 1867 enfranchised all borough householders, and that of 1884 all county householders. In 1918 all men over 21 and women over 30 were enfranchised. Women over 21 have voted since

1928. Plural voting, whereby certain electors might vote in more than one constituency, did not end until the abolition of the university seats in 1948.

Francis, Sir Philip (1740-1818). Politician and pamphleteer, who may have written the Letters of *Junius. He was first clerk in the War Office (1762-72) and was then sent to India as a member of the newly created ruling council. He came into conflict with the governor general Warren *Hastings, with whom he fought a duel (1780). On his return to England he became an MP (1784) and played a prominent part in the impeachment of Hastings.

frankalmoign (Anglo-Norman: free alms). Land held by the church freely except for such services as praying for the souls of the lord and his heirs. Originating in Anglo-Saxon times, it was not abolished until 1925.

Franklin, Sir John (1786-1847). Explorer of the Arctic, who discovered the *northwest passage. A professional naval officer, Franklin led two major North American expeditions (1819-22, 1825-27) before being appointed lieutenant governor of Van Dieman's Land (1837-43). In command of the *Erebus* and *Terror*, he sought the northwest passage in 1845 but, together with all the other members of the expedition, perished on the voyage.

frankpledge. A system devised by Norman lawyers in the 11th century for the preservation of law and order, based on the Anglo-Saxon *tithing. All free men over the age of 12 years were made members of frankpledges (or tithings), often consisting of households. Members of frankpledges were answerable for the conduct of their associates.

Fraser, Simon, 12th Baron Lovat (?1667-1747). *Jacobite. He first gained notoriety through his violent efforts to secure the succession to the title of his kinsman, Lord Lovat, who died in 1696. He later took to Jacobite intrigue, but won a pardon by keeping the Frasers loyal in the 1715 rising. He finally secured the title of Lord Lovat in 1730

but was executed for supporting the 1745 rising.

Free Church of Scotland. The church formed at the *disruption of 1843 in opposition to patronage and state interference in the Church of Scotland. In 1900 the majority of members united with the United Presbyterian Church to form the United Free Church, which in turn reunited with the Church of Scotland in 1929.

free companies. Bands of mercenaries in the *Hundred Years' War (1337-1453). First appearing after the battle of Poitiers (1356), they were composed of soldiers from several European countries, including England and France, and were often led by younger or illegitimate sons of the nobility. Established in castles, they sometimes dominated whole regions and caused widespread destruction by pillaging, especially during lulls in the fighting. Attempts by successive French kings to eradicate free companies, which both sides employed, were only temporarily successful until the final establishment of peace made them redundant.

freehold. A form of land tenure. Under *feudalism freeholders were those who held land by *knight service or by *socage tenure. The services attached to these tenures were at an early date commuted to money payments. These rents were fixed and thus constituted a decreasing burden. Lands held in knight service also bore the various feudal incidents, but in practice the free tenures had become hardly distinguishable from absolute possession well before they were finally abolished by the Long Parliament (1640-60). The unfree tenures, notably *copyhold, were finally converted into freehold by the Property Act (1922).

Freetown. The capital of Sierra Leone. In 1787 a group of English abolitionists (see slavery) chose the site, with its natural harbour, as a settlement for freed African slaves, appropriately naming it Free Town. It became a flourishing port and was incorporated into Sierra Leone in 1893.

free trade. International trade that is carried on without the imposition of tariffs, import quotas, etc. Advocated by Adam *Smith, free trade took place in association with *laissez-faire, gradually replacing *mercantilism from the 18th century onwards. Pitt the younger's financial policies included elements of free trade, and tariffs were reduced in the 1820s by Robinson and Huskisson. Peel further contributed to the movement, his measures culminating in the repeal of the *corn laws (1846). Gladstone, while chancellor of the exchequer, virtually completed the process by 1860. Joseph Chamberlain attempted unsuccessfully to gain acceptance for tariffs in the years 1903-06. The policy of free trade came under pressure after World War I, and in the face of adverse trading conditions was finally abandoned with the introduction of a general tariff in 1932; the policy of *imperial preference exempted most goods from the dominions and colonies. Since World War II Britain's trade policies have been influenced by the international General Agreement on Tariffs and Trade (GATT), of which it is a signatory, and by successive free trade arrangements within Europe: the *European Free Trade Association and then the *European Economic Community.

French, John, 1st earl of Ypres (1852-1925). Field marshal, who commanded the *British Expeditionary Force (1914-15) in World War I. He did not work harmoniously with either his French and Belgian allies or *Kitchener and was criticized for his indecision and failure to coordinate his troops. Under his command British casualties were high, especially at *Ypres, and he was replaced by *Haig in Dec 1915. He thereafter commanded home forces and was lord lieutenant of Ireland (1918-21).

French Revolutionary and Napoleonic Wars (1792-1815). The conflict arising from the threat that the example of the French Revolution posed to the established powers of Europe and from Napoleon's attempt to dominate the Continent. British involvement, under

Pitt the younger's leadership, was brought about by the French invasion of the Austrian Netherlands, a move that threatened Britain's maritime security. On 1 Feb 1793 France declared war, and in the summer the duke of York began an abortive campaign in Flanders, which dragged on until the British, retreating into Germany, were evacuated from Bremen in March 1795. In Aug 1793 Admiral Hood established an allied force at Toulon, and in the following year a fleet under the command of Jervis made conquests in the West Indies. In European waters Howe won the victory of the *Glorious First of June and Corsica was captured. In 1795 the first coalition began to disintegrate, and although Britain then acquired the overseas Dutch possessions of Pondicherry, Trincomalee, Ceylon, Malacca, Amboina, and Banda, in Europe it was threatened by invasion. A French expedition to Ireland, which was on the point of rebellion, in Dec 1796 was frustrated only by bad weather, but, in spite of mutinies at *Spithead and the *Nore, the 1797 invasion plans of France and its allies were thwarted by victories—Jervis' off Cape *St Vincent and Duncan's off *Camperdown. A second coalition of Britain, Russia, Turkey, Naples, Portugal, and Austria was negotiated in 1798-99, while Nelson defeated Napoleon at *Aboukir Bay in Aug and Minorca was captured in Nov. An allied invasion of Holland failed in Oct 1799, and victories in Italy earlier in the year were reversed by Napoleon's Italian campaign in 1800. The second coalition fell apart in the following year, and British successes in the Far and Middle East were offset by the hostility of the league of *armed neutrality in the Baltic. Nelson's bloody victory at *Copenhagen brought an armistice with the league, and in 1802 Addington, who had succeeded Pitt, negotiated the treaty of *Amiens.

When Napoleon's continental aggression brought a renewal of war with Britain (18 May 1803) Addington planned only for defensive action, and Britain was well prepared for the projected

French invasion. Pitt, however, resuming the leadership in May 1804, negotiated (1804-05) a third coalition with Russia, Austria, Sweden, and Naples, which frustrated Napoleon's plans, and in Oct 1805 Nelson secured the great victory at *Trafalgar. Nevertheless, in 1805-06 Napoleon reached the pinnacle of his power, defeating the Austrians and Russians at Ulm and Austerlitz (1805), the Prussians at Jena and Auerstädt (1806), and the Russians at Friedland (1807); in 1806 he initiated the *continental system against Britain and in 1807-08 gained control of Portugal and Spain. The ensuing *Peninsular War, in which British forces were led by Wellesley (later the duke of *Wellington), seriously weakened French resources, which were further undermined by Napoleon's disastrous invasion of Russia (1812). In 1813 Europe allied against Napoleon for the last time. He was routed at *Leipzig (1813) and, after his return from exile on Elba, finally defeated in the *Waterloo campaign (1815). The post-Napoleonic settlement of Europe was arranged at the congress of *Vienna (1814-15), at which the victorious powers negotiated the treaties of *Paris.

friendly (or benefit) **societies**. Groups of individuals associated to provide mutual insurance during times of sickness or distress. Benefit societies have existed since the early 17th century and in their origins are similar to the *cooperative movement. Members have been protected by legislation since 1792, and a national register has been kept since 1846.

frith (Old English: peace). The condition of peace and security in a kingdom. Frith-guilds were voluntary associations formed in southern England in the 10th century. They were divided into groups of a hundred freemen, subdivided into groups of ten, and were collectively responsible for maintaining law and order.

Frobisher, Sir Martin (c. 1535-1594). Sailor, who tried to discover the northwest passage to China. Frobisher reached Labrador and Baffin Land (Frobisher Bay) in 1576, exploring the area again in search of gold in 1577 and 1578. He commanded a squadron against the Spanish armada (1588).

Frontinus, Sextus Julius (1st century AD). Governor of Roman Britain (74-78). During his governorship Frontinus conquered the *Silures and founded the camp and town of Caerwent. He was also a distinguished writer on engineering and military science.

Fry, Elizabeth (1780-1845). Prison reformer. Mrs Fry, a Quaker minister, was horrified when visiting Newgate prison (1813) by the conditions under which women prisoners and their children lived. In 1817 she formed an association to improve such conditions, and for the rest of her life campaigned for prison reform in Britain and Europe. She travelled widely, promoting voluntary efforts and persuading governments to make improvements. She also helped raise standards in British hospitals and founded hostels for the homeless.

Fulford, battle of (20 Sept 1066). A battle outside York between Harold Hardraada, king of Norway, and the forces of Edwin, earl of Mercia, and Morcar, earl of Northumbria. The English armies, seeking to oppose the invasion of Hardraada and *Tostig, were decisively defeated. Consequently, the military potential of the English king Harold II against the Normans at the battle of Hastings was weakened.

fyrd. During the Anglo-Saxon period, a local military force in which all free men were obliged to serve. A fyrd seldom fought beyond the borders of the shires in which it was raised. See also militia.

G

Gaelic. A Celtic language of the Goidelic group. Records of Irish Gaelic, which is a national language of the Republic of Ireland, date back to the 5th century AD. Scots Gaelic was introduced to

Scotland by the *Scots of Dalriada. Its use spread throughout Scotland except the southeast, but its long retreat before the Scots variant of the English tongue was under way by the 12th century. By the late middle ages it was regarded as the distinctive language of the Highlanders and had diverged widely from its Irish ancestor.

Gage, Thomas (1721-87). Soldier and colonial governor. He served under Braddock in America (1751-56) and became commander in chief, North America, in 1763. As governor of Massachusetts (1774-75) Gage took an unyielding line following the *Boston tea party, precipitating the engagements at *Lexington (1775) and *Bunker Hill (1775), which initiated the American Revolution.

Gainsborough, Thomas (1727-88). Painter. He preferred to paint landscapes but found portraits more lucrative and often compromised by placing his figures on a landscape background, as in *Mr and Mrs Andrews* (c. 1750). His later works include *The Blue Boy* (c. 1770).

Gaitskell, Hugh (1906-63). Labour Party leader. An MP from 1945 to 1963, he was chancellor of the exchequer (1950-51). Leader of the opposition (1955-63), succeeding *Attlee, he maintained party unity while, notably, opposing unilateral nuclear disarmament.

Gallipoli expedition (1915). A British attempt in *World War I to end the deadlock of trench warfare in France by forcing a passage through the Dardanelles and forcing Turkey out of the war. The first, purely naval, operation failed in March. Five divisions were landed in April and five more in Aug. Despite the valour of the British and Australian troops, who suffered heavy casualties, the expedition was abandoned in Dec. Churchill, who was blamed for the expedition, resigned from the cabinet in Nov 1915.

galloglasses (Gaelic: foreign warriors). Heavily-armed mercenaries in the service of the Irish. Many of them came from west Scotland, settling in Ireland from the mid-13th century. Originally employed by Ulster lords against the English, they subsequently served Anglo-Irish masters and the government of the *Pale. In the 16th century they fought as pikemen but ceased to exist after the failure of *O'Neill's revolt (1603).

Gambia, The. A country in the Gambia river valley, West Africa, surrounded on three sides by Senegal, and a former British crown colony. The first British settlement was established on James Island in 1661. Administered from Sierra Leone (1807-43, 1866-88), it was a crown colony from 1843 to 1866 and from 1888. Self-governing since 1963, it gained independence in 1965 with Sir Dawda Jawara (1924-) as prime minister. It is a member of the Commonwealth.

Gandhi, Mohandas Karamchand (1869-1948). Indian nationalist and spiritual leader, known as Mahatma ("Great Soul"). As leader of the Indian National Congress he adopted a policy of noncooperation (*satyagraha*) with the British government in India to achieve Indian independence. In 1930-32 he attended the abortive *Round Table conferences in London, subsequently retiring to his ashram at Wardha. In 1942, together with other Congress leaders, he was imprisoned for demanding immediate British withdrawal in return for support against Hitler. After the war he took part in the negotiations for independence. He was assassinated by a Hindu fanatic, who opposed his advocacy of friendship between Hindus and Muslims.

Gardiner, Stephen (c. 1490-1555). Bishop of Winchester (1531-51, 1553-55). He was secretary to Wolsey and, after the cardinal's fall, to Henry VIII. He supported the king's rejection of papal authority in England but became an opponent of doctrinal change and of Thomas *Cromwell. Imprisoned in Edward VI's reign, following Mary's accession (1553) he became lord high chancellor, supporting the queen's efforts to restore papal supremacy in England.

Garrick, David (1717-79). Actor and theatre manager. During his acting career (1741-76) he excelled in both tragedy and comedy, especially in Shakespeare. He wrote and adapted many plays for the Drury Lane theatre, of which he was manager (1747-76), and made innovations in scenery, costumes, and lighting.

Garter, Order of the. The most ancient order of *knighthood in Europe, founded by Edward III in 1348, and modelled on King Arthur and the knights of the Round Table. The motto of the order and its emblem, the blue garter, are said to derive from an occasion on which *Joan of Kent lost her garter at a ball and had it returned to her by Edward with the words "Honi soit qui mal y pense" ("Evil to him who evil thinks"). Membership is at the sole discretion of the sovereign, and each knight has a stall in St George's Chapel, Windsor.

Gascony. An area of SW France, roughly that between the Pyrenees and the river Garonne, within the duchy of *Aquitaine. The English often called Aquitaine by the name of Gascony, while the French called it Gayenne, which formed the northern part of the duchy.

gavelkind. Tenure of land in return for the payment of rent (gavel) rather than performance of services. Common in Kent, but occurring elsewhere, gavelkind land was not subject to the law of primogeniture but was inheritable by all heirs.

Gaveston, Piers (d. 1312). Son of a Gascon knight and the notorious favourite of Edward II. He was created earl of Cornwall (1307) and was keeper of the realm (1307-08). The barons twice (1308, 1311) forced Edward to banish Gaveston, who was finally seized by Robert de Beaumont, earl of Leicester, and beheaded.

gebur. An Anglo-Saxon peasant, or *ceorl. The gebur might have originated as a serf, who was given a yardland (generally approximating to 20 acres) in return for specified and often burdensome labour services and rents. His land and tools reverted to his lord on his death.

geld. A land tax raised by Anglo-Saxon kings from the late 10th century (see Danegeld) and continued by the Norman kings often for military purposes. Assessment was based on the number of *hides or *ploughlands owned, the amount payable for each being decided by the king.

geneat. A high-ranking *ceorl, who paid rent for his land and performed services for his lord that were suitable to his standing, such as serving as a horseman. The word means companion, so geneatas probably originated as members of the lord's household. See also gebur; kotsetla.

General Strike (3-13 May 1926). A general strike called by the Trades Union Congress in an unsuccessful attempt to support coalminers, who were already on strike against threatened wage cuts. The strike was not strictly "general" since only workers in certain key industries (e.g. railways, docks, electricity, gas) were called out. It was remarkable for the relatively good relations between the strikers and police and volunteers manning public services. The strike provoked retaliatory legislation against *trade unions, and its failure strengthened the moderate tradition in their leadership.

General Surveyors, Court of. A court established in 1542 to control crown lands. It arose out of an early Tudor government office, which was expanded by Thomas Cromwell to audit the accounts of lands acquired by the crown as a result of such processes as *attainder.

Geoffrey of Brittany (1158-1186). Fourth son of Henry II. He joined his brothers' unsuccessful rebellion against their father in 1173. In 1182 he turned on his brother Richard in Poitou and died while plotting another intrigue —once more against his father—from the court of Philip II Augustus of France.

Geoffrey of Monmouth (c. 1100-1155). Chronicler. His *Historia regum Britanniae* is a source of Arthurian legend but has little historical value. It begins with the settlement of Britain by *Brut, a descendant of Aeneas, and culminates in the conquests of King *Arthur.

Geoffrey Plantagenet (d. 1212). An illegitimate son of Henry II, who was bishop of Lincoln (1173-82), chancellor (1182-89), and then archbishop of York (1189-1207). He joined his halfbrothers Henry, the young king, and Richard in rebellion against their father (1173-74) but remained loyal to Henry in 1189. His appointment as archbishop was opposed by the chapter, with which he was intermittently in dispute until forced to flee abroad (1207) after objecting to a tax on church property.

George, St (4th century). Patron saint of England from the 14th century. Very little is known of George's life, although he may have been martyred in Palestine. Early venerated in the east as a soldier saint, he was popular with the crusaders. The story of the dragon and George's martyrdom under Diocletian is a late medieval myth. Feast day: 23 April.

George I (1660-1727). Elector of Hanover (1688-1727) and king of Great Britain and Ireland (1714-27). A Protestant and the great-grandson of James I, he was the first Hanoverian to rule Britain (see Settlement, Act of). He married his cousin, *Sophia Dorothea of Celle, in 1682 but divorced her 12 years later, imprisoning her for life on a charge of adultery. George did not endear himself to the British. He never learnt English, clearly preferred Hanover to Britain, and had three unpopular mistresses. Two of them were implicated in the scandal that followed the collapse of the *South Sea Company, and only Walpole's skill saved the king from disgrace. George left the administration of Britain to his ministers, usually Whigs, but was himself a shrewd diplomat, with a good understanding of European politics, as well as a brave soldier. In spite of his failure to win the hearts of his subjects, the easy suppression of the *Jacobite risings in 1715 and 1719 showed their preference for the Hanoverian monarchy.

George II (1683-1760). King of Great Britain and Ireland and elector of Hanover (1727-60). Son of George I and Sophia Dorothea of Celle, he married *Caroline of Ansbach (1705), a devoted wife despite her husband's infidelities. As prince of Wales George quarrelled openly with his father and made his home at Leicester House a centre of political opposition to the court. As king he relied heavily on the advice of his ministers and Queen Caroline; it was she who persuaded him to keep *Walpole in office and to support Walpole's cautious policies of peace and economy. After Caroline's death (1737) George ceased wholeheartedly to support Walpole, after whose resignation in 1742 *Carteret gained royal favour by his support for Hanoverian interests. George and Carteret led Britain into the War of *Austrian Succession (1740-48), a move that was criticized as involving Britain in a war merely to protect Hanover. Parliamentary protests led to Carteret's resignation (1744), and in 1746 George was obliged to accept *Pitt the elder as chief minister (1746). He subsequently withdrew from active involvement in politics, and his reign was a landmark in the development of constitutional monarchy. George was a discriminating patron of musicians, notably Handel, and a keen soldier, acquitting himself bravely at *Dettingen (1743), the last occasion on which a British monarch appeared in battle.

George III (1738-1820). King of Great Britain and Ireland (1760-1820), succeeding his grandfather George II. George, whose father Frederick Louis, prince of Wales, died in 1751, was taught by *Bute, the great influence on his youth and his unpopular chief minister (1762-63), fully to exercise royal powers of government. Obstinately pursuing this aim, he was nevertheless forced in the politically unstable 1760s to acknowledge the reality of party politics. In 1770 Lord *North came to power and until 1782, in spite of vociferous opposition, complied with George's determination to suppress the *American

Revolution. After North's resignation and the death in office of his successor, Rockingham, George was forced to accept a coalition that included Charles James *Fox (1783). In the same year, however, he was instrumental in the fall of the government, over a bill to reform the East India Company, and in the appointment of Pitt the younger. In 1788 George suffered a serious bout of the insanity, attributed to porphyria, that culminated in permanent incapacity in 1811 and the regency of the prince of Wales (later George IV). His political involvement declined in the 1790s but in the years 1801 to 1807 he effectively prevented *Catholic emancipation.

George IV (1762-1830). King of the United Kingdom (1820-30). Eldest son of George III, he was prince regent (1811-20) during the mental illness of his father. Clever, indolent, selfish, and lying, George was a man of fashion and extravagant artistic tastes, disreputable sexual morals, and, later, physical grossness (he was nicknamed prince of whales). Introduced to dissolute society by the Whig politician Charles James Fox, in 1785 he "married" Mrs Maria Fitzherbert (1756-1837). Since she was a Roman Catholic the marriage was invalid, but their relationship continued until 1811. In 1795 George was married, legally, to *Caroline of Brunswick and they had a daughter Charlotte (1796-1817). In 1796 he deserted Caroline, who lived a life of some indiscretion on the Continent (see delicate investigation). His attempt to divorce her in 1820, after excluding her from his coronation, caused considerable scandal. Allied since youth to the Whigs (in opposition to his father), George was forced after assuming the regency to accept a Tory government. He was succeeded by his brother William IV.

George V (1865-1936). King of the United Kingdom (1910-36). Second son of Edward VII, he served in the navy from 1877 to 1892, when he became heir apparent following the death of his elder brother the duke of Clarence. Created prince of Wales (1901), he made tours of the empire. He visited India for the second time in 1911 after becoming king (and emperor of India) and held a memorable coronation *durbar. His political influence was seen in the choice of *Baldwin as prime minister (1923) and in the decision to form a *national government (1931). George won great loyalty and affection—demonstrated at his Silver Jubilee (1935)—by his devotion to royal duty, especially in World War I, and family life (he married *Mary of Teck in 1893). He was a stamp collector and an expert shot. He adopted the surname *Windsor in 1917 and was succeeded by his eldest son, who became Edward VIII.

George VI (1894-1952). King of the United Kingdom (1936-52) and the last emperor of India until 15 Aug 1947. Second son of George V, Prince Albert (as he was then known) served in the navy and air force (1909-19) and was present at the battle of Jutland. As duke of York (from 1920), he was involved in youth work. Called to the throne on the abdication of his brother *Edward VIII, George performed his royal duties with great conscientiousness (overcoming the handicap of a severe stammer) and became a symbol of British resistance during World War II. George married (1923) Lady Elizabeth Bowes-Lyon (see Elizabeth, the Queen Mother) and was succeeded by his elder daughter, Elizabeth II.

George of Denmark (1653-1708). Consort of Queen Anne, whom he married in 1683, second son of Frederick III of Denmark. He served as nominal head of the army and the navy (1702-08).

Gerald of Wales (Latinized name: Giraldus Cambrensis; died c. 1220). Welsh writer. Son of a Welsh princess and a Norman baron, he studied at Paris and Oxford. An enthusiastic traveller and observer, his best-known work is the Gemma ecclesiastica, a lively description of the manners and morals of the clergy. He also wrote on a variety of other subjects, including Ireland, Wales, and the education of princes.

Germain, George Sackville. *See* Sackville, George Sackville Germain, 1st Viscount.

Germanus, St (c. 378-448). Bishop of Auxerre (his birthplace) from 418, who twice visited Britain (429, 447) to combat the Pelagian heresy. He is also said to have aided the Britons, and taught them the war cry "Alleluia", in their victory over the Picts and Saxons (447). Feast day: 31 July.

Ghana. *See* Gold Coast.

Ghent, treaty of (24 Dec 1814). The peace treaty that ended the *Anglo-American War of 1812. Although it confirmed Britain's possession of Canada, the treaty was a compromise in which Britain and the USA agreed to restore conquered territories and to set up commissions to settle the US-Canadian frontier.

Gibbon, Edward (1737-94). Historian. Gibbon is remembered for his classic *The History of the Decline and Fall of the Roman Empire* (1776-88). It deals with the last centuries of Roman supremacy and the early history of the Christian Church, which Gibbon blamed for the Empire's fall.

Gibbons, Grinling (1648-1721). Dutch carver, all of whose work was carried out in England. The finest wood carver of the baroque era, Gibbons is remarkable for the enormous complexity of his designs and skill in execution. His best surviving work is the carved room at Petworth house in West Sussex.

Gibbons, Orlando (1583-1625). Composer. He was educated at Oxford and Cambridge and in 1623 became organist of Westminster abbey. His works include service settings, anthems, madrigals, and instrumental music.

Gibraltar. A self-governing British crown colony at the western entrance to the Mediterranean Sea. Known as "the Rock", this strategic site was captured from Spain in 1704. British possession was confirmed by the treaties of Utrecht (1713), Paris (1763), and Versailles (1783), but Spain has constantly pressed its claim to Gibraltar. Gibraltar voted overwhelmingly in 1967 to remain British, and from 1969 to 1985 Spain closed its frontier with the colony.

Giffard, Walter (d. 1279). Archbishop of York from 1266. He became bishop of Bath and Wells in 1264 and was chancellor (1265-66) following Simon de Montfort's death at Evesham. He was reputed to be zealous in the reform of ecclesiastical abuses. From 1272 to 1274 and in 1275 he acted as a regent for Edward I.

Gilbert, Sir Humphrey (c. 1539-1583). Soldier and explorer. The stepbrother of Sir Walter Raleigh, Gilbert enthusiastically supported overseas exploration and colonization. In 1566, in *Discourse on a North-West Passage to India*, he proposed a voyage in search of the passage, but Elizabeth I rejected the scheme and Gilbert was sent instead to quell rebellion in Ireland (1567-70). In 1578 he finally set sail for North America but was forced to return when his fleet broke up. On a second voyage, in 1583, he claimed Newfoundland for England. He drowned in a storm on the return journey.

Gilbert and Ellice Islands Colony. A former British crown colony comprising a group of Pacific islands. In 1892 the islands were declared a protectorate of Britain and in 1915, at the islands' request, were annexed as a British colony. The Ellice Islands (now Tuvalu) became a separate colony in 1975 and independent in 1978. In 1979 the Gilbert Islands became fully independent as Kiribati.

Gilbertines. A monastic order founded in 1131 by St Gilbert (c. 1083-1189) of Sempringham (Lincolnshire). It was established in his native village as a small community for women. The number of recruits grew rapidly and a rule was drawn up in 1148. It borrowed extensively from Cistercian and Augustinian models and was designed for double communities of canons and nuns, served by lay brethren and sisters. Never a large order, the Gilbertines were confined to England (most of their priories being in eastern England). Only four priories had incomes over £200 at the dissolution.

Gildas, St (6th century). Monk and author of *De excidio et conquestu Britanniae* ("The Ruin of Britain"). This polemical work, which castigates the sins of contemporary British society and attacks five kings in Britain, including *Maelgwn Gwynedd, constitutes a crucial historical source for an understanding of conditions in Roman Britain. Feast day: 29 Jan.

gilds. *See* guilds.

gin drinking. The excessive consumption of gin was pronounced, especially in London, from the 1720s to the 1750s. From about 1720 cheap corn facilitated the manufacture of cheap gin, and by 1736 there were about 7000 unlicensed gin (or dram) shops in London. Attempts to control the trade by legislation (1729, 1733, 1736, 1743) failed until public opinion, aroused by Hogarth's *Gin Lane*, forced parliament to pass the more effective Gin Act (1751). This increased taxation and banned retailing of spirits by distillers and shopkeepers, cutting consumption rapidly and dramatically.

Ginkel, Godert de, 1st earl of Athlone (1644-1703). Soldier, born in the Netherlands, who came to England in 1688 with William of Orange (later *William III). He fought in Ireland against the Jacobite supporters of the former King James II, capturing Athlone and winning the victory of *Aughrim in 1691. He completed the conquest of Ireland by taking Limerick. Created earl of Athlone in 1692, he later fought under Marlborough.

Giraldus Cambrensis. *See* Gerald of Wales.

Gladstone, William Ewart (1809-98). Prime minister. Entering politics as a Tory, Gladstone was an MP from 1832 until 1895 (except for 1846) and held junior office under Peel (1834-35). In Peel's second ministry, he was president of the board of trade (1843-45) and secretary for the colonies (1845-46), remaining a member of the Peelite

Conservatives until 1865. Chancellor of the exchequer (1852-55) in Aberdeen's coalition, he cut duties but failed in his aim to end income tax because of the expense of the Crimean War. He served again as chancellor of the exchequer (1859-65) in Palmerston's second administration, when he further reduced taxes and established the Post Office Savings Bank (1861). On Palmerston's death, Gladstone continued as chancellor under Russell until Jan 1866, succeeding Russell as leader of the *Liberal Party in 1867.

During his first ministry (1868-74) Gladstone unsuccessfully attempted to pacify Ireland by disestablishing the Irish Church (1869) and passing the first *Irish Land Act (1870). The government also introduced *Cardwell's army reforms and was responsible for the *Ballot Act (1872), the *Judicature Act (1873), and *Forster's Education Act (1870). In opposition (1874-80), Gladstone strongly attacked his rival *Disraeli's imperialist policies and scored a striking personal success with his Midlothian election campaign (Nov-Dec 1879). His second ministry (1880-85) was notable for the second Irish Land Act (1881) and the third *Reform Act (1884), which enfranchised agricultural labourers, but this was overshadowed by defeat in the first *Boer war (1881) and the death of General *Gordon at Khartoum (1885). Irish affairs dominated Gladstone's third ministry (Feb-July 1886). An unsuccessful bill for Irish *home rule, to which Gladstone had been converted in 1885, led to the resignation of Joseph Chamberlain and the splitting of the Liberals (*see* Unionists). Prime minister for the last time from 1892 to 1894, Gladstone succeeded in passing a home rule bill through the Commons (1893), but resigned when it was defeated in the Lords. He died of cancer in 1898.

Glanville, Ranulf de (d. 1190). Sheriff of York (1163-70) and then justiciar (1180-89). The *Treatise on the Laws and Customs of England* has been attributed to him. Distrusted by Richard I, he was removed from office in 1189 and died on crusade in Acre.

Glastonbury legends. Myths associating Glastonbury abbey in Somerset with King Arthur and St Joseph of Arimathea. In an effort to attract pilgrims, and funds to rebuild the abbey, Glastonbury's 12th-century monks claimed that the bodies of Arthur and his queen Guinevere were buried in the abbey grounds. In the 13th century they also told the story that Joseph of Arimathea had come to Glastonbury in the 1st century with the Holy Grail and had built a church there.

glebe. The land held by the incumbent of a parish church. It was originally intended to be large enough to support the parish priest, but additional taxes were soon found to be necessary for his support.

Glencoe, massacre of (13 Feb 1692). The killing of about 38 MacDonalds of Glencoe by forces led by Capt. Robert Campbell of Glenlyon. These forces had been quartered on the MacDonalds and had accepted their hospitality. The victims were probably killed because of their cattle-raiding activities and their alleged Roman Catholicism (in fact they were probably Episcopalians), as well as for their Jacobite sympathies and their delay in taking an oath of allegiance.

Glorious First of June (1794). A naval battle during the French Revolutionary War, a British victory, fought west of Ushant. Admiral Lord Howe attacked a French fleet of 26 ships with the aim of seizing the valuable convoy it was protecting. Although the convoy escaped safely to Brest, six French ships of the line were captured and a seventh sunk.

Glorious Revolution (1688–89). The events that brought about the removal of *James II from the throne and his replacement by his daughter Mary and her husband William of Orange. James' unconstitutional rule provoked seven statesmen to invite William to land an army in England. He did so, and James fled to France. On their acceptance of the *Declaration of Rights (Feb 1689),

incorporated into the subsequent *Bill of Rights, they became joint sovereigns as William III and Mary II.

Gloucester. A city and the county town of Gloucestershire. It was an important Roman town, founded in about 97 AD and called Glevum, and later the capital of Mercia. The oldest part of the present-day cathedral is Norman and occupies the site of the Abbey of St Peter, founded in 681; Edward II is buried there.

Gloucester, duke of. *See* Humphrey, duke of Gloucester.

Gloucester, Statute of (1278). One of a series of enactments between 1275 and 1290 designed to centralize administration in the hands of the crown. The statute forbade the exercise of any franchise, or privilege, until title to it had been proved before the royal judges. Its provisions were clarified in the statute *quo warranto (1290).

Godden versus Hales (1686). A legal action brought against Sir Edward Hales (d. 1695) by his servant Godden. Hales, a Roman Catholic, was convicted of holding an army command without taking the oath prescribed by the *Test Act. Hales appealed to the Court of King's Bench and the judges confirmed the king's right to dispense with the Test Act and introduce Roman Catholics into civil and military offices (*see* dispensing power).

Goderich, Frederick John Robinson, Viscount (and 1st earl of Ripon) (1782–1859). Prime minister (1827–28). As F. J. Robinson, he was president of the Board of Trade (1818–23) and chancellor of the exchequer (1823–28), helping to dismantle the navigation laws to achieve freer trade. Created Viscount Goderich, he became prime minister in Aug 1827 but, unable to control the disintegrating Tory party, resigned in Jan 1828. Lord Ripon from 1833, he held office under Grey (1830–34) and Peel (1841–46).

Godiva (or **Godgifu**), **Lady** (11th century). The wife of *Leofric, earl of Mercia. According to legend, Leofric agreed to her request that he remit unpopular taxes only on condition that she rode naked through the streets of Coventry, with which she complied. The account appears first in the *Flores Historiarum* of the 13th-century chronicler *Roger of Wendover.

Godolphin, Sidney Godolphin, earl of (1645–1712). Politician, who served Charles II, James II, and Anne. In 1702 he became lord treasurer, proving an able financial administrator, who gave his patron *Marlborough firm financial support in the War of the *Spanish Succession. He played an important role in the passage of the Act of *Union (1707), but in the same year was replaced by *Harley as the queen's chief adviser. Godolphin subsequently became more closely identified with Whig policies and was dismissed from office in 1710.

Godwin, William (1756–1836). Radical philosopher and novelist, who influenced Wordsworth, Coleridge, and Southey. His *Inquiry Concerning Political Justice* (1793) embodied French Revolutionary ideas and he put forward his social theories in the novel *The Adventures of Caleb Williams* (1794). In 1797 Godwin married Mary *Wollstonecraft, a pioneer feminist.

Godwine (d. 1053). Earl of Wessex. The Anglo-Saxon Godwine was appointed earl of Wessex by *Cnut and rapidly achieved a dominant position in English politics. In 1042 he procured the accession of *Edward the Confessor, who married his daughter *Edith. Thereafter, Godwine and his family virtually controlled the kingdom and led the resistance to Edward's Norman advisers. Briefly outlawed in 1051, Godwine invaded England with his son Harold (1052), and Edward was forced to reinstate the family. Godwine was succeeded as earl by Harold, who became *Harold II of England on Edward's death.

Gold Coast. A former British colony in West Africa. The Gold Coast, which was the source of the lucrative slave trade, originally consisted of the forts along the coast (1821). British control was extended to include most of southern

Ghana in 1874 and the northern areas in 1896 after the defeat of the *Ashanti. It became a colony in 1906 and, as Ghana, gained independence in 1957 with Kwame *Nkrumah as prime minister.

Golden Jubilee (1887). A celebration throughout the British Empire, marking 50 years of Victoria's reign. The gathering for the occasion in London of colonial premiers made possible the first colonial conference (*see* imperial conferences). The Imperial Institute (now the Commonwealth Institute) was founded in London to commemorate the Jubilee.

Goldsmith, Oliver (1728–74). Irish dramatist, poet, and novelist. He arrived penniless in London in 1756 and rapidly rose to fame, his best-known works being *The Vicar of Wakefield* (1766), *The Deserted Village* (1770), and *She Stoops to Conquer* (1773). A heavy gambler, he died owing £2,000.

gold standard. A monetary system in which a country's paper currency (in Britain's case, sterling) is valued in terms of gold, which is freely traded; implicit is the right to demand gold for paper money. In Britain during the French Revolutionary and Napoleonic Wars (1792–1815), the *Bank of England suspended the payment of gold for bank notes, but a gold standard was maintained thereafter until 1914. By the end of the 19th century all the major powers were on a gold standard, which functioned throughout the world. The system could not be maintained in World War I, during which trade in gold was restricted. In 1925 Britain adopted the gold bullion standard, by which gold in bulk was bought and sold at the pre-1914 parity, mainly for external settlements; bank notes, however, could not be exchanged for gold. The run on the pound during the depression year of 1931 led to the abandonment of the gold standard by the national government.

Good Parliament (April–July 1376). The parliament, summoned at a time of military failure in France (*see* Hundred Years' War) and heavy taxation, that attacked the profligate court party. As a result the chamberlain, Lord Latimer, and a financier accused of corruption, Richard Lyons, were tried in parliament (see impeachment) and Alice *Perrers, mistress of Edward III, was expelled from court. Parliament's case was presented by Sir Peter de la Mare, who thus became the first speaker. Its acts were annulled in 1377.

Goodwin's case (1604). The annulment by Chancery of the election as MP for Buckinghamshire of Sir Francis Goodwin, because as an outlaw he was barred by royal proclamation, and the seating instead of Sir John Fortescue. The Commons protested, and the result was a compromise by which both men stood down. Thereafter the Commons' claim to control its own election returns, which had no basis in law or precedent, was not contested.

Gordon, Charles George (1833-85). British general. After serving in the Crimean War and the Chinese war of 1859-60 Gordon commanded Chinese forces against the rebel Taipings (1863-64), earning the sobriquet Chinese Gordon. In 1874 he was appointed governor of the equatorial provinces of the Sudan by the khedive of Egypt but, frustrated in his attempts to abolish the slave trade, resigned in 1876. He was again governor from 1877 to 1880. In 1884 he was dispatched by the British government to evacuate Egyptian forces from Khartoum during the *Mahdi's revolt, but, after enduring a ten-month siege, was killed shortly before the arrival of a relief force. The dilatoriness with which Gladstone's government responded to Gordon's dilemma was condemned by Queen Victoria and a substantial section of the British public.

Gordon, Lord George (1751-93). MP (1774-81), who achieved notoriety through his part in provoking the *Gordon riots. He was subsequently acquitted of high treason. He then became an increasingly eccentric supporter of various causes, protesting against the treatment of sailors and criminals and about imagined threats to Protestantism. In 1788 he was imprisoned for five years for libel, the harsh sentence reflecting the fear that he would again stir up popular disorder rather than the seriousness of his crime.

Gordon, George, 6th earl and 1st marquess of Huntly (c. 1563-1636). Scottish noble, who led the intrigues of the northern earls in the Roman Catholic interest against James VI. Huntly was imprisoned in 1588-89, murdered the earl of Moray in 1592, and defeated the royal forces at Glenlivet in 1594. The king forgave Huntly's lawlessness and even made him a marquess in 1599, but after succeeding to the English throne he was strong enough to curb Huntly's power in the north.

Gordon riots (2-9 June 1780). Anti-Catholic riots in London, which began after Lord George *Gordon presented a petition to parliament against the Roman Catholic Relief Act (1778). The rioters caused widespread destruction until the army and the militia were called in. About 300 people were killed in the riots and Gordon was charged with, and later acquitted of, high treason.

Goschen, George Joachim Goschen, 1st Viscount (1831-1907). A banker and MP from 1863 to 1900, when he was created viscount, Goschen was a Liberal cabinet minister (1866, 1868-74). A Liberal *Unionist after the party split over Irish home rule (1886), he became, under Salisbury, chancellor of the exchequer (1887-92), converting the *national debt (1888) and introducing a *death duty (1889). From 1895 to 1900 he was first lord of the admiralty.

governor. 1. The representative of the crown (not of the British government) in a dominion or colony. **2.** See guardian.

Gowrie "conspiracy" (5 Aug 1600). An attack on James VI of Scots at Gowrie house, to which he alleged he had been lured. In the ensuing confusion John Ruthven, 3rd earl of Gowrie, and his brother Alexander were killed. The king accused the earl of attempted kidnapping, but some held that he invented the plot to justify the elimination of his enemies.

The mystery has never been solved. *See also* Ruthven raid.

Grafton, Augustus Henry Fitzroy, 3rd duke of (1735-1811). First lord of the treasury (Aug 1766-Jan 1770). Grafton assumed full responsibility as prime minister only after *Pitt the elder's illness and resignation (1767-68). With a quarrelling cabinet, preoccupied with the *Wilkes affair, Grafton could not implement his conciliatory policy towards the American colonists. Subsequently, he served as a minister (1771-75, 1782-83) under North and Rockingham.

Graham of Claverhouse, John, 1st Viscount Dundee (1648-89). Soldier. After service in Dutch and French armies Claverhouse joined (1678) the forces of Charles II operating against the covenanters in southwest Scotland. He acted harshly on occasion, but his sobriquet "Bloody Clavers" was not fully deserved. In 1688 he was created Lord Dundee and in the following year he led a Highland rising in the Jacobite interest. Although victorious at *Killiecrankie "Bonny Dundee" was mortally wounded.

grand alliance. 1. (1689) An alliance formed between Austria, the Netherlands, England, Spain, and a number of German states following the invasion of the Palatinate by Louis XIV of France. The subsequent War of the Grand Alliance is sometimes also called the War of the League of Augsburg, an ineffective alliance formed against Louis XIV's expansionist policy in 1686 by Austria, Sweden, Spain, Bavaria, Saxony, and the Palatinate. Fighting, known in England as King William's War, continued intermittently both in Europe and overseas until 1697, when the treaty of Rijswick brought temporary peace. 2. (1701) An alliance of England, Austria, and the Netherlands, organized by William III of England and later joined by Prussia, Portugal, and Savoy. It aimed to prevent the union of the French and Spanish crowns—the issue of the War of the *Spanish Succession, which followed.

grand assize. A judicial proceeding, instituted by Henry II in about 1179, in which a jury of 16 knights determined the title to disputed land. It was an alternative to *trial by battle and was abolished in 1833.

Grand Remonstrance (1641). A comprehensive statement, drawn up by *Pym and other parliamentary leaders, defining parliament's stance in the struggle against the authoritarian rule of Charles I. The Remonstrance (effectively a manifesto of extremist parliamentarians) listed the reforms already enacted by the *Long Parliament, while calling for further action by the king on outstanding grievances. It urged the replacement of the king's "evil counsellors" (said to be plotting to advance Roman Catholicism) by ministers to be approved by parliament. The power of the bishops, too, should be curbed and the church reformed by a synod of Protestant churchmen. After passing the House of Commons by a mere 11 votes the Remonstrance was printed only to be rejected by Charles, who denied the need for any reform of the church or of his ministers. The Grand Remonstrance —one of the major English constitutional documents in its assertion of parliamentary claims—led to a hardening of divisions between parliamentarians and royalists, the threat to the church driving many moderates into the royalist camp.

Granville, Earl. *See* Carteret, John.

Granville, Granville George Leveson-Gower, 2nd Earl (1815-91). Liberal politician. An MP from 1836 to 1846, when he succeeded to the earldom, he held cabinet posts over the period 1851-86, notably that of foreign secretary (1851-52, 1870-74, 1880-85). He was a close political associate of Gladstone and took a leading part in the decision to dispatch *Gordon to Khartoum (1884).

Grattan, Henry (1746-1820) Irish statesman. From 1775 he led the patriot party in the Irish parliament, for which in 1782 he succeeded in gaining legislative independence (Grattan's parliament, 1782-1800). In a series of brilliant speeches he opposed the projected *union between England and Ireland, which, however, he failed to prevent. From 1805 he sat in the English parliament, concentrating his energies on the campaign for *Catholic emancipation.

Gravelines, battle of. 1. (13 July 1558) A battle during the war between Spain and France (1547-59), in which England, following Mary I's marriage to Philip of Spain, was an ally of the Spaniards. After losing Calais to the French (Jan 1558) England gave naval support to the Spanish troops during their counterattack at Gravelines, east of Calais. The guns of the English fleet played a material part in the Spanish victory—an early instance of naval strength intervening in a land engagement. **2.** (29 July 1588) The naval battle in which the Spanish *armada was finally defeated.

great cause (1291-92). The adjudication by Edward I of England of the claims of the 13 *competitors to the Scottish throne. Edward gave judgment in favour of *John Balliol.

Great Contract (1610). A proposal by Robert Cecil, earl of Salisbury, to place government revenue on a firmer basis by commuting the crown's feudal revenues for a fixed annual sum voted by parliament. Negotiations were protracted but eventually broke down because of James I's reluctance to surrender part of his *prerogative and because of quarrels between crown and parliament over religious questions. Royal feudal dues remained in force until 1643.

great council. A meeting of the lords spiritual and temporal by personal writ of summons from the sovereign. Under Henry I (reigned 1100-35) there were 27 such assemblies to dispense feudal justice and to advise the king. Their composition was settled by *Magna Carta (1215), which assigned them the function of granting extraordinary taxation. Great councils continued to be summoned even after the development of *parliament. Edward IV and Henry VII each summoned at least five. They discussed matters of high policy, often in time of war or rebellion, and some authorized the imposition of financial aid in advance of parliamentary grant. Mary summoned a great council in 1553 to announce her proposed marriage to Philip of Spain. The last one was called in 1640 by Charles I.

Great Exhibition (1851). An exhibition of industrial products from Britain and the Continent held in the specially constructed *Crystal Palace in Hyde Park, London. It was planned and opened by Prince Albert and over 100 000 objects were displayed.

great plague (1665). The last major outbreak of bubonic *plague in Britain. Beginning in London in late 1664, it reached its height in Aug and Sept 1665. Over 68 000 Londoners died in 1665 and striking descriptions of the plague-stricken city are found in Pepys' diary and Defoe's *Journal of the Plague Year* (1722).

great seal. The premier seal of England. Introduced by Edward the Confessor, the great seal of each sovereign has always been in the custody of the lord chancellor operating in *Chancery. Its use was to authenticate royal decisions; it alone could issue orders requiring full legal backing, such as grants of land, appointment to office, and treaties with foreign powers, although normally a warrant from either the *privy seal or *signet was required first. It is round and double-sided, showing the sovereign crowned and enthroned on one side and mounted on the other. It is still used for sealing all public acts of state.

great trek. The movement of over 12 000 Afrikaners from the Cape, South Africa, in the 1830s. They trekked north to find new lands free from British control and settled *Natal, the *Orange Free State, and the *Transvaal republic.

Gregory I, St (c. 540-604). Pope (590-604). A monk, theologian, and one of the greatest of the medieval popes, Gregory sent *Augustine as missionary to Kent in 596. Feast day: 12 March.

Grenada. The southernmost of the *Windward Islands. Discovered by

Columbus (1498), who named it either Ascención or Concepción, the island initially attracted French settlers. The British captured it in 1762, during the Seven Years' War, lost it in 1779, and regained it in 1782. A West Indies Associated State from 1967, it became an independent member of the Commonwealth in 1974.

Grenville, George (1712-70). MP (1741-70), who was allied with his brother in law *Pitt the elder but stayed in office after Pitt's fall, as treasurer of the navy (1757-62), secretary of state (May-Oct 1762), and first lord of the admiralty (Oct 1762-April 1763). Succeeding *Bute as first lord of the treasury (1763-65), Grenville pursued rigid financial economies. His government initiated the *North Briton prosecution (1763) and introduced taxation of the American colonies with the *Stamp Act.

Grenville, Sir Richard (1542-91). Naval commander. A cousin of Sir Walter Raleigh, Grenville is best known for his dramatic attempt to vanquish the Spanish fleet (1591) as second in command of the *Revenge*. After hand-to-hand fighting with 15 Spanish vessels off the coast of the Azores, the *Revenge* was defeated and its surviving crew captured. Grenville died later of his wounds.

Grenville, William Wyndham, Baron (1759-1834). Prime minister. George Grenville's son, he was home secretary (1789-91) and foreign secretary (1791-1801) under Pitt the younger (his cousin). He subsequently moved into alliance with Charles James *Fox and finally broke with Pitt in 1804. Grenville was prime minister in the predominantly Foxite Ministry of *All the Talents (1806-07). He later led the conservative Whig elements and, from 1822, formally supported Liverpool's administration.

Gresham, Sir Thomas (?1519-1579). Merchant and financier, who founded the *Royal Exchange (1566) and Gresham College (1575), in London. He was appointed ambassador to the Netherlands in 1559 and subsequently became financial agent to the crown.

Gresham's law, which states that coins made of inferior metal will drive "good" coins of the same value out of circulation because the latter will be hoarded, was erroneously attributed to him in 1857.

Grey, Charles Grey, 2nd Earl (1764-1845). Prime minister (1830-34). A Whig MP (1786-1807), Grey joined (1793) the radical Society of the Friends of the People, campaigning for parliamentary reform, and introduced an unsuccessful franchise bill (1797). A friend of Charles James Fox, Grey helped manage Warren Hastings's impeachment and strongly opposed Pitt's foreign and domestic policies during the 1790s. Grey became first lord of the admiralty in 1806 and, on the death of Fox, foreign secretary in the Ministry of *All the Talents but resigned in protest against George III's demand for a pledge not to introduce *Catholic emancipation. In opposition (1807-30) Grey was a vehement critic of the Tories' repressive policies but subsequently refused to cooperate with Canning. As prime minister he once more took up the cause of parliamentary reform and introduced a reform bill (1831). Following its defeat, he called a general election, and on being returned to power passed a new bill through the Commons only to see it defeated in the Lords. Grey resigned but returned in a few days (May 1832) armed with a promise from William IV to create sufficient new peers to ensure the passage of the bill. The first *Reform Act (1832) proved the beginning of the extension of the franchise to the British people. Grey resigned in 1834 because of cabinet disagreements over his Irish policy and retired from politics.

Grey, Lady Jane (1537-54). A granddaughter of Henry VIII's younger sister Mary. Lady Jane Grey, a devout Protestant and a gifted scholar, was married against her will (1553) to Lord Guildford *Dudley, son of the earl of *Northumberland. Northumberland, determined to retain his power after the king's death, persuaded Edward to name Jane as his successor. An innocent pawn in the plot, Jane was proclaimed queen on 9 July 1553, but within nine days Northumberland's forces had been dispersed by troops loyal to Mary Tudor. Jane's life was initially spared, but *Wyatt's rebellion (1554) convinced Mary that, as the focal point of Protestant opposition, Jane and her husband should be executed.

Grey, Reginald de, 3rd Baron Grey of Ruthin (c. 1362-1440). Governor of Ireland (1398), who later served *Henry IV and *Henry V as councillor and military commander. He led campaigns against *Owain Glyndŵr in 1402 and 1409 and played a prominent part in the later stages of the *Hundred Years' War.

Grey of Fallodon, Edward Grey, Viscount (1862-1933). Liberal MP (1885-1916), who was foreign secretary for 11 years (1905-16), the longest continuous tenure of that office in British history. He dealt with the Morocco crises of 1905-06 and 1911 (see Algeciras conference; Agadir crisis). He took Britain into World War I, remarking "The lamps are going out all over Europe; we shall not see them lit again in our lifetime". He led negotiations in the secret treaty of London (1915), which allied Italy with Britain, France, and Russia.

Griffith, Arthur (1872-1922). Irish nationalist. He campaigned for Irish independence from 1898 and formed *Sinn Féin in 1905. He gave up the presidency of Sinn Féin (1917) to *De Valera, under whom he became (1919) vice president of the republic declared by the *Dáil Éireann. With Michael *Collins, he negotiated the 1921 Anglo-Irish treaty establishing the *Irish Free State and was elected president of the Irish republic (1922).

Grindal, Edmund (?1519-1583). Archbishop of Canterbury. Chaplain to Edward VI, during the *Marian reaction he went to Frankfurt, where he was influenced by Calvinism. He was appointed bishop of London (1559), archbishop of York (1570), and archbishop of Canterbury (1575). His refusal to suppress Puritan meetings ("prophesyings") resulted in his suspension in 1577.

Griqualand East. A highland area of east Cape Province, South Africa. Settled by the Griquas from *Griqualand West (1862), it remained autonomous until incorporated into Cape Colony (1880).

Griqualand West. An area in north Cape Province, South Africa. Settled by the Griquas (c. 1800), it attracted outside interest with the discovery of diamonds (1867) and was annexed by Britain (1871), which integrated it into Cape Colony (1877-80).

Grosseteste, Robert (c. 1175-1253). Bishop of Lincoln from 1235. Of humble origins, Grosseteste became a distinguished scholar, with wide interests. He strove to improve pastoral care in his diocese and opposed the appointment of foreign priests to English livings.

Gruffudd ap Cynan (c. 1055-1137). King of Gwynedd (1081-1137). Gruffudd ap Cynan, whose childhood was spent in Ireland, made a first attempt to claim his inheritance in 1075. In 1081 his alliance with *Rhys ap Tewdwr ensured victory at the battle of *Mynydd Carn. The royal expedition of 1114 failed to curb his power and further territorial gains were made by his sons *Owain and *Cadwaladr. He is traditionally regarded as a formulator of bardic regulations.

Gruffudd ap Llywelyn (d. 1063). Welsh king. He had gained control of the kingdoms of Gwynedd and Powys by 1039 and Deheubarth, and probably Gwent and Morgannwg, following his victory over Gruffudd ap Rhydderch in 1055. He led numerous raids into the borderlands and formed an alliance with Aelfgar of Mercia. Following an attack on Rhuddlan by Earl Harold he was slain in 1063.

Gruffudd Hiraethog (d. 1564). Bard and herald, who had many disciples among prominent Welsh bards in the late 16th century. He compiled manuscript copies of Welsh pedigrees and a Welsh dictionary and collection of proverbs.

guardian (or **governor**). In Scotland, a regent who governed the country during the minority or absence of the monarch. The most famous were the six guardians appointed on the death of Alexander III to rule in the name of the infant Queen Margaret, the Maid of Norway.

Guelph (or **Welf**). A German family, members of which became rulers of the Brunswick duchies in Lower Saxony. The Brunswick-Lüneburg branch—best known as the house of *Hanover—ruled Britain from 1714 to 1901.

Guernsey. The second largest of the *Channel Islands. Under the English crown since 1066, the bailiwick of Guernsey, which includes Alderney and the smaller islands, has its own parliament and laws, based on the *Approbation des Lois* (1580-81).

guilds (or **gilds**). Originally, Anglo-Saxon associations of families (*frithgilds*) formed to provide mutual protection. Guilds became important after the Norman conquest as general associations of townsmen, the purpose of which was to provide protection for trading interests and to assist in the administration of towns. From the 12th century craft guilds—associations of craftsmen practising a common craft—developed on similar lines, protecting the monopoly of their members and controlling the apprenticeship system. The monopolistic power of the guilds came under attack from the 16th century, and legislative efforts to control this power, together with the rise of capitalist entrepreneurial production, led to the gradual break-up of the guild system. The present-day *livery companies derive from the medieval guilds.

Guinness, Edward Cecil, 1st earl of Iveagh (1847-1927). Philanthropist and brewer. Guinness (earl, 1919) contributed generously to housing projects in Dublin and London, and to medical research, as well as bequeathing Kenwood House, London and its art collection (the Iveagh Bequest) to the nation.

gunpowder plot. A conspiracy to blow up the Houses of Parliament and James I on 5 Nov 1605. It was led by Robert *Catesby, whose co-conspirators included Robert Winter, John Wright, and Guy *Fawkes, all staunch Roman

Catholics. The group secured a cellar under the House of Lords, in which about 30 barrels of gunpowder were secreted (March 1605). The plot was uncovered when an anonymous letter of warning to stay away from parliament was sent to a Catholic MP. Guy Gawkes was arrested in the cellar on 4 Nov, and the conspirators were subsequently executed.

Gurkhas. A people of Nepal and a major source of manpower for Britain's Indian army. The Gurkhas, who were organized into separately numbered regiments after the Indian mutiny, were deemed to be the finest native troops in the British Empire. In 1947 they were divided between the British army and the army of newly independent India.

Guthrum (d. 890). King of Denmark and East Anglia. Viking invader of England. His invasion of Wessex was repelled by *Alfred the Great at Edington (878). Guthrum accepted baptism and in a formal peace was allowed to settle in eastern England (*see* Danelaw) as an equal power.

Guyana. *See* British Guiana.

Gwent. A Welsh kingdom in southeast Wales, between the rivers Wye and Usk. The Normans, led by William fitz *Osbern, secured lands and built castles in Gwent and had, by 1086, established themselves as far west as Caerleon.

Gwyn, Nell (1650-87). Actress and mistress of Charles II. Between 1665 and 1670 she acted numerous comic roles at Drury Lane. As Charles' mistress she shunned involvement with politics.

Gwynedd. A kingdom in northwest Wales, including *Anglesey and Snowdonia, and also the lands to the east of the river Conway (designated Gwynedd Is Conway or the *Perfeddwlad). The dynasty governing this kingdom claimed descent from *Cunedda and the royal residence was established first at Degannwy and later at Aberffraw, in Anglesey. Prominent rulers included *Maelgwn Gwynedd, *Cadwallon, *Rhodri Mawr, *Gruffudd ap Llywelyn,

*Owain Gwynedd, *Llywelyn ap Ior-
werth, and *Llywelyn ap Gruffudd.

H

habeas corpus (Latin: you may have the
body). A writ, originating in the 13th
century, that required anyone detaining
an individual to produce him or her in
court within a specified period and to
furnish reasons for the detention. In
medieval times habeas corpus (the opening words of the Latin writ) was
employed largely as a weapon in the
conflict between rival courts and systems
of justice (e.g. between common law and
equity), but from the reign of Henry VII
it was increasingly used to protect
individuals against arbitrary imprisonment. The Habeas Corpus Act (1679)
laid down procedures for the issue of the
writ, imposed penalties for officials
ignoring it, and closed certain loopholes
in its use. The act covered only criminal
charges, but in 1816 its provisions were
extended to cover cases of civil detention. Further adjustments, limiting cases
where habeas corpus could be denied,
were made by the Administration of
Justice Act (1960). Habeas corpus was
suspended during the *Jacobite
rebellions (1715, 1745) and during the
French Revolutionary War (1794).

Hadrian's wall. A wall built by the
Romans to mark the northern frontier of
Britain. Erected in the years 122-27,
except for a western extension in the
mid-2nd century, it extends for 117 km
(73 mi). It was originally built of stone
3 m (10 ft) thick, 3.5 m (15 ft) high, and,
in the west, of turf 6 m (20 ft) thick,
3.6 m (12 ft) high. A parapet walk linked
castles every 1475 m (1620 yd), with
intermediate fortlets. On its northern
side the wall was guarded by a ditch 3 m
(10 ft) deep and 9 m (30 ft) wide, with a
similar ditch behind. Some 17 garrison
forts served the wall, the best-preserved
being at Housesteads. The wall was
breached and severely damaged by the

Picts in 196, 296, and 367 and was finally
abandoned in 383.

Haig, Douglas Haig, 1st Earl (1861-
1928). Commander in chief (1915-18) of
the *British Expeditionary Force in
World War I. His strategy of attrition
resulted in appalling casualties, notably
in the battles of the *Somme (1916) and
*Ypres (1917). As president of the
British Legion after 1921 he organized
Poppy Day.

Hailsham, Quintin Hogg, Baron
(1907-). Conservative politician and
lawyer. A cabinet minister-(1956-64),
Hailsham renounced his viscountcy in
1963 as part of an unsuccessful bid to
succeed Macmillan as Conservative
leader. He was created a life peer in 1970
on assuming the office of lord chancellor, which he held until 1974 and from
1979 to 1987.

**Haldane, Richard Burdon Haldane, 1st
Viscount** (1856-1928). Lawyer and politician, best known for his military
reforms. A Liberal MP from 1885 until
1911, when he was created a viscount,
Haldane was secretary for war (1905-
12). His reforms provided for the
mobilization of an expeditionary force
(with reorganized reserves) at the start
of World War I and created the Territorial Force (later Territorial Army).
He also created the Imperial General
Staff (1909). He was lord chancellor
from 1912 to 1915, when he was dismissed on the ground of alleged German
sympathies, and again, having joined the
Labour Party, in 1924. Also a philosopher, he wrote *The Pathway to Reality*
(1903).

Hales' case. *See* Godden versus Hales.

Halidon Hill, battle of (19 July 1333). A
battle in which an army led by the
Scottish guardian, Sir Archibald
Douglas, unsuccessfully attacked the
forces of Edward III of England and
Edward Balliol in an attempt to relieve
Berwick. The guardian and five Scottish
earls were killed in the battle, and
Berwick then surrendered.

Halifax, Charles Montagu, 1st earl of
(1661-1715). Statesman and outstanding

financier. He became a lord of the treasury in 1692 and initiated the national debt by proposing a government loan of £1 million. With a further loan in 1694 he established the Bank of England. In the same year he joined the Whig *junto and became chancellor of the exchequer, devising in 1695 a scheme of currency reform. In 1697 he became first lord of the treasury and leader of the House of Commons, but Tory pressure forced him to resign in 1699. Created Baron Halifax in 1700, and an earl in 1714, on the succession of George I, he returned to office as first lord but died in the following year.

Halifax, Edward Frederick Wood, 1st earl of (1881-1959). Statesman. Halifax served as a Conservative MP (1910-25) and as a cabinet minister (1922-24, 1924-25). He was then raised to the peerage as Baron Irwin and appointed viceroy of India, where he remained until 1931. Returning to the cabinet (1932), Halifax (created Viscount Halifax in 1934 and earl in 1944) was foreign secretary (Feb 1938-Dec 1940), supporting Neville Chamberlain's *appeasement policy. During World War II he was ambassador in Washington (1941-46).

Halifax, George Montagu Dunk, 2nd earl of (1716-71). Politician, great nephew of Charles Montagu, 1st earl of Halifax. As president of the Board of Trade (1748-61), Halifax fostered North American commerce. The town of Halifax in Nova Scotia was named in his honour. He is best remembered for taking a leading part, while secretary of state (1762-65), in the government's efforts to silence *Wilkes by use of a general warrant (1763). Wilkes was awarded damages against Halifax in 1769.

Halifax, George Savile, 1st marquess of (1633-95). Statesman and writer, whose moderate political views earned him the nickname the Trimmer. He was an opponent of Charles II's pro-French policies and demonstrated his political tolerance by opposing the anti-Catholic *Test Act (1673) and the second *exclusion bill (1680). He was appoin-

ted lord privy seal in 1682 and served briefly as lord president of the council (1685) under James II, being dismissed. After an unsuccessful attempt (1688) to mediate between James and William of Orange he became a supporter of William. From 1689 to 1690, in the office of lord privy seal, he served the new rulers William and Mary as their chief minister. Halifax's political views are outlined in his book *The Character of a Trimmer* (1688). He is represented by Jotham in Dryden's *Absalom and Achitophel.*

Hall (or Halle), Edward (c. 1498-1547). Historian, lawyer, and MP. His *Union of the Noble and Illustre Famelies of Lancastre and York* (1542), completed (1550) by Richard Grafton (c. 1513-c. 1572), was used by Shakespeare for several of his history plays.

Hall's case (1581). A case arising from the suing for debt in 1576 of Edward Smalley, the servant of an MP, Arthur Hall. Smalley had himself arrested while parliament was sitting so that Hall could gain his release on the ground of parliamentary privilege. Chancery, however, refused to issue the required writ of privilege and, although the Commons then ordered Smalley's release, they demanded that the debt be paid. Hall refused, and the affair was only resolved when Hall's wife made good the debt. He subsequently published two pamphlets attacking the Commons, who expelled him from the House (1581).

ham. A settlement or village in Anglo-Saxon England. "Ham" originally meant home or dwelling but gradually became applicable to groups of dwellings. As an element in modern place names it indicates Anglo-Saxon origin or influence.

Hamilton, Emma, Lady (?1761-1815). Mistress of Horatio *Nelson. In 1791 she married Sir William Hamilton (1730-1803), British ambassador in Naples, where she first met Nelson (1793). She became his mistress in 1798 and in 1801 gave birth to their daughter Horatia. Imprisoned for debt (1813-14), she died penniless in France.

Hamilton, James Hamilton, 3rd marquess and 1st duke of (1606-49). Scottish royalist, who in 1638 negotiated with the *covenanters on Charles I's behalf. He was created a duke in 1643. His failure to prevent the covenanters from helping the English parliament during the Civil War caused the king to suspect his loyalty and to imprison him (1644-46). In 1648 he led the Engagers (*see* Engagement), but was captured after the battle of *Preston and executed in London.

Hamilton, James Hamilton (or **Douglas**), **4th duke of** (1658-1712). Scottish noble. He succeeded to the title in 1698 on the resignation of his mother Anne, duchess of Hamilton. In the Scottish parliament Hamilton led the Jacobites, who sought support by posing as patriotic *cavaliers opposed to English domination and closer union. His inconsistency greatly damaged the Jacobite cause. Hamilton was killed in a duel.

Hamon, Robert fitz (11th century). Norman lord. Holding extensive lands in Gloucestershire, he led the successful onslaught, in the last decade of the 11th century, on the kingdom of *Morgannwg. He built a castle at Cardiff and the lands occupied by his followers in the Vale of Glamorgan formed the shire-fee of the newly constituted lordship of Glamorgan.

Hampden, John (1594-1643). Parliamentary leader noted for his unyielding opposition to the arbitrary government of Charles I. Hampden was imprisoned in 1627 for refusing to subscribe to a *forced loan, while his refusal in 1635 to pay the assessment of *ship money levied on his property led to widespread resistance to the tax. As a member of the *Long Parliament he played an important part in the impeachment of Strafford. After the outbreak of the Civil War Hampden led a parliamentary detachment at the battle of Edghill, but died of wounds received at an engagement at Chalgrove Field.

Hampton Court conference (1604). A meeting called in response to the *millenary petition (1603) to discuss Puritan requests for reforms in the Anglican church. These included changes in the episcopacy and the prayer book. Most of the Puritans' demands were rejected by James I with the exception of their call for a new translation of the Bible. The *Authorized Version of the Bible, which appeared in 1611, was the most important result of the conference.

Hampton Court palace. One of the residences of the UK monarch, in Richmond-upon-Thames, London. Hampton Court was originally built by Cardinal Wolsey, who gave it to Henry VIII in the 1520s. Henry made substantial additions to it, adding most notably the Great Hall. In the 1690s it was again extensively remodelled by Wren for William III. However, only Fountain Court with the main garden façade were completed to his designs.

hanaper, clerk of the. A Chancery official who recorded fees paid on the writs that began every action at common law. He was so named because the writs, and the returns to them, were kept in a wickerwork box called a hanaper (or hamper). The office was abolished in 1852.

Handel, George Frederick (1685-1759). Composer of the late baroque period. Born in Saxony, Handel became musical director of the court of the elector of Hanover (later George I of England) in 1710 but almost immediately left for England, where he settled. He wrote many operas, oratorios, the most famous being the *Messiah* (1741), and occasional music, including *Music for the Royal Fireworks* (1749).

Hankey, Maurice, 1st Baron (1877-1963). Public servant. Secretary to the Imperial Defence Committee (1912-38), he created the cabinet secretariat (1916), remaining secretary of the cabinet until 1938. Subsequently, he served (1839-42) in wartime cabinets.

Hanover, house of. The sovereigns of Great Britain, Ireland, and the United Kingdom (1714-1901). The dynasty (of the *Guelph family) was named after the

German state of Hanover (known alternatively as Brunswick-Lüneburg), the rulers of which were electors of the Holy Roman Empire. The Act of *Settlement (1701) ensured the Hanoverian succession to the English (subsequently British) crown. The elector George accordingly succeeded (1714) as George I. In 1837 the personal union between Britain and Hanover (since 1815 a kingdom) ended, the crown of Hanover passing to Victoria's uncle, Ernest, duke of Cumberland. The British dynasty ended with Victoria's death in 1901; the dynastic name of her successor Edward VII was *Saxe-Coburg.

Hanoverian succession. *See* Settlement, Act of.

Hansard. The official reports of proceedings and debates of the Houses of Parliament, named after the Hansard family of printers. The unofficial publication of parliamentary reports was begun by *Cobbett in 1803. Their publication was taken on by T. C. Hansard (1776-1833) in 1811 and, as *Hansard's Parliamentary Debates*, was continued by his family until 1889 (with government support from 1855). The government finally took over publication in 1909. The reports continued to be generally known as *Hansard* and in 1943 the name was restored to the title page.

Hanse (German: association). A league of German trading towns. In the 13th century the German Baltic ports, such as Lübeck, Hamburg, and Cologne, were the centre of European commerce, and several established companies in London. After combining into a single company in 1282, the London Hanse, at the *Steelyard, became a major trading centre. It was superseded in the 16th century by the *Merchants Adventurers.

Harcourt, Sir William (1827-1904). Liberal MP (1868-98). He was home secretary (1880-85) in Gladstone's second ministry and, as chancellor of the exchequer (1886, 1892-94, 1894-95), introduced *death duties (1894). He was Liberal leader (1896-98).

Hardie, (James) Keir (1856-1915). Labour leader, largely responsible for the foundation of the *Labour Party. A Lanarkshire coalminer from the age of ten, Keir Hardie, after being dismissed as an agitator (1878), became a union organizer (1879) and secretary of the Scottish Miners' Federation (1886). Following his conversion to socialism he strongly advocated the creation of a labour party instead of reliance on the cooperation of the Liberal Party to achieve socialist aims. He was an independent labour MP (1892-95), the first chairman of the *Independent Labour Party (1893-1900), and helped establish the Labour Representation Committee (1900). Again an MP (1900-15), he was the first leader of the parliamentary Labour Party (1906-07).

Harfleur, siege of (19 Aug-22 Sept 1415). The siege, during the Hundred Years' War, of Harfleur, a strategically important town at the mouth of the river Seine. It was Henry V's first military undertaking after he resumed the war against France. Because of Harfleur's strong fortifications and an outbreak of dysentery among the English the port was able to hold out for nearly six weeks before capitulating to Henry.

Hargreaves, James (d. 1778). Carpenter and weaver, who in 1765 invented the *spinning jenny. Named after his wife, it accelerated spinning in the textile industry by using eight spindles driven by a large wheel. After suffering mob violence from hand-spinners who feared for their livelihood, Hargreaves moved in 1768 to Nottingham, where he successfully operated a small mill.

Harlech, siege of (1468). The siege of Harlech castle by William *Herbert, on behalf of the Yorkists, during the Wars of the Roses. Jasper *Tudor, who held it, had fled to Ireland, and Harlech had to be captured if its Lancastrian links with Ireland and Scotland were to be severed. Its capture, in Aug 1468, is commemorated in the song "March of the Men of Harlech".

Harley, Robert, 1st earl of Oxford and Mortimer (1661-1724). Statesman. He entered parliament (1689) as a Whig but, with St John (later Lord Bolingbroke), transferred his allegiance to the Tories following the accession of Anne (1702). He was secretary of state (1704-08), chancellor of the exchequer (1710), and lord high treasurer (1711-14). The treaty of *Utrecht, which followed secret negotiations with the French, constituted the chief act of his administration. Following quarrels with Bolingbroke he was dismissed (1714). His remarkable collection of books was subsequently bought by the British Museum, forming the Harleian collection.

Harold I Harefoot (d. 1040). King of England (1035-40). Illegitimate son of *Cnut, Harold became regent of England on the death of his father (1035) while *Harthacnut, Cnut's legitimate son and claimant to the throne, was absent in Denmark. Following the murder of another royal claimant, Alfred the Aetheling, in 1036, Harold was recognized as king (1037).

Harold II (?1020-66). King of England (Jan-Oct 1066). Second son of Earl *Godwine, Harold was exiled in the anti-Godwine reaction of 1051 but was restored, after invading England, in 1052. In 1053 he succeeded Godwine as earl of Wessex and thereafter dominated the court and English politics. While at the court of William, duke of Normandy (1064), he swore to aid his accession to the English throne, but on the death of *Edward the Confessor he himself became king. He was defeated and killed by William at the battle of *Hastings.

Harthacnut (?1019-42). King of England (1040-42). The only legitimate son of *Cnut, Harthacnut ruled Denmark from 1028. Unable to take control of England on Cnut's death (1035) because of the Norwegian threat to Denmark, Harthacnut allowed the throne to be taken by his half-brother *Harold I. On Harold's death (1040) Harthacnut became king. His brief reign was marked by political violence and the persecution of Harold's supporters.

Hartington, marquess of. See Devon-

shire, Spencer Compton Cavendish, 8th duke of.

Harvey, William (1578-1657). Physician famous for his discovery, published in 1628, of the circulation of the blood. He was physician extraordinary to James I and attended Charles I in the Civil War. He became warden of Merton College in 1645.

Hastings, battle of (14 Oct 1066). The decisive initial battle of the Norman conquest, fought at Senlac hill, 9 km (5 mi) from Hastings. News of the Norman invasion reached Harold on 1 Oct, shortly after his victory at *Stamford bridge. After a forced march from York to Kent, the English met Duke William's army, marching on London from its base at Hastings castle, at Senlac hill. The English army defended the ridge throughout the day, finally being overwhelmed by the Normans' archers, cavalry, and superior discipline. Harold was killed (traditionally by an arrow in the eye) along with his two brothers. William built Battle abbey on the site of his victory.

Hastings, Francis Rawdon-Hastings, 1st marquess of (1754-1826). Soldier, politician, and (1813-22) governor general of India. As a close friend of George IV, Hastings (then Lord Moira) served in the Ministry of *All the Talents (1806-07). His major achievement was in India; his campaigns pacified Nepal (1814-16) and assured control over central India (1817-19).

Hastings, Henry, 3rd earl of Huntingdon (1535-95). Heir presumptive to the crown through his mother, who was descended from George, duke of Clarence, brother of Edward IV. A Puritan, he was given charge of Mary Queen of Scots (1569-70) and, as president of the north from 1572, reimposed order after the northern rebellion.

Hastings, John Hastings, 2nd Baron (1262-1313). Claimant to the Scottish throne in 1290 as grandson of Ada, third daughter of David, earl of Huntingdon (David I). Unsuccessful, he subsequently served Edward I on Irish,

Scottish, and Gascon campaigns and became his lieutenant in Aquitaine in 1302.

Hastings, Warren (1732-1818). Colonial administrator, who laid the foundations of British India. Arriving in India in 1750 as a clerk of the *East India Company, Hastings became a member of the Bengal Council (1761) and later, following a period in England (1764-68), of the Madras Council (1768). He became governor of Bengal in 1771 and the first governor general in 1774. He made many legal and administrative reforms, especially in the period 1771-74, upon which later British rulers built, while respecting Indian customs and culture. He achieved peace with the Maratha states (1782) and with Hyder Ali, ruler of Mysore (1784). However, he came into conflict with the crown-appointed council (see Regulating Act) and fought a duel with Sir Philip *Francis in 1779. Hastings was also censored for the hanging for forgery of Maharaja Nandakumar, who had made allegations of corruption against Hastings. He returned to England in 1785, amid accusations of partiality and high-handedness, and was impeached for corruption in 1788. The trial before the House of Lords, conducted by Burke, Fox, and Sheridan, continued for seven years and ended in 1795 with Hastings' acquittal.

Hatfield house. A country house in Hertfordshire, built in 1607-11 for Robert Cecil, 1st earl of Salisbury, and still the home of his descendants. It was constructed with bricks taken from the 15th-century Old Palace (built for Cardinal Morton), of which only the Great Hall remains and which was used by Henry VIII and Elizabeth I.

Hatton, Sir Christopher (1540-91). Lord chancellor (1587-91). A favourite of Elizabeth I, he first attracted her attention by his skilful dancing. He supported *Leicester in pursuit of a bold anti-Spanish foreign policy and played a leading part in the trials of Roman Catholic conspirators, including *Babington. He took part in the trial of Mary Queen of Scots (1586) and, as lord

chancellor, supported Archbishop Whitgift's opposition to Puritanism.

Hawke, Edward Hawke, 1st Baron (1705-81). Naval commander. Hawke commanded the home fleet (1748-52), the western fleet (1755-56), and then the Mediterranean fleet (1756). His successful blockade of Brest and subsequent victory at *Quiberon Bay (1759) helped frustrate French plans for an invasion of Britain. He served as first lord of the admiralty (1766-71) and in 1768 was promoted admiral of the fleet.

Hawkins (or Hawkyns), Sir John (1532-95). Seaman and slave-trader, who largely reconstructed the Elizabethan navy and helped to weaken Spain's maritime power on the eve of the attempted Spanish invasion. His third slave-trading voyage (1567-69), on which he was accompanied by *Drake, a relative, came into conflict with Spanish ships and exacerbated the ill feeling between Spain and England. Hawkins became treasurer (1577) and later comptroller of the navy, and as a rear admiral he was the navy's third in command against the Spanish *armada. He died on an expedition to raid the Spanish West Indies.

Hawkins (or Hawkyns), Sir Richard (1560-1622). Naval commander, the son of Sir John Hawkins. He participated in the defeat of the *armada (1588). In 1593 he set off to voyage round the world; he plundered Valparaiso but was captured by the Spanish at San Mateo Bay and imprisoned until ransomed in 1602.

Hawksmoor, Nicholas (1661-1736). Architect. He was employed by *Wren in 1679, assisting him at *St Paul's cathedral. He also worked with Vanbrugh at Blenheim palace and Castle Howard. On the death of Wren (1723) he became surveyor general of Westminster abbey, designing its west towers. His own original style of English baroque is evident in the churches he built in London, notably Christ Church, Spitalfields (1714-29).

Hawley-Shakell case (1378). A case arising from the escape from the Tower of two squires, Robert Hawley and John Shakell. They took *sanctuary in Westminster abbey, but Hawley was murdered by the constable of the Tower on the altar steps. In the outrage that followed John of Gaunt was, wrongly, implicated.

Haxey's case (1397). A case arising from the presentation by Thomas Haxey (d. 1425) of a parliamentary bill condemning royal extravagance. Richard II forced its withdrawal and a humble apology from the Commons, and Haxey was condemned to death as a traitor. The case marked the beginning of the royalist reaction against the lords *appellant.

Heads of the Proposals (1647). A list of demands formulated by senior officers of the New Model Army as a basis for compromise with Charles I at the end of the Civil War. The proposals included biennial parliaments, religious toleration, and parliamentary control of the armed forces together with the power to nominate ministers for a period of ten years. Despite their moderation, Charles made no response to the demands and subsequently concluded his *Engagement with the Scots to establish Presbyterianism in England in return for their support.

hearth tax. A tax levied at the rate of two shillings on every fire hearth from 1662 to 1689 (1690 in Scotland). It formed part of an attempt by the government to replace surviving feudal dues with a regular source of revenue. The tax's unpopularity led to its abandonment in favour of the *window tax.

Heath, Edward (1916-). Prime minister (1970-74). An MP from 1950, Heath held various ministerial and Cabinet posts (1951-64). He became leader of the Conservative Party and the opposition in July 1965. As prime minister he achieved Britain's entry into the EEC in 1973. He lost the Conservative leadership to Margaret Thatcher in Feb 1975.

Hebrides (or **Western Isles**, or **Isles**). A group of islands off the west coast of Scotland. Christianized in the second half of the 6th century, the Hebrides came under Viking control from the 8th century until 1266, when they were ceded by Norway to Scotland by the treaty of *Perth. They remained largely outside the rule of central government until the 17th century. *See also* Isles, lords of the).

Hedgeley Moor, battle of (25 April 1464). A battle of the Wars of the Roses, in which the Lancastrians were defeated by the Yorkist Lord Montagu after the return in 1463 of Margaret of Anjou to Scotland. This defeat and that shortly afterwards at Hexham destroyed Lancastrian resistance to Edward IV.

Heligoland (or **Helgoland**). A West German island near the mouth of the River Elbe. Ceded to Britain at the congress of Vienna (1814) as a North Sea naval base, Heligoland was transferred to Germany in 1890 in exchange for Zanzibar and other East African territories. It was a German naval base in World Wars I and II and, while under British control (1945-52), was used by the RAF for bombing exercises.

hell-fire clubs. Eighteenth-century clubs devoted to debauchery. The name is applied especially to the Hell-Fire Club led by Francis *Dashwood. Dashwood and his friends, who included John *Wilkes, gathered in the village of Medmenham, near West Wycombe in Buckinghamshire. In caves under the church (and allegedly in the church itself) and the nearby ruined Medmenham abbey, these so-called monks of Medmenham engaged, it was said, in orgies that included devil worship. The accusations have now been shown to be baseless.

Henderson, Arthur (1863-1935). Labour MP for most of the period 1903-35. As party secretary (1911-34) Henderson helped draft the *Labour Party constitution (1918). A member of the war cabinet (1916-17), he became home secretary in 1924 and was foreign secretary from 1929 to 1931. Briefly party leader in 1931, he won the Nobel peace prize in 1934 for his work for disarmament.

Hengist (d. ?488). Traditionally, leader, with his brother *Horsa, of the first Anglo-Saxon invasions of England. Hengist, probably a Jute, is said by Bede to have come to Britain at the invitation of *Vortigern in 449, to have revolted, and to have seized Kent. The Kentish kings, however, later claimed descent from Aesc (or Oisc), said to have been Hengist's son, and it is likely that he, not Hengist, established the Kentish kingdom. The names Hengist and Horsa mean "gelding" and "horse" respectively, and it has been suggested that the brothers were mythological figures associated with Germanic cults, in which horses played an important role.

Henrietta Anne, duchess of Orléans (1644-70). Youngest child of Charles I and Henrietta Maria. She married Philippe, duke of Orléans, in 1661 and helped to negotiate the secret treaty of *Dover (1670) between England and France. Shortly after her return to France she died suddenly, of peritonitis.

Henrietta Maria (1609-69). Queen consort of Charles I, mother of Charles II and James II, and daughter of Henry IV of France. Her staunch Roman Catholic beliefs made her unpopular in England. She supported Charles during the Civil War, raising funds for him in the Netherlands, but was finally obliged to flee to France (1644), where she lived for most of the rest of her life.

Henry I (1068-1135). King of England (1100-35). Youngest son of William the Conqueror and Matilda, he married twice: first (1100) to Matilda of Scotland (niece of Edgar Aetheling), by whom he had a son William and daughter Matilda, and second (1121) to Adelaide of Louvain. His presence at the death in the New Forest of his brother William II Rufus enabled him to seize the Treasury at Winchester while his elder brother Robert was still on crusade. Robert received Normandy in compensation but Henry invaded the duchy in 1105, conquering it and capturing his brother

at the battle of *Tinchebrai. He subsequently twice went to war with France (1111-13, 1116-20), emerging victorious from both confrontations, and twice invaded Wales (1114, 1121). Henry clashed with Archbishop *Anselm over lay investiture in 1100 but eventually arranged a compromise, enabling Anselm to return from the Continent in 1107.

Henry's reign is remarkable for the growth and rationalization of the royal administration and judicial systems. Of particular note is the work in developing the role of the Exchequer by his justiciar *Roger of Salisbury, one of a number of men of talent but lowly birth whom Henry raised to greatness to counterbalance the power of the barons. The Charter of Liberties (1100) promised to preserve the rights of the individual from arbitrary encroachment and the *Leges Henrici Primi* (Laws of Henry I) provide a comprehensive record of contemporary legal custom.

Henry's last years were dominated by the problem of the succession following the death in the *White Ship in 1120 of his only son Prince William. In 1127 the king exacted from the barons an oath of allegiance to his daughter Matilda, but his death was followed by the accession of his nephew *Stephen and a period of anarchy. Henry was buried in the church of the monastery founded by him at Reading.

Henry II (1133-89). King of England (1154-89), the first *Angevin king. He was the son of Matilda, daughter of Henry I, and of Geoffrey Plantagenet, Count of Anjou. His extensive continental inheritance, which included Normandy, Brittany, and Anjou, was substantially enhanced by his marriage (1152) to Eleanor of Aquitaine, and by the treaty of Winchester (1153) he was recognized as heir to the English king Stephen. Henry dealt effectively to end the anarchy of his predecessor's reign, razing illegally built baronial castles (*see* adulterine castles) and introducing, with the help of a team of able administrators, a number of remarkable legal reforms.

The Assize of *Clarendon (1166), which established the jury system, and the introduction of possessory *assizes and the *grand assize contributed greatly to the centralization of government and form a milestone in the development of the judicial system. Henry received the homage of Malcolm III of Scotland, who restored Northumberland, Westmorland, and Cumberland to England, subdued the Welsh, and obtained the submission of the Irish kings. However, his reign was darkened by the tragic events resulting from the appointment in 1162 of his chancellor Thomas *Becket as archbishop of Canterbury. Their dispute over the relative rights of church and state led to Becket's exile and subsequent murder at Canterbury, a crime of which Henry was absolved at the compromise of *Avranches (1172). His reign was further marred by the rebellions of his quarrelsome sons: in 1173-74 *Henry, the young king, Geoffrey, and Richard, with the support of disaffected barons and of Scotland, rebelled against their father; in 1189 he was defeated in battle by Richard in alliance with Philip II Augustus of France. Shortly afterwards he died at Tours.

Henry III (1207-72). King of England (1216-72). The son of King John and Isabella of Angoulême, he married Eleanor of Provence in 1236. They had three children, Edward (I), Edmund, and Beatrice. Nine years old at his accession, during the first *Barons' War, the leading figures in his minority were successively, William *Marshal, 1st earl of Pembroke (until his death in 1219) and Hubert de *Burgh. In 1227 he declared himself of age. His ineffectual government, financial mismanagement, and dependence upon foreign favourites (see Poitevins) provoked baronial opposition. The *Marshal rebellion (1233-34) forced him to dismiss Peter des *Roches and Peter des *Rivaux, but the Savoyard relations of his wife Eleanor of Provence (whom he married in 1236) aroused further anger. When Henry demanded an exorbitant sum to fulfil a promise to finance papal wars in Sicily in return for the Sicilian crown for his son Edmund the conflict came to a head. The barons issued the *Provisions of Oxford limiting the king's power, and Henry's renunciation of these led to the outbreak of the second Barons' War (1264). In May of that year the baronial leader Simon de *Montfort captured the king and his son Edward at the battle of *Lewes and ruled England until his death at *Evesham in Aug 1265. In the last years of his reign Henry played little part in government, which was largely in the hands of Edward.

Henry IV (1367-1413). King of England (1399-1413). Eldest surviving son of *John of Gaunt and Blanche of Lancaster, he was created earl of Derby in 1377 and duke of Hereford in 1397 but was known as Henry Bolingbroke (because he was born at Bolingbroke castle, Lincolnshire) until becoming king. He married Mary de Bohun in 1380 and Joan of Navarre in 1401. In 1386 he joined the lords *appellant in opposition to Richard II, but not until 1398 was the king able to banish Bolingbroke. When, in 1399, after the death of John of Gaunt, Richard seized his estates, Bolingbroke invaded England, landing at Ravenspur (July), and received Richard's surrender (Aug). In Sept Richard abdicated and the usurper became king. Henry's position was threatened by a series of revolts, notably the rebellion of Owain Glyndŵr in Wales (1400-09), which was joined by Henry *Percy, earl of Northumberland, and his son Hotspur. Hotspur was killed in battle in 1403, but in 1405 Northumberland, with Thomas Mowbray, duke of Norfolk, and Richard Scrope, archbishop of York, raised another rebellion. This Henry was able to foil, but the danger was not entirely over until 1408, when the crown defeated a third insurrection by Northumberland at *Bramham Moor. The threat of a French invasion now also receded, but Henry's last years were troubled by the ambitions of his son Prince Henry. In 1410 the prince, with the backing of the increasingly powerful

Beaufort faction, ousted the king's chancellor Thomas Arundel, archbishop of Canterbury. He was restored in 1412, but illness further eroded the king's strength and led to his early death.

Henry V (1387-1422). King of England (1413-22), son of Henry IV and Mary de Bohun. He was created prince of Wales in 1399 and spent many years fighting the Welsh, notably *Owain Glyndŵr. In 1415 he resumed the *Hundred Years' War against France, demanding the restoration of English domains in France and claiming the French throne. His first campaign led to the capture of *Harfleur and the great English victory at *Agincourt (1415). His alliance with Burgundy and with the emperor Sigismund greatly strengthened his hand in negotiating the treaty of *Troyes (1420), by which the French king Charles VI made Henry his heir and regent of France and betrothed him to his daughter Catherine of Valois. Henry died of dysentery two months before the death of Charles, leaving his infant son *Henry VI, as heir to his claims in France.

Henry VI (1421-71). King of England (1422-61, 1470-71). Only son of Henry V and Catherine of Valois, Henry succeeded to the throne while still an infant and a council of regency, headed by his uncles *John of Lancaster, and *Humphrey, duke of Gloucester, governed during his minority (1422-37). Henry was crowned at Westminster in 1429 and in Paris, as king of France (see Troyes, treaty of), in 1430. He had no military or administrative skills and suffered recurrent bouts of insanity, which encouraged the feuds between leading magnates that dominated his reign. The conflict between Gloucester and Henry *Beaufort, bishop of Winchester, gave way after their deaths (1447) to the power struggle between the king's chief minister Edmund *Beaufort, duke of Somerset, and *Richard, duke of York. In 1453-54, during a phase of Henry's mental illness, York obtained the protectorship, but after the king's recovery Beaufort was again in the ascendant. In 1455 the conflict between their two houses, Lancaster and York, erupted in the Wars of the *Roses, during which Henry was dominated by his wife *Margaret of Anjou, whom he married in 1445. After the Yorkist victories of 1461 the king was deposed by York's son Edward (IV) and fled to Scotland. Returning in 1464, he was captured in the following year and imprisoned. In Oct 1470, however, Warwick the kingmaker secured Henry's restoration (or readeption), which lasted until April 1471, when Edward returned to reclaim the throne. Henry was imprisoned in the Tower, where, after *Tewkesbury, he was murdered.

Henry VII (1457-1509). The first Tudor king of England (1485-1509), son of Edmund Tudor, earl of Richmond, and Margaret Beaufort. Born during the Wars of the Roses, he went into exile in Brittany after the collapse of the Lancastrian cause in 1471. In 1485 he invaded England, landing at Milford Haven in Wales, and defeated and killed Richard III at *Bosworth Field on 22 Aug. In Oct he was crowned and in Jan 1486 he married Elizabeth of York, thus uniting the houses of Lancaster and York. However, Yorkist plots, notably those of Lambert *Simnel and Perkin *Warbeck, continued to threaten his position for most of his reign. In 1489 Henry negotiated the treaty of *Medina del Campo with Spain, which arranged for the marriage of his elder son Arthur to Catherine of Aragon, and in 1496 and 1506 respectively, the *intercursus magnus and *intercursus malus with the Netherlands. He also established peace with Scotland (1499), subsequently (1503) marrying his daughter Margaret to James IV. Henry introduced few innovations in government but his shrewd and resolute rule restored order after the Wars of the Roses. His efficient, although sometimes unscrupulous, management of finances left a healthy surplus to his successor, his second son Henry VIII.

Henry VIII (1491-1547). King of England (1509-47) and Ireland (1540-47).

Second son of Henry VII and Elizabeth of York, he became heir to the throne on the death (1502) of his elder brother Arthur and, shortly after succeeding to the throne, married Arthur's widow *Catherine of Aragon. The first half of his reign was dominated by his desire for a glorious foreign policy. In 1512, in alliance with his father in law Ferdinand of Aragon, he went to war with France, capturing Tournai in the battle of the *Spurs, while a Scottish invasion was soundly defeated at *Flodden (1513). By 1515 Cardinal *Wolsey had come to the fore, determined to pursue Henry's aim to make England a power to be reckoned with in Europe. The diplomatic coup of the treaty of London (1518) was followed by Henry's meeting with Francis I of France at the splendid *field of the cloth of gold (1520). In the following year, however, the French alliance was abandoned for one with the emperor Charles V, and England embarked on a war that served none of its interests. Its expense provoked opposition in the country to Wolsey's financial demands, and by 1527 England was close to bankruptcy.

Henry, whose daughter Mary was born in 1516, was by now obsessed with his lack of an heir—a failure he blamed on his marriage to his brother's widow, a liaison prohibited by canon law and for which a papal dispensation had been necesssary. After falling in love with *Anne Boleyn he sought an annulment of his marriage to Catherine from Pope Clement VII. The pope, however, was the virtual prisoner of Catherine's nephew, the emperor Charles, and, following a hearing of the case before a legatine court presided over by Cardinals Wolsey and Campeggio, was constrained to refuse Henry's request (1529). In the same year Wolsey fell from power, to be replaced by Sir Thomas *More. The "king's great matter" remained in stalemate until the rise of Thomas *Cromwell, who was responsible for a spate of legislation (1532-36) that brought about the break with Rome and the elevation of Henry to the supreme headship of the English church (see

Reformation). By Jan 1533 Henry was free to marry Anne, and later in the year she gave birth to the future queen Elizabeth. An heir was still denied him, and in 1536 Anne was executed. By her successor as queen, *Jane Seymour, the king at last had a son, Edward (1537). Jane died in childbirth, and Henry did not remarry until 1540, when Cromwell, pursuing alliance with German Protestant rulers, arranged a union with *Anne of Cleves. The king found her uncongenial and blamed Cromwell, who went to the block for treason. In the same year Henry married *Catherine Howard, whose unfaithfulness brought about her execution in 1542. Finally, he married *Catherine Parr.

In his last years he turned once more to war with France. Boulogne was captured and the Scots were defeated at *Solway Moss (1542), but the enterprise placed the government of his successor Edward VI in severe financial straits.

Henry, the young king (1155-83). Son of Henry II. He was crowned (1170) in his father's lifetime. In 1173 he joined the baronial rebellion against the king but made his peace in 1174. In 1183 he and his brother Geoffrey led a rebellion in Aquitaine against their brother Richard (I).

Henry of Almaine (or of Cornwall) (1235-71). Son of *Richard, earl of Cornwall. He played an ambivalent role in the second *Barons' War and acted as arbiter of the dictum of *Kenilworth. In 1268 he took the cross and was murdered by Guy and Simon (the younger) de *Montfort, while attending Mass in a church at Viterbo.

Henry of Blois (d. 1171). Half-brother of King *Stephen. He became abbot of Glastonbury in 1126 and bishop of Winchester in 1129. He played a crucial role during his brother's reign, mediating between Stephen and the empress Matilda.

Henry of Huntingdon (?1084-1155). Chronicler and archdeacon of Huntingdon. He wrote the *Historia Anglorum* (from the Roman invasions until 1154).

Henry of Lancaster, 1st duke of Lancaster (?1299-1361). Soldier, nephew of Thomas of Lancaster. Henry fought with distinction in the first stages of the Hundred Years' War. Also a close adviser of Edward III, he was employed by the king in diplomatic missions, helping, notably, to negotiate the treaty of *Brétigny (1360). His daughter Blanche married *John of Gaunt.

Hepplewhite, George (d. 1786). Furniture designer, whose work, influenced by the *Adam brothers, was more delicate and classical than that of his contemporary *Chippendale. Hepplewhite's style book, *The Cabinet-Maker and Upholsterer's Guide*, was published in 1788-89.

Heptarchy. The seven English kingdoms that existed from the 6th to 9th centuries: *Northumbria, *East Anglia, *Essex, *Mercia, *Wessex, *Sussex, and *Kent. The most powerful king of the seven was entitled *bretwalda and acknowledged by the others as overlord.

Herbert, Arthur, earl of Torrington (1647-1716). Naval commander. Herbert served in the Dutch Wars in 1666 and against Mediterranean corsairs (1669-71, 1678-83) and commanded the fleet that conveyed William of Orange to England in 1688. First lord of the admiralty (1689-90), he was court-martialled (1690) for caution in engaging a French Channel fleet at the battle of *Beachy Head. Although acquitted, he never again held command.

Herbert, William, 1st earl of Pembroke (d. 1469). A scion of Raglan, Gwent, who actively supported the Yorkists in the Wars of the Roses. He gained lands and offices and, after 1461, became Edward IV's chief counsellor. After leading a successful siege of *Harlech castle (1468) he was made earl of Pembroke. He was highly esteemed by the Welsh bards, who regarded his execution by the Lancastrians in 1469 as a national catastrophe.

Herbert, William, 3rd earl of Pembroke (1580-1630). Poet. Patron of Ben Jonson and Inigo Jones, he was lord chamberlain (1615-25). The first folio of Shakespeare's works was dedicated (1623) to Pembroke and his brother Philip. In 1617 he became chancellor of Oxford University, and Pembroke College was named after him.

heregeld. *See* Danegeld.

Hereward the Wake (11th century). Leader (1070-71) of a revolt against William the Conqueror. Possibly a tenant of the abbey of Peterborough, Hereward and his followers sacked the abbey, perhaps in protest against the appointment of a Norman abbot. He fled to the Isle of Ely, and a band of other refugees, including *Morcar, gathered round him. In 1071 King William besieged the Isle, but Hereward escaped. His later life is obscure, but he may have been reconciled to William. He became the subject of many legends and is the hero of Charles Kingsley's last completed novel, *Hereward the Wake* (1866).

heriot. A death duty paid by villeins to the manorial lord. The heirs of a deceased villein who had no war-gear (heregeatu) to return to the lord were obliged to give his best beast. Heriots were the equivalent of the *reliefs paid by free men.

Herrings, battle of the (12 Feb 1429). A battle of the Hundred Years' War. An English convoy, protecting salt-herring provisions for the English army besieging Orléans, was surprised at Rouvray by French and Scottish forces. The English, under Sir John Fastolf, entrenched and repulsed their attackers.

Hertford, synod of (673). A general council of the English church. Summoned by *Theodore of Tarsus, it regulated monastic and episcopal discipline, created the basis for a central ecclesiastical administration, and forbade divorce, except for adultery, and the remarriage of a divorced man.

Hervey, John Hervey, Baron (1696-1743). Politician and pamphleteer. A Whig MP (1725-33), he was lord privy seal (1740-42). He is best remembered, however, as a court wit, whose *Memoirs of the Reign of George the Second* (published 1848) are a revealing portrait of early-18th-century political life. He acquired notoriety as Sporus in Pope's "Epistle to Dr Arbuthnot".

Hesilrige (or Haselrig), Sir Arthur (d. 1661). Parliamentarian. He took a prominent part in the impeachment of Charles I's minister Strafford (1641) and was one of the *five members whom the king attempted to arrest in 1642. He fought throughout the Civil War and was a leading *Independent. Following the dismissal of the Long Parliament (1653) he became an opponent of Oliver Cromwell and withheld support from Richard Cromwell in 1658. He backed Monck in his opposition to the dissolution of parliament but not the restoration of Charles II. Arrested, he died in the Tower.

Hexham, battle of (15 May 1464). A battle of the Wars of the Roses, resulting in a victory for a Yorkist force under Lord Montagu (d. 1471). The Lancastrian army of Henry Beaufort, 3rd duke of Somerset, was caught in camp near Hexham in Northumberland and obliged to surrender. Somerset himself was immediately executed.

Hicks Beach, Michael, 1st Earl St Aldwyn (1837–1916). Conservative MP from 1864 to 1906, when he was created a viscount (earl, 1915). Nicknamed Black Michael, he first entered the cabinet in 1876 and served in all Conservative cabinets until 1902, notably as chancellor of the exchequer (1885–86, 1895–1902).

hidage. An assessment of tax and military service due from each *shire, based on the number of *hides in the shire. The 10th-century *Burghal Hidage* lists the hides in southern *burhs and stipulates that each hide must supply one man to defend his burh. The *Tribal Hidage* is an 8th-century document, which assesses the taxable capacity of Mercia and its client states.

hide. An Anglo-Saxon unit of land of a size considered sufficient to support a peasant and his household. A hide is thought to have been abut 120 acres in the eastern shires (where it came to be called a *ploughland) but as little as 40 acres in Wessex. Hides are the basic units of assessment for taxation and military service.

High Church. The party within the Church of England that emphasized church authority, ritualistic worship, the sacraments, and the continuity of the Church with Catholicism. Leading Elizabethan High Churchmen, such as Richard *Hooker, were opponents of the *Puritans. Their successors, such as Archbishop *Laud, identified closely with the Stuart monarchs. After the *Glorious Revolution most High Churchmen became *nonjurors, and the party declined. The *Oxford movement resurrected High Church beliefs in *Anglo-Catholicism. *Compare* Latitudinarians.

High Commission, Court of. An ecclesiastical court developed after Henry VIII became head of the English church in 1534. The court, which had the power to inquire into offences against the Act of *Supremacy and Act of *Uniformity, attracted opposition from Puritans and lawyers by its arbitrary procedures (*see* prohibition, writ of). It was used by the early Stuarts to enforce the prerogative in nonspiritual matters, an abuse that led the Long Parliament to abolish it in 1641.

high commissioner. The diplomatic representative of one *Commonwealth country in another, equivalent to an ambassador to any other foreign country.

Highland Host (1678). A force quartered for some weeks in parts of southwest Scotland to suppress the *covenanters. Many who had little sympathy with the covenanters objected to this use of Highlanders against Lowland Protestants, but about a third of the Host in fact consisted of Lowlanders.

Highlands of Scotland. Geographically, all Scotland north of a geological fault running from the Clyde Estuary in the west to Stonehaven in the east. Historians, however, generally exclude the eastern coastal plains and the northern isles (Orkneys and Shetlands) from the Highlands, which they thus confine to the area that remained Gaelic in language and culture until the 19th century. Under the *clans much of the Highlands (especially the west and the Hebrides) remained outside the effective control of central government until the 18th century.

Hild (or **Hilda**) (614-80). Abbess of Whitby from 657. Grandniece of Edwin, king of Northumbria, she was baptized in 627. She displayed a remarkable talent for organization and in 649 became superior of a nunnery near Hartlepool. She founded a community at Whitby in 657 and at the synod held there in 664 defended Celtic practices in the Anglo-Saxon church (see Whitby, synod of).

Hill, Octavia (1838-1912). Housing reformer. With help from friends, notably John Ruskin, in 1865 she began to acquire dilapidated houses in London for rehabilitation and letting to the poor. Her work expanded until ultimately she was managing some 6000 dwellings. She was also cofounder of the *National Trust.

Hill, Sir Rowland (1795-1879). Inventor of the postage stamp and the *penny post. Originally a schoolmaster, in 1837 Hill proposed a uniform postal system in which mail was prepaid by adhesive stamps (rather than payment by the addressee on receipt). Overcoming official opposition, he secured the adoption of his scheme in 1840. After being dismissed (1842) from the post office by the new Conservative government Hill became chairman of a railway company. He returned to the post office in 1846 and was its secretary from 1854 to 1864.

Hilliard, Nicholas (c. 1547-1619). Portrait miniaturist. The first English painter of international stature, Hilliard painted many exquisite portraits of Elizabeth I and her court. He also wrote a treatise on his genre called *The Art of Limning*.

Hingston Down, battle of (838). A battle in the Tamar valley in Cornwall, in which Egbert, king of Wessex, defeated the Britons and their Danish allies. After his victory Egbert annexed Cornwall to Wessex.

Hoare, Sir Samuel, Viscount Templewood (1880-1959). Conservative MP (1910-44; viscount, 1944). Hoare was secretary for India (1931-35) and foreign secretary (1935), resigning following criticism of the *Hoare-Laval pact. In office again from 1936 to 1940 (home secretary, 1937-40), he supported *appeasement. He was then ambassador to Spain (1940-44). An advocate of penal reform, he wrote *The Shadow of the Gallows* (1951).

Hoare-Laval pact (Dec 1935). A proposal for ending the Italian-Ethiopian war, submitted by *Hoare, the British foreign secretary, and Pierre Laval (1883-1945), the French premier. Italy invaded Ethiopia in Oct 1935 and the League of Nations, ordering sanctions against Italy, invited Britain and France to draft settlement proposals. Hoare and Laval, judging no state would go to war over Ethiopia, proposed that Italy be permitted to annex Ethiopian territory. Facing uproar in Britain, however, the cabinet repudiated the plan. Hoare resigned.

Hobbes, Thomas (1588-1679). Political theorist. He spent much of the period 1610-37 abroad, meeting Galileo, Descartes, and Gassendi. In the *Leviathan* (1651), written in exile during the Civil War period, he argued that human beings, because they are inherently selfish, require an absolute ruler to whom complete obedience must be given. This belief enabled him to accept the government of the Interregnum—as that of the established authority—after he returned to England in 1651.

Hobhouse, John Cam, Baron Broughton de Gyffard (1786-1869). Radical politician, writer, and friend of Byron. Hobhouse, an MP for most of the period 1820-51, served in Melbourne's cabinet (1835-41) as president of the India Board, holding the same office under

Russell (1846-52). He invented the term "His Majesty's Opposition", with its implication that the party out of office remained loyal to the crown.

Hobson, Jack Atkinson (1858-1940). Economist. He argued that unemployment was caused mainly by excessive savings and that the resulting domestic underconsumption motivated imperial expansion to find compensating markets. He advocated sharply graduated taxation, more social services, and the nationalization of monopolies.

Hogarth, William (1697-1764). Painter and engraver, best known for his series *A Rake's Progress* (1735) and *Marriage à la Mode* (1745), satirizing the follies of his age. His *Gin Lane*, an exposure of the social evil of *gin drinking, was one of numerous engravings the technical virtuosity of which ensured a large public for his work. Hogarth was also a notable portrait painter. He campaigned successfully for copyright legislation for designers' works, embodied in the so-called Hogarth's Acts (Engraving Copyright Acts 1734, 1766).

Holbein the younger, Hans (?1498-1543). German painter. One of the greatest portraitists northern Europe has produced, Holbein was well known long before he began living in London in the 1530s. He painted many members of Henry VIII's court and some of these, especially his *Thomas More* (1526) and *Anne of Cleves* (c. 1539), together with his earlier portraits of Erasmus, are among his masterpieces.

Holinshed, Raphael (c. 1520-c. 1580). Chronicler. He continued the printer Reginald Wolfe's (d. 1573) universal history, publishing it as the *Chronicles of England, Scotland, and Ireland* (1577). A second enlarged edition provided material for Elizabethan dramatists, notably Shakespeare.

Holland, Henry Richard Fox, 3rd Baron (1773-1840). Politician and writer, whose London home, Holland House, was notable as a centre of Whig society. Holland (Henry *Fox's grandson and Charles James *Fox's nephew) served in

the Ministry of *All the Talents (1806-07) and as chancellor of the duchy of Lancaster in the cabinets of Grey (1830-34) and Melbourne (1835-40). His writings include *Memoirs of the Whig Party* (1852).

Holles, Denzil Holles, 1st Baron (1599-1680). One of the *five members of the Long Parliament whom Charles I attempted to arrest in 1642. He fought at Edgehill and Brentford for the parliamentarians but, advocating peace with the king, he broke with Cromwell and fled to France. Following the Restoration he was made a peer (1661).

Holme, battle of the (902). A battle, fought probably in East Anglia, between the forces of *Edward the Elder and an alliance of Edward's rebellious kinsman Aethelwold and the Danish army of Northumbria. The latter, although victorious, lost their king and Aethelwold. The battle demonstrates the confused state of contemporary Anglo-Danish relations.

Holy Island. *See* Lindisfarne.

Holyroodhouse. A palace in Edinburgh the building of which was begun (c. 1498-1501) by James IV of Scots in the outer courtyard of Holyrood abbey, where Scottish kings had often stayed. It was completely rebuilt in the years after 1671, only the tower house of the earlier building being retained.

homage. 1. The act of submission made by a feudal tenant to his lord. Kneeling, the tenant gave his joined hands to be clasped by his lord, whom he undertook to serve. *See also* fealty. **2.** The tenants of a manor who assembled in the *court baron.

Home Guard. An unpaid part-time defence force, originally of volunteers, formed in 1940 under the threat of German invasion. Composed of civilians exempt from military service because of their age or occupation, the Home Guard by 1943 numbered some two million fully armed men. Its duties included the manning of anti-aircraft batteries. Disbanded at the end of the war, volunteers were again recruited from 1951 to 1957.

Home Office. A government department with responsibility for those domestic affairs not specifically assigned to other departments. The Home Office originated in 1782 with the reallocation of duties between the offices of the two secretaries of state—the Southern and Northern Departments—on the basis of home and foreign affairs respectively (compare Foreign and Commonwealth Office). The responsibilities of the Home Office, headed by the secretary of state for home affairs (the home secretary), now include responsibility for public order, ensuring the efficiency of police forces (with direct responsibility for the Metropolitan Police) and fire services, prisons and treatment of offenders, civil defence, community relations, broadcasting, immigration, naturalization, and the conduct of elections. The home secretary is also the official channel of communication between monarch and subjects and between Britain and the government of the Channel Islands and the Isle of Man.

Home of the Hirsel, Alexander (or Alec) Frederick Douglas-Home, Baron (1903–). Prime minister (1963–64). A Conservative MP (1931–45, 1950–51, 1963–74), as earl of Home he was commonwealth secretary, (1955–60) and foreign secretary (1960–63). Renouncing his earldom, he became, as Sir Alec Douglas-Home, prime minister (in succession to Macmillan) in Oct 1963 but lost the general election of Oct. 1964. He was leader of the opposition until July 1965, when *Heath succeeded him, and served as foreign secretary (1970–74). He received a life peerage in 1974.

home rule. The movement to repeal the Act of Union (1801) between Britain and Ireland and give the latter a parliament responsible for domestic affairs. In 1870 the Home Government (from 1873 Home Rule) Association was formed, and in 1874 some 59 Irish MPs committed to the cause were returned to Westminster under the leadership of Isaac *Butt. In the 1886 election the Irish party at Westminster, led now by *Parnell, held the balance of power between the Conservatives and Liberals and with Gladstone's conversion to home rule supported the Liberals; but Gladstone's bill was defeated by the defection of the Liberal Unionists. Gladstone returned to power in 1892, and a second home rule bill passed the Commons but was defeated in the Lords (1893). In 1910 the Irish party once again held the balance of power and supported the Liberals in return for a promise of home rule. The bill passed the Commons in 1912 and, since bills could now only be delayed for two years by the Lords, went onto the statute book in 1914, to be suspended for the duration of the war. A modified bill was passed in 1920 (the Government of Ireland Act), providing separate parliaments for northern and southern Ireland (see Ireland under British rule).

Homildon Hill, battle of (14 Sept 1402). A battle fought between the English and the Scots in Northumberland. Sir Henry Percy (Hotspur) defeated the Scots, who were raiding the north, and captured 80 Scottish nobles, including their leader, the 4th earl of Douglas.

Hong Kong. A British crown colony on the coast of south China. The colony consists of Hong Kong Island (ceded by China in the treaty of *Nanking in 1842), the Kowloon Peninsula (ceded in 1860), and the New Territories (held on a 99-year lease granted by China in 1898). It was occupied by the Japanese (1941–45) during World War II. Hong Kong will be returned to China in 1997.

Honorius (d. 653). Archbishop of Canterbury, consecrated by Paulinus at Lincoln in 627. He was a pupil of Pope Gregory the Great. He oversaw a rapid expansion of Christianity in England.

honour. The sum of lands held by a tenant in chief. The honour originated as a centre of military command in the period of the Norman conquest, but within a century often encompassed estates scattered throughout the kingdom. The honourial court was held at the "head" of the honour, which was usually its largest castle.

Hood, Samuel Hood, 1st Viscount (1724-1816). Naval commander. Hood held command in North America (1767-70) and, during the American Revolution, commanded the rear at the battles of Chesapeake (1782) and Dominica (1782). He served as a lord of the admiralty (1788-93) and was commander in chief in the Mediterranean (1793-94), during the French Revolutionary War, in which he occupied Toulon (1793) and Corsica (1794).

Hooke, Robert (1635-1703). Physicist with wide scientific interests. He became professor of geometry at Gresham College in 1665 and surveyor of London in 1667, designing *Bedlam, among other buildings. A gifted instrument maker, he invented the balance spring used in watches. His study of elasticity led to his formulation of Hooke's law, described in the *Micrographia* (1665).

Hooker, Richard (c. 1554-1600). Theologian. His *Treatise on the Laws of Ecclesiastical Polity*, written at the end of his life, was an apology for Anglicanism, defending episcopacy and the Elizabethan settlement. It attacked the Puritans' literal interpretation of the Bible and expressed the idea of a fundamental natural law, stemming from God, in the light of which all human and religious laws should be made. Hooker's emphasis on reason influenced theories of civil as well as ecclesiastical government.

Hopton, Ralph Hopton, Baron (1596-1652). Royalist commander. His Puritan background led him to support parliament against Charles I, but he shifted his allegiance to the royalists in 1642, when parliament took control of the *militia. As lieutenant general of western England Hopton led a number of royalist victories in the southwest, notably at Stratton (May 1643) and Lansdown (July 1643), where he was badly wounded. In 1646 he was forced to surrender to Gen. Fairfax at Torrington and retired into exile.

Horsa (d. 455). Anglo-Saxon leader, said by Bede to have come to Britain with his brother *Hengist and to have been killed in battle at Aegelsthrep (perhaps Aylesford in Kent).

Hospitallers. A military order of knighthood, called in full the Knights of the Order of the Hospital of St John of Jerusalem. Originating in the 11th century, it offered military protection and hospital care to Christian pilgrims in Jerusalem during the *crusades. The English houses of the order date from the mid-12th century and the head house was the priory of Clerkenwell. The Hospitallers' headquarters moved to Cyprus after the fall of Acre (1291) and subsequently to Rhodes and then Malta; they are now in Rome. They were rivals of the *Templars.

Hotspur. *See* Percy, Sir Henry.

housecarle. A member of the highly trained military bodyguard kept by the Danish kings of England from 1016. They were part of the royal household and were paid out of the heregeld (*see* Danegeld).

House of Commons. The lower chamber of *parliament, representing the "communities", or counties and towns (*compare* House of Lords). Its origin lay in the requirement that taxation must be consented to by those who have to pay it. The summoning of nonbaronial representatives to parliament occurred in 1213, 1254, and 1258, when shire representatives attended, and in 1265 Simon de *Montfort's parliament included borough representatives. By the end of the 14th century taxation was being granted "by the Commons, with the advice and consent of the Lords". Nevertheless, for most of the middle ages the Commons were an adjunct to parliament rather than a part of it. They met separately and were represented in the parliament chamber by their speaker, elected from 1376 but often the servant of the crown rather than of the Commons until the 17th century. It was only in 1547 that the Commons acquired a permanent meeting place—the secularized chapel of St Stephen in Westminster. During the 16th century the House increased in importance, but it was far from winning the initiative or even from representing opposition to the crown. Its influence was limited both by the Lords and by court faction. Free speech, regular parliaments, and control over taxation were not achieved until the Glorious Revolution (1688-89), and even then the Lords remained the more important forum for political debate. *Patronage gave the crown and the peers extensive influence over the membership of the Commons until the end of the 18th century. Even after the first *Reform Act (1832) the membership of the Commons was still overwhelmingly aristocratic, and *cabinets often contained more peers than commoners. Important themes in the history of the Commons in the 19th century were the importance of the Irish members, consequent on the Act of Union (1801) and Roman *Catholic emancipation (1829), and the widening of the electoral *franchise. In the long run these resulted in a decline in the power of the crown in its choice of ministers and of the Lords to delay or obstruct legislation. At the same time, however, the development of party political organizations and party discipline has reduced the independence of individual members of the Commons. Thus, although parliamentary control increasingly means control of the Commons, a party winning a general election with a very small majority has a reasonable expectation of passing even controversial legislation and of surviving for its full term of office.

The House of Commons has always been larger than the Lords, containing the lesser clergy until the development in the 15th century of the Lower House of Convocation, two representatives from each county, and, by Henry VII's reign, 300 burgesses representing the towns. The number of members of parliament (MPs) has tended to become larger: in 1800, after union with Ireland, there were 658 MPs, and in 1885, following the Reform Act (1884) the number rose to 670. In 1918 it rose again to 707 but, after the creation of the Irish Free State (1920), fell to 615. Since 1949 boundaries of constituencies have been

determined by the principle that each should contain approximately 65 000 voters, and since 1983 there have been 650 MPs.

House of Lords. The upper or second chamber of *parliament (compare House of Commons). The phrase was not used before the 16th century, partly because a parliament meant primarily the king and the lords together and partly because it was not until the 16th century that the non-noble members of what was originally a special session of the *curia regis were excluded. The king was always present until the reign of Henry VI, and the royal throne was the salient feature of the parliament chamber. The king summoned whom he wished to give him advice, and the *peerage (the lords temporal), which had developed by the reign of Edward I, carried no automatic right of summons. From the *Model Parliament (1295) all the bishops (the lords spiritual) were summoned. At first a large number of abbots were also summoned, but this was reduced to only 27 after the reign of Edward III. The number of lay lords varied from 49 (1295) to 73 (1453) but had shrunk to 36 by Henry VII's reign because of the effects of the Wars of the Roses on the noble population. By the beginning of the Tudor period the non-noble judges and household officers had either ceased to attend or played no effective part in the deliberations of the House. The House was abolished together with the monarchy in 1649, and when restored it embodied a changed view of the peerage —the result of the abolition during the Civil War of feudal tenures. Peerages now became the reward for political service, and there was a steady increase in the size of the House. By the end of the 17th century there was a membership of 220. The 1719 peerage bill attempted to limit the creation of new peers, in order to maintain a permanent Whig majority, but was defeated in the Commons. A further large increase came at the end of the 18th century. The Union with Scotland (1707) added 16 peers and the Union with Ireland (1801) added 28.

The first real clash between the two Houses came over the reform bill of 1831, which the Tory Lords violently opposed and was only passed under threat of the creation of enough new peers to ensure the bill's passage. There were other clashes, for example over the *Municipal Corporations Act (1835) and later over *home rule for Ireland. Conflict over the legislative programme of the Liberal government of 1906, which occasioned Lloyd George's famous description of the House of Lords as "Mr Balfour's poodle", came to a head with the Lords' rejection of the finance bill (1909). Again under threat of the creation of new peers the *Parliament Act (1911) was passed, which removed the Lords' veto on money bills and left only a delaying power on most other legislation. The Parliament Act (1949) reduced the period of delay.

Howard. See Norfolk, dukes of.

Howard, Charles, 1st earl of Carlisle (1629-85). Convert to Protestantism, who fought for the parliamentarians at the battle of *Worcester (1651) and later became a member of Cromwell's Council of State (1653). He commanded against the Scots (1654) and led Cromwell's bodyguard, before being appointed lord lieutenant of Cumberland and Westmorland (1660). Created earl of Carlisle (1661), he served under Charles II as ambassador to Russia, Sweden, and Denmark (1663-64) and later as governor of Jamaica (1677-81).

Howard, Charles, 1st earl of Nottingham and 2nd Baron Howard of Effingham (1536-1624). Naval commander. He served as ambassador to France (1559) and later as lord chamberlain (1574-85). As lord high admiral (1585-1618) he commanded the English naval forces against the Spanish *armada (1588) and himself led the centre during the engagement. He later fought alongside the earl of Essex at Cádiz (1596). Howard also served as commissioner at the trials of Mary Queen of Scots (1586),

Essex (1601), and the conspirators in the gunpowder plot (1606).

Howard, Ebenezer (1850-1928). Pioneer town planner, who, rejecting the suburban expansion of existing towns, proposed garden cities—new communities within green belts. He put his ideas into effect at Letchworth from 1903 and Welwyn from 1919.

Howard, Henry, 1st earl of Northampton (1540-1614). Second son of Henry Howard, earl of *Surrey. A Roman Catholic, Howard antagonized Elizabeth I by his association with Mary Queen of Scots and was imprisoned (1583). Following the accession of James I he was created earl of Northampton (1604), lord privy seal (1608), and the trial of Raleigh (1603) and Guy Fawkes (1605). He erected a monument at Westminster to Mary Queen of Scots.

Howard, John (1726-90). Prison reformer. As high sheriff of Bedfordshire (1773), Howard found appalling conditions in the gaols and was especially shocked by the inhumanity of gaolers whose living depended on fees extorted from prisoners. For the rest of his life Howard campaigned against such evils. He made extensive tours of English prisons, producing reports, as well as visiting the Continent. He died of gaol fever in Russia.

Howard, Thomas, 1st earl of Suffolk and 1st Baron Howard de Walden (1561-1626). Son of Thomas Howard, 4th duke of *Norfolk. He fought against the armada (1588) and took part in the expedition to Cádiz (1596), being created Baron Howard de Walden. Under James I he was lord chamberlain (1603-14) and lord high treasurer (1614-18). In 1619 he was fined £7,000 and imprisoned for ten days for embezzlement, but was subsequently restored to royal favour.

Howard, William, 1st Baron Howard of Effingham (?1510-1573). Lord high admiral. After several diplomatic missions to Scotland and France he was found guilty (1541) of concealing the treason of his niece *Catherine Howard but was later pardoned. He was subsequently lord high admiral (1554-73) and was raised to the peerage for leading the defence of London against *Wyatt's rebellion.

Howe, Richard Howe, 4th Viscount and Earl (1726-99). Naval commander, brother of William *Howe. Howe commanded in the first naval action of the Seven Years' War in 1755, fought at the battle of Quiberon Bay in 1759, and served as a lord of the admiralty (1762-65). In 1782 he relieved Gibraltar and was first lord of the admiralty from 1783 to 1788, when he was created Earl Howe. In 1794 he won his greatest victory—that of the *Glorious First of June—against the French in the English Channel.

Howe, William Howe, 5th Viscount (1729-1814). Soldier, brother of Richard *Howe. He fought with distinction in North America during the *Seven Years' War and returned to the Continent at the outbreak of the American Revolution. Victorious at Bunker Hill (1775), he became commander in chief in the following year. He was victorious at Brandywine and Germantown (1776) but resigned after Burgoyne's defeat at Saratoga (1778).

Howel Dda. See Hywel Dda.

Hubert Walter (d. 1205). Archbishop of Canterbury from 1193, who was also justiciar (1193-98) under Richard I and chancellor (1199-1205) under King John. He accompanied Richard on the third crusade and on his return (1193) raised the king's ransom by means of the first tax for secular purposes. Hubert was virtual ruler of England after Richard's final departure for the Continent (1194), introducing financial and judicial reforms. He became papal legate in 1195. His influence continued under King John, whose accession Hubert helped to secure.

Hudson, Henry (d. 1611). Navigator. On his first two voyages (1607, 1608) he tried in vain to find a northeast passage to China. In 1609 he set out on a third expedition, in search of the northwest passage, and sailed 240 km (150 mi) up the Hudson river. On his fourth and last voyage he discovered Hudson Bay (1610) and spent the winter there. In the following spring his crew mutinied and abandoned Hudson and eight other members of his crew in a small boat, in which they died.

Hudson's Bay Company. A company, incorporated in 1670, that had exclusive rights over all territory draining into Hudson's Bay, named Rupert's Land in honour of the company's first governor, Prince Rupert. It engaged chiefly in the fur trade. It was not able to compete effectively against the French until the British conquest of Canada in the Seven Years' War (1756-63). Subsequent rivalry with the Northwest Company broke into violence, ended only by the enforced amalgamation of the two companies, in 1821, under the name of the Hudson's Bay Company. It lost its monopoly in 1859.

hue and cry. The general alarm that a witness to a crime was duty bound to raise in order that its supposed perpetrator might be apprehended. Failure to raise or to participate in the hue and cry was a punishable offence in a statute of 1275, and the custom survives in the obligation to assist the police in apprehending a suspected criminal.

Huggins, Godfrey, 1st Viscount Malvern of Rhodesia (1883-1971). Prime minister of Southern Rhodesia (1933-53) and of the *Central African Federation (1953-56). A doctor, Huggins was elected (1923) to the Legislative Council of Southern Rhodesia and in 1933 became prime minister. A staunch advocate of the Federation, he later became its first prime minister.

Hull, Kingston upon. A port on Humberside. The port was given its first charter in 1299. From the 14th century, when the English cloth trade began to flourish, Hull was an important mercantile centre. In 1642 Charles I was denied entry to Hull, the first resistance to the king in the Civil War, during which the city was twice besieged.

Humble Petition and Advice (25 May 1657). A constitutional proposal, framed by the second parliament of the Protectorate in reaction against the *major generals. Cromwell rejected the title of king urged upon him in its first clause but approved other changes: he was given the right to nominate his successor and an "Other House" comprising between 40 and 70 members; in addition, the powers of the Council of State were curbed.

Hume, David (1711-76). One of the most influential philosophers of his age, noted for his rigorous empiricism. Hume combined religious scepticism with Toryism, both of which probably contributed to his failure to gain any academic post in his native Scotland. His greatest work was perhaps his first, the *Treatise of Human Nature* (1738-40), although he revised and extended his ideas in subsequent works. In his lifetime, however, his fame rested on his *History of England* (1754-62).

Hume, Joseph (1777-1855). Radical politician. A Scot, Hume was an MP from 1812 to 1855, initially a Tory and from 1818 a radical. With *Place, he was instrumental in repealing the *Combination Acts (1824) but, in common with some other radicals, was bitterly opposed to factory legislation limiting working hours in factories. He was devoted to prudent public spending —retrenchment, which, after peace and reform, became the third slogan of radicalism.

Humphrey, duke of Gloucester (1391-1447). Youngest son of Henry IV, known as the Good Duke Humphrey because of his patronage of learning. He was named as protector by Henry's will but in the council of regency during Henry VI's minority (1422-37) was subordinate to his brother *John of Lancaster, except during John's absences in France. Over the next two decades Gloucester was involved in a feud with his uncle Henry *Beaufort, bishop of Winchester, clashing particularly over policies towards France. Gloucester's influence came to an abrupt end in 1447, when he was accused of treason. He died before his trial.

hundred. From Anglo-Saxon times to the 19th century, a unit of local government common south of the river Tees. A subdivision of the shire, it corresponded to the *wapentakes of the Danelaw. Varying in size from area to area, hundreds may have originated from the grouping of a hundred *hides; they emerged as administrative units in the 10th century. Hundred courts, which met every four weeks, had jurisdiction in cases relating to local issues and apportioned taxes. The term survives today in the *Chiltern Hundreds.

Hundred Years' War (1337-1453). A prolonged but intermittent conflict between England and France. The causes of the war lay in the dispute over the territorial limits and extent of English sovereignty in the English domains in France; France's concern at the strength of English commercial influence in Flanders, and French support of Scotland's struggle for independence; and the claim of English monarchs, through the mother of Edward III—Isabel of France—to the French crown.

War broke out when Philip VI of France confiscated Gascony from Edward III. Edward retaliated by supporting Flemish rebels against Count Louis, a French ally, and by invading northern France. At the same time he renewed his claim to the French throne. The English naval success at *Sluys (1340) was followed by the great victory of *Crécy (1346), and Edward went on to take Calais (1347). A seven-year truce followed. The second phase of the war (1355-1396) began with English raids in northern France, Languedoc, and Normandy. Edward, the Black Prince, won a decisive victory at Poitiers (1356), but Edward III failed to follow up this advantage. In 1360 he agreed to the treaty of *Brétigny, by which he gained Calais, Ponthieu, and an enlarged Gascony in exchange for giving up his claim to the French throne. Intermittent fighting followed, notably in Aquitaine, where France aided rebels against the

Black Prince, and at La Rochelle (1372) France decisively defeated the English navy. In 1387, however, the English defeated a Franco-Castilian invasion fleet off Margate. The peace of Paris (1396) arranged Richard II's marriage to the French king's daughter and confirmed England in the possession of Calais and part of Aquitaine. Some 20 years of uneasy peace, punctuated by intermittent conflicts, followed until 1415, when Henry V, encouraged by a France weakened by civil war, renewed the English claim to the French crown. The final phase of the war began with Henry's invasion of Normandy, the fall of *Harfleur, and the great English victory at *Agincourt, all in 1415. By 1419 the English conquest of Normandy was complete. The treaty of *Troyes (1420) reflected England's strength; it arranged Henry's marriage to Catherine of Valois and made him heir to the French throne. Despite Henry's premature death in 1422 English conquests continued until Charles (VII) and Joan of Arc led a French revival and defeated the English forces besieging Orléans (1429). By 1450 the French had driven the English out of Normandy, winning a notable victory at *Formigny, and by 1453, after the battle of Castillon, had taken the last English stronghold, Bordeaux. The war was effectively over, England retaining only Calais on the French mainland.

hunger marches. Demonstrations by unemployed workers in the 1920s and 1930s. As early as 1922 a march from Glasgow to London took place, and in the post-1929 Depression many were organized (mostly by the communist-led National Unemployed Workers' Movement) from depressed areas to London. The marches, especially the *Jarrow march, had a powerful propagandist effect.

Hunne's case (1514-15). A case arising from the death in 1514 in the bishop's prison at St Paul's of a London merchant-taylor, Richard Hunne, who was awaiting trial for heresy. The church alleged that he died a suicide, of guilt, and proceeded to burn his body. His friends, however, claimed that he had been arrested for paying a *mortuary and was murdered. The bishop's chancellor Dr Horsey was subsequently charged by a coroner's court with the murder and arrested, upon which the church objected that the lay courts had no jurisdiction over ecclesiastics (see benefit of clergy). The case, which revealed the considerable anticlericalism that existed on the eve of the Reformation, was twice debated before Henry VIII, ending in compromise. Horsey was not prosecuted but was obliged to pay a fine and leave London.

Hunt, Henry (1773-1835). Radical politician, known as Orator Hunt. A farmer's son, who became a brewer and maker of blacking, Hunt emerged as the best-known extremist leader in the post-1815 agitation for parliamentary reform. He was present at *Spa Fields and was imprisoned after the *Peterloo massacre. He was an MP (1830-33).

Huntingdon, Selina Hastings, countess of (1707-91). Founder of the Calvinistic Methodist sect, the Countess of Huntingdon's Connexion. She sought originally to evangelize fellow aristocrats within the Church of England but, facing the Church's hostility to Methodists, ultimately established, with *Whitefield, her own "Connexion", now part of the United Reformed Church.

Huntly, 1st marquess of. See Gordon, George.

Huskisson, William (1770-1830). President of the Board of Trade (1823-27), who promoted freer trade by modifying the *Navigation Acts. His resignation, as a leading Canningite liberal Tory, from Wellington's cabinet (1828) hastened the breakup of the old Tory party. He was run over and killed at the opening of the Manchester and Liverpool railway.

husting. 1. The temporary platform from which, prior to the Ballot Act (1872), the nomination of candidates for parliament was made, and on which they addressed the electors. By extension, "hustings" denotes proceedings at parliamentary elections in general. 2. The platform, at the upper end of the Guildhall, on which sat the mayor and aldermen of the City of London.

Hutchinson, Lucy (1620–?1680). Writer, the author of the *Life of Colonel Hutchinson* (published 1806), a biography of her husband John Hutchinson (1615–64), which vividly portrays the times they lived in. A Baptist, she also wrote *On Principles of the Christian Religion* (1817).

Huxley, T(homas) H(enry) (1825–95). Biologist. He developed an interest in natural history while serving as assistant surgeon on an expedition to Australia (1846–50). He subsequently became a staunch supporter of Darwinism. In his essays on philosophy and theology Huxley coined the term "agnostic" to describe his own religious opinions.

Hyde, Anne, duchess of York (1637–71). Daughter of Edward Hyde, earl of *Clarendon, she married James, duke of York (later James II) in 1660 despite the opposition of Charles II and her father. Only two of their eight children survived infancy—Mary (II) and (Queen) Anne.

Hywel (or Howel) Dda (d. 950). Welsh king and legislator. Grandson of *Rhodri Mawr, Hywel ap Cadell, known as Hywel Dda (Hywel the Good), governed the kingdoms of *Gwynedd, *Powys, and *Deheubarth. Aware of the Viking threat, he pursued a policy of cooperation with the English kings, especially Athelstan. In 1928 he went on pilgrimage to Rome. The earliest surviving manuscripts of *Cyfraith Hywel* (the Laws of Hywel) were compiled in the late 12th century, but Hywel is traditionally regarded as having been responsible for their codification at an assembly held at Whitland (Dyfed).

I

Iceni. A British tribe, whose territory covered present-day Norfolk and Suffolk. Their chief town was Venta Icenorum (Caistor-next-Norwich). They accepted Roman rule soon after the invasion and regarded themselves as free allies of the Romans. When Prasutagus, their king, died (61 AD) the Roman officials cruelly mistreated his widow *Boudicca and her daughters. The tribe rose in revolt and destroyed Colchester, London, and St Albans. The revolt was crushed by the Roman governor Suetonius Paulinus.

Icknield way. A prehistoric trackway between southwestern England and the Wash, on the east coast. Parts of it still survive, notably the *Ridgeway in Berkshire. It provided an important route for the Saxon tribes, particularly the Mercians, in the 5th and 6th centuries AD.

Ida. King of Bernicia, who, according to the *Anglo-Saxon Chronicle*, reigned from 547 to 560. He was the founder of the dynasty of Northumbrian kings. He established the centre of his power at *Bamburgh, which he fortified with a wall. He seems to have exercised control over all Northumbria, although on his death his son Aelle became king only of *Deira.

Idle, battle of the (616). A battle in south Yorkshire, at a crossing on the river Idle, in which Raedwald, overlord of the southern English, killed Aethelfrith, king of Northumbria, and installed Edwin of Deira, the first Christian king of Northumbria.

Illtud, St (c. 475–c. 525) Celtic monk. Born in Brittany, Illtud travelled extensively along the western seaways. He established in the Vale of Glamorgan the monastery of Llanilltud Fawr, renowned as a centre of learning, and his disciples included St *Gildas, St Samson of Dol, and St *David.

impeachment. A trial in which the Commons act as prosecutors and the Lords as judges. The practice dates from the reign of Edward III. It was revived in the early 17th century, when it became a weapon in the struggle between king and parliament. But it was always a clumsy and ineffective procedure, which served to frighten rather than punish. Between 1628 and 1806, when it was last used, ineffectively, against Henry *Dundas, 1st Viscount Melville, only one defended impeachment (of Henry *Sacheverell in 1710) resulted in a conviction, and this rebounded on the government. The impeachment of Warren Hastings lasted seven years (1788-95), and ended in acquittal.

imperial conferences. Conferences of the prime ministers of the self-governing colonies (or *dominions as they were defined at the 1907 conference) and leading British ministers to discuss matters of mutual interest, especially defence and trade. Generally held in London, the first four meetings—called colonial conferences—were held in 1887, 1897, 1902, and 1907, when they were renamed imperial conferences (1911, 1917-18, 1921, 1923, 1926, 1930, and 1937). The 1926 imperial conference laid down the doctrine of the British *Commonwealth of Nations and the imperial conferences gave way in 1944 to meetings of Commonwealth heads of government. *See also* Ottawa conference.

Imperial Defence, Committee of (CID). A British government committee concerned with the coordination of defence strategy for the Empire. Developed in 1902-04 under the chairmanship of the prime minister, with the aim of establishing relative levels of naval and military expenditure, the CID remained largely an advisory body. It was superseded in 1947 by the cabinet defence committee.

imperialism. The policy of extending, usually by conquest, the rule of a state over other countries or peoples for the purposes of economic gain and national aggrandizement. Imperialism became an important element of British foreign policy in the late 19th century, advocated especially by Joseph *Chamberlain, and dominated international affairs in the decades before World War I. Imperialism involved an obligation to provide

responsible administration of the territories of the *British Empire, but these were to be largely self-supporting and provide Britain with raw materials, markets for its manufactured goods, and opportunities for investment. Imperialism gave way after World War I to the idea of a *Commonwealth of equal nations.

imperial preference. An arrangement, associated particularly with the British Empire, by which special preferential tariff rates are given to one another by the countries forming part of an empire. Imperial preferences began to be introduced in 1919, but only after Britain introduced (1932), during the Depression, tariffs on food imports were preferences established on a significant scale. At the *Ottawa conference (1932) Britain agreed not to tax most goods imported from its colonies, which reciprocated the arrangement except when it endangered home producers. The General Agreement on Tariffs and Trade (GATT), signed by all the Ottawa signatories, prevented an extension of imperial (Commonwealth, from 1958) preferences, which were phased out after Britain joined the EEC.

Imperial War Cabinet. The *cabinet that was created in March 1917 under *Lloyd George's chairmanship to enable *dominion leaders to participate in the prosecution of World War I and to plan the peace under the aegis of the British government. The Nov 1918 session agreed on dominion participation in the Paris Peace Conference. This, in turn, led to dominion self-representation in the *League of Nations. The Imperial War Cabinet was under no parliamentary control and, lacking any enduring unity or purpose, disbanded after the war.

impositions. Import duties levied by the crown on its sole authority. Their legality was challenged during the reign of James I in *Bate's case, but was upheld by the Court of Exchequer. They were confirmed by statute in 1641.

impressment. The forcible recruiting of able-bodied men, often paupers or criminals, to serve in the army or navy. An irregular and on occasion illegal form of conscription, impressment was used to man the New Model Army and also, during the 18th century, the Royal Navy. Public concern forced the authorities to abandon impressment early in the 19th century, but it is still legal.

impropriation. The transference, which took place after the *dissolution of the monasteries, of *tithes to laymen. *See also* vicar.

Inchiquin, earl of. *See* O'Brien, Murrough, 1st earl of Inchiquin.

income tax. A tax levied directly on the income of individuals. It was first levied in 1799, at a rate of two shillings in the pound, by Pitt the younger, as a temporary measure to help finance the French Revolutionary War. It continued to be levied, except in the year of peace 1802-03, until 1816. Reimposed by Peel in 1842 to balance cuts in customs duties, it continued to be levied on a temporary basis while becoming a permanent feature of the economy. By the end of the 19th century it was a major source of revenue. In the 20th century income tax came to be regarded as an instrument of social reform as well as a source of revenue. Asquith in 1907 introduced a lower rate for earned income and Lloyd George's people's budget (1909) restored child allowances (first introduced by Pitt) and pioneered supertax (later surtax) on higher incomes. After World War I a variety of personal allowances were adopted, with progressive rates on increments of income.

Indemnity and Oblivion, Act of (1660). An act of parliament giving legislative effect to the general amnesty promised by Charles II in the Declaration of *Breda. Fifty individuals were specifically excluded from the operation of the act, of whom 14—the 13 *regicides and Sir Henry *Vane the younger—were executed.

indenture. A contract or deed between two or more parties. Originally, the document of indenture was copied, two or more times, on a single parchment, each copy being divided by a word or phrase. The copies were then separated, being cut along the dividing word. Their authenticity could thus subsequently be established by matching the cuts. Indentures were commonly used to bind apprentices, retainers, servants, and soldiers. *Compare* deed poll.

Independent Labour Party (ILP). A socialist organization founded in 1893 under the leadership of Keir *Hardie. The ILP helped to establish the Labour Representation Committee (1900), which became the *Labour Party in 1906. After individuals became eligible to join the Labour Party directly rather than through the ILP (1918), ILP influence waned. Disaffiliated from the Labour Party following policy disagreements (1932), it was represented in parliament by a steadily declining number of MPs, the last losing his seat in 1959.

Independents. In the 17th century, nonconformists who rejected both episcopacy and Presbyterianism, believing in the autonomy of local church congregations. The main Independent groups were the *Congregationalists and the *Baptists, along with smaller and more radical groups, such as the *fifth monarchy men and Anabaptists. The Independents dominated the *New Model Army.

India. A country in southern Asia that was under direct British rule from 1858 to 1947. The Government of *India Act (1858), which followed the *Indian mutiny, finally transferred the responsibility for the administration of India from the *East India Company (formed 1600) to the crown. Responsibility for India lay with the secretary of state for India, advised by a Council of India; day-to-day administration was monitored by the India Office. However, control was largely in the hands of the viceroy, who was assisted by the Indian Civil Service. In 1858 the British committed themselves to the policies of support for the Indian princes and to noninterference in religious matters; they also promised racial equality, but the British Raj was,

British India on the eve of the mutiny (1858)

on the contrary, characterized in the 19th century by the maintenance of racial barriers between the British ruling elite and the Indians. Economically, agriculture was developed and industrialization begun, and by 1914 some 56 326 km (35 000 mi) of railway had been built, linking the rural areas with the towns.

The Indian Army twice went into *Afghanistan (1878, 1919) to maintain British influence there, and in 1901 the *Northwest Frontier Province was created to settle the northern border disputes. By 1886 *Burma had been annexed to British India. Under Lord *Curzon, viceroy from 1899 to 1905, the government of India reached the height of its indifference to local opinion with the partition of *Bengal. As a result many Indians turned to the newly formed Indian National Congress, which by 1906 was calling for self-government. In World War I Indians contributed significantly to the allied effort, but their political rewards were meagre. The reforms introduced by the India Act (1919) were regarded by many Indians as insufficient, and *Gandhi intensified his campaign of noncooperation (satyagraha). In 1930-32 a series of *Round Table conferences was held in London, and the resulting India Act (1935) gave Indians a large measure of self-government. Congress won the 1936 elections and took office but its members resigned in 1939, when the viceroy Linlithgow failed to consult its leaders before declaring India at war with Germany. The 1946 elections showed the strength of Jinnah's Muslim League, and Mountbatten, who was appointed viceroy in 1947 to oversee the transfer of power into Indian hands, decided to create a separate state for the Muslims. Thus, in Aug 1947, Pakistan and India came into independent nationhood. Jawaharlal *Nehru became the first prime minister of India, which is a member of the Commonwealth.

India Acts. Legislation (1784-1937) that regulated the administration of *India. The Government of India Acts (1784, 1813, 1833, 1853) progressively limited the power of the *East India Company, which by the 1858 act lost all its administrative responsibilities to the crown. The India Councils Acts (1861, 1892, and 1909) established and extended the functions of executive and legislative councils of central and provincial governments and, following the *Montagu-Chelmsford Report, the Government of India Act (1919) created a two-house legislature. The Government of India Act (1935) gave a large measure of

self-government to India, envisaging a quasi-federal system, which formed the basis of independent India's constitution (1950).

Indian mutiny (1857-58). A rebellion against British rule, originating in the Bengal army of the East India Company but supported by part of the civilian population in upper and central India. The underlying cause of the revolt was widespread antagonism to the religious and economic westernization of the subcontinent. The mutiny, however, was precipitated by the introduction of the new Enfield paper cartridge, the end of which had to be bitten off prior to its loading. The cartridges were allegedly greased with animal fat and hence were regarded by Muslims and Hindus as unclean. In May 1857 mutineers seized Meerut, Delhi, and nearby towns and by mid-June the revolt had spread to the Ganges valley. Captured Europeans were massacred. The 40 000 European troops in India managed to save the situation largely because the entire Punjab remained loyal. Sir Colin Campbell retook Delhi (Sept 1857) and *Lucknow (March 1858), civilian support for the mutineers ebbed away, and the rebels were gradually reduced. Savage reprisals were taken, ringleaders being blown from the mouths of cannon. The mutiny led to the passing of the *India Act (1858), transferring possession of the East India Company's territories and forces to the crown. The proportion of Europeans to Indians in the Indian army was also greatly increased.

indirect rule. A system of colonial administration, introduced from 1900 by *Lugard in Nigeria, whereby British officials ruled "indirectly" through the existing chiefs and the traditional system of government. It became the blueprint of British colonial administration and was used extensively in its African colonies.

industrial revolution. A term, first popularized by Arnold Toynbee in 1882, to describe the economic and social transformation of Britain during a period

England before the industrial revolution (c. 1700)

England after the industrial revolution (c. 1850)

conventionally dated from about 1740 to 1850. Economically, the most important aspects of the industrial revolution were a change from domestic production to production in factories under capitalist control, the introduction of water and,

above all, steam power to drive machines, and a surge of innovation that transformed several major industries.

Why the industrial revolution began in Britain is still a matter for dispute. As early as 1500 Britain had a preindustrial economy, producing cloth for export rather than primary products, and thus a cumulative process may have begun. Among other factors encouraging industrialization were the relative political stability that followed the Glorious Revolution of 1688-89, together with a constitution that emphasized individualism, the development of a strong banking and credit system from the 17th century, and the inventiveness and enterprise that had come to be associated with nonconformity (see nonconformists). There were, too, abundant raw materials, in the form of coal, iron, and wool, while an overseas colonial empire complemented an expanding domestic market.

There were major changes in the textile industry, the *iron and steel industry, and in mining, as well as in mechanical engineering and pottery. The textile industry was notable for a series of inventions, which, together with the trend towards factory organization and capitalist control in the cotton industry, ensured its rapid growth to become the leading industrial sector from the 1740s. The iron industry demonstrated the overwhelming importance of new raw materials, as coke replaced charcoal, and the new dominance of coal as a power source led to a marked relocation of industry as new industrial regions grew up on the coalfields of northern and western Britain. Steam engines, perfected by James *Watt in 1769, pumped out water from the coalmines, drove the new machinery, and propelled locomotives and steamships. Change in some industries, such as the woollen or shipbuilding industries, was less rapid, however.

The revolution caused vast social changes because it initiated a major move from the land to the industrial towns and cities (see also agrarian revolution) and created an industrial working class, often suffering hardship and sometimes fiercely opposed to employers. The Revolutionary and Napoleonic Wars, as well as stimulating the growth of industrialism, aggravated social unrest, but by the mid-19th century it was clear that a political revolution would not accompany the economic transformation.

Ine (d. after 726). King of Wessex (688-726). After succeeding *Caedwalla in 688, Ine established himself as the strongest Saxon king of his generation. His great law code is the fullest and most significant royal legislation before that of Alfred and reveals both the growing prestige and sophistication of kingship and Ine's own statesmanship in the synthesis of old and new customs. He abdicated, retiring to Rome, in 726.

infangtheft. The right held by a manorial lord or a borough to bring to justice any thief caught within his jurisdiction and in possession of stolen property. Outfangtheft was the right of a lord to bring to justice one of his tenants caught elsewhere in possession of stolen property. These rights, which originated before the Norman conquest, were commonly one of the privileges granted by 12th- and 13th-century charters. Their importance was eroded by the development of royal justice.

injunction. 1. An order made by an English court. If interlocutory, injunctions are temporary and are issued pending trial of an action; if perpetual, they follow the suit. **2.** An instruction to the clergy issued by the crown as the supreme head of the church (or by Thomas *Cromwell as vicegerent). Such injunctions were issued in 1536, 1538, 1547, and 1559.

Inkerman, battle of (5 Nov 1854). A costly engagement of the Crimean War, arising from the Russians' attempt to break the Anglo-French investment of their fortress, Sebastopol. Inkerman was a "soldiers' battle", a series of disconnected encounters between individual units in which strategy played little part. The allied lines held, and the Russians withdrew to their defences, having lost some 12 000 men. Allied casualties numbered some 3500.

Inns of Court. Associations that have the exclusive right to call barristers to the Bar (or confer the rank of barrister).

Their origin is uncertain, but they existed in the 14th century, and by 1400 the four that still exist were in being, all in London: Lincoln's Inn, Gray's Inn, the Inner Temple, and the Middle Temple. Their curriculum was wide, and from the 15th to the 19th centuries they were much patronized by sons of gentlemen seeking a general education. Their governing bodies are called benchers (or Masters of the Bench).

Serjeants' Inn, abolished in 1877, was an association of *serjeants at law (or serjeants of the coif).

inquest. A legal or judicial inquiry, especially one made by a jury in a civil or criminal case. It was originally a general term for all official inquiries. The *Domesday survey, for example, was sometimes referred to as the Great Inquest. Perhaps the best-known application of the term in the middle ages is to Henry II's Inquest of Sheriffs (1170), a wide-ranging investigation of the conduct of royal officials and lay and ecclesiastical landowners who had profited at the expense of local inhabitants.

Instrument of Government (16 Dec 1653). The constitution that established the *Protectorate. Drawn up by John *Lambert and the council of officers, it vested executive authority in a lord protector—Cromwell—and a Council of State, and provided for triennial parliaments comprising 460 members elected in reformed constituencies. Cromwell was granted £200,000 per annum to cover the cost of government, together with the means to finance the army. It was superseded by the *Humble Petition and Advice.

intercursus magnus (Latin: great exchange; Feb 1496). A political and commercial treaty between Henry VII and Philip, duke of Burgundy. It was negotiated at the time of Perkin *Warbeck's bid for the English throne, and the signatories undertook not to aid each other's enemies. The commercial clauses covered every aspect of trade between England and the Netherlands, which the treaty was designed to encourage. Compare intercursus malus.

intercursus malus (Latin: bad exchange; April 1506). A trade agreement between Henry VII and Philip, duke of Burgundy. Negotiated at Falmouth, after Philip had been forced by storms in the Channel to take refuge in England, the treaty, unlike the earlier *intercursus magnus, was more favourable to England than to the Netherlands, permitting the English to sell cloth freely throughout the Netherlands, except in Flanders. However, Philip died before the treaty was ratified.

interdict. In the Roman Catholic Church, an ecclesiastical punishment prohibiting participation in the sacraments. Pope Alexander III (reigned 1159-81) placed Scotland under an interdict for the expulsion of the bishop of St Andrews, and Innocent III placed England under an interdict (1208) during his quarrel with King *John.

Interregnum. The period of republican government under the *Commonwealth and *Protectorate, falling between the reigns of Charles I and Charles II. Beginning in Jan 1649 with the execution of Charles I, the Interregnum ended with the restoration of Charles II in May 1660.

Intolerable Acts (1774). Legislation passed by the British parliament in retaliation for the *Boston tea party in the American colonies. They comprised the Boston Port Bill, which closed Boston harbour until the owners of the destroyed tea had been compensated; the Massachusetts Government Act, which revoked the colony's charter; the Quartering Act, which empowered the new governor, Gen. Gage, to billet troops in colonists' homes; and the Administration of Justice Act, which allowed British officials to return home to face trial for capital offences. The dissident colonists also regarded the *Quebec Act as a retaliatory measure.

Invergordon mutiny (1931). A mutiny by men of the Atlantic fleet at Invergordon in protest against threatened pay cuts. The crisis passed when the Admiralty promised to revise the proposed cuts. The mutiny caused such alarm on the exchange markets that the government was provoked into taking sterling off the gold standard.

Inverlochy, battle of. 1. (1431) The battle, fought near present-day Fort William, in which royal forces under the earls of Mar and Caithness were routed by Highlanders supporting the imprisoned earl of Ross (lord of the isles). 2. (2 Feb 1645) The battle in which an army of Highlanders and Irish under the marquess of Montrose inflicted a major defeat on a covenanters' army of Campbells and some Lowland troops.

investiture contest. A controversy over the right of secular rulers to invest a bishop or abbot with the symbols of his office, the ring and pastoral staff. The practice was first condemned by Pope Gregory VII in 1075 as an unwelcome secular interference in the appointment of ecclesiastics. In England Henry I reached a compromise with Archbishop *Anselm in 1106, whereby he gave up investiture while retaining his right to receive *homage from bishops in respect of their estates.

Iona, monastery of. A monastery founded by St Columba in 563 on the island of Iona, west of Scotland. It became the centre of the Celtic church and a source of missionary activity among the northern English during the 7th century. On his accession, Oswald of Northumbria, who had been baptized in Iona while in exile, invited Ionan monks to convert his people (634). The monks founded the monastery of *Lindisfarne. *Aidan, Fihan, and *Colman, three great Ionans, became bishops in the Northumbrian church. One of the first objects of Viking attack, Iona was sacked in 795 but quickly rebuilt. In the 9th century, after further attacks, St Columba's relics were moved to Ireland. The monastery was again rebuilt in the middle of the 11th century. It adopted the Benedictine rule in about 1203 and survived until the Reformation.

IRA. See Irish Republican Army.

Ireland, conquest of. By the 12th century Ireland was culturally unified but politically divided into a number of autonomous regions or kingships (see Connaught; Leinster; Meath; Munster; Ulster). The king of Leinster in the 1160s, *Dermot MacMurrough, on being defeated and deposed by his rivals, sought support from outside Ireland. He applied to Henry II of England for permission to recruit from his subjects and with Henry's approval enlisted the services of the Norman warriors who had recently conquered south Wales. Their leader Richard de *Clare agreed to participate and an advance party under Robert FitzStephen landed near Wexford in 1169. The next year de Clare himself arrived and after taking Waterford married Dermot MacMurrough's daughter. The Normans, and their Irish allies, then captured Dublin (1170). An attack by the Irish high king, *Rory O'Connor, was successfully repelled in 1171. Later in 1171 Henry II, alarmed at the prospect of Norman power outside his jurisdiction, arrived in Ireland. He brought with him a papal bull (from the English pope *Adrian IV) granting him the lordship of Ireland. In 1171-72 he received the submission not only of the Normans but of every important Irish chief and king except Rory—who submitted later. For the rest of the century and throughout the 13th century the Anglo-Normans proceeded to conquer the rest of Ireland, failing only to subdue the northwest and southwest. See Ireland under English rule.

Ireland under English rule. The Anglo-Norman conquest of Ireland, except the southwest and northwest, was complete by 1300. In the 14th and 15th centuries some land was reconquered by the native Irish and many of the Anglo-Normans were assimilated into Irish society. By the 16th century English rule was confined to a small area around Dublin known as the English *Pale. In 1541 Henry VIII was proclaimed king of Ireland, and under the Tudors English authority expanded once more. By 1603, after much warfare, the whole island was

Normans: BUTLER

Irish: O'NEILL

O'DOHERTY

McDONNELL

O'DONNELL

ULSTER

O'FLYNN

O'NEILL
L. Erne

L. Neagh

O'DOWD

O'ROURKE

O'CARROLL

L. Conn

O'CONNOR

NUGENT

O'REILLY

IRISH

CONNAUGHT

L.
Ree

O'NEILL

SEA

DE BURGH
L. Corrib

O'FLAHERTY

O'KELLY

TYRRELL

MEATH

PALE

O'SHAUG-
HNESSY

L. Derg

O'DEMPSEY

DUBLIN

ATLANTIC

OCEAN

CLARE

O'BRIEN

BUTLER

McGILLIPATRICK

LEINSTER

O'TOOLE

MacMURROUGH

FITZGERALD

BUTLER

CLARE

MUNSTER

BUTLER

FITZGERALD

O'SULLIVAN

O'DONOVAN

km 0   80
mi 0   50

The five ancient kingdoms of Ireland, family territories, and the English Pale

under the crown's jurisdiction. Various areas were planted (*see* plantation of Ireland) with English settlers, most successfully in the north. Less successful was the introduction of Protestantism, which was never accepted by the majority. In the 17th century two massive land transferences, after the Cromwellian and Williamite wars, left most of the Irish Catholics landless. In the later 18th century the repressive *Penal Code against Catholics was relaxed and in 1782 the Irish parliament, an all-Protestant institution, was allowed greater freedom from Westminster (see Grattan, Henry. After the 1798 rebellion (see Irish rebellion), however, union between Britain and Ireland was arranged, and in 1801 the Irish parliament was dissolved. With the achievement (1829) of *Catholic emancipation and the extension of the franchise a movement developed to press for a measure of Irish independence. At first it seemed that constitutional methods would suffice to achieve this aim, but attempts to pass *home rule bills were frustrated. It also became clear that the northeast of Ireland, many of the inhabitants of which were descended from British settlers, was unwilling to withdraw from the United Kingdom (see Ulster Unionists). The Government of Ireland Act (1920) proposed partition with the establishment of separate parliaments in the northeast and south. It proved unacceptable to the south, where armed resistance forced the British to concede virtual independence by the Anglo-Irish treaty in 1921. The six northeastern counties, however, immediately withdrew from the new *Irish Free State, opting for self-government within the UK (see Northern Ireland).

Ireton, Henry (1611–51). Parliamentary commander, the son in law of Oliver Cromwell. He commanded the left-flank cavalry at Naseby (1645) and was captured, later escaping. He signed the death warrant of Charles I. During Cromwell's Irish campaign he was second in command, he died of a fever while besieging Limerick.

Irish famine. The starvation and death of large numbers of Irish people (1847–51) following a blight (1845) that ruined the potato crop, the staple diet of the population. The shortage of food combined with the inability and unwillingness of the government to provide adequate relief caused the death of about one million Irish from starvation and disease; a further million emigrated, many to the USA.

Irish Free State. The state created by the Anglo-Irish treaty, signed on 6 Dec 1921. The southern 26 counties of Ireland, the Irish Free State, were granted dominion status within the Empire. Dedicated Republicans repudiated the treaty and fought a civil war in southern Ireland against the Free State forces but were defeated in 1923. The first president of the state was W. T. *Cosgrave who held office until 1932, when he was replaced by De *Valera and his Fianna Fáil party. In 1937 the Irish Free State was renamed Éire (Irish: Ireland). It was a member of the Commonwealth until 1949, when it became the Republic of Ireland. Compare Northern Ireland.

Irish Land Acts. A series of acts passed in response to agitation by Irish tenants for land rights. 1. (1870) An act that provided compensation for eviction and for improvements carried out by tenants. 2. (1881) An act guaranteeing fair rents, fixity of tenure, and freedom to sell (the three Fs). 3. (1885) An act —Ashbourne's Act—that advanced £5 million (increased in 1888 and 1891) for the purchase of land by tenants. 4. (1903) An act—Wyndham's Act—by which landlords were offered bonuses to sell their lands.

Irish Land League. An organization formed to achieve land reform in Ireland. Founded in 1879 by Michael *Davitt, its most famous tactic was organized ostracism (see boycotting) of unpopular landlords and their agents. After Gladstone's 1881 *Irish Land Act the League's immediate aims were achieved, and it disbanded.

Irish rebellion 1. (1641) A rising of Gaelic Irish in Ulster. After the *flight of the earls (1607) northern Ireland was settled with British, who ousted many of the local inhabitants from their lands (see plantation of Ireland). In Oct 1641 the Gaelic Irish in Ulster rose in rebellion and massacred thousands of settlers. They then allied with the previously loyal Roman Catholic Anglo-Irish in the rest of Ireland, and a governing council was established

(1642). The rebellion was eventually subdued (1649-50) by Oliver Cromwell. 2. (1798) A rising led by the *United Irishmen. The society pressed for an independent Irish Republic and sought military aid from France, with which Britain was at war; it also enlisted the support of the *Defenders, a Catholic agrarian organization. By 1798 the movement had been penetrated by government informers and was in danger of being destroyed. Consequently the United Irishmen rose in rebellion in May before the landing of a French expedition. The rising, which was confined largely to Ulster and Wexford, was soon crushed. It impressed upon Pitt the younger the necessity for settling the affairs of Ireland and led to the union of Britain and Ireland in 1801.

Irish Republican Army (IRA). A militant organization that evolved from the Irish Republican Brotherhood (see Fenian Society), a 19th-century revolutionary movement desiring an independent Irish republic. The IRA was formed in 1919 and its successful campaign against British forces resulted in the establishment of the *Irish Free State in 1921. The IRA then split between those who accepted or rejected the treaty; the latter group, keeping the name IRA, continued to demand the unification of all Ireland in one republic. Defeated in the south in 1923, this group was later outlawed, and the movement was generally inactive until the present troubles began in 1968. In 1969 the IRA split into the Officials, who want a socialist republic of all Ireland, and the Provisionals, who are concerned only with expelling the British from the north.

Irish Republican Brotherhood. See Fenian Society.

Ironsides. A regiment of parliamentary cavalry, formed during the Civil War and notable for its discipline and religious fanaticism. The nucleus of the regiment was raised by Cromwell at Huntingdon in 1643 and formed part of the forces of the *Eastern Association. Composed largely of independent small-farmers ("godly men"), the regiment

first won renown at *Marston Moor (1644), at which their commander Cromwell was nicknamed Ironside by Prince Rupert—an epithet subsequently transferred to his men. The Ironsides were a major factor in the parliamentary victory in the Civil War.

Irvine, agreement at (7 July 1297). The submission, by the future Robert I of Scots and other Scottish leaders in the name of the whole community, of the realm of Scotland to Edward I of England.

Irving, Sir Henry (1838-1905). Actor and theatre manager, born John Henry Brodribb. Noted for his interpretation of Shakespearean roles, Irving's famous partnership with Ellen *Terry began at the Lyceum Theatre (1878). He subsequently became manager of the Lyceum, and in 1895 he was knighted, the first actor to be so.

Irvingites. See Catholic Apostolic Church.

Isaacs, Rufus Daniel, 1st marquess of Reading (1860-1935). Barrister and politician. While attorney general (1910-13) he was implicated in the *Marconi affair. In 1913 he became lord chief justice, an office that in 1918-19 he combined with being ambassador to the USA. He was viceroy of India (1921-26) and in 1931 served briefly as foreign secretary under Ramsay *MacDonald.

Isabel of Angoulême (d. 1246). Queen consort of England (1200-16) as the second wife of King John. After John's death she married (1220) her former betrothed Hugh of Lusignan, count of La Marche. In 1241 she joined her son Henry III in war against the French king. They were defeated, and in 1244 Isabel fled to the abbey of Fontevraud, where she remained until her death.

Isabel of France (1292-1358). Queen consort (1308-27) of Edward II, daughter of Philip the Fair of France. She was soon alienated from her husband because of his attachment to Piers *Gaveston and later to the *Despensers. In 1325, while in France, she became the mistress of Roger de *Mortimer. In Sept

1326 Isabel and Mortimer landed at Harwich and, joined by other nobles, marched against the king, forcing him to surrender. Despenser was immediately executed and the king deposed and later murdered. From 1327 to 1330 the queen and Mortimer ruled in the name of the young king Edward III. But in Oct 1330 Edward had Mortimer and his mother seized at Nottingham. Mortimer was hastily tried and executed and the queen forced to retire on a yearly allowance of £3,000.

Isabel of France (1389-1409). Queen consort of England (1396-99) as the second wife of Richard II. She was the daughter of Charles VI of France and her marriage to Richard ended the war between the two countries. After Richard's deposition (1399) she returned to France but attempted to rejoin him several times. Not convinced of his death until 1406, she then remarried; her second husband was Charles, later duke of Orléans.

Isabel of Gloucester. *See* Avice of Gloucester.

Isle of Ely. A small raised area of the *Fens, on which stands the city of Ely. Its name derives from the fact that it was surrounded by marsh until the creation of the Bedford level by draining in the mid-17th century. It was the scene of *Hereward the Wake's final stand against William I in 1071 and of that of the rebels in the second *Barons' War (1264-67).

Isle of Man. An island in the Irish Sea. Inhabited by Celts from the 6th to 9th centuries, the island retains many Celtic characteristics although the Vikings settled here in the 10th century. Ceded to Alexander III of Scotland in 1266 (*see* Perth, treaty of), it was a pawn in the Anglo-Scottish disputes of the 14th century. In 1405 it was granted to Sir John *Stanley, whose descendants were lords of Man until 1736. In 1765 the British government bought the lordship of Man, which passed to the British crown. The island retains home rule with its own legislative assembly —*Tynwald—presided over by the

sovereign's representative, the lieutenant governor.

Isles, lord of the. The title adopted by the chief of the most powerful clan of the Scottish Isles (or *Hebrides), the MacDonalds. It first appears in the 14th century. The expansion of the lordship soon made it a major threat to the Scottish crown, especially as the lords sometimes sought English support. The lands of John, the 4th lord, were forfeited by James IV in 1493, but attempts to restore the lordship continued until the mid-16th century.

Italian bankers. *See* Lombards.

Iveagh, 1st earl of. *See* Guinness, Edward Cecil, 1st earl of Iveagh.

J

Jacobinism. In Britain, radicalism that was sympathetic to the French Revolution. The name refers to the Jacobin Club, the extreme radicals in the French Revolution. The government of Pitt the younger regarded radicals, such as *Paine, *Tooke, and members of the *Corresponding Society, as advocates of Jacobinism in Britain and acted with increasing severity against social or political unrest. It suspended *habeas corpus (1794-1801) and introduced such legislation as the *Combination Acts.

Jacobites. Supporters of the deposed James II and his heirs, active for almost 60 years after the Glorious Revolution of 1688-89. Their name derives from the Latin Jacobus, James. Early Jacobite resistance was in Scotland and Ireland. A Highland rising in James' support collapsed after the battle of *Killiecrankie (1689). James himself was in Ireland (March 1689-July 1690), leaving after defeat at the battle of the Boyne; his forces finally surrendered at Limerick in Oct 1791, and Irish Jacobitism was crushed. In England politicians, even non-Jacobites, maintained contacts with James and his son *James Edward Stuart, the old pretender, until the Hanoverian succession (1714) ended any chance that James Edward could become king peacefully. Open Jacobite rebellion in 1715-16 (the Fifteen) failed: an English rising was crushed at *Preston (Nov 1715), while the more serious Scottish rising, begun in Sept 1715, ended in Feb 1716 after one indecisive battle at *Sheriffmuir. The Whigs seized the opportunity to establish their political supremacy, claiming Tories were Jacobite sympathizers. An invasion attempt by the 2nd duke of *Ormonde failed in 1719, and *Atterbury's plot (1722) completed the ruin of the English Jacobites. The final Jacobite effort was the rebellion (1745-46) of *Charles Edward Stuart, the younger pretender —the Forty-Five. The last Stuart, cardinal duke of *York, died in 1807.

Jamaica. A West Indian island and former British crown colony. Discovered by Columbus in 1494, Jamaica was a Spanish possession until conquered by the English in 1655. It became a centre for buccaneers, traders, and slave merchants. The abolition of *slavery in 1833 contributed to economic difficulties and was followed by an insurrection (1865). A crown colony from 1866, Jamaica moved progressively towards self-government, becoming a fully independent member of the Commonwealth in 1962.

James I (1394-1437). King of Scots (1406-37), second son of Robert III. En route to France, James was captured by the English (c. 1406); he was released in 1424 after reaching an agreement with the English and marrying Princess Joan, a cousin of Henry V. Back in Scotland James first destroyed the power of the family of Robert Stewart, 1st duke of *Albany, who had controlled the country during his captivity. He incurred the resentment of the great lords and earned a reputation for greed because of his attempts to recover lost royal property and because of his determination to impose the royal will on all men, however high their rank. James was also an accomplished musician and poet, the probable author of The Kingis Quair

(The King's Book). He was murdered by descendants of Robert II, who hoped to seize the throne, but he was succeeded by his six-year-old son, James II.

James I of England. See James VI of Scots.

James II (1430-60). King of Scots (1437-60), son of James I. During his minority he and his family were sometimes little better than pawns in the hands of various Scottish factions, but in 1449 the Douglases helped him overthrow the power of the Livingstons and assume his full royal powers. James subsequently quarrelled with the Douglases and personally murdered the 8th earl (1452) and confiscated the 9th earl's estates (1455). They may have been plotting against the crown, but James may simply have wished to overthrow this powerful family of royal descent. Like his father, the king earned a reputation for ruthlessness and greed. While laying siege to Roxburgh castle, which was in English hands, he was accidentally killed by a bursting cannon and was succeeded by his young son, James III.

James II (1633-1701). King of England, Scotland, and Ireland (1685-88). Second surviving son of Charles I and Henrietta Maria, he was created duke of York in 1634. During the Civil War he escaped to the Netherlands (1648) and then went to France (1649), fighting with distinction in the 1650s in French and Spanish campaigns. After the restoration of his brother Charles II he was appointed lord high admiral and fought personally in the second and third *Dutch Wars. In 1660 he married Anne *Hyde, by whom he had two daughters—the future queens Mary II and Anne. In the late 1660s he became a Roman Catholic, and in 1673, unwilling to swear the anti-Catholic oath imposed by the *Test Act, resigned all his offices. The widespread alarm at his religious convictions was intensified by his second marriage (1673), to Mary of Modena. In 1678 James was the focus of the fabricated *popish plot, and between 1679 and 1681 parliament made three attempts to exclude him from the succession (see exclusion bills). Agitation against James subsequently quietened. He was made high commissioner for Scotland and then restored to the Admiralty. In 1685 he succeeded without opposition. However, after the ruthless suppression of *Monmouth's rebellion (1685) he embarked on provocative pro-Catholic policies. Following the decision in the case *Godden versus Hales (1686) Catholics were admitted to high office; the *Declaration of Indulgence (1687) granted toleration to both Catholics and nonconformists. Anxiety for the future of Protestantism intensified with the birth in 1688 of a Catholic heir to the throne—Charles Edward Stuart, the old pretender. In the following month the *seven bishops, prosecuted for refusing to read James' second Declaration of Indulgence from the pulpit, were acquitted and on the same day William of Orange was invited by seven prominent personalities to lead an army to England. William landed at Torbay in Nov, and James, deserted by most of his officers, fled to France. In 1689 he launched in Ireland a campaign to regain the crown but was defeated by William at the *Boyne (1690). James died, an exile, at Saint-Germain.

James III (1451-88). King of Scots (1460-88), son of James II. After the death of his mother, Mary of Gueldres (1463), the young king fell into the hands of the Boyds. In 1469 he married Margaret of Denmark and assumed royal power, but his authority was challenged by factious nobles and members of his family, abetted by the English. It was said that he alienated men of rank by supporting those of low status who shared his artistic tastes. In 1479 he feared that his brothers, more popular than he, were conspiring against him. The earl of Mar died in custody, possibly murdered; but the duke of Albany escaped and won English recognition as king of Scots. In 1484 the king successfully defeated Albany's attempt to seize the throne, but he lost Berwick castle to the English. James III was finally defeated at Sauchieburn and killed by

rebellious nobles, led by his son and heir —James IV.

James IV (1473-1513). King of Scots (1488-1513). An energetic and attractive ruler, he had wide-ranging cultural and scientific interests. He managed to extend his power without alienating the nobility, suppressing, notably, the lordship of the *Isles. His taste for military adventure was displayed in his invasion of England in 1496 in support of Perkin *Warbeck. In 1502 he made peace with England and in 1503 married Henry VII's daughter, *Margaret Tudor. When Henry VIII invaded France in 1513 James felt obliged by the Franco-Scottish alliance to invade England, where he was killed at *Flodden. One legitimate son survived him—his successor James V—and he had five illegitimate sons.

James V (1512-42). King of Scots (1513-42), son of James IV and Margaret Tudor. Until a Scottish parliament granted the young king full powers in 1524 his reign was troubled by disputes between various factions. James angered many by his insistence on strict obedience to royal authority and by his use of the law to forfeit property to the crown—sometimes used vindictively against his personal enemies. After some hesitation he chose the French rather than the English alliance and at the beginning of 1537 he married Madeleine, daughter of the French king. She died six months later, and in 1538 James married Mary of Guise-Lorraine. He died shortly after being defeated by the English at *Solway Moss and was succeeded by his infant daughter, Mary.

James VI of Scots and I of England (1566-1625). King of Scots (1567-1625) and of England and Ireland (1603-25). James, the first *Stuart king of England, was the son of *Mary Queen of Scots and her second husband, Henry, Lord *Darnley. When James succeeded to the Scottish throne in 1567, following his mother's enforced abdication, he was only 13 months old. His long and troubled minority saw a succession of regents. Religious and aristocratic factions made various attempts to secure the king's person, and civil war raged until 1573 when the earl of Morton took control of Scotland. In 1586 by the treaty of Berwick James was awarded an English pension; and his cousin Elizabeth I promised not to oppose his claims to the English succession unless he provoked her by his actions in Scotland. This sufficed to ensure James' acquiescence to his mother's execution in 1587 and his neutrality when the Spanish armada sailed against England in the following year. In 1592 James consented to an act of parliament establishing Presbyterianism in Scotland; with the support of Presbyterians he was finally able to subdue the Roman Catholic earls of the north. James did much to improve the system of civil government in Scotland and took the first steps towards initiating a regular system of taxation. He married Anne of Denmark in 1589.

When James succeeded to the English throne in 1603, he made it clear that there would be no fundamental alteration to the Elizabethan church settlement and that he believed the Anglican church and the monarchy to be interdependent. His slogan was "no bishop, no king". One manifestation of the frustration of the religious minorities was the Roman Catholic inspired *gunpowder plot of 1604.

James' experience in Scotland failed to prepare him adequately for the English throne. He was soon in conflict with his parliaments (1604-11, the 1614 *Addled Parliament, and 1621-22) on the question of the extent of his sovereignty and its refusal to grant what he considered adequate revenue. On occasion he sought financial independence by means of extraparliamentary levies. His liking for attractive young men, notably such court favourites as Robert *Carr and George Villiers (duke of *Buckingham), alienated many Englishmen. Soon after his accession James made peace with Spain, realizing England could no longer afford the crippling costs of war. He aspired to the role of the peacemaker of Europe, acceptable to both Catholics and

Protestants. His efforts were ruined both by the strength of Protestant opinion in Britain and by the reluctance of Spain to form an alliance with him. After the outbreak of the Thirty Years' War (1618) on the Continent, James had to settle for a treaty with the Dutch and a French marriage alliance for his heir Charles.

James Edward Stuart, the old pretender (1688-1766). Son of James II and Mary of Modena. Taken to France at the Glorious Revolution (1688), he was proclaimed James III and VIII on his father's death in 1701. He attempted, unsuccessfully, to invade Scotland with French troops in 1708, but in the 1715 *Jacobite rising he landed safely after the victory of his followers at Sheriffmuir. By Feb 1716, however, he was forced to flee. He settled in Italy, remaining there during the 1745 rising of his son *Charles Edward Stuart, and was buried in St Peter's Basilica, Rome.

Jameson raid (29 Dec 1895-2 Jan 1896). An abortive invasion of the *Transvaal led by Dr Leander Starr Jameson (1853-1917), a colleague of Cecil *Rhodes. Its aim was to overthrow the Afrikaner government of Paul *Kruger. However, it resulted in a worsening of Anglo-Boer relations and led finally to the second *Boer War (1899-1902).

Jane Seymour (1509-37). Queen consort of England (1536-37), as the third wife of Henry VIII. A former lady in waiting to her predecessors Catherine of Aragon and Anne Boleyn, Jane Seymour was married privately to the king in May 1536. She died giving birth to Henry's only male heir Edward (later Edward VI).

Jarrow march (1936). The best-remembered of the *hunger marches of the depression years. Led by their Labour MP, Ellen Wilkinson (1891-1947), 200 shipyard workers marched to London from Jarrow as a demonstration against the massive unemployment in the area.

Jarrow monastery. A monastery, on the bank of the river Tyne, founded by St Benedict Biscop in 681 on land granted by King Ecgfrith of Northumbria. Its famous library, furnished with books and relics brought by Benedict from Rome, was one of the finest of its time. The great Bede died here, having written his works, including a history of the abbots of Jarrow, in the library.

Jeffreys of Wem, George Jeffreys, 1st Baron (c. 1645-1689). Judge. Already notorious for his cruelty in the trials that followed the *popish plot (1678), as lord chief justice (1682-85) Jeffreys presided over the savage *bloody assizes that followed the unsuccessful *Monmouth rebellion (1685). He was subsequently appointed lord chancellor but after the overthrow of James II was arrested, dying in the Tower.

Jellicoe, John Jellicoe, 1st Earl (1859-1935). Admiral of the fleet. He was criticized for excessive caution at the battle of *Jutland, but later events showed that his tactics were justified. Despite his own reservations he organized an efficient system of naval *convoys in 1917 but, coming into conflict with Lloyd George, was dismissed at the end of the year. He was governor of New Zealand (1920-23).

Jenkins' Ear, War of (1739-48). A conflict between Britain and Spain. It was ostensibly over the maltreatment by the Spanish of a British seaman, Capt. Jenkins, but was in fact caused by the British attempt to break the Spanish monopoly of trade with South America. The capture by Admiral *Vernon of Porto Bello (1739) was followed by his unsuccessful raid on Cartagena (1741), after which the war became absorbed in the wider struggle of the War of the *Austrian Succession (1740-48).

Jersey. The largest of the *Channel Islands and the nearest to France. Under the English crown since the Norman conquest (1066), the bailiwick of Jersey has its own parliament and laws, based on the *Grand Coutumier de Normandie* (1539). The crown is represented by the bailiff.

Jervis, John, Earl St Vincent (1735-1818). Naval commander. Jervis served in Wolfe's expedition to North America (1759-60) and helped three times to

relieve Gibraltar (1780-82) and to capture Martinique and Guadeloupe (1794). His greatest victory was in 1797, when he defeated the Spanish fleet off *Cape St Vincent, for which he was granted an earldom. As first lord of the admiralty (1801-04), he introduced naval reforms and opposed the policy of armed neutrality. He returned to active service in command of the Channel fleet (1806-07).

Jesuits. Members of the Society of Jesus, founded by St Ignatius Loyola in 1534 to promote Roman Catholicism and oppose heresy. Entering England in 1580, they were implicated in plots to place *Mary Queen of Scots on the English throne and were involved in the *gunpowder plot (1604-05). Successive attempts were made to expel them and they suffered under the penal laws against Catholics. The order was dissolved by Pope Clement XIV in 1773, and although restored in 1814 it was not recognized in England until 1829 (see Catholic emancipation).

Jews. A Semitic people, claiming descent from the ancient Israelites. Jewish communities were first established in England after the *Norman conquest. During the 12th century they played an increasing role in the economy as money lenders (see usury) both to the king and to lay and ecclesiastical lords; others served as doctors, jewellers, and tradesmen. Although the Jews were nominally under royal protection antisemitism, fired by the popular misbelief that they sacrificed Christian children and by crusading fervour, was prevalent in the late 12th century. In 1189-90 a wave of pogroms spread through England, culminating in the massacre of 150 Jews in York. In the 13th century they were taxed increasingly heavily, being subject to *tallage, and their estates were also frequently confiscated for alleged currency and financial offences. By the end of the 13th century many Jews were impoverished and some had fled the country, and in 1290 those that remained were expelled by *Edward I. They were formally readmitted in 1655, during the

Protectorate, but did not gain political equality until the middle of the 19th century. They were first admitted to the House of Commons in 1858 and to the Lords in 1885 (see Rothschild, Lionel de).

jingoism. A term derived from the expression "by jingo", used in a music-hall song written in support of Disraeli's stand against Russia in 1878. Thereafter jingoism acquired a pejorative sense, meaning a belligerent and chauvinistic stance in matters of foreign policy.

Joan (d. 1237). An illegitimate daughter of King John, betrothed to *Llywelyn ap Iorwerth of Gwynedd in 1204. In 1211 she negotiated favourable terms for Llywelyn after his defeat by John. She later acted as a mediator between Gwynedd and *Henry III.

Joan of Kent (1328-85). Countess of Kent, whose beauty and mildness earned her the sobriquet Fair Maid of Kent. She married (1361) Edward, the Black Prince, her second husband, and their younger son became Richard II. In 1376, when rioting Londoners besieged John of Gaunt's palace, he sought refuge with Joan at her home in Kennington.

Joan of Navarre (c. 1370-1437). Queen consort of England (1401-13), as the second wife of Henry IV. Daughter of Charles the Bad of Navarre, she was formerly married to John IV, duke of Brittany. She was imprisoned (1419-22) for alleged witchcraft.

Joan of the Tower (1321-62). Queen consort (1329-62) of David II of Scots, whom she married in 1327, and youngest daughter of Edward II of England. After David's capture at *Neville's Cross (1346), Edward III allowed Joan to visit her husband in the Tower of London. She later separated from him and lived in England.

John (1166-1216). King of England (1199-1216). Youngest and favourite son of Henry II (who nicknamed him Lackland because he possessed no lands) and *Eleanor of Aquitaine. He was married twice: first (1189) to *Avice of Gloucester and second (1200) to *Isabel

of Angoulême. By his second wife he had two sons, Henry and Richard. John's reign saw the loss of much of the *Angevin empire. After divorcing his first wife, he married the betrothed of the count of La Marche. The count appealed to Philip II Augustus of France, who in 1202 declared all John's possessions in France forfeit. In the ensuing conflict Normandy was lost in 1204 and within two years Anjou, Maine, and Brittany had all followed. John did not mount a serious offensive to regain the lost territories until 1213, when he allied with the emperor Otto IV. The cause collapsed, however, at *Bouvines in the following year.

John's reign also witnessed confrontation with the church. After the death of the archbishop of Canterbury Hubert Walter in 1205 John's own nominee to succeed him was passed over in favour of Stephen *Langton, the papal candidate. John refused to allow Langton into England, and in 1208 the pope placed the kingdom under interdict. The dispute ended in 1213, when England and Ireland became papal fiefs, but not before the pope had excommunicated John (1209) and threatened to depose him and to sanction the imminent French invasion. John also faced the opposition of his own barons, who regarded his rule, in particular the methods used in raising royal revenue, as despotic, and in 1215 he was forced to issue *Magna Carta. However, civil war was not thus averted and John died at Newark during the subsequent *Barons' War.

John Balliol (c. 1250-1313). King of Scots (1292-96). Chosen King by Edward I of England from among the *competitors, Balliol had had little previous contact with Scotland, but held lands in England and France. As king he was caught between the excessive demands of Edward as his feudal superior and the growing determination of his Scottish advisers to defy such English demands. Resistance to Edward brought about defeat at *Dunbar (1296) and John resigned his kingdom to the English king. Held prisoner by Edward until

1299, he then lived in France until his death. His eldest son, *Edward Balliol, later claimed the Scottish throne. *See also* Anglo-Scottish Wars.

John Bull. The personification of an Englishman. The character was invented by John Arbuthnot (1667-1735), a physician and witty political pamphleteer, in his *History of John Bull* (1712). During the 19th century John Bull's cartoon characteristics, such as the Union Jack waistcoat, were steadily developed.

John of Gaunt, duke of Lancaster (1340-99). Fourth son of Edward III, who was virtual ruler of England from about 1371 until 1399. Born at Ghent, he inherited the dukedom of Lancaster through his first wife Blanche (d. 1362). He subsequently married (1371) Constance of Castile (d. 1394) and (1396) his mistress Catherine *Swinford. His four children by Catherine, born before their parents' marriage, were legitimized in 1397, and from the oldest, John *Beaufort, Henry VII was descended. John served in the Hundred Years' War from 1367 to 1374, assuming control of government as his father became increasingly infirm. A supporter of the Lollards, but probably only for political reasons, he used their leader John Wycliffe to maintain his position against the party of prelates who opposed him. In the years immediately following the *peasants' revolt (1381), for which John's policies have been blamed, he successfully kept the peace between the supporters of the young Richard II (reigned 1377-99) and the opposition to the crown led by Thomas of Woodstock, earl of Gloucester. During John's absence (1386-89) in (unsuccessful) pursuit of his claim through his second wife to Castile, England came close to civil war. John reconciled the opposing factions on his return, but when he died in 1399 the king was deposed—by John's own son, who ascended the throne as Henry IV.

John of Lancaster, duke of Bedford (1389-1435). Third son of Henry IV and, for most of Henry VI's minority, regent of France and protector of England (1422-35). He generally left English affairs to his brother *Humphrey, duke of Gloucester, while he ruled in France with some success until Joan of Arc rallied the French at Orléans (1429). He had Joan burned as a witch. His last years were troubled by Humphrey's attacks on his administration of France.

John of Salisbury (c. 1115-1180). Regarded as one of the most learned men of his day, he served as secretary to Archbishop Theobald of Canterbury after studying at Paris and Chartres. Between 1164 and 1170 he was forced to live abroad because of his friendship with Becket. In 1176 he became bishop of Chartres and attended the third Lateran Council in 1179. He is the author of many works, notably the *Policraticus*.

Johnson, Samuel (1709-84). Literary critic, essayist, and poet, best known for his *Dictionary of the English Language* (1755) and *The Lives of the Most Eminent English Poets* (1779-81). In 1763 he met James *Boswell, who became a close friend and wrote Johnson's biography.

Johnston, Sir Harry Hamilton (1858-1927). Explorer and administrator, who did much to promote British colonial acquisitions in Africa. In 1883, Johnston penetrated the Congo basin alone and in 1884 led an expedition to Mount Kilimanjaro. From 1885 he held a succession of consular posts, including those of consul to Portuguese East Africa (1889), commissioner for south central Africa (1891-96), consul general to Tunisia (1897-99), and special commissioner to Uganda (1899-1901). He was the author of more than 40 books on Africa.

joint-stock company. A company in which several people with limited liability own a share. Joint-stock companies date from the 17th century. After the failure of the *South Sea Company in 1720 legislation restricted the formation of joint-stock companies, which became *limited liability companies and might only be formed by royal charter or act of parliament. Restrictions on their formation were relaxed during the 19th century.

Jones, Inigo (1573-1652). The first known great English architect, whose surviving work includes the Queen's House, Greenwich (1617-35), and the Banqueting Hall, Whitehall (1619-22). Also a designer of masques, including those of Ben Jonson, he is credited with introducing the proscenium arch and movable scenery to the English stage.

Jonson, Ben (1572-1637). Dramatist and poet. A contemporary of Shakespeare, who acted in some of his plays, Jonson satirized society in such comedies as *Volpone* (1606) and *The Alchemist* (1610). He also wrote masques, staged by Inigo Jones, for the court of James I.

Jordan, Mrs (1762-1816). Actress, who was the mistress of the duke of Clarence (later William IV). Born Dorothy (Dorothea) Bland, she became a leading London actress under the name of Mrs Jordan. She and William lived together from 1790 to 1811, during which time she bore him ten children.

Judicature Act (1873). A statute remodelling the higher courts. The act (including amendments in 1876 and 1880) set up a Supreme Court of Judicature, comprising the Court of Appeal and the High Court of Justice. The three divisions of the High Court—Queen's Bench, Common Pleas, and Exchequer; Chancery; and Probate, Admiralty, and Divorce—embodied what had formerly been separate courts. The House of Lords was confirmed as the final appeal court.

Junius, letters of. Brilliant and vicious attacks on political personalities, published in the London *Public Advertiser* (Jan 1769-Jan 1772). The 70 letters, signed "Junius", followed others published from 1767 under different pseudonyms. They concentrated on Grafton, but other victims included George III. Junius' identity remains unknown; Sir Philip *Francis, later Warren Hastings' most bitter enemy, is the likeliest candidate.

junto. A small group of people holding (or seeking) political power (from Spanish *junta*, council). In British history, the term is applied to the group of Whigs in power under William III (1696-97) and Anne (1708-10). Allied to Marlborough and Godolphin, this junto included Lords (John) *Somers, (Thomas) *Wharton, and *Halifax, Charles Spencer (3rd earl of *Sunderland from 1702), and Sir Robert Walpole.

jury. A body of persons, which came to number 12, sworn to give a verdict on evidence presented in a court of law. Its Anglo-Saxon forerunners include the *wager of law, but the jury was a Norman institution, dating from the Assize of *Clarendon (1166), which directed jurors to present crimes and suspected criminals to the justices in *eyre. Trial by jury in civil cases dates from the institution of the *grand assize in about 1179. Following the abolition of *trial by ordeal (1215) the jury system was greatly extended, becoming compulsory for some cases in 1275.

justice general of Scotland. The chief judge in criminal cases. The office was held by successive earls of Argyll from 1514 to 1628. Since 1837 it has been combined with the office of lord president of the Court of Session. See Justiciary, Court of.

justice of the peace (JP). A person appointed by the lord chancellor with statutory power to try certain cases (e.g. assault, motoring offences) in a magistrate's court and to commit more serious cases to a higher court. JPs were first so named in 1361, when the conservators of the peace, dating from the 13th century, were given judicial powers in matters relating to the keeping of the peace in boroughs and counties. They formerly acted through *quarter sessions and *petty sessions.

justiciar. The chief officer of the crown for two centuries following the Norman conquest, charged with governing the country in the king's absence. *Odo of Bayeux and Ranulf *Flambard exercised the powers of justiciar, but were not named as such, and the office was properly established with Henry I's appointment of *Roger of Salisbury. It reached the height of its prestige in the late 12th century, when the Angevin kings were preoccupied with their continental territories. With the decline of the Angevin empire the office lessened in importance and no justiciar was appointed from 1234 to 1258, when it was revived in the *Provisions of Oxford. The last justiciar was Hugh le *Despenser, who was killed at Evesham (1265).

Justiciary, Court of. The central criminal court of Scotland, organized on a permanent basis in 1672, when some of the lords of session (see Session, Court of) were appointed commissioners of justiciary to act as judges with the *justice general and justice depute.

Jutes. A Germanic people who, together with the *Angles and the *Saxons, formed part of the wave of invaders of Britain in the 5th century. According to Bede the Jutes settled in Kent, the Isle of Wight, and parts of Hampshire, and although their origin is unclear early brooches and pottery in Kent have affinities with Jutland and Frisia. Early Kentish laws and agricultural organization, however, suggest strong links with the Franks. Kent retained idiosyncratic customs for centuries (e.g. the *lathes of Kent).

Jutland, battle of (31 May and 1 June 1916). A naval battle in the North Sea during World War I. While in pursuit of *Beatty's battlecruisers, the German fleet under Admiral Scheer was outflanked by the British Grand Fleet under the command of *Jellicoe. Two engagements took place before the German fleet escaped under the cover of darkness. The British were disappointed at the inconclusive result of this encounter and by the fact that British losses were heavier than those of the Germans. Nevertheless, this was an important strategic victory for Britain, because the German fleet remained in port for the rest of the war.

K

Kaffraria. Land between the Keiskama and Kei rivers on the eastern coast of South Africa, annexed by Britain in 1847 as the crown colony of British Kaffraria. From 1857 Whites were allowed to settle here, and in 1865 it was incorporated into *Cape Colony.

Kaunda, Kenneth (1924–). President of Zambia since 1964. A teacher by profession, Kaunda was imprisoned (1959) for his activities in the Zambia African National Congress. On his release he formed the United National Independence Party (1960), which helped negotiate Zambia's independence in 1964.

Kay, John (18th century). A Lancashire reedmaker who patented a weaving device, the flying shuttle, in 1733. The shuttle "threw" the fabric mechanically across the loom, thus requiring one weaver in place of two. This was the first of the major textile inventions of the *industrial revolution. Ruined by litigation to protect his patent, Kay emigrated to France, where he was last heard of in 1778.

Kean, Edmund (1789–1833). Actor. Kean entered the theatre after an insecure childhood and was soon recognized as one of the greatest tragic actors of all time, famous especially for his naturalistic acting in Shakespearean roles. He died shortly after collapsing while playing Othello.

Keats, John (1795–1821). Romantic poet. His lyrical verse is characterized by sensuous imagery and includes the odes "On Melancholy" and "To a Nightingale" and the epic poem *Hyperion*. Keats died of tuberculosis at the age of 25.

Kemble, Fanny (1809–93). Actress. Niece of Sarah Siddons and the theatrical manager Charles Kemble (1775–1854), she became a favourite on the London stage in such leading roles as Juliet, Portia, and Lady Teazle. She also wrote plays, poems, and volumes of reminiscences about the theatre.

Kemp (or Kempe), John (?1380-1454). Chancellor and archbishop. Elected bishop of Rochester in 1419, he was transferred first to Chichester and then (1421) to London. A member of the council of regency for Henry VI, he was appointed chancellor and archbishop of York in 1426. Because of his support for Cardinal *Beaufort against Humphrey, duke of Gloucester, he had to resign the great seal in 1432. In 1450, however, he was again chancellor and two years later became archbishop of Canterbury.

Kenilworth, dictum of (31 Oct 1266). A declaration of terms between Henry III and the rebellious barons (see Barons' Wars). It made void the acts of Simon de Montfort, declared the king's powers restored, and stated the ways in which the barons (the *disinherited) might legally recover the lands that had been seized from them by the crown after its victory at Evesham.

Kenilworth, siege of (June-Dec 1266). The offensive launched by Henry III and his son Edward on Kenilworth castle, the strongly fortified home of the de *Montforts and refuge of some of their supporters after the barons' defeat at Evesham. At the end of Oct the dictum of *Kenilworth offered peace terms but the besieged earls, hoping for aid from Simon de Montfort the younger in Normandy, did not surrender until Dec.

Kenneth I MacAlpin (d. 858). King of Scotia (c. 843-858). Kenneth succeeded his father Alpin as king of the Scots of Dalriada in 841. He drove out the Viking pirates and completed the conquest of the Picts by about 850. He united the Picts with the Scots in the kingdom of Scotia, or Alba, and moved his capital to Scone. Kenneth is said to have invaded Lothian six times and to have suffered invasions by the British of Strathclyde and the Vikings.

Kenneth II (d. 995). King of Scotia (971-95). A brother of King Dubh (killed 966), Kenneth recognized Edgar, king of England, as his lord in 973. Edgar granted him Lothian, which in practice was already in Scottish hands. Kenneth was killed in a feud, perhaps by his successor, Constantine III.

Kenneth III (d. 1005). King of Scotia (997-1005). A grandson of Malcolm I, Kenneth murdered his predecessor, Constantine III. Kenneth, who may have ruled jointly with his own son Giric, was killed by Malcolm II.

Kensington palace. A royal palace in Kensington, London. It was bought by William III in 1689 and rebuilt by Sir Christopher Wren in the 1690s. Further additions were designed by Hawkesmoor and Kent.

Kent. A kingdom founded by Aesc (see Hengist) and probably settled by Frankish *Jutes after the conquest of the Britons (494). Kent was the first English kingdom converted to Christianity (597), which, together with Kentish power in southern England, waned after King *Aethelbert died (616). Kent was divided (686-690) and fell under Mercian domination (c. 762). It was finally absorbed by Wessex (825).

Kent, William (1684-1748). Artist, landscape gardener, and architect who became one of the leading exponents of the Palladian style in English architecture. His best-known surviving works are the Horse Guards buildings in Whitehall, London, and Holkham hall, Norfolk. In garden design, Kent began the transformation from 17th-century formality to the naturalistic style, which "Capability" *Brown developed.

Kenya. A country in East Africa and a former British protectorate. In the European scramble to seize Africa Kenya fell into Britain's zone (1889). From 1890 it was controlled by the British East Africa Company and in 1895 was placed under the crown. It became a colony in 1920. The move towards self-government was hindered by the *Mau Mau rebellion (1952-59), but independence was achieved in 1963 with Jomo *Kenyatta as prime minister. Kenya became a republic and a member of the Commonwealth in 1964.

Kenyatta, Jomo (c. 1894–1978). African nationalist, the first president of Kenya (1964–78). Imprisoned (1953–60) for taking part in the *Mau Mau rebellion, he became president of the Kenya African National Union on his release and led Kenya to independence in 1963.

Keppel, Augustus Keppel, 1st Viscount (1725–86). Naval commander. Keppel accompanied Anson on his voyage round the world in 1740 and became commander in chief of the grand fleet in 1778. In 1779 he was court-martialled for alleged mishandling of an engagement against the French off Ushant (1778) but was completely cleared. A Whig MP (1761–80), he served as first lord of the admiralty (1782–83).

Kett's rebellion (1549). An insurrection in Norfolk led by Robert Kett (or Ket). The rebellion was directed against the *enclosure by landowners of common pasture lands to raise their own sheep. The rebels—numbering some 16 000 —proposed the abolition of private ownership of land and achieved some short-lived success before being suppressed by forces under the earl of Warwick (later duke of *Northumberland). Kett was hanged.

Keynes, John Maynard Keynes, 1st Baron (1883–1946). Economist. He attended the Paris peace conference after World War I, and in *The Economic Consequences of Peace* (1919) argued that the war reparations imposed on Germany would have severe social consequences. In *The General Theory of Employment, Interest and Money* (1936) he advocated his view, which has profoundly influenced successive government policies, that budgets should be used to determine production and thereby maintain full employment. He played an important part in the Bretton Woods conference, in New Hampshire, USA (1944), which founded the International Monetary Fund.

Keys, House of. A body of 24 members that forms the elective branch of the legislature (*see* Tynwald) of the Isle of Man. The origins of the name are not clear, but it appears as early as 1422.

The Manx popular name is *Yn Kiare as Feed,* the Four and Twenty.

Khaki election (Oct 1900). A general election called by Salisbury's Conservative-Unionist government. It hoped to obtain a renewed majority through popular enthusiasm for recent *Boer War victories (and was so named because of the army's new khaki combat uniform). The government marginally increased its majority but without recovering all the support lost since the 1895 election.

Khama, Sir Seretse (1921–80). President of Botswana (1966–80). Son of the Bamangwato chief, Seretse Khama forfeited his right to succeed by marrying an Englishwoman, Ruth Williams. Restored to the chieftainship in 1963, he led Bechuanaland to independence as Botswana in 1966.

Khartoum. The capital city of the *Sudan. Khartoum was the seat from 1830 of the British-supported Turko-Egyptian government of the Sudan. When the *Mahdi overran the Sudan Gen. *Gordon was ordered to withdraw British forces but he dug in at Khartoum hoping for British reinforcements. He was killed and the town destroyed (1885). It was rebuilt by *Kitchener after Britain had reconquered the Sudan (1898) and became the seat of the Anglo-Egyptian government.

Khyber pass. A strategically important pass between Afghanistan and the Indian subcontinent. During the 19th century, as part of the northwest frontier, it was a focal point of conflict between the British and the hill peoples of the region.

Kidd, William (1645–1701). Scottish sea captain and pirate, known as Captain Kidd. Following colonial service as a privateer against the French (1690–95) Kidd was appointed (1695) to head an expedition against pirates in the Indian Ocean. However, he turned to piracy himself, moving between the East and West Indies. The hope of a pardon induced him to return to New York (1699), but he was arrested on arrival and sent to London, where he was convicted of murder and piracy and hanged. The archetype of the romantic pirate of literature, Kidd left behind him legends of buried treasure, which has yet to be discovered.

Kildare, earls of. *See* Fitzgerald.

Kilkenny, Statutes of (1366). Legislation passed by the parliament of Ireland at Kilkenny. The 14th century saw a revival of Irish power, not only by reconquest but by the assimilation of Anglo-Normans into Irish society. The 35 statutes were designed to halt this process and included a ban on inter-marriage with the Irish and on the adoption of the Irish language, dress, or legal system. They were repealed in 1613, having proved unenforceable.

Killiecrankie, battle of (27 July 1689). A battle fought between the Jacobites, under Viscount Dundee, and the troops of William III, under Maj. Gen. Mackay, on the Pass of Killiecrankie in Scotland. Mackay retreated, but Dundee later died of injuries he received in the foray.

Kilmainham treaty (1882). An informal agreement between the government and *Parnell, leader of the home rule party in Ireland. Parnell, who had been imprisoned in 1881 for making speeches to incite violence, was released from Kilmainham gaol, and the government, further to the *Irish Land Act (1881), promised further concessions to tenants. In return Parnell promised to call off violent agitation.

Kilsyth, battle of (15 Aug 1645). The battle, fought in Stirling, in which *Montrose defeated the *covenanters, the last of his six successive major victories over them. After the battle no covenanting army remained in arms in Scotland, and their regime temporarily collapsed.

Kimberley. A city in Cape Province, South Africa. It rapidly grew in impor-tance after the discovery of diamonds here in 1871 and was taken over by Cape Colony in 1880. During the second *Boer War (1899-1902) Kimberley was besieged by the Boers for four months

until relieved by Gen. John *French (later 1st earl of Ypres) on 15 Feb 1900.

King and Country debate (9 Feb 1933). A debate in the Oxford University Union that resulted in the resolution that "this House will in no circumstances fight for King and Country". The resolution, which was widely publicized, probably indicated the widespread commitment to *disarmament in the years following World War I, rather than a lack of patriotism.

king consort. *See* prince consort.

King Philip's War (1675-76). An uprising of the Wampanoag and Narraganset Indians in New England. Its name derived from that of the Wampanoag chief, known as King Philip. The colonists destroyed the Indian forces in two engagements, at Great Swamp (1675) and Hadley (1676).

King's (or Queen's) Bench, Court of. A division of the High Court of Justice. Dating from Edward I's time, the Court of King's Bench (so called because the king commonly sat there) was one of the three courts administering the *common law (the others were the Courts of Common Pleas and Exchequer). The *Judicature Act (1873) merged the three courts into the Queen's (or King's) Bench Division.

King's Bench prison. A former prison, in Southwark, London. Dating from the 14th century, originally for prisoners of the Court of *King's Bench, it became a debtors' prison. Renamed Queen's Bench Prison (1842) and later a military gaol, it was demolished in 1879.

king's court. *See* curia regis.

king's evil. Scrofula, or tuberculosis of the lymphatic glands. During the middle ages popular belief attributed to royalty the hereditary power of curing the disease by touching the victim. Intro-duced to England from France by Edward the Confessor, the custom of touching sufferers was revived by James I. Under Charles II a religious cere-mony was frequently linked with the custom, which was last practised in England by Queen Anne.

king's friends. Politicians who, from the 1760s to the 1780s, backed the desire of George III for government that was not dominated by parties. Many were *placemen (including semiprofessional administrators, such as Charles Jenkinson, 1st earl of *Liverpool). Their opponents, chiefly Whigs, such as *Burke, saw them as corrupt accomplices in the king's attempt to subvert constitutional rule.

Kingsley, Charles (1819-75). Novelist and clergyman. In his early works Kingsley preached the ideals of the *Christian Socialist movement. However, he achieved greater popularity with his later novels, which include the historical adventure story *Westward Ho!* (1855) and the children's classic *The Water Babies* (1863).

king's peace. *See* monarchy.

Kingston-upon-Thames, treaty of (12 Sept 1217). The peace treaty, ending the first *Barons' War, between Louis of France (later King Louis VIII), who had been offered the English crown by the baronial rebels, and the supporters of Henry III. It granted a general amnesty to the rebels, whom Louis undertook not to aid further. Shortly afterwards he was paid 10,000 marks to leave the country promptly. The moderation of the treaty prepared the way for the establishment of unity after the strife of King John's reign.

King William's War. *See* grand alliance.

Kipling, Rudyard (1865-1936). Writer. He was born in India, the setting for most of his highly successful tales and poems, which include *Barrack Room Ballads* (1892) and the children's stories *The Jungle Books* (1894, 1895). He was awarded the Nobel prize in 1907.

Kiribati. *See* Gilbert and Ellice Islands Colony.

Kirkby, John (d. 1290). Bishop of Ely from 1286. A clerk of Chancery under Henry III, he became a member of the royal council in 1276. In 1282 he toured England to beg for gifts and loans to finance Edward I's wars, his success being recognized by his appointment (1284) as treasurer. In the following year he undertook an inquiry—Kirkby's quest—into debts owed by individuals throughout the country to the crown. He was a notorious pluralist.

Kirk o' Field. A collegiate church in Edinburgh founded in 1510. The Church was in ruins by 1567, when Lord Darnley, husband of *Mary Queen of Scots, was murdered in a house on the site.

Kirk Party. The party of extreme *covenanters who seized power in Scotland in 1648 after the defeat of the Engagers in England. The party showed itself more radical in its policies than the earlier covenanter regimes; it soon split into factions.

Kitchener of Khartoum and of Broome, Horatio Herbert Kitchener, 1st Earl (1850-1916). Soldier. He served in Egypt and the Sudan from 1883 to 1899 and after defeating the dervishes at *Omdurman he re-established British authority in the Sudan. In South Africa as chief of staff and commander in chief, he helped moderate the terms of the Boers' surrender (1902). He was commander in chief in India (1902-09). Appointed secretary for war (1914), he created a "new army" of 70 divisions and supported increased munitions production, but he proved unable to delegate authority or to cooperate with politicians. By 1916, when he was drowned while travelling to Russia, his powers had been effectively reduced by Lloyd George.

Kneller, Sir Godfrey (?1646-1723). Portrait painter. Born in Germany, he came to England in 1675 and became principal painter to Charles II. He painted portraits of nine monarchs, over 40 members of the Whig Kit-Cat Club, and a series called the *Hampton Court Beauties*, commissioned by William III.

knight. The mounted warrior of medieval Europe. There is much debate over the knight's introduction into England, but it is likely that he was a Norman innovation. A man became a knight, or was dubbed for knighthood, in a ceremony in which he was invested, by his father or lord, with a set of arms. In return for field service for a stated period, garrison duty, payment of feudal incidents, and a general obligation to give counsel and aid to his lord a knight received land—the *fee. In the late 11th and early 12th centuries most knights were relatively humble professional fighting men, who held only one or two fees, but their status rose during the 12th century as they were called upon to serve in local and central government. The rising cost of military equipment and the chivalric code (see chivalry) further enhanced their prestige and status. Changes in the techniques of warfare and its increasing specialization and professionalism, combined with the needs of English kings for an army for long-term campaigns, reduced the military importance of knights. However, the wealthier knights continued to play an important part in the politics and administration of medieval England. See also feudalism.

knighthood (or **chivalry**), **order of**. A fraternity of knights. Military orders of knights bound by a religious rule, such as the *Hospitallers and the *Templars, emerged in the 12th century, during the crusades. The crusading orders formed the model for the royal orders of knighthood, such as the Orders of the *Garter, founded by sovereigns in the 14th and 15th centuries to honour, and retain the loyalty of, their barons. In the 17th, 18th, and 19th centuries the orders of knighthood were revived in the form of orders of merit, societies to which persons are admitted as a mark of honour.

Knox, John (?1512–1572). The dominant figure in the establishment of the *Church of Scotland. Knox became a priest but by 1546 was supporting the Protestant cause. His association with the murderers of Cardinal David *Beaton led to forced labour in French galleys (1547–49). After his release he became a leading radical Protestant preacher in England but fled when Roman Catholicism was restored there in 1553 and ministered to a congregation of English

exiles in Geneva. There he came under the influence of John Calvin. Knox visited Scotland in 1555–56, and in 1559 returned there and emerged as the leading reformed minister, renowned for his energy, strength of character, and forceful preaching. He was appointed minister of Edinburgh in 1560. His opposition to Mary Queen of Scots, both as a Catholic and as a woman ruler, was frequently and strongly expressed, but he was in some ways a more moderate and flexible man than is often thought. His acceptance of bishops in the church undermines the common assumption that he was the founder of Scottish Presbyterianism. His History of the Reformation (first edition 1560) is a historical source of outstanding value, although it tends to over-emphasize his own role in events.

kotsetla. In the 11th century, a *ceorl, or free peasant, who owed one day's labour a week to his lord and extra days at harvest time. In return he was permitted to farm a small share of the common. See also gebur; geneat.

Kruger, Paul (1825–1904). Afrikaner statesman, president of the Transvaal (1883–1900). He led the Afrikaners in the first *Boer War against the British and gained virtual independence for the Transvaal at the *Pretoria convention (1881). As president he resisted the demands of the mostly British Uitlanders (Afrikaans: outlanders, foreigners) for political equality with the Afrikaner. This policy led to the second Boer War, during which Kruger escaped to Europe. He died in Switzerland.

Kruger telegram (3 Jan 1896). A congratulatory message sent to *Kruger, president of the Transvaal, by the German emperor, William II, following the defeat of the *Jameson raid.

L

Labouchère, Henry du Pré (1831–1912). Radical journalist and politician. Initially a diplomat at St Petersburg and Dresden, in 1877 Labouchère founded the campaigning weekly *Truth*. He was also co-proprietor of the *Daily News*. A Liberal MP (1865-66, 1867-68, 1880-1906), he was barred from cabinet office by Queen Victoria because of his attacks on members of the royal family.

Labourers, Statute of (1351). A statute designed to reverse the effects on wages of the labour shortages resulting from the *black death. Employers were not to raise wages above the rates that were standard prior to the outbreak of the plague and all landless men aged 60 or under were obliged to accept work at these rates. The statute was unpopular both with landowners, who were prevented from competing for labour that continued in short supply, and with labourers. It contributed to the outbreak of the *peasants' revolt (1381).

Labour Party. A political party formed in 1906 from the Labour Representation Committee (LRC) and reorganized in 1918. Working-class political activity developed after the failure of *Chartism in the mid-19th century. The *trade unions influenced and supported sympathetic Liberal and Conservative politicians, and in 1874 two trade unionists were elected Liberal MPs, beginning a tradition of "Lib-Lab" association. In the 1880s socialist groups, such as the Marxist-inclined Social Democratic Federation (SDF; established in 1881) and the *Fabian Society (1884), began to influence the trade union movement, and Keir *Hardie initiated the campaign for the formation of a separate labour party. Hardie (and two others) were elected independent MPs in 1892, and the *Independent Labour Party (ILP) was founded in 1893 to work for independent parliamentary representation for the unions. In 1900 a number of unions, the ILP, the SDF, and the Fabians established a Labour Representation Committee (1900) to promote a separate parliamentary labour party. Working-class representation in local government was meanwhile increasing.

In 1906, when 29 LRC candidates were elected MPs (with another 25 Lib-Labs), the LRC changed its name to Labour Party, forming a parliamentary group (which most Lib-Labs soon joined). Labour entered the wartime coalition (1915-18), and in 1918 the party was reorganized by Arthur *Henderson, with the help of Sidney *Webb. Provisions were made for the formation of local constituency parties, allowing individual membership as well as the affiliation of unions and socialist societies. The party formally adopted a socialist policy of "common ownership of the means of production". From 1922 Labour's middle-class element increased, and the party came to replace the Liberals as one of the two major parties. Labour formed a minority government under Ramsay *MacDonald in 1924, and again from 1929 to 1931. MacDonald then formed the *national government and was expelled from the Labour Party.

Labour was represented in the coalition government of World War II (1940-45), after which it formed its first majority administration, under *Attlee (1945-51). The postwar Labour government implemented *nationalization policies and established the *National Health Service. The party was led by *Gaitskell from 1955 to 1963 and was again in office under Harold *Wilson (1964-70, 1974-76) and James Callaghan (1976-79).

Ladysmith. A town in Natal province, South Africa, named after the wife of Sir Harry Smith (1787-1860), governor of Cape Colony (1847). Founded in 1850, Ladysmith was besieged by the Boers in the second *Boer War for four months until relieved by Sir Redvers Buller on 28 Feb 1900.

Lagos. The capital city of *Nigeria and of Lagos State, situated on the Bight of Benin. An important slaving port in the 19th century, Lagos became a British colony in 1861. A centre from the 1840s for freed slaves returning from Brazil, the West Indies, and Sierra Leone and for Christian missionaries, Lagos acquired a diverse population. It became the capital of the protectorate of Southern Nigeria (1906) and then of all Nigeria (1914).

Laing, Alexander Gordon (1793–1826). Explorer in Africa. Laing began his African travels in 1822 and was engaged in the early conflicts between the Ashanti and Europeans in West Africa (1823). In 1825 he launched an expedition to discover the source of the *Niger but was murdered by Arabs upon his arrival at Timbuktu.

Laing's Nek. A pass in Natal, South Africa. In the first *Boer War British troops under Sir George Pomeroy Colley (1835–81) were defeated by Transvaal Boers entrenched here (28 Jan 1881).

laird. A Scottish variant of "lord". Originally the term denoted any tenant in chief, but it came to be used to denote the lesser, untitled, tenants in chief (the "small barons"). Later the term often referred to any landed proprietor. A bonnet laird was a proprietor whose estate was so small that he worked it himself as a farmer (the term refers to his customary humble headdress).

laissez-faire (French: let them act). A policy of noninterference by the government in economic affairs. Advocated by Adam *Smith, it was widely accepted by the early 19th century. However, its excesses, especially in the exploitation of workers and growth of *monopolies, led to its gradual erosion by government regulation. *See also* free trade; Manchester school.

Lambert, John (1619–83). Parliamentary military commander. After leading the parliamentary cavalry at the battle of *Marston Moor (1644) he assumed command of the army in the north and, with Cromwell, defeated the Scots at *Preston (1648). In 1651, again with Cromwell, Lambert routed Charles II's armies at *Worcester. Lambert was head of the council of officers that proclaimed Cromwell lord protector in 1653 but lost his influence in 1657, when he opposed the constitutional amendments contained in the *Humble Petition and Advice. He was prominent in the military govern-

ment that secured power after Cromwell's death and commanded the army that attempted, unsuccessfully, to halt *Monck's advance from Scotland. After the Restoration, he spent the remainder of his life in prison.

Lambeth, treaty of (4 May 1212). An agreement between King John and Renaud of Dammartin, count of Bologne, by which each promised not to make a separate peace with France. Renaud, whose county had been seized by Philip II Augustus of France, was given several fiefs in England and an annuity. In return, he brought other continental princes, notably the count of Flanders, into the coalition that John hoped would help him to regain his *Angevin possessions.

Lancaster, house of. A royal dynasty descended from the second son of Henry III—Edmund, created earl of Lancaster in 1267. The first earls, especially *Thomas and *Henry, who was created 1st duke of Lancaster in 1351, played prominent roles in English politics. On Henry's death the title and Lancastrian possessions passed to his son in law *John of Gaunt. His son Henry Bolingbroke, who was denied his inheritance and exiled by Richard II, became King *Henry IV on Richard's deposition in 1399. His son Henry V and grandson *Henry VI continued the line, but the Lancastrian succession was disputed from 1455 by the house of *York (*see also* Roses, Wars of the). On Henry VI's death (1471) the dynasty ended in the male line, although the Tudor Henry VII could trace a Lancastrian descent through his mother Margaret *Beaufort.

Lander, Richard (1804–34). Explorer of West Africa. He accompanied Hugh *Clapperton on his expedition to Northern Nigeria (1825) and in 1830, with his brother John Lander (1807–39), traced the course of the *Niger from Bussa to the sea. In 1834 Richard was fatally wounded by tribesmen while on a trading mission on the Niger.

Lanfranc (d. 1089). Archbishop of Canterbury from 1070. Born in Pavia, he was a noted theologian and teacher.

A close adviser of William the Conqueror, he visited Pope Gregory VII in Rome in 1076 and persuaded him to withdraw his demand that William pay homage to him. He also preserved the king's rights to ecclesiastical patronage and in 1072 he attempted to unify the English church by asserting the primacy of Canterbury over York. He was a key supporter of William Rufus during the rebellion of 1088.

Langland, William (c. 1330-c. 1400). Poet. Born in the Malvern Hills, he settled in London after taking minor orders. The masterpiece attributed to him, *The Vision concerning Piers the Plowman*, is an alliterative poem that exists in three versions. It is a theological discussion, and the author, while maintaining a belief in the Christian message, castigates the clergy for their lax morals and worldliness.

Langley, Edmund de, 1st duke of York (1341-1402). Fifth son of Edward III. He became earl of Cambridge in 1362 and duke of York in 1385. Between 1367 and 1372 he fought with his brother *Edward, the Black Prince, on the Continent. He was the leading member of Richard II's council of regency, but when Henry of Lancaster invaded England in 1399 Langley gave him his support.

Langport, battle of (10th July 1645). A battle of the Civil War. Following their decisive victories at *Marston Moor and *Naseby the New Model Army met and defeated Charles I's army of the west at Langport, in Somerset. Bristol fell two months later, and a royalist defeat in the first Civil War became unavoidable.

Langside, battle of (13 May 1568). A battle in which Mary Queen of Scots and Bothwell were finally defeated by their Scottish opponents. Mary was subsequently imprisoned in Lochleven castle and forced to abdicate.

Langton, Stephen (d. 1228). Archbishop of Canterbury. After studying in Paris, he served at the papal court and was made a cardinal in 1206. His appointment as archbishop in 1207 was opposed

by King John until 1213. Langton played a considerable role in the drafting of the Magna Carta (1215) but was suspended shortly afterwards for his unwillingness to promulgate sentences of excommunication against the barons. He left England for Rome but returned in 1218.

Lansbury, George (1859-1940). Labour MP (1910-12, 1922-40). He served in Ramsay *MacDonald's government (1929-31), succeeding him as leader of the Labour Party and opposition (1931-35). A pacifist, Lansbury opposed sanctions against Italy and resigned the leadership, being succeeded by *Attlee.

Lansdowne, Henry Petty-Fitzmaurice, 3rd marquess of (1780-1863). MP from 1803 to 1809, when he succeeded as marquess of Lansdowne, who was chancellor of the exchequer (1806-07) in the Ministry of *All the Talents. He entered the cabinet of the liberal Tory premiers Canning and Goderich (1827-28) and belonged to every Whig, or Liberal, cabinet in the period 1830-63, twice refusing the premiership.

Lansdowne, Henry Petty-Fitzmaurice, 5th marquess of (1845-1927). Irish peer and Liberal, who was an opponent of Gladstone's Irish policy, becoming a Liberal *Unionist and then a Conservative. Grandson of the 3rd marquess, he was governor general of Canada (1883-88) and viceroy of India (1888-94). As secretary for war (1895-1900) he was severely criticized for Britain's unreadiness for the second *Boer War. His appointment as foreign secretary in 1900 was widely objected to, but he remained in the post until 1905, negotiating the *Anglo-Japanese alliance (1902) and the *entente cordiale with France (1904). Conservative leader in the House of Lords (1903-16), he joined Asquith's wartime coalition. He provoked bitter public hostility for suggesting, in a letter to the *Daily Telegraph* (29 Nov 1917), a compromise peace with Germany.

Lansdowne, William Petty, 1st marquess of (and 2nd earl of Shelburne) (1737-1805). Statesman. As Lord Shelburne (from 1761) he was president of the board of trade under George Grenville (April-Sept 1763). Becoming a follower of *Pitt the elder (Lord Chatham), he was secretary of state in the Chatham-Grafton ministry (Aug 1766-Oct 1768) but resigned because of opposition to his advocacy of conciliation to the American colonists. Following the fall of Lord North in 1782 Shelburne was again secretary of state, under *Rockingham (March-July 1782), and after Rockingham's death was prime minister (July 1782-Feb 1783). He completed the negotiation of the treaty of Versailles, which concluded the American Revolution, but was then defeated by Charles James Fox and Lord North and never held office again. Shelburne, who was created marquess of Lansdowne in 1784, was distrusted by his contemporaries, who called him Malagrida, or the Jesuit, but he was notable for his patronage, at Bowood House, of such reformers as Jeremy Bentham, Richard Price, and Joseph Priestley.

La Rochelle. A fortified harbour on the Atlantic coast of France, which was a refuge of persecuted French Protestants (Huguenots). In 1627 George Villiers, 1st duke of Buckingham, led an unsuccessful expedition to relieve the besieged Huguenots and in 1628 was assassinated as he was about to set sail on a second attempt. The French recaptured La Rochelle in 1629.

lathes of Kent. Units of local government, unique to Kent. According to the Domesday Book they were six in number, each consisting of several *hundreds. The *geld was assessed on the basis of the lathes.

Latimer, Hugh (c. 1485-1555). Bishop of Worcester (1535-39). A noted preacher with a social conscience and Protestant leanings, Latimer became one of Henry VIII's chief advisers. In 1539, however, he opposed the firmly Catholic six *articles and resigned. Briefly restored to favour in Edward VI's reign, on Mary's accession he was imprisoned in the Tower. Refusing to acknowledge Catholic doctrines in debate at Oxford,

he was burnt at the stake with *Ridley for heresy.

Latitudinarians. The name given by conservative Anglicans from the mid-17th century to clerics who adopted a nondogmatic attitude to church authority, doctrine, and practice. George I and George II advanced the Latitudinarians to oppose the power of the Tory *High Church party (see Bangorian controversy).

Laud, William (1573-1645). Archbishop of Canterbury; with Wentworth the chief proponent of the policy of *thorough that characterized the *eleven years' tyranny of Charles I. He was made a royal chaplain in 1611 and became an intimate of the duke of Buckingham. A privy councillor from 1627, he was appointed bishop of London in 1628 and archbishop of Canterbury in 1633. He zealously imposed religious uniformity and, while raising standards in the Anglican ministry, provoked the hostility of Puritans. The attempt by Laud and the king to impose Anglican practices on the Scots caused the *Bishops' Wars, and in 1640 Laud was impeached by the Long Parliament. He was not tried until 1644 and, although found not guilty by the Lords, was executed after passage in the Commons of a bill of *attainder.

Laudabiliter. See Adrian IV.

Lauderdale, John Maitland, 2nd earl and 1st duke of (1616-82). Member of the *cabal under Charles II. A Scotsman and grandson of Baron *Maitland, during the Civil War he helped negotiate the *Solemn League and Covenant (1643) with the parliamentarians and the *Engagement (1647) with Charles I. Joining the royalist camp, he was captured at the battle of Worcester (1651) and imprisoned until 1660. After the Restoration he was secretary for Scottish affairs (1660-80) and earned widespread hatred for his ruthless enforcement of royal and episcopal power. He was created duke in 1672.

Law, (Andrew) Bonar (1858-1923). Prime minister (1922-23). Born in Canada and brought up in Scotland,

Law was a Conservative MP from 1900 to 1923. He became party leader in opposition in 1911 and backed Ulster resistance to *home rule. He was colonial secretary in Asquith's wartime coalition (May 1915-Dec 1916). As chancellor of the exchequer (1916-19) in *Lloyd George's war cabinet he introduced war bonds and in the postwar coalition was lord privy seal (1919-21). In March 1921 Law retired because of ill health (being succeeded by Austen *Chamberlain as party leader). He returned to politics in the following year, when his opposition to the coalition helped bring about Lloyd George's resignation. Resuming the party leadership and becoming prime minister (Oct), he was again forced to resign because of illness (May 1923).

Lawrence, Sir Thomas (1769-1830). Painter, who succeeded Reynolds as official portrait painter to George III in 1792 and became immensely fashionable. In 1818 he was sent by the prince regent to the congress of Aix-la-Chapelle to paint the portraits of the heads of state and military leaders assembled there. These portraits are now hung at Windsor castle.

Lawrence, T(homas) E(dward) (1888-1935). Soldier and writer, known as Lawrence of Arabia because of his military leadership in the Arab revolt (1917-18) against the Turks in World War I. Lawrence was a delegate at the Paris peace conference (1919), the decisions of which on Arab affairs he condemned, and later served as adviser to the Colonial Office (1921-22). Disillusioned with public affairs, he joined the RAF under the pseudonyms of Ross and then Shaw and later the Tank Corps. He was killed in a motorcycle accident. His account of the Arab revolt was published in *Seven Pillars of Wisdom* (1926).

League of Nations. An assembly, established in 1920 under the treaty of *Versailles, for the peaceful settlement of international disputes. Its name was coined by Lowes Dickinson. Its 58 founder members included the UK and all members of the British Empire, and the League's first secretary general was Sir Eric Drummond (later 16th earl of Perth; 1876-1952). It was weakened by the refusal of the USA to join and the withdrawal of several members, and failed in the 1930s to halt either Japanese or Italian aggression and rearmament. It achieved some successes, however, especially through the work of the International Labour Organisation and the International Court of Justice and in the administration of mandated territories (see mandate). In 1946 its functions were transferred to the *United Nations.

leet. In East Anglia, a unit of local government dating from the 11th century or earlier. It was a subdivision of a *hundred and consisted of a small group of villages. It was responsible for collecting its share of the *geld and had its own court.

Leeward Islands. The northern islands of the Lesser Antilles in the Caribbean Sea, colonized by several European countries and the USA. The name was also applied (1871-1956) to British possessions in the group: St Kitts-Nevis-Anguilla, Antigua, Montserrat, and the British Virgin Islands. The first two became associated states within the *Commonwealth (1967), while the latter remain British dependencies.

legal aid. Assistance in meeting the cost of legal advice and representation, provided from public funds to an individual whose income falls below a certain level. The facility became general with the Legal Aid and Advice Act (1949), but a number of previous acts, including the Criminal Appeals Act (1907) and the Poor Prisoners' Defence Act (1930), conferred legal aid in special circumstances.

legion, Roman. A brigade of 5000 heavy infantry with about the same number of auxiliary troops. Claudius invaded Britain in 43 AD with an army of four legions. These remained as the army of occupation, reinforced at times by additional legions. They were stationed at Caerleon-on-Usk, Wroxeter, Chester, and Lincoln. The legionary bases provided a focus of Roman life.

Leicester, Robert Dudley, 1st earl of (?1532-1588). A favourite of Elizabeth I. Fifth son of John Dudley, duke of *Northumberland, he was made a privy councillor in 1559 and, after the death of his wife Amy *Robsart (for which rumour held him responsible), was a strong candidate for the queen's hand. She refused him, but he nevertheless retained her favour and was created earl of Leicester in 1564. In 1578 he married Lettice, widow of the 1st earl of Essex. A Puritan, he counselled a pro-Protestant foreign policy and led a disastrous expedition (1585-87) to aid the Dutch in their revolt against Spain. His character was lampooned in *Leicester's Commonwealth* (1584), probably written by a Roman Catholic.

Leinster. A province of east and southeast Ireland, one of the five ancient kingdoms of Ireland (*see also* Connaught; Meath; Munster; Ulster). For most of the Celtic period it was the weakest of the kingdoms and its kings were never high kings of Ireland. Leinster's last king, *Dermot MacMurrough, was banished by the high king Rory O'Connor in 1166; his invitation to the Anglo-Normans to invade Ireland as his allies began its conquest.

Leipzig, battle of (16-19 Oct 1813). A massive engagement, known also as the battle of the Nations, in the closing stages of the Napoleonic War. Napoleon, defeated by a combined British, Austrian, Russian, Prussian, and Swedish army, 325 000 men strong, was forced to abandon the French conquests in Germany, with the loss of 68 000 men out of his army of some 185 000; allied losses numbered 55 000.

Lely, Sir Peter (1618-80). Dutch portrait painter. He came to London in 1641 and served Charles I, Cromwell, and Charles II, who knighted him (1679). His works include two famous series, the *Windsor Beauties* (Hampton Court) and the *Flagmen* (Greenwich).

lend-lease. An arrangement whereby the USA provided the allies with military supplies during World War II. In March 1941, when the USA was still neutral, Congress authorized the leasing or lending of defence articles to nations whose defence the president deemed vital to the security of the USA. The UK, the Soviet Union, and others received aid worth almost $50,000 million (then about £12,000 million), of which the UK received about $27,000 million. In return, it supplied about £1,896 million in reciprocal aid. Lend-lease was ended on 2 Sept 1945, the day on which the victory over Japan was celebrated.

Lennox, Charles, 1st duke of Richmond (1672-1723). Illegitimate son of Charles II by Louise de Kéroualle, duchess of Portsmouth. After changing his religion and his politics Lennox became a supporter of William III. In 1714 he became lord of the bedchamber to George I.

Lennox, Charles, 3rd duke of Richmond and Lennox (1735-1806). Grandson of the 1st duke, who was a minister under Rockingham, Shelburne, and (1784-95) Pitt the younger. Richmond sympathized with the American colonists and, unsuccessfully, introduced (1780) a bill for parliamentary reform.

Lennox, Matthew Stewart, 4th earl of (1516-71). Scottish magnate. In 1545 his title was forfeited after he had acted as an agent for the English. It was restored in 1564, and in the following year his son Lord Darnley married Mary Queen of Scots. After Darnley's murder in 1567 Lennox retired to England. He was appointed regent of Scotland for James VI in 1570, but was killed shortly afterwards in a skirmish with supporters of Mary.

Leofric (d. 1057). Earl of Mercia from about 1032. Created earl by *Cnut, Leofric was a rival of *Godwine. He played an important part in the politics of *Edward the Confessor's reign, supporting the king against Godwine in 1051. Thereafter, although territorially very powerful, he had little political influence. His wife was Lady *Godiva.

Leslie, Alexander, 1st earl of Leven (?1580-1661). Scottish military commander. After spending 30 years in the army of Gustavus (II) Adolphus of Sweden, Leslie returned to lead the Scots in the *Bishops' Wars, defeating the English troops at the battle of Newburn (1640). During the Civil War he commanded the Scots army that invaded England in support of the parliamentarians and fought at the battle of Marston Moor (1644). He accepted Charles I's surrender at Newark (1646) and later handed the king over to parliament. He fought for the Scottish royalists at Dunbar (1650) and was imprisoned by the parliamentarians (1651-54).

Leslie, David, 1st Baron Newark (d. 1682). Soldier. Leslie commanded the Scottish cavalry at *Marston Moor and defeated Montrose at *Philiphaugh. But he was defeated by Cromwell at *Dunbar and *Worcester and was then a prisoner in England (1651-60).

Lesotho. *See* Basutoland.

Levant Company. A company formed in 1592 from the amalgamation of the Turkey Company (founded in 1581) and the Venice Company (founded in 1583). It traded with the Levant—the lands bordering the east Mediterranean, then a part of the Ottoman (Turkish) Empire. Tin for the making of bronze cannon and cloth were exported, in return for currants, wine, cotton, and silk. The company retained its monopoly until 1825.

Levellers. A radical faction of parliamentarians, active between 1645 and 1649, originating among MPs and strongly supported in the lower ranks of the New Model Army. Led by John *Lilburne, the Levellers campaigned against social distinctions (hence their name). They wanted to replace the monarchy and the nobility with a sovereign parliament elected by manhood suffrage. They also pressed for religious toleration and the dismantling of church establishments. Their programme was embodied in the *Agreement of the People* (1647). Even after its final suppression by Cromwell

in 1649 the movement continued to influence radical thought.

Lewes, battle of (14 May 1264). A battle fought between the rebel barons, led by Simon de Montfort, and Henry III (see Barons' Wars). The royal army, with Prince Edward commanding the right flank and Richard of Cornwall the left, greatly outnumbered the baronial force but was surprised by Simon, who took advantage of an unguarded hill to gain a superior position. His victory was decisive; the royalist army was scattered and Henry, Edward, and many of the king's earls were captured. On the day following the battle the mise of *Lewes was agreed.

Lewes, mise of (15 May 1264). A peace agreement that followed the barons' defeat of the royalists in the battle of *Lewes. Castles captured by the royalists were to be returned and imprisoned baronial supporters were to be released. Prince Edward and Henry of Almaine were held hostage as a guarantee of the royalists' fulfilment of the mise's terms.

Liberal Party. One of the two major political parties from the 1860s until the 1920s. Succeeding the *Whig grouping, the Liberal Party emerged in the 1860s and encompassed *radicals and former *Conservatives (notably the followers of Peel), as well as Whigs. The party, dominated by *Gladstone from 1867 until 1894, championed free trade and reform and practised restraint in foreign affairs. In 1886 Gladstone's commitment to Irish *home rule disaffected a large number of Liberals, and some 78 so-called Liberal *Unionists, led by Joseph Chamberlain, were returned at the following election and allied with the victorious Conservatives. The Liberals were out of office until 1892 and again, under *Rosebery, *Harcourt, and *Campbell-Bannerman successively, from 1895 until 1905, when Campbell-Bannerman became prime minister. In 1908 he was succeeded by *Asquith, whose government introduced legislation of fundamental importance. His leadership of the wartime coalition was successfully challenged by *Lloyd

George in 1916, causing the disintegration of the Liberal Party into two factions (see also coupon election). In 1922 it relinquished to the Labour Party its position as one of the two major political parties. The Liberals briefly (1931-32) served in the *national government and subsequently joined the coalition government of World War II. In spite of electoral revivals under Joseph Grimond (1913- ; leader 1956-67) and Jeremy Thorpe (1929- ; leader 1967-76), the party, advocating reform policies based on a belief in individual freedom, has not been able to break the political dominance of the Labour and Conservative Parties. David Steel (1938-) became its leader in 1976.

liberty. Freedom from royal jurisdiction or the area in which that freedom is exercised. Thus the liberty to hold *courts leet might be granted to a manorial lord and the territories of the marcher lords were termed liberties.

Licensing Act (1662). An act passed for two years to prevent the publication of seditious writings. It forbade the printing of books or pamphlets that did not conform with the teachings of the Church of England and required that all publications be licensed and registered with the *Stationers' Company. It was subsequently extended to 1679 and in 1685 was renewed until 1694. Thereafter censorship was maintained by severe laws of libel.

Lilburne, John (?1614-1657). Leader of the *Levellers. In 1638 he was imprisoned for smuggling Puritan pamphlets into England. Released by the Long Parliament, he fought for the parliamentarians in the Civil War until 1645, when he resigned in opposition to the *Solemn League and Covenant. His criticism of parliament and the army led to his frequent imprisonment. Acquitted of treason in 1649, he was banished in 1652 and on his return again tried and, amid popular rejoicing, acquitted. During his final term of imprisonment (1653-55) he became a Quaker.

Limerick, treaty of (3 Oct 1691). The terms of the final surrender of the *Jacobite forces at Limerick in Ireland in 1691. Its military articles, allowing James II's supporters to leave the country, were honoured; but the civil articles, promising de facto religious toleration, were broken by the later *Penal Code.

limited liability company. A company the owners (shareholders) of which are liable, should the company be unable to meet its debts, only for the share they hold in it. Limited liability was first allowed for certain types of company in 1720, after the collapse of the *South Sea Company, and has been available to all companies since 1862. See also joint-stock company.

Linacre, Thomas (c. 1460-1524). Humanist and physician. An associate of John *Colet, he taught Sir Thomas *More and Erasmus at Oxford. He was one of Henry VIII's physicians and helped found the College of Physicians (1518).

Lincoln. A city and the county town of Lincolnshire. It was an important Roman town, named Lindum Colonia, lying on both Ermine Street and the Fosse Way, and during the Danish occupation it was one of the five boroughs of the Danelaw. Lincoln castle was built mostly in 1068, by William I, and the cathedral, with its three towers, around the beginning of the 13th century. Lincoln received its first charter in 1154 and was made a *staple town in 1326. The first railway arrived in 1846.

Lincoln, Assize of (1202). Judicial proceedings, held at Lincoln. Its records are the earliest to survive in their entirety. The assize provides an interesting insight into the criminal patterns of the day. Of particular note are the high proportion of violent crime to the size of the population and the sparing use of capital punishment.

Lincoln, battles of. 1. (2 Feb 1141) The battle in which King *Stephen was defeated, and captured, by forces supporting the empress Matilda. The victory gave Matilda a brief ascendancy in the wars with Stephen, which lasted until she was routed at Winchester in Sept. 2.

(20 May 1217) The battle of the first *Barons' War in which the forces of the future Louis VIII of France and the barons, besieging Lincoln castle, were defeated in the streets of the city by supporters of the young Henry III.

Lincoln, earl of. See Pole, John de la.

Lindisfarne. An island off Northumbria, also called Holy Island since the 11th century on account of the many saints associated with it. In 635 St *Aidan arrived from Iona with a group of Celtic monks and established a monastery on the island, which became a missionary centre and a bishopric. From Lindisfarne monks went to build new churches in southern Scotland and northern England, but many withdrew to Iona when Lindisfarne accepted the Roman discipline after the synod of *Whitby (664). The missionary activity of St *Cuthbert, bishop of Lindisfarne (685-87), spread the fame of Lindisfarne throughout Western Europe. The famous Lindisfarne Gospels, written in about 700 and now in the British Museum, are dedicated to St Cuthbert. The monks fled when they were attacked by the Danes (793, 875), and the last bishop of Lindisfarne, Eardulf, transferred his see to Chester-le-Street (875). From 1082 until the *dissolution of the monasteries in the 1530s there was a Benedictine priory on Lindisfarne.

Lindsey. An Angle kingdom, from which derived (until 1974) the administrative division of Lincolnshire known as the Parts (region) of Lindsey. It was ruled by Northumbria from the mid-7th century and by Mercia from 678 and was overrun by the Danes in 841.

Liverpool, Charles Jenkinson, 1st earl of (and 1st Baron Hawkesbury) (1729-1809). One of the *king's friends, who was secretary to the Treasury (1763-65), secretary at war (1778-82), and president of the board of trade (1768-1801).

Liverpool, Robert Banks Jenkinson, 2nd earl of (1770-1828). Prime minister (1812-27). Son of the 1st earl of Liverpool, Liverpool entered the House of Commons as a Tory MP in 1790 before being called to the Lords, as Lord Hawkesbury, in 1803 (2nd earl of Liverpool from 1808). He served in successive cabinets from 1801 to 1812 as foreign secretary (1801-03), home secretary (1804-06, 1807-09), and secretary for war and the colonies (1809-12), before succeeding Perceval as prime minister on the latter's assassination. The early years of his premiership encompassed the defeat of Napoleon and were followed by the post-1815 period of political and social unrest, including *Spa Fields and the *Peterloo massacre, which the cabinet countered with such repressive measures as the *Six Acts. Liverpool's experiences in public life marked him with a deep antirevolutionary conservatism, but he moved towards a more liberal Toryism in 1822, reconstructing the government to include *Canning and backing the reforms of *Peel at the Home Office and *Huskisson at the Board of Trade. He was succeeded as prime minister in 1827 by Canning.

livery and maintenance. The practice of receiving the livery (or uniform) of a lord and of a lord maintaining (or interfering in) the litigation of his followers by illegal means, such as corruption or coercion. Maintenance became an abuse associated with the keeping of indentured retainers by lords during the late middle ages. Frequent and largely unsuccessful attempts were made to legislate against these threats to public order, which only finally disappeared with the development in the 17th century of a standing army. See also bastard feudalism.

livery companies. The London trade or craft associations, such as those of the weavers, mercers, and vintners, which, successors of the *guilds, dominated the City's political and economic life in the late middle ages. Their members wore distinguishing ceremonial dress (or livery). They began to control trades in the mid-13th century and thereafter exercised increasing power over monopolies, apprenticeships, and all aspects of commercial organization. Immensely wealthy, they engaged in charitable and educational activities, founding such schools as St Paul's and Merchant Taylors. In 1878, with the Corporation of the *City of London, they founded the City and Guilds of London Institute. There are now 84 City Companies, the Great Twelve and the 72 Minor Companies.

Livingstone, David (1813-73). Scottish missionary and explorer of Africa. Livingstone qualified in medicine at Glasgow University and after his ordination in 1840 set out for Bechuanaland (now Botswana). In three major expeditions he traced long stretches of the Zambesi and discovered Lake Ngami (1849), the Victoria Falls (1855), and Lake Nyasa (1859; now Lake Malawi). In 1866 he began his quest for the source of the Nile, during which he had his famous encounter at Ujiji with Sir Henry Morton *Stanley (1871). He died in the Ilala district of what is now Zambia, where his heart was buried. His remains were interred in Westminster Abbey.

Lloyd George, David, 1st Earl Lloyd-George of Dwyfor (1863-1945). Prime minister (1916-22). Born in Manchester of Welsh parents, Lloyd George, following the death of his father, a schoolmaster, in 1864, was brought up in Caernarfonshire by his mother and her brother Richard Lloyd, whose name he later added to his father's surname George. After qualifying as a solicitor (1884), Lloyd George entered the Commons (1890) as Liberal member for Caernarfon Boroughs, a seat he held uninterruptedly until 1945, when he was created an earl. By 1899 he had secured a reputation as a fiery spokesman for Welsh causes and as a leader of radical Liberalism, proving an outspoken opponent of the second *Boer War (1899-1902).

As president of the board of trade (1905-08) in Campbell-Bannerman's cabinet Lloyd George was responsible for the Merchant Shipping Act (1906), the Patents Act (1907), and for setting up the Port of London Authority (1908). Under *Asquith, who became prime minister on Campbell-Bannerman's death in 1908, Lloyd George, as chancellor of the exchequer (1908-15), provoked fierce opposition from established interests by his reforming zeal. In particular, his people's budget of 1909 aroused great controversy; ambitious schemes of social reform, together with naval rearmament, were to be paid for by a land tax, higher death duties, and a supertax on incomes over £3,000. The rejection of the budget by the Lords precipitated a constitutional crisis, which was resolved only after two elections in 1910 and the reduction of the powers of the Lords by the *Parliament Act (1911).

In Asquith's wartime coalition cabinet Lloyd George proved an outstandingly successful minister of munitions (1915-16). However, after serving briefly as secretary for war (1916), he became disillusioned with Asquith's direction of the war and helped manoeuvre his downfall (Dec 1916). He replaced Asquith as head of a coalition that was dominated by Conservatives after many prominent Liberals had followed Asquith out of office. As prime minister Lloyd George, aided by a small war cabinet but wielding almost dictatorial powers, led Britain to victory in 1918 despite clashes with *Haig and the chief of the imperial general staff, Gen. Sir William Robertson (1860-1933). Almost immediately he appealed to the country in the *coupon election, which gave the coalition a massive but predominantly Conservative majority.

Success at the Paris peace conference, where he resisted pressures to impose draconian terms on Germany, was offset by economic difficulties at home resulting from the reintegration of four million servicemen into peacetime employment. Continuing violence in Ireland (1919-21), culminating in the establishment of the Irish Free State (1921) on terms that alienated many Conservatives, weakened Lloyd George's position, which was further undermined by revelations about the sale of honours for contributions towards campaign expenses. In 1922 the withdrawal of Conservative support forced his resignation.

The Liberals were reunited under Asquith (1923-26) and Lloyd George (1926-31), but continued to lose support at elections. Lloyd George never returned to office, although he was approached by Churchill in 1940. Remembered as a great radical reformer, who helped lay the foundations of the welfare state, and as the man who led Britain to victory in *World War I, Lloyd George remained distrusted by many, especially among those Liberals who never forgave him for ousting Asquith in 1916.

Llywarch Hen (6th century). Welsh leader, involved in events of the 6th century in northern Britain. A cycle of 9th-century tales were focused on him but were located in the kingdom of *Powys.

Llywelyn ap Gruffudd (d. 1282). Prince of Wales. He was the second son of *Gruffudd ap Llywelyn and attained ascendancy in Gwynedd after the death (1246) of his uncle *Dafydd ap Llywelyn by imposing himself as overlord on other independent Welsh rulers. In 1267 Llywelyn was acknowledged officially as *prince of Wales by Henry III in the treaty of *Montgomery, and he established an autonomous feudal principality. Legal and other problems forced him into war against Edward I in 1277, after which he lost many of his lands. He joined his brother *Dafydd ap Gruffudd in a second war in 1282 and was killed near Builth. He was buried in Cwm Hir abbey.

Llywelyn ap Iorwerth (d. 1240). Prince of Gwynedd and grandson of *Owain Gwynedd. He conquered the territory of his uncle Dafydd in 1194 and established his supremacy in Gwynedd east and west of the river Conwy. In 1205 he married Joan, illegitimate daughter of King John of England. He strengthened outlying regions of Gwynedd and gradually assumed overlordship over other independent Welsh rulers, which was confirmed by the treaty of *Worcester (1218). He developed close ties

with marcher lords and, in 1230, took the title prince of Aberffraw and lord of Snowdonia. In 1238 he forced his vassals to acknowledge his legitimate son *Dafydd ap Llywelyn as his successor. He laid the basis of the Welsh feudal principality established by his grandson, *Llywelyn ap Gruffudd, and is regarded as having been the most powerful and successful ruler of independent rulers in medieval Wales.

Local Government Acts. Legislation modernizing and democratizing local government. The 1888 act established *county councils, large towns becoming county boroughs with equivalent powers. It was followed in 1894 by an act creating, within the counties, urban and rural districts and elected parish councils. The 1929 act transferred poor relief from boards of guardians to counties and county boroughs. The 1972 act (effective 1974) introduced a reorganized two-tier county and district system in England and Wales. A 1973 act (effective 1975) created Scottish regions, island areas, and districts.

Locarno, treaty of (1 Dec 1925). A pact of nonaggression between France, Germany and Belgium, guaranteed by Britain and Italy.

Locke, John (1632-1704). Philosopher. He was confidential adviser to Lord Ashley (later earl of *Shaftesbury) from 1667 and joined the Royal Society in the following year. On the fall of Shaftesbury (1675) he was forced to leave the country and went to Holland, returning after the Glorious Revolution (1688-89) to become a commissioner of appeals. His works include *An Essay concerning Human Understanding* (1690), which pioneered empiricism and sought to examine the extent of human thought, and *Two Treatises of Government* (1690), in which he denied the *divine right of kings and argued that in fulfilment of a social contract rulers were obliged to preserve the liberties of citizens.

Lollards. Religious reformers who adopted and further developed the ideas of John *Wycliffe. The name, derived probably from the Dutch for "mumbler" (of prayers), was applied to Wycliffe's followers after 1380. The Lollard criticisms of ecclesiastical abuses and their unorthodox views, particularly rejecting transubstantiation (see Eucharist), aroused controversy. Their attacks on the worldliness of the church and the lives of luxury enjoyed by churchmen earned them the hostility of the authorities, temporal as well as ecclesiastical. Following the enactment of the statute *de heretico comburendo* (1401), which made heresy a political crime, punishable by death, the Lollards also campaigned for constitutional reform. Under Sir John *Oldcastle they participated in an abortive rebellion (1413-14). A statute of 1430, limiting the franchise to the owners of land worth at least 40 shillings a year, disenfranchised large numbers of the Lollard supporters, who came mainly from the poorer classes. Lollard ideas influenced the thought of the Bohemian reformer, John Huss, who in turn influenced Martin Luther. In England the Lollards' most notable contribution was that they preached in English and popularized the English translation of the *Bible.

Lombards. A term applied in the middle ages to bankers, moneylenders, and pawnbrokers, many of whom were from Lombardy or elsewhere in north Italy. Italian bankers played an important part in financing the crown in the 13th and 14th centuries. In return for their loans, such firms as the Riccardi of Lucca and the Frescobaldi of Florence received substantial gifts (see usury) and a variety of business privileges. Dislike for these advantages, their power, and their association with unpopular government policies culminated in the expulsion of the Frescobaldi by the lords *ordainers (1311). The strain of heavy royal borrowing brought the collapse of the Riccardi in 1294 and of the Bardi and Peruzzi of Florence in the mid-14th century. Many Italian bankers occupied premises in what became Lombard Street, in London.

London. The capital city of the United Kingdom. London's history seems to have begun with the Romans, who made Londinium the administrative centre of their British province. In the political chaos that followed the Roman withdrawal the Angles and Saxons established the seven kingdoms and London's importance was correspondingly reduced. After the unification of England in the 10th century London again became a city of prime importance. In the 11th century Cnut built a palace a few miles up river, and next to it Edward the Confessor founded the minster that became *Westminster abbey. The city's prominence was made permanent by the Norman conquest, which fixed England's international orientation towards central Europe, as opposed to Scandinavia.

The gradual bureaucratization of the king's government throughout the medieval period meant that parts of it stopped following the king on progress around the country and became permanently established at Westminster. This development gave London its political importance, but it was the development of trade that gave it its economic significance. Until the 17th century England's most important exports were wool and woollen goods, and an overwhelming proportion of these—some 90 per cent in the 16th century—went through the port (Pool) of London. Stimulated by this, and by the population explosion of the 16th century, London began to expand. In this it was aided by the remarkable degree of political stability, which made defensive town walls increasingly unnecessary. Having a population of less than 35 000 in 1500, it had exceeded 100 000 by the end of the 16th century, making it probably the largest city in Europe. It then continued to expand steadily until the industrial revolution produced another population explosion—London's population exceeded one million towards the end of the 18th century, was over 2.5 million by 1851, 6.5 million in 1901, and 8 million in 1951. Since then the population has declined to the present figure of just over 7 million.

The physical expansion of London was initially to the west. The empty spaces between the City and Westminster were developed in the 17th century (Covent Garden, the Strand) and then those to the north, beginning with the area around Bloomsbury. The 19th century saw the most rapid period of London's expansion, with the London conurbation reaching out to swallow up what were originally small villages (Chelsea, Hampstead) and marshland (Pimlico). In addition came the health hazards produced by dense population —London suffered epidemics of cholera until the development of an effective sewage system at the end of the 19th century—and by smog, largely produced by coal fires, until the 1950s. The entire face of the old city was radically altered with the disastrous fire of 1666, which necessitated an almost complete rebuilding. The results lasted until the Blitz of World War II and subsequent demolitions.

The centre of London is still divided by its two main functions, the mercantile interests dominating the City, with the political and administrative centres concentrated on Whitehall. The West End has also succeeded in establishing itself as the cultural centre of the country. The old docklands, the original source of London's wealth, fell into decline at the beginning of the 20th century, largely because the river is no longer deep enough for modern ships. *See also* City of London, Corporation of the.

London Bridge. A bridge over the Thames from the City of London to Southwark. The existence of a bridge across the Thames was one of the earliest reasons for London's importance. The Romans appear to have been the first to bridge the river, and a succession of wooden structures followed until the first stone bridge was built in the 12th century. This was covered with houses and shops on the medieval pattern until the 18th century. The bridge was rebuilt in 1831 by John Rennie the elder (1761–1821) and again replaced in 1969.

London Company. A company, incorporated in 1606, that founded the first permanent settlement in America —Jamestown in Virginia (1607). The settlement barely survived by subsistence agriculture, which was supplemented by tobacco sales after the company was reincorporated as the Virginia Company in 1609. On the verge of bankruptcy, the colony relinquished its charter to the crown in 1624.

Londonderry, siege of (17 April–30 July 1689). The siege of some 30 000 Protestants in Londonderry, Ulster, by the forces of James (II) during his campaign to regain the throne. Although suffering privations that reduced the garrison by two-thirds the Protestants held out until relieved after 105 days.

longbow. A light bow made of yew. Probably of Welsh origin, longbows were introduced to England in the 12th century. They were particularly effective in the *Hundred Years' War, contributing to English victories at *Crécy, *Poitiers, and *Agincourt. They enjoyed several advantages over *crossbows: they were lighter and more accurate and could be fired more rapidly. Longbows were best deployed in a V-shaped formation, which protected the centre of the army.

Longchamp, William (d. 1197). Bishop of Ely from 1189, when he was also appointed chancellor of England. Becoming justiciar and papal legate in 1190, he administered England in Richard I's absence until Prince John engineered his fall from power in 1191. He continued to serve the king abroad, helping to negotiate Richard's release from captivity in Germany in 1193. He was reinstated as chancellor but left England with Richard in 1194, never to return.

Long Parliament (1640–60). The parliament summoned by Charles I after his defeat in the second Bishops' War. It impeached the king's ministers *Strafford and *Laud; secured passage of the *Triennial Act and a bill preventing its dissolution without its own consent; abolished the Courts of *Star Chamber and *High Commission and the Councils of the *North and the *Marches; declared *ship money illegal and, while according Charles *tunnage and poundage, did so for only two months. In Dec 1641 parliament presented the *Grand Remonstrance to the king, who in Jan 1642 attempted to arrest the *five members. A struggle for control of the armed forces culminated in parliament's passage of the *militia bill. The *nineteen propositions followed in June, and in Aug war broke out.

Divided over whether to abolish episcopacy (see Root and Branch Petition), in 1643 parliament summoned the *Westminster Assembly in an attempt to settle the religious issue. Presbyterians came to the fore but clashed with the Independents in the *New Model Army, which dominated events after 1645. In 1648 the Long Parliament was purged by Col *Pride, and its *Rump proceeded to establish the *Commonwealth. In 1653 Cromwell expelled the Rump, which was not recalled until 1659, after the fall of the Protectorate. Its full membership was restored by *Monck, and in 1660 it dissolved itself to be succeeded by the *convention parliament, which restored the monarchy.

lord chamberlain of the household. The officer responsible for the management of the royal household. The office originated in that of the medieval *chamberlain. From 1843 until 1968 he was responsible also for the censorship of plays. See also lord great chamberlain.

lord great chamberlain. A hereditary office created in 1133, when it was conferred on Aubrey de Vere (d. 1141). The lord great chamberlain has largely ceremonial duties in the Houses of Parliament and at coronations.

lord (high) chancellor. Originally, the king's chief secretary (see chancellor). Usually an ecclesiastic, he had custody of the *great seal and developed an important judicial role, administering equity in *Chancery. Under Wolsey the office was politically powerful. The lord chancellor is still speaker of the *House of Lords, in which he sits on the woolsack, and president when it sits as the final Court of Appeal. He is the chief law officer of the government, generally a member of the cabinet, and a privy councillor.

lord high steward. An officer of the crown, originating in the household of the Norman dukes, who presided over a court of justice. The office became hereditary in the family of the earls of Leicester and on the death of Simon de Montfort (1265) passed to the earls and dukes of Lancaster and thence, after the accession of Henry IV to the throne, to the crown (1407). Subsequently a lord high steward was appointed for a special occasion, such as the impeachment of a peer. See also lord steward of the household; steward.

lord lieutenant. An officer appointed to take charge of the county *militia. The office became a regular part of local government under Elizabeth I, and the lord lieutenant is still the chief representative of the crown in the counties. His military responsibilities ended in 1871. Viceroys of Ireland were also called lord lieutenants.

lord protector. See Protectorate.

lord steward of the household. An officer of the royal household whose main responsibility was for the supervision of household servants. Formerly held by a peer who was a member of the political party in power, since 1924 the office has been in the gift of the monarch. Its function is performed by a permanent subordinate officer.

Lostwithiel, battle of (2 Sept 1644). A battle of the Civil War, in which the royalists defeated the parliamentarians. Charles I, commanding in person, surrounded the army of Lord Essex at Lostwithiel, in Cornwall, and forced the infantry to surrender. This and other victories in 1644 placed Charles in a position to launch a direct attack upon London.

Loudoun, John Campbell, 1st earl of (1598–1663). A leading opponent of

Charles I's ecclesiastical policies in Scotland during the 1630s. As lord chancellor of Scotland (1641-60) Loudoun acted as an intermediary (1642-47) between the king and the Scottish parliament. After the Scottish breach with England, Loudoun supported Charles II, taking part in the battle of Dunbar (1650), but failed to gain royal favour after the Restoration.

Loudun Hill, battle of (May 1307). A battle, fought in Ayrshire, in which *Robert the Bruce defeated the forces of Edward II of England under Aymer de Valence. It marked the beginning of the campaign that led to Bruce's recovery of Scotland.

Louviers, treaty of (15 Jan 1196). A peace treaty between Richard the Lionheart and Philip II Augustus of France. Richard conceded the Norman region of Vexin while regaining lands east of the Seine and in Berry.

Lovell, Francis Lovell, 1st Viscount (1454-?1487). Lord chamberlain (1483-85). After the death of Richard III he raised a rebellion in the north against the new king Henry VII and then supported the claims of the pretender Lambert *Simnel. He was reported killed at the battle of *Stoke (1487) but possibly escaped and died in hiding at home.

Lovett, William (1800-77). A leader of *Chartism. A founder of the London Working Men's Association (1836), Lovett was chief author of the *People's Charter* (1838). He was imprisoned (1839-40), for publishing a pamphlet denouncing police severity. A moderate, he subsequently fell out with the more extreme Chartist leaders.

Lower Britain. One of the two provinces (*compare* Upper Britain) into which Britain was divided by *Septimius Severus. The province had its capital at York.

Lucan, George Charles Bingham, 3rd earl of (1800-88). Soldier. Lucan, who succeeded to his title in 1839, accompanied the Russian troops during the Russo-Turkish War of 1828. At the battle of *Balaclava (1854), at which he commanded a cavalry division, his misreading of orders from the commander in chief Lord Raglan led to the abortive *charge of the Light Brigade. He was promoted to field marshal shortly before his death.

Lucknow, relief of (1858). An episode during the Indian mutiny. Lucknow, besieged by mutineers, was first relieved by Gen. Henry Havelock. His forces were insufficient to disperse the enemy and were themselves imprisoned within the town until relieved by Maj. Gen. Sir Colin *Campbell.

Lucy, Richard de (d. 1179). A supporter of King Stephen, who later became a trusted minister of Henry II. As justiciar (1153-79), he helped draw up the constitutions of *Clarendon (1164) and was excommunicated by Becket. He defeated a rebellion of Henry's sons in 1173. Shortly before his death he resigned the justiciarship and retired to his abbey of Westwood.

Luddites. Early 19th-century workmen who destroyed factory machinery. The name derives from the signature "Ned Ludd", used on a workmen's manifesto (the original Ned Ludd being reputedly a Leicestershire youth who broke some machinery in 1799). Organized Luddite activity broke out in textile factories in Nottinghamshire, Derbyshire, Leicestershire, and Yorkshire in 1811-12 and was renewed in 1816. The government, fearing a revolutionary conspiracy (and having no effective police forces), repressed Luddite rioting harshly; in 1813 some 17 men were executed at York. Luddism (like earlier machine-smashing episodes) was a desperate attempt to preserve jobs, thought to be threatened by the new machines of the industrial revolution, at a time of economic distress provoked by the Napoleonic War.

Ludford Bridge, rout of (12-13 Oct 1459). An encounter, during the Wars of the Roses, at Ludford in Shropshire between Yorkists and Lancastrians. The Yorkists were routed and the Lancastrians went on to sack Ludlow castle, the home of Richard, duke of York. He, his son Edward, and their supporters were obliged to flee.

Ludlow, Edmund (c. 1617-1692). Parliamentarian during the Civil War, who was a judge at the trial of Charles I and signed the king's death warrant (1649). Prominent during the Commonwealth (1649-53), he opposed the Protectorate and after Cromwell's death (1658) tried to reunite the republican party. Following the Restoration he fled to Switzerland. There he wrote his memoirs, which are an important historical source (published 1698).

Lugard, Frederick Lugard, 1st Baron (1858-1945). Colonial administrator, notably in Northern Nigeria, where he introduced his policy of *indirect rule. After leaving Sandhurst Lugard served in Afghanistan, the Sudan, and Burma in the 1880s and subsequently in Buganda and Nigeria. He was high commissioner of Northern Nigeria (1900-06) and governor general of all Nigeria (1914-19). He was also governor of Hong Kong (1907-12).

M

Mabinogi, Four Branches of the. A medieval prose romance. These mythological tales, written down in the late 11th century (with surviving texts dated c. 1300-25), preserve traditions transmitted orally over many centuries. The Four Branches, Pwyll, Prince of Dyfed, Branwen, Daughter of Llŷr, Manawydan, Son of Llŷr, and Math, Son of Mathonwy, locate heroic and legendary figures in the Welsh countryside.

Macadam, John Loudon (1756-1836). Road engineer. Born in Scotland, Macadam began experimenting with road building at his estate in Ayrshire, before being appointed surveyor general of the Bristol roads in 1815. There he put his discoveries into practice, creating a wear-resistant surface, impervious to water, by using successive layers of small hard stones; a traffic-compacted firm road resulted. In 1827 Macadam was appointed surveyor general of metropolitan roads. "Macadamizing" became almost universal in Britain and western Europe by 1900.

Macaulay, Thomas Babington, 1st Baron (1800-59). Politician and historian; son of Zacharay *Macaulay. A barrister and an MP (1830-34, 1839-47, 1852-56), Macaulay eloquently advocated the 1832 reform bills and served in India (1834-38). He was subsequently secretary for war (1839-41) and paymaster general (1846-47). His *History of England* from 1688 to 1820 (5 vols, 1849-61), unfinished at his death, expounded the Whig interpretation of history.

Macaulay, Zachary (1768-1838). Philanthropist and one of the leaders of the movement to abolish *slavery. He was the father of Thomas Babington *Macaulay. Zachary Macaulay was governor of Sierra Leone, the freed slave settlement in West Africa, from 1793 to 1799. With *Wilberforce and Sharp he helped form the Sierra Leone Company to finance the settlement and was its secretary (1799-1808). He edited the *Christian Observer* (1802-16), the organ of the antislavery movement, and was prominent in the Anti-Slavery Society from 1823.

Macbeth (c. 1005-1057). King of Scots (1040-57). Son of Finlaech, mormaer (earl) of Moray, and probably a grandson of Malcolm II, Macbeth asserted his claim to the throne against Duncan I, whom he killed near Elgin. In 1045 he killed Crinan, Duncan's father, in battle, but in 1057 he was himself killed by Duncan's son, Malcolm Canmore. Both Macbeth and his wife, Gruoch, gave generously to the church, and in 1050 he made a pilgrimage to Rome.

McCarthy, Justin (1830-1912) Irish politician and writer. A journalist and novelist, he began his career in politics in the 1870s as a home rule MP. In 1890 he sided with the majority of Irish MPs in repudiating Parnell and led this faction of the party at Westminster from 1890 to 1896.

MacDonald, Flora (1722-90). The Scottish woman who won popular renown for helping Charles Edward Stuart escape capture after *Culloden, for which she was imprisoned. In 1774 she emigrated to America but returned to Scotland in 1779.

MacDonald, (James) Ramsay (1866-1937). The first Labour prime minister. A Scot, of illegitimate birth, MacDonald became a journalist in London. Initially active in the Social Democratic Federation, he joined the *Independent Labour Party in 1894. He was the first secretary of the Labour Representation Committee (1900-05) and of the Labour Party (1906-12). Elected an MP in 1906, he became leader of the parliamentary Labour Party (1911) but resigned (Aug 1914) in opposition to World War I, losing his seat in 1918. He returned to parliament in 1922, becoming leader of the party and the opposition. MacDonald was prime minister and foreign secretary from Jan to Nov 1924, his minority government falling when it lost Liberal support. Prime minister again (without an overall majority) in June 1929, he faced the crisis engendered by the world economic depression. In Aug 1931, after his cabinet split over proposed cuts in unemployment benefits, MacDonald formed, with Conservatives and Liberals, a *national government. He was denounced as a betrayer of Labour and expelled from party membership. Leading a tiny National Labour Party, he remained prime minister, backed by the Conservatives, until succeeded by *Baldwin in June 1935. MacDonald became lord president of the council but lost his parliamentary seat in Nov 1935. Re-elected (Feb 1936), he retired in May 1937.

Macdonald, Sir John (1815-91). Canadian statesman. A lawyer, Macdonald led the movement for Canadian federation. He was the first prime minister of the Dominion of Canada (1867-73), and held office a second time from 1878 until his death. He helped originate the Canadian Pacific Railway.

MacGregor (or Campbell), Robert (1671-1734). A Highland cattle dealer, known as Rob Roy, who became notorious through his exploits as a cattle thief and his exactions of protection money from cattle owners.

Mackenzie, William Lyon (1795-1861). Leader of a rebellion in Upper Canada (1837-38). Mackenzie, a Scottish-born radical journalist and politician, dissatisfied by his failure to secure reforms, led a revolt that aimed to establish a provisional govenment in Toronto. His insurrection, following *Papineau's, was soon suppressed. He was pardoned in 1849 and thereafter sat in the united Canadian legislature (1851-58).

Macmillan, (Maurice) Harold (1894-1986). Prime minister (1957-63). Macmillan (a publisher) was a Conservative MP (1924-29, 1931-45, 1945-64), but as a critic of the government's economic policies in the 1930s and an opponent of *appeasement he did not achieve office until World War II, under Winston Churchill. He was later minister of housing (1951-54), minister of defence (1954-55), foreign secretary (1955), and chancellor of the exchequer (1955-57). Following the *Suez crisis Macmillan succeeded Eden as prime minister (Jan 1957) and won the election of 1959 with the slogan "You have never had it so good". The aims of his government included independence for former colonies (expressed in his "wind of change" speech in Africa), the maintenance of close Anglo-American relations, and entry into the EEC. In 1963, however, France vetoed British membership of the EEC and, in spite of his achievement in helping to negotiate the *nuclear test-ban treaty (1963), Macmillan's political problems further increased with the *Profumo scandal. When illness temporarily incapacitated him (Oct 1963), Macmillan retired and became earl of Stockton in 1984.

Mad Mullah (1864-1920). The British nickname for the Somali *dervish, Mohammed ibn Abdullah, who waged a holy war (*jihad*) against the British in Somaliland from 1899 until his death.

Madog ap Maredudd (d. 1160). King of Powys. The last ruler of an united kingdom of Powys, he was defeated by *Owain Gwynedd at the battle of Coleshill (1150). Territory in Ial (Yale) surrendered to Owain was recovered in 1157, when Madog supported the royal expedition led by Henry II against Owain Gwynedd.

Madog ap Owain Gwynedd (c. 1170). A legendary figure, associated with *Owain Gwynedd's court. He is believed to have sailed across the Atlantic (c. 1170) and discovered America. This legend exercised considerable influence from the 16th century, when the story was included in Richard Hakluyt's *Voyages* (1582). In the late 18th century John Evans, a Caernarfonshire preacher, explored the upper reaches of the Missouri in his search for reputed Welsh-speaking Indians (called the Padoucas, an anglicized form of Madogwys), the descendants of Madog.

Maelgwn Gwynedd (died c. 547). Ruler of Gwynedd, a descendant of *Cunedda. Severely criticized by St *Gildas for his many nefarious deeds, including murder, he retreated, at one stage, into a monastery and patronized several religious centres.

Mafeking. A town in Cape Province, South Africa. During the second *Boer War Mafeking, besieged by the Boers, held out under Sir Robert *Baden-Powell from 12 Oct 1899 to 17 May 1900, when it was relieved by Col (later 1st Viscount) H. C. O. Plumer (1857–1932).

Magersfontein, battle of (11 Dec 1899). A battle of the second *Boer War. The Boers dug in around Magersfontein Hill in the north Cape Colony and severely defeated a British force, which, commanded by Lord Methuen (1845–1932), was attempting to seize the hill and relieve nearby *Kimberley.

Magna Carta. The Great Charter sealed by King John after his meeting with the barons at Runnymede on 15 June 1215. Violent baronial opposition to John's disastrous foreign policy and what was regarded as his arbitrary rule was chan-

nelled by Archbishop Langton into a demand for constitutional restraints on royal power. The resulting document redefined many feudal practices, but the term "Great" does not imply contemporary recognition of any special constitutional significance, referring rather to the charter's unusual length. Nevertheless it came subsequently to be regarded as a milestone in British constitutional history, especially by the parliamentarians in the 17th century.

Magna Carta comprises a preamble and 63 clauses. The most famous guarantee every free man security from illegal interference in his person or property (39) and justice to everyone (40). The king was not to levy scutage or aids (except for three) without reference to the "common council" of the realm (12), and other feudal incidents were limited. Further, the church was to be "free", the power of sheriffs was restricted, and the liberties of the boroughs were confirmed. The charter was to be enforced by a council of 25 barons, which, if the king reneged on his promises, would declare war on him. Magna Carta was condemned by Pope Innocent III and failed to prevent the outbreak of the first *Barons' War, but it was reissued with some changes in 1216, 1217, and 1225. The four extant copies of the original are in Salisbury Cathedral, Lincoln Cathedral, and (two) the British Library.

Mahdi, the (1844–85). The title (meaning the guided one) of Muhammad Ahmad, the Muslim leader who founded the Mahdiya brotherhood in Islam. He proclaimed a holy war (*jihad*) to purify Islam (1881) and overran the Sudan, besieging and capturing *Khartoum and killing Gen. Gordon. He then established a theocratic state with its capital at *Omdurman.

main plot (1603). A conspiracy to replace James I as sovereign with Lady Arabella *Stuart, James' cousin and an English descendant of Henry VII. The plot failed, and its instigator Henry Brooke, 8th Baron Cobham (d. 1619), together with Sir Walter *Raleigh, whom Cobham implicated, were imprisoned in the Tower; the other plotters were executed. The conspirators of the main plot were tried together with those of the contemporary *bye plot, as if the latter was an offshoot (which it was not) of the former—hence their names.

mainprise (Anglo-Norman: take into the hand). A writ ordering a sheriff to accept an undertaking from pledges, or main-pernors, to present an accused person in court for trial. It was issued only in the case of minor offences and was the forerunner of the modern system of *bail.

Maitland of Thirlestane, John, 1st Baron (1543-95). The most influential of the advisers of James VI of Scotland from the mid-1580s until 1592. Many of his policies were continued by the king after Maitland's fall. His grandson was the 1st duke of *Lauderdale.

major generals. Between 1655 and 1657, officers responsible for direct military rule in England and Wales. In March 1655 a royalist uprising led Cromwell to divide the country into 11 districts, each commanded by a major general. They controlled the local militia as well as their own troops, exacted fines from royalists, and suppressed all gatherings, pastimes, and institutions that might foster sedition or injure public morals. Their puritanical zeal made them greatly detested and the parliament elected in 1656 soon terminated their rule (see Humble Petition and Advice).

Majuba Hill, battle of (27 Feb 1881). A battle of the first *Boer War. The Boer troops of Piet Joubert surrounded a British force, which, under Sir George Pomeroy Colley, was occupying Majuba Hill, and virtually annihilated it.

Malawi. See Nyasaland.

Malaya. A peninsula in southeast Asia. British influence spread throughout Malaya in the 19th century. Treaties were made with the rulers of Perak (1873), Selangor (1874), Negri Sembilan (1876), and Pahang (1888), which formed the Federated Malay States in 1895, and of Johore (1885), *Brunei (1888), Perlis (1907), and Kedah, Kelantan, and Trengganu (all 1909), the

Unfederated Malay States, which became British protectorates. After occupation by the Japanese in World War II, all the states save Brunei formed (1946) the Union of Malaya. Reconstituted as the Federation of Malaya in 1948, it became an independent member of the Commonwealth in 1957.

Malaysia. A southeast Asian federation within the Commonwealth, consisting of the former Federation of *Malaya and of *Sarawak and Sabah (see North Borneo). The federation came into being in 1963 and included *Singapore until 1965.

Malcolm I (d. 954). King of Scotia (943-54). Son of Donald II, Malcolm succeeded on the abdication of his second cousin, Constantine II. He invaded England as far as the Tees in about 950 but was probably chiefly occupied in suppressing rebellions by the men of Moray, by whom he was eventually killed.

Malcolm II (c. 954-1034). King of Scotia (1005-34). Malcolm, the son of Kenneth II, gained the throne by killing his predecessor, Kenneth III. He sought to extend his kingdom southwards and after the battle of Carham in 1018 recovered Lothian from the English. Shortly afterwards Malcolm's grandson, later Duncan I, became the last king of Strathclyde and the southwest was thus joined to the Scottish kingdom. In 1031 an English invasion forced Malcolm to submit to Cnut, and he may have lost control of much of northern Scotland to the men of Moray.

Malcolm III Canmore (c. 1031-1093). King of Scots (1058-93). Malcolm fled to England when Macbeth murdered his father, Duncan I, and was brought up at the English court. With English help he defeated Macbeth in 1054 (at Dunsinane, in Shakespeare's play) and killed him three years later. Malcolm undertook five invasions of England, being killed during the last of them. His first wife was Ingibjorg, daughter of the earl of Orkney, and his second, St *Margaret. He was succeeded by his brother, Donald III.

Malcolm IV (1141-65). King of Scots (1153-65), eldest son of Henry (son of David I). Rebellions in the north and the Hebrides soon after the accession of the child king may reflect resentment at the strength of Norman influence under his grandfather. Later risings may indicate discontent at his becoming the vassal of Henry II of England in 1163. His nickname, the Maiden, reflects devotion to celibacy (he never married) rather than weakness. Malcolm was succeeded by his brother William I.

Maldon, battle of (Aug 991). A battle between Englishmen under Byrhtnoth and the Danes under Anlaf. The battle was the subject of a poem in Old English, composed by an eyewitness, which commemorates the heroism of the English, who were, however, defeated.

malignants. A name given by the parliamentarians to supporters of Charles I. Royalists were first so called in the Grand Remonstrance (1641), which also used the term delinquent to describe a follower of the king.

Malory, Sir Thomas. Translator and author of the *Morte d'Arthur* (1470), the epic prose work relating the Arthurian legends. He is tentatively identified with Sir Thomas Malory, a knight from Newbold Revell in Warwickshire.

Malplaquet, battle of (11 Sept 1709). A battle in the War of the *Spanish Succession. The combined German and British forces under *Marlborough defeated the French but lost about 16 000 men. Although this victory enabled the allies to take Mons, the heavy casualties strengthened the hands of the peace party in Britain.

Malta. A Mediterranean island. It was the property of the Knights of St John from 1530 until captured by Napoleon Bonaparte in 1798. Malta sought British help and was annexed to the crown in 1814. An important naval base, it was besieged in World War II and awarded the George Cross. The island obtained self-government in 1947 and became an independent member of the Commonwealth in 1964.

Malthus, Thomas Robert (1766-1834). Economist. In his *Essay on the Principle of Population as It Affects the Future Improvement of Society* (1798) he argued that the increase in population could not be matched by a similar quantitative increase in production, that population was limited only by natural disasters, such as famine, and that a growing population will get poorer. Malthus' ideas influenced Darwin, as well as 19th-century economists, notably Ricardo, and also stimulated social reform.

Manchester, Edward Montagu, 2nd earl of (1602-71). Parliamentary general in the Civil War. He was in command at *Marston Moor (1644) but was accused by Cromwell of incompetency at *Newbury (1644) and resigned (1645). He opposed the trial of Charles I and retired from public life until the Restoration.

Manchester martyrs. Three Fenians executed in 1867 for killing a British policeman in Manchester while rescuing two other Fenians from a prison van. In England they are remembered as the Manchester murderers.

Manchester school. A group of advocates of *laissez-faire economics and *free trade, active during the period 1820-50. Influenced by the ideas of David *Ricardo, its leaders included Richard *Cobden and John *Bright, who were both prominent members of the Anti-Corn-Law League (see corn laws).

mandate (or **mandated territory**). A former German or Turkish colony that was administered by one of the victors of World War I by mandate (direction) of the *League of Nations. Britain obtained Tanganyika and part of Togoland and the Cameroons from Germany and Palestine, Iraq, and Transjordan from Turkey. South Africa, Australia, New Zealand, Belgium, and France also won mandates. This system was replaced in 1946 by the UN system of *trust territories.

Manning, Henry Edward, Cardinal (1808-92). Anglican priest, who after his conversion (1851) from *Anglo-Catholicism to Roman Catholicism, rose to become archbishop of Westminster. Succeeding *Wiseman, Manning was archbishop from 1865 until his death, and was created cardinal in 1875. Although authoritarian in matters of doctrine, he was keenly interested in social questions, and supported trade-union rights.

manor. A landholding unit in medieval England. It was normally, although not always, divided into two: the *demesne, land kept under the lord's direct control and cultivated for his profit, and the tenants' holdings, land granted in return for service, whether free (i.e. for money rent) or unfree (i.e. for labour provided on the lord's demesne). The proportion of demesne and tenanted land varied; some manors had no demesne, others no landholding tenants. Nor was it always coterminous with a village: some manors comprised several villages or one village might be divided between several manors. The lord of a manor exercised jurisdiction over his tenants in the *court baron and some also held *courts leet. The manor's origin is unclear but manors were certainly present in the late Anglo-Saxon period and almost all were created before 1289. They retained their integrity as territorial, legal, and administrative units until the early modern period, and vestiges of the manorial system still exist.

Mansel, John (d. 1256). Counsellor to Henry III. After a distinguished military career in Italy and France he rose to a position of trust in Henry III's household. He became keeper of the great seal (1246) and was entrusted with many diplomatic missions. He was one of the king's representatives on the council of 15 established by the *Provisions of Oxford and remained the king's counsellor throughout the Barons' War.

Mansfield, William Murray, 1st earl of (1705-93). Lord chief justice (1756-88). He earned great unpopularity for his strict interpretation of the laws of seditious libel, notably in the cases brought as a result of the letters of *Junius. He delivered the *Mansfield judgment on slavery.

Mansfield judgment (1772). A legal judgment, delivered by Lord *Mansfield, that declared *slavery illegal in England. The pronouncement arose in the case of James Somersett, one of over 10 000 Black slaves in England, who had escaped from his master.

manumission. The granting of the status of a free man, or *franchise, to a *villein. Freedom was usually obtained by payment (quit rent) to the lord, who gave the villein his freedom (see quit claim) in a ceremony performed before the sheriff in court.

Maori Wars (1860-72). Wars fought by the New Zealand Maori against the encroachment, in contravention of the treaty of *Waitangi (1840), of British settlers on their land in North Island. In a series of wars (1860-61, 1863-64, 1864-72) the Maori were pushed out of Tataraimaka and Waikato by British troops and local militia. Maori fanatics, believing themselves impervious to bullets, fought a guerrilla war (1864-72), but by 1872 the Maori were left with only Maori King Country in the west of North Island.

Mar, John Erskine, 1st or 6th earl of (d. 1572). Scottish noble, who served Mary Queen of Scots until she married *Bothwell. In 1566 he became guardian of the infant Prince James, who was crowned James VI the following year. Mar was one of the insurgent leaders who received the surrender of Mary at Carberry Hill (1567). As regent (1571-72) he was much influenced by the earl of *Morton, who succeeded him in 1572.

Mar, John Erskine, 6th or 11th earl of (1675-1732). Leader of the 1715 *Jacobite rising in Scotland. He embraced the Jacobite cause after being dismissed from office by George I. The rebellion failed partly because of his incompetent leadership. After his defeat at *Sheriffmuir he fled to France, and his title was forfeited.

March, earls of. See Mortimer.

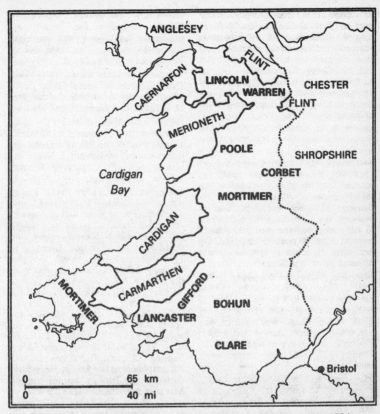

The chief marcher lordships of Wales and the counties created in 1284

Marches of Wales. The areas on the Welsh–English border and on the southern Welsh coast where lordships were established following the Norman conquest. The process whereby marcher lordships were founded was set in motion in the late 11th century, with significant developments in Brecon and in Glamorgan. The Marches were extended in the late 13th century with the creation of lordships in northeast Wales as a result of the conquests of Edward I. A lordship was normally divided into an Englishry and Welshry. The Englishry, comprising lowland areas, contained the castle, the military and administrative centre; the manor, an agricultural unit providing for the maintenance of the lord's household; and the borough, the commercial centre the privileges of which were often based on those conferred on Hereford by William *Fitzosbern. Welsh customs survived to a far greater extent in the Welshry, located in the upland regions. *See also* Principality.

Marconi affair (1912–13). A political scandal that followed the announcement (March 1912) by the (Liberal) government that it proposed to employ the British Marconi Company to establish an "imperial wireless chain". Certain ministers were then accused of influencing the deal in order to gain from Marconi shares, and the subsequent parliamentary investigation found that *Lloyd George (chancellor of the exchequer) and Sir Rufus *Isaacs (attorney-general) had imprudently but not corruptly bought American (not British) Marconi shares. The Liberal majority, against bitter Conservative opposition, voted to accept their apologies (June 1913).

Margaret (?1283-1290). Queen of Scots (1286-90). Known as the maid of Norway, Margaret was the granddaughter of Alexander III by his daughter Margaret and Erik, king of Norway. Six *guardians ruled Scotland in her name, but she died while being brought from Norway to Scotland. On her death the right to the crown was disputed by 13 *competitors.

Margaret, duchess of Burgundy (1446-1503). Sister of Edward IV, whose marriage (1468) to Charles the Bold of Burgundy strengthened the house of York with a Burgundian alliance. She supported Lambert Simnel and Perkin Warbeck, pretenders to the throne of Henry VII, but was subsequently pardoned.

Margaret, St (c. 1046-1093). Queen consort of Malcolm III Canmore of Scots, granddaughter of Edmund Ironside of England. Margaret, a pious and determined woman, worked to bring the practices of the church in Scotland into line with Roman usages and brought Benedictine monks to Scotland. She was canonized in 1249. Feast day: 10 June.

Margaret of Anjou (1430-82). Queen consort of Henry VI from 1445, daughter of Réné, duke of Lorraine and Anjou, and a powerful figure in the Lancastrian camp during the Wars of the *Roses. In 1461, after the Lancastrian defeat at *Towton, she escaped into exile in Scotland. She returned in 1470, in alliance with the earl of Warwick, restoring Henry. In the following year her and Warwick's forces were finally defeated at the battle of *Tewkesbury,

where her son Edward was killed. Shortly afterwards she herself was imprisoned and Henry was murdered. Ransomed in 1476 by Louis XI of France, she retired to Anjou.

Margaret of Denmark (c. 1457-1486). Queen consort of James III of Scots, whom she married in 1469, and daughter of Christian I of Denmark and Norway. Margaret was noted for her piety.

Margaret of France (?1282-1318). Daughter of Philip III of France and queen consort of Edward I, whom she married in 1299 as part of a treaty between the two kings.

Margaret Tudor (1489-1541). Queen consort of James IV (1503-13), and eldest daughter of Henry VII of England. After the death of James at Flodden (1513) Margaret became regent and guardian of her infant son, James V. In 1514 she married Archibald *Douglas, 6th earl of Angus. Forced to surrender the regency to John Stewart, 1st duke of *Albany (1515), she fled to England but after her return (1517) again became embroiled in the conflict between the pro-English and pro-French parties vying for control of the king. Divorced from Angus in 1527, she subsequently married Albany. The Stewart (or *Stuart) claim to the English throne was based on the family's descent through Margaret from Henry VII.

Marian reaction. The restoration of the Roman Catholic faith in England during the reign of *Mary I. The reversal of the Reformation began in 1553 with the repeal of Edward VI's Act of *Uniformity. Soon after, all married clergy were removed from their benefices. In Nov 1554 Cardinal *Pole arrived in England as papal legate and absolved England from schism. Parliament then repealed all existing antipapal legislation and revived the old heresy laws but made no attempt to restore monastic property. In 1555 a synod restored Catholic doctrine and ceremonial and the persecution of committed Protestants was begun. Bishops Hooper, Latimer, and Ridley and Archbishop Cranmer were burned between 1555 and 1556, and an estimated

270 others had suffered a similar fate by 1558.

marischal. See marshal.

Marlborough, John Churchill, 1st duke of, (1650-1722). Soldier, who is generally acknowledged to have been one of the foremost strategists and military administrators in British history. Son of Sir Winston Churchill, an MP, Marlborough entered the army in 1667 and rose rapidly through the officer ranks, serving with distinction at Tangier (1668-70) and during the third Dutch War (1672-73). From 1675, when he married Sarah Jennings (1660-1722), lady in waiting to Princess (later Queen) Anne, he developed links with the court. In 1682 he was created a Scottish peer and in 1685 Baron Churchill in the English peerage. He played a leading role in the suppression of *Monmouth's rebellion (1685) but in 1688 abandoned James II for William of Orange and, following William's accession to the throne, was rewarded with the earldom of Marlborough (1689). In 1690 Marlborough was appointed a privy councillor, but his relations with William III became strained and in 1691 he was dismissed, to be briefly imprisoned in the following year upon an unfounded treason charge. On the succession of Anne (1702), at the outset of the War of the *Spanish Succession, Marlborough was appointed captain general of the British forces and supreme commander of the allied forces, as well as being granted a dukedom (1702). His wife became an intimate of Queen Anne and mistress of the robes. In 1704 Marlborough won the spectacular victory of *Blenheim, following it with the victories of *Ramillies (1706), *Oudenarde (1708), and *Malplaquet (1709). This last, however, was a costly success, and at home relations between the duchess and Queen Anne were cooling. Despite further victories on the Continent, in 1711 Marlborough was dismissed from all his posts on a charge of embezzlement and went to live abroad. In 1714 he was reinstated by George I, one of his greatest admirers, but in 1718 he was incapacitated by a stroke and resigned.

Marlborough, Statute of (1267). The statute, passed after the second *Barons' War, that confirmed many of the measures introduced by the Montfortians, notably the *Provisions of Westminster. It included clauses, still in force, for the regulation of *distress.

Marlowe, Christopher (1564-93). Elizabethan poet, dramatist, and government spy. His plays, including Tamburlaine (1590) and Doctor Faustus (1604), are brilliant dramatic studies of psychological conflict. Marlowe was killed in a tavern brawl.

Marprelate tracts. Extreme-Puritan attacks, printed between 1587 and 1589, on the bishops of the Anglican church. Martin Marprelate (mar a prelate) was a pseudonym adopted by the author. In 1592 John *Penry was convicted for their authorship and hanged.

marque, letters of. Licences granted by the sovereign to fit out an armed ship in time of war. They were used, especially in the 16th century, to distinguish *privateers from pirates. James I was unwilling to grant them, but they did not disappear until the abolition of privateering by the Declaration of *Paris (1856).

marquess. A rank of the *peerage, standing below a duke and above an earl. It was first conferred in 1385 on Robert de Vere, 9th earl of *Oxford. The oldest surviving marquessate ·is Winchester, created in 1551. A woman holding the rank is called a marchioness.

marriage. See wardship and marriage.

Marriage Act (1753). The act that made void all marriages other than those celebrated in a church or by special licence. Formerly a marriage was valid under the common law if the parties consented to marriage in the presence of witnesses or if it was celebrated by a person in priest's orders. Clandestine marriages, sometimes of minors, were commonly celebrated—for a sum—in the district of the *Fleet prison (hence being termed Fleet marriages) by persons pretending to be priests. The Marriage Act, or Lord

Hardwicke's Act, was designed to end such abuses. However, it stipulated that a marriage to be valid must be celebrated by the Church of England, and, until the Marriage Act (1837), marriages between Roman Catholics and nonconformists (except Quakers) were not valid if celebrated according to their own rites. (*See also* Royal Marriages Act.)

Married Women's Property Acts (1870, 1882). Two statutes that granted basic property rights to married women and were thus important landmarks in the *women's movement. Previously all property within marriage legally belonged to the husband. The first act only gave women the right to keep their earnings, but the second allowed them to keep property they had owned on marriage or acquired later.

marshal. One of the chief officers of the royal household, initially entrusted with the military affairs of the sovereign. His functions were later shared between the earl marshal, the high office of state held hereditarily from the 13th century by the earls and later the dukes of Norfolk, and the knight marshal, who presided, with the steward, over the court of the *Marshalsea. The office of marshal (or marischal) of the Scottish court became hereditary in the Keith family in the early 14th century; it became extinct in 1716.

Marshal, William, 1st earl of Pembroke and Striguil (d. 1219). Regent (1216-19). He inherited the earldom through his marriage to Isabel, daughter of Richard de *Clare, earl of Pembroke and Striguil (1189). He fought in France with Henry II and in 1170 was given charge of the young prince Henry. He went on crusade from 1183 to 1187 and served in the government of Richard I. As King John's chief adviser from 1213, he counselled moderation during the crisis over *Magna Carta. Appointed regent for Henry III in 1216, he expelled Louis of France from the kingdom in the following year and restored order after the first *Barons' War.

Marshall plan. The informal name for the European Recovery Programme

(1948-51), financed by the USA after World War II. Publicly proposed in June 1947 by Gen. George Marshall (1880-1959), the US secretary of state, the programme ultimately involved $12,000 million in "Marshall aid" for economic reconstruction. The Soviet Union refused to participate. The plan, implemented by the Organization for European Economic Cooperation, facilitated the postwar economic growth of West Europe.

Marshal rebellion (1233-34). A rebellion led by Richard Marshal, 3rd earl of Pembroke and Striguil (d. 1234), against control of royal government by the *Poitevins. Richard was supported by many marcher and Anglo-Irish lords and by *Llywelyn ap Iorwerth of Gwynedd. Open warfare, chiefly in Wales and Ireland, was brief but fierce and ended with Richard's murder by royalists in Ireland. The English bishops brought about a reconciliation between Henry III and the rebels, and the Poitevins were deprived of power.

Marshalsea. 1. A court, originally held before the steward and marshal of the royal household, that heard cases concerning disputes between members of the household. It dealt primarily with trespasses committed within 12 mi (the "verge") of the monarch's court, and with debts. It was renamed the Court of the Verge in 1612 and Palace Court (referring to Whitehall palace) in 1630; it was abolished in 1849. 2. A prison in Southwark for those convicted in the court of the Marshalsea. After 1601 it confined chiefly debtors and was abolished in 1842.

Marston Moor, battle of (2 July 1644). A battle, fought near York during the Civil War, between parliamentary armies, commanded by Cromwell, Manchester, and Sir Thomas *Fairfax, and a royalist army led by Prince Rupert. The battle, ill-managed on both sides, ended with the rout of the royalists, who suffered crippling losses, with 4000 men killed and 1500 captured.

Martello towers. Fortifications containing cannon, built (1804-12) along the eastern and southern coasts of England as a defence against Napoleon's threatened invasion. They took their name and function from a tower at Cap Mortella, Corsica, which had been attacked (1794) by British forces.

martial law. The use of military courts (without trial by jury) to try civilians. Examples are the proceedings against the rebels of the *Pilgrimage of Grace (1536) and the *northern rebellion (1569). Its use to levy the forced loan of 1627 was a grievance in the *Petition of Right (1628), and it has subsequently been authorized only in 1803, 1833, and (in Ireland) 1920.

Martineau, Harriet (1802-76). Writer. Brought up as a Unitarian, she wrote fiction and gained a wide readership for her popularizations of history, economics, and the positivist philosophy of the Frenchman Auguste Comte (1798-1857); her books include *History of England during the Thirty Years' Peace, 1816-46* (1849). She also became an enthusiastic advocate of mesmerism.

Marvell, Andrew (1621-78). Puritan poet and politician. He was tutor in the Fairfax and Cromwell families, and in 1657 became Milton's assistant in the Latin secretaryship to the Council of State. As an MP (1659-78) he violently attacked Charles II and his ministers in pamphlets and verse satires.

Mary (1631-60). Princess royal of England and princess of Orange. Mary was the eldest daughter of Charles I and, by her marriage (1641) into the Dutch house of Orange, mother of William of Orange, later William III of England.

Mary (1542-87). Queen of Scots (1542-67), daughter of James V and Mary of Guise. In 1548 Mary was sent to France and in 1558 she married the heir to the French throne, who succeeded as Francis II in the following year. He died in 1560, and Mary returned to Scotland in 1561. Although remaining a Roman Catholic she tacitly accepted the Protestant Reformation, which had just taken place. Mary's marriage to her cousin, Lord *Darnley, in 1565 led to an unsuccessful rebellion by many who had previously supported her. Mary soon recognized that Darnley lacked both intelligence and morality and became estranged from him. Jealous of the influence he thought *Rizzio, her French secretary, had over her, Darnley and some Protestant lords murdered him in 1566. Mary may well have had no knowledge of the mysterious plottings that led to the murder of Darnley (*see* casket letters), which followed in 1567, but her subsequent marriage to the earl of *Bothwell, who was believed to have been involved in the murder, turned opinion against her. Deserted by her army at *Carberry Hill, Mary was imprisoned and forced to abdicate. She escaped in 1568 but was defeated at *Langside and fled to England. There she was held captive, as in Catholic eyes she and not Elizabeth was rightful queen of England. Eventually her complicity in the *Babington plot to murder Elizabeth led to her execution.

Mary I (1516-58). Queen of England and Ireland (1553-58). Daughter of Henry VIII and Catherine of Aragon, Mary succeeded her brother, Edward VI, after rallying support against the Protestant claimant, Lady Jane Grey. In common with her mother, Mary was a devout Roman Catholic, and after her accession she set about reversing the Protestant tide in England. She failed to comprehend the English hostility to Catholic Spain, and the news of her proposed marriage to her Spanish cousin, *Philip (in 1554), sparked off three insurrections. With great personal courage Mary quelled these revolts and then embarked on a more aggressive religious policy (*see* Marian reaction). She officially reconciled England to Rome and re-enacted the old heresy laws and ecclesiastical courts. She earned the nickname Bloody Mary for her execution of Protestants; in 1555, the first year of religious persecution, 90 Protestants lost their lives. The total eventually exceeded 300. Drawn by her marriage into war with France, she lost Calais, the last English possession on the

Continent, in 1558. She died childless, having failed to produce the longed-for Catholic heir to the English throne, and was succeeded by her Protestant sister, *Elizabeth I.

Mary II (1662-94). Queen of England, Scotland, and Ireland (1689-94). Daughter of James II and Anne Hyde, Mary married William of Orange in 1677. Despite her father's conversion to Roman Catholicism she remained a loyal Protestant. During the Glorious Revolution of 1688-89 she insisted that her husband should share her throne, and they were crowned jointly in 1689. A gracious and sincere woman, she played little significant part in the making of political decisions. During William's prolonged absences from England due to the war with France, Mary assumed with dignity the duties of head of state. She died childless.

Mary of Gueldres (d. 1463). Queen consort of James II of Scots (1449-60), and daughter of Arnold, duke of Gueldres. Mary acted as regent during the minority of her son, James III, and she founded Trinity College Church, Edinburgh.

Mary of Guise (1515-60). Queen consort of James V of Scots (1538-42), whom she married after the death of her first husband. On James' death in 1542 Mary successfully opposed the pro-English policies of the earl of Arran, who as governor ruled in the name of her infant daughter Mary Queen of Scots. She succeeded Arran in 1554 but, although a woman of considerable political skill, she ultimately failed in her aim of keeping Scotland loyal both to France and to Catholicism. Her attempts in 1559 to suppress the Protestant reformers provoked them into open rebellion. Once they gained English military help her cause was lost, but she died suddenly just before her enemies triumphed.

Mary of Modena (1658-1718). Queen consort and second wife of James II (1685-88), whom she married in 1673. At the Glorious Revolution (1688) she fled to France with her only surviving child, James Francis Edward (the old pretender).

Mary of Teck (1867-1953). Queen consort (1910-36) of George V. She married George in 1893, having formerly been engaged to his elder brother Albert, duke of *Clarence. She was Queen Victoria's choice as future queen.

Mary Tudor (1496-1533). Youngest daughter of Henry VII and queen consort of Louis XII of France. She married Louis in 1514 after the annulment of her earlier betrothal to the future emperor Charles V. When Louis died in 1515 Mary was secretly married to Charles Brandon, 1st duke of Suffolk (d. 1545). Their grandchild was Lady Jane Grey.

Masham, Lady Abigail (d. 1734). A favourite of Queen Anne, supplanting Sarah Churchill, duchess of Marlborough, to whom she was related. She exerted considerable influence over Anne, securing a peerage for her husband Samuel (1st Baron) Masham (d. 1758). She was instrumental in the dismissal of Robert *Harley, 1st earl of Oxford, in 1714, and supported the Jacobites in 1715.

Mashonaland. The NE part of Zimbabwe, home of the Shona-speaking people. First settled by Whites in 1890, it was administered by Cecil Rhodes' *British South Africa Company until 1923, when it became with *Matabeleland the self-governing colony of *Southern Rhodesia.

Massachusetts Bay Company. A company incorporated in 1629 to trade and colonize in the area that became (1630) the Massachusetts Bay Colony. Under John Winthrop (1588-1649) the colony's theocratic government was distrusted in England, and the colony's charter was revoked in 1684.

Master of the Rolls. The most important of the lord chancellor's assistants in the court of *Chancery, so called because he was responsible for the records, orginally on rolls of parchment. In the 18th century he became a second judge in Chancery. Since 1881 he has been a judge of the Court of Appeal.

Matabeleland. The southern part of Zimbabwe, home of the Matabele people. Rhodes' *British South Africa Company administered the territory from 1889 and mined the valuable minerals. The Matabele rose in two unsuccessful revolts (1893-94, 1896). In 1923 it became, with *Mashonaland, the self-governing colony of Southern Rhodesia.

Matapan, battle of Cape (28-29 March 1941). A naval battle of World War II. The British Mediterranean fleet under Admiral Cunningham engaged the Italian main fleet, which was intent on attacking British convoys from Egypt to Greece. The Italian fleet was forced to turn for home and lost five ships, while the British lost only one aircraft.

Matilda (or Maud), Empress (1102-67). Only daughter of Henry I. She married twice: first (1114) the emperor Henry V (d. 1125) and second (1128) Geoffrey of Anjou. After the death of Henry's heir William in the sinking of the *White Ship the English barons did homage to Matilda as their future queen (1127). However, on the king's death in 1135 *Stephen of Blois took the throne. Matilda invaded the kingdom in 1139, established a stronghold in the west country, and held Stephen prisoner for a few months in 1141. Her cause subsequently weakened and in 1148 she returned to Normandy. Her son, however, became Henry II, the first *Plantagenet king of England.

Matilda of Boulogne (d. 1152). Queen consort of King Stephen (1135-52) and daughter and heiress of the count of Boulogne.

Matilda of Flanders (d. 1083). Queen consort of William the Conqueror (1053-83) and daughter of Baldwin V, count of Flanders. She was excommunicated for marrying William, her cousin, but the sentence was revoked in 1059.

Matilda of Scotland (d. 1118). Queen consort of Henry I from 1100; daughter of Malcolm III of Scots and granddaughter of of Edmund Ironside. Known as Good Queen Maud, she was a strong supporter of Archbishop Anselm and the church.

Matthew Paris (c. 1200-1259). Chronicler. As a Benedictine monk at St Albans he succeeded Roger of Wendover (1236) in revising and extending from 1235 until 1259 the monastery's *Chronica Majora*. His accurate coverage of the period makes it a particularly valuable historical source.

Mau Mau rebellion (1952-57). An uprising among the Kikuyu of Kenya in pursuit of national independence of Britain. Mau Mau (the origins of the name are unknown) was a secret society, whose members perpetrated atrocious acts of violence against both Whites and Blacks. Jomo Kenyatta, the first prime minister of independent Kenya, was imprisoned (1953-59) as a Mau Mau leader.

Mauritius. An island state, east of Madagascar, and a former British colony. Colonized by the French in the early 18th century, it was taken by Britain in 1810 and became independent and a member of the Commonwealth in 1968.

Mayflower. The ship in which the *pilgrim fathers sailed to America. Crowded with over a hundred passengers, the *Mayflower* left Plymouth, England, in the autumn of 1620. After a voyage lasting two months the ship reached Cape Cod instead of Virginia as originally planned. Depositing the settlers at the place they later named New Plymouth, the *Mayflower* returned in the following April to England.

Maynooth, St Patrick's College. The principal Roman Catholic seminary in Ireland. It was founded in 1795 by Pitt the younger in an attempt to conciliate Catholic opinion and also to avoid priests being educated in France, then at war with England. The proposal to give it a permanent endowment in 1845 caused Gladstone's resignation as president of the board of trade and led to a major political crisis.

mayor. The chairman or chairwoman of a district council having *borough status.

The mayor of the *City of London and some other cities is called the lord mayor.

meal tub plot (1679). A fictitious plot against Charles II. During the panic engendered by the *popish plot Thomas Dangerfield (?1650–1685) alleged that evidence of a conspiracy to prevent the accession of James, duke of York, to the throne was hidden in a meal tub belonging to Mrs Elizabeth Cellier, a midwife. When Dangerfield's claim was discredited he claimed that the plot was fabricated by Roman Catholics to conceal a genuine popish plot. Dangerfield died shortly after being convicted of perjury.

Meath. A county of east Ireland, one of the five ancient kingdoms that controlled Ireland until the arrival of the Anglo-Normans (*see also* Connaught; Leinster; Munster; Ulster). It wrested dominance from Ulster in the 6th century and, from *Tara (where excavations have revealed a significant civilization), controlled most of Ireland. Meath subsequently lost its separate distinction and became a county of the province of Leinster.

Medina del Campo, treaty of (March 1489). A treaty between England and Spain, by which each guaranteed the other's territorial claims in France. It also arranged for the marriage of Prince Arthur, heir to the English throne, and *Catherine of Aragon.

Medway, battle of the (43 AD). A battle between the Roman invaders led by Aulus Plautius and the Britons led by *Caractacus and Togodumnus. The Romans crossed the river Medway and took the Britons by surprise. The Britons scattered and fled after the two-day battle. Togodumnus was killed but Caractacus survived to continue the struggle against the invaders.

Melbourne, William Lamb, 2nd Viscount (1779–1848). Prime minister (1834, 1835–41). A Whig MP from 1806, he lost his seat in 1812 and was not re-elected until 1816. As a supporter of the moderate Toryism of *Canning, he served under him as secretary for Ireland in 1827. He held the same post under

Wellington (1828) but resigned with other Canningites later in the year. After succeeding to his title in 1829, he held his first cabinet post, as home secretary (1830–34) in *Grey's Whig ministry. Indolent by nature, he proved unexpectedly industrious in office and firmly suppressed radical and working-class discontent. On the resignation of Grey, Melbourne formed his first ministry (July 1834). Its disunity led Melbourne to offer his resignation in Dec, but he was recalled in the following year. His second administration continued Grey's programme of reform, with the *Municipal Corporations Act (1835), but was troubled by economic depression, Chartist discontent, and the furore over the *corn laws. Perhaps Melbourne's most significant achievement was the tact with which he instructed the youthful Queen Victoria in her duties after her accession in 1837 (*see* bedchamber crisis). His marriage (1805) to Lady Caroline Ponsonby (1785–1828), best known for her love affair with Lord Byron, ended with their formal separation in 1825. Melbourne was subsequently twice named in divorce cases.

Melville, Andrew (1545–1622). Scottish Presbyterian leader. After returning to Scotland from Geneva in 1574 Melville undertook the reform of the Scottish universities and, in the Second Book of *Discipline, pressed Presbyterian reforms on the Church of Scotland. These were resisted by James VI, who gradually succeeded in establishing royal control over the church. In 1606, after James had succeeded to the English throne, Melville was summoned to London and arrested. Freed from imprisonment in 1611, he spent the rest of his life teaching in France.

Menzies, Sir Robert (Gordon) (1894–1978). Prime minister of Australia (1939–41, 1949–66). He became attorney general in 1934 and, as leader of the United Australia Party, prime minister in 1939. He resigned in 1941 and formed the Liberal Party in 1944. During his second term of office he encouraged industrial growth and strengthened military links with the USA. In 1965 he became lord warden of the Cinque Ports.

mercantilism. An economic and cultural philosophy of the 16th and 17th centuries, reflecting the emergence of economies based on commerce. Mercantilists attached great importance to the attainment of a net inflow of precious metals and imports were discouraged by duties. The policy was also marked by aggressive nationalism towards overseas colonies (see Navigation Acts). Walpole's reforms of 1722, when over a hundred export duties, as well as tariffs on the import of raw materials and semifinished goods, were abolished, saw the beginning of a move away from mercantilism, which was attacked by Adam *Smith in *The Wealth of Nations* (1776). Under his influence *free-trade replaced mercantilism by the mid-19th century.

mercenaries. Soldiers serving for pay in the forces of a foreign power, formerly a traditional component of the English army. Mercenaries were used to supplement the feudal *array levied after the Norman conquest and were extensively employed until the development of a standing *army in the 17th century. The British government last hired mercenaries during the Crimean War, when German, Italian, and Swiss legions entered the British service. See also free companies.

Merchants, Statute of (1285). An act intended to expedite the payment of debts. It provided for the committal of the debtor to prison and the forfeiture of his chattels and, if necessary, his lands to the creditor. It was designed to encourage foreign merchants to trade in England. It supplemented the statute of Acton Burnell (1283), devised at the home at Acton Burnell, near Shrewsbury, of the chancellor Robert Burnell (d. 1292). It was repealed in 1863.

Merchants Adventurers. A trading company, incorporated in 1407, that by the mid-16th century controlled three-quarters of English foreign trade, supplanting the *Hanse. Its continental mart was at first in Bruges. In 1446 it moved to Antwerp, in 1493 to Calais, and in 1496 back to Antwerp. Transferring to Hamburg in 1567, it again obtained a Dutch base in the 1580s. It was subsequently attacked for exercising monopoly and lost its charter in 1689.

Mercia. A kingdom established by the *Angles, who began to settle in the Trent valley in central England late in the 5th century. The name derives from the Old English *Merce*, boundary people, for Mercia was situated between the Anglo-Saxon settlements in the east and south and the British tribes driven westwards. The leader of the first settlers of Mercia was possibly Icel, ancestor of the Mercian dynasty. The first recorded king was Cearl. Mercia became strong under *Penda (632-54) and reached the height of its power under *Offa (757-96). After 670 Mercian kings were also overlords of England south of the Humber (see bretwalda). In the 9th century the kingdom of Mercia was overthrown by the Danish invaders and divided between the Danes and Wessex (877).

Merciless Parliament (1388). A parliament summoned by the lords *appellant, so called because of the severity of the punishments imposed on five of Richard II's supporters. All were sentenced to death following an appeal of treason, and although three escaped abroad two—Sir Robert Tresilian, chief justice of the king's bench, and Sir Nicholas Brembre, lord mayor of London—were executed.

Merthyr rising (1831). A rising of miners and ironworkers in Merthyr Tydfil. Suffering poverty and falling wages, they were incited by the ferment caused by the parliamentary reform bill to take possession of the town for three days. Confrontation with the military forces before the Castle Hotel left about 16 dead. One leader, Richard Lewis (Dic Penderyn), was condemned to death.

Merton, Statute of (1235). A statute, the earliest in the statute book, issued after a meeting of the great council at Merton Priory in Surrey. It upheld the right of a lord of a *manor to enclose common land and, in contradiction of canon law, the principle that a child born before the marriage of his or her parents remained illegitimate after their marriage.

Merton, Walter de (d. 1277). Chancellor (1261-63, 1272-74) and bishop of Rochester from 1274. He is founder of Merton College, Oxford.

mesne tenure. In feudal law, the holding of land of a lord by a mesne, or middle, lord, of whom an inferior tenant then held it. This process is called subinfeudation.

Mesopotamian campaign. A British campaign during World War I in that part of the Ottoman (Turkish) Empire corresponding to present-day Iraq. Britain wished to secure access to the vital Persian oil supplies. In 1914 and 1915 the advance towards Baghdad was slow but generally successful. After the *Gallipoli disaster the campaign became more intense but received a severe setback in April 1916, when Gen. Sir Charles Townshend (1861-1924) and 10 000 soldiers were captured by the Turks at Kut al-Amara. Substantial reinforcements were sent to Mesopotamia, bringing the total number of troops to 300 000. Gen. Sir Stanley Maude (1864-1917) took Baghdad in March 1917 and speedily occupied the rest of the region. Critics believed that this campaign stemmed from political and imperial rather than military considerations.

Methodists. In England, a Christian denomination originating at Oxford University in 1729 from the society known as the "Holy Club", the principal members of which were John and Charles *Wesley and George *Whitefield. The Methodists' ministry began in 1738. Their open-air meetings and evangelical enthusiasm earned them some hostility from Anglicans. Concentrating on sections of society neglected by the Church of England, Methodists emphasized individual salvation and the love of God. Local societies were formed (1744) and an annual conference was established. In 1784 John Wesley established the annual conference of Methodists as a corporate body, although it was still

officially a society within the Church of England. The final break was made in 1795, from which date the sacraments were administered in all Methodist chapels. Secessionist groups included the New Connexion (1797), the Independent Methodists (1805), the Primitive Methodists (1810), the Bible Christians (1815), the Wesleyan Methodist Association (1835), and the Wesleyan Reformers (1849). All except the Independent and Calvinistic Methodists and the Wesleyan Reformers were united as the Methodist Church of Great Britain in 1932.

In Wales, methodism was a separate revivalist movement, characterized by Calvinist theology, evangelical zeal, and a Presbyterian government. The Welsh Methodist leaders were almost all Anglican clergymen. Howell Harris (1714-73) and Daniel Rowland (1713-90) experienced religious conversion in 1735. In 1737 they began field-preaching and the organization of societies. The third leader, William Williams (1717-91), was the movement's hymnist. Its organization survived the schism of 1750, when Harris for a time broke away, and in 1811 the Methodists separated from the Church of England as a fully fledged sect. The Methodist revival also strengthened the old dissenting sects; in the 19th century the Welsh were almost entirely nonconformist.

Methuen treaty (1703). A commercial agreement between England and Portugal. Negotiated by the English special envoy to Portugal, John Methuen (d. 1706), the treaty permitted the import of English textiles into Portugal in return for a preferential rate of duty on port wine, a third lower than that levied on French wines. The treaty was cancelled in 1836.

Middle Anglia. An Anglo-Saxon province between Mercia and East Anglia, probably corresponding to parts of Leicestershire, Cambridgeshire, Lincolnshire, and Northamptonshire. It was under Mercian control by the mid-6th century. Peada (d. 656), the son of King Penda of Mercia was appointed ealdorman of Middle Anglia in 653 and introduced Christianity to the province.

Middle Party. An alliance of lay and spiritual lords formed in 1316 under the leadership of Aymer de *Valence, earl of Pembroke. Less hostile to Edward II than the lords *ordainers, they nevertheless supported the *Ordinances. By 1321, following the rise of the Despensers, the group dissolved.

Middlesex. The territory of the Middle *Saxons. It was incorporated in *Essex by the early 7th century. In the 10th century it became a shire.

Middlesex, Lionel Cranfield, earl of (1575-1645). Lord treasurer. After holding a series of household posts he became a privy councillor (1620), lord treasurer (1621), and earl of Middlesex (1622). He introduced measures to reduce royal expenditure, incurring the enmity of Buckingham and the future Charles I, who had him impeached (1624). He was pardoned in 1625.

Middleton, Charles Middleton, 2nd earl of (?1640-1719). Scottish statesman. He became joint secretary for Scotland in 1682 and secretary of state for England in 1684. Chief adviser to James II in exile at Saint-Germain, he became a Roman Catholic in 1703.

Midlothian campaign (1879-80). A speaking tour undertaken by *Gladstone. Emerging from semiretirement to oppose Disraeli's foreign policy, Gladstone (hitherto MP for Greenwich) became candidate for Midlothian, held by the Conservatives. He made an unprecedented Scottish pre-election tour (Nov-Dec 1879), addressing crowds at huge meetings. The campaign demonstrated the potential of a direct appeal to electors by a national leader: the Liberals won the April 1880 general election and Gladstone, gaining the Midlothian seat, again became prime minister.

Mildenhall treasure. A hoard of Romano-British silver discovered (1942) on a farm near Mildenhall in Suffolk. It was probably buried during Saxon raids in the 4th or 5th century. The treasure comprises 34 silver dishes, spoons, and goblets—probably the heirlooms of a rich family—and is now in the British Museum.

militia. The people's army, originating in the Anglo-Saxon *fyrd. In 1181 the Assize of *Arms gave the militia statutory recognition, and under this and succeeding laws conscript levies were raised chiefly by *impressment. In the 16th century the local militia was placed under the *lord lieutenants. On the eve of the Civil War control of these so-called *trained bands became an issue between king and parliament. In 1642 the Long Parliament passed the Militia Ordinance, which empowered it to appoint the lord lieutenants and thereby assume sovereign powers. On the Restoration the Militia Act (1661) restored control of the militia to the king and acts of 1662 and 1663 reorganized it. The inadequate training of the militia led to the Militia Act (1757), which empowered the government to conscript all males of military age for three years' service, although only a few battalions were raised under this statute. The militia finally ceased to exist with the establishment of the Territorial Army in 1907.

Mill, James (1773-1836). Writer and exponent of *utilitarianism, father of John Stuart Mill. *Bentham's leading disciple, he was a leading member of the *philosophical radicals, a group that propounded economic and political liberalism. His books include *History of British India* (1817) and *Elements of Political Economy* (1821), which was influenced by David *Ricardo and in turn influenced Karl Marx. From 1819 he worked for the East India Company in London.

Mill, John Stuart (1806-73). Philosopher and economist, son of James Mill. An empiricist, he defined his methods of enquiry in *A System of Logic* (1843), modified the theory of *utilitarianism (*Utilitarianism*, 1863), and defended individual freedom (*On Liberty*, 1859; *Subjection of Women*, 1861). These and his works on political economy, notably *Principles of Political Economy* (2 vols,

1848), exerted considerable influence. In common with his father, he worked for the East India Company (1823-58) and was also a Liberal MP (1865-68).

millenary petition (April 1603). A petition, presented by the Puritans to James I, said to have the support of a thousand ministers. The list of practices objected to included the sign of the cross during baptism, confirmation, the surplice, the ring in marriage, and bowing at the name of Jesus. At the subsequent *Hampton Court conference (1604) James refused any relaxation in church practices.

Milner, Alfred Milner, 1st Viscount (1854-1925). Colonial administrator and financier. His success as director general of accounts in Egypt (1889-92) led to his appointment as chairman of the Board of Inland Revenue (1892-97). As high commissioner in South Africa (1897-1905), with his "kindergarten" of able young men from Oxford he re-established the South African economy and administration after the second Boer War. Ennobled in 1901, he served in Lloyd George's war cabinet (1916-18) and as colonial secretary (1918-21), in which post he headed a mission to Egypt that recommended Egyptian independence (granted 1922).

Milton, John (1608-74). Poet. He wrote some of the greatest verse in the English language, including the lyrics *L'Allegro* and *Il Penseroso* (1632), sonnets, and the magnificent epic poems *Paradise Lost* (1667) and *Samson Agonistes* (1671). During the 1640s he took up the Puritan cause, defending personal and political liberties in a series of revolutionary pamphlets that included four tracts in defence of divorce (1643-45) and the *Areopagitica* (1644) in support of a free press. In 1649 he became Latin secretary to Cromwell's Council of State, retaining the post until the Restoration, in spite of his blindness.

mines acts. Legislation to protect coal-mine workers. Prior to 1842 the exploitation of women and child miners included cases of four-year-olds working under ground. The Mines Act (1842), which was carried through parliament by Lord Ashley (later *Shaftesbury), prohibited the employment under ground of women, girls, and boys under ten years of age. The Coal Mine Inspection Act (1850) provided for the inspection of mines, and in the following year the Royal School of Mines was founded to train inspectors. Subsequent legislation introduced safety regulations, including the requirement that managers of mines possess a certificate of competency (1872). In 1908 the underground shift was limited to eight hours by the Coal Mines Regulation Act, the first time that the working hours of men were regulated. The working day of underground mine workers was finally reduced to seven and a half hours in the Coal Mines Act (1930), having been established at seven in 1920 only to be raised again to eight after the *general strike (1926). In 1938 a Coal Commission was given responsibility for coal and mines and in 1946 the Coal Industry Nationalisation Act established a National Coal Board to control all coal-mining and its assets. *See also* factory acts.

ministerial responsibility. The constitutional principle that . ministers are responsible to parliament (effectively, the House of Commons) for their, and their department's, actions. In early *cabinet government ministers continued to be responsible to the sovereign. As executive power shifted during the later 18th century from the sovereign to the cabinet, ministers became answerable to parliament, both individually and collectively. A minister therefore may have to resign if the cabinet (able to command the Commons) does not support his or her action; occasionally, a minister may choose to resign, as a personally honourable course, even when colleagues do not regard the action criticized as demanding resignation. Conversely, a significant defeat in the Commons demands the collective resignation of ministers.

Minorca. The second largest of the Balearic Islands. Ceded to Britain by Spain by the treaty of Utrecht (1713), which concluded the War of the Spanish

Succession, Minorca was taken by the French (1756) during the Seven Years' War but restored to Britain by the treaty of Paris (1763). Regained by Spain in 1783, it was again captured by the British in 1798. The treaty of Amiens (1802) finally restored the island to Spain.

minster. Originally, a large church that was attached to a monastery (e.g. York minster, Westminster). The term remained in use after the dissolution of the monasteries in the 16th century.

Mint, Royal. The place in which the *coinage is manufactured under the authority of the Treasury. Athelstan made .the earliest regulations governing coining in about 928. Originally in the Tower of London, the Royal Mint was transferred to Tower Hill in 1811 and to Llantrisant, South Wales, in 1968, when decimal currency was introduced. The Royal Mint also manufactures medals and decorations, seals, and some foreign coins.

Minto, Gilbert John Elliot Murray Kynynmond, 4th earl of (1845-1914). Public servant. Minto served as governor general of Canada (1898-1904). As viceroy of India (1905-10), he was partly responsible for the *Morley-Minto reforms (1909).

mise. The process in the *writ of right whereby a tenant "placed" himself at the mercy of the judgment of the *Grand Assize. It also referred to certain taxes levied in Wales and to an agreed settlement (e.g. mises of *Amiens and *Lewes).

missionary societies. Societies set up to organize and finance Christian evangelization in Africa. Although Roman Catholic missionaries were sent to West Africa in the 16th and 17th centuries their activity was largely unsuccessful, and large-scale missionary activity in British West Africa began in the early 19th century. The Church Missionary Society (founded 1799) was the major missionary body in Sierra Leone from 1807 and in Nigeria from 1842. The Wesleyan Missionary Society (founded 1813) followed, and Roman Catholic

missions were established in both French and British West Africa in the 1860s. In South Africa the major missionary body from 1810 was the London Missionary Society (founded 1795), for which Robert Moffat (1795-1883) extended evangelization into Rhodesia (1859). The Universities' Mission to Central Africa was active in the 1850s, its most famous missionary being David *Livingstone; Scottish Presbyterians constituted the other important missionary body in central Africa. The missionaries, whose objectives were to introduce Christianity and suppress the slave trade, played an important educational role in Africa.

Model Parliament (Nov 1295). The parliament summoned by Edward I to obtain aid for his wars. It received its sobriquet during the 19th century because it was more representative than any previous parliament. It did not, however, serve as a model for the future. It was attended by 7 earls, 41 barons, the archbishops and bishops, 70 abbots and heads of religious houses, archdeacons, 1 proctor for the clergy of each chapter, 2 proctors for the clergy of each diocese, 2 knights from each shire, and 2 representatives from each city and borough.

monarchy. A form of government in which the supreme power is vested in a single person, usually a king or queen. The origins of the English monarchy lie in the struggles for supremacy among the seven kingdoms of the *Heptarchy and the dominance of successive overlords (see bretwalda). *Athelstan established effective rule of all England in 926, and Alfred (reigned 871-99), the greatest of the Anglo-Saxon kings, emerged as a national hero. However, political unification was not achieved until the reign (1017-35) of the Dane, Cnut. The Anglo-Saxon monarchy had no extensive legal rights or standing army. The duties of a king were to defend the people, to uphold the law, and to administer justice. Kings were bound by tribal custom, and the laws they promulgated with the advice of the *witan were declaratory rather than legislative. But gradually shires and shire courts developed as instruments of royal administration, and crime came to be an offence against the king's peace rather than a wrong against a private person. At the same time the peripatetic *royal household assumed administrative functions. The monarchy gained enormously from the circumstances of the Norman conquest (1066) and from the contribution of religious ideas expressed in the *coronation. The anointed king took on a sacerdotal character reflected in such practices as touching for the *king's evil (continued until Queen Anne). To these were added the resources in land and military service due to the king as feudal overlord. However, medieval monarchy was intensely personal, and a monarch's success depended on a combination of character, military skill, and successful exploitation of the royal estates. Thus, the monarchy only gradually became hereditary. Dynastic rivalry dominated the 15th century (see Roses, Wars of the) and the Tudor monarchs were persistently troubled by plots and the question of the succession. The Tudors, however, gained much from their exploitation of the mystique of kingship ("your majesty" replaced "your grace" as the title of address), from their manipulation of anticlericalism into a doctrine of the royal supremacy, and from their appropriation of church land. The problems of the early Stuarts were partly personal, partly the result of inflation, the inadequacies of a medieval financial system, and the difficulty of ruling Scotland as well as England. The execution of Charles I led to the only period in which England has not been a monarchy. Its restoration brought restrictions on monarchical power, but many historians would regard the Glorious Revolution (1688-89) as a greater constitutional watershed than the Civil War. There were nevertheless large areas of executive power that kings could still exploit through the resources of *patronage and "influence". These were utilized in particular by George I and George II. The waning of the executive power of the monarchy is illustrated in many incidents of the long reign of *Victoria. It is now a focus of historic tradition and pageantry and of the ideals of national goodwill and public service. See also parliament.

monasticism. The withdrawal of men and women from secular society in order to devote themselves to a religious life. Early monasticism in Britain followed the rule of St Benedict of Nursia. It was introduced to southern England by St *Augustine and to Northumbria by St Wilfred in the late 7th and early 8th centuries. Best known of the monasteries founded in the 8th century were those of *Jarrow and *Iona. Monasticism was temporarily destroyed by the Danish invasions of the 9th century, but in the 10th century a remarkable monastic revival took place. Encouraged by King *Edgar, its leading personalities were St *Dunstan and St *Oswald. The Cistercians opened their first house in England in 1128, the Dominicans in 1221, and the Franciscans in 1224. The monasteries acquired extensive lands and considerable wealth, and the ideals of austerity and sacrifice that motivated their foundation were debased. They became an object of anticlericalism, and their *dissolution, in the wake of the Henrician Reformation, provoked relatively little opposition.

Monck, George, 1st duke of Albemarle (1608-70). General and statesman. After helping suppress the *Irish rebellion in Ulster (1642-43), he returned to fight for Charles I in the Civil War and was captured at Nantwich (1644). After the king's defeat in 1646 the parliamentarians, recognizing Monck's abilities, gave him command in Ireland. He subsequently assisted Cromwell's campaign in Scotland (1650-51), of which he was then appointed commander in chief. In the politically uncertain times following Cromwell's death Monck sided with the *Rump of the Long Parliament against the army and in 1659 began to march south. Entering London in Feb 1660, he brought about the recall of those MPs excluded from the Long Parliament in 1648 by Pride's purge.

Under Monck's influence the restored Long Parliament dissolved itself, having arranged for the election of the *convention parliament, which recalled Charles II. Monck was created duke of Albemarle for his services, and captain general, and he subsequently played a prominent role in the second *Dutch War (1665-67).

Monmouth, James Scott, duke of (1649-85). Illegitimate son of Charles II. After 1662 rumours abounded that he would be legitimized and made heir to the throne. He was an energetic military commander and gained immense popularity as the Protestant candidate for the throne, but Charles refused to legitimize him. Ambitious and reckless, Monmouth then embarked on intrigues (see Rye House plot) and was forced into exile. He returned to lead the *Monmouth rebellion and was captured, tried, and executed.

Monmouth rebellion (1685). A shortlived uprising against James II led by the duke of *Monmouth. Monmouth landed at Lyme Regis with about 150 men and denounced James as a usurper. Supporters from Wiltshire, Devon, and Somerset joined him, but the king's army cornered him at Bridgewater and, attempting to break out across *Sedgemoor, Monmouth's untrained troops were slaughtered. Survivors were savagely punished by Judge *Jeffreys at the *bloody assizes.

monopoly. A market dominated by a single producer or trader. Monopolies in trade were granted to companies during the middle ages (see staple). They became an abuse during the 16th century, when the crown granted monopolies, not only to regulate trade and raise revenue, but also to favour individuals, who frequently increased the price of a commodity to make large profits. In spite of parliamentary opposition the practice was continued by James I and Charles I. Most industrial monopolies were abolished by the Long Parliament, but many commercial monopolies continued until after the Glorious Revolution (1688-89). Monopolies have

been subject to legislation since 1948, when the Monopolies Commission was set up to investigate individual monopolies and assess their effect on the public interest.

Mons Graupius, battle of (83 AD). The battle in which *Agricola, the Roman governor, defeated the Caledonians at the unidentified Mons Graupius in the valley of Strathmore, central Scotland, during his campaign to crush local tribes and gain control of the Scottish Lowlands.

Montagu-Chelmsford report (1918). Proposals for constitutional reform in British India, named after the secretary for India Edwin Montagu (1879-1924), and the viceroy Lord Chelmsford (1868-1933). It followed Montagu's announcement (1917) that Britain intended the "progressive realization of responsible government". The Government · of *India Act (1919) accordingly introduced partially responsible provincial government and new central legislative bodies.

Montagu, Charles, 1st earl of Halifax. See Halifax, Charles Montagu, 1st earl of.

Montagu (or Mountagu), Edward, 1st earl of Sandwich (1625-72). Admiral. He joined the parliamentary army in 1643 and fought at Marston Moor (1644), Naseby (1645), and the capture of Bristol (1645). He was a general at sea from 1656 but assisted in the Restoration, conveying Charles II from Holland to England in 1660. For these services he was granted the earldom of Sandwich. He was killed in an explosion at sea during the third Dutch War.

Montagu, Lady Mary Wortley (1689-1762). Writer. For long a leading figure in English society, she is remembered for her published Letters. She tried unsuccessfully to popularize smallpox inoculation in England, after learning of it in Turkey, where her husband was ambassador (1716-18).

Montfort, Simon de, earl of Leicester (c. 1208-1265). Leader of the baronial opposition to Henry III. Born in

Normandy, Simon landed in England in 1230 with a claim through his English grandmother to the earldom of Leicester, a title in which he was formally invested in 1239. A year before he had married Eleanor, sister of Henry III. He served the king in Poitou in 1242 and as lieutenant of Gascony from 1248 to 1252, when he was forced to resign following a revolt against his administration. In 1258 he emerged as the leader of the baronial reform party and was one of the 24 who drew up the *Provisions of Oxford. After the failure in 1264 of the mise of *Amiens to settle the dispute with the king, the barons went into armed revolt (see Barons' Wars). Simon won the victory at *Lewes in 1264, capturing Henry and his son Edward. As virtual ruler of England, he summoned a parliament famous for its inclusion of burgesses as representatives of certain boroughs (see House of Commons). Soon after, however, Prince Edward escaped, gathered an army, and defeated and killed Simon at *Evesham.

Montfort the younger, Simon de, earl of Leicester (1240–71). Second son of the elder Simon de Montfort. He defended Northampton against the royalists in 1264 but was defeated and taken prisoner. Released after the mise of *Lewes, he escaped abroad following the battle of *Evesham. With his brother Guy de Montfort (d. 1288) he murdered *Henry of Almaine at Viterbo in 1271 and died shortly after being excommunicated.

Montgomery, treaty of (1267). A treaty between Henry III and *Llywelyn ap Gruffudd of Gwynedd, which made Llywelyn *prince of Wales and marked his highest peak of achievement before the Edwardian conquest in 1282–83. Henry III recognized his rule over Gwynedd and his overlordship of independent Welsh rulers outside the Marches.

Montgomery of Alamein, Bernard Law Montgomery, 1st Viscount (1887–1979). Field marshal. In World War II he led the Third Division at *Dunkirk and as commander of the Eighth Army won the battle of *Alamein (1942), forcing the

Axis armies back upon Tunis. He commanded the ground forces during the *Normandy invasion (1944) and thereafter the British-Canadian 21st Army. Following the German surrender he was in command of the occupation forces in Germany before serving as chief of the Imperial General Staff. From 1951 to 1958 he was deputy supreme commander of NATO forces.

Montreal. The largest city and main port of Canada, in south Quebec, strategically situated on the St Lawrence river. Founded by French settlers in 1642, Montreal surrendered to the British in 1760 during the Seven Years' War. Montreal was occupied by the American revolutionaries in 1775 but fierce resistance forced their retreat in the following year.

Montrose, James Graham, 5th earl and 1st marquess of (1612–50). *Covenanter leader in the 1630s, who became the leading supporter of the king in Scotland during the Civil War. His conversion to the royalist cause was prompted both by personal ambition and his belief that the covenanters wished to restrict royal power too much. Created a marquess in 1644, he led a brilliant royalist campaign in Scotland. He was at first successful —scoring victories at Tippermuir, Aberdeen, Inverlochy, Auldern, Alford, and Kilsyth—but had to rely almost entirely on Irish and Highland troops because few Lowlanders would join him. His power was broken by the defeat at *Philiphaugh in Sept 1645. He then went into exile until 1650, when he returned to rally support for the royalist cause, an attempt that led to his defeat at *Carbisdale and his execution.

Moore, Sir John (1761–1809). Soldier, who originated modern light-infantry training. During the *Peninsular War Moore led a historic midwinter retreat 402 km (250 mi) to *Coruña, where he was mortally wounded during a victorious encounter with the French.

moot. From Anglo-Saxon times, public assemblies held in all communities from the shire downwards to decide legal and administrative issues requiring the presence of witnesses. Inhabitants of an area had a duty to attend the local moot. The term moot point, a topic that demands discussion, survives.

Moray, James Stewart (or Stuart), earl of (c. 1531-1570). An illegitimate son of James V of Scotland. Lord James joined the Protestant Party in Scotland in rebellion in 1559 and took a leading part in bringing about its triumph in 1560. On the return of Mary Queen of Scots, his half-sister, to Scotland in 1561 he came to dominate the regime, pursuing a moderate pro-English and Protestant policy. He was created earl in 1562. Moray opposed Mary's marriage to Darnley in 1565, but his attempted rebellion was easily defeated. After Mary's abdication he was appointed regent but was assassinated in 1570.

Moray risings. A series of revolts in Moray during the 12th century. The land of Moray (in northeast Scotland) was anciently an independent Pictish kingdom ruled by an independent *Mormaer* (great steward). The mormaer Angus led a rebellion against David I in 1130 in resistance to the expansion of Scottish rule. Although he was defeated and killed rebellions against the imposition of royal authority continued throughout the 12th century.

Morcar, earl of Northumbria. Mercian nobleman. He aided the Northumbrian revolt against *Tostig, whom he succeeded as earl in 1065. The invading forces of Harold Haardraada and Tostig defeated Morcar at *Fulford (1066), but he was saved by King Harold's victory over his enemies at Stamford Bridge (1066). Nevertheless, Morcar came too late to support Harold at Hastings. He recognized the accession of William I but in 1068 rebelled against the king. He was pardoned but in 1071 joined the revolt of *Hereward the Wake and was imprisoned. On his deathbed William ordered the release of Morcar (1087), but he was arrested again by William II and died in prison.

More, Hannah (1745-1833). Writer, who, after early success as a fashionable playwright, abandoned the stage for philanthropic work. She established village schools as well as writing many improving books and tracts that emphasized acceptance of the established social order.

More, Sir Thomas (1478-1535). Lord chancellor of England (1529-32), scholar, and saint. He trained as a lawyer, entered parliament in 1504, and succeeded Wolsey as lord chancellor. He resigned in opposition to Henry VIII's religious policies and was arrested for refusing to swear the oath to the Act of *Succession and thereby deny papal supremacy. He was convicted on the perjured evidence of Sir Richard Rich after a remarkable self-defence and was executed. He was canonized in 1935. He was a renowned scholar and a friend of Erasmus, his writings including *Utopia* (1516), a description of an ideal society.

Morgan, Sir Henry (1635-88). Welsh buccaneer. An early colonist in Jamaica, having helped seize it from Spain, Morgan organized buccaneering raids on Spain's American possessions. He was charged with piracy for attacking Panama in 1671, after peace had been concluded between England and Spain, but was later acquitted, knighted, and appointed lieutenant governor of Jamaica.

Morgannwg. A Welsh kingdom between the rivers Nedd and Usk. Called Glywysing until the 8th century, it was renamed after its ruler Morgan. Iestyn ap Gwrgant, the last Welsh ruler of Morgannwg, was defeated by Robert fitz *Hamon, whose territorial acquisitions, in the coastal lowlands, led to the establishment of the lordship of Glamorgan.

Morley-Minto reforms (1909). Measures that increased Indian participation in the British government of India, named after the secretary for India, Viscount Morley (1838-1923), and the viceroy Lord *Minto. Elected members—with separate Hindu and Muslim representation—joined the viceroy's council and the legislative council as well as the provincial councils, which received greater powers.

Morris, William (1834-96). Artist, designer, craftsman, poet, and socialist propagandist, who deeply influenced developments in the decorative arts. Morris condemned capitalism and industrialism and, inspired by medieval models, preached realization of human potential through craftsmanship. His designs for fabrics, wallpapers, tapestry, and printing typefaces achieved a lasting popularity.

Morrison, Herbert, Baron (1888-1965). Labour MP (1923-24, 1929-31, 1935-59; life peer, 1959), minister of transport (1929-31), and later home secretary (1940-45), who served in the war cabinet (1942-45). He was also a member of the London County Council from 1922 to 1945. Under Attlee he was lord privy seal (1945-51), overseeing domestic policies, and then foreign secretary (1951). He twice unsuccessfully sought the party leadership (1935, 1955).

Mort d'Ancestor, Assize of. A judicial proceeding, or the writ giving rise to it, by which a person might be reinstated in possession of land taken by a feudal lord on the death of the claimant's ancestor. First mentioned in records in 1176, it was abolished in 1833. *See also* assizes.

Mortimer, Edmund de, 3rd earl of March (1351-81). Marshal of England (1369-77). The Yorkist claim to the throne during the Wars of the Roses derived from his marriage to Philippa, daughter and heiress of Lionel, duke of Clarence, Edward III's third son (*see* York, house of). In 1379 he was created lieutenant of Ireland.

·Mortimer, Edmund de, 5th earl of March (1391-1425). He was recognized as heir presumptive by Richard II but when the king abdicated in 1399 March was superseded by Henry Bolingbroke (Henry IV). In spite of unsuccessful risings on his behalf led by Henry *Percy, 1st earl of Northumberland, in 1405 and by the earl of Cambridge in 1415 (*see* Cambridge plot), he remained loyal to the crown and fought with Henry V in

France. He was created lieutenant of Ireland in 1423.

Mortimer, Roger de, 4th earl of March and Ulster (1374-98). Son of Edmund *Mortimer, 3rd earl of March. In 1385 he was declared heir presumptive to the throne by Richard II, whose niece Eleanor Holland he married in 1388. He died in Ireland, where he was serving as lord lieutenant.

Mortimer, Roger de, 6th baron of Wigmore (c. 1231-82). A prominent marcher lord, who was a member of the council of barons in 1258 but after 1261 supported Henry III against Simon de Montfort. He was an active opponent of Llywelyn ap Gruffudd in Wales.

Mortimer, Roger de, 8th baron of Wigmore and 1st earl of March (?1287-1330). Virtual ruler of England (1327-30). He was lieutenant (1317) and the justiciar (1319) in Ireland. In 1321 he took up arms against Edward II and the royal favourite Hugh le *Despenser and was imprisoned in 1322. He escaped to France in 1324 and became the lover of Edward's estranged queen *Isabel. In 1326 they invaded England, bringing the young prince Edward with them, and in 1327 Mortimer engineered the king's deposition and probably his murder. In 1328 he was created earl of March, but his influence over Edward III was short-lived. In Oct 1330, at Edward's instigation, he was arrested at Nottingham castle and hanged at Tyburn.

Mortimer's Cross, battle of (2 Feb 1461). The battle of the Wars of the Roses in which Edward, son of Richard, duke of York, routed a Lancastrian army under the earls of Pembroke and Wiltshire at Mortimer's Cross, Herefordshire. Owen Tudor was captured and beheaded and Edward marched to London, where he was proclaimed king Edward IV.

mortmain. Land held inalienably by a corporation, usually the church. The consequent loss of feudal benefits to lay lords gave rise to the Statute of Mortmain (1279), which limited grants of land to the church.

Morton, James Douglas, 4th earl of (c. 1525-1581). Regent of Scotland. In 1563 he became lord chancellor under Mary Queen of Scots and in 1566 was responsible for the murder of her secretary *Rizzio. Involved in the assassination of Lord *Darnley (1567), he then led the forces that defeated Mary's army at- *Langside (1568). He was regent from 1572 until 1578, when he was briefly ousted from power, and then again until condemned by Lennox for Darnley's murder and executed. His government was notably efficient.

Morton, John, Cardinal (c. 1420-1500). Chief minister to Henry VII, having already served under Edward IV and Henry VI. He became archbishop of Canterbury in 1486 and chancellor in 1487. In 1491 he helped raise a benevolence for a proposed invasion of France, arguing that an extravagant man could afford to give generously, while a careful one, having presumably saved, could also afford to be open-handed (alternatives known as Morton's fork).

Morton, Thomas (1564-1659). Bishop of Chester (1616), Lichfield and Coventry (1618), and then Durham (1632). He published several works against Roman Catholicism, including *Apologia catholica* (1605) and *A Catholic Appeal* (1609). An opponent also of nonconformity, he was impeached (1641) by the Long Parliament and imprisoned.

Morton, William Douglas, 6th or 7th earl of (d. 1606). One of the murderers of Rizzio (1566), secretary to Mary Queen of Scots. He had charge of Mary in Lochleven castle after *Carberry Hill (1567) and was involved in the plot that effected the overthrow of James Stewart, earl of Arran (1585). He succeeded to the earldom of Morton in 1588, the 5th earl being John Maxwell (1553-93), who lost the title on his exile (1587) but held it again in 1592: thus Douglas is the 6th or 7th earl.

mortuary. A gift claimed by a parish priest on the death of a parishioner on the assumption that the deceased person was likely not have paid all ecclesiastical tithes and other dues owed during his lifetime. Traditionally his second best beast was surrendered, but mortuaries came to be paid in the form of fees that were sometimes exorbitant, provoking opposition (see Hunne's case). In 1529 limits were placed on mortuaries, although they continued to be levied until the 18th century.

Mosley, Sir Oswald (Ernald) (1896-1980). Politician, who founded (1932) the *British Union of Fascists (BUF). An MP from 1918 to 1931, he sat at first as a Conservative, then as an Independent, and lastly as a member of the Labour Party. He created a short-lived (1931-32) New Party before forming the BUF. During World War II he was imprisoned (1940-43) and subsequently sought to return to politics through the Union Movement, a right-wing organization that he founded in 1948.

Mountbatten. A family descended from the German Prince Alexander of Battenberg (1823-88). His son Prince Louis (1854-1921) married (1884) a granddaughter of Queen Victoria and in 1917, after anglicizing his name to Mountbatten, was created marquess of Milford Haven. His fourth child was Louis, 1st earl *Mountbatten of Burma.

Mountbatten of Burma, Louis Mountbatten, 1st Earl (1900-79). A great-grandson of Queen Victoria. He was supreme allied commander in Southeast Asia (1943-45). As viceroy of India (1947) he oversaw the transfer of power to *India and Pakistan, serving as governor general (1947-48). From 1952 to 1954 he was commander in chief of the Mediterranean fleet and then (1955-59) first sea lord. He became an admiral in 1956. He was murdered in Ireland by the IRA.

Mountjoy, Charles Blount, 8th Baron (and earl of Devonshire) (1563-1606). Soldier and friend of *Essex, who escaped involvement in Essex's rebellion. In Ireland, as lord deputy (1601-03) and lord lieutenant (1603) he suppressed *O'Neill's revolt.

Mowbray, John, 3rd duke of Norfolk (1415-61). A supporter of the Yorkist cause (apart from a brief commitment to the Lancastrians in 1459-60) during the Wars of the Roses. He is mentioned in the *Paston letters as the claimant to the Pastons' castle of Caistor, which his son, John Mowbray, 4th duke of Norfolk (1444-76), seized in 1469. The Pastons recovered it in 1476.

Mowbray, Thomas, 12th Baron Mowbray and 1st duke of Norfolk (d. 1399). Son of John de Mowbray (d. 1368) and Elizabeth, granddaughter of the earl of Norfolk. He took part in the defeat of Robert de Vere, 9th earl of *Oxford, at *Radcot Bridge (1388) and was one of the lords *appellant. He was subsequently reconciled to Richard II and was appointed governor of Calais (1391), where he probably connived at the murder of Thomas of Woodstock, duke of Gloucester, in 1397. After being accused of treason by the duke of Hereford (later Henry IV) he was banished from England for life (1398) and died in Venice.

mule. A spinning machine, invented (1779) by Samuel *Crompton, which played an important part in the development of the cotton industry during the industrial revolution. The mule (thought to have been so named because it was a "cross" betwen the *spinning jenny and water frame) spun a fine yet strong thread. At first employed in the home, it came into increasing use in factories after 1790, as it could be powered either by steam or water.

mund. In the Anglo-Saxon period, the peace to which every freeman was entitled in his home. He had the right to appeal to the king's court against any breach of this peace by strangers.

Munich agreement (29 Sept 1938). A pact, signed in Munich by Britain, Germany, France, and Italy, that settled Germany's demands on Czechoslovakia. The agreement, imposed upon Czechoslovakia (which was unrepresented at Munich), was largely the work of Neville *Chamberlain, pursuing a policy of *appeasement. (France, unlike Britain, was allied to Czechoslovakia, but nevertheless ᴀᴄquiesced.) Czechoslovakia

surrendered to Germany one-fifth of its territory and a quarter of its population (mostly from the Sudeten German-speaking border areas), great economic resources, and its defence fortifications. Further areas of Czechoslovakia were subsequently allocated to Hungary and Poland. The agreement was described by Chamberlain as "peace with honour...peace for our time". Six months later Germany invaded and occupied the rest of Czechoslovakia.

Municipal Corporations Act (1835). The first major reform of city and town government. Urban government, like parliamentary representation, had been slow to respond to changed economic and social conditions, and included many ancient *boroughs (some with corrupt self-perpetuating *corporations), while new industrial areas had only parish status. The act established uniform corporations elected by ratepayers (i.e. directly elected councillors and indirectly elected aldermen and mayors), which became the vehicles for developing the scope of Victorian local government.

municipium. The first stage in the romanization of provincial communities. Municipia were not common in Britain, where local government depended more on the pre-Roman cantons. *Verulamium, however, became a municipium. The government of the municipium was by an assembly (see ordo) the members of which were called decurions. See also colonia.

Munster. A province of southwest Ireland and one of the five ancient kingdoms that controlled Ireland from the 5th century AD to the Norman conquest (see also Connaught; Leinster; Meath; Ulster). The kingship alternated between the O'Briens and MacCarthys. In the 11th century its king, *Brian Boru of the O'Briens, became the first effective high king of Ireland. The Normans conquered most of Munster in the 13th century but never subdued the extreme southwest, which remained independent until the 17th century.

murage. A toll levied for the maintenance of a town's walls (Latin *murus*, wall).

murder fine. A fine first ordered by William I in an attempt to prevent the assassination of Norman settlers. The fine, originally of 40 marks payable to the king and six marks to the victim's family, was paid by the hundred in which the murder took place unless it could produce the murderer within five days or, from the reign of Henry I, could prove that the murdered man was English (see Englishry). It was abolished in 1340. See also wergild.

Murdock, William (1754-1839). Scottish-born engineer, who invented gas lighting. He first used coal gas for lighting in 1792. He developed production techniques and made gas lighting a practicable commercial proposition by 1802, when he lit the exterior of Boulton's and Watt's Soho works.

Murray, Lord George (1694-1760). Jacobite commander, who, as one of Charles Edward Stuart's leading generals, largely ensured the Jacobite victories at *Prestonpans (1745) and Falkirk (1746). After commanding the right wing at *Culloden, he escaped abroad and died in exile.

Murray, James (1721-94). General. He served in Wolfe's Quebec expedition (1759) and was appointed governor of Quebec (1760) and of Canada (1763). He became governor of Minorca in 1774, surrendering the port to French and Spanish troops in 1782. He was court-martialled, but acquitted.

Muscovy Company. A trading company founded in 1555, by a group of merchants that included Sebastian Cabot, to trade with Russia. The company was the outcome of the Russian contacts made by Richard *Chancellor in his search for a northeast passage (1553-54). The company exported cloth and firearms in return for fish oil, furs, timber, and other primary products. Its monopoly was ended in 1698, but the company survived until the Russian Revolution.

Mutiny Act (1689). The first of a long series of acts, passed at first every six months and then annually, which sanctioned the existence of a standing *army by providing for the punishment of mutiny and desertion. The temporary nature of the acts emphasized the need for regular parliaments. In 1879 the Mutiny Act was replaced by the Army Discipline and Regulation Act, which gave way in 1917 to the Army and Air Force (Annual) Acts.

Myddelton, Sir Hugh (?1560-1631). Welsh goldsmith, who became famous for his New River project designed to improve London's water supply (1609). Completed in 1613, it comprised a canal 61 km (38 mi) long that carried water from springs in Hertfordsire to a reservoir called New River Head.

Mynydd Carn, battle of (1081). A battle, fought at an unidentified site on the borders of Dyfed, in which *Gruffudd ap Cynan, seeking to re-establish himself in Gwynedd, and *Rhys ap Tewdwr, king of Deheubarth, defeated Gruffudd's northern rivals and Caradog ap Gruffudd of Morgannwg.

Myton, battle of (20 Sept 1319). A battle, fought at Myton-in-Swaledale in Yorkshire, in which an ill-armed and untrained force led by William Melton, archbishop of York, was decisively defeated by the Scots under Sir James Douglas. The ecclesiastical complexion of the English army inspired John *Barbour (in the Bruce) to describe it as "the chapter of Myton". As a result of the Scottish victory Edward II abandoned the siege of Berwick.

N

nabob. A nickname, in the 18th and early 19th centuries, for a man who had made a fortune in India. The term derives from nawab, the title of certain Mogul princes, and came to be applied to any very wealthy person. A female nabob was called a nabobess.

Nanking, treaty of (29 Aug 1842). The treaty that terminated the *Opium War (1839-42) between Britain and China. China agreed to pay Britain an indemnity, ceded Hong Kong to Britain, and opened five so-called "treaty" ports (Canton, Amoy, Foochow, Nangpo, and Shanghai) to British traders. By a subsequent treaty in 1843 British citizens were no longer subject to Chinese law.

Napier, Sir Charles James (1782-1853). Soldier. Napier served under Moore in the Peninsular War and was severely wounded at *Coruña (1809). In 1841 he was given command of Upper and Lower Sind and, during the next four years, suppressed rebellion and established a civil government. In 1850 he returned to England, and devoted himself to writing on Indian and military subjects.

Napier of Magdala, Robert Cornelis Napier, 1st Baron (1810-90). Commissioned in the Bengal engineers (1826), Napier served in the first and second Sikh Wars (1845, 1848) and helped relieve Lucknow (1858) during the Indian mutiny. In 1867-68 he conducted what was regarded as a model campaign in Ethiopia, for which he was raised to the peerage. He subsequently became commander in chief in India (1870) and governor of Gibraltar (1876).

Napoleonic War. *See* French Revolutionary and Napoleonic Wars.

Naseby, battle of (14 June 1645). An engagement during the Civil War. Some 7500 royalists, commanded by Charles I and Prince Rupert, were decisively defeated by nearly twice the number of parliamentarians, commanded by Cromwell and Sir Thomas Fairfax; about 5000 royalists were taken prisoner. Naseby, the first major success of the *New Model Army, prompted the surrender of Leicester, Bristol, Winchester, Basing House, and Chester to parliament and brought the first stage of the Civil War to a close.

Nash, John (1752-1835). Architect and town planner. Nash, the best-known Regency architect, worked for the Prince Regent (later George IV) in replanning the West End of London, laying out Regent's Park (1811) and the original Regent Street (1813-20). His other work included the enlarging of Buckingham palace and rebuilding the Brighton pavilion.

Nash, Richard (1674-1762). Dandy, who was known as Beau Nash. He was a gambler before settling in *Bath, which he established as a leading English spa. He exerted considerable influence on upper-class manners and fashion.

Natal. A province of southeast South Africa and a former British colony. Home of the Zulu people, it was settled by British traders from 1823. It was annexed by Britain in 1843, following the arrival of the Boers (*see* great trek), many of whom then moved on to the Transvaal. Natal became a colony in 1856 and, with the addition (1897) of Zululand and Tongaland, part of the Union of South Africa in 1910.

national anthem. The official patriotic hymn of a country, which, in Britain, is "God Save the King (or Queen)". The tune was already a long-established patriotic song (author and composer unknown), which had been performed on public occasions since 1745, the year of Charles Edward Stuart's Jacobite rebellion. Official regulations for its performance were issued in 1933.

National Assistance Board (NAB). The government body formerly (1948-66) responsible for administering state financial aid to those in need. The National Assistance Board took over from the Assistance Board (named from 1934 to 1940 the Unemployment Assistance Board), set up in 1934 as part of the process by which a noncontributory benefit system replaced the poor law. The NAB was replaced in 1966 by the Supplementary Benefits Commission. *See also* national insurance.

national debt. The money borrowed by the government, from creditors either at home (the internal debt) or abroad (the external debt). It originated (1692) during the wars with France, but was formally instituted with the founding of the *Bank of England (1694). Conversions of the national debt began, unsuccessfully, with that undertaken by the *South Sea Company (1720) and capital redemption with Walpole's *sinking fund ('1717).

national government (1931–40). A coalition government formed by the Labour prime minister Ramsay *MacDonald to combat the national economic crisis. It comprised Conservatives, Liberals, and MacDonald's Labour supporters who called themselves the National Labour Party; the majority of Labour MPs repudiated MacDonald's leadership and went into opposition. In Oct 1932 the Liberals, too, split: the Liberal Nationals under Sir John Simon continued to support the government, while the rest, under Herbert Samuel (who had suggested the formation of a national government in 1931), joined the opposition. The government's economic policies, including the introduction of *tariffs (1932), contributed little to the country's recovery, which was achieved largely by more favourable trading conditions. MacDonald's successors as prime ministers were Stanley *Baldwin (June 1935) and Neville *Chamberlain (May 1937). In May 1940 Churchill's wartime coalition replaced the national government.

National Health Service. A comprehensive health service that was established in 1948 under the National Health Service Act (1946). Such a service was proposed in the *Beveridge Report (1942), and Aneurin Bevan was responsible, as minister of health in the Labour government (1945–51) for its implementation. The service, which was reorganized in 1974, is financed partly out of *national insurance (to which employers and employees contribute) but mainly out of taxation.

national insurance. A national system of insurance providing funds to finance the *National Health Service (NHS) and social security benefits. Old-age pensions were introduced by Lloyd George in 1908, but these were noncontributory and means-tested. The National Insurance Act (1911) provided for unemployment and sickness insurance. The former applied initially only to certain industries, but was gradually extended to most employers, while the latter was compulsory, financed by contributions from employers, employees, and the state. The lower-income groups covered by sickness insurance were provided in 1925 with old-age pensions, which were then established on a national basis and financed by additions to sickness contributions. A comprehensive system of social security based on national insurance was put forward in the *Beveridge Report (1942) and became effective with the National Insurance Act (1946) and the establishment of the NHS (1948).

nationalization. The compulsory purchase of industrial and commercial enterprises from their private owners by the state. Nationalization was adopted as an aim of the Labour Party in 1918, and began to be implemented by the first majority Labour administration (1945–51). The Bank of England and the coal, gas, electricity, and railway industries were among those affected.

national service. The conscription of civilians into the armed services or industry immediately prior to and during World War II. Cold War conditions led to the retention of national service in peacetime (1947–62); men on reaching the age of 18 became liable for two years' military service (later reduced to 18 months).

National Trust. A voluntary body, founded in 1895 and incorporated in 1907, holding buildings of architectural or historic interest, or land of natural beauty, in the UK in order to guarantee their preservation for the public benefit. Relying for funds chiefly on individual and corporate members and income from visitors, the Trust acquires properties by gift, purchase, or (since 1946) from the state. The separate National Trust for Scotland dates from 1931.

Nations, battle of the. See Leipzig, battle of.

NATO. See North Atlantic Treaty Organization.

Nauru. An independent island republic in the western Pacific. Annexed by Germany in 1888, it became a joint *mandate of Britain, Australia, and New Zealand in 1920 and was administered by Australia until gaining independence in 1968; it is a special member of the Commonwealth.

Navarino, battle of (20 Oct 1827). A naval engagement during the Greek War of Independence, in which the Turkish-Egyptian fleet was defeated by a combined force of British, French, and Russian ships. This was the last fleet action carried out wholly under sail. Vice Admiral Sir Edward Codrington, who had launched the attack on his own initiative, was censured and recalled to London by the British government.

Navigation Acts. Legislation designed to give English shipping a monopoly in the colonial trade. Earlier regulations (1382, 1485, 1540) were intended only to protect English shipping, but in the 17th century ordinances were issued specifically to increase revenues from the colonial trade. The ordinance of 1650 forbade foreign ships to trade in England's colonies and that of 1651 specified that colonial goods must be carried in English or colonial ships, of which at least 75% of the crew were to be English. The Navigation Act (1660), based on the earlier ordinances, further required that certain colonial goods were to be shipped only to England. This system of *mercantilism was directed against the Dutch but further acts (1663, 1672, 1696) proved difficult to enforce and were repealed in 1849 and 1854.

navy. The warships, together with their crews and supporting administration, of a nation. The origins of the Royal Navy lie in the fleet created by Alfred the Great (reigned 871-99) in defence against the Danish invasions. From the 11th to the 16th centuries the *cinque ports and mercenaries supplied the navy, which was then enlarged and rendered more efficient by Henry VIII (reigned 1509-47). His work was continued by the Stuarts, and in the second half of the 17th century Samuel *Pepys, the diarist, introduced administrative reforms of fundamental importance. The Glorious Revolution (1688-89) gave parliament almost complete control of the navy, which retained its command of the seas until superseded by the US navy in World War II. The navy was administered by a navy board from 1546 until 1832, when the Board of *Admiralty was instituted, to be merged in 1964 with the Ministry of Defence.

Nechtansmere, battle of (20 May 685). The battle in which King Bruide and the Picts annihilated King Ecgfrith's Northumbrian army, thwarting his attempt to subjugate them.

Nehru, Jawaharlal (1889-1964). The first prime minister of independent India (1947-64). In 1919 he joined *Gandhi's Indian National Congress and in 1929 became its president. He served several prison sentences for his refusal to cooperate with the British (the policy termed *satyagraha*) and played a prominent role in the negotiations for Indian independence.

Nelson, Horatio Nelson, Viscount (1758-1805). Admiral, who held command throughout the French Revolutionary War and in the early stages of the Napoleonic War. In 1794, at Calvi, he lost the sight in his right eye but went on to play a distinguished role at Cape *St Vincent (1797) and, after losing his right arm, to win the battle of *Aboukir Bay (1798); for this victory he was made Baron Nelson of the Nile. In 1799 he put down a rebellion in Naples, where he became the lover of Emma, Lady *Hamilton, and conducted from Palermo the blockade of Malta. Ill health forced his return to England in 1800, but in 1801 he was appointed second in command of an expedition to the Baltic, where he defeated a superior Danish fleet at the battle of *Copenhagen (1801). Created a viscount, in 1803 he was given command in the Mediterranean and blockaded Villeneuve in Toulon for two years. The French escaped (March 1805), and Nelson spent six months in pursuit, crossing to the West Indies and back again. Eventually he caught up with the combined French-Spanish fleet off Cape *Trafalgar, and in a single day's fighting virtually annihilated his opponents. He himself was mortally wounded by a sharpshooter. He is buried in St Paul's.

Nennius (late 8th-early 9th centuries). Welsh chronicler, who compiled the *Historia Britonum*. Based on earlier sources and chronicles (most of which are now lost), it includes references to King *Arthur. Its veracity has been questioned.

Neville, George (d. 1476). Archbishop of York from 1465. He was the youngest brother of Warwick the kingmaker, after whose victory at Northampton (1460) Neville was appointed chancellor. In 1467 he was deprived of the chancellorship because of the quarrel between his brother and Edward IV, and after the king's victories of Barnet and Tewkesbury (1471) he was imprisoned for three years.

Neville, Richard, earl of Warwick and Salisbury (1428-71). A politician whose influence during the Wars of the *Roses earned him the sobriquet kingmaker. He was the son of Richard, earl of Salisbury, and married Anne Beauchamp, heiress to the earldom of Warwick, which Neville inherited in 1449. He supported Richard, duke of York, at the first battle of *St Albans in 1455, but after the rout at *Ludford Bridge in 1459 was forced to flee abroad. He returned in 1460 and fought at *Northampton, *St Albans, and *Towton, helping Edward, duke of York, secure the throne as Edward IV. Confirmed in the offices of lord chamberlain and warden of the Cinque Ports, he wielded enormous power until, following Edward's marriage (1464) to Elizabeth Woodville, he lost the friendship of the king. In France in 1469 Warwick began to intrigue with his son in law (and the king's brother) George, duke of Clarence, and after victory at Banbury briefly captured Edward. Forced to flee, in 1470 they returned to proclaim Henry VI king. Edward fled to Flanders but returned the following year to defeat and kill Warwick at *Barnet.

Neville's Cross, battle of (17 Oct 1346). A battle, fought outside Durham, in which David II of Scots was heavily defeated and captured by a northern English force. The defeat effectively ended the involvement of the Scots in the early stages of the *Hundred Years' War, as allies of the French.

Nevis. *See* St Kitts.

New Brunswick. A maritime province of Canada. It was settled by the French in the early 17th century as part of Acadia, which was ceded to Britain (who called it *Nova Scotia) by the treaty of Utrecht (1713). Many *United Empire Loyalists settled here in 1784, when it became a separate colony. It was incorporated into the Dominion of Canada in 1867.

Newbury, battles of. Two battles of the Civil War, fought in Berkshire. 1. (20 Sept 1643) A battle that was inconclusive, but in which the royalists, commanded by Charles I, suffered heavily, withdrawing towards Oxford. The parliamentary commander, Lord *Essex, achieved his immediate aim of taking Reading. 2. (27 Oct 1644) A battle in which three parliamentary armies attempted to capture a small royalist force under Charles. Their failure to do so prompted the parliamentarians to merge their forces into the *New Model Army.

Newcastle, Thomas Pelham-Holles, 1st duke of (1693-1768). Inheriting immense estates from his uncle John Holles (1662-1711), whose name he added to his own, Newcastle became the supreme political manager, perfecting the use of official *patronage (and his own money) to maintain "Whiggery". Secretary of state from 1724, he led the *broad-bottom administration with his brother Henry *Pelham, whom he succeeded as first lord of the treasury (1754-56). He again became first lord in July 1757, working with Pitt the elder until Pitt's fall (Oct 1761). In May 1762 Newcastle was driven out of office by the king's favourite *Bute. He was lord privy seal under Rockingham (1765-66).

Newcastle, William Cavendish, duke of (1592-1676). Royalist. As Charles I's northern commander, he took virtually all Yorkshire (June 1643) but, after

*Marston Moor (July 1644), withdrew to the Continent. He helped finance the royal cause, spending over £900,000.

Newcastle programme. Policy aims approved by the Liberals (under Gladstone) at the Newcastle party conference (Oct 1891). They included Irish home rule, disestablishment of the Welsh and Scottish churches, triennial parliaments, reform of the land law and rural local government, and the introduction of liability by employers to pay compensation for industrial accidents.

Newcomen, Thomas (1663-1729). Inventor of the atmospheric steam engine. Newcomen's engine, which he developed in partnership with Thomas *Savery, came into use in 1712. Newcomen engines were widely employed in draining mines (and adapted for some industrial processes) until supplanted by those of *Watt.

New Delhi. The capital of India, since 1912. George V announced the city's foundation in 1911, and it was carefully planned 5 km (3 mi) south of Old Delhi, chiefly by Sir Edwin Lutyens (1869-1944), to complement the monuments of Old Delhi.

New England. The northeastern corner of the USA, comprising the states of Maine, New Hampshire, Vermont, Massachusetts, Rhode Island, and Connecticut. It was named by Capt. John Smith (1580-1631), who explored the area, in 1614 and the earliest settlers were Puritans, including the *pilgrim fathers.

New Forest. A woodland region of Hampshire that has been reserved as a crown property since 1079. Its original function was to serve as the king's hunting ground, and William (II) Rufus was killed (perhaps murdered) here by an arrow while hunting. The oaks of the New Forest were formerly used to build Britain's naval fleet.

Newfoundland. The most easterly province of Canada, claimed for Britain by Sir Humphrey *Gilbert in 1583. Despite constant disputes with the French, Newfoundland remained a British colony

for 300 years and in 1949 was the last province to join the Dominion of Canada.

Newgate. A prison in the City of London, established in the 12th century and used until 1881 to house criminals of all kinds. Executions took place here, rather than at *Tyburn, from 1783. Destroyed in the great fire (1666), Newgate was twice rebuilt and finally pulled down in 1902. The *Old Bailey occupies its site.

New Guinea. The largest island in the Pacific Ocean. It was visited by Europeans from the 16th century, and in 1828 the Dutch took possession of the west (West Irian, now in Indonesia). The southeast became a British protectorate in 1885, in which year the Germans annexed the northeast. British New Guinea was renamed Papua in 1906, when Australia gained control of it. In 1914 the Australians conquered the German colony, which, as the Territory of New Guinea, became, under Australian administration, a League of Nations mandate (1920) and then a UN trust territory (1946). Papua and New Guinea were united under Australian administration and obtained self-government in 1973. Papua New Guinea became an independent member of the Commonwealth in 1975.

New Hebrides. An island group in the southwest Pacific Ocean. The islands began to attract European settlers in the 19th century, and in 1906, to protect their own interests, Britain and France formed a condominium to govern the islands jointly. The New Hebrides became independent as the Vanuatu Republic in 1980.

New Lanark. An experiment in industrial management, conducted at the New Lanark textile mills by Robert *Owen and his partners (1800-29). Owen demonstrated that the provision of humane working conditions, together with model housing and schools, was compatible with financial profitability.

Newman, John Henry, Cardinal (1801-90). Religious leader, converted from

Anglicanism to Roman Catholicism. Vicar of St Mary's Oxford, the University church (1828-43), Newman became a leading figure in the *Oxford movement through his powerful writings and sermons. Gradually convinced, however, that the Church of England was not truly catholic, he became a Roman Catholic (1845), being created a cardinal in 1879. He published a classic spiritual autobiography, *Apologia pro vita sua* (1864).

Newmarch, Bernard de (11th century). Norman lord. Occupying several manors in Herefordshire, he was prominently involved in the conquest of the kingdom of Brycheiniog. Following the defeat and death of *Rhys ap Tewdwr in 1093, Bernard built a castle and established a borough at Brecon, the administrative centre of his new lordship.

New Model Army. The force established in Feb 1645, during the Civil War, by the Long Parliament. It was initially composed of some 20 000 men, under the command of Sir Thomas Fairfax. Designed to supersede the uncoordinated parliamentary forces of the early years of the Civil War, the army, by its cohesion and professional standards, was a prime factor in the final defeat of Charles I. It was reduced in size in 1649, 1651, and 1655 but continued to form the basis of the government of the Interregnum until 1660, when most of the troops, discontented over arrears of pay and conscious of their general unpopularity, welcomed the restoration of Charles II.

Newport rising (1839). A rising among the textile workers of Montgomeryshire and the miners and ironworkers of Monmouthshire and east Glamorganshire. The resort to physical force at Llanidloes in April was followed in Nov by a march on Newport by contingents led by John Frost (a delegate at the Chartist convention), Zephaniah Williams, and William Jones. From the Westgate Hotel, the military fired on the mob leaving several dead. The three leaders were condemned to die, but their sentence was commuted to transportation.

Newport treaty (1648). Terms for peace negotiated at Newport, on the Isle of Wight, between Charles I and parliamentary leaders following the royalist defeat in the second phase of the Civil War. Parliament disregarded the *Vote of No Addresses, hoping to reach agreement with Charles over the head of the army, but the meetings proved futile as by now the army was fully in control of events.

New South Wales. A federal state of *Australia. It was the original penal colony for British convicts between 1788 and 1840 and expanded rapidly as free settlers also arrived. A crown colony, it initially comprised the whole continent except Western Australia. Tasmania, South Australia, Victoria, Queensland, the Northern Territory, and New Zealand became separate colonies between 1825 and 1863. New South Wales was granted representative government in 1842 and became a member of the newly created Commonwealth of Australia in 1901.

Newton, Sir Isaac (1642-1727). Mathematician and physicist. He discovered the law of gravitation, inspired, it was said, by observing an apple falling from a tree to the ground. He also defined force in his laws of motion, invented calculus, probably independently of Leibniz, and showed that white light comprises rays of light of different colours. His *Philosophia naturalis principia mathematica* (1687)—the *Principia* —was a landmark in the history of science. Newton was an MP (1689, 1701-02) and warden (1696) and then master (1700) of the mint.

New Zealand. An archipelago in the southern Pacific Ocean. Its islands began to be colonized after the foundation of New South Wales (1788), but only with the formation of the New Zealand Company (1839) under the auspices of Edward Gibbon *Wakefield did regular colonization begin. Formal annexation followed the treaty of *Waitangi (1840) with the Maori inhabitants of the islands. Representative institutions were established in New Zealand in 1852, and ministerial responsibility was granted four years later. The colony's early years were troubled by the *Maori Wars, which did not seriously threaten the colonists but resulted in the decimation of the Maoris and the breakdown of their tribal structure. The economy of New Zealand was greatly boosted by the discovery of gold in 1861 and the subsequent gold rushes. The country maintained close imperial ties, assisting Great Britain during the second *Boer War (1899-1902) and both world wars. It became a dominion in 1907 but only assumed legal equality with the UK as a member of the Commonwealth in 1947 (16 years after being empowered to do so by the Statute of *Westminster).

Nicholson's Nek, battle of (30 Oct 1899). A battle of the second *Boer War that ended with the surrender of some 800 British soldiers. The siege of *Ladysmith followed.

Nigeria. A country in West Africa and a former British colony. British slave traders visited Nigeria from the late 15th century. The trade was abolished in 1807, following which a number of British missionaries and explorers penetrated Nigeria. *Lagos, annexed in 1861, was the first British colony in Nigeria, which was divided in 1906 into the Colony (of Lagos) and Protectorate of Southern Nigeria (allocated to Britain at the *Berlin Conference) and the Protectorate of Northern Nigeria (formerly chartered to the Royal Niger Company). United in 1914, Nigeria was administered by a system of *indirect rule. In 1954 it became a federation under a governor general and in 1960 gained independence within the Commonwealth; it became a republic in 1963.

Niger river. The major river of West Africa. Rising in Sierra Leone, it sweeps 4200 km (2600 mi) round to a vast delta on the coast of Nigeria. Its chief tributary is the Benue. Navigable 1600 km (1000 mi) from its mouth, it was first explored by *Park (1795, 1805) and the *Lander brothers (1830).

Nightingale, Florence (1820-1910). Pioneer of modern nursing. Appointed (1854) superintendent of nurses in British

military hospitals in Turkey during the Crimean War, she helped to remedy their scandalous conditions and was named the Lady with the Lamp by the soldiers. A fund in her honour financed the establishment of the first modern nursing school, at St Thomas's Hospital, London.

Nile, battle of the. See Aboukir Bay, battle of.

Nile, river. The longest river in the world, 6648 km (4132 mi). The White Nile rises south of the equator and flows northwards through the East African lakes system to *Khartoum to join the Blue Nile, which rises in Ethiopia. The Nile flows on into the Mediterranean. It was explored by *Burton, *Speke, and Grant in the mid-19th century.

nine-power treaty. See Washington conference.

nineteen propositions (1 June 1642). Demands made of Charles I by the Long Parliament. The propositions included the demands that parliamentary approval should be required for the appointment and dismissal of all officers of state, anti-Catholic legislation should be strictly enforced, the church should be reformed on lines directed by parliament, parliament should control the militia, and the king should hand *delinquents over to parliament. The king's rejection of the propositions led directly to the outbreak of the Civil War.

Ninian, St (c. 360-c. 432). Missionary. Son of a Cumbrian chieftain, he was educated in Rome and consecrated bishop by the pope (394). He then set out to convert Scotland, working from the monastery of Whithorn, which he founded in 397. He and his followers may have travelled also to Ireland and Wales.

nisi prius. A trial at nisi prius was one that might be held at an *assize. The term appeared in a clause of the Statute of *Westminster (1285), providing that a trial would be held at Westminster "unless before that" (*nisi prius*) it had taken place at an assize.

nithing. A person disgraced for life, a form of public condemnation by Anglo-Saxon and Norman kings. Edward the Confessor used it against *Swein for fratricide. It was last resorted to by William II, who threatened to use nithing against those who evaded military service (1088).

Nkrumah, Kwame (1909-72). The first president of Ghana (1957-66). In 1947 he formed the Convention People's Party, which gained independence from the British for the former *Gold Coast Colony in 1957. He was deposed in a military coup in 1966.

nonconformists (or **dissenters**). Protestants who do not conform to the doctrines or practices of the Church of England. In common with Roman Catholics, Protestant recusants were liable to penalties (see penal laws) under Elizabeth I and James I. Nonconformist sects, such as the Brownists (see Browne, Robert) and Barrowists (see Barrow, Henry), were penalized also by the Conventicle Act (1593; see conventicle). During the Civil War the nonconformist *Independents (chiefly *Congregationalists and *Baptists) gained increasing influence on the parliamentary side, to the detriment of the Presbyterians (see Westminster Assembly). However, the post-Restoration Act of Uniformity (1662) identified Presbyterians as nonconformists. The other harsh measures of the Clarendon code and the *Test Acts gave rise to further nonconformist colonization of North America, especially by the *Quakers. Many Presbyterians and Baptists became *Unitarians during the 18th century; the *Methodists became a nonconformist sect in 1795. Nonconformist championship of religious and civil liberty came to be associated with the Whigs, and later with the Liberal and Labour Parties. See also Puritanism.

Non-Intervention Committee (1936). An international body set up in London, at the suggestion of Britain and France, to maintain an agreement by all the European powers not to intervene on either side in the Spanish Civil War (1936-

39). The committee was disregarded from the first by Germany and Italy and subsequently by other powers, including the Soviet Union.

nonjurors. Anglican clergy and laymen who refused to take the oath of allegiance to William and Mary in 1689 (see Glorious Revolution) because such an oath would violate the oath sworn previously to James II. Archbishop Sancroft was the most prominent of the nonjurors, who included 8 bishops and 400 clergy. They were deprived in 1690 and for several decades consecrated their own bishops and held illegal services before being gradually reabsorbed into the Church of England. The nonjurors based their position on their belief in *nonresistance and the *divine right of kings.

nonresidence. The holding of a benefice by an absentee clergyman. The practice was widespread at various times from the middle ages. Puritan opposition to nonresidence was voiced in the *millenary petition (1603), and it was forbidden in the Book of *Canons (1604). By the 18th century nonresidence was again rife, over half of all clergymen being nonresident by 1810. Following a report of the Ecclesiastical Commissioners in 1836 a permanent commission was established to reform the allocation of revenues, which effectively reformed the abuse. See also pluralism.

nonresistance. The doctrine of passive obedience to authority, even if that authority is unjustly exercised. A fundamental doctrine of the Church of England, it was intensively preached under Charles I. After the Restoration an oath of nonresistance was required by the *Corporation Act (1661). See also divine right of kings.

Nonsuch palace. A palace founded in 1538, by Henry VIII, at Cuddington in Surrey. It was intended as the greatest showpiece of Henrician court architecture and as a rival to Francis I's Chambord. Unfinished at Henry's death, it was completed by private hands in Mary's reign and demolished in 1670.

Nore mutiny (May 1797). The mutiny of the British North Sea fleet anchored at the Nore in the Thames estuary. The revolt, which followed the *Spithead mutiny, was largely a protest against the barbarity of lower-deck conditions. After holding out for some four weeks, the mutineers surrendered. Their leader, Richard Parker, was hanged.

Norfolk, Roger Bigod, 4th earl of (d. 1270). Earl marshal of England from 1246. A leader of the baronial opposition to Henry III, he helped draft the *Provisions of Oxford. In 1259, however, after disputes among the barons, he gave his support to the king until Henry repudiated the Provisions in 1264, when Bigod again joined the baronial cause.

Norfolk, John Howard, 1st duke of (?1430–1485). Yorkist magnate, known as Jack of Norfolk. He served Edward IV on a number of campaigns against the Lancastrians (see Roses, Wars of the) and as ambassador to France. He was a loyal follower of *Richard III, who made him admiral, earl marshal, high steward, and duke of Norfolk in 1483. He was killed at *Bosworth.

Norfolk, Thomas Howard, 3rd duke of (1473–1554). Brother in law of Henry VII. He was appointed lord high admiral n 1513, and in the same year led the English vanguard at the battle of *Flodden, commanded by his father, the 2nd duke (earl of *Surrey). As earl of Surrey (1514–24) he served as lord lieutenant of Ireland (1520–21), returning to England to lead the anti-Wolsey faction. In 1529, on Wolsey's fall, he became president of the Privy Council. He presided at the trial of his niece *Anne Boleyn and was responsible for the arrest of Thomas *Cromwell (1540). Imprisoned during the reign of Edward VI, he was restored to favour under Mary. His son was the poet Henry Howard, earl of *Surrey.

Norfolk, Thomas Howard, 4th duke of (1536–72). Son of Henry Howard, earl of *Surrey. He was lieutenant in the north (1559–60). In 1569 he was arrested for his part in the *northern rebellion.

Subsequently released, in 1571 he was involved in *Ridolfi's plot and executed.

Norham, treaty of (1209). The treaty by which William I of Scots agreed, under threat of an English invasion, to pay £10,000 to John of England; his two daughters were given to John to be married to the king's son and an English noble respectively.

Normandy. A former province in north France, on the English Channel. In 1066 the duke of Normandy became King William I of England. After his death he was succeeded in Normandy by his eldest son Robert *Curthose, but by 1091 his second son William II of England had occupied much of the duchy. Robert was finally defeated by Henry I at *Tinchebrai (1106). In 1202 Philip II Augustus of France invaded Normandy, conquering the entire duchy, apart from the Channel Islands, in 1204. England did not formally cede Normandy to France until the treaty of *Paris (1259). In the *Hundred Years' War Edward III occupied the province in 1346, but it was restored to France by the treaty of *Brétigny (1360). The renewal of the war under Henry V resulted in the reconquest of almost all Normandy by 1420. In 1449 Charles VII of France invaded it, captured Rouen, and won the battle of *Formigny (1450). This victory finally ended English rule in Normandy. See also Normans.

Normans. A ruling dynasty, descended from the Viking Rollo, whose rule over territories that formed the nucleus of later *Normandy was recognized by Charles the Simple in 911. Duke William II claimed the English throne in 1066 on the death of Edward the Confessor (who had probably promised him the crown) and defeated and killed Harold II at Hastings. William (I) the Conqueror, as he is called, and his sons William II and Henry I established the Anglo-Norman state in England. Under William I and again under Henry I, after he had defeated his eldest brother Duke Robert Curthose at Tinchebrai (1106), the duchy and kingdom were ruled as one. Norman rule was harsh but largely successful until the misfortunes of Stephen, son of William I's daughter, and last of the line.

Norman yoke. A phrase applied to Norman rule by those believing that the Norman conquest led to the overthrow of free democratic institutions and their replacement by despotic and autocratic government. It was a powerful political myth in the parliamentary struggles of the 17th century, when the Anglo-Saxon witan was equated with parliament and the Norman kings with the Stuarts.

North, Frederick North, Lord (1732-92). Prime minister (1770-82), during the *American Revolution. His ministry was characterized by his loyalty to George III, often against his own better judgment. He abolished (1770) duties under the American Import Duties Act (1767), except on tea. In 1774, however, after the *Boston tea party (1773), the government retaliated with the *Intolerable Acts, which led to armed resistance (1775) and the American Declaration of Independence (1776). North attempted to resign after the military defeats at Saratoga (1777) and Yorktown (1781) but was dissuaded from doing so by George; North finally resigned in March 1782. He again held office, with Charles James *Fox, from April to Dec 1783. He succeeded as 2nd earl of Guildford in 1790.

Northampton, Assize of. See Clarendon, Assize of.

Northampton, battle of (10 July 1460). A battle of the Wars of the Roses, in which the Lancastrians were heavily defeated by the earl of March (later Edward IV). Many prominent Lancastrians were killed and Henry VI was captured.

Northampton, 1st earl of. See Howard, Henry.

Northampton, treaty of. See Edinburgh, treaty of.

North Atlantic Treaty Organization (NATO). A military alliance formed in April 1949 by Belgium, Britain, Canada, Denmark, France, Iceland, Italy, Luxembourg, the Netherlands, Norway, Portugal, and the USA; Greece and Turkey became members in 1952, West Germany in 1955, and Spain in 1982. In Europe the NATO forces are under the Supreme Allied Commander Europe, and defence is coordinated by the North Atlantic Council of Ministers, the Defence Committee, and the Military Committee.

North Borneo. A British dependency (1881-1963) on the island of *Borneo. Acquired (1878) by what became (1881) the British North Borneo Company, it became a protectorate in 1888 and a crown colony in 1946. In 1963, as the state of Sabah, it became part of Malaysia.

North Briton. A periodical published weekly from June 1762 to April 1763 by John *Wilkes. Its name is a reference to the earl of *Bute, a Scot (i.e. a North Briton), who was a prime object of the journal's attacks. No. 45 (23 April 1763) of the *North Briton* alleged that the king's speech, proroguing parliament, contained a lie. George *Grenville's government began proceedings, by general *warrant, for seditious libel. Wilkes won the ensuing legal case, which established the illegality of general warrants.

northeast passage. The sea route between the Atlantic and the Pacific through Siberian waters. In the 16th century the *Muscovy Company sponsored voyages in search of the passage, which was also sought by *Hudson. However, the first through passage was not made until 1878-79, by the Swede Nils Nordenskjöld. See also northwest passage.

Northern Ireland. The six northeastern counties of Ireland, which formed part of the Irish province of Ulster until Ireland was partitioned by the Government of Ireland Act (1920). Northern Ireland was a self-governing province of the UK, and its parliament at Stormont had powers over all domestic legislation. Control of foreign policy and certain other matters remained at Westminster, where Northern Ireland is represented by 17 MPs. The *Ulster Unionist party always had a majority at Stormont and ruled uninterruptedly from 1921 to 1972, opposed by a Roman Catholic minority, which desired some form of union with the Republic of Ireland. This minority experienced discrimination in local government, employment, and housing, and in the late 1960s a civil rights campaign began to make protest marches. Extremist Unionist reaction to these caused riots, and in Aug 1969 the British army was introduced to keep the peace. From 1970 the army has been attacked by the *Irish Republican Army, and there have also been many sectarian attacks· between the two communities, Protestants and Catholics. In 1972 Stormont was suspended and direct rule from Westminster imposed.

northern rebellion (1569-70). A rising inspired initially by the resentment felt by Thomas Howard, 4th duke of *Norfolk, at the influence at court of the Cecils. Norfolk sought Spanish assistance for his plan to release Mary (Queen of Scots) but almost immediately submitted to Elizabeth I. Leadership of the revolt then passed to the great northern families, the Percys of Northumberland and the Nevilles of Westmorland, who demanded the restoration of Catholicism and of Mary to the Scottish throne. Government troops easily imposed order on the north, suppressing a subsequent rising led by Leonard Dacre; some 800 rebels were executed.

Northern Rhodesia. A British dependency (1889-1964), administered first by Rhodes' *British South Africa Company (1889-1924) and then as a protectorate (1924-53). From 1953 to 1963 it was a member of the *Central African Federation and, as Zambia, became an independent republic and a member of the Commonwealth in 1964. *See also* Southern Rhodesia.

Northern Territory. The north central region of Australia. Formerly part of New South Wales, it was annexed to South Australia (1863-1907) and became a separate territory of the Commonwealth of Australia in 1911. A federal administrator ruled the territory until

power was transferred (1977-79) to a legislative assembly and cabinet.

Northumberland, John Dudley, duke of (?1502-1553). A powerful member of Edward VI's privy council, who overthrew the protector Somerset (1551) to become virtual ruler of England. He rose to prominence in the wars of the last years of Henry VIII's reign and was created Viscount Lisle in 1542 and earl of Warwick in 1547. He became duke of Northumberland shortly before engineering Somerset's second arrest for treason in 1551. Northumberland's government advanced the Protestant *Reformation, with the revised *Book of Common Prayer (1552) and Cranmer's 42 *articles and initiated effective financial reforms. A man of intense ambition, Northumberland persuaded the king to name Lady Jane *Grey (Northumberland's daughter in law) as his successor. She was proclaimed queen on Edward's death, but Northumberland lost the support of the council and was arrested for treason in opposing the succession of Mary I. His attempt to save his life by announcing his conversion to Roman Catholicism failed, and he was executed.

Northumbria. A kingdom of the Angles, north of the Humber, which was created by the amalgamation of *Bernicia and *Deira in the 6th century. Northumbria extended its power over the southern English (see bretwalda) from 585 to 671, during the reigns of *Edwin, *Oswald, and *Oswy. This power was challenged by the rise of *Mercia in the 7th century, and defeat by the Picts at *Nechtansmere (685) broke the Northumbrian attempt to subject the north. Northumbrian monastic art and learning, notably at *Jarrow, exerted a considerable influence on Europe in the late 7th and 8th centuries. Ruled by the Danes from 867 to 872, they subsequently established the Kingdom of *York, and the rest of Northumbria was divided among several chiefs; it became an earldom in the 11th century.

Northwest Frontier Province. The northwestern region of the Punjab. This area, inhabited by turbulent Pathan tribes and predominately Muslim in religion, commanded the Khyber pass and the Afghan frontier with India. Strategically important to the defence of India, it was annexed by Britain in 1849. Created a separate province of India in 1901, it became part of Pakistan after the partition of India in 1947.

northwest passage. The Arctic sea route from the Atlantic to the Pacific Oceans. Explorers including Sir Martin Frobisher, Henry Hudson, and Sir John Franklin searching for a short route from Europe to the east opened up the northern regions of Canada but found no ice-free channel. Amundsen was the first to navigate the passage (1903–06) in the Gjöa, and the Canadian coastguard vessel St Roch made the first single-season journey. See also northeast passage.

Norwich crusade (1383). An English expedition to Flanders. Led by Henry le *Despenser, bishop of Norwich, the crusade was ostensibly launched in support of pope Urban VI against the followers of the Avignon antipope Clement VII. However, it was also intended to protect the English wool trade in Flanders, threatened by the French during the Hundred Years' War. The campaign was a complete failure.

Nottingham, Daniel Finch, 2nd earl of (1647–1730). First lord of the admiralty (1681–84) under Charles II. Nottingham proposed a regency following the flight of James II but later served William III as secretary of state (1688–93). He helped carry the *Toleration Act (1689). He subsequently served Anne as secretary of state (1702–04). Lord president of the council (1714–16) under George I, he lost his office for urging lenient treatment of Jacobite rebels.

Nottingham, Heneage Finch, 1st earl of (1621–82). Judge and politician. In 1660 he became solicitor general and in 1670 attorney general. In 1673 he was appointed lord keeper of the seals and subsequently (1674) lord chancellor. He was the model for Amri in Dryden's Absalom and Achitophel.

Nova Scotia. A maritime province of Canada. Settled by the French in the early 17th century, the territory (which included present-day Nova Scotia, Cape Breton Island, Prince Edward Island, and New Brunswick) was disputed for over a hundred years by French settlers, who called it Acadia, and the English, who called it Nova Scotia. Formally ceded to the British by the treaty of Utrecht (1713), Nova Scotia was a founding province of the confederated Dominion of Canada in 1867.

Novel Disseisin, Assize of. A judicial proceeding, or the writ giving rise to it, by which a person wrongfully dispossessed (or disseised) of a freehold might recover it. It was so called because initially only newly arisen cases of disseisin were heard. See also assizes.

nuclear test-ban treaty (1963). An international agreement between the Soviet Union, the UK, and the USA that banned nuclear testing by its signatories in the atmosphere, space, and under water. Many other countries (but not France or China) subsequently signed the treaty.

nuclear warfare. A potential form of warfare employing the fission of a heavy atomic nucleus or the fusion of two light nuclei. Atomic (or fission) bombs were developed jointly during World War II by Britain and the USA and were used for the first (and only) time (Aug 1945) against the Japanese cities of Hiroshima and Nagasaki, causing unprecedented damage and loss of life from blast and atomic radiation. The hydrogen (or fusion) bomb has never been used in war but has been tested by the USA, Soviet Union, Britain, France, and China. Nuclear missiles are generally regarded as the "great deterrent"; if ever used, they will have failed in their purpose.

Nuffield, William Morris, 1st Viscount (1877–1863). Motor-car manufacturer and philanthropist. Morris produced his first car in 1913 and subsequently introduced mass production into Britain. His benefactions include Nuffield College, Oxford, and the Nuffield Foundation, established to promote "health...social wellbeing...and education".

Nyasaland. A British protectorate (1891-1964). Nyasaland had no valuable minerals and few European colonists, although missionaries were active in the late 19th century. From 1953 to 1963 it joined its wealthier neighbours Northern and Southern Rhodesia in the *Central African Federation, which was dissolved largely because of opposition to it in Nyasaland. As Malawi, it became an independent member of the Commonwealth in 1964.

Nyerere, Julius (1922-). President of Tanzania. He led his country to independence in 1962, when he became president first of *Tanganyika (1962-64) and then of Tanzania.

O

Oastler, Richard (1789-1861). Social reformer, nicknamed the factory king. A Yorkshire estate manager and Tory radical, he began to expose the scandal of child factory labour in 1830 and campaigned for the ten-hour working day (see factory acts). He was also a vigorous opponent of the Poor Law Amendment Act (1834). From 1840 to 1844 he was imprisoned for debt in Fleet prison, where he wrote *Fleet Papers* (3 vols, 1841-43).

Oates, Titus (1649-1705). Clergyman, who, with Israel Tonge (1621-80), invented the *popish plot (1678). Oates was dismissed for misconduct from a number of posts before becoming chaplain to the Protestants in the household of the Roman Catholic duke of Norfolk. Encouraged by Tonge, he subsequently (1677) infiltrated Catholic circles, even becoming a Catholic and entering the Jesuit college at Valladolid in search of information detrimental to Catholics. Oates' testimony of a popish plot was later found to contain inconsistencies, and in 1685 he was convicted of perjury. Pilloried, flogged, and imprisoned for

life, he was released in 1689, after the accession of William III.

oath-helpers. Persons produced in a medieval court of law by a man charged with a crime to testify to his innocence.

O'Brien, James Bronterre (1805-64). Chartist leader. An Irish-born radical journalist and theoretician, he was editor (1831-35) of the *Poor Man's Guardian* and became one of *Chartism's most outspoken leaders. In 1850 he helped found the socialist National Reform League.

O'Brien, Murrough, 1st earl of Inchiquin (1614-74). Irish general. Brought up a Protestant, he fought vigorously for the English in the Irish rebellion of 1641, earning himself the sobriquet Murrough of the burnings. During the English Civil War he submitted to the parliamentarians in 1644 but later (1648) sided with Charles I. After Cromwell's suppression of the Irish, O'Brien went to France (1650), returning finally to Ireland in 1663.

O'Brien, William (1852-1928). Irish nationalist, journalist, and MP (1885-86, 1887-92, 1910-18). As editor of *United Ireland* (1881) he promoted the aims of the *Irish Land League. He was imprisoned several times for his nationalist activities.

Occasional Conformity, Act of (1711). An act designed to prevent *nonconformists from receiving communion in the Anglican Church simply so as to qualify themselves for civil or military office. A £40 fine and disqualification from office were imposed upon those who, after receiving the Anglican sacrament, attended nonconformist services. The act was generally evaded and was repealed in 1719.

O'Connell, Daniel (1775-1847). Irish nationalist. A formidable barrister, he founded the *Catholic Association in 1823 to press for the right of Roman Catholics to sit in parliament. This was achieved in 1829, the year following O'Connell's election as MP for Co. Clare (see Catholic emancipation). O'Connell then mobilized support for repeal of the

Act of Union, forming the Repeal Association in 1840. Always a pacifist, he lost the allegiance of the more revolutionary *Young Ireland group, but is still revered in Ireland as the "Liberator".

O'Connor, Feargus (Edward) (1796-1855). Irish Chartist. He became an MP in 1832, but was unseated (1835) and joined the Chartists. He founded his journal the *Northern Star* in 1837 and was imprisoned for seditious libel in 1840. Following the failure of his Chartist petition (1848) he became insane (1852).

Odo (d. 1097). Bishop of Bayeux. Half-brother of William I, he became bishop in 1049 and was created earl of Kent after the Norman conquest. He acted as regent while William was in Normandy, but in 1082 he was imprisoned, for obscure reasons, until William's death. He led baronial opposition to William II and was forced to return to Normandy in 1088. Thereafter he served Robert Curthose, duke of Normandy, and died on the first crusade. He probably commissioned the *Bayeux tapestry.

O'Donnell, Hugh Roe (c. 1571-1602). Lord of Tyrconnell. He was imprisoned by the English administration but made a sensational escape (1591) and in 1594 joined *O'Neill's revolt. After their defeat at Kinsale (1601) O'Donnell fled to Spain, where he was poisoned by an English agent.

O'Donnell, Rory, 1st earl of Tyrconnell (1575-1608). Irish chief, brother of Hue Roe. During 1602 he waged guerrilla warfare in Connaught until Dec, when he became chief of his clan and submitted to the English. Although James I made him earl of Tyrconnell (1603) he continued to resist English authority over his territory. He left Ireland with O'Neill in 1607, and died in Rome. Their departure—the *flight of the earls—left Ulster open to British colonization.

Offa (d. 796). King of Mercia (757-96), crowned after seizing power in the civil war that followed the death of his cousin Aethelbald. Offa consolidated Mercian

power over the southern English (see bretwalda) as well as extending Mercian influence to the north. His daughters married the kings of Wessex and Northumbria, and Offa's special power in England was recognized by Pope Adrian I. Adrian referred to him as the "king of the English" and agreed to the creation of an archbishop at Lichfield, which freed the Mercian church from the control of Canterbury in Kent. Offa negotiated a commercial treaty with the future emperor Charlemagne on equal terms. He may have built *Offa's dyke and struck a new *coinage, issuing the silver penny, which bore his name and title.

Offa's dyke. An earthwork, 113 km (70 mi) long, supposedly built by *Offa (d. 796), king of Mercia, to mark the boundary between his kingdom and the Welsh tribes. It replaced an earlier boundary, Wat's dyke, which was built in the reign (716-57) of Offa's predecessor, Aethelbald.

Ogham (or **Ogam**). An alphabetic script found in stone inscriptions, usually on standing memorial stones, in Ireland and areas of Cornwall and Wales settled by the Irish. Of obscure origin, it dates from the 4th to the 8th centuries and consists of 20 letters, comprising one to five long or short strokes.

Oglethorpe, James Edward (1696-1785). Army officer, politician, and founder of the colony of Georgia in America. Moved by the sufferings of imprisoned debtors, Oglethorpe, with other philanthropists, obtained a charter (1732) to establish Georgia as a colony offering paupers a new life and forming a southern defence for British America. His banning of slavery in Georgia, however, aroused bitter opposition. Returning to Britain in 1743, he became an MP.

O'Higgins, Kevin Christopher (1892-1927). Irish nationalist. In 1918 he was elected a *Sinn Féin MP and in 1921 sided with Arthur Griffith in supporting the Anglo-Irish treaty, which established the *Irish Free State. Minister of justice from 1923, he was assassinated in 1927.

Oisin (or Ossian). A mythical figure in Gaelic literature. He features in romantic tales set in the 3rd century AD. In the 18th century James Macpherson (1736-96) "translated" several of his poems —the Ossianic sagas—but these have been shown to be Macpherson's own inventions.

O'Kelly, Sean Thomas (1883-1966). President of Ireland (1945-59). An early member of Sinn Féin, he followed De Valera in repudiating the Anglo-Irish treaty in 1921. He was in successive Fianna Fáil governments (1932-45) before becoming president.

Olaf Guthfrithson (d. 941 AD). King of Dublin from 934, succeeding his father, and effective leader of the Norsemen on the east coast of Ireland. After sporadic warfare against the Irish he aided his kinsmen in Deira (Northumbria) but was defeated in 937 by Athelstan. He was killed in an obscure battle in Scotland.

Olaf Sitricson (d. 981 AD). King of Dublin (945-80) and York (940-44, 949-52). For most of his life he alternated between military campaigns in Ireland and Deira (Northumbria). After 953 he remained in Ireland, based at Dublin until his defeat at *Tara by the Irish in 980. He died in Iona.

Old Bailey. A street in the City of London, site of the Central Criminal Court, established in 1834, to which it has given its name. The court, which occupies the site of the former *Newgate prison, tries offences committed in Greater London.

Oldcastle, Sir John (d. 1417). *Lollard leader, one of the few from the ranks of the gentry. He was convicted of heresy (1413) and imprisoned in the Tower. He escaped and, after organizing an unsuccessful rising, went into hiding. Three years later he was captured and executed.

ombudsman. An official who investigates citizens' complaints of maladministration by government departments. Of Swedish origin, in Britain the term is applied to the parliamentary commissioner for administration (established in 1967), health service commissioner (1972), and commissioners for local administration in England and Wales (1974).

Omdurman. A town in the *Sudan, which after the fall of nearby *Khartoum in 1885 to the British Nile expeditionary force became the capital of the *Mahdi and then of his successor the Khalifa. The defeat of the Khalifa's main force by an Anglo-Egyptian army under Kitchener at the battle of Omdurman (2 Sept 1898) facilitated the reconquest of the Sudan.

O'Neill, Con, 1st earl of Tyrone (c. 1483-c. 1559). Irish chief. In 1542 he visited England and was created earl of Tyrone, a submission that undermined his authority in Ireland. His son, Shane O'Neill, expelled him from his lands in 1556.

O'Neill, Daniel (?1612-1664). Irish royalist soldier in the Civil War. Impeached and imprisoned (1642) in the Tower for participating in army plots, he escaped and fought with Prince Rupert at *Newbury (1643, 1644), *Marston Moor (1644), and *Naseby (1645). In 1649 he had temporary command of the Ulster army and subsequently worked for Charles II in exile.

O'Neill, Hugh, 3rd baron of Dungannon and 2nd earl of Tyrone (c. 1540-1616). Irish chief, known as the Great O'Neill. He lived in England in the 1560s, returning to Ireland as a government protégé against a rival chief of the O'Neills. He served the government in the 1580s but in 1594 rebelled (see O'Neill's revolt). Although pardoned in 1603, he resented the encroaching English administration in Ulster and fled to the Continent in 1607 (see flight of the earls), dying in Rome.

O'Neill, Owen Roe (c. 1590-1649). Irish soldier. Nephew of Hugh O'Neill, he was in Spanish service for 30 years. He returned to Ireland in 1642 and led the Irish Catholic forces until his death.

O'Neill, Sir Phelim (1604-53). Irish rebel. In 1641, he was expelled from the Irish parliament and played an important part in the Irish rebellion. He held the military command until eclipsed by the arrival of Owen Roe O'Neill in 1642. He was executed by English parliamentary forces.

O'Neill, Shane, 2nd earl of Tyrone (c. 1530–1567). Irish chief. Passed over by his father (Con O'Neill) for succession, he promptly expelled him and seized the chieftainship (1556). A man of stupendous pride and restless violence, he enjoyed virtual autonomy in Ulster until his death.

O'Neill's revolt (1594–1603). A revolt led by Hugh *O'Neill, 2nd earl of Tyrone, in alliance with Hugh Roe *O'Donnell. O'Neill's Fabian tactics won him a great success at Yellow Ford (1598) but the Irish were defeated while attempting to join a Spanish force that arrived at Kinsale in 1601. Two years later O'Neill submitted and was pardoned by James I.

Ontario. A province of Canada, extending from the Great Lakes to Hudson Bay. The French and English disputed its possession until 1763, when it was gained by Britain by the treaty of Paris. It was a thinly populated wilderness until the *United Empire Loyalists arrived (1784) after the American Declaration of Independence. Called Upper Canada in 1791, when it became a separate colonial province, it was renamed Ontario following incorporation into the confederated Dominion of Canada in 1867.

Opium War (1839–42). A conflict between Britain and China arising from Chinese attempts to suppress the smuggling of opium, in which many British merchants were engaged. Following the refusal by the Chinese government to pay compensation for opium that they had confiscated fighting broke out, in which a British force bombarded Canton. The treaty of *Nanking concluded the conflict.

Oporto, battle of (12 May 1809). A battle during the Peninsular War, in which a surprise attack by a British force under Wellesley (later duke of Welling-ton) inflicted 6000 casualities on Marshal Soult's army and forced its retreat. The French were dispossessed of the vital harbour of Oporto and evacuated the whole of northern Portugal.

Opposition. The largest party in parliament opposed to the government. As late as the mid-19th century systematic opposition carried lingering implications of disloyalty to the crown. As government became firmly party based and independent of the monarch this view was replaced by recognition of "Her Majesty's Loyal Opposition", with a state-salaried leader, as the alternative government.

Orange Free State. A province in South Africa. Settled by the Afrikaners in 1836 following the *great trek, the region was annexed by Britain in 1848 as the Orange River Sovereignty. Its independence was acknowledged at the *Bloemfontein convention (1854), but the Orange Free State was again annexed by the British in 1900, during the second *Boer War. Renamed the Orange River Colony, it obtained self-government in 1907 and joined the Union of South Africa in 1910.

Orange Order. An Irish sectarian society, named after William of Orange (king of England, 1688–1702) and pledged to maintain the Protestant succession. It was formed in 1795 as a counterorganization to Catholic agrarian movements but was quiescent until the emergence in the 1880s of the home rule movement, which it vehemently opposed. After 1920 it continued as a ginger group to the *Ulster Unionist Party, all senior Unionist politicians being expected to become members. It survives today as the bastion of Protestant unionism in the north.

ordainers, lords. The committee of 21 spiritual and lay lords, led by Thomas, earl of Lancaster, that Edward II was forced to appoint in 1311. They demanded reforms set out in 41 *Ordinances (1311).

order in council. An order made by the sovereign with the advice of the Privy

Council. Orders in council are issued either by the prerogative powers of the crown, independent of any statutory authority, or by virtue of the power given by a statute to the government of the day to make detailed orders and regulations. They have been used, especially in the 19th century, to avoid parliamentary discussion of controversial issues, a notable example being Cardwell's army reforms in Gladstone's first ministry.

Ordinances (1311). The 41 enactments of the lords *ordainers, designed to give the barons control of government. Edward II was required to obtain baronial consent before leaving the country, the banishment of his favourite Piers Gaveston was renewed, his Italian bankers, the Frescobaldi, were expelled, and greater parliamentary control of his finances was established. Central and local officials were to be responsible to the barons, and parliament was to meet at least once a year. The Ordinances were revoked by the Statute of York (1322).

Ordnance, Board of. An office, formed in the 16th century, to supply munitions for the navy and army. Its head was the master, later master general of the ordnance. In 1855 its powers were taken over by the secretary for war.

ordo. The governing body of a provincial town (see colonia; municipium) in the Roman Empire. It fulfilled the functions of a senate, and its members were called decurions. It was a permanent executive body and was consulted by the magistrates, who were elected by the citizens.

Ordovices. A Celtic tribe in northwest Wales. The Ordovices fiercely resisted the Romans and unlike the *Silures in southeast Wales were never romanized. The containment of this tribe was one of the prime military objectives of the Roman authorities.

Orkneys. An archipelago off the northeast tip of Scotland. Colonized by Vikings in the 9th century and subsequently ruled by Norway and Denmark, the islands came to Scotland in 1472 as security for the dowry (which was never paid) of James III's wife, Margaret of Denmark. Between the islands of Pomona (or Mainland), Hoy, and South Ronaldsay lies the naval anchorage of *Scapa Flow.

Orléans, siege of (Sept 1428–May 1429). The English siege of Orléans, which was held by supporters of the dauphin. Led by Thomas Montacute, 4th earl of Salisbury, and, after his death under William de la Pole, 4th earl of Suffolk, it was one of the turning points of the later stages of the *Hundred Years' War. The French relief was led by Joan of Arc.

Ormonde, James Butler, 12th earl and 1st duke of (1610–88). Anglo-Irish magnate. He became a royal ward after the death of his father (1619) and was educated as a Protestant. He commanded royalist forces in Ireland during the Civil War and went into exile in 1650, after being defeated by Cromwell. After the Restoration he was made duke of Ormonde and lord lieutenant of Ireland, a post he held from 1661 until he fell from royal favour in 1669. In 1670 Colonel *Blood seized the duke and attempted to hang him at Tyburn. He was again lord lieutenant from 1677 to 1684.

Ormonde, James Butler, 2nd duke of (1665–1745). Soldier, who supported William of Orange in 1688 and served under him in Ireland and in Europe. Queen Anne made him lord lieutenant of Ireland (1703–05, 1710–11) and, after *Marlborough's recall in 1711, commander in chief. A firm Tory, he opposed the accession of George I (1714) and was attainted. He participated in the Jacobite rising (1715) and spent the rest of his life in exile. In 1719 he led a Spanish invasion fleet that hoped to restore the Stuarts, but failed.

Ormonde, Thomas Butler, 10th earl of (1532–1614). Anglo-Irish magnate. Educated as a Protestant, he earned the favour of Elizabeth I and throughout his life remained staunchly loyal to the crown. He was able to establish his power firmly in southwest Ireland after the defeat (1583) of his rival, the earl of Desmond (see Desmond revolt).

O'Rourke's revolt (1590-91). The rising of the O'Rourkes, an Irish tribe in Leitrim. Opponents of the new English authority in the late 16th century, the O'Rourkes rose in rebellion when they were attacked by government troops after Sir Brian O'Rourke aided the survivors among the Spanish armada (1588). The revolt was suppressed; Sir Brian fled to Scotland but was handed over to the English and executed.

Osborne case (1908-09). A legal action brought by W. V. Osborne, secretary of the Walthamstow branch of the Amalgamated Society of Railway Servants, to stop the union from making compulsory levies for Labour Party funds. The decision, that compulsory levies on union members for political purposes was illegal, was upheld by the law lords. Labour finances were severely affected as a result, and 16 Labour MPs found themselves without salaries, a predicament that led to the introduction in 1911 of payment of MPs. The Trade Union Act (1913) legalized union political funds financed by levies, although allowing individuals to opt out.

Ossian. See Oisin.

Ossory, earl of. See Butler, Thomas.

Ostmen. The Norsemen (or *Vikings) who arrived in Ireland on raids in the late 8th century. They consolidated themselves in the 9th century, but their inland expansion was checked at *Clontarf in 1014.

Oswald, St (d. 642). King of Northumbria (633-42). He restored the fortunes of the Northumbrian kingdom by defeating *Cadwallon near Hexham in 633 and reuniting the kingdoms of Deira and Bernicia. He revived Christianity by inviting *Aidan to be bishop of Lindisfarne. He died in battle against Penda, king of Mercia.

Oswin (d. 651). King of Deira (642-51). Made king after the death of his cousin *Oswald, Oswin was noted for his piety and generosity. He was assas-

sinated at Gilling (Yorkshire) on the orders of Oswald's brother *Oswy.

Oswy (d. 670). King of Northumbria (651-70). Succeeding his brother Oswald as king of Bernicia (642), Oswy instigated the assassination of *Oswin of Deira (651) and reunited Northumbria, at first as a subordinate to Penda, king of Mercia. After defeating Penda (655), however, he became *bretwalda. Oswy's support of Wilfrid at the synod of *Whitby ensured the victory of the Roman over the Celtic church in Britain.

Ottawa conference (21 July-20 Aug 1932). The Imperial Economic Conference, held in Ottawa, at which *imperial preferences were negotiated. The 12 Ottawa Agreements established preferential tariff rates between Britain and its dominions and between the dominions themselves.

Otterburn (or Chevy Chase), battle of (15 Aug 1388). A battle in which a Scottish force under the 3rd earl of *Douglas (who was killed) decisively defeated an English army under Henry *Percy (who was captured). It is the subject of two ballads, those of Otterbourne and Chevy Chase.

Oudenarde, battle of (11 July 1708). A battle of the War of the Spanish Succession between allied armies, commanded by *Marlborough and Prince Eugene of Savoy, and the French under the duc de Vendôme. The French, attacked in the flank, barely extricated themselves from complete encirclement, losing some 18 000 men to the allies' 3000.

outfangtheft. See infangtheft.

outlawry. The act of placing outside the protection of the law a person who has failed to face a charge of felony. Before the Norman conquest an outlaw was said to be caput lupinum (to have a "head like a wolf's") and might be killed by anyone with impunity. During the reign (1327-77) of Edward III, however, only the sheriff was empowered to put an outlaw to death. The outlaw's goods were forfeited to the crown and his lands to his lord. In later times outlawry was used in civil actions, especially for debt, and deprived a person of the right to sue. Long obsolete, it was abolished in civil proceedings in 1879 and in criminal proceedings in 1938.

Overbury murder (1613). The crime that occasioned the downfall of James I's favourite, Robert *Carr, earl of Somerset. Sir Thomas Overbury·(1581-1613) opposed Somerset's marriage with Frances Howard, the divorced countess of Essex, for which they had him imprisoned and then poisoned. The Somersets were imprisoned.

Overton, Richard (mid-17th century). Pamphleteer and satirist. He published anonymous attacks on bishops and, in 1646, on the *Westminster Assembly. Twice imprisoned for his activities as a *Leveller, he fled to Flanders in 1655.

Owain ap Gruffudd (or **Owain Gwynedd**) (c. 1100-1170). Ruler of Gwynedd, succeeding his father *Gruffudd ap Cynan in 1137. Having established his authority, he acquired lands in northeast Wales following his defeat of *Madog ap Maredudd in 1150. Despite his submission to Henry II in 1157 he was in a dominant position in Wales and was frequently supported by *Rhys ap Gruffudd.

Owain Glyndŵr (or **Owen Glendower**) (c. 1354-c. 1416). Lord of Glyndyfrdwy and Cynllaith Owain in north Powys, whose quarrel over land with Reginald de Grey, lord of Ruthin, in 1400 sparked off a popular revolt against Henry IV that lasted until 1415. He planned to divide the kingdom between Edmund Mortimer, Henry Percy, and himself, allied with France, and styled himself prince of Wales (1404). After 1406, when he proposed an independent Welsh church and two university colleges, the revolt began to wane. The whereabouts of his death are not known, but he became a national hero, a symbol of Welsh national fervour at a time of stress and oppression.

Owain Gwynedd (died c. 1170). Prince of Gwynedd (1137-70), who made his principality the most powerful in Wales and established a leadership maintained during the ensuing struggles for Welsh independence. In 1157 he did homage to Henry II after defeat by the English king. In 1165, however, he helped to defeat Henry's invasion of South Wales. The wisdom of Owain's rule was proclaimed by the Welsh bards.

Owen, Robert (1771-1858). Socialist and pioneer of the *cooperative movement. Born in Wales, he established a model community for his employees in the mills of *New Lanark. His theories for transforming society along cooperative lines were put into practice in such experimental communities as New Harmony, Indiana (1825), Orbiston, near Glasgow (1826), Ralakine, Co. Cork (1831), and Queenswood, Hampshire (1839). He helped secure passage of the *Factory Act (1819), but his attempt to organize trades unionism (see trade union) on a national basis through his Grand National Consolidated Trades Union (1834) failed.

Oxford, 1st earl of. See Harley, Robert, 1st earl of Oxford and Mortimer.

Oxford, Robert de Vere, 9th earl of (1362-92). A favourite of Richard II. He was created marquess of Dublin in 1385, the first English marquess, and duke·of Ireland in 1386. Accused of treason (1387) by Thomas of Woodstock, duke of Gloucester, leader of the lords *appellant, Oxford raised an army and marched on London. He was defeated by Henry Bolingbroke at *Radcot Bridge and escaped to the Continent, where he died.

Oxford movement. A religious movement, widely influential within the Church of England between 1833 and 1845. It was initiated by a sermon on "National Apostasy" preached on 14 July 1833 by John Keble (1792-1866). He, in common with the movement's other leaders, J. H. *Newman, R. H. Froude (1803-36), and E. B. Pusey (1800-82), was a Fellow of Oriel College Oxford. They rejected the Protestant element in Anglicanism in favour of its pre-Reformation Catholic tradition and denied parliament's right to supervise the Church. Their views, notably in a series of *Tracts for the Times* (hence the movement's alternative name, Tractarianism), aroused bitter controversy. Newman became a Roman Catholic in 1845; Keble and Pusey remained Anglicans, and the movement developed into *Anglo-Catholicism.

Oxford Parliament. 1. (1258) The parliament summoned at Oxford by Henry III in the hope of financial aid. This the barons agreed to give in return for the king's consent to major reforms to be drafted by a committee of 24 (*see* Provisions of Oxford). **2.** (1681) The fourth and last parliament of Charles II. Convened in Oxford to escape intimidation by the London mob, it debated the sensitive and long-standing issue of the *exclusion of James, duke of York, from the succession. A compromise solution failed and parliament was dissolved within a week.

oxgang. A unit of arable land in the Danelaw. It was one-eighth the size of a *ploughland and was probably equivalent to the amount of land that could be farmed by one ox from a team of eight.

oyer and terminer (Anglo-Norman: to hear and determine). A commission issued from the 13th century to justices to hear *pleas of the crown. Originally, special justices, outside the slow-functioning *eyre, were commissioned for this purpose but oyer and terminer gradually became a commission of the justices of *assize.

P

Padarn, St (mid-6th century). Celtic monk, born in southeast Wales. Padarn is associated with a group of churches in mid- and west Wales. His main foundation was at Llanbadarn Fawr in Ceredigion, which survived the Norman conquest and was described by *Gerald of Wales (1188).

Paine, Thomas (1737–1809). Libertarian pamphleteer and revolutionary. His *Rights of Man* (1790–92), which counter attacked *Burke's *Reflections on the French Revolution*, greatly influenced contemporary English radicals. He was forced to flee to France and was convicted *in absentia* of sedition and outlawed.

Palace of Westminster. The seat of *parliament. The original palace, main residence of the English monarchs from Edward the Confessor to Henry VIII and the building in which parliament met from the 13th century, was largely burnt down in 1834. The New Palace of Westminster, usually called the Houses of Parliament, was built (1840–67) on the same site by Sir Charles Barry (1795–1860). The adjacent Westminster Hall was the chief law court until the courts on the Strand were completed in 1870.

Palatinate (or County Palatine). Territories the rulers of which were granted extensive liberties and privileges in medieval England. The two lay English palatinates of Chester (created after the Norman conquest) and Lancaster (1351) were originally frontier zones between England and Wales and Scotland, as was the ecclesiastical palatinate of Durham. Other palatinates were also briefly established at Ely and Tipperary (1328). Their lords exercised quasi-regal authority, which was not completely abolished until the 19th century.

Pale, the English. That area in Ireland in which the Crown's writ ran, that is where English law and the royal administration were respected. The extent of the Pale varied: in the mid-14th century it comprised Dublin, Louth, Meath, Trim, Kilkenny, and Kildare, but subsequently it progressively shrank until the Tudors reasserted the English presence in the 16th century.

Palestine. A region in the Middle East, between the Mediterranean and the river Jordan, and a former British *mandate. It was captured (1917–18) from the Ottoman (Turkish) Empire by Allenby and became a British mandate in 1920. The *Balfour declaration (1917) committed Britain to the establishment of a Jewish homeland in Palestine. Subsequent Jewish immigration gave rise to violence against both the Jews and British from Palestinian Arabs, and in 1939 Britain placed limitations on Jewish immigration and land purchase. Illegal immigration of survivors of the Nazi holocaust led to further conflict between Arabs and Jews, and in 1947 the UN recommended the partition of Palestine. This was rejected by the Arabs, and in May 1948 Britain renounced its mandate. On the same day the Jews established the independent state of Israel.

Palladius (c. 400–c. 440). Missionary to Ireland. There is slight evidence that he visited Ireland before St Patrick and that his mission was unsuccessful. Palladius is often confused with St Patrick and may not have existed.

Palmerston, Henry John Temple, 3rd Viscount (1784-1865). Prime minister (1855-58, 1859-65). An Irish peer, Palmerston entered the Commons as a Tory in 1806 and served in the minor office of secretary at war (1809-28). As a Canningite and supporter of parliamentary reform, he served in the Whig administrations of Grey and Melbourne as foreign secretary (1830-41), when he resolutely supported British interests and liberal causes abroad: he was instrumental in the achievement of Belgian independence (1830-31), formed the *quadruple alliance (1834) against the pretenders to the Spanish and Portuguese thrones, supported Turkey against Russian and then Egyptian encroachment, and declared the *Opium War on China (1840). As foreign secretary again (1846-51), under Russell, his outspokenness won him popular support in the country (especially with his support of *Don Pacifico) but antagonized Russell and others, and he was dismissed for recognizing, without consulting his colleagues, the overthrow by Louis Napoleon of the Second Republic of France. As home secretary under Aberdeen (1852-55), he promoted factory legislation and prison reform under the influence of *Shaftesbury. On Aberdeen's resignation, Palmerston formed his first ministry, bringing the Crimean

War to a successful conclusion and suppressing the Indian mutiny. His second administration was a strong one, with Russell as foreign secretary and Gladstone as chancellor of the exchequer. Abroad, the government recognized the new kingdom of Italy, transferred the Ionian islands to Greece, and maintained neutrality during the American Civil War; at home, it cut government expenditure and reduced taxes and duties.

Pandulf (d. 1226). Bishop of Norwich from 1216. Born in Rome, he was a clerk at the papal court of Innocent III and was given the task of resolving the quarrel between the church and King John over the appointment in 1207 of Stephen *Langton to the see of Canterbury. He promulgated John's excommunication in 1209 but secured his submission in 1213. He was papal legate from 1218 until 1221, when he returned to Rome.

Pankhurst, Emmeline (1858-1928). Feminist. In 1903 she formed the Women's Social and Political Union to campaign for female suffrage and, becoming a militant, was frequently imprisoned, notably in 1913 after Lloyd George's house was bombed. She died shortly before all adult women were granted the *franchise. Her daughters Dame Christabel Pankhurst (1880-1958) and Sylvia Pankhurst (1882-1960) also took part in the *women's movement.

pannage. The right of a tenant to graze swine in the woodlands of a manor. From the 11th century lords of the manor granted this right in exchange for a payment, also known as pannage.

Papineau, Louis Joseph (1786-1871). French-Canadian politician and rebel. Papineau was speaker of the Lower Canada assembly (1815-37) and, after failing to secure better conditions for French Canadians, led an unsuccessful rebellion (1837). Pardoned in 1847, he later sat in the united Canadian legislature (1850-54). The rebellions of Papineau and William Lyon *Mackenzie led to Lord *Durham's appointment in 1838 as governor general.

parage (French: equality of rank). A form of feudal land tenure by which the eldest son and heir transferred part of his inheritance to his younger brothers without placing conditions of service or homage on them. It was common in England's French possessions.

Paris, declaration of (16 April 1856). An agreement among the great powers of Europe aimed at regulating maritime law in times of war. Among its main provisions was the safeguarding of neutral goods carried by enemy ships and the abolition of privateering (*see* privateers).

Paris, treaty of 1. (1259) A treaty between Louis IX of France and Henry III of England, also called the treaty of Abbeville. It formalized the loss under King John of most of the *Angevin empire: Henry renounced his claims to Normandy, Maine, Anjou, and Poitou and retained Gascony—but only as a vassal of the French king—and territories in Aquitaine. **2.** (1303) A treaty between Edward I and Philip IV of France, who sought peace with England after his defeat by the Flemings at Courtrai. Philip's daughter Isabel was betrothed to Edward's son, the future Edward II, and the English king regained his French territories and paid homage for Gascony. **3.** (10 Feb 1763) The peace treaty ending the Seven Years' War and redefining British, French, and Spanish colonial territories. Britain made substantial gains, receiving Quebec, Cape Breton Island, Grenada, St Vincent, Dominica, Tobago, Senegal, Florida, and Minorca. France recovered Guadeloupe, Martinique, and a few minor territories elsewhere in the West Indies and in India. Spain received Havana from Britain, and Louisiana west of the Mississippi from its former ally France. Britain was thus established as the world's leading colonial power. **4.** (30 May 1814) The treaty imposed on France by the allies after Napoleon's abdication. It established France's frontiers as those of 1792, before the outbreak of the French Revolutionary and Napoleonic Wars, and restored to France some of the colonies annexed by Britain. **5.** (20 Nov 1815) The treaty concluded after Napoleon's final defeat at Waterloo. France was reduced to its 1790 frontiers, surrendered the Saar, agreed to pay an indemnity of 700 million francs, and accepted the allied occupation of its northern and eastern fortresses. **6.** (30 March 1856) An international treaty ending the Crimean War. Under its provisions Russia ceded southern Bessarabia to Moldavia and abandoned its claim to act as the protector of Orthodox Christians living under Turkish rule; the Danube was declared open to the trading vessels of all nations; and the Black Sea was neutralized. Russia was thus debarred from maintaining a Black Sea warfleet. Turkish independence was guaranteed (15 April) by Britain, France, and Austria.

parish. 1. A district under the religious care of a priest. Parishes in England date from at least the 7th century. Initially they were often coterminous with the estate of a lord, who controlled the appointment of a priest (*see* advowson) and was sometimes entitled to the ecclesiastical income of the parish, chiefly *tithes. Following the Lateran Council (1179), however, the bishops had greater control over the parishes in their dioceses. The creation of new parishes, in response to the growth of population and changes in its distribution, is the responsibility of the *Church Commissioners. **2.** The smallest unit of local government. Parishes became units of civil administration in the 16th century, when they were made responsible for the highways and for administering the *poor law. The boundaries of civil and ecclesiastical parishes, at first corresponding, increasingly diverged with the growing complexity of local government, especially in the 19th century. The powers of the parish councils are now limited to such matters as maintaining bus shelters and footpaths. The ancient custom of "beating the bounds" (or marking the boundaries) on 25 April and the Monday, Tuesday, and

Wednesday before Ascension Day (the Rogation Days) is still practised in some parishes.

Parisii. A British tribe living in the East Riding of Yorkshire and round the Humber. They were related to the Parisii of Gaul.

Park, Mungo (1771-1806). Explorer of the *Niger river in West Africa. A surgeon by profession, Park was sent by the African Association to explore the Niger in 1795. From the mouth of the Gambia he travelled along the Niger to Ségou in modern Mali and covered a further 129 km (80 mi) before being forced to turn back. He recorded his adventures in *Travels in the Interior Districts of Africa* (1797). On his second expedition (1805) he again reached Ségou but was drowned at the Bussa Rapids.

Parker, Matthew (1504-75). Archbishop of Canterbury from 1559. He became master of Corpus Christi College, Cambridge (1544), and dean of Lincoln (1552). Deprived of his position under Mary I, he was appointed archbishop of Canterbury by Elizabeth I. He achieved his aim of a compromise between Catholicism and Calvinism in the 39 *articles (1562) and provoked increasing Puritan opposition, especially with his *Advertisements* (1566; *see* vestiarian controversy). A leading scholar, Parker commissioned the Bishops' *Bible (1568).

parliament. The supreme legislature, comprising the sovereign, the *House of Lords, and the *House of Commons, which sits in the *Palace of Westminster. It emerged from the *curia regis in the 13th century, as an assembly summoned by the king to settle matters of unusual importance. These were at first largely judicial in character. Other functions were to give advice and to raise taxation, and because the latter required consent the assemblies became representative. The *Model Parliament of 1295 is usually regarded as establishing the right of bishops, abbots, lay lords, and the representatives of the boroughs and shires all to be summoned, but for most

of the middle ages a parliament meant primarily the king and the Lords, with the Commons meeting separately. Parliaments were for the most part irregular, occasional, and brief. Frequent parliaments were undesirable, because they implied extraordinary taxation, as early in the 15th century to meet the expenses of the Percy and Owain Glyndŵr revolts, or crisis in the body politic, as in the 1530s (*see* Reformation) or in the 1620s (*see* James I; Charles I). The legislative function of parliament, although clearly understood in the 14th century, remained limited until the modern period (*see* act of parliament). Regular parliaments were assured after the Glorious Revolution (1688-89), but both Houses were dominated by the landed aristocracy until well into the 19th century. Together with the widening of the electoral *franchise (*see also* Reform Acts), the Commons became more representative and, with the Parliament Act (1911), its supremacy was assured.

Parliament Act (1911). A statute that curtailed the powers of the *House of Lords, asserting the legislative supremacy of the Commons. It was provoked by the Lords' rejection of the Liberal *people's budget (1909). The Lords, who passed the Parliament Act under the threat of the creation of a sufficient number of Liberal peers to secure its passage, lost the power to reject public legislation, except bills to extend parliament's life. In the case of other public bills they were permitted only delaying powers—one month for money bills and two years for other public bills (reduced to one year by the Parliament Act, 1949). Parliament's maximum duration was reduced from seven years (*see* Septennial Act) to five.

parliamentarians. Supporters of the parliamentary cause against Charles I during the *Civil War (*compare* royalists). They are also called roundheads, a reference to the short-hair of the apprentices who demonstrated against the king at Westminster in 1641. The parliamentarians united those who opposed the king's exercise of royal *prerogative and

the various Protestant groups that were
offended by the *Arminianism of Archbishop Laud. During the Civil War the
parliamentary cause was strongest in the
south and east.

Parnell, Charles Stewart (1846–91). Irish
nationalist. A Protestant Anglo-Irish
landowner, he was elected an MP in
1875 and replaced *Butt as leader of the
Irish *home rule MPs (1878). His
obstructive tactics in parliament, notably
the filibuster, effectively drew attention
to Irish grievances. He became (1879)
the first president of the *Irish Land
League, which boycotted unpopular
landlords, and in Oct 1881 Parnell was
arrested for inciting agrarian violence.
He was released in the following year
according to an agreement with the
authorities, known as the *Kilmainham
treaty, by which Parnell, in return, was
required to curb agrarian unrest. The
1885 election gave the Irish the balance
of power at Westminister, and in 1886,
with Gladstone now converted to home
rule, Parnell extended support to the
Liberal government. The publication in
The Times (18 April 1887) of a letter
underplaying the gravity of the *Phoenix
Park murders, and purporting to be from
Parnell, led to the appointment of a
commission (1888) to investigate his and
his colleagues' responsibility for violence
in Ireland. The letter proved to be a
forgery and Parnell was vindicated.
However, after being cited in the
*O'Shea divorce case he was forced to
resign the party leadership (1890). Spur-
ned by his party and the public, he died
in 1891.

Parsons (or **Persons**), **Robert** (1546–
1610). Jesuit. He accompanied Edmund
*Campion on his mission to England in
1580 but after Campion's arrest in the
following year returned to the Continent.
In Spain (1588–97) he wrote anti-
Protestant pamphlets. His most famous
book was *The Christian Directory*
(1585).

Passchendaele. See Ypres, (third) battle
of.

Paston letters. A collection of over a
thousand letters, comprising the private
correspondence of the Paston family of
Norfolk in the 15th century. They reveal
the life style of a middle-class family as
well as comment on current affairs at the
time of the Wars of the Roses. Most of
the letters, which relate also to the
Pastons' neighbour Sir John *Fastolf,
are in the British Library.

Patay, battle of (18 June 1429). The
battle, following the siege of Orléans, in
which the English under John Talbot
(1st earl of Shrewsbury) and Sir John
Fastolf were heavily defeated (and
Talbot was captured) by the French
commanded by Joan of Arc.

patent rolls. Records of royal grants of
privileges, offices, lands, etc., that is of
letters patent (or letters overt) affixed
with the great seal. Dating from 1201,
they are still maintained (by the clerk of
the crown in Chancery), but do not now
record patents of invention, which are
registered in the Patent Office.

Patrick, St (5th century AD). The patron
saint of Ireland. As a boy he was
captured by Irish raiders from his
Romano-British family and taken as a
slave to north Ireland. After six years he
escaped to the Continent, became a priest
and then a bishop and in about 450
returned to Ireland with a missionary
party, spending the rest of his life there.
Feast day: 17 March.

patriot king. A concept advocated by
Viscount *Bolingbroke in *The Idea of a
Patriot King* (written in 1738). Bolingbroke's king would rule benevolently
through ministers freely chosen and
without party allegiance. It was later
wrongly assumed that George III
borrowed his early similar ideas directly
from Bolingbroke's treatise, which was
written for George's father Frederick,
prince of Wales.

Patriots. Those Whig factions opposing
*Walpole in the 1730s and early 1740s.
Representing trading interests, they
called for war against Spain to protect
Britain's West Indian trade. They
included John *Carteret, *Chesterfield,
and Richard Temple, Viscount Cobham
(1669–1749), and the "Boy Patriots" (or

"Cobham's cubs")—ambitious young men, such as *Pitt (later earl of Chatham) and George *Grenville.

patronage. The right of control of appointment to an office or privilege, especially in the public service but also to an ecclesiastical benefice (see advowson). The use of patronage as a political weapon belongs especially to the 18th century. It became available to the crown owing to the expansion of the Treasury, the Customs and Excise, and also of the army and navy at the end of the 17th century. The presence of office holders in the House of Commons —there were 113 out of a total membership of 513 in 1701—gave the crown a valuable means of parliamentary management (see placemen). The art of government consisted largely in the most effective distribution of the offices, titles, sinecures, pensions, contracts, and commissions at the disposal of the government. Other patronage, not in the hands of the crown but in those of the great landowners, embraced parliamentary boroughs (see rotten borough), ecclesiastical livings, the economic dependence of local tradesmen, and the traditional loyalty of tenants, all of which might be mobilized for or against the government. Reforms from the Civil List Act (1782) onwards much reduced its importance. See also civil service.

Paulinus, St (d. 644). Roman missionary in England. Arriving in England in 601, he assisted Augustine in Kent, where he was consecrated bishop in 625. He then travelled to Northumbria, where he converted King Edwin (627) and was appointed bishop of York. His work subsequently extended beyond the boundaries of Northumbria to Lindsey and East Anglia. He left the north after the death of Edwin at Hatfield Chase (632) and became bishop of Rochester. In 634 he became archbishop. Feast day: 10 Oct.

pavage. A tax levied from the reign (1272-1307) of Edward I to finance the paving of streets. From the late middle ages boroughs were empowered by royal charters to impose this tax on goods entering or leaving the town.

Pax Britannica. The maintenance of peace under British rule. The notion, analogous to the Pax Romana established under the Roman Empire, was popularized by Palmerston during the 1840s and 1850s and became a commonplace of imperial thought thereafter.

Paxton, Sir Joseph (1801-65). Engineer and architect. Initially employed as a gardener at *Chatsworth, Paxton is most notable for designing the *Crystal Palace, built for the Great Exhibition of 1851.

peace, commission of the. An authority, first issued in the 12th century to laymen, to maintain public order. Regularized by the Statute of *Winchester (1285), in the 14th century these agents of the crown were authorized to try cases and became known as *justices of the peace (JPs). A commission of the peace was also held by justices of *assize, whereby JPs were obliged to attend them at the regional assizes.

Pearse, Patrick Henry (1879-1916). Irish nationalist. He joined the Irish Republican Brotherhood in 1914. In the Easter Rising (1916) he was commander-in-chief of the Irish forces and proclaimed the Irish Republic. After holding out for a week against the British he surrendered, was court martialled, and executed.

peasants' revolt (1381). Widespread risings, among artisans as well as peasants, provoked by a variety of social and economic grievances, notably against the Statute of *Labourers and a series of *poll taxes. The revolt was most serious in Kent, where the rebels under Wat *Tyler seized Rochester castle, and in Essex. The two groups joined forces and marched on London, entering the City on 13 June and destroying, among other property, John of Gaunt's manor of the Savoy. On the 14th Richard II agreed at Mile End to the demands of the Essex men (including a general pardon, abolition of villeinage, liberty to trade, and the fixing of a land rent at four pence per acre). At the same time the Kentish rebels occupied the Tower of London and executed the chancellor and archbishop of Canterbury, Simon of Sudbury, and the treasurer Sir Robert Hales. On the 15th, at Smithfield, Richard met the men of Kent and during the encounter Wat Tyler was killed by the mayor of London, William Walworth. Encouraged by Richard, who showed great presence of mind, the peasants dispersed. Elsewhere, revolts occurred most seriously in East Anglia, where the rebels were ruthlessly crushed by the bishop of Norwich. By Sept the government was firmly in control and Richard's promises had been withdrawn.

Peckham, John (d. 1292). Archbishop of Canterbury from 1279. A Franciscan friar, he studied in Paris and lectured in Rome before becoming archbishop. At a provincial council at Reading in 1279 he offended Edward I by asserting the rights of church courts.

Peel, Sir Robert (1788-1850). Prime minister (1834-35, 1841-46). Son of a rich cotton manufacturer, Peel, a Tory MP from 1809, became undersecretary for war and the colonies in 1810 and was secretary for Ireland (1812-18) under Liverpool. An outstanding home secretary (1822-27, 1828-30), Peel carried through wide-ranging reforms of the criminal law and the prison system and established the Metropolitan Police Force (1829). In 1829, having previously opposed Catholic emancipation, he antagonized many Tories by introducing legislation that enabled Catholics to become MPs. His *Tamworth manifesto (1834) laid the foundations of modern Conservatism by accepting the principle of reform where necessary. His first administration (Nov 1834-April 1835) was brief, but his second ministry provided efficient government and benefited finance and trade. The reduction or abolition of most import duties, together with the control of paper money by the Bank Charter Act (1844), brought prosperity, despite the reintroduction of income tax. Legislation was passed to protect factory and mine workers.

However, poor harvests in England and the failure of the Irish potato crop in 1845 led Peel, contrary to his election pledge to repeal the *corn laws (1846). The measure split the Conservatives and Peel was forced to resign. Peel and his followers subsequently supported Russell's Whig government and free trade.

peerage. In order of rank, *dukes, *marquesses, *earls, *viscounts, and *barons. The peerage originated in the tenants in chief, those who held land direct from the Norman kings. Although of different ranks they enjoyed the same privileges, notably the right to be tried by their "peers" (Latin *pares*, equals), which was last claimed in 1936 and abolished in 1948. The peers collectively comprise the lords temporal of the *House of Lords. The hereditary peers are divided into the peers of England, created before the union with Scotland (1707), peers of Great Britain, created after 1707 and before the union with Ireland (1801), peers of the UK, created since 1800, peers of Scotland, created before 1707, and the Irish peers. Since 1876 the lords of appeal in ordinary (the law lords) have been life peers. Since 1958 life peerages have also been conferred on men and women of distinction. The Peerage Act (1963) allowed certain hereditary peerages to be disclaimed for life and permitted hereditary peeresses to sit in the House of Lords.

peerage bill. *See* House of Lords.

Pelagius (c. 360-c. 420). Monk, who originated Pelagianism, a heresy asserting that man could attain salvation by the exercise of his own will, without the help of divine grace. Pelagius was a Briton, from Wales or Ireland, who taught in Rome in about 400. His doctrines were attacked by St Jerome and St Augustine of Hippo, and Augustine formulated the doctrine of divine grace partly in opposition to Pelagius' views.

Pelham, Henry (1696-1754). MP from 1717, who was given office by Walpole in 1730 as paymaster of the forces. He was first lord of the treasury (1743-54), and from Nov 1744 (after John

*Carteret's departure) until his death led the *broad-bottom administration. He was personally a colourless figure but expertly managed parliament with his brother, the duke of *Newcastle.

Pembroke, earls of. *See* Herbert; Marshal.

Penal Code. A series of laws (1695-1727) designed to suppress the practice of Roman Catholicism and restrict the material wealth and participation in public life of the Catholics in Ireland. The acts included measures prohibiting Catholics from voting, sitting in parliament, holding office, and buying land or inheriting it from Protestants. Furthermore, land was to be divided among all the sons of a deceased Catholic rather than descending to one of them. Most were repealed in the late 18th century, although Catholics were not allowed to sit in parliament until 1829 (*see* Catholic emancipation).

penal laws. Legislation against *recusants, especially Roman Catholics, passed in the 16th and 17th centuries. A series of acts were passed between 1571 and 1593, introducing penalties for those who refused to attend Church of England services ranging from proscription of worship to disqualification from office. These were extended in 1606 and 1610, but the penal laws were implemented, according to the temper of the times, with varying degrees of strictness. Repeal occurred gradually with successive *Toleration Acts.

Penda (d. 655). King of Mercia. In 633, in alliance with Cadwallon, king of Gwynedd, he defeated and killed Edwin of Northumbria. A pagan, Penda greatly expanded Mercia, and his influence extended over the East Angles, the Middle Angles, and the West Saxons. Frequently at war with Northumbria, he was killed by *Oswy at the battle of the Winwaed, an unidentified river near Leeds.

Peninsular War (1808-13). The struggle between French and British armies for control of Spain and Portugal, which constituted Britain's principal involvement on land during the Napoleonic War. After the Spanish rebelled against Napoleon's attempt to establish his brother Joseph Bonaparte as king of Spain, Britain seized the chance to establish a foothold on the Continent by landing a force under Wellington (then Sir Arthur Wellesley). During the ensuing conflict, Wellington, aided by Spanish and Portuguese guerrillas (the term "guerrilla", the Spanish for "little war", originated in this campaign), conducted hard-fought and dispersed campaigns that eventually tied down some 300 000 French troops. Napoleon's withdrawal of forces from the Iberian peninsula for the Russian campaign (1812) allowed Wellington to drive the remaining French armies back into France by the end of 1813. *See also* Albuera, battle of; Coruña, battle of; Oporto, battle of; Salamanca, battle of; Talavera, battle of; Vitoria, battle of.

The term Peninsular War is sometimes also applied to the similar struggle (1702-13) in which the British tried to place the Austrian candidate, Charles III, on the throne of Spain (*see* Spanish Succession, War of the).

Penn, William (1644-1718). One of the founders of Quakerism. He became a Quaker at the age of 21, and in 1681 Charles II granted him a charter to a large tract of land in America. There, Penn established his colony of Pennsylvania, embodying in its constitution his beliefs in peace and religious freedom.

penny post. A uniform postal system of prepaid letters, introduced (1840) at the instigation of Rowland *Hill with the issue of the first adhesive stamp (the Penny Black). Previously, letters had been carried at varying, often exorbitant, rates for which cash had usually been demanded on delivery. The new system, which was cheap and well organized, had wide social and economic effects. The basic rate of one penny (0.24 p) continued unchanged until 1918.

Penruddock's rising (March 1655). A royalist rebellion against the government of the Protectorate. Led by Col John Penruddock (1619-55), the rebels entered Salisbury and proclaimed Charles II king. The Cromwellians swiftly crushed the rebellion, executed its leaders, and imposed the rule of the *major generals on England.

Penry, John (1559-93). Puritan writer. A native of Brecknockshire, he was dissatisfied with the condition of the Anglican Church in Wales. He wrote three treatises advocating a reform of the clergy and a better preaching ministry, which were presented to parliament (1587, 1588) and the Council in the Marches (1588). Charged with the authorship of the *Marprelate tracts, he was convicted of treason and hanged in 1593.

Pepys, Samuel (1633-1703). Diarist, naval administrator, and MP. He is best known for his diary, kept from 1660 until 1669, which provides a remarkable documentary of Charles II's London. It was written in Thomas Shelton's system of shorthand, in six volumes, and was first deciphered in 1819.

Perceval, Spencer (1762-1812). Prime minister (1809-12). A barrister, Perceval was a Tory MP from 1796. He was appointed solicitor general in 1801 and attorney general in 1802, serving under Addington and then Pitt the younger. He was chancellor of the exchequer from 1807 until 1809, when he succeeded Portland as prime minister. Often wrongly regarded as a nonentity, he pursued the war against Napoleon with courage, despite divisions and incompetence inside his cabinet and military disasters. At home, unrest resulting from economic distress (including *Luddite activity) was severely repressed. Perceval was shot dead (11 May 1812)—the only British prime minister ever to be assassinated—in the lobby of the House of Commons by John Bellingham, a bankrupt.

Percy, Henry, 1st earl of Northumberland (1342-1408). Warden of the Scottish Marches, who captured Berwick in 1378 and won the battle of *Homildon Hill in 1402. He led a rebellion against Henry IV in 1403, in which his son and namesake was killed, and joined Sir Edmund de Mortimer and Owain Glyndŵr against the king in 1405. Forced to flee to Scotland, he later invaded England and died on the field of *Bramham Moor.

Percy, Sir Henry (1364-1403). Son of Henry Percy, 1st earl of Northumberland. He gained a reputation as a soldier in France and on account of his daring and impetuosity was nicknamed Hotspur. In 1399 he supported Henry Bolingbroke's claim to the throne but in 1403 joined his father's rebellion against the king. He was killed at the battle of *Shrewsbury. His exploits are celebrated in Shakespeare's *Henry IV*, Part 1.

Percy, Henry, 4th earl of Northumberland (1446-89). Great chamberlain from 1482. He betrayed Richard III at the battle of *Bosworth and was subsequently murdered by a mob while attempting to enforce a royal subsidy.

Perfeddwlad, four cantrefs of. A Welsh region comprising territory lying between the rivers Conway and Dee in north Wales and consisting of the four cantrefs (hundreds) of Rhos, Rhufoniog, Dyffryn Clwyd, and Tegeingl (or Englefield). Control of this land, also known as Gwynedd Is Conwy, was contested for many years by the kingdoms of Gwynedd and Powys and in the 13th century by the principality of Gwynedd and the realm of England.

Perrers, Alice (d. 1400). Mistress of Edward III. In 1376 the Good Parliament brought charges of corruption against her but the sentence of banishment was later reversed. At Edward's deathbed in 1377 she stole the rings from his fingers before finally fleeing the court.

Perth, treaty of (2 July 1266). The treaty by which Magnus IV of Norway ceded the Hebrides and the Isle of Man to the Scots, who had already largely conquered them.

Peterborough, Charles Mordaunt, 3rd earl of (1658-1735). A leading supporter of William III, who was made first lord of the treasury in 1689. As commander of an Anglo-Dutch force during the War of the Spanish Succession, he won a series of brilliant victories in Spain (1705-07), including the capture of Barcelona (1705).

Peterloo massacre (16 Aug 1819). The dispersal by force of an open-air mass meeting in Manchester during the post-1815 campaign for parliamentary reform. A lull had followed the events of 1816-17 (including *Spa Fields and the *Blanketeers), but economic distress, especially among Lancashire handloom weavers, provoked renewed agitation (1819). A rally at St Peter's Field, Manchester, attracted 50 000-80 000 people. After the meeting began the magistrates took alarm and ordered the local yeomanry to arrest the speaker, Henry ("Orator") *Hunt. Harried by the crowd, the troopers drew their sabres, and the magistrates sent in a hussar detachment. Panic resulted; 11 civilians died and hundreds were injured, many by sabre-cuts. The affair, nicknamed the "Peterloo massacre" in ironical reference to the battle of Waterloo, became a symbol of repression. The government replied with new legislation (the *Six Acts), aimed against potentially revolutionary activity.

Peter's pence. An annual tax for the support of the papacy levied from the early 10th century at the rate of a penny on every English householder. It was later levied as a lump sum of £200 a year for the entire country, until its abolition in 1534.

Petillius Cerialis, Quintus. Governor of Roman Britain (71-74 AD). He defeated the Brigantes after heavy fighting and overran much of Yorkshire and Lancashire. He probably established York (Eboracum) as a legionary garrison base, although this has been assigned to the governorship of Agricola.

Petitioners. Supporters of the demand by Anthony Ashley Cooper, 1st earl of *Shaftesbury, for the summons of the parliament elected in Aug 1679 and then prorogued (until Oct 1680). Following the crisis over the *exclusion bills Shaftesbury organized nationwide petitions for parliament's recall, but these were met by counterpetitions from court

supporters abhorring the campaign. "Abhorrers" and "petitioners" were quickly replaced as party labels by *Tory and *Whig.

Petition of Right (1628). A declaration of the "rights and liberties of the subject", conceived by *Coke in response to the conflict between Charles I and parliament over the extent of the royal prerogative. It stated parliamentary grievances and forbade the levying of taxes without parliamentary consent, arbitrary imprisonment, forced *billeting, and *martial law. Charles eventually assented to the Petition but insisted that he was merely confirming ancient rights and not conceding new ones.

Petty Bag Office. An office of the Court of Chancery. The clerks of the office kept records of, for example, liveries granted in the Court of Wards and Liveries and of specifications for patents, which they kept in petits (small leather bags). It was abolished in 1889.

petty sessions. Meetings of two or more justices of the peace at regular intervals in particular localities to supplement the work of *quarter sessions. They had to do with *minor offences, the poor law, local highways, and the granting of licences of all kinds. Since 1949 they have been called magistrates' courts.

Philip, Prince, duke of Edinburgh (1921-). Husband of Elizabeth II (whom he married in 1947). Born Prince Philip of Greece and Denmark, a grandson of George I of Greece and great-great-grandson of Queen Victoria of the UK, he was brought up in Britain. He joined the navy, serving throughout World War II, and in 1947 acquired British nationality as Philip *Mountbatten. He was created duke of Edinburgh in 1947 and a British prince in 1957.

Philip II (1527-98). King of Spain (1558-98) and of England as the husband (1554-58) of Mary I. The marriage, which took place in Winchester, was extremely unpopular in England. The Spanish alliance drew the country into war with France in 1557, which brought the loss of Calais—England's last continental possession (1558). Mary's death did not end Habsburg designs on England, against which Philip sent the Spanish *armada in 1588.

Philiphaugh, battle of (13 Sept 1645). The battle in which the royalist marquess of Montrose and his army were surprised and routed near Selkirk by Lieut. Gen. David Leslie and part of the Scottish army.

philosophical radicals. Followers of *Bentham's ideas on legal, political, and social reform. They included James *Mill and David *Ricardo, as well as politicians, such as Joseph *Hume, and administrative reformers, such as Sir Edwin *Chadwick.

Phoenix Park murders (6 May 1882). The murder, while they were perambulating in Phoenix Park, Dublin, of the new chief secretary for Ireland, Lord Frederick *Cavendish, and the permanent undersecretary, Thomas Burke (1829–82). They were hacked to death with surgical knives by extreme Irish nationalists called the Invincibles. The publication on 18 April 1887 by *The Times* of a letter, said to be written by *Parnell, implying approval of this crime was shown by a special commission on violence in Ireland (1888–89) to be a forgery.

Picquigny, treaty of (29 Aug 1475). A treaty between Edward IV and Louis XI of France, by which Edward agreed to withdraw his troops from France in return for a large cash payment and an annual pension. It was ratified on a bridge over the river Somme at Picquigny near Amiens.

Picts. A name given by the Romans to tribes living in Scotland north of the Forth and speaking a partly Celtic and partly non-Celtic language. By the late 6th century there was a single kingdom of the Picts. For a time they dominated the Scots of *Dalriada but were weakened in the mid-9th century by Norse raids, and the Scots under Kenneth I MacAlpin overran their kingdom.

piepowder court (or **Court of Piepoudre**). A court that administered the law merchant at a *fair, market, or seaport. Its name is derived from the French *pied poudré*, dusty foot, pedlar, either because such courts worked quickly (as fast as the dust fell from the feet) or because of the dusty feet of the suitors. They were abolished in 1971.

Pilgrimage of Grace (1536–37). A series of risings against Henry VIII that originated as a protest in Lincolnshire against the dissolution of the smaller monasteries. These rebellious supporters of traditional religion were joined by feudal magnates opposed to the extension of royal control over the north and by peasants worried by the *enclosure of arable lands for pasture. The unrest spread to Yorkshire, where Robert *Aske led the forces opposed to the king. The rebels did not coordinate their efforts, and no pitched battle took place. Their leaders were arrested and executed, and royal authority was restored by Feb 1537.

pilgrim fathers. The founding settlers of *New England. The expedition was initiated by a group of English Puritans, who chose exile to avoid religious persecution, but these refugees made up less than a third of the final party of 102. The pilgrim fathers left England for North America in the *Mayflower* in 1620 and established a flourishing colony in New Plymouth, Massachusetts.

Pinkie, battle of (10 Sept 1547). The battle, fought east of Edinburgh, in which the duke of Somerset, protector of England, with about 16 000 men routed a larger Scottish army under the earl of Arran, governor of Scotland.

Pipe Rolls. Exchequer records of the accounts of the sheriffs and other royal officials. Both royal income and the sheriff's expenses were itemized for each county. Dating, with few breaks, from 1130 to 1832, they are the longest series of English public records.

Pitcairn Islands. An isolated British dependent territory in the South Pacific, consisting of Pitcairn Island and three uninhabited islands. The island's population is largely descended from mutineers from the *Bounty* (1790) and women from Tahiti.

Pitt the elder, William, 1st earl of Chatham (1708-78). Statesman, known as the Great Commoner, who, as war leader (1756-61), ensured the establishment of British imperial power. An MP from 1735, Pitt developed his reputation for superb oratory in opposing Walpole and then Carteret. Demanding maritime war against France to defend British trade, he denounced involvement in the European aspect of the War of the *Austrian Succession as primarily benefiting Hanover. He incurred George II's enmity but gained public popularity. Pitt supported the *broad-bottom administration (1744), but was refused office until 1746, when he became paymaster general but still exerted no real influence. Denied advancement after Henry Pelham's death (1754), he openly criticized the government, now—under Newcastle—facing renewed war with France, and was dismissed (1755).

The *Seven Years' War, however, finally gave Pitt his opportunity. After military failures, Newcastle resigned in Nov 1756. Pitt, appointed secretary of state, took over direction of the war and implemented his maritime strategy. He concentrated on driving the French from North America—a policy that culminated in the capture of Quebec and other triumphs of the "Year of Victory" (1759). In India, the British became masters of Bengal following Clive's victory at Plassey (1757). At home, however, by 1760 war-weariness had developed; the new king, George III, was also determined on peace. Pitt, now demanding action against France's ally Spain, found himself isolated in the cabinet, and resigned (Oct 1761). Dogged by increasingly severe attacks of depression and gout, Pitt never again exercised decisive political power. In July 1766, created earl of Chatham, he became lord privy seal (with Grafton as nominal prime minister) but was totally incapacitated by depression throughout

1767-68, resigning in Oct 1768. His subsequent public activity was intermittent and mainly devoted, during the *American Revolution, to pleading for reconciliation with the colonists. However, he always rejected the idea of American independence, the theme of his last speech in the House of Lords. Collapsing before he had finished speaking, he died a month later.

Pitt the younger, William (1759-1806). Prime minister (1783-1801, 1804-06), son of William Pitt the elder. He was elected an MP in 1781 and two years later became Britain's youngest ever prime minister at the age of twenty-four. His *India Act (1784) effectively placed the East India Company under government control; he also sought to ease the tension in Canada by dividing it into (French) Lower Canada and (British) Upper Canada (1791). His financial measures were particularly successful, especially the reduction of *customs duties and, by the introduction (1786) of a *sinking fund, of the national debt. Pitt abandoned his former commitment to parliamentary reform at the outbreak of the French Revolution, fear of the influence of which also provoked the suspension of *habeas corpus (1794). As war leader Pitt negotiated three European coalitions (1793, 1798, and 1805) against France (see French Revolutionary and Napoleonic Wars) and introduced *income tax to help meet costs. In 1800 he secured passage of the bill for the *union of Great Britain and Ireland, but resigned in 1801, when George III denied *Catholic emancipation. He returned to office after Addington's resignation. Napoleon's victories over Britain's allies at Ulm and Austerlitz in 1805 reputedly shattered Pitt's already fragile health. He died in February 1806; his last words are said to have been "Oh, my country! How I leave my country!"

Place, Francis (1771-1854). Political radical. A leather-breeches maker, he was dismissed after organizing a strike and subsequently opened a tailor's shop. He campaigned against the sinking fund

(1816-23) and in 1824 secured the repeal of the *Combination Acts, thus opening the way for the trades union movement. He was also active in the campaign to secure passage of the *Reform Act (1832). He later helped Lovett draw up the People's Charter, although he was basically out of sympathy with the Chartists.

Place Acts. Legislation designed to exclude *placemen, used to sustain a government's parliamentary majority, from the House of Commons. The Act of settlement (1701) stipulated that all placemen were to be removed from the Commons at the Hanoverian succession. However, the Regency Act (1706) exempted holders of offices created before 24 Oct 1705. Subsequent bills, in 1709-10, were rejected by the Lords, but further categories of office holder were excluded in 1716 (pensioners) and 1742 (certain civil servants). Most effective were the acts forming part of Burke's "economical" reforms of 1782—Crewe's Act disenfranchised the crown's revenue officers, through whom control of certain boroughs was formerly maintained, and Clerk's Act excluded from the Commons anyone holding a government contract.

placemen. Those MPs, especially in the 17th and 18th centuries, who held offices of profit under the crown. Placemen included ministers, but the term increasingly referred to backbenchers receiving financial inducements, such as official posts (often merely sinecures) and pensions, to encourage them to support the government. The *Place Acts sought to remove the abuse. See also patronage.

plague, bubonic. An infectious disease caused by a bacterium transmitted to man by rat fleas. Past outbreaks in Europe resulted in catastrophic death rates. Following the *black death (1348), epidemics of plague occurred at intervals in the 17th century but were largely confined to London. During the last of these, the *great plague (1665-66), 70 000-100 000 are estimated to have died.

Plaid Cymru (Welsh: Party of Wales). A Welsh political movement, founded in 1925 as Plaid Genedlaethol Cymru (Welsh Nationalist Party). It aims at the separation of Wales from the UK to preserve the culture, language, and economy of Wales. Gwynfor Evans won the Carmarthen by-election in 1966 to become the party's first representative in parliament.

Plantagenet, house of. A royal dynasty descended from the counts of Anjou and probably taking its name from the nickname of Geoffrey (1113-51), count of Anjou, who was said to wear a sprig of broom (*plante genêt*) in his cap. The first three Plantagenet kings—Henry II, son of Geoffrey and Matilda, Richard I, and John—are usually styled *Angevins. The right of succession of the following kings (Henry III, Edward I, Edward II, Edward III, and Richard II) was undisputed, but in 1399 Henry Bolingbroke, claiming the throne as the son of Edward III's third son John of Gaunt, deposed his cousin Richard II to become Henry IV. In the 15th century there were two branches of the dynasty, the house of *Lancaster (Henry IV, Henry V, and Henry VI) and the house of *York, which claimed the throne through the rights of Anne de Mortimer, great-granddaughter of Lionel (third son of Edward III), who married Richard, earl of Cambridge, father of Richard, duke of York. One of his sons became Edward IV and another, the last Plantagenet king, Richard III. See also Roses, Wars of the.

plantation of Ireland. In the 16th and 17th centuries, the settlement of Ireland by English and Scottish families, encouraged by the English government as a means of anglicizing the country and securing its allegiance. The Tudor plantations in Leix and Offaly and parts of Munster lacked sufficient settlers. After the *flight of the earls in 1607 most of Ulster was confiscated and settled with English and Scots families; the city of London participated by colonizing Londonderry. These predominantly Presbyterian inhabitants survived and prospered and their descendants remained a distinctive identity in Ulster. Later in the 17th century there were further land confiscations called plantations in Wexford, Longford, and Leitrim, but no accompanying large-scale immigration from Britain. See also Ireland under English rule.

Plassey, battle of (23 June 1757). The battle in which Robert *Clive, commanding forces of the East India company, defeated the army of Siraj-ud-Dawlah, ruler of Bengal, who was assisted by French gunners. Clive's troops numbered 3200, of whom two-thirds were Indian; his opponents totalled some 50 000. The battle ensured British supremacy in Bengal.

pleas of the crown. Cases, usually of serious crimes involving a breach of the king's peace, reserved for jurisdiction in the royal courts by late Anglo-Saxon kings. Such pleas could be heard in lesser courts only by special royal dispensation.

Plimsoll line. A loading mark painted on merchant ships, indicating the amount of freeboard essential for a ship's safety. It is named after Samuel Plimsoll (1824-98), an MP and campaigner for seamen's rights, through whose efforts the line became obligatory with the passage of the Merchant Shipping Act (1876).

ploughland. A unit of land of uncertain area but probably approximating to the area of land that could be ploughed by one team of eight oxen. It probably amounted to a hundred acres. Use of the term was usually restricted to the *Danelaw, in which it replaced the *hide.

Plunket, St Oliver (1629-81). Roman Catholic archbishop of Armagh, who was arrested during the panic caused by the *popish plot in England and executed on bogus charges. He was canonized in 1976.

Plunket, William Conyngham Plunket, 1st Baron (1764-1854). Irish politician. In 1798 he became an MP in the Irish parliament and opposed the union with Britain. Nevertheless he accepted the office of solicitor general in 1803 and attorney general in 1805. As an MP at Westminster in 1807 and from 1812 he used his brilliant oratorical powers to campaign for Catholic emancipation. He was lord chancellor of Ireland from 1830 to 1841.

pluralism. The simultaneous holding of more than one ecclesiastical benefice. It was forbidden by statute in 1529 but remained common, especially in the 18th century, until effectively prohibited in 1838. See also nonresidence.

pocket borough. See rotten borough.

Poitevins. The Poitevin followers of Peter des *Roches and Peter des *Rivaux, who aroused baronial opposition in 1233 (see Marshal rebellion) because of their abuse of power and disregard of feudal conventions. Their importance in the royal administration has probably been exaggerated.

Poitiers, battle of (19 Sept 1356). A battle in the *Hundred Years' War. The French engaged the forces of Edward, the Black Prince, which had been raiding central France. The English were victorious and captured John II of France, thereby strenthening their negotiating position at *Brétigny.

Pole, Edmund de la, earl of Suffolk (?1472-1513). Yorkist. Suffolk lived at court until 1499, when he fled abroad. He was persuaded to return but again fled to the Continent in 1501. Eventually handed over to Henry (1506) by Philip, archduke of Burgundy, he was confined to the Tower, being executed by Henry VIII in 1513.

Pole, John de la, earl of Lincoln (c. 1464-1487). Lord lieutenant of Ireland from 1484, who was named as Richard III's heir. After Henry VII seized the crown (1485) Lincoln supported the conspiracy of Lambert Simnel and was killed at the battle of Stoke.

Pole, Margaret, countess of Salisbury (1473-1541). Daughter of George, duke of Clarence (Edward IV's brother), and wife of Sir Richard Pole (d. 1505). She became governess to Mary, daughter of Henry VIII, but quarrelled with the king when he married (1534) Anne Boleyn.

Dismissed, she was reinstated after Anne's death (1536) but, following the attack on Henry's policies published by her son Reginald *Pole, she was accused of treason and executed.

Pole, Michael de la, 1st earl of Suffolk (d. 1389). Adviser to Richard II. He became chancellor in 1383 and earl of Suffolk in 1385. In the following year he was impeached by parliament for corruption and imprisoned. Richard restored him to power, but in 1387 the threat of a treason charge (see appellant, lords) forced him to flee to France. He died in exile.

Pole, Reginald, Cardinal (1500–58). Archbishop of Canterbury from 1556. His disapproval of Henry VIII's assumption of supremacy over the English church forced him to leave England in 1532. In 1536 he published an attack on the king's antipapal policies, *Pro ecclesiasticae unitatis defensione*, which was the cause of an act of attainder against his family in 1539. Created cardinal (1536), in exile he undertook diplomatic missions for the pope, returning to England as papal legate (1554) after the accession of Mary. As archbishop he zealously furthered the *Marian reaction and died only 12 hours after the queen.

Pole, Richard de la (d. 1525). The last Yorkist pretender to the throne of England. He was forced into exile by Henry VII and died fighting for Francis I of France at the battle of Pavia.

Pole, William de la, 4th earl and 1st duke of Suffolk (1396–1450). Grandson of Michael de la Pole, he played a distinguished part in the Hundred Years' War against France (1415–31) and then became a powerful political figure. He was an opponent of the war party led by Humphrey, duke of Gloucester, and helped arrange the marriage of Henry VI to Margaret of Anjou. Instrumental in the overthrow of Gloucester (1447), he was created duke in 1448 but was impeached in 1450 after ceding Anjou and Maine to France. He was banished by Henry but was seized by his enemies

while crossing the Channel and was beheaded at sea.

police. A force organized for the maintenance of law and order; a constabulary. There were no effective police forces before the 19th century, the law being enforced by *constables appointed by justices of the peace (JPs). In London the *Bow Street Runners date from the mid-18th century, and the Middlesex Justices Act (1792) established a small police force to assist the magistracy. Peel's Metropolitan Police Act (1829) set up the first effective organization—a force of a thousand men, which began its duties in London on 29 Sept 1829. The Municipal Corporations Act (1835) called upon boroughs to establish similar forces, and in 1839 the JPs were authorized to do likewise in the counties. The County and Borough Police Act (1856) made the maintenance of police forces obligatory and, in spite of the opposition of those who argued that England was becoming a police state, provided for inspectors of constabulary to report to the Home Office. After the Local Government Act (1888) the county councils shared control of police forces with the JPs. The Police Act (1919) standardized police pay and conditions, but the country's police forces remained uncentralized.

poll tax. A tax, introduced in 1222, on every individual over 14 years of age; the name derives from the Middle High German *polle*, head. Its levy in 1377, 1379, and 1381 was widely evaded, and the government's despatch of commissioners to ensure the collection of arrears provoked the *peasants' revolt (1381); the tax was then abandoned.

Pondoland. The southeastern coastal region of Transkei, South Africa, home of the Mpondo people. The area was annexed to Cape Colony in 1894.

poor laws. The laws designed to provide relief for the poor. An act of 1536 provided relief for the "impotent poor" but compelled "sturdy beggars" to work. Relief was funded by voluntary subscription and administered by the parish. In 1552 parish registers of the poor were introduced, and in 1563 and 1597 justices of the peace were given powers to raise compulsory funds. Administration was regularized by the Poor Law Act (1601), which introduced a poor relief rate on property owners. The Act of *Settlement (1662) permitted parish overseers to send vagrants back to their native parishes. From 1723 the Workhouse Test Act obliged the poor to enter workhouses to obtain relief, but Gilbert's Act (1782) excluded the able-bodied poor from the workhouse and forced parishes to provide work or outdoor relief for them. After 1795 the *Speenhamland system was widely adopted. Increased hardship among agricultural workers and heavy expenditure on outdoor relief in the early 19th century resulted in the Poor Law Amendment Act (1834). The act created 600 unions of parishes, managed by boards of guardians elected by ratepayers. Outdoor relief ceased, all paupers being forced into the workhouse, in which conditions were deliberately harsh. New attitudes to poverty in the 20th century resulted in the introduction of insurance schemes (see national insurance), which provided a comprehensive social security network that replaced the poor laws.

Pope, Alexander (1688-74). Poet. He became well known with the publication of *Essay on Criticism* (1711) and the mock epic *The Rape of the Lock* (1712). He later wrote political satire, fiercely attacking Walpole's supporters. He also wrote the philosophical poem *An Essay on Man* (1733-34).

popish plot (1678). A fictitious Jesuit plot to assassinate Charles II, massacre Protestants, and place the Roman Catholic James, duke of York, on the throne. Invented by Titus *Oates and Israel Tonge (1621-80), the plot caused widespread panic. The duchess of York's secretary was found to have taken part in treasonable correspondence with France, giving the plot credibility, and about 35 were executed, including St Oliver *Plunket, primate of Ireland.

Porteous riots (8 Sept 1736). Riots in Edinburgh. Following the execution of

a smuggler, Andrew Wilson, the city guard under Capt. John Porteous fired on a threatening crowd, killing several people. Porteous was condemned to death but reprieved by Queen *Caroline, whereupon a mob seized and hanged him.

Portland, William Henry Cavendish Bentinck, 3rd duke of (1738-1809). Prime minister. Portland was nominal prime minister in the Fox-North coalition (1783). As home secretary (1794-1801), under Pitt the younger, he used his repressive powers generally with moderation. His second premiership (1807-09) was vitiated by economic and military difficulties and—despite his ability to reconcile differences—rivalries among ministers.

Portsmouth, Louise Renée de Kéroualle, duchess of (1649-1734). Mistress of Charles II. A French Roman Catholic, she was greatly disliked by the English but maintained her influence from 1671 until Charles' death in 1685. Their son was Charles *Lennox, duke of Richmond.

Potsdam conference (17 July-2 Aug 1945). A meeting towards the end of World War II, held at Potsdam, near Berlin, between Stalin, Truman, and Churchill (who was replaced by his successor Attlee). It arranged for the allied foreign ministers to draw up peace treaties for Germany's allies. Soviet predominance in eastern Europe was recognized by the cession of Königsberg and the continued endorsement of the Oder-Neisse line as Poland's frontier with Germany.

Powys. A kingdom, described as the Paradise of Wales in tales featuring *Llywarch Hen, that emerged from the tribal lands of the Cornovii based at Wroxeter. Regarded as the gateway to Wales, it was frequently threatened from the east, and lands now located in English counties were lost following the encroachments of the Mercians in the period leading up to the construction of *Offa's dyke (late 8th century). The rulers of Powys often fought against those of *Gwynedd and contested possession of the *Perfeddwlad. *Madog ap Maredudd was the last ruler of an intact Powys, and his successors ruled over either Powys Fadog (northern Powys, corresponding to part of the later Denbighshire) or Powys Wenwynwyn (southern Powys, corresponding to later Montgomeryshire).

Poynings' Law (1494). An act named after Sir Edward Poynings (1459-1521), lord deputy of Ireland (1494-95). It stipulated that statutes passed by the Irish parliament were valid only if approved by the English parliament. The law soon became a grievance to Irish parliamentarians desiring legislative freedom but was not repealed until 1782 (see Grattan, Henry).

Praemunire, Statutes of. 1. (1353) The statute that forbade appeals to foreign courts in cases within the jurisdiction of the king's courts. It was directed against appeals to Rome in ecclesiastical patronage cases (see advowson). 2. (1365) The statute that forbade appeals specifically to the papal court. 3. (1393) The statute that forbade any suits concerning patronage from being heard by the pope and forbade bulls of excommunication or provision to enter England. Those convicted of the offence lost the protection of, and his lands were forfeited to, the crown. See also Provisors, Statutes of.

pragmatic sanction. An edict pronounced by a ruler or government. The best-known pragmatic sanction is that promulgated by the emperor Charles VI in 1713. It settled the succession to the Habsburg lands on his daughter Maria Theresa. Almost all the major European states, including Britain (1731), acceded to the edict in return for certain concessions. However, after Charles' death Prussia abrogated its agreement, giving rise to the War of the *Austrian Succession (1740-48), in which Britain supported Maria Theresa.

prerogative. The powers and privileges that the law recognizes as belonging to the sovereign. In the middle ages the royal prerogative reflected the feudal pre-eminence of the king, especially as leader in war, sole owner of land, and the fount of justice. In the 16th century its scope was much extended to cover executive powers. Elizabeth I claimed that parliament had no right to initiate discussion of the religious settlement, her marriage, or the succession question because such discussions infringed her prerogative. In the early 17th century the first two Stuart kings came into conflict with parliament over the extent of especially their fiscal prerogative (see forced loan; monopoly; ship money; tunnage and poundage), many of which were condemned by the *Long Parliament. The *Bill of Rights (1689) restricted the prerogative by guaranteeing regular parliaments, abolishing the *dispensing and *suspending powers of the crown, and securing the independence of judges. The royal veto was last used in 1707, but George III was still able to use his influence on cabinet members to prevent Roman *Catholic emancipation for as long as he reigned. In the 19th century the effects of parliamentary reform (see Reform Acts) reduced the crown's freedom of action in the choice of ministers. In its present-day exercise of the prerogative —including the rights to be sued, to make war and peace, to summon and dissolve parliament, and to make coins —the crown usually acts on the advice of a responsible minister. See also monarchy.

Presbyterianism. A form of Protestant Christianity, which rejected episcopacy but substituted an even stronger, oligarchical, form of church government through presbyteries, at parish level, diocesan synods, and a national assembly. It was adopted in Scotland after the Reformation in 1560, but never found much support in England, except among clerical intellectuals like *Cartwright. It had its heyday in the years 1640-45, when Scottish influence on the Long Parliament was at its height. In the Solemn League and Covenant (1643) parliament pledged itself, although in ambiguous terms, to introduce Presbyterianism into the English church and set up the *Westminster Assembly (the Westminster Confession (1645) is still the official statement of Presbyterian doctrine). But the legislation (1647-48) setting up a Presbyterian church was permissive, not mandatory, and the New Model Army, disliking presbyters as much as bishops, purged the Presbyterian leaders from parliament in 1647 and 1648. Thereafter the use of the term Presbyterian is confused, and it was often attached to laymen whose attitude was merely conservative or moderate; most of them became Anglican again, without notable hypocrisy, in 1660. The Presbyterians survived as a small but important element in English nonconformity, especially among the wealthy urban middle class, but they were virtually taken over by the *Unitarians in the 18th century. The Presbyterian Church of England, established in 1876 and merged in the United Reformed Church in 1972, was effectively a missionary church organized from Scotland. Scotland has always remained substantially loyal to Presbyterianism, and it is the creed of the *Church of Scotland.

Preston, battle of (17-19 Aug 1648). The battle in which the army of the Scottish Engagers, invading England under the duke of Hamilton, was cut off from Scotland by Cromwell and completely dispersed in a series of running fights.

Prestonpans, battle of (21 Sept 1745). An engagement during the *Jacobite rebellion of 1745, in which some 2500 Highlanders under Charles Edward Stuart and Lord George Murray routed a similar number of regular troops commanded by Sir John Cope and Col James Gardiner. It was this success that encouraged Charles Edward to commence his ill-fated march upon London.

Pretoria convention (3 Aug 1881). The agreement between the UK and the Transvaal that ended the first *Boer War (1880-81). The convention recognized the independence of the Transvaal, subject to British suzerainty and with stipulations on native rights.

Price, Richard (1723-91). Economist, philosopher, and political radical. Born near Bridgend (Glamorganshire), he became a Presbyterian minister in London. He advised *Pitt the younger on the national debt and his Northampton Tables laid the foundation for scientific actuarial calculation. His political treatises are best remembered, his *Observation on the Nature of Civil Liberty* (1776) being a formative influence on the American Revolution. An advocate of civil rights and parliamentary reform he greeted the French Revolution in a commemorative sermon that drew from *Burke his *Reflections on the Revolution in France* in answer.

Pride, Thomas (d. 1658). Parliamentary colonel in the Civil War. On 6 Dec 1648, on the orders of the army council, he carried out "Pride's purge", the arrest or exclusion of about 140 MPs. Those who remained—the *Rump—voted that Charles I be brought to trial. Pride was a judge at the trial and signed the king's death warrant.

Priestley, Joseph (1733-1804). Scientist, philosopher, and Presbyterian minister. His work on electricity was encouraged by the American scientist and statesman Benjamin Franklin; his discoveries in chemistry included oxygen (1774). In sociopolitical thought he anticipated *utilitarianism, and his theological views exerted a considerable influence on Unitarianism. His support of the French Revolution forced him to emigrate to America in 1794.

prime minister. The head of the government and leader of the political party with the majority, or largest number, of seats in the House of Commons. Sir Robert *Walpole is generally regarded as the first prime minister. As first lord of the treasury (1721-42), he presided, in the frequent absence of the Hanoverian kings, over the developing institution of the *cabinet. In the later 18th century *Pitt the younger firmly established the role of prime minister as head of the cabinet, upon which, during the 19th century, political power was increasingly concentrated at the expense of the *monarch. The 20th century has witnessed an enhancement of the prime minister's dominance in the cabinet. He or she appoints and dismisses ministers and is the link between the sovereign and cabinet. The prime minister continues to be the first lord of the treasury, but the functions of this office are carried out by the *chancellor of the exchequer. No peer has been prime minister since 1902.

Primrose League. A Conservative organization founded in 1883 by Lord Randolph *Churchill and other *Fourth Party members to promote their ideals of Tory democracy. The name commemorates Disraeli, the primrose having reputedly been his favourite flower.

prince consort. The title conferred on Prince Albert, husband of Queen Victoria, in 1857. The queen had hoped that he might be called king consort, by analogy with *queen consort, but kings must be regnant, and another title had to be found. The title became so much associated with him that it is unlikely ever to be conferred upon anyone else.

Prince Edward Island. A maritime province of Canada. It was discovered by Jacques Cartier in 1534 and, named Île St Jean, was settled by the French in 1719. Britain obtained it by the treaty of Paris (1763), when it became part of *Nova Scotia. A separate colony from 1769, it received its present name in 1799, in honour of Edward, duke of Kent (Queen Victoria's father). It was settled by Scottish colonists under Lord Selkirk in 1803 and joined the Dominion of Canada in 1873.

prince of Wales. A title first assumed officially by *Llywelyn ap Gruffudd in 1267 following the treaty of *Montgomery. It had been first adopted by his uncle *Dafydd ap Llywelyn. In 1301 Edward of Caernarfon, eldest son of Edward I, was given the title and lands of the *Principality and since then the title has almost continually been vested in the heir apparent to the throne.

Principality. Those areas of Wales held directly by the English crown, rather than the *Marches of Wales. Government of the area was provided for by the Statute of *Rhuddlan (1284) but, strictly, it dates from the creation (1301) of Edward of Caernarfon as *prince of Wales.

printing. The multiple reproduction of a text or picture. Printing from movable type, invented by Johann Gutenberg in Germany in the 1440s, was introduced to England in 1476 by William *Caxton. Notable printers in the 17th century include Robert Baker, who printed the Authorized Version of the Bible (1611), and William and Isaac Jaggard, who were responsible for the first folio edition of Shakespeare (1623). The 18th century saw the work of the great typefounders William Caslon (1692-1766) and John Baskerville (1706-75). Mechanization dates from the 19th century, the steam-powered press being introduced in 1814 and rotary printing in 1866. Phototypesetting, introduced in the 1950s, has now revolutionized printing.

prisage. The right of the sovereign to take a certain part of cargoes of imported wine. It was converted into a customs duty by Edward I and lasted until 1809 (1832 in the duchy of Lancaster).

prison reform. The improvement of the notorious conditions of prisons, such as *Newgate, was begun in the late 18th and early 19th centuries with the humanitarian work of John *Howard and Elizabeth *Fry. James Mill, notably in an article on prisons in the *Encyclopaedia Britannica* (1823), advocated prison sentences as an alternative to *capital punishment. Peel's Gaol Act (1823) obliged each county to have a gaol (which was to accord with a specified plan and to be inspected regularly), to classify prisoners for work, and to teach prisoners to read and write. An act of 1835 instituted a centralized system of prison administration and inspection. The ending of *transportation prompted much prison building in the mid-19th century, beginning with Pentonville in London (1842). Penal servitude was introduced in 1853 (and abolished in 1948). The Youthful Offenders Act (1854) introduced reformatories, which were the forerunners of the Borstal system of rehabilitating juvenile offenders (established in 1908). In 1877 prisons were placed under the Home Office, which appointed prison commissioners to supervise the prisons. The home secretary took over their powers in 1963.

privateers. Owners or captains of privately commissioned ships permitted under government licence (letters of marque) to attack enemy vessels. Without such authorization they were pirates. *Drake and *Hawkins both engaged in privateering, which continued into the 19th century (see Paris, declaration of).

Privy Council. The governing body of the realm, presided over by the sovereign, for much of the 16th and 17th centuries. It emerged in the 1530s from the larger king's council. Its register dates from 1540 and it had its own seal from 1556. Its members were the great officers of state and of the household, meeting regularly, wherever the sovereign might be, to deal with the concerns of government, whether matters of high policy or administrative trivia. In the 18th century the *cabinet took over the functions of the Privy Council, which now retains only formal duties, membership being granted to those who have attained high political office. The lord president of the council is a member of the cabinet. The Judicial Committee of the Privy Council, created in 1833, is the final court of appeal from ecclesiastical courts and from dependencies overseas.

privy seal. The seal used from the 11th century to authorize proceedings in Chancery or the Exchequer. Its use increased as that of the *great seal became more formalized. It was employed to seal instructions to royal officials and to foreign courts and was the seal associated with conciliar business in late medieval times. The Privy Seal Office was abolished in 1884, but the lord privy seal, while having no special duties, is a member of the cabinet. See also signet.

prize. A ship or property captured at sea by virtue of the rights of war. The first government regulations concerning prize were enacted under the Commonwealth of England (1649-53), when graded shares in the proceeds of captured ships, or prize money for sunk ships, were apportioned among the victorious crew. The payment of such prize bounty was not abolished until after World War II.

proclamation. A declaration in writing of the royal will, issued on the advice of the council and under the *great seal. Proclamations were widely used, especially by Protector Somerset and by Elizabeth I, in the 16th century, when they often amended, modified, extended, or even anticipated statutes. In 1610, however, a legal decision by Sir Edward *Coke established that legislation could not be created by royal proclamation. Their modern uses include proroguing, dissolving, or summoning parliament, declaring war, peace, or states of emergency, and appointing public holidays.

Profumo, John (Dennis) (1915-). Conservative MP. He was forced to resign as secretary of state for war (1963) following the discovery of his relationship with Christine Keeler, a woman who had also had an affair with the Soviet naval attaché. The potential security risk and subsequent misleading answers to questions in parliament caused a scandal that damaged the standing of Harold Macmillan's government.

prohibition, writ of. An order from a superior court halting a case in an inferior court and removing it to another. Many were issued by the judges of the common law courts to challenge the jurisdiction of the Court of *High Commission in the late 16th and early 17th centuries.

Propositions of Newcastle (14 July 1646). Parliamentary conditions for peace, presented to Charles I while he was a prisoner of the Scots at Newcastle. The 19 clauses included acceptance of the National *Covenant, the abolition of episcopacy, parliamentary control of the armed forces, and the punishment of leading royalists. Charles temporized, hoping to profit from a breach between parliament and the Scots. The latter, however, came to terms with parliament and withdrew from England (Feb 1647).

prorogation of parliament. The termination of a session of parliament and the announcement of the date of the next session. Any uncompleted business must be introduced *ab initio* (from the start) after the intervening recess.

protectorate. An overseas territory to which Britain, generally by treaty with its ruler, gave protection. The former protected states, which included *Aden, *Nigeria, *Uganda, and *Zanzibar, were administered as *crown colonies.

Protectorate (16 Dec 1653–25 May 1659). The period of the Interregnum during which England was governed by a protector. After Oliver *Cromwell's expulsion of the *Rump, *Barebones Parliament failed to fulfil the requirements of the army leaders for an effective legislature. At *Lambert's instigation the Barebones members were induced to transfer their powers to Cromwell. The military leaders drafted a new constitution, the *Instrument of Government, and Cromwell was appointed lord protector.

In foreign affairs, the Protectorate saw the conclusion of the first *Dutch War, an alliance with France against Spain, and the conquest, in 1655, of Jamaica, in the Spanish West Indies. Cromwell obtained Dunkirk in return for assisting France against the Spanish in Flanders, and an Anglo-French force defeated the Spanish in the battle of the *Dunes (1658). At home, Cromwell introduced reforms in administration and education as well as measures to achieve a Puritan church (*see* Triers and Ejectors). The Protectorate, however, permitted toleration and is notable for measures that allowed the *Jews to return to England.

The Protectorate was also marked by failure to achieve a satisfactory balance between the powers of the protector,

parliament, and the army. Failing to reach a working relationship with his first parliament (1654–55), Cromwell dissolved it. *Penruddock's rising (March 1655) led Cromwell to institute direct military rule (*see* major generals), but this also proved unsatisfactory. In the *Humble Petition and Advice Cromwell's second parliament (1656–58) offered him the title of king; he rejected it, but the protector's powers were again increased. Constructive legislation was impossible in a parliament deadlocked in constitutional uncertainty, and when Cromwell's opponents sought to use it to undermine the Protectorate he dissolved it. National bankruptcy seemed imminent. Before Cromwell could find a way out of the impasse he died (Sept 1658). Under his son Richard the Protectorate survived only another eight months before Richard lost control of the army and was forced to resign (*see* Restoration).

province (Latin: *provincia*). An administrative division of the Roman Empire. Augustus (reigned 27 BC–14 AD) reorganized the Roman Empire, dividing the provinces into two classes, senatorial and imperial. *Britain was at first one imperial province. *Septimius Severus divided it into two, Upper and Lower Britain, and Diocletian (reigned 284–305) into four, Britannia Prima, Britannia Secunda, Maxima Caesariensis and Flavia Caesariensis. Theodosius the Great (reigned 379–95) added a fifth province, Valentia, which was partly in Wales.

Provisions of Oxford (1258). The government reforms issued by the committee of 24 appointed by the *Oxford Parliament. Executive power was invested in the king and a council of 15, to which a newly appointed justiciar (Hugh Bigod) was made responsible. Parliament was to meet three times a year and would elect a standing commission of 12. Local administration was placed in the hands of the council, which immediately initiated an investigation into local government. The Provisions were finally annulled by the dictum of

*Kenilworth (1266) after the second Barons' War. *See also* Provisions of Westminster.

Provisions of Westminster (1259). The reforms issued by the parliament that met at Westminster in Oct 1259. They resulted from the deliberations of the council of 15 and commission of 12 established in 1258 by the more radical *Provisions of Oxford. The measures gave greater protection to subtenants in feudal courts, limited the obligation to attend courts, and reformed abuses in the laws of *wardship, *distress, and *Englishry. The provisions were reissued in 1263 and were contained in the Statute of *Marlborough (1267). The Westminster parliament also issued a series of administrative measures, including the provision of councillors permanently attendant on the king and the establishment of a financial committee to inquire into royal funds and of a system of inquiry into complaints about local government.

Provisors, Statutes of. 1. (1351) The statute that empowered the crown to exclude papal provisions to English benefices, confirming the king's power over ecclesiastical appointments. **2.** (1390) A statute that reinforced the measure of 1351 by forbidding papal nominations. *See also* Praemunire, Statutes of.

Prynne, William (1600-69). Puritan pamphleteer. In 1633 he published *Histrio Mastix: The Players Scourge, or, Actors Tragoedie* (1633), which condemned the theatre and was thought to insult by implication Queen Henrietta Maria, a stage enthusiast. Imprisoned and his ears partly amputated, he continued to produce pamphlets in prison, attacking Archbishop Laud and other Anglican churchmen. In 1637 what was left of his ears was removed. Released by the Long Parliament in 1640, he later turned against the parliamentarians and was imprisoned (1650-53). He supported the Restoration.

Public Record Office (PRO). The national archive of government, administration, and the law courts, established in 1838. The two PRO branches, in Chancery Lane and (since 1977) at Kew, London, are open to all researchers (modern state documents, e.g. cabinet minutes, are generally subject to a 30-year embargo). Very old records at Chancery Lane include the *Domesday Book.

Purcell, Henry (1659-95). Composer. A choirboy at the Chapel Royal, he became composer in ordinary for the violins in 1677 and organist of Westminster Abbey in 1679. One of the greatest of English composers, his compositions include odes for royal occasions, the opera *Dido and Aeneas* (1689), music for plays, songs, sacred music, and instrumental music.

Puritanism. The extreme Protestant movement in England during the 16th and 17th centuries. The term covers a range of doctrines and attitudes and never had a precise definition. Puritans were united only in their demand for further purification of the reformed English church from elements that they regarded as Roman Catholic, superstitious, or lacking in scriptural authority. Puritan theology was basically Calvinist. English refugees from the Marian persecution studied in Geneva and other Calvinist centres and were responsible for the translation of the *Bible known as the Geneva Bible (1560). The Puritans opposed the dogma, ritual, and organization of the Elizabethan church. Archbishops *Parker and *Whitgift both took measures against them, the latter provoking the violently anti-episcopal *Marprelate tracts (1588-89). James I convened the *Hampton Court conference (1604) to examine Puritan doctrine and was antagonized by the Puritans' hostility towards episcopacy. Polarization in the English church hardened as Charles I and Archbishop *Laud tried to impose their own brand of High Church uniformity (*see* Arminians); the Puritan faction was increasingly identified with the parliamentary opposition to the monarchy and allied itself with Scottish *Presbyterianism in order to resist the bishops. More extreme Puritan sects burgeoned during the upheaval of the Civil War (see Fifth Monarchy Men; Levellers) and were well represented in the *New Model Army. In the 1640s and 1650s the Puritan emphasis on preaching, observance of the Sabbath, moral strictness, and abstinence from pleasure prevailed. There was iconoclasm in the churches, and Puritan forms of worship and ecclesiastical organization replaced the Anglican liturgy and episcopacy. After 1660, although such Puritan spokesmen as *Milton and *Marvell continued their opposition to the new settlement, Puritanism was subsumed into nonconformity (see nonconformists).

purveyance. An ancient royal right of demanding provisions, goods, and services from the districts through which the court passed, at prices fixed by royal officers. Payment was made by Exchequer *tallies, which could be rendered in lieu of tax payments. Exploitation of the right led to discontent under Elizabeth and the early Stuarts, and it was abolished in 1657.

Putney debates (Oct-Nov 1647). Discussions conducted in Putney church by the council of the New Model Army and attended by two officers and two *agitators from each regiment. They revealed a deep divergence of views between the two groups, with Cromwell and Ireton resisting the radical demands of the ranks, among whom there was strong support for the Levellers.

Pym, John (?1584-1643). Parliamentary statesman. He first entered parliament in 1614 and became prominent in the 1620s, taking part in the impeachment of Buckingham (1626). During the personal rule (1629-40) of Charles I he joined other Puritans in the Providence Island Company. A leading member of the *Long Parliament, he was largely responsible for maintaining its unity, threatened by differences between republicans and those who desired above all else to avoid civil war. He participated in the impeachments of Strafford (a former friend) and Laud and in

drafting the *Grand Remonstrance. In 1642 he was one of the *five members whom Charles attempted to arrest. Pym is also important for his imposition, after the outbreak of war, of what became the land tax.

Q

quadruple alliance 1. (2 Aug 1718) An alliance formed between Britain, France, the Netherlands, and Austria to compel Spain to abide by the treaty of *Utrecht (1713) and to counteract Spanish attempts to supplant Austrian power in Italy. After hostilities, in which Spain gave its support to an unsuccessful *Jacobite invasion of England, Spain complied with the demands of the alliance (1720). 2. (20 Nov 1815) An alliance between Britain, Austria, Russia, and Prussia, formed in 1813 to overthrow Napoleon and renewed after his final defeat in 1815. The signatories bound themselves to remain in alliance for 20 years after the prospective peace settlement. The agreement was renewed simultaneously with the signing of the treaty of *Paris (Nov 1815). In 1818, during the Congress of Aix-la-Chapelle, the alliance was extended to include France. It effectively disintegrated at the Congress of Verona (1822). 3. (22 April 1834) An alliance, negotiated by Palmerston, between Britain, France, Portugal, and Spain. It forced the pretenders to the thrones of Portugal and Spain to leave their countries.

Quakers (or Society of Friends). A *nonconformist sect founded by George *Fox, who began his ministry in 1647. Their name derived from the spiritual "trembling" experienced during meetings. The Quakers' renunciation of creeds, paid ministers, formal services, and oathtaking made them targets of religious persecution. They were tolerated under the Protectorate but suffered the penalties imposed by the *Clarendon code. In 1681 William *Penn founded Pennsylvania as a Quaker refuge. After the Toleration Act (1689) they became increasingly involved in humanitarian activities. In the 18th century they campaigned against *slavery, and in the early 19th century the Quaker Elizabeth *Fry was a leading prison reformer. Many Quakers were imprisoned as conscientious objectors during World Wars I and II.

quarter sessions. Meetings of the *justices of the peace of a shire four times a year. They were instituted in 1363. In addition to extensive criminal jurisdiction, from the 16th century they administered the laws concerning bridges, roads, gaols, houses of correction, wages, prices, licensing of alehouses, and many other functions of local government. They were abolished in 1971. See also petty sessions.

Quatre-Bras, battle of (16 June 1815). The battle in which the British, under Wellington, defeated the French, under Marshal Ney. *Waterloo followed two days later.

quattuorviri (Latin: four men). In the Roman Empire, the chief magistrates of a *municipium. They exercised the functions performed in a colonia by the *duoviri, being responsible for the administration of law and building programmes.

Quebec. The largest province of Canada. First explored and settled in the 16th and 17th centuries, by the Frenchmen Jacques Cartier and Samuel de Champlain, Quebec was a French colony, known as New France, until the British capture of the territory (1760), during the Seven Years' War. In 1791 it became a colony, which was known as Lower Canada until it eventually joined the Canadian confederation as the province of Quebec in 1867.

Queen Anne's Bounty. A fund established by Queen Anne in 1704. She surrendered her revenues from *first fruits and tenths to the fund, which was to be used for the benefit of poorer beneficed clergy. In the 19th century the fund also received parliamentary grants and private donations. In 1948 the administration of the fund passed to the *Church Commissioners.

queen consort. The wife of a king, as opposed to a queen regnant, who rules in her own right. A queen consort enjoys a separate ceremony at the coronation of a king. See also prince consort.

Queen's Bench, Court of. See King's Bench, Court of.

Queensberry, John Sholto Douglas, 8th marquess of (1844-1900). Patron of boxing, who supervised the compilation of the Queensberry Rules of boxing (1867). Tried in 1895 for publishing "defamatory libel" about Oscar Wilde, Queensberry's acquittal, and the evidence in the case, led to Wilde's conviction for homosexual practices.

Queensland. A state in northeast Australia. Formerly part of New South Wales, it became a separate colony in 1859 and joined the Commonwealth of Australia in 1901.

quia emptores (1290). The statute that provided that purchasers (emptores) of land should owe accompanying feudal incidents not to the middle tenant (see mesne tenure), from whom it was acquired (subinfeudation) but to the superior lord, of whom the middle tenant held the land.

Quiberon Bay, battle of (20 Nov 1759). A naval battle during the Seven Years' War, in which the British were victorious over the French. A French fleet of 26 ships, which had been assembled to cover a planned invasion of Britain, was driven by Hawke into Quiberon Bay, Brittany. Thirteen French vessels were lost or beached and the invasion was abandoned.

quit claim. The release by a lord of all claims that he might have against a villein, who in compensation for lost services paid a quit rent. See manumission.

quo warranto. A writ issued by the Court of King's Bench against a person usurping any office or privilege, asking "by what authority" he did so. Edward I instituted a general quo warranto inquiry into the jurisdictions of barons and corporations in 1278. The statute quo warranto (1290) allowed a defendant to base his claim on long user, in addition to the already established defence of royal grant. After the Restoration Charles II issued writs of quo warranto against many corporations.

R

radar (radio detection and ranging). A device whereby the position and range of distant objects, such as ships or aircraft, may be established by means of radio waves. Radar, which was developed by British scientists led by Sir Robert Watson-Watt (1892-1973), revolutionized the conduct of air warfare and was widely used by the RAF, the Luftwaffe, and British and German ground defences during most of World War II.

Radcot Bridge, battle of (19 Dec 1387). A battle in which a force under *Richard II's favourite, Robert de Vere, earl of Oxford, was defeated by the lords *appellant, Henry Bolingbroke, earl of Derby, and Thomas, duke of Gloucester. The outcome deprived Richard of any chance of defeating his enemies by force and was followed by the attack on his ministers in the *Merciless Parliament.

radicals. Advocates of fundamental political and/or social change. The term "radical" has been applied to various politicians and movements since the end of the 18th century. It was first used to describe reformers ranging from Benthamite *philosophical radicals to left-wing Whigs, such as Sir Francis *Burdett, and populist demagogues, such as Henry *Hunt. After the parliamentary reform of 1832 radicals formed a vigorous force, urging further reforms, and were distrusted by such establishment Whigs as *Melbourne. Radicalism became a major element in the *Liberal Party and was especially associated with religious nonconformity. Joseph *Chamberlain carried this tradition into the Liberal Union-Conservative alliance,

in which it met Randolph *Churchill's strain of Tory democracy.

Raedwald (d. 627). King of East Anglia. The only East Anglian ruler to become *bretwalda, Raedwald protected *Edwin from *Aethelfrith of Northumbria, whom he defeated at the battle of the river Idle (616). Only nominally a Christian, it is probably Raedwald who is commemorated by the *Sutton Hoo ship burial.

Raffles, Sir (Thomas) Stamford (1781-1826). Founder of *Singapore. An official of the East India Company, he persuaded his employers to acquire Singapore island, then almost uninhabited, from its Malay owners (1819). He initiated its development into an international commercial centre, before retiring because of ill health (1824). A distinguished oriental scholar, botanist, and zoologist, he founded (1825) the Zoological Society in London.

Raglan, Fitzroy James Henry Somerset, 1st Baron (1788-1855). Soldier, who commanded British forces during the early stages of the Crimean War. Raglan fought, and was wounded, at Waterloo and, after serving as military secretary at the Horse Guards (1827-52), succeeded Wellington as commander in chief of the forces. In 1854 he took command in the Crimea. His leadership, notably an ambiguous order that resulted in Cardigan's ill-fated *charge of the Light Brigade at Balaclava, was strongly criticized. Raglan died after the failure in June 1855 of the assault on Sebastopol.

ragman rolls. The returns from the commissions of enquiry, held in 1274-75, which investigated the administration of *eyres. They appeared ragged because of the many seals that hung from them. The name was later applied to other similar documents, particularly those recording the homage performed (1297) by Scottish barons and clergy to Edward I.

railways. Horse-drawn railways were common by the 18th century in British collieries, but around 1800 Richard *Trevithick pioneered the steam-powered railway locomotive. This was developed by George *Stephenson, who engineered the world's first public locomotive railway—the Stockton and Darlington, opened in 1825. Horses were soon widely superseded by reliable locomotives, modelled on Stephenson's *Rocket* (1829). By 1830 a flourishing economy and increasing investment capital fostered a vast railway network, which was developed somewhat haphazardly between 1830 and 1870. The first cheap rapid transport system revolutionized society, despite opposition, and attracted heavy speculative investment. By 1850 freight had overtaken passenger transport, and *canals and *roads could not compete. The first underground railway was built in London in 1863. Fierce rivalry between companies led to consolidation, but the government, fearing monopolies, prevented major amalgamations. Legislation from 1840 was instrumental in achieving a remarkable safety record on the railways.

Assuming control of railways during World War I, the government in 1921 compulsorily amalgamated 123 railways into four groups to facilitate their economical operation. Despite increased competition from roads, and economic depression, the railways continued to expand and in World War II provided invaluable military transport. The consequent deterioration of the railways and financial strains led to the nationalization of all railways in 1947. They were divided into six regions (excluding Northern Ireland), and in 1955 a modernization programme was begun that included replacing steam by Diesel and electric locomotives; in 1963 many branches lines were closed.

Raleigh, Sir Walter (?1552–1618). Courtier and explorer. In the 1580s he organized several voyages of discovery along the Atlantic seaboard of North America, but an attempt to colonize a region named Virginia (in honour of Queen Elizabeth, the Virgin Queen) was unsuccessful. In 1592 Raleigh fell out of favour with the queen after marrying Elizabeth Throgmorton, one of her ladies in waiting, and in 1595 set off on a fruitless search for the legendary Eldorado supposedly to be found in Guyana. On his return he played a distinguished part in the *Cádiz expedition (1596) and also fought the Spanish in the Azores (1597). In 1603, however, Raleigh was accused of conspiring against James I and was imprisoned in the Tower (see main plot). There he remained until 1616, when he was released for the purpose of undertaking a second voyage in search of Eldorado. The expedition ended in the English destruction of a Spanish settlement, and on his return to England Raleigh was executed. His literary works include *The Discovery of the Empire of Guyana* (1596), the *History of the World* (1614), and poetry.

Ramillies, battle of (23 May 1706). A battle of the War of the Spanish Succession, the culminating engagement of Marlborough's 1706 campaign in Flanders. The French forces under Villeroi were decisively outmanoeuvred by Marlborough's skilful use of feint attacks, which enabled him to throw in his main force where least expected. French losses amounted to 15 000, five times those of the allies. Ramillies and a further 12 towns held by the French and in the Netherlands were then taken in swift succession.

ransom. A sum or price demanded for the release of a prisoner or for the restoration of captured property. The practice was widespread in the middle ages for, under feudalism, knights were obliged to pay for the release of their lord if he was captured in war. The most celebrated example of ransom in British history is the 150,000 marks demanded by the emperor Henry VI for the release of *Richard I.

rapes of Sussex. Subdivisions of the *hundreds originating in the roping or measuring out of the land. Unlike the *lathes of Kent, they had no judicial significance, but were merely geographical.

rationing. A system of controlling the national consumption of foodstuffs, introduced in Britain towards the end of World War I and during World War II. In World War I rationing was not introduced until 1918 and then relied largely upon the cooperation of retailers. The more affluent frequently ignored the system, and ration coupons were rarely checked against sales. A far stricter system of national rationing was established in Jan 1940. A basic ration of essential foodstuffs, such as meat, fats, sugar, eggs, and cheese, was guaranteed on surrender of the appropriate coupon, while a more flexible "points" system covered a further range of foodstuffs, such as tinned fruit, as well as clothing. The system continued after the war, until 1954.

Rebecca Riots (1842–44). Disturbances in Wales. The rioters, many disguised as women, destroyed turnpike tollhouses and gates—taking their name from the biblical prophecy that Rebekah's seed should "possess the gate of those which hate them" (Genesis 24.60). Protest against the *Poor Law Amendment Act (1834) was an underlying factor.

rector. *See* vicar.

recusants. Those—both Roman Catholics and Protestants—who refused to attend the services of the Church of England. By the Acts of *Uniformity of 1552 and 1559 they were liable to a fine of 1s for each weekly nonattendance. In 1581 the fine was increased to £20 per month. *See also* penal laws.

Red Ensign. The flag of the mercantile marine. It dates from the 16th century, when it became the flag carried by the centre vessels of a war fleet, the van and the rear carrying white and blue ensigns respectively. In 1864 the white ensign was designated the flag of the Royal Navy, while the red was restricted to the mercantile marine.

Redmond, John (1856–1918). Irish politician. Elected an MP in 1880 he supported Parnell and led the minority pro-Parnellite faction in the Irish party from 1890 to 1900. In 1900 the split was healed under Redmond's leadership and

in 1910 he allied his party with the Liberals in order to achieve *home rule.

Red River Rebellion (1869–70). A revolt in Canada, led by Louis Riel (1844–85). The rebellion was an attempt by *métis* (people of mixed French-Canadian and Indian descent) to resist the incorporation of the Northwest Territories into the Dominion of Canada. An expedition under *Wolseley restored order, and Riel was exiled for five years.

reeve. In Anglo-Saxon England, an official having a local jurisdiction under his lord. The shire reeve (*see* sheriff) administered justice and collected revenues in the counties for the king. Manorial reeves acted as farm managers, organizing the year's work on the demesne, managing the lord's sheep and cattle, and supervising the villeins in their labour on the lord's land.

Reform Acts. Three measures of electoral reform in the 19th century. **1.** (1832) An act originated by the Whig government of Lord Grey in response to widespread unrest. The first reform bill was introduced in March 1831. It was defeated by the Tories in April and the government resigned. The general election returned the Whigs, who introduced a second reform bill in June. In Oct the Lords rejected it, and riots, notably at Bristol, ensued. A third bill, introduced in Dec, met obstruction in the Lords. Only after William IV, in response to Grey's resignation and popular agitation, threatened to create sufficient new peers to override the opposition did the bill become law. The act disenfranchised most *rotten boroughs, and the released seats were redistributed among the counties and previously unrepresented boroughs. The *franchise was extended in the counties from the freeholders of property worth 40 shillings a year to £10 copyholders and £50 short-leaseholders and tenants at will; in the boroughs £10 householders were granted the vote. The electorate in England and Wales was increased immediately by some 50%, but the vote had been extended only to the prosperous middle class. Scottish and Irish reform acts increased representation from 45 to 53 and 100 to 105 seats respectively; the vote was extended to £10 householders in the boroughs. 2. (1867) An act, sponsored by Derby's Conservative government and largely the work of Disraeli, that extended the franchise to another 938 000 voters (bringing the total to some two million). It extended the vote to £5 leaseholders and £12 occupiers in the counties and to all householders and rentpayers paying £10 per annum in the boroughs. Some 45 parliamentary seats were redistributed. 3. (1884) An act, introduced by Gladstone's government in response to radicals' demands, that extended the household franchise to the counties; the total electorate thus increased from about three to about five million. A separate measure (1885) redistributed parliamentary seats to achieve an exact correspondence throughout the country between population and representation.

Reformation. The Reformation was a religious and political movement in 16th-century Europe, inspired by a wish to reform the Roman Catholic Church and resulting in the establishment of Protestant churches in several countries. In England and Wales, dissatisfaction with the pre-Reformation *church facilitated the break with Rome, itself the outcome of the refusal of Pope Clement VII to allow *Henry VIII to divorce Catherine of Aragon. The king, desperate for a male heir and in love with Anne Boleyn, made a series of abortive representations to Clement, whose own hands were tied by his subjection to Catherine's nephew, the emperor Charles V. In 1529 Henry summoned parliament, and in a series of statutes, which were largely the work of Thomas *Cromwell, papal authority in England was destroyed. In 1533 an Act of *Annates suspended payment of first fruits, while the Act in *Restraint of Appeals (to Rome) permitted Henry's divorce from Catherine and marriage to Anne. Princess Mary was declared illegitimate by the Act of *Succession, and by the Act of *Supremacy the king became the "supreme head" of the English church (1534). In 1536 the *dissolution

of the monasteries was set in motion. The mildly Lutheran ten *articles of religion (1536) were replaced by the Catholic six articles (1539), a demonstration of the religious conservatism of the Henrician Reformation. The king's death in 1547 permitted the more radical reformers, led by Archbishop *Cranmer, to introduce Protestantism into the English church. The six articles and accompanying heresy laws were repealed (1547), and an Act of *Uniformity required use of the *Book of Common Prayer (1549). A second, more Protestant, prayer book was issued in 1552, followed in 1553 by the 42 articles. Edward's death gave rise to the shortlived *Marian reaction (1553–58), after which Elizabeth I established a moderate but firmly Protestant church. The Elizabethan settlement was embodied in an Act of Supremacy, which defined the sovereign as the supreme governor of the church, and an Act of Uniformity, which imposed the second Edwardian prayer book (1559), and the 39 articles (1563).

In medieval Scotland heresy was rare, but in the 1520s Lutheran ideas began to spread from the Continent, the first Protestant martyr being burned in 1528. In the 1530s the political pattern that was to dominate the Scottish Reformation began to emerge: Catholicism became identified with alliance with France, while Protestantism became identified with friendship with England, which under Henry VIII had broken with Rome. By the 1540s Lutheran ideas were being replaced by the more radical teachings of Calvin, and under the governorship from 1554 of Mary of Guise the religious grievances of Protestants combined with political fears that Scotland was becoming a satellite of France. When in 1559 Mary of Guise attempted to suppress Protestant preachers they and their powerful lay supporters, the lords of the *Congregation, rose in arms against Catholicism and France. Military deadlock between the two sides followed but was broken by English intervention in 1560. With the withdrawal of both French and English troops power was in the hands of the

Congregation, and the Reformation parliament of 1560 proceeded to ban the saying of Mass, reject papal authority, and accept a reformed, basically Calvinist, confession of faith. As the Reformation had been carried out in Scotland in defiance of the crown it presented a major threat to royal authority, and a church was born that was frequently to claim independence of the state. See Church of Scotland.

regalia. The accoutrements of royalty, especially the apparatus of a coronation. The most important items of the English regalia are the three crowns, the oldest of which dates from Charles II, the others being the Imperial State Crown made for Queen Victoria in 1838 and the Imperial Crown of India made for George V; the king's sceptres; the two orbs; the sword of state; the ampulla and spoon; the spurs of chivalry; the coronation ring; the state trumpets; and the bracelets or armills. In 1637 Colonel *Blood attempted to steal them from their home in the Tower of London. The regalia of Scotland (the crown, sceptre, sword of state, and mace) are in Edinburgh castle.

regency. The delegation of all or some royal powers to a person or persons during the minority, illness, or absence of the monarch or as a precaution against such eventualities. The Regency Act (1811) named the prince of Wales (from 1820 George IV) prince regent, with limited powers, after the onset of the final illness of his father George III. The Regency was a distinctive period in British history, having a characteristic style in architecture and furniture. Influenced by classicism and lightened by ornamentation, the Regency style is seen at its best in the *Nash terraces of Regent's Park in London and the seafront squares in Brighton.

regicide. The killing of a king; or a person who kills him. The 59 signatories of the death warrant of Charles I in 1649 were termed regicides. They included Oliver *Cromwell, Henry *Ireton, and Thomas *Pride.

registration of births, marriages, and deaths. Such registration has been carried out on a compulsory civil basis in England and Wales since 1837 and in Scotland since 1855. Establishment of government-maintained centralized population records (superseding local, inevitably incomplete, church registers) resulted from a growing realization that accurate data were essential for improved administration. See also Census Act.

Regni (or **Reginenses**). A British tribe. Their territory covered parts of present-day Hampshire and Sussex; their chief town was Chichester. Under the leadership of their king, Cogidubnus, they submitted to the Romans in the mid-1st century AD; the remains of his palace at Fishbourne show the extent of Roman influence.

Regulating Act (1773). An act aimed at extending government control over the East India Company by making the newly created post of governor general (although a Company appointment) subject to a government-appointed council. The system proved unworkable (see Hastings, Warren; India Acts).

Reith, John Charles Walsham Reith, 1st Baron (1889-1971). The first general manager (1922) and director general (1927-38) of the *British Broadcasting Corporation, the early development of which he greatly influenced. An MP during World War II, he was minister of information and then of transport (1940) and minister of works (1940-42).

relief. The sum of money payable to a feudal lord before an heir could inherit his estates. Reliefs, especially those demanded by the crown, were often exorbitant and *Magna Carta (1215) limited their amounts.

remembrancers. Three officers of the Exchequer. The queen's (or king's) remembrancer is concerned with the recovery of penalties and debts due to the crown and now has largely ceremonial duties. The posts of lord treasurer's remembrancer and remembrancer of the first fruits were abolished in 1833 and 1838 respectively.

Remigius (d. 1092). Bishop of Dorchester (later Lincoln) from 1067. He was a monk at the Norman abbey of Fécamp before accompanying the army of William the Conqueror to England in 1066. Appointed bishop of Dorchester, the see was transferred to Lincoln in 1072, where Remigius founded the cathedral.

Remonstrance of the Army (Nov 1648). A petition presented by the army council to parliament during the Civil War. Among its demands was a call for the trial of Charles I. Parliament, however, continued to negotiate with the king, and in Dec the army seized Charles and purged parliament (see Pride, Thomas).

Rennie, John (1761–1821). Civil engineer. Rennie, a Scot, opened a business in London in 1791. He designed and constructed bridges (including Waterloo Bridge, 1810–17, and the rebuilt London Bridge, completed 1831), docks (Hull docks and East and West India docks, London) and canals (Kennet and Avon canal).

reparations. The imposition of indemnities upon Germany by the allied powers following World Wars I and II. After World War I the payment of reparations was stipulated by article 232 of the treaty of Versailles and was fixed by the London Conference (1921) at £6,600 million. The figure proved unrealistic and was modified in 1924 and again in 1929, until finally, in 1932, reparations were cancelled. In contrast to these arrangements, it was agreed at the Potsdam conference that reparations following World War II should be exacted from Germany in the form of capital equipment, such as industrial plant, to aid in the recovery of the war-damaged economies of the allies.

Requests (or Poor Men's Causes), Court of. A court of equity that dealt exclusively with the pleas of poor men and afforded some protection against, for example, enclosures and rack-renting. Originating in the 14th century, it was institutionalized in 1497 and sat at Westminster from 1516. At the end of the 16th century it was accused of encroaching on the jurisdiction of the common-law courts and it did not sit after 1642.

Restoration (1660). The reinstatement of the English monarchy under Charles II after the collapse of the *Protectorate. The confusion following Richard Cromwell's downfall led most except diehard republicans to favour the restoration of the Stuarts. The *Rump was totally discredited and effective power lay with Gen. *Monck, who took measures to dissolve parliament while discreetly advising the exiled king about the constitutional guarantees necessary to make his return acceptable (see Breda, Declaration of). The *convention parliament voted for Charles' recall and he landed in May 1660 to an enthusiastic reception. A religious settlement (see Clarendon code) was made by the subsequent *cavalier parliament (1661–79).

In art and literature "Restoration" often refers to the period 1660–1700, during which a new cosmopolitanism, sensuality, and gaiety, epitomized in *Lely's portraits and *Wycherley's comedies, were characteristic.

Restraint of Appeals, Act in (1533). The act that prevented appeals to Rome in testamentary and matrimonial disputes. By asserting that the king had supreme jurisdiction in both temporal and spiritual matters, the act effectively brought papal authority in England to an end. It enabled Cranmer to annul Henry VIII's marriage to Catherine of Aragon and validate his marriage to Anne Boleyn. See Reformation.

retainers. The personal retinue of medieval lords and kings. In the Anglo-Saxon period they fulfilled a predominantly military function, but they subsequently also acted as judges and counsellors. They always formed an influential group in baronial and royal policies, and late medieval kings made frequent but largely unsuccessful attempts to limit their number, prestige, and power. See also bastard feudalism; livery and maintenance.

Reynolds, Sir Joshua (1723-92). Artist. The leading portrait painter of his day, his subjects included Gibbon, Burke, and Fox. In 1768 he became the first president of the Royal Academy.

Rhodes, Cecil John (1853-1902). South African statesman, born in Britain. A vicar's son, he went to South Africa for the benefit of his health. He made a fortune in diamond mining and, after completing his education at Oriel College, Oxford, founded the De Beers Company (1880). In 1887 he formed the *British South Africa Company (incorporated 1889) to develop the region north of the Transvaal (subsequently named Rhodesia in his honour). He had entered Cape politics in 1880 and was premier from 1890 to 1896, when he was forced to resign following the *Jameson raid (1895). He established 170 Rhodes scholarships at Oxford University for students from the British Empire, the USA, and Germany.

Rhodesia. *See* Northern Rhodesia; Southern Rhodesia.

Rhodesia and Nyasaland, Federation of. *See* Central African Federation.

Rhodri Mawr (d. 878). King of Gwynedd, Powys, and Seisyllwg, as a result of the propitious marriage alliances of himself and his father, Merfyn Frych. He was threatened by the Vikings and the Saxons: in 856 he defeated and killed Gorm, the Viking leader, but in 878 was killed in battle by the Saxons.

Rhuddlan, Robert of (d. 1088). Norman lord. Renowned for his ruthlessness, Robert built a castle and established a small borough at Rhuddlan. Dominating the greater part of the *Perfeddwlad, he initially supported *Gruffudd ap Cynan but later captured him and briefly gained control of *Gwynedd west of the river Conway.

Rhuddlan (or Wales), Statute of (1284). The legal and administrative arrangements made by Edward I for the conquered territories of *Llywelyn ap Gruffudd. New government centres were established at Caernarfon and Carmarthen and five new counties

(Anglesey, Caernarfon, Merioneth, Cardigan, and Carmarthen) were formed, in addition to Flint. English officers were introduced and castles and boroughs built. English criminal law was made compulsory but Welsh civil law was allowed to continue until its abolition in 1536-43 (*see* Union of England and Wales).

Rhys ap Gruffudd (or Yr Arglwydd Rhys) (1132-97). Lord of Deheubarth. Son of *Gruffudd ap Rhys, he had established himself as sole ruler of Deheubarth by 1155. He submitted to Henry II in 1158 but was recognized as the dominant Welsh ruler, especially after the death of *Owain Gwynedd in 1170 and his appointment, by the king, as justice of south Wales in 1172. An *eisteddfod* was held at Cardigan in 1176 under his auspices.

Rhys ap Tewdwr (d. 1093) Lord of Deheubarth. Having gained possession of Deheubarth in 1075, he further secured his hold over this territory at the battle of *Mynydd Carn. He probably formed an alliance with William I in 1081. He was killed near Brecon while resisting the Norman advance into the area under Bernard de *Newmarch.

Ricardo, David (1772-1823). Economist. In the influential *Principles of Political Economy and Taxation* (1817), he argued the labour theory of value, that the amount of labour used in the production of goods determines their exchange ratio. As an MP (1819-23), he was prominent in the free trade movement.

Riccio, David. *See* Rizzio, David.

Rich, Richard, 1st Baron (d. 1567). Lord chancellor (1548-51). His provision, while solicitor general, of false evidence at the trial of Sir Thomas *More was instrumental in securing More's conviction for treason (1535).

Richard I, Coeur de Lion (1157-99). King of England (1189-99), whose military exploits earned him the sobriquet Lionheart and made him a hero of medieval legend. Third son of Henry II and Eleanor of Aquitaine, as duke of Aquitaine he twice took up arms against his father: in 1173-74, when he joined his brothers in revolt, and in 1189, when he allied with Philip II Augustus of France against Henry. In 1190 Richard set out on the third *crusade and on his way to the Holy Land captured Messina, acknowledging Tancred of Lecce as king of Sicily rather than the emperor Henry VI. He went on to take Cyprus, where he married (1191) Berengaria of Navarre. After taking part in the siege of Acre, Richard defeated Saladin at Arsuf, which gave him Joppa, and advanced on Jerusalem. He failed to take the city and in 1192 concluded a three-year truce with Saladin. Captured on his way home by Duke Leopold of Austria, he was handed over to the emperor Henry VI, who demanded a ransom of 150,000 marks and Richard's acknowledgement of Henry as his overlord. In 1194, most of this huge ransom paid, he returned to England—only his second visit—but within weeks had left for ever. In his last years he was engaged intermittently in war with Philip II Augustus and died from wounds received while attacking the castle at Châlus. Richard's campaigns placed a heavy burden on England's finances and began the break-up of the *Angevin empire. His absences abroad led to a significant growth in the independence of the administration and of the baronial party with which Richard's successor John was to come to blows.

Richard II (1367-1400). King of England (1377-99). Son of Edward, the Black Prince, and Joan of Kent, he was married twice: first to Anne of Bohemia and, after her death in 1394, to Isabel of France. Richard's reign was dominated by his uncle *John of Gaunt. In 1381 Richard presented a brave face to the rebels in the *peasants' revolt, but his inability to control his magnates led to conflict between them. In 1386, while John of Gaunt was absent in Spain, a faction led by Thomas of Woodstock, earl of Gloucester, induced parliament to impeach Richard's chancellor Michael de la *Pole. A commission of government was then constituted and, when

Richard declared it illegal, parliament, at the behest of the lords *appellant led by Gloucester, outlawed Richard's favourites, including de la Pole and Robert de Vere, 9th earl of Oxford (1388). Following Gaunt's return in 1389 more amicable relations were established, but in July 1397 Richard moved to avenge his friends. Gloucester was murdered at Calais, and other appellants were subsequently executed or banished. Such actions courted disaster, but Richard took his fatal step in 1399, when, after the death of John of Gaunt, he confiscated his estates. This provoked John's son Henry Bolingbroke, to invade England while Richard was in Ireland. Returning in August, the king surrendered at Conway. He abdicated in the following month and died a few months later in prison at Pontefract. He may have starved himself to death, but there is no evidence that he was murdered, as represented in Shakespeare's *Richard II*.

Richard III (1452-85). King of England (1483-85). Son of Richard Plantagenet, duke of York (d. 1460), and Cicily Neville, he was created duke of Gloucester in 1461 and married Anne Neville, daughter of Warwick the king-maker, in 1472. He remained loyal to his brother Edward IV during the Wars of the Roses, fleeing the kingdom with him in 1470 and returning to fight by his side at *Barnet and *Tewkesbury. He subsequently earned a considerable reputation as a soldier in the border country of the north. However, on the death of his brother in 1483 Richard became protector for the 12-year-old *Edward V, whom he imprisoned with Edward's younger brother in the Tower of London. He then had the leaders of the hostile Woodville faction arrested and, later, executed. After declaring Edward IV's marriage invalid, and Edward's sons illegitimate, Richard was proclaimed king (June 1483). The two young princes disappeared, perhaps murdered at Richard's instigation. In the autumn of the same year the king dealt successfully with a rising in the west country led by Henry Stafford, duke of Buckingham, who was executed. In Aug 1485, however, Henry Tudor, earl of Richmond, led a second, successful, attempt to overthrow the king, defeating and killing Richard at the battle of *Bosworth Field to become Henry VII.

Richard, the usurper, received a bad press from Tudor apologists, and the tradition of Richard's villainy, portrayed most notably in Shakespeare's *Richard III*, has continued to the present day. He appears, however, to have been a potentially competent ruler, and in his short reign fostered trade and initiated financial reforms. There is no evidence that he was a hunchback (or "crouchback"), although contemporary portraits suggest that he had one shoulder higher than the other.

Richard, earl of Cornwall (1209–72). Second son of King John. After service in France he joined the baronial opposition to the foreign influence at the court of his brother Henry III. Reconciled with the king in 1239, he was regent (1253–54) during Henry's absence abroad. He was elected king of the Romans (Holy Roman Empire) in 1257 but never fully succeeded in establishing his authority. During the second Barons' War he fought for Henry and was captured at Lewes (1264), being held until 1265.

Richard, 3rd duke of York (1411–60). Grandson of Edmund de Langley and also of Roger de *Mortimer and a descendant through both of Edward III. He was lieutenant in France (1436–37, 1440–45) and married (1438) Cicily, daughter of Ralph Neville, 1st earl of Westmorland. An enemy of Edmund Beaufort, duke of Somerset, he was dispatched (1447) to be lieutenant in Ireland. In 1452 he led a force to London in an attempt to displace Somerset, which he eventually achieved in 1453. York held the protectorship during Henry VI's illness (1454–55), but Somerset was then reinstated. Consequently, York and the Nevilles took up arms (see Roses, Wars of the) and defeated the royal forces at St Albans, where Somerset was slain. Although again named protector (1455) York's position was undermined by Queen Margaret and when, in 1459, he again attempted to seize power, he was attainted. Following the Yorkist victory at Northampton (1460) York claimed, and was granted, the succession. Shortly afterwards, he was killed by Queen Margaret's forces at Wakefield. Two of his sons became kings of England —as Edward IV and Richard III.

Richmond, dukes of. See Fitzroy, Henry; Lennox.

Ridgeway. A prehistoric track along the Berkshire Downs from Avebury to the Thames.

riding. The third part of a shire. An administrative division of the Danelaw, the word derives from Old Norse, via the Old English *thriding*, third part. In Yorkshire ridings survived as separate units of local government until the reorganization of local government in 1974.

Ridley, Nicholas (c. 1500–1555). Bishop of Rochester (1547) and then London (1550). He contributed to the compilation of the Book of Common Prayer (1549) and was a representative of the more extreme Protestant view during Edward's reign. His support for Lady Jane *Grey cost him his bishopric when the Catholic Mary became queen (1553) and, refusing to acknowledge Catholic doctrines in debate at Oxford, he was burned at the stake, together with Latimer, for heresy.

Ridolfi plot (1570–71). A Roman Catholic conspiracy, conceived by an Italian banker, Roberto Ridolfi (1531–1612), and supported by Spain, to murder *Elizabeth I and place Mary Queen of Scots on the English throne. The plot was discovered while Ridolfi was abroad, but one of the conspirators, Thomas Howard, 4th duke of *Norfolk, was executed.

right, writ of. A writ sent in response to a person's claim to land that was in the possession of another. Its recipient, either the sheriff or the parties' lord, was obliged to restore the land to the plaintiff or hear the case. The defendant chose whether the dispute was to be decided by *trial by battle or by the *grand assize.

Riot Act (1715). An act passed after the *Jacobite riots in 1715. It provided that if riotous assemblies of 12 or more persons failed to disperse after the reading by a local government officer of a proclamation ordering them, in the name of the sovereign, to do so, they would be guilty of a felony, punishable by death; hence the expression "to read the Riot Act".

Ripon, George Frederick Samuel Robinson, 1st marquess of (1827-1909). Son of Viscount Goderich. A Christian Socialist, he was a Liberal MP from 1853 to 1859, when he succeeded as 2nd earl of Ripon (marquess, 1871). While lord president of the council he was largely responsible for the settlement with the US government (1871) of claims arising from the *Alabama case. As viceroy of India (1880-84) his sympathy towards Indian political aspirations aroused controversy at home. In 1886 he became first lord of the admiralty and he later led the Liberal Party in the House of Lords (1905-08).

Ripon, treaty of (26 Oct 1640). The treaty that ended the second *Bishops' War. It was virtually a royal surrender —the Scots were to remain in possession of Northumberland and Durham and to receive £850 a day until the issue was finally settled. Charles I, under Scottish pressure, summoned the *Long Parliament to conclude the peace.

Rivaux, Peter des (d. 1258). One of the *Poitevin favourites of Henry III. The king was forced to dismiss him from the office of treasurer following the Marshal rebellion (1234).

River Plate, battle of the (Dec 1939). A naval engagement between the German pocket battleship *Graf Spee*, which had sunk eight ships in the South Atlantic, and the British cruisers *Ajax*, *Achilles*, and *Exeter*. After being driven into Montevideo, the *Graf Spee* was scuttled.

Rivers, Anthony Woodville, Baron Scales and 2nd Earl (1440-83). Yorkist supporter of Edward IV and guardian of his son, the future *Edward V. After Edward IV's death Edward V was imprisoned in the Tower and Rivers was executed for treason by the future *Richard III. His *Dictes and Sayenges of the Phylosophers* (1477) was the first book printed in England by *Caxton.

Rizzio (or Riccio), David (1533-66). Italian secretary and adviser to Mary Queen of Scots. He went to Scotland in 1561 and soon entered her service, initially as a musician. Mary's husband, Lord Darnley, whom she married in 1565, became jealous of Rizzio and conspired with Scottish noblemen for his murder. He was dragged from the queen's presence and stabbed to death.

roads. The three periods of systematic road building in British history, *Roman Britain, the *industrial revolution, and the 20th century, have a developed economy, sound engineering knowledge, and suitable vehicles in common. Extensive track networks (see Icknield way; Ridgeway) existed in ancient Britain, but the Romans built the first road system, on which they travelled in two- or four-wheeled chariots capable of high speeds. The network, which eventually comprised at least 8047 km (5000 mi), centred on London and connected the *colonia, legionary fortresses, and the tribal capitals. It bore little relation to local needs, being essentially strategic (see Ermine Street; Foss Way; Watling Street). After the withdrawal of the Romans the roads declined until the 16th century, when *parishes were made responsible for the maintenance of their roads; Scotland adopted a similar system in 1669. Gen. George *Wade built the first modern government-sponsored road network in Britain (1726-37) in the Scottish Highlands for military purposes. The introduction of *turnpikes brought the first major road-building projects since the Romans, fostering the development of road engineering in the 18th century with the work of especially *Telford and *Macadam. British roads declined with the expansion of *railways after 1830 until scientific developments facilitated the manufacture of cars in the late 19th century. The far-sighted Highway Act (1835) invested responsibility for roads in highway boards, and with the development of local government in the late 19th century *county councils became the highway authorities. Increasing motor transport at the turn of the century led to the establishment of the Road Board (1909), which was superseded by the Ministry of Transport in 1920. A system of trunk roads was developed following legislation in 1939 and 1944, and motorways were thus classified in 1949. The Ministry of Transport was merged into the Department of the Environment in 1970.

Robert (I) the Bruce (1274-1329). King of Scots (1306-29). Son of Robert Bruce, earl of Carrick, and grandson of one of the *competitors for the Scottish throne in 1290-92. Robert fought for the English against John Balliol, king of Scots, in 1296, but in 1297 he joined Sir William *Wallace's rising against them. In 1298 he was appointed one of the guardians of the realm but submitted to the English in 1302-05. In 1306 he murdered John Comyn (King John's nephew) and had himself inaugurated as king. The forces he gathered were soon defeated by the English and Robert was forced into hiding. But in 1307 he renewed his campaign and gradually recovered much of the country from the English, a process that culminated in his great victory at *Bannockburn. Fighting continued, however, until in 1327 an invasion of England persuaded the English to recognize Scottish independence by the treaty of Edinburgh (1328). He was succeeded by his son, David II. See also Anglo-Scottish Wars.

Robert II (1316-90). King of Scots (1371-90). Son of Walter, steward of Scotland, and Marjory, daughter of Robert I. Robert helped to rule Scotland in the absence of David II in France, and was guardian during David's captivity in England. On succeeding David he proved weak and incompetent, partly owing to increasing ill health. He

was succeeded by his son, Robert III. See also Stuart, house of.

Robert III (c. 1337-1406). King of Scots (1390-1406). Eldest son of Robert II and Elizabeth Mure. Although baptized John he assumed the name Robert on his succession. Robert showed little capacity or energy as a king, and power passed largely into the hands of his brother, the duke of *Albany. He was succeeded by his son, James I.

Robert II Curthose, duke of Normandy (?1054-1134). Eldest son of William the Conqueror. He rebelled against his father in 1077 and three years later secured the succession to Normandy. He rebelled again in 1082 but succeeded to the dukedom on William's death (1087). Claiming the throne of England, he made war on his brothers, William II Rufus in 1094 and Henry I in 1101. In 1106 he was defeated by Henry at the battle of *Tinchebrai and remained in prison until his death.

Robert, earl of Gloucester (d. 1147). An illegitimate son of Henry I, who supported the claim to the throne of his half-sister Matilda in 1135. He invaded England with her in 1139 and captured King Stephen at Lincoln in Feb 1141. A few months later he was himself taken prisoner and exchanged for the king. His death from fever at Bristol effectively ended Matilda's bid for the throne.

Roberts of Kandahar, Pretoria, and Waterford, Frederick Roberts, 1st Earl (1832-1914). Soldier whose conduct of the later stages of the second Boer War largely ensured victory for Britain. Roberts served during the Indian mutiny, in which he won the Victoria Cross (1858), and commanded a division and then the force sent to Kandahar during the Afghan War (1878-80; see Afghanistan). He was then commander in chief of the Madras army (1881-85) and in India (1885-93) before becoming commander of the forces in Ireland (1895). As commander in chief of imperial forces in South Africa (1899-1900), he directed the campaign that achieved the capture of Pretoria, for which he was granted an earldom. Returning home, he served as commander in chief of the forces until the post was abolished in 1904.

Robin Hood. A legendary outlaw, a popular hero of ballads by the 14th century, whose story may be based on historical facts. The pipe roll of 1230 mentions a Robin Hood, a fugitive in Yorkshire, where the probably 14th-century *Lytell Geste of Robin Hood* (printed c. 1420) also locates him. Some later writers, however, place him and his followers' exploits (directed chiefly against the local sheriff and the wealthy) in Sherwood Forest, Nottinghamshire; he is sometimes dated to the 12th century and referred to as the earl of Huntingdon. It has been suggested that he was one of the 13th-century *disinherited followers of Simon de Montfort, but the ballads are also consistent with the peasant unrest prevalent in the 14th century.

Robinson. *See* Goderich, Frederick John Robinson, Viscount; Ripon, George Frederick Samuel Robinson, 1st marquess of.

Rob Roy. *See* MacGregor (or Campbell), Robert.

Robsart, Amy (1532-60). Wife of Elizabeth I's favourite Robert Dudley (later earl of *Leicester). She was found dead with a broken neck, having apparently fallen down stairs. It was rumoured that Dudley and possibly also Elizabeth, wishing to marry, were responsible for her death.

Rochdale Pioneers. Forerunners of the modern *cooperative movement. A group of workmen, they opened a cooperative shop in Toad Lane, Rochdale, in 1844. Adapting Robert *Owen's ideas, they invented the dividend system, sharing profits among society members according to purchases made.

Roches, Peter des (d. 1238). Bishop of Winchester from 1205. A *Poitevin favourite of King John, he was very unpopular with the English. In 1234, under pressure from the barons, Henry III confined him to purely spiritual duties.

Rockingham, Charles Watson-Wentworth, 2nd marquess of (1730-82). Leader of a group of *Whigs who opposed the war with the American colonists. He succeeded to the Whig leadership of the duke of Newcastle in 1762 and became first lord of the treasury in July 1765. His administration, lasting until July 1766, repealed the *Stamp Act imposing duties on the American colonists but passed a Declaratory Act asserting Britain's sovereignty over the colonies. In opposition he advocated conciliation towards America and after Lord *North's resignation again became first lord (March 1782). His government initiated peace negotiations with the Americans, secured the legislative independence of the Irish parliament, and began to implement Edmund *Burke's "economical" reforms. Rockingham died suddenly in office (July 1782).

Rodney, George Brydges Rodney, 1st Baron (1719-1792). Naval commander whose many exploits included his capture of St Lucia and Grenada (1762) and the victory of *Cape St Vincent and relief of Gibraltar (1780). In 1782 he scored a notable victory over the French at the battle of the *Saints.

Roger of Salisbury (d. 1139). Bishop of Salisbury. A Norman priest, he entered the household of *Henry I and became chancellor (1101) and bishop of Salisbury (1102). Thereafter, he was the most powerful and influential of Henry's administrators and was responsible for many administrative and financial reforms. In 1135 he was appointed justiciar by Stephen, but in 1139 his enemies among the barons brought about his arrest and removal from office.

Roger of Wendover (d. 1236). Chronicler. A Benedictine monk at St Albans, he compiled *Flores historiarum*, which, beginning with the Creation, extends to 1235. It is a valuable source for the history of the period in which Roger lived.

Roman Britain. The Roman *province of Britain, established in 43 AD (*see* Roman conquest), fell into two distinct areas, the civil zone south of a line from

Roman Britain, with the territories of the British tribes

the Humber to the Mersey and the military zone north of this line. The civil zone showed an uneven distribution of population and civilization. Parts of the country show evidence of a numerous and wealthy population while other areas, notably the Midlands, seem to have been sparsely populated. There were a number of towns in the civil zone, five of municipal status, and all linked by an efficient road system. According to Tacitus by the governorship of Agricola the British population had begun to acquire Roman civilization and Latin became the language of communication between most sections of the population. Town life flourished and local government developed as the romanized British aristocracy were encouraged to participate. Trade and industry expanded rapidly during the period of consolidation. Pottery and metalwork were noteworthy, with the potteries of the Nene valley exporting all over the island. The period of consolidation is marked by the increase in estates with farm-houses, the whole complex being called a *villa.

The military zone shows none of the characteristics of the civil zone. Nearly 40 000 men were maintained in the province based in three legionary fortresses at York, Chester, and Caerleon with smaller auxiliary forts in disturbed areas or along the border. Over a hundred forts were constructed in Britain, although not all were in existence at the same time. In the military zone the British tribes were far less affected by Roman civilization.

The period of decline began shortly before 350. The Pictish tribes to the north made incursions across Hadrian's wall, Saxon pirates made raids on the southeast coast, and a line of forts was constructed for defence. In 367-68 there seems to have been extensive destruction by a combination of Saxon and Pictish forces. The British defences were weakened by the ambitions of governors of Britain who led their troops across the Channel to claim the imperial throne. In 410, in the face of barbarian pressure at a number of points on the northern frontier of the empire, the emperor Honorius severed connection with the British province. The period of Roman decline and the rise of the Saxon kingdoms (see heptarchy) is one of the most obscure periods of British history.

Roman Catholics. In England after the *Reformation, Roman Catholics, in common with other *recusants were liable to fines under the Acts of *Uniformity (1552, 1559), although these penal-

ties were not often enforced until the excommunication of Elizabeth I (1570). Roman Catholic and *Jesuit involvement in the *northern rebellion (1569), *Ridolfi plot (1571), *Throckmorton plot (1583), and *Babington conspiracy (1586), which aimed to place Mary Queen of Scots on the English throne, resulted in a series of anti-Catholic *penal laws (1571-93). Catholicism continued to be strong in the north and west of England, and from 1598 Catholics were organized under their own archpriest. The recusancy laws were reinforced in James I's reign following the *bye plot (1603) and the *gunpowder plot (1604-05), but under Charles I, through the influence of his Catholic wife Henrietta Maria, they were lightly enforced. The first post-Reformation Catholic bishop was appointed in 1623, and in 1634 Maryland was founded as a Catholic colony; most Catholics supported Charles during the Civil War. They were tacitly tolerated during the Commonwealth and the Protectorate but were again persecuted after the Restoration. The first *Test Act (1673) excluded Catholics from all civil and military offices while the second, which followed the *popish plot (1678), excluded Catholics from parliament. James II's openly pro-Catholic policies were largely responsible for the *Glorious Revolution (1688), which brought further restrictions on Catholics. Although Catholicism was unofficially tolerated by the Hanoverians, the Roman Catholic Relief Act (1778), under which Catholics were enabled to acquire landed property, provoked the *Gordon riots, and Irish Catholics continued to be subject to the *Penal Code. *Catholic emancipation was not obtained until 1829, when Catholics were admitted to parliament and all property-owning restrictions were removed. The present English Catholic hierarchy was established in 1850, provoking considerable controversy, but the last major anti-Catholic legislation was repealed in 1871, when the University Tests Act allowed Catholics (and nonconformists) to take degrees and hold office in the universities.

In Ireland, the Catholic church was recognized in the 1937 constitution as having a special position in the country; this clause was repealed after a referendum in 1973.

Roman conquest. The Romans first came to Britain in 55 and 54 BC, when Julius *Caesar made two inconclusive raids. These were followed by a century of trading contact during which, as archaeological evidence shows, Roman influences on the upper classes in the south of Britain increased. Augustus contemplated an invasion, and Caligula led an army as far as Boulogne. However, it was not until 43 AD that Claudius determined on conquest. Four legions and auxiliary troops were sent under the command of Aulus Plautius, governor of Pannonia. They landed at Richborough (Rutupiae) in Kent and marched inland. They were virtually unopposed until they reached the *Medway, where the Britons resisted for two days. Claudius himself then came to Britain and entered Colchester, where he received the surrender of a number of tribes. The south of England was quickly conquered and by 48 the governor Publius Ostorius Scapula was campaigning in Wales. The revolt of *Boudicca (61) temporarily halted the progress of the conquest, but under the governorship of *Agricola (78-84) the Romans advanced well into the Scottish Highlands. However, the expense of maintaining a Roman presence there was regarded by the imperial government as unjustified, and most of Agricola's northern conquests were abandoned. In 122 the northern frontier of the province was established by the construction of *Hadrian's wall, which remained the main barrier to invasion from Scotland, despite the construction further north of the *Antonine wall (142). In the south of England the Roman conquest was completed during the governorship of Agricola, and archaeological evidence indicates few military installations in the civilian zone after this date. See also Roman Britain.

Romney, George (1732-1802). Portrait painter, best known for his portraits of Lady Hamilton. Building up a fashionable clientele, he rivalled Reynolds in popularity but never attained the distinction of his great contemporary.

Root and Branch petition (1640). A petition, demanding the abolition of episcopal church government, debated by the Commons in Feb 1641. The resulting Root and Branch bill was designed to abolish episcopacy "with all its dependencies, roots and branches". The bill, which only received a second reading, rallied pro-episcopal feeling behind the king.

Rory O'Connor (d. 1198). King of Connaught (1156-86, 1186-91) and the last high king of Ireland (1166-75). His seizure of *Dermot MacMurrough's territories brought an Anglo-Norman force to Ireland on Dermot's behalf (1170). Defeated near Dublin (1171), Rory subsequently submitted (1175) to Henry II of England and was recognized by the English as high king. He was briefly ousted from Connaught in 1186 and in 1191 retired to a monastery.

Rosebery, Archibald Philip Primrose, 5th earl of (1847-1929). Prime minister (1894-95). He served in Gladstone's second ministry, first as undersecretary at the Home Office, with responsibility for Scottish affairs (1881-83), and then as lord privy seal (1885), with a seat in the cabinet, where he was largely responsible for the creation of the Scottish Office. Foreign secretary under Gladstone in 1886, he became first chairman of the London County Council in 1889, returning as foreign secretary (1892-94) in Gladstone's fourth administration. A firm Liberal Imperialist, Rosebery established a protectorate over Uganda (1894). Succeeding Gladstone as prime minister (Mar 1894), Rosebery failed to carry Liberal legislation through the House of Lords, except for the budget in 1894, which was notable for the introduction of *death duties. Plagued by cabinet disputes, Rosebery resigned in June 1895, after defeat in the Commons, and relinquished the Liberal leadership in 1896. He subsequently became a successful racehorse owner and wrote a number of political biographies.

Roses, Wars of the (1455-85). Dynastic wars fought between the houses of *Lancaster and *York for the English crown, the name deriving from their supposed use as badges of the red and white roses respectively. Both families claimed royal right by descent from Edward III: the Lancastrians (represented by Henry VI) by direct male descent from *John of Gaunt, fourth son of Edward III, and the Yorkists (represented by *Richard, duke of York) in the female line from Lionel, Edward's third son (see Plantagenet, house of). The long minority (1422-37) of Henry VI allowed the development of baronial factions on the regency council, and his incompetent personal rule, punctuated by bouts of insanity, further contributed to the decline of respect for the king and to the increasing power of great magnates, such as the Beauforts and their opponents Richard, duke of York, and Richard *Neville, earl of Warwick (the kingmaker). Mismanagement of and defeat by France in the *Hundred Years' War further contributed to unrest, and it was widely believed that William de la *Pole, 1st duke of Suffolk, a supporter of Henry Beaufort, had made a shameful and treacherous peace with France through the influence of the queen *Margaret of Anjou. At the same time baronial struggles were reflected in increasing disorder in the counties as local government officials came under the domination of the magnates, and local feuds were taken up at a national level (see bastard feudalism).

Open warfare between the factions broke out in a skirmish at the first battle of *St Albans in 1455. Henry VI was injured and Edmund Beaufort, 2nd duke of Somerset, was killed. Although in the ascendant, York did not claim the crown until 1460, when he was recognized as Henry's heir and the king's own son Edward, prince of Wales, was disinherited. York was killed shortly afterwards at *Wakefield, but in 1461 his son Edward, after his victory at *Mortimer's Cross, seized the crown as Edward IV and crushed the Lancastrians in a series of battles at *Towton, *Hedgeley Moor, and *Hexham. Edward's support of the Woodville family after his secret marriage (1464) to Elizabeth Woodville aroused the opposition of his brother George, duke of *Clarence, and his most powerful supporter, Warwick the kingmaker. Their alliance briefly restored Henry VI to the throne in 1470, and Edward fled to the Low Countries. On his return in 1471 he destroyed the Lancastrians at *Barnet (where Warwick was killed) and *Tewkesbury (where Edward, prince of Wales, was killed); Henry VI was killed in the Tower of London shortly afterwards.

War was resumed after the death of Edward IV in 1483, when his brother Richard, duke of Gloucester, seized the throne as *Richard III and Edward's son *Edward V disappeared. Richard was defeated and killed at *Bosworth in 1485 by Henry Tudor, earl of Richmond, supported by a group of disaffected Yorkists. As *Henry VII he defeated a Yorkist revolt, centred on Lambert *Simnel, at *Stoke in 1487, which ended the conflict apart from a few abortive pro-Yorkist plots.

The civil wars lasted for more than 30 years. However, they were not continuous but a series of outbreaks between periods of armed peace or, as was the case for much of Edward IV's reign, comparative harmony.

Ross, Sir James Clark (1800-62). Arctic explorer, nephew of Sir John *Ross, whom he accompanied on his first and second Arctic expeditions. In 1831, Ross discovered the north magnetic pole, and in his Antarctic expedition of 1839-43 he approached to within 257 km (160 mi) of the south pole.

Ross, Sir John (1777-1856). Arctic explorer. Ross commanded three Arctic expeditions (1818, 1829-33, 1850) and published extensive accounts of his voyages (1819, 1835). In 1850 led an unsuccessful expedition to search for Sir John Franklin.

Rotherham, Thomas (1423-1500). Archbishop of York from 1480 and chancellor of England (1474-83). He took part in diplomatic missions to the courts of France and Burgundy. After Edward IV's death he was deprived of the chancellorship by Richard III and briefly imprisoned.

Rothschild, Lionel Nathan de (1808-79). Banker, who was the first person of the Jewish faith to become an MP. Elected in 1847, and five times re-elected, he was not allowed to take his seat, owing to the wording of the parliamentary oath (taken "on the true faith of a Christian"), until 1858. His son Nathan, Baron Rothschild (1840-1915), was the first peer of the Jewish faith.

rotten borough. A borough constituency so decayed that it was altogether disfranchised by the *Reform Act (1832). Examples are Gatton, which was a gentleman's park, Old Sarum, which was a green mound, and Dunwich, which had for centuries been submerged under the North Sea. In these and many other boroughs a single landowner was able to nominate MPs, or had the seat "in his pocket"—hence the term pocket (or nomination) borough.

Rough Wooing. The immensely destructive English invasions of Scotland in 1544 and 1545, ordered by Henry VIII after the failure of negotiations to marry his son Prince Edward to Mary Queen of Scots.

roundheads. *See* parliamentarians.

Round Table conferences (1930-32). Three conferences held in London to seek agreement on constitutional change for British India. At the first conference (1930-31) the Indian princes agreed to all-Indian federation and Britain granted responsible government to the provinces. No progress was made at the second conference (1931) because of *Gandhi's insistence upon communal representation in an Indian assembly. Following the third conference (1932) Britain issued proposals that resulted in the Government of *India Act (1935).

Roundway Down, battle of (13 July 1643). A battle of the Civil War fought 3 km (2 mi) north of Devizes in Wiltshire between royalist troops under Lord Wilmot (?1612-1658; later 1st earl of Rochester) and the western parliamentary army commanded by Sir William *Waller. The parliamentarians suffered a disastrous reverse, losing all their cannon and much of their ammunition and baggage.

Rowlandson, Thomas (1756-1827). Artist and caricaturist. From about 1781, Rowlandson steadily developed as a political and social satirist, especially of low life in London, as in *The English Dance of Death* (1815-16). His other work includes *Vauxhall Gardens* (1784) and *The Tours of Dr Syntax* (1812-20).

Royal Academy. An institution for the promotion of painting, sculpture, and architecture. It was founded (with George III's encouragement) in 1768 and its first president was Joshua *Reynolds. Since 1869 its home has been at Burlington House, Piccadilly, where it holds its summer exhibitions (of work by its members, associate members, and other living artists) and winter exhibitions and maintains its teaching schools.

Royal Air Force (RAF). The most recently established of the three British armed services. Formed on 1 April 1918 from the amalgamation of its predecessors, the Royal Flying Corps and the Royal Naval Air Service, during the 1930s the RAF was built up as an independent bomber and antibomber force and from 1937 received priority over both the army and the Royal Navy in the allocation of defence funds. In 1964 the RAF, with the other armed services, was placed under the Ministry of Defence.

Royal Exchange. An institution in the City of London, between Cornhill and Threadneedle Street. Founded by Sir Thomas *Gresham as a meeting place for merchants and bankers, it was modelled on the Antwerp exchange. The original structure (built 1566-71) was destroyed in the Fire of London (1666), rebuilt (1667-69), again destroyed by fire (1838), and again rebuilt (1842-44).

royal household. The sovereign's retinue. Originally, its functions were domestic, but by the 12th century it was the mainspring of government. The great departments of state, such as the Treasury, the Exchequer, and the common law courts, originated in the household, but went "out of court" in the middle ages. The *Chamber and *Wardrobe remained government institutions until the 1530s. By the end of the 16th century the household consisted of the departments of the *lord steward (below stairs) and the *lord chamberlain (above stairs), responsible for the physical wellbeing of the sovereign and for court ceremonial respectively. Some offices became sinecures. The link between the royal household and national finance ended in 1782, but as late as 1839 the *bedchamber crisis demonstrated the political significance of the household. *See also* curia regis.

Royal Institution. An organization for the promotion of scientific knowledge, founded in 1799 and incorporated in 1800. It rapidly became a leading research centre, establishing laboratories in which Sir Humphry Davy, Michael Faraday, and other 19th-century pioneers worked. It is also known for its lectures for members and for children.

royalists. Supporters of Charles I from 1640 to 1649 and, following his execution, of his son Charles (II). They are also called cavaliers, originally a derogatory name for the gallants who rallied to the king's cause. The royalists emerged as an identifiable party during the breakdown of relations between the king and the Long Parliament, in which they constituted the supporters of episcopacy against the *Root and Branch petition (1641). Similarly, in the country at large they were united by support for the established church, as well as for the crown, against which many felt unable to take up arms. Representatives of all sections of society were numbered among the royalists, who, however, included most of the great landowners

and peers and virtually all Roman Catholics. Geographically, after the outbreak of war, the king's cause was strongest in the north and the west. Following their defeat an ordinance of general pardon and oblivion was passed (1651), in spite of which many royalist estates were confiscated. A tax of 10% on royalist incomes was imposed after the royalist *Penruddock's rising (1655). With the *Restoration most royalists recovered their estates, the exception being those who had mortgaged or sold their property in return for indemnity. The parliament of 1661-79, which consolidated the Restoration, is sometimes called the cavalier parliament. *Compare* parliamentarians.

Royal Marriages Act (1772). An act laying down conditions for marriages of the royal family. The act was instigated by George III after two of his brothers, the duke of Cumberland and the duke of Gloucester, married commoners without his approval. It specifies that members of the royal family cannot contract valid marriages without the sovereign's consent, unless they are over 25 and give 12 months' notice to the Privy Council.

Royal Pavilion. A small residence in Brighton bought for the prince regent (later George IV). Built in a conventional picturesque style in 1784, it was remodelled by Nash after 1818 in a remarkably eclectic combination of classical and eastern styles, employing minarets and onion-shaped domes.

Royal Society. The principal British scientific society. The Society emerged from meetings, dating from 1645, of scientists, philosophers, and other thinking persons. Formally established in 1660, it was granted its first royal charter in 1662. Early fellows (members) included Sir Christopher Wren, Samuel Pepys, and Sir Isaac Newton (who was president from 1703 to 1727). Fellowship of the Royal Society has become one of the world's highest scientific distinctions. *Compare* British Academy.

Rubens, Sir Peter Paul (1577-1640). Flemish painter. He came to England in 1629 as an envoy of Philip IV of Spain and negotiated a peace treaty for which he was knighted by Charles I (1630). He subsequently decorated the ceiling of the Whitehall banqueting hall (completed c. 1634).

Rump. Those members of the *Long Parliament who retained their seats after *Pride's purge (6 Dec 1648) and declared the *Commonwealth of England. Increasingly corrupt and ineffective, the Rump (or remnant of the Long Parliament) refused dissolution until Cromwell's soldiers ejected it (20 April 1653), replacing it with the *Barebones parliament. This expulsion ("the interruption") caused lasting hostility between soldiers and civilians on the republican side. However, in 1659, after the collapse of the Protectorate, the army reconvened the Rump to fill the legislative vacuum. It proved meddlesome and intransigent and was once again expelled. *Monck effected its recall and, as demands for a full and free parliament grew, forced the Rump to readmit members excluded by Pride's purge. In March 1660 parliament dissolved itself and in April the *convention parliament assembled to effect the Restoration.

Runneymede. A meadow on the south bank of the Thames, near Egham in Surrey, where on 15 June 1215 King John met his rebellious barons and agreed to the *Magna Carta.

Rupert, Prince (1619-82). The leading royalist commander in the *Civil War. Son of Frederick V, Elector Palatine, and Elizabeth of Bohemia (sister of Charles I), Rupert grew up in exile with his family in the United Provinces and, becoming a soldier of fortune, joined Charles I in 1642. He became famous for leading daring cavalry actions. He held command at *Edgehill (1642), won a series of victories in 1643-44, but was outmanoeuvred at *Marston Moor (1644) and *Naseby (1645). After surrendering Bristol he was dismissed from his post in 1645 and banished from England by parliament in 1646. In the 1650s he turned to piracy, preying on Commonwealth ships, and after the Restoration was given naval commands against the Dutch. He also interested himself in scientific experiments and introduced mezzotint printing into England.

Russell, Bertrand Russell, 3rd Earl (1872-1970). Philosopher, grandson of Lord John Russell. His early work on mathematical logic was published in *Principles of Mathematics* (1903) and *Principia Mathematica* (1910-13), which he wrote with Alfred North Whitehead (1861-1947). His later works include *The Analysis of Matter* (1927) and the best-selling *History of Western Philosophy* (1945). Imprisoned in 1918 for pacifism, he was increasingly engaged in political activities. He became an opponent of nuclear weapons and helped found the *Campaign for Nuclear Disarmament (1958). In 1950 he won the Nobel prize for literature.

Russell, Lord John, 1st Earl Russell (1792-1878). Prime minister (1846-52, 1865-66). Whig MP from 1813, Russell advocated parliamentary reform (*see* Reform Acts) from 1819 and promoted the abolition of the *Test and *Corporation Acts (1828). Paymaster general under Grey and Melbourne (1830-34), he was largely responsible for drafting the 1831 reform bill. Home secretary (1835-39) and secretary for war and the colonies (1839-41) in Melbourne's second ministry, he carried through municipal reform (1835) and the Act of Union (1840) with Canada. After *Peel's fall, Russell was prime minister (July 1846-Feb 1852). Although preoccupied with famine in Ireland and with Chartism, he enacted factory legislation and a major Public Health Act (1848). Becoming a minister in Aberdeen's coalition (1852), he unsuccessfully proposed further franchise reform. He supported the *Crimean War but resigned in Jan 1855 over its mismanagement; colonial secretary under Palmerston (Feb-July 1855), he resigned after criticism of his share in peace negotiations. In Palmerston's second cabinet, he became foreign secretary (June 1859). Together with Palmerston, he promoted

Italian unification, but their stance during the American Civil War (including the *Alabama affair) brought a momentary risk of Anglo-American hostilities, and attempts to prevent the 1864 Prussian-Danish war failed. Russell (created earl, 1861) succeeded Palmerston as prime minister in Oct 1865, retiring after defeat of his government's franchise bill in June 1866.

Rutherford, Ernest Rutherford, 1st Baron (1871-1937). New Zealand-born physicist. Working on the nature of radioactivity, he discovered that an atom has a positively charged dense core—the nucleus. He was professor of experimental physics and director of the Cavendish Laboratory at Cambridge (1919-37) and was awarded the Nobel prize in 1908.

Ruthven, battle of (20 June 1306). A battle in which the English under Aymer de Valence decisively defeated a small Scots army under Robert the Bruce. In spite of attempts to rally his forces, Bruce was forced to flee and many of his followers were imprisoned or executed.

Ruthven raid (1582). The abduction in Aug 1582 of the young James VI of Scotland by an extreme Protestant faction led by William Ruthven, 1st earl of Gowrie (?1541-1584). The kidnappers wished to free the king from the influence of Esmé Stuart, duke of Lennox, who was feared to be plotting the restoration of Catholicism. James escaped in June 1583 and pardoned Gowrie, who, however, was executed in 1584 after being involved in a further plot. See also Gowrie *conspiracy".

Rye House plot (1683). A conspiracy to assassinate Charles II and his brother James, duke of York, as they travelled from Newmarket races to London past Rye House in Hertfordshire. The plot aborted but was betrayed to the government. *Monmouth, Algernon *Sidney, and several prominent Whigs were implicated.

Ryswick, peace of (20 Sept 1697). The peace settlement, signed by the plenipotentiaries of France, England, the Netherlands, Spain, and the Holy Roman Empire, that concluded the War of the Grand Alliance (1688-97). Louis XIV of France surrendered most of the territorial gains he had made since the treaty of Nijmegen (1676) and recognized William III as king of England and Anne as his successor. The settlement tipped the balance of European power in favour of the Habsburgs of Spain and the Empire.

S

Sabah. See North Borneo.

sac and soc. See soke.

Sacheverell, Henry (c. 1674-1724). Preacher of High Church and Tory views. In 1709 he delivered two inflammatory sermons against the ideals of the Glorious Revolution (1688-89) and was impeached by the Whig government and suspended from preaching for three years (1710). Popular protests and the fall of the Whigs in Oct 1710 led to his appointment to the living of Selattyn.

Sackville, George Sackville Germain, 1st Viscount (1716-85). Politician and soldier. Originally Lord George Sackville, he adopted the surname Germain in 1770 and became Viscount Sackville in 1782. An MP (1741-82), he rose in the army to become a general but was cashiered after the battle of Minden (1759), during the Seven Years' War, for refusing to go into the attack when ordered. He returned to public life under George III, who thought him unjustly condemned.

St Albans. See Verulamium.

St Albans, battles of. Two battles of the Wars of the Roses. 1. (22 May 1455) A battle caused by the struggle for power that followed the conclusion of the protectorate of Richard, duke of York. It was a convincing victory for the Yorkists. Henry VI was wounded and several Lancastrian nobles were killed. 2. (17 Feb 1461) A battle in which Queen

Margaret and the Lancastrians defeated the forces of Warwick the kingmaker. They rescued Henry VI but were unable to prevent the accession of Edward IV ten days later.

St Brice's day, massacre of (13 Nov 1002). The slaughter of Danes resident in England. Fearing Danish plots against him, *Aethelred II ordered the massacre, which provoked the Danish invasion of 1003.

St Ffagan, battle of (8 May 1648). The only major battle of the Civil War fought in Wales, near St Ffagan on the western outskirts of Cardiff. An army, led by rebellious parliamentarians in Pembrokeshire, planned to capture Cardiff but was heavily defeated by Cromwell's troops under Col Thomas Horton, who had moved south from Brecon to combat them.

Saint-Germain, treaty of (10 Sept 1919). The peace treaty imposed on Austria after World War I. The treaty confirmed the dissolution of the former Austro-Hungarian empire by distributing many of its territories (including the German-speaking areas of the Sudetenland and South Tyrol) between Czechoslovakia, Italy, Poland, Romania, and Yugoslavia. Austria itself was effectively prohibited from forming a union with Germany.

St Helena. An island in the South Atlantic and a British colony. Successfully resisting Dutch claims, the British *East India Company controlled this important pre-Suez port from 1659 until 1834, when Britain established direct government. Napoleon I was exiled here from 1815 until his death (1821).

St John, Henry. *See* Bolingbroke, 1st Viscount.

St Kitts (or St Christopher). An island in the West Indies. Settled originally by the English (1628), it was formally ceded to Britain in 1783, after years of dispute with the French. In 1871, together with its dependency Nevis, it became part of the *Leeward Islands. St Kitts and Nevis became with Anguilla a West Indies Associated State in 1967.

St Lucia. One of the *Windward Islands. After crushing the resistance of the indigenous Caribs, French and English settlers disputed possession of St Lucia throughout the 17th and 18th centuries. The island was finally ceded to Britain by the treaty of Paris (1814). It gained independence in 1979.

St Vincent. One of the *Windward Islands. French, English, and Dutch settlers arrived in the 18th century, the English finally gaining possession of the island in 1783. The indigenous Caribs revolted in 1795 but were crushed and deported. St Vincent became a West Indies Associated State in 1967 and gained full independence in 1979. As secretary of state for the colonies (1775-82) he bore the major responsibility for Britain's war effort during the American Revolution.

Sackville, Thomas, 1st earl of Dorset (c. 1530-1608). Privy councillor, who conveyed to Mary Queen of Scots her death sentence. In 1598 he succeeded Lord Burghley as lord high treasurer. He also contributed to two major verse works, *A Mirror for Magistrates* (1563) and *Tragedy of Gorboduc* (1561), the first tragedy in English.

Saints, battle of the (12 April 1782). A naval engagement between the French and British off Dominica. The British, under Rodney and Hood, captured or destroyed seven enemy vessels and inflicted some 3000 casualties upon the French, as well as capturing de Grasse, the French admiral.

Salamanca, battle of (22 July 1812). A battle of the Peninsular War, a major British victory. Facing a French army of 40 000 under Marshal Marmont, Wellington, with equal forces, inflicted 15 000 casualties on his enemies at a cost of 5000 of his own troops, and opened the way to Madrid.

Salesbury, William (c. 1520-1584). Welsh Protestant scholar. He was the chief translator of the New Testament into Welsh (1567), in which he was assisted by Bishop Richard *Davies. He also completed a *Welsh-English*

Dictionary (1547) and a collection of Welsh proverbs (1547) and is generally acknowledged to be the most noteworthy Welsh scholar of his age.

Salisbury, 1st earl of. *See* Cecil, Robert.

Salisbury, Robert Arthur Talbot Gascoyne-Cecil, 3rd marquess of (1830–1903). Prime minister (1885–86, 1886–92, 1895–1902). A Conservative MP (1853–68), he first held office as secretary for India (1866–67) under Derby but resigned over the second reform bill. Succeeding to the title in 1868, he was again secretary for India from 1874 to 1878 and then foreign secretary (1878–80) in Disraeli's second administration. He played a prominent part in resolving the Eastern crisis and accompanied Disraeli to the congress of Berlin (1878). Conservative leader after Disraeli's death (1881), he was prime minister of a minority government from June 1885 until Jan 1886. His second ministry, with Liberal Unionist support, saw the extension of British rule in Africa, while at home the *Local Government Act (1888) established county councils. His third administration, a Conservative-Liberal Unionist coalition, was dominated by the second *Boer War (1899–1902) and, at home, by his clashes with Joseph *Chamberlain.

Salvation Army. A religious movement. Founded (1865) by William *Booth in Whitechapel, London, as the Christian Revival Association (1865), it took the name Salvation Army, with an organization on military lines, in 1878. The Army's unorthodox revivalism and militant teetotalism aroused initial hostility, but it became increasingly respected for its outstanding social work. It now operates in some 70 countries.

Samuel, Herbert Samuel, 1st Viscount (1870–1963). Liberal leader. An MP (1902–18, 1929–37), Samuel held government offices (1905–16), serving briefly as home secretary (Jan–Dec 1916) in Asquith's coalition government. In 1925–26 he headed the commission that reported on the coal industry. Samuel joined the *national government (whose formation he inspired), again as home secretary, in Aug 1931, but resigned in Sept 1932, leading the Liberal opposition until 1935. Created viscount in 1937, he led the Liberals in the Lords from 1944 to 1955.

Sancroft, William (1617–93). Archbishop of Canterbury. He became Charles II's chaplain (1660), dean of St Paul's (1664), and archbishop of Canterbury (1678). As leader of the *seven bishops he opposed James II's pro-Catholic *Declaration of Indulgence but refused to acknowledge William and Mary, becoming a *nonjuror.

sanctions. In international relations, measures taken by one state, or group of states, against another that has violated international law. Such sanctions consist usually of economic measures, such as embargo. The idea of sanctions as a means of imposing international peace was developed by the League of Nations, notably—and unsuccessfully—against Italy after its invasion of Ethiopia (1935–36). The best-known subsequent example of sanctions is probably those employed by the UK and the UN against Rhodesia (see Southern Rhodesia) following its unilateral declaration of independence (1965). Their effectiveness remains in dispute.

sanctuary. A place in which a person might take refuge to escape prosecution for an offence. From soon after the introduction of Christianity fugitives were able to claim sanctuary in any church or churchyard (and later also in certain other places, e.g. Whitefriars in London). After 40 days they were obliged to swear their *abjuration of the realm. The right of sanctuary was abolished for criminals in 1623 and for civil offenders in 1723.

Sand River Convention (1852). An agreement on the independence of the *Transvaal. Britain, abandoning attempts to control Afrikaners settled beyond the Vaal after the *great trek, recognized their independence on condition that slavery was banned.

Sandwich, John Montagu, 4th earl of (1718–92). Politician, who, as first lord of the admiralty (1771-82) during the American Revolution, was held responsible for the navy's disastrous unpreparedness for war. Earlier, he had shown himself to be a competent administrator, chiefly at the Admiralty. The sandwich, with which he sustained himself during long hours at the gaming table, is named after him.

Saratoga, battle of (1777). A battle of the American Revolution, in which the British were decisively defeated. The army of Gen. Burgoyne, numbering some 5000 men, was cut off by an American force under Gates and obliged to surrender (17 Oct). The outcome encouraged the French to recognize the United States and to send it military aid, and thus virtually assured American victory.

Sarawak. A state of Malaysia since 1963 and a former British protectorate and colony. Originally part of the sultanate of Brunei in Borneo, Sarawak was granted in 1841 to James Brooke (1803-68), who became rajah. The third rajah, Sir Charles Vyner Brooke (1874-1963), ceded Sarawak to Britain in 1946.

Savery, Thomas (c. 1650-1715). Inventor of the first steam engine (1698). Savery's machine—a steam vacuum pump, for draining water from coalmines—was limited to operation at low pressures and was improved by *Newcomen.

Saxe-Coburg, house of. The sovereigns of the United Kingdom and British Empire from 1901 to 1917. *Albert, consort of Victoria (who was the last sovereign of the house of *Hanover), was a prince of the German duchy of Saxe-Coburg and Gotha (family name: Wettin). Their son Edward VII (1901-10) was therefore the first British sovereign of the house of Saxe-Coburg. His successor George V, however, changed the name to *Windsor. Victoria's second son had meanwhile inherited Saxe-Coburg and Gotha (1893), Edward having renounced his rights to it.

Saxons. A Germanic people who, together with the *Angles and *Jutes, invaded and settled in Britain in the 5th

century. The Saxons, who had for long made pirate attacks on the English coast, which the forts of the Saxon Shore —644 km (400 mi) from the Wash to the Solent—were designed to protect, originated in Schleswig and along the north German Baltic coast. In England they settled especially in western and southern regions, as their early kingdoms of *Wessex, *Essex, *Middlesex, and *Sussex testify.

Saye and Sele, William Fiennes, 1st Viscount (1582-1662). A Puritan member of the House of Lords, who participated in the 1630s in enterprises to establish colonies in New England. A critic of Charles I's policies as a result of his religious convictions and commercial interests, in the *Long Parliament Saye supported the faction that sought not to remove the king but to transfer his powers to parliament. He took little part in the politics of the Interregnum and became lord privy seal at the Restoration.

Scapa Flow. A sheltered expanse of sea in the Orkney Islands and an important naval base in World Wars I and II. The Germans scuttled the Grand Fleet, interned here, in 1919. In World War II a causeway was built to block the eastern approaches, linking several islands.

Schism Act (1714). An act forbidding nonconformists to teach or to keep a school. It was almost entirely ineffective and was repealed in 1719.

Scone. A palace near Perth in Scotland. Originally the site of the coronation of the Scottish kings, it was largely demolished in the 19th century to make way for a country house and park. The stone of Scone, on which the Scottish kings sat at their coronation, was seized by Edward I of England in 1296 and is now housed in Westminster abbey.

Scotia. Originally, Ireland but, from the 9th century, the kingdom created in Scotland north of the Forth by Kenneth I MacAlpin. Later, Scotia came to mean all Scotland. *See also* Scots.

Scots. Originally, the inhabitants of Ireland. They began to settle in western coastal areas of Britain in the 4th and 5th centuries, and many Scots from *Dalriada settled in modern Argyllshire. In about 500 Fergus, king of Dalriada, moved to Argyllshire, the colony having become more important than, and taken the name of, the parent kingdom. Through their conquest of the Picts in the 9th century and their later expansion into Lothian and Strathclyde the kings of Scots gave their name to the kingdoms of *Scotia and, later, of Scotland.

Scott, Robert Falcon (1868-1912). Naval officer and explorer in the Antarctic. He reached the south pole on 18 Jan 1912, only to find that Roald Amundsen's Norwegian expedition had reached it 33 days earlier. Scott and his companions died of cold and hunger on the journey back to their base. A search party found their bodies and Scott's diaries in Nov 1912.

Scott, Sir Walter (1771-1832). Novelist and poet. His Romantic narrative poems, including *Marmion* (1808), brought him wide popularity, but he became one of the first best-selling writers with the Waverley series of novels (1814-32).

scutage. A payment made by a *knight to the king in commutation of services owed for his fee. The term derives from the Latin *scutum*, shield, part of the knight's accoutrement.

SEATO. *See* South-East Asia Treaty Organization.

Sebastopol, siege of (Oct 1854-Sept 1855). The siege of the fortified naval base of Sebastopol during the Crimean War. The Russian forces were surrounded in the town by 50 000 British and French troops soon after their arrival in the Crimea. Resisting all Russian attempts to break out, the allied armies ringed the fortress with trenches and after a massive bombardment forced the defenders to evacuate the ruined town.

Sedgemoor, battle of (6 July 1685). The battle that ended *Monmouth's rebellion against James II. Monmouth's undisciplined forces met the royal army near Bridgewater and were defeated.

seignory. A manor or lordship held of a feudal lord (seigneur) by a tenant, or the rights, such as feudal incidents, possessed by the lord. No new seignories were created after the statute *quia emptores (1290).

select committees. An aspect of the procedure of the *House of Commons. Comprising not more than 15 members, select committees are appointed to consider particular matters and cease to exist once they have reported. They are less formal and less partisan than *standing committees and may receive oral and written evidence. Often concerned with finance, they were widely used in the 19th century.

Self-Denying Ordinance (1645). The proposal by Cromwell's parliamentary supporters that no MP or peer should hold an army commission. The ordinance, which was a response to parliament's military reverses in 1644, was designed as a means of relieving ineffective officers of their command. *Essex and *Manchester lost their commissions, but Cromwell's military successes ensured his re-appointment.

seneschal. *See* steward.

Septennial Act (1716). The act fixing the life of a parliament at a maximum of seven years (instead of three, as previously). Devised to bolster Whig power, it ultimately promoted governmental stability and the authority of the House of Commons. The *Parliament Act (1911) reduced a parliament's life to a maximum of five years.

Septimius Severus, Lucius (146-211). Roman emperor (193-211). In 208 he came to Britain to supervise an invasion of Scotland. Roman losses were severe and peace was made (210). Severus divided the province into Lower and Upper Britain and supervised a substantial repair of *Hadrian's wall.

sequestration. The seizure of the income from a church benefice or other estate. During the Civil War this money-raising measure was extensively used by parliament against active royalists.

serf. An unfree peasant. A serf was tied to the land, which he tilled in return for paying a fee in cash or kind and providing services to his lord. He enjoyed certain rights that distinguished him from a slave (see slavery).

serjeant. A feudal tenant who performed a specialized service for his lord in return for land. His actual duties varied enormously. He might bear his lord's standard, perform ushering duties, or look after the falcons. The practice of making the holding of land dependent on such services was rare by the beginning of the 13th century.

serjeant at law. A person appointed from the 14th century to present a suitor's case in court (compare attorney at law). Also called the Order of the Coif (in reference to the white cap fastened under the chin, which they wore), serjeants had their own inn (see Inns of Court). They were superseded by kings' counsels in the 17th century and the order was abolished in 1870.

Session, Court of. The supreme civil court of Scotland, which emerged in the 15th century and was formally established as the College of Justice in 1532. The judges, the senators of the College of Justice, are more commonly referred to as the lords of session.

Settlement, Acts of. 1. (1652) An act passed following Cromwell's suppression of the *Irish rebellion (1641). A hundred named leaders of the revolt, together with anyone who had participated in its early stages and who had killed an Englishman except in battle, lost their lives and estates. Other leaders of the Irish army lost two-thirds of their estates, and anyone who had not demonstrated "constant good affection" to the English lost one-third and was liable for transportation to Connaught or Clare. The severity of the act was lessened by further legislation in 1662. **2.** (1662) A *poor law designed to control vagrancy. It enabled parish overseers to compel a person not born in their parish and having no land or work to return to his native parish. **3.** The act that secured the Hanoverian succession to the thrones of England and Ireland. It stipulated that if William III and his sister in law Anne died without heirs, the throne should pass to *Sophia, electress of Hanover, or her Protestant descendants. The act also required the sovereign to be a member of the Church of England and not to leave England or make war to protect foreign possessions without parliamentary approval. It also debarred foreigners from office and parliament. In 1714, on the death of Queen Anne, George I of Hanover succeeded to the thrones of Great Britain (Scotland having united with England in 1707) and Ireland.

seven bishops, trial of the (1688). The trial of Archbishop *Sancroft and six other bishops. James II ordered that his *Declaration of Indulgence, permitting liberty of worship, should be read on two successive Sundays (20 May and 27 May 1688 in London, 3 and 10 June elsewhere) in all Anglican churches. A meeting held by Sancroft resulted in a petition of protest being presented to the king on 18 May. The bishops were imprisoned and tried for seditious libel but were found not guilty, a verdict widely welcomed.

Seven Years' War (1756–63). A conflict between Prussia, Britain, and Hanover on one side and Austria, France, Russia, Saxony, Sweden, and Spain on the other (see diplomatic revolution). Britain's involvement was brought about by its struggle with France for supremacy in India and North America, and the war was precipitated by the French attack on Minorca. The continental conflict was provoked by the invasion of Saxony by Frederick the Great of Prussia and ended with the treaty of Hubertusburg (1763), which established Prussian supremacy. Overseas, *Clive, in India, and *Wolfe, in North America, won a series of victories for the British, whose position as the leading colonial power was established by the treaty of *Paris (1763).

Severus, Lucius Septimius. See Septimius Severus, Lucius.

Sexby, Edward (d. 1658). Parliamentarian, who served in Cromwell's army. He was one of the *agitators who took part in the *Putney debates and was sent on diplomatic missions to France and Spain. An opponent of the Protectorate, he took part in *Penruddock's rising (1655) and fled to Flanders. Returning in 1657, he was arrested and died in the Tower. He wrote *Killing No Murder* (1657), an apology for tyrannicide directed against Cromwell.

Seychelles. An archipelago in the Indian Ocean. Strategically situated but remote, the Seychelles were ceded to Britain by France in 1814 and formed a dependency of *Mauritius until 1903. They became a crown colony until they achieved independence in 1976.

Seymour, William, 1st marquess and 2nd earl of Hertford and 2nd duke of Somerset (1588-1660). Grandson of Edward Seymour (the protector). He was imprisoned for marrying Arabella *Stuart in 1610 without James I's consent and escaped to France; he was allowed to return in 1615. He supported Charles I during the Civil War, attended him during his imprisonment, and welcomed Charles II to England at the Restoration in 1660.

Seymour of Sudeley, Thomas Seymour, Baron (c. 1508-1549). Diplomat and soldier, lord high admiral of England from 1547. He married (1547) Henry VIII's widow, Catherine Parr, and, after her death (1548), attempted to obtain the hand of Princess Elizabeth. He also encouraged opposition to his elder brother Somerset with the aim of assuming his role as protector, and was convicted of treason and executed.

Shackleton, Sir Ernest (1874-1922). Antarctic explorer, who led an expedition to within 155 km (97 mi) of the south pole in 1909. His second expedition was notable for a 1500-km (800-mi) voyage in a whaleboat after his ship, the *Endurance*, was crushed by ice (1916). He died in Antarctica.

Shaftesbury, Anthony Ashley Cooper, 1st earl of (1621-83). Politician. He served (1653-54) on Cromwell's Council of State, but took part in the Restoration of Charles II and, as Baron Ashley,

became chancellor of the exchequer (1661) and a member of the *cabal. He criticized the severity of the *Clarendon code, desiring toleration of nonconformists. As lord chancellor (1672-73), however, he supported the anti-Catholic *Test Act (1673) and was dismissed. In 1677-78, after attempting to force the dissolution of parliament, he was imprisoned. Following his release he secured passage of *habeas corpus and supported the *exclusion bill (1679), attempting at the time of the *popish plot to have the duke of York prosecuted for recusancy. In 1681 he was arrested for treason but the case against him was dismissed. After trying unsuccessfully to organize a revolt he fled to Holland (1682). He is portrayed as Achitophel in Dryden's *Absalom and Achitophel*.

Shaftesbury, Anthony Ashley Cooper, 7th earl of (1801-85). Social reformer. Shaftesbury (Lord Ashley, 1811-51), a prominent evangelical Christian, became leader (1832) of the so-called "ten-hour movement" for limiting by statute factory working hours. He was the driving force behind successive *factory acts (1833-50), which limited hours for women and children, and, effectively, for many men. Shaftesbury also helped achieve the *Mines Act (1842), banning underground employment of females and small boys.

Shakespeare, William (1564-1616). Dramatist and poet regarded as the greatest writer in English literature. He was born and educated in Stratford-upon-Avon, had joined the Lord Chamberlain's Men as an actor and playwright by 1592, and became one of the landlords of the new Globe theatre in 1598. Shakespeare's chief English history plays, for which *Holinshed is the main source, are *Henry VI*, parts 1-3, *Richard III* (1589-92), *Richard II*, *Henry IV*, parts 1-2 (1594-97), *Henry V* (1599), *Macbeth* (1599), and *Henry VIII* (1612-13).

Shaw, George Bernard (1856-1950). Dramatist and socialist. Irish-born, Shaw settled in England in 1876 and began writing plays in the early 1890s.

His works include the four *Plays: Pleasant and Unpleasant* (1898), *Pygmalion* (1912), and *St Joan of Arc* (1923). He was awarded the Nobel prize in 1925 and was a leading member of the *Fabian Society.

Shelburne, 2nd earl of. *See* Lansdowne, William Petty, 1st marquess of.

Sheraton, Thomas (1751-1806). Furniture designer. In common with Chippendale and Hepplewhite, he exercised a wide influence through his style books (1791, 1803). His neoclassical designs are firm yet delicate and are notable for their use of marquetry decoration.

Sheridan, Richard Brinsley (1751-1816). Dramatist, MP, and orator. Sheridan remains famous for brilliant comedies like *The School for Scandal* (1777). Politically, he was a faithful ally of Charles James *Fox.

sheriff. A royal official who, from the early 11th century, came to replace the *earl as the king's chief agent in the *shire. The sheriff (or shire reeve) was responsible for financial administration, the collection and local assessment of royal taxes, and the supervision of royal estates. He also sat in the shire court —although he did not preside over it until after the Norman conquest. Abuse of their powers by sheriffs led to an inquest (1170), following which many were dismissed. The office lost its importance by the 16th century, and the sheriff's duties now comprise chiefly the supervision of parliamentary elections, executing writs, and the summoning of jurors.

Sheriffmuir, battle of (13 Nov 1715). An engagement during the Fifteen Rebellion between 10 000 *Jacobite rebels under the earl of Mar and 3300 loyalist Scots under the duke of Argyll. After an indecisive action, in which each side suffered about 500 casualties, Mar retreated. His rising collapsed and he later abandoned his followers.

ship money. A tax imposed by Charles I during the 'eleven years' tyranny. In 1634 Charles, in accordance with ancient right, levied ship money from the mari-time towns and shires to meet naval expenses. In 1635, however, he extended the tax to inland areas and continued to do so annually until 1640. In 1635 John *Hampden refused to pay, and in the subsequent test case the judges pronounced in favour of the crown (1638). Ship money was made illegal by the *Long Parliament in 1641.

shire. A unit of local government that originated in 8th- and 9th-century Wessex. The shire system, which replaced the Roman *provinces, was later extended to cover the whole of England. A shire usually took its name from its principal city. The king's interest was represented by an *ealdorman and later by a *sheriff, who presided over the shire court and was responsible for the militia (*see* fyrd). The shires were replaced after the Norman conquest by the *counties.

Short Parliament (13 April-5 May 1640). The parliament summoned by Charles I to grant him funds for the *Bishops' Wars. However, after the *eleven years' tyranny its members, under the eloquent leadership of *Pym, were determined to discuss and obtain redress for the nation's grievances before voting the king any money. Charles, therefore, abruptly and unwisely dissolved parliament. *See also* Long Parliament.

Shrewsbury, battle of (21 July 1403). A battle fought at Hateley Field (present-day Battlefield), north of Shrewsbury, between the forces of Henry IV and an army of rebels led by Sir Henry *Percy (or Hotspur). The royal army won a decisive victory, in which Hotspur was killed.

Shrewsbury, Charles Talbot, 12th earl and duke of (1660-1718). Brought up as a Roman Catholic, he became an Anglican in 1679 and was one of the seven signatories of the letter inviting William of Orange to take the English throne in 1688. He subsequently served William as secretary of state (1689-90, 1694-98) but then withdrew from politics until 1710. As lord high treasurer on the death of Queen Anne (1714) he secured the peaceful succession of the Hanoverian George I.

Shrewsbury, Elizabeth Talbot, countess of (1518-1608). Builder of Hardwick Hall in Derbyshire and of the original *Chatsworth, on the estates of her second husband Sir William Cavendish (d. 1557). Known as Bess of Hardwick (her father was John Hardwick of Hardwick), she and her fourth husband, George Talbot, 6th earl of Shrewsbury (d. 1590), were entrusted with the custody of Mary Queen of Scots in 1569.

Shrewsbury, John Talbot, 1st earl of (?1388-1453). Soldier, who fought in the Hundred Years' War during the reigns of Henry V and Henry VI; the earldom of Shrewsbury was one of the several honours he received in reward. His bravery earned him the sobriquet, the English Achilles, and his death at the battle of *Castillon contributed to the English failure to maintain their claims in France.

Shrewsbury, parliament at (Jan 1398). The parliament that, after being adjourned by Richard II to Shrewsbury following its session in 1397 at Westminster, repealed the acts of the *Merciless Parliament. It also established a committee of 18 to examine the accusation of treason made by Henry Bolingbroke against Thomas *Mowbray, duke of Norfolk, and a second committee to hear outstanding petitions.

Siddons, Mrs Sarah (1755-1831). Actress. Born Sarah Kemble, sister of John Philip and Charles Kemble and aunt of Fanny *Kemble, she began acting as a child. She married another actor, William Siddons, in 1773. Her London stage success began in 1782, and she became the leading actress of her day, especially in such tragic roles as Lady Macbeth. She retired in 1812.

Sidmouth, 1st Viscount. *See* Addington, Henry, 1st Viscount Sidmouth.

Sidney, Algernon (1622-83). Republican politician. He fought for parliament in the Civil War and was elected to the Long Parliament in 1646. He withdrew from politics after Cromwell's dis-

solution of the Rump in 1653, and after the Restoration he lived in exile on the Continent. Returning to England in 1677, he continued to oppose the monarchy and was arrested after the *Rye House plot (1683). He was convicted, perhaps unjustly, of high treason and executed. His *Discourses concerning Government* were published posthumously (1698).

Sidney, Sir Philip (1554-86). Soldier, statesman, and poet, admired as the ideal English gentleman of his age. He met Penelope Devereux, the Stella of his sonnet sequence *Astrophel and Stella* (1582), in 1575 and a year later held his first position at court. He was sent on several diplomatic missions and was killed while fighting at Zutphen. His literary works, which include *Arcadia* (1580) and the *Defence of Poesie* (1595), established him as a leading Elizabethan writer.

Sierra Leone. A West African state, originating as a home for freed slaves. Members of the British abolition movement established a settlement at Free Town (1787-88), forming the Sierra Leone Company in 1791. A crown colony from 1807, which was extended inland, becoming a protectorate in 1896, Sierra Leone gained independence in 1961.

signet. A small seal, used in the middle ages by the king's secretary and later by secretaries of state, to seal certain documents. Dating from the reign (1307-27) of Edward II, until 1851 signets sealed every warrant for the use of the *privy seal or *great seal.

Silchester. The site of a Romano-British town, 11 km (18 mi) north of Basingstoke in north Hampshire. Called Calleva Atrebatum by the Romans, Silchester was the capital of the *Atrebates during the 3rd and 4th centuries. The site, abandoned following the Romans' departure from Britain, remained deserted, and thus complete excavation and archaeological investigation has been possible.

Silures. A Celtic tribe in southeast Wales, which offered strong resistance to the Roman forces. The eventual submission and romanization of the Silures was accompanied by the establishment of a legionary fortress at Isca (Caerleon) in about 75 AD and a town at Venta Silurum (Caerwent)—"the market of the Silures".

Simnel, Lambert (c. 1475-1535). Son of a baker who, under the influence of a priest named William Symonds, claimed to be Edward Plantagenet, son of George, duke of *Clarence. He was crowned as Edward VI in Dublin in 1487. Henry VII removed the real Edward from prison and paraded him through the streets of London. When the rebel forces landed they found no support in England and were defeated at *Stoke, outside Newark. Simnel ended his days as a turnspit in the king's kitchens.

Simon, John Simon, 1st Viscount (1873-1954). Lawyer and politician. A Liberal MP (1906-18, 1922-40; viscount, 1940), Simon led the "Liberal Nationals" supporting the 1930s *national government. He was foreign secretary (1931-35), home secretary (1935-37), chancellor of the exchequer (1937-40), and lord chancellor (1940-45).

Singapore. An island south of Malaysia. A British trading post was established here (1819) by Sir Stamford *Raffles for the East India Company. Incorporated into the *Straits Settlements in 1824, Singapore became a major international port. In 1946 it became a crown colony and attained self-government in 1959. It joined the Federation of Malaysia in 1963 before becoming fully independent in 1965.

sinking fund. A fund into which a certain amount of government revenues is paid for the purpose of redeeming the *national debt. Walpole established the first sinking fund in 1717, and by 1727 the national debt was reduced from £54 million to £47.5 million. However, the fund's initial success was undermined by its use to cover expenditures not provided for by revenue from taxation. Thus, in 1786, Pitt the younger established a new sinking fund, to be controlled by inde-

pendent commissioners. £1 million per annum was paid into it but, because of the high cost of the French Revolutionary and Napoleonic Wars, this sum could only be raised by borrowing, at high rates of interest. New funds were established in 1875 and 1923.

Sinn Féin (Irish: We Ourselves). An Irish nationalist political party, founded in 1905 by a Dublin journalist, Arthur *Griffith. With the continuing failure of the home rule movement, it became increasingly republican. In 1917 the party began to win by-election seats and in the general election in 1918, under *De Valera's leadership, won an overwhelming majority in Ireland (except in the northeast). The Sinn Féin MPs declined to go to Westminster, proclaimed a parliament in Ireland in 1919, and set up an alternative administration. After violent disturbances Britain conceded virtual independence, but not republican status, in 1921. Elements of Sinn Féin followed De Valera in continuing to press for a full republic and in 1926 many of these joined his new constitutional party, *Fianna Fáil, leaving a rump of Sinn Féin diehards behind. Until the present troubles in 1968 the organization existed as the political wing of the republican movement. In 1969 Sinn Féin followed the split in its military wing, the *Irish Republican Army, into Officials and Provisionals.

Siward (d. 1055). Danish soldier, who was created earl of Northumbria by Cnut in 1041. He brought political stability to the troubled province and defended it from Scottish invasion, extending his territories to the west at the expense of the kingdom of Strathclyde. He supported Edward the Confessor against *Godwine in 1051.

Six Acts (1819). Six parliamentary statutes, passed after the Peterloo massacre and designed to suppress radicalism. They included measures against the holding of public meetings of more than 50 persons and extending newspaper stamp duties.

slavery. The legal ownership of one person by another. A slave has no rights or property and his function is to provide services for his master (*compare* serf). Slaves existed in Anglo-Saxon England but as a class had largely died out by the 12th century. The importation of slaves, generally from Africa, began in the 16th century (*see* Atlantic triangle), and, although slavery was declared illegal in England in 1772 (*see* Mansfield judgment), the slave trade was an integral part of Britain's colonial system until several years into the 19th century. The Quakers were among the first to oppose slavery and, largely owing to the efforts of the Abolition Society (founded 1787), led by *Wilberforce and *Clarkson, the slave trade was abolished in 1807. However, the emancipation of slaves did not, as had been hoped, follow automatically. In 1823 the Anti-Slavery Society was formed, and finally, in 1833, slavery was abolished throughout the British Empire.

Sluys, battle of (24 June 1340). The main naval engagement between England and France in the Hundred Years' War. The French fleet gathered in the Zwyn estuary in an attempt to prevent Edward III's fleet from landing in Flanders. English archers and men-at-arms defeated the French and destroyed their fleet, but Edward failed to follow up his victory with a decisive campaign on land.

Smiles, Samuel (1812-1904). Author, remembered for such books as *Self-Help* (1859), which asserted that the humblest individual could succeed, by hard work. Smiles' works, inspired by *utilitarianism, were widely popular in his lifetime.

Smith, Adam (1723-90). Scottish economist and philosopher. In *An Inquiry into the Nature and Causes of the Wealth of Nations* (1776), Smith attacked *mercantilism, arguing for a system of "natural liberty" based on the free division of labour and largely unimpeded by government interference. Smith's principles underlay 19th-century *laissez-faire and remain profoundly

influential in modern theories of free enterprise.

Smith, F(rederick) E(dwin), 1st earl of Birkenhead (1872-1930). Lawyer and politician. A Conservative MP (1906-18), Smith had outstanding intellectual abilities and was famous as an orator. He was attorney general (1915-18), serving notaby as chief counsel for the crown in the trial of Sir Roger Casement; lord chancellor (1919-22), as which he introduced important reforms in land law; and secretary for India (1924-28).

Smith, Ian (Douglas) (1919-   ). Rhodesian politician. He became prime minister of *Southern Rhodesia in 1964, after the dissolution of the Central African Federation. In 1966, after the UK refused independence without an assurance of Black majority rule, he made a unilateral declaration of independence (UDI). In 1979 he was forced to concede majority rule and resigned.

Smuts, Jan Christian (1870-1950). South African and Commonwealth statesman. A Boer general in the second *Boer War, Smuts helped negotiate the peace of *Vereeniging (1902). He played an important part in the establishment of the Union of South Africa (1910) and served in the British war cabinet (1917-18). He was prime minister of South Africa (1919-24, 1939-48). An outstanding advocate of international cooperation, Smuts suggested (1920) the replacement of the name British Empire with that of Commonwealth (1926).

Soane, Sir John (1753-1837). Architect. His classically simple buildings include the Bank of England (1792-1833; since rebuilt), Dulwich College Art Gallery (1811-14), and his own house in Lincoln's Inn Fields, London (1812-14), now Sir John Soane's Museum.

socage. A form of land tenure, in which a tenant owed any of a variety of (nonmilitary) services in return for land. The term now refers to freehold tenure.

Society for Promoting Christian Knowledge (SPCK). A society founded in 1698 by a parson, Thomas Bray, and four laymen to promote charity schools, to circulate Christian literature, and to foster Christianity in the colonies. The society's publishing activities are extensive both in Britain and abroad.

Society of Friends. See Quakers.

soke. The right of private jurisdiction (also called "sac and soc", synonyms used alliteratively) over a specified group of free men, or the district under such jurisdiction. It originated in the Danelaw, but by 1100 most great lords had this authority.

Solemn League and Covenant (25 Sept 1643). An agreement between the covenanters and the Long Parliament. To the English the *Covenant was the price to be paid for Scottish military aid against Charles I in the *Civil War, and by a separate treaty the covenanters undertook to send an army of 21 000 men into England. To the covenanters the agreement was an attempt to impose Presbyterianism in England and Ireland, to maintain the constitutional liberties won by the Scottish and English parliaments, and to provide permanent links between the two. The failure of the English fully to implement the Covenant caused increasing tension between the allies. The English regarded the Engagers' invasion of England in 1648 as freeing them from any obligation to adhere to the Covenant (see Engagement), and continuing Scottish demands that it be implemented helped to provoke the Cromwellian conquest of Scotland (1650-51).

Solway Moss, battle of (24 Nov 1542). A battle in which an invading English force decisively defeated the Scots. James V, already ill, died on hearing the news.

Somaliland, British. Territory in the Horn of Africa that became a British protectorate in 1884. The *Mad Mullah waged a holy war (jihad) against the British in Somaliland (1900-20). Occupied by the Italians (1940-41), it subsequently merged with the former Italian Somaliland and became independent Somalia in 1960.

Somerled (or Sumerled) (d. 1164). Lord of the Isles. He obtained control of Argyll and in 1154 rebelled unsuccessfully against Malcolm IV of Scots. In 1156-58 Somerled seized most of the Hebrides from the Norse king of Man and won recognition from the king of Norway. He was killed in an attack on Renfrew castle.

Somers, John Somers, Baron (1651-1716). Lawyer, who took part in the successful defence of the *seven bishops and entered parliament in 1689, being appointed attorney general (1689) and lord keeper of the great seal (1693). By 1696 he was leader of the Whig *junto and chief adviser to William III. He became lord chancellor in 1697 but was dismissed in 1700. He returned to power only briefly under Queen Anne, as lord president of the council (1708-10).

Somerset, earl of. See Carr, Robert.

Somerset, Edward, 6th earl and 2nd marquess of Worcester (1601-67). Royalist commander in the Civil War and inventor. He defended South Wales for Charles I and was imprisoned for a short time for failing in a mission to raise troops in Ireland. Following the Restoration (1660) he devoted himself to his mechanical inventions, which included a steam-driven device capable of raising a column of water 12 m (40 ft).

Somerset, Edward Seymour, 1st earl of Hertford and duke of (c. 1506-1552). Lord protector and virtual ruler of England during the first two and a half years (1647-49) of the reign of his nephew Edward VI. Seymour was the brother of *Jane Seymour, Henry VIII's third wife. He invaded Scotland and pillaged Edinburgh in 1544, while lord lieutenant of the north, and successfully defended Boulogne in 1545. As lord protector he subdued the Scots at the battle of *Pinkie (1547) and initiated the Edwardian *Reformation with an Act of *Uniformity enforcing use of the first *Book of Common Prayer (1549), provoking Roman Catholic risings in the west. A peasants' revolt (see Kett's rebellion) over land enclosure drew Somerset's sympathy, but he thus incurred the enmity of powerful landowners, who turned to his arch rival the earl of Warwick (see Northumberland, John Dudley, duke of). Imprisoned in 1549, he was released in the following year but was finally overthrown by Northumberland in 1551 and executed.

Somme, battle of the (1 July–18 Nov 1916). A series of Anglo-French assaults on well-established German positions in northeastern France during World War I. *Haig believed that a powerful offensive might win the war and favoured a massed frontal attack perhaps because of the inadequate training of *Kitchener's "new army". Persistence, bravery, and a particularly daring night operation by the Fourth Army nearly enabled the allies to break through the German lines. Tanks were used for the first time in these engagements, but with limited success. Casualties were heavy—Britain suffered 420 000, France 204 000, and Germany 670 000 (according to one estimate). No strategic gains were made.

Sophia (1630–1714). Electress of Hanover and granddaughter of James I through her mother Elizabeth (the Electress Palatine). Her Protestant descendants were named as heirs to the English throne by the Act of *Settlement (1701). She was the wife from 1658 of Ernest Augustus, who became elector of Hanover in 1692.

Sophia Dorothea of Celle (1666–1726). Wife of the future George I and mother of George II. Married in 1682, she was accused of adultery with the Swedish Count Königsmarch in 1694, divorced, and imprisoned in Ahlden castle until her death.

South Africa. An independent republic consisting of the four provinces of *Natal, the *Cape of Good Hope, *Transvaal, and the *Orange Free State. The Cape, first settled by the Dutch East India Company in 1652, was ceded to Britain in 1814. Thousands of Boers, settlers of Dutch descent, made the *great trek northwards in the 1830s, away from British authority. They established republics in Natal, the Transvaal, and the Orange Free State. Natal was annexed by Britain in 1843, but the Boers fought to maintain their independence in the Transvaal and the Orange Free State (see Boer Wars). These disadvantaged communities were transformed by the discovery of diamonds in 1867 in *Griqualand West and of gold in 1886 in the Transvaal. The gold mines were developed largely with British capital but the so-called uitlanders (foreigners, mostly British) were not given political rights by the Afrikaners. The British won the consequent second Boer War (1899–1902) and in 1910 the four provinces were united in the self-governing Union of South Africa, a British *dominion. The policy of apartheid (separate development of the White and non-White populations), introduced (1948) by the Nationalist Party, was condemned by members of the Commonwealth, from which South Africa resigned in 1961.

Southampton, Henry Wriothesley, 3rd earl of (1573–1624). Courtier, soldier, and patron most notably of Shakespeare. He gave £1,000 on one occasion alone to Shakespeare, who dedicated *Venus and Adonis* (1593) and *The Rape of Lucrece* (1594) to him. Southampton accompanied the earl of *Essex on expeditions to Cádiz and the Azores (1596, 1597) and in 1599 to Ireland. In 1601 he took part in Essex's conspiracy against Elizabeth I, organizing a performance at the Globe Theatre of Shakespeare's *Richard II*—which portrays the deposition of a king. He was imprisoned until the accession of James I (1603).

Southampton plot. See Cambridge plot.

Southcott, Joanna (1750–1814). Religious fanatic. A Devonshire farmer's daughter, she began "prophesying" in 1792 and moved to London in 1802, attracting thousands of followers. She died shortly after announcing that she was about to give birth to a "Prince of Peace". Her box, said to contain directions for the attainment of happiness, is retained by her followers.

South-East Asia Treaty Organization (SEATO). A military alliance formed in 1954 to implement the South-East Asia

Collective Defence Treaty. The Pacific counterpart of NATO, the alliance consisted of Australia, Britain, France, New Zealand, Pakistan (until 1973), the Philippines, Thailand, and the USA. It was dissolved in 1977.

Southern Rhodesia. A former British colony in southern Africa. Rhodesia was administered from 1889 by the *British South Africa Company (founded by Cecil *Rhodes, after whom Rhodesia was named). It was divided (1911) into *Northern Rhodesia and Southern Rhodesia, the latter becoming a self-governing colony in 1923. From 1953 to 1963 it formed part of the *Central African Federation and in 1964 was renamed Rhodesia. Power remained with the White minority, whose demands for independence were refused by Britain without an assurance that Black majority rule would be introduced. Thus, in 1965, the prime minister Ian Smith issued a unilateral declaration of independence (UDI), to which Britain responded with the imposition of (ineffective) economic sanctions. Subsequent negotiations broke down, but in 1974 the guerrilla warfare conducted by sections of the Black nationalist movement forced Smith to initiate talks with its leaders. The subsequent transitional government, which was committed to Black majority rule, failed, under Bishop Muzorewa, to obtain the support of the Patriotic Front (the two arms of which—the Zimbabwe African People's Union (ZAPU) and the Zimbabwe African National Union (ZANU)—fought the guerrilla war), and the 1979 Commonwealth Conference called for an all-party meeting to solve the crisis. This was held at Lancaster House, London (1979-80), and resulted in the appointment as governor of Lord Soames. Elections were held under his supervision, and Rhodesia became independent Zimbabwe, with Robert Mugabe (1925-), leader of ZANU/PF, as its first prime minister, in 1980. It is a member of the Commonwealth.

South Sea Company. A *joint-stock company founded in 1711 to trade, chiefly in slaves, with Spanish America.

In 1720 its offer to take over a large part of the national debt was accepted by parliament and was followed by an enormous rise in the value of its shares. The subsequent slump—or "burst" of the South Sea bubble—ruined many investors and implicated three ministers on charges of corruption. The scandal touched even George I, two of whose mistresses were involved, but the day was saved by Walpole. The subsequent Bubble Act (1720) restricted the formation of joint-stock companies.

Spa Fields riots (2 Dec 1816). Disorders provoked by demands for parliamentary reform. To promote the reform campaign Henry Hunt was to address a mass meeting at Spa Fields, London. Before Hunt arrived, other more violent agitators led part of the crowd towards the City. One citizen was wounded. The lord mayor led police in breaking up the mob.

Spanish Succession, War of the (1701-14). A European war provoked by the death in 1700 of the childless Charles II of Spain. His throne was claimed by Philip, grandson of Louis XIV of France, and in 1701 the French invaded the Spanish Netherlands. A *grand alliance was formed between Britain, the Dutch Republic, and the Holy Roman Emperor, joined later by Portugal and certain German states. Between 1704 and 1709, under the leadership of the duke of *Marlborough and Prince Eugene of Savoy, the allies achieved a series of victories, including *Blenheim (1704), *Ramillies (1706), *Oudenarde (1708), and *Malplaquet (1709). Britain also captured Gibraltar (1704), Minorca (1708), and Nova Scotia (1710). By 1711, the Tories, opposed to the war, were in power, and Marlborough was recalled. Peace was ratified by the treaties of *Utrecht (1713-14).

SPCK. See Society for Promoting Christian Knowledge.

Speenhamland system. A method of poor relief. The system, originally devised by Berkshire justices, meeting as local government administrators at Speenhamland (Newbury) in 1795, was subsequently adopted almost throughout England and Wales. Farm labourers' wages were supplemented, from parish rates, on a scale depending on wheat prices and family size. This well-intentioned "outdoor relief" encouraged low wage rates and pauperized labourers. The 1834 Poor Law Amendment Act abolished it. *See also* poor laws.

Speke, John Hanning (1827-64). Explorer, who discovered the main source of the *Nile. After discovering, with *Burton, Lake Tanganyika, Speke independently reached and named Lake Victoria (July 1858), assuming it to be the source of the Nile. Leading his own expedition, with James Grant (1827-92), Speke found the river's outlet from the lake (July 1862).

Spencer, Herbert (1820-1903) Social philosopher. He applied Darwin's theory of evolution to social development and in *A System of Synthetic Philosophy* (9 vols, 1862-96) presented a philosophical system embracing metaphysics, biology, psychology, sociology, and ethics. His work had considerable influence in Europe, America, and in the Far East.

Spenser, Edmund (c. 1552-1599). Elizabethan poet. He combined political service in Ireland with writing poetry, his first major work being *The Shepheardes Calender* (c. 1579). He invented the nine-line "Spenserian stanza" for his allegorical poem in six volumes, *The Faerie Queene* (1590, 1596).

spinning jenny. A machine, patented (1770) by *Hargreaves, for spinning a number of threads simultaneously. It extended the principle of the spinning wheel by carrying several spindles (ultimately 120) vertically—the idea is said to have come to Hargreaves when he saw a spinning wheel, knocked over by his daughter Jenny, fall on its side. In the 1780s the spinning jenny began to be superseded by the *mule for spinning cotton, but its adaptation to wool ensured its survival well into the 19th century.

Spithead mutiny (April 1797). A mutiny of the Channel fleet provoked by the appalling nature of lower-deck conditions. Within a few days the mutineers' demands were substantially granted, which encouraged rebels in the subsequent more serious *Nore mutiny.

Spurs, battle of the (1513). A battle between the invasion force led by Henry VIII, aided by the emperor Maximilian and continental mercenaries, and the French at Guinegate. The French were routed by the 30 000 strong English force and the cavalry fled the field, many allegedly losing their spurs, which gave the battle its name.

squire (originally: **esquire**). In the later middle ages, a young man of good birth attendant upon a knight; hence, later, a man of gentle birth entitled to bear arms (the word derives from the Latin *scutarius*, shield bearer). By the 17th century the squire was the principal landowner of a neighbourhood, and usually the lord of the manor. In many parishes he was the patron of the ecclesiastical living and had a large and well-appointed pew in the parish church. In the 19th century the term squireship was widely used of the country gentry as a whole, and the term squarson was coined to describe clergy who were landed proprietors. The abbreviation of esquire (Esq.) came to be written after a man's name as a title of respect.

Sri Lanka. *See* Ceylon.

St. *See* Saint.

Stair, Viscount and earl of. *See* Dalrymple.

Stamford Bridge, battle of (25 Sept 1066). A battle, fought near York, in which Harold II decisively defeated and killed Harold Hardraada, king of Norway, and *Tostig, the English king's exiled brother, who had recently defeated the Mercians at *Fulford. Harold then marched south to face the Normans at *Hastings.

Stamp Act (1765). An act that imposed stamp duty on legal documents and newspapers in the American colonies. Introduced by George Grenville to help finance the colonies' defence, it was violently opposed in America and was repealed by Rockingham in 1766. The controversy questioned the right of the British parliament to tax the colonies, a right that was asserted in the subsequent Declaratory Act (1766).

Standard, battle of the (22 Aug 1138). The battle, during the anarchy of King Stephen's reign, in which the invading army of David I of Scots was defeated by an Anglo-Norman force led by William, count of Aumale. Fought on Cowton Moor, north of Northallerton in Yorkshire, the battle received its name from a mast, carried by the English on a cart and bearing the banners (Old French *estandard*, banner) of St Peter of York, St John of Beverley, and St Wilfrid of Ripon.

standing committees. An aspect of the procedure of the *House of Commons. As early as 1571 there was a permanent committee for "matters of religion" and in 1581 a similar committee was appointed to deal with disputed election returns. Meetings are usually when the House is not sitting and membership is between 16 and 50 and in proportion to party strength in the House. *Compare* select committees.

Stanhope, Charles Stanhope, 3rd Earl (1753–1816). Radical politician, scientist, and inventor. Pitt the younger's brother in law, he was nicknamed "Citizen Stanhope" because of his sympathy for the French Revolution. He experimented with electricity and steam propulsion for ships, and his inventions included a printing press and a microscope lens.

Stanhope, Lady Hester (1776–1839). Traveller. A niece of Pitt the younger, she kept house for him (1803–06). After travelling in North Africa, she settled in the Lebanon (1814), practising astrology and leading a life of some eccentricity. She died heavily in debt and alone.

Stanhope, James Stanhope, 1st Earl (1673–1721). As English commander in Spain (1708–10), Stanhope captured Port Mahon (Minorca) in 1708. Appointed secretary of state on George I's accession in 1714, he helped defeat Jacobitism and

secure the Hanoverian succession. He maintained the treaty of Utrecht through European alliances, notably the *quadruple alliance (1718). Strain over the scandal of the *South Sea Company (although he was not personally implicated in its collapse) caused his premature death.

Stanley, Sir Henry Morton (1841–1904). Explorer and journalist. Born in Wales (as John Rowlands), he emigrated to America in 1859, taking US citizenship. A brilliant journalist, he was sent by the *New York Herald* to search for *Livingstone, apparently lost in central Africa. On finding him, at Ujiji in Nov 1871, Stanley uttered the famous words "Dr Livingstone I presume". In his greatest expedition (1874–77) Stanley crossed Africa from Zanzibar to the Atlantic, tracing the Congo's course (and also confirming *Speke's discoveries). He helped establish for Belgium the Congo Free State (now Zaïre). Again crossing central Africa (1887–89), from west to east, he helped lay the foundations of what became Uganda and Kenya. Resuming British nationality, he was a Liberal Unionist MP (1895–1900).

Stanley, Sir John (d. 1414). Founder of the house of Stanley, lords of the *Isle of Man. Granted to him in 1405, the lordship remained in the family until 1736.

Stanley. *See* Derby, earls of.

Stannaries. The tin-mining districts of Devon and Cornwall. The working of precious metals was a royal prerogative, and the workers in these areas had an ancient right to sue and be sued, except in cases of land, life, and limb, in their own courts. The privilege was confirmed by Edward I in a charter of 1305. The Stannary Court was not abolished until 1897.

staple. A town on the Continent or in England, Wales, or Ireland to which the sale of products to foreign merchants was restricted. From the reign of Edward I the so-called merchants of the staple were required to fix their trade, chiefly in wool, on one continental town. The staple changed frequently—Dordrecht was the first, but was subsequently succeeded by, among other towns, Antwerp, Bruges, and Middelburg. In 1326 some 14 home staples were created and, after the system had been temporarily abandoned, the Statute of Staples (1354) fixed their number at 15: Bristol, Canterbury, Carmarthen, Chichester, Cork, Drogheda, Dublin, Exeter, Lincoln, London, Newcastle, Norwich, Waterford, Winchester, and York. In 1363 the continental staple was revived and from 1392 was permanently at Calais, to which the home staples channelled goods. The importance of the staple lessened with the decline in the wool trade, which gave way to the cloth trade (dominated by the *Merchants Adventurers) in the late 15th century. A continental staple continued to exist (moving to Middelburg after the loss of Calais in 1558 and thence to Bruges) until the export of wool was forbidden in 1617.

Star Chamber. A court of law, sitting in the Star Chamber at Westminster palace, that evolved from the king's council in its function of hearing subjects' petitions. It was brought to prominence by Henry VII, who used it to curb the disorder that continued after the conclusion of the Wars of the Roses. He and, subsequently, Wolsey and Cromwell extended its jurisdiction (1487, 1529, 1539), encouraging plaintiffs to bring their grievances before it in the first instance rather than to regard it merely as a court of appeal. Its unpopularity arose from its association with the maintenance of royal authority, and its extensive use by Charles I during his years of rule without parliament brought about its abolition by the *Long Parliament.

Stationers' Company. A book-trade guild, formed in 1403 by the association of scriveners, limners, bookbinders, and stationers. Its charter, granted in 1557, ensured control of almost all printing and publishing in England by requiring that anyone, other than a member of the company, wishing to publish a book must first obtain the company's

authorization. The exclusive right (established before the end of the 16th century) of a member to print a particular book was the origin of *copyright.

Steele, Sir Richard (1672–1729). Writer and politician. Steele is remembered for his essays, especially in the vein of social comedy, which he contributed to his periodicals—the *Tatler* (1709–11) and the *Spectator* (1711–12, founded with *Addison).

Steelyard. A German trading area established west of London bridge on the north side of the Thames during the late 13th century by the *Hanse merchants. The steelyard (a mistranslation of German *Stal*, sample, + *Hof*, courtyard) was demolished in 1863 and Cannon Street station now occupies the site. Other steelyards were established during the 15th century at Boston and King's Lynn.

Stephen (?1097–1154). King of England (1135–54), during a period known as the anarchy. Son of Stephen, count of Blois, and Adela, daughter of William the Conqueror, he married Matilda of Boulogne and they had two children, Eustace and William. Stephen was brought up at the court of his uncle Henry I. Before his death in 1135 Henry secured a pledge from his magnates, including Stephen, to support the accession of his daughter *Matilda, whose husband was Geoffrey of Anjou. When the king died, however, Stephen seized the crown with the support of the church and those Norman nobles who opposed Geoffrey's Angevin connections. Stephen's ineffective rule soon alienated his supporters, and in 1138 Robert, earl of Gloucester, Matilda's half-brother, rebelled. Shortly afterwards the Scots invaded England and, although defeated at the battle of the *Standard, took Northumberland, Carlisle, and later Durham. In 1139 Matilda herself invaded England and before long controlled most of the west. In 1141 Stephen was captured at *Lincoln and held for several months, being exchanged for Gloucester after the rout of *Winchester. Stephen's victory at

Faringdon (1145) was a turning point, and Matilda, her cause weakened by her own unpopularity and Gloucester's death (1147), withdrew in 1148. The last years of Stephen's reign were relatively peaceful, but, quarrelling with the church, he failed to obtain acknowledgement of his son Eustace as his successor. By the treaty of *Winchester (1153), following Eustace's death, Matilda's son was recognized as the future king, succeeding in 1154 as Henry II.

Stephenson, George (1781–1848). Inventor of the first practicable railway locomotives. A self-educated colliery engineman, Stephenson was appointed (1821) engineer to the Stockton and Darlington mineral railway (opened Sept 1825, with his engine *Locomotion*). He became (1826) engineer for the first all-steam railway, the Liverpool and Manchester (opened Sept 1830), for which he built his *Rocket* in 1829.

steward (or seneschal). The keeper of a court of justice who served as an officer of the crown (see lord high steward) or of a feudal lord. The steward of a lord of a manor was responsible for all financial and legal matters and presided over the manorial court.

Stewart, house of. See Stuart, house of.

Stigand (d. 1072). Archbishop of Canterbury from 1052. He found his position repeatedly under papal attack (his predecessor, the Norman Robert of Jumiège, had been outlawed but was still living) and was excommunicated. He survived the Norman conquest but was deposed by the king in 1070 and imprisoned.

Stirling Bridge, battle of (11 Sept 1297). The battle in which the Scots under William *Wallace and Andrew Moray defeated an English army, inflicting heavy losses and briefly freeing most of Scotland from English rule. Moray was mortally wounded in the battle. See also Anglo-Scottish wars.

Stoke, battle of (16 June 1487). The battle outside Newark in which royalist forces broke Lambert *Simnel's rising against Henry VII. The rebel force, consisting of English and Irish Yorkists

and German mercenaries, was scattered and most of the Yorkist leaders were killed. Simnel was captured.

Stow, John (d. 1605). Antiquary best known for A *Survey of London* (1598, 1603).

Stonehenge. A megalithic monument on Salisbury Plain. Begun in Neolithic times and remade several times, Stonehenge was completed about 1400 BC. Its outer circle and inner horseshoe formations of massive standing stones form Europe's finest Bronze Age sanctuary. Although its exact purpose is still unknown, the alignment of certain stones with sunrise at the winter and summer solstices is significant.

Stopes, Marie (1880–1958). Pioneer of *birth control. Initially a scientist, she turned to the study of marital problems in about 1916, opening the first British clinic for contraceptive advice in 1921. Her books *Married Love* (1918) and *Wise Parenthood* (1918) provoked great controversy but ultimately had worldwide influence.

Strafford, Thomas Wentworth, 1st earl of (1593–1641). At first an opponent of Charles I's policies, Wentworth subsequently accepted high office. He became lord president of the north (1628), a privy councillor (1629), and then lord deputy of Ireland (1632). An unpopular autocrat, he earned a reputation for ruthless efficiency in pursuit of an anglicized Ireland and was, together with William *Laud, the chief exponent of the method of government known as *thorough. Faced with the Scottish revolt of 1639 (see Bishops' Wars) against Laud's ecclesiastical policies, Charles turned to Wentworth for guidance. He was recalled from Ireland, made the king's principal adviser, and led an English army against the Scots. In 1640 he was created earl of Strafford. In Nov 1640 Strafford was impeached for high treason by the *Long Parliament, whose leaders regarded him as an apostate, and executed in May 1641.

Straits Settlements. A former crown colony (1867–1946) that comprised

Penang, Malacca, *Singapore, and Labuan. The territories were all established or acquired by the East India Company.

Strathclyde. A British kingdom in southwest Scotland, which was frequently involved in conflicts between the Scots, Picts, and English from the 6th to the 11th centuries. A strong power in the area during the second half of the 7th century, Strathclyde retained its independence until defeated by the Northumbrians and Picts (756). Plundered by Vikings (870), Strathclyde submitted to England (c. 920) and was finally (c. 1020) incorporated into Scotland.

Strongbow, Richard. See Clare, Richard de.

Stuart (or Stewart), house of. The ruling dynasty of Scotland from 1371 to 1714 and of England from 1603 to 1714. The Stewart (Stuart is the French form of the name, which became accepted in England) dynasty took its name from the office of steward of Scotland. David I granted the office to Walter fitz Alan (d. 1177), whose family was Breton in origin, and it became hereditary. In 1316 another Walter (1293–1326), the sixth steward, married Marjory, daughter of Robert I. Their son succeeded to the throne as Robert II in 1371. The Stewarts gained the English throne through the marriage of James IV to Margaret Tudor, daughter of Henry VII of England, in 1503. Their granddaughter *Mary Queen of Scots had a strong claim to the English throne from 1558, either in succession to Elizabeth I or in place of her if (as many Roman Catholics argued) Elizabeth was illegitimate. The claims of Mary's son James VI were even stronger, for he was descended from Margaret Tudor through his father, Lord *Darnley, as well as through his mother. Elizabeth refused to acknowledge James openly as her heir, but, as James I of England, he succeeded her in 1603 without difficulty. After the execution of Charles I in 1649 the monarchy was abolished in England, but the Scots proclaimed his son King Char-

les II and in 1651 crowned him. English conquest promptly drove him into exile until the monarchy was restored in 1660. In the revolution of 1688–89 James II and VII was dethroned and the claims of his son James Edward Stuart, the old pretender, were ignored. The last reigning monarch of the Stuart dynasty was thus Queen Anne, James II's daughter, who died in 1714. On the death of the old pretender's eldest son, Charles Edward Stuart, the young pretender, in 1788 the Stuart claim passed to the old pretender's younger son, Henry, cardinal duke of *York, and was extinguished on his death without heirs in 1807. See also Jacobites.

Stuart, Lady Arabella (1575–1615). A claimant to the English throne as the great-granddaughter of *Margaret Tudor. She was the focus of the *main plot (1603), and James I, her cousin, fearing that she might marry a foreign ruler, had her imprisoned in 1609. On her release (1610) she secretly married William Seymour (later duke of Somerset), also a claimant to the throne, and they were both imprisoned. He escaped to Belgium, but Arabella's attempt was foiled and she was returned to the Tower, where she died.

subinfeudation. See mesne tenure.

subsidy. A tax granted to the crown by parliament, in addition to customary revenue. Subsidies originated in Edward I's taxes of a tenth or fifteenth of movable property and under the Tudors were levied on movables and land. Import and export duties, such as *tunnage and poundage, were also called subsidies, and the term came to be applied to any parliamentary tax.

Succession, Acts of. Legislation of Henry VIII that established the succession to the throne. 1. (1534) An act that declared that Henry VIII's (second) marriage to *Anne Boleyn was "undoubted, true, sincere and perfect" and that their children should succeed to the throne. It also declared Mary, Henry's daughter by Catherine of Aragon, a bastard, and empowered the king to demand from any subject an oath to maintain its provisions. 2. (1536) An act that, replacing that of 1534, provided for the succession of the children of Henry's recent marriage to *Jane Seymour. 3. (1544) An act that settled the order of the succession of Henry's three children: Edward (VI), Mary (I), and Elizabeth (I).

Sudan. A country in NE Africa and a former Anglo-Egyptian condominium. It was ruled by the khedive of Egypt from 1821, with the assistance from 1869 of British administrators. Conquered (1881–85) by the *Mahdi, who besieged and killed Gen. *Gordon in Khartoum (1885), the Sudan was reconquered by the British under *Kitchener and in 1898 became a condominium. It became independent in 1956.

Suez Canal. A canal, 165 km (103 mi) long, connecting the Mediterranean Sea with the Red Sea. Designed and built by the Frenchman Ferdinand, vicomte de Lesseps, it was opened in 1869. In 1875 Britain, at Disraeli's initiative, acquired a controlling interest in the Suez Canal Company, and in 1888 Britain became guarantor of its neutral status. When, after the withdrawal of British troops, Egypt nationalized the company (1956) a joint Anglo-French force attacked Egypt. They were forced, in the face of strong international opposition, to withdraw.

Suffolk, earls of. See Pole, de la.

suffragettes. See women's movement.

Sumerled. See Somerled.

Sunday school movement. A Christian education movement. Robert Raikes (1735–1811) established the movement in 1780, when he arranged for illiterate children in Gloucester to be instructed in reading and the catechism on Sundays. The movement expanded rapidly among all denominations, and as secular education improved during the 19th century Sunday schools placed increasing emphasis on religious instruction.

Sunderland, Charles Spencer, 3rd earl of (1674–1722). Son of Robert Spencer, 2nd earl of *Sunderland. He was the first member of the Whig *junto to be brought into Queen Anne's government, as secretary of state (1706–10), an appointment obtained largely by the influence of his father in law, the duke of Marlborough. Enjoying George I's favour, he became lord privy seal in 1715 and first lord of the treasury, supplanting *Walpole, in 1718. With James, 1st Earl *Stanhope, Sunderland led George's ministry until forced to resign (1721) after the *South Sea Company crashed.

Sunderland, Robert Spencer, 2nd earl of (1640–1702). Politician notable for his lack of principle, and his skill, in political management. Secretary of state (1679–81), he was dismissed for supporting the exclusion of James, duke of York, from the succession. He worked his way back into favour and was again secretary of state (1683–88). After James' succession he became an enthusiastic advocate of the king's pro-Catholic policies, professing Roman Catholicism himself. After the Glorious Revolution he ingratiated himself with William III and re-embraced Protestantism. In due course he emerged as one of the king's advisers and persuaded him to govern with the Whig *junto (1696–97). Sunderland was lord chamberlain in 1697 from April to Dec, when he resigned under pressure from a hostile House of Commons.

Supremacy, Acts of. 1. (1534) The act that established Henry VIII in place of the pope as supreme head of the Church of England. It gave him control over all ecclesiastical appointments, income, and doctrine. The measure was repealed during the *Marian reaction (1553–58). 2. (1559) The act that established Elizabeth I as supreme governor of the Church of England. See also Reformation.

surplice. A white liturgical vestment worn by priests in the Church of England and the Roman Catholic Church. Its obligatory use after the Reformation precipitated the 16th-century *vestiarian controversy.

Surrey, Henry Howard, earl of (1517–47). Soldier and poet. Author of lyric verse and elegies, Surrey was responsible, with Sir Thomas Wyatt (?1503-1542), for introducing the sonnet form into England from Italy. Son of the 3rd duke of *Norfolk, Surrey served in the Scottish campaign of 1542 and in France and Flanders (1543-46). Caught up in the rivalry between the Howards and the Seymours, he was tried and executed on a flimsy charge of "treasonable ambition".

Surrey, Thomas Howard, earl of (and 2nd duke of Norfolk) (1443-1524). Soldier. He fought for Richard III at Bosworth (1485), where he was wounded and captured. Imprisoned in the Tower by Henry VII, he was later restored to royal favour and was lord treasurer (1501-22). As lieutenant general of the north he defeated the Scots at *Flodden (1513) and was created duke of Norfolk (1514). In 1517 he quelled a riot of London apprentices.

suspending power. A royal *prerogative right to suspend a statute, as by the *Declarations of Indulgence issued by Charles II and James II. The Bill of Rights (1681) declared it illegal. See also dispensing power.

Sussex. The kingdom of the south *Saxons. In 477 the Saxon Aelle landed in southeast England and defeated the Britons to become king of Sussex, with his sovereignty extending as far north as the Humber. Sussex fell finally to Wessex in the 9th century.

Sutton Hoo. The site, near Woodbridge in Suffolk, of a grave (or cenotaph, as no body has been found), which is probably that of *Raedwald, a 7th-century king of East Anglia. The barrow, discovered in 1939, contained a 24-metre boat and a wealth of golden artefacts and other treasure.

Swaziland. A kingdom in southern Africa and a former British protectorate (1903-68). It was ruled jointly by the Transvaal and Britain from 1894 until 1903. In 1968 it became independent and a member of the Commonwealth.

Sweyn I Forkbeard (d. 1014). King of Denmark (?985-1014). With the Nor-

wegian Olaf Tryggvason, Sweyn invaded England in 994 and again, in retaliation for the massacre of *St Brice's day, in 1003. Following his third invasion, in 1013, he was rapidly accepted as king by the *Danelaw. He subdued much of southern England, and the surrender of London made him effective ruler of all England. His sudden death brought about the restoration of *Aethelred II.

Sweyn II Estrithson (c. 1020-75). King of Denmark (1047-75). In 1069 Sweyn aided English rebels against William the Conqueror and briefly captured York. He returned with a fleet to the Humber in 1070 and raided Peterborough, but a treaty with William effected his withdrawal.

Swift, Jonathan (1667-1745). Irish clergyman, poet, pamphleteer, and satirist. As a reward for his pamphleteering in support of the Tory Party and the established church, he was appointed dean of St Patrick's, Dublin (1713). He rallied Irish patriotism with his "Drapier's Letters" (1724-35), which opposed *Wood's halfpence, and satirized society, politics, and mankind in general in his masterpiece, Gulliver's Travels (1726).

Swinford (or Swynford), Catherine (d. 1403). Third wife of John of Gaunt. The widow of Sir Hugh Swinford, she became John's mistress in the 1370s and had four children by him. In 1396, following the death of his second wife, John and Catherine married, and in 1397 their children, surnamed *Beaufort, were legitimized. Henry VII was among their descendants.

T

Taff Vale judgment (1901). A legal judgment that, for a time, established the principle that trade unions could be sued for damages. The Taff Vale Railway Company sued the Amalgamated Society of Railway Servants for losses sustained during a strike and was awarded damages of £23,000. Thus the view that union funds were protected under the Trade Union Act (1871) was rejected. Union anger at the judgment was a potent factor in the development of the Labour Party. In 1906, however, the Trade Disputes Act effectively reversed it by giving the unions immunity from actions for tort.

Talavera, battle of (27-28 July 1809). A battle during the Peninsular War. It was a costly British victory, in which Sir Arthur Wellesley (later duke of Wellington), commanding 19 000 of his own troops and 34 000 Spanish (who took little part in the fighting), defeated 40 000 French under Joseph Bonaparte and Marshals Victor and Jourdan. British casualties numbered some 5300 as against French losses of 7200.

Talbot. See Shrewsbury, earls and countess of.

Taliesin (late 6th century). Welsh poet. A contemporary of *Aneirin, he sang in praise of the generosity, hospitality, and other heroic qualities of Urien, ruler of Rheged (modern Galloway and Cumbria), and other prominent northern Britons. The surviving text appears in the *Book of Taliesin* (c. 1275), a collection of the works of different authors.

tallage. A tax levied at the will of a lord, especially that imposed by the crown, often to finance military campaigns, on tenants on the ancient demesne. It was abolished in 1340.

Tallis, Thomas (1505-85). Composer. With William *Byrd he became joint organist at the Chapel Royal. In 1575 Elizabeth I granted the two composers a monopoly of the right to print music. Tallis' compositions include Masses, motets, services, secular vocal music, and some instrumental music.

tally. A stick, used in the middle ages by royal officials, on which notches were cut to represent sums of money. The tally was cut, then split into two pieces. The smaller one was kept by the Exchequer as a record of the transaction and the larger one (the stock, hence Stock Exchange) served as a receipt. Tallies continued in use until 1826.

Tamworth manifesto (1834). An election address by *Peel (then prime minister) to his Tamworth constituents in preparation for the 1835 election. It is regarded as marking the emergence of the *Conservative Party from the old Tory grouping. Peel declared his acceptance of the Reform Act (1832) and belief in moderate reform, while recognizing and balancing the rights of landed interests, trade, and industry.

Tanganyika. A former British *mandate. The colony of German East Africa, it was conquered by Britain in World War I and became a British mandate in 1920. It became independent in 1961 and in 1964 joined with *Zanzibar to become Tanzania, a member of the *Commonwealth.

tank. A self-propelled armour-plated military vehicle with caterpillar tracks, first proposed by Sir Ernest Swinton (1868-1951) in Oct 1914 as a counter to German machine-gun fire in *World War I. The War Office rejected the scheme, but *Churchill and the Admiralty supported it. Tanks were used at the *Somme (1916), but their significance in breaking the deadlock of trench warfare only became evident at Cambrai (1917).

Tanzania. See Tanganyika; Zanzibar.

Tara. A hill in Co. Meath, the site of the religious and political centre of Ireland until the 7th century. On its summit is a pillar stone believed to have been the coronation stone of the kings of Tara. In 980 AD the Irish defeated the Norsemen under Olaf Sitricson here.

Taverner, John (c. 1495-1545). Composer. He was choirmaster and organist at Cardinal College (now Christ Church), Oxford, but in 1530 was dismissed, having been imprisoned for heresy. He subsequently gave up composition and became an agent for Thomas Cromwell in the dissolution of the monasteries. His works include Masses, Magnificats, and motets.

Tehran conference (28 Nov-1 Dec 1943). A meeting during World War II, held at Tehran in Iran, between Churchill, Roosevelt, and Stalin. Its purpose was to discuss the Anglo-American plan for the invasion of France ("Operation Overlord") and to coordinate a simultaneous Russian offensive.

Tel-el-Kebir, battle of (13 Sept 1882). The battle in which Sir Garnet Wolseley decisively defeated Egyptian nationalists led by Arabi Pasha. The engagement brought to a successful conclusion the six-week-long Egyptian campaign of 1882.

Telford, Thomas (1757-1834). Civil engineer. A Scot, initially a stonemason, Telford moved to London in 1782 and by 1787 had begun his career as a builder of bridges (especially in iron), canals, roads, and other public works. His achievements included the *Ellesmere canal (1793-1805), *Caledonian canal 1803-23), Shrewsbury-Holyhead road and Menai suspension bridge (1814-25), and St Katharine's docks, London (1826-28).

Templars. A military order of *knighthood, called in full the Poor Knights of Christ and of the Temple of Solomon, which was founded in 1118 by Hugo de Payens, a French knight, to protect pilgrims to the Holy Land. The head house of the English branch of the order was the Temple Church, south of the Strand in London. The original building, the Old Temple, erected in about 1128, was replaced by the New Temple in 1184. The Templars' wealth provoked jealousy and accusations, chiefly in France, of immorality and heresy. In 1308 the pope ordered the confiscation of the Templars' property, with which Edward II of England complied, and in 1312 the order was dissolved—to the benefit of its rivals, the *Hospitallers, who were granted most of the Templars' estates.

Temple, Richard Temple Grenville, 1st Earl (1711-79). A supporter of John Wilkes. Temple (George *Grenville's brother) was closely allied to his brother in law, Pitt the elder, and held office as first lord of the admiralty (1756-57) and lord privy seal (1757-61); he later quarrelled with Pitt (1766). Temple

backed Wilkes in the *North Briton* affair.

Temple, Sir William (1628-99). Diplomat and author. He served Charles II on major diplomatic missions in Brussels and The Hague, where he carried through the *triple alliance between England, Holland, and Sweden (1668). In 1677 he negotiated the marriage of *Mary, daughter of the future James II, with William of Orange (later *William III of England). Temple was the author of three volumes of political and literary essays (1680, 1692, 1701).

Tennyson, Alfred, 1st Baron (1809-92). Poet. His work included *In Memoriam* (1850), written after the death of his friend Arthur Hallam (1811-33), and his Arthurian poems *Idylls of the King* (1859). He became poet laureate in 1850.

Terry, (Alice) Ellen (1847-1928). Actress, one of the most popular stage performers of her time. Her famous partnership with Henry Irving began in 1878 and lasted for 24 years. She is also remembered for her correspondence with George Bernard Shaw.

Test Acts. 1. (1673) An act designed to exclude nonconformists from civil and military office. Office holders had to receive the Anglican communion, swear allegiance to the monarch and affirm the monarch's supremacy as head of the Church of England, and repudiate the Roman Catholic doctrine of transubstantiation (*see* Eucharist). Evasion by Protestant nonconformists was frequent (*see* Occasional Conformity, Act of). Despite the long-term bad effects of imposing a religious test upon candidates for secular office, the Test Act was not repealed until 1829. **2.** (1678) An act, passed after the *popish plot, that excluded Roman Catholics, except the duke of York (later James II), from parliament. **3.** (1681) In Scotland, an act that required all government officials to be believers in the Protestant faith.

Tettenhall, battle of (5 Aug 910). A battle, fought in Staffordshire, between Edward the Elder of Wessex and the invading Danes of the Kingdom of *York in which the latter were decisively defeated. As a result the Northumbrian threat to southern England was removed for many years.

Tewkesbury, battle of (4 May 1471). A battle of the Wars of the Roses. Despite the death of their ally, Warwick, at *Barnet, Queen Margaret and her son Edward crossed from France, raised a Lancastrian army, and made for Wales. They were overtaken by Edward IV at Tewkesbury, where they were routed and many Lancastrian leaders, including Prince Edward, were killed in battle or subsequently executed. Margaret was captured shortly afterwards and imprisoned. The victory was decisive for Edward IV, whose throne was not seriously challenged again.

thegn (or **thane**) (Old English: one who serves). A noble of Anglo-Saxon England, having a *wergild six times greater than that of a *ceorl. A thegn held his estates, which were hereditary, in return for service to his lord. The duties of the king's thegns included attendance at the *witan, military service, and administration in both central and local government. The importance of the king's thegns was undermined in the 11th century by the *housecarles of the Danish sovereigns, and many thegns were impoverished by the time of the Norman conquest because the estates of a deceased thegn were divided among all his sons.

Theobald (d. 1161). Archbishop of Canterbury from 1138. Theobald was twice forced to leave England following conflict with King Stephen, whom, however, he later reconciled to the future Henry II. He commended his protegé Thomas *Becket to Henry as chancellor and hoped that Becket would succeed him (which he did) as archbishop. Theobald was deeply interested in both civil and canon law. He left a greatly strengthened English church.

Theodore of Tarsus (?602-690). Archbishop of Canterbury from 668. Theodore reorganized church government in England. Summoning the first synod of the whole English church at *Hertford in 673, he established Canterbury's authority in a united English church and laid the foundations of its parochial system.

third penny. A term used in the Domesday Book to refer to the ancient custom by which an earl took one third of the profits of justice collected in the shire court.

Thistlewood, Arthur. See Cato Street conspiracy.

Thomas, earl of Lancaster (c. 1277-1322). Leader of the lords *ordainers, son of Edmund of Lancaster (who was the brother of Edward I) and Blanche of Artois. Lancaster was responsible for the death of Piers *Gaveston, favourite of Edward II, in 1312. Two years later, following the king's disastrous defeat at Bannockburn, Lancaster became virtual ruler of England. His administration, however, was as feeble as Edward's and was additionally troubled by Lancaster's feud with Earl *Warenne. By 1318, following the rise of the *Middle Party, the king had regained control, but Lancaster's opposition to Edward was revived by the growing influence of the *Despensers. He secured their banishment in 1321, but in 1322 Edward took up arms against him and Lancaster was defeated at *Boroughbridge and executed.

Thomas of Brotherton, earl of Norfolk (1300-38). Marshal of England from 1316. Eldest son of Edward I, by his second wife Margaret, Thomas was the half-brother of Edward II. An able soldier, he fought against the Scots, notably at Newcastle (1317). In 1319 he acted as warden of England during the absence of Edward II, but in 1326 he was among those who condemned Edward II's favourites, the *Despensers, and supported the deposition of Edward by Mortimer and Queen Isabel. During the reign of Edward III he was active in arraying Welsh soldiers for the king's wars.

Thomas of Woodstock, earl of Buckingham and duke of Gloucester (1355-97). Leader of the lords *appellant, youngest son of Edward III. He led the opposition to the government of his nephew Richard II and was the dominant figure in the *Merciless Parliament (1388), which condemned a group of the king's favourites. In 1397 Richard took his revenge. Thomas was arrested and died, presumably murdered, in Calais.

Thorkell the Tall (early 11th century). Danish warrior, who, after leading the invasion of 1009, served the Anglo-Saxon king Aethelred II from 1012. In 1015 Thorkell supported the invasion of *Cnut, who created him earl of East Anglia. During Cnut's absence in 1019 Thorkell acted as regent.

thorough. The term given to the thoroughgoing authoritarian policies of *Laud and *Strafford during the *eleven years' tyranny of Charles I. It is also sometimes applied to the government of Cromwell.

Throckmorton plot (1583). A plot, revealed under torture by one of the conspirators, the Roman Catholic Francis Throckmorton (1554-84), to place *Mary Queen of Scots on the English throne in place of Elizabeth I. The conspiracy planned a Spanish-backed invasion of England by English Catholic exiles led by the Frenchman, Henri, duc de Guise. Its discovery led to the execution of Throckmorton and the expulsion of the Spanish ambassador Mendoza.

Tichborne claimant. Arthur Orton (1834-98), an ex-butcher claiming to be Sir Roger Tichborne, missing heir to a baronetcy and its accompanying fortune. Losing an action to establish his claim (1872) and subsequently (1874) convicted of perjury, Orton served ten years' imprisonment. The sensational affair riveted public attention.

Ticonderoga, battle of (8 July 1777). A battle during the American Revolution, in which the fort of Ticonderoga was seized by the army of Gen. John Burgoyne. This success tempted Burgoyne into a risky advance, his retreat being cut off at *Saratoga.

Tinchebrai, battle of (28 Sept 1106). The battle in which *Robert II Curthose, duke of Normandy, was defeated by his younger brother Henry I of England. Henry was thus able to establish his rule over Normandy, and Robert and his ally, the count of Mortain, were captured and imprisoned for life.

Tiptoft, John, earl of Worcester (c. 1427-1470). Constable of England (1462-67, 1470), who had a reputation for ruthlessness that earned him the sobriquet Butcher of England. A Yorkist, on the restoration of Henry VI he was captured and beheaded. He was also a scholar and patron of learning.

Tirel, Walter. Lord of Poix, in Picardy, and of the manor of Langham, in Essex. It was alleged, although he denied it, that his arrow killed William Rufus in the New Forest in 1100.

tithe. The payment of one-tenth of the earnings or produce of an inhabitant of a parish for the upkeep of the church. Originally voluntary, tithes were first enforced in the mid-10th century, and they became an important item in the income of parish priests (see vicar). The payment of tithes was widely resented and became a political issue during the Interregnum, when *Barebones Parliament (1653) sought to abolish them. They were also bitterly resented by the Roman Catholic majority in Ireland and formed one of the grievances of the *Whiteboys. A series of Tithe Acts (1836-91) replaced tithes with rent charges dependent on corn prices; these charges were abolished in 1936. Similar acts were later passed for Scotland and Ireland.

tithing. A subdivision of a *hundred. It originally corresponded to ten households, whose members were responsible to the king for each other's good behaviour. It formed the basis of *frankpledge.

Tobago. An island in the Caribbean Sea, which together with *Trinidad forms an independent unitary state within the *Commonwealth. A former British colony, it gained its independence in 1962.

Tobruk, battle of (May-June 1942). A battle during the North African campaign of World War II, an Axis victory that exposed Egypt to the threat of German occupation. Tobruk, the focus of much bitter fighting since its capture by the British in Jan 1941, finally fell, after a month's fighting, to the Afrika Korps under its commander Rommel on 20 June; 33 000 British troops were taken prisoner. It was recaptured in Nov 1942.

toleration acts. Legislation granting rights of citizenship to *nonconformists, who suffered discrimination under the *Clarendon code (1661-65). The Toleration Act (1689) allowed English nonconformists their own places of worship, teachers, and preachers; in Scotland Presbyterianism was finally established in 1690. However, English nonconformists remained excluded from public office, although they were able to qualify for municipal offices by occasional conformity with Anglicanism (see Occasional Conformity, Act of). From 1727 annual indemnity acts effectively allowed nonconformists municipal office, but the *Corporation Act was not repealed until 1828. See also Bradlaugh, Charles; Jews; Roman Catholics.

toll. See turnpike.

Tolpuddle martyrs. Six trade unionists, farm labourers from the Dorset village of Tolpuddle, who were transported to Australia in 1834. *Trade unions had been legal since 1824, but their use of secret rituals heightened government alarm at unrest associated with developing union activity. The labourers —George and James Loveless, John and Thomas Stanfield, James Brine, and James Hammett—were prosecuted for having administered "illegal oaths" for "seditious" purposes. Convicted, they were sentenced to transportation for seven years. Despite widespread public protests, including a monster trade-union petition, the men were not pardoned until 1836.

Tone, (Theobald) Wolfe (1763-98). Irish nationalist. Inspired by the French Revolution, Tone and other Protestant radicals founded the *United Irishmen in 1791 with the aim of establishing an independent Irish republic. Banished from Ireland in 1795, in France he organized an expedition against Ireland, which, dispersed by a storm, failed to land (1796). Tone eventually arrived in Ireland too late to assist the Irish rebellion of 1798 and was captured and sentenced to death, but committed suicide.

Tonga. An island kingdom in the south Pacific. A British protectorate from 1900, it became an independent member of the Commonwealth in 1970.

Tooke, John Horne (1736-1812). Politician and philologist. He was born John Horne, adding the name of his friend William Tooke to his own in 1782. He supported John *Wilkes in his struggle to take his seat in parliament, organizing with Wilkes the Society for Supporting the Bill of Rights. The two men later quarrelled, and in 1771 Horne formed the Constitutional Society. In 1778 he was imprisoned for proposing to raise a subscription for the American colonists, in revolt against England. He subsequently supported Pitt the younger against Charles James Fox and twice unsuccessfully contested Fox's constituency, Westminster (1790, 1796). Horne Tooke's great philological work, *The Diversions of Purley*, was first published in 1786 (enlarged version, 1798).

Tories. A political grouping that emerged in the 1680s and became the *Conservative Party in the 1830s. The term is still applied to present-day Conservatives. "Tory" derives from the Irish *toraidhe*, outlaw, and was originally applied abusively to the *Abhorrers of the attempt (by those later called *Whigs) to exclude the Roman Catholic James, duke of York, from the succession to the throne. The Tories complied with the Glorious Revolution, which overthrew James, but became associated with the *Jacobite rebels and, following the

Hanoverian succession (1714), were excluded from office until the reign of George III. A new Tory party emerged under *Pitt the younger and held power almost uninterruptedly from 1783 to 1830. Opposed to the French Revolution, following the harsh period of the Revolutionary and Napoleonic Wars the Tories became repressive under the leadership of Lord *Liverpool, and the name Tory became synonymous with reaction. A liberal Tory period, associated with George *Canning, in the 1820s led to a split in the party between liberal and more right-wing elements. Under *Peel its development into the Conservative Party began.

Torrington, earl of. See Herbert, Arthur.

Tory Democracy. See Fourth Party.

Tostig (d. 1066). Earl of Northumbria. A son of Earl *Godwine. Tostig became earl of Northumbria on *Siward's death (1055). His ruthless measures provoked a rebellion in 1065 and led to his replacement as earl by *Morcar. Tostig fled to Flanders and in 1066 raided the south coast before allying himself with the Norwegian King Harald III Hardraade in the latter's invasion of Britain. He was killed at the battle of *Stamford Bridge.

tournament (or **tourney**). A martial combat between knights, introduced into England from France in the 11th century. Mock battles (*mêlées*) between groups of horsemen were succeeded by jousting, in which two mounted knights, their squires acting as seconds, entered the lists (the walls of the jousting ground) and charged each other with lances. By the early 15th century a central wooden barrier prevented the horses from colliding and special armour was developed to reduce injury. Fighting on foot, using a variety of weapons, became popular in the 16th century. Tournaments developed elaborate ceremonial, colourful pageantry, and complex rules. Blunted weapons were usually used, but loss of life and private vendettas were frequent. See also chivalry.

Tower of London. A royal fortress built to protect London. Although it is likely that a defensive structure of some sort existed before the Normans, it was William I who erected the first stone castle, the White Tower, begun in 1078. As control of London and London's trade was crucial for control of the entire country, much effort was put into making the castle as strong as possible. Advances in the techniques of warfare necessitated constant rebuilding and strengthening. New inner and outer defences, containing 19 towers, were gradually added in the 12th and 13th centuries. The external defences outside the moat were added at the beginning of the 16th century. However, the gradual pacification of England, carried out largely under the Tudors, meant that the Tower was becoming increasingly redundant, and from the 16th century onwards its main function was as a prison (prisoners executed here include Sir Thomas More, Anne Boleyn, and Strafford and Laud). Equally the rapid expansion of London meant that the Tower could no longer defend it adequately. It ceased being a royal residence in the 17th century, when comfort finally supplanted security in the minds of the monarchs, since when its main function has been as a museum (the *regalia are here) and tourist attraction.

Townshend, Charles (1725-67). Chancellor of the exchequer (1766-67). He was responsible for the American Import Duties Act (1767), which imposed duties on lead, glass, paper, painters' colours, and tea imported to America from Britain. Bitterly resented by the colonists, it was repealed in 1770.

Townshend, Charles Townshend, 2nd Viscount (1674-1738). Politician and agriculturalist. Walpole's brother in law, Townshend became secretary of state (with James *Stanhope) in 1714; dismissed in 1717, he returned to office in 1720. In 1721, in Walpole's ministry, Townshend became responsble for foreign policy (with, until 1724, *Carteret). To maintain the treaty of Utrecht Townshend allied Britain with France and Prussia in the league of Hanover (1725). After Walpole took control of foreign policy in 1729 Townshend resigned (1730). He retired to improve his Norfolk estates and was nicknamed "Turnip" Townshend for his introduction of turnips into crop rotation.

Townshend, George Townshend, 4th Viscount and 1st Marquess (1724–1807). Lord lieutenant of Ireland (1767–72). He took control of parliamentary management from the *undertakers (Anglo-Irish leaders) by creating a "Castle" party of Irish MPs relying on the viceroy's government (in Dublin castle) for offices and honours. He was also a talented caricaturist.

Towton, battle of (29 March 1461). A battle of the Wars of the Roses, fought in a snowstorm near Tadcaster in Yorkshire. The Lancastrians were defeated, suffering heavy casualties, and the Yorkists under Edward IV went on to take York. Henry VI and Queen Margaret fled to Scotland.

Tractarianism. See Oxford movement.

Trade, Board of. The name formerly borne by the government department dealing with matters affecting trade, now called the Department of Trade. A permanent board of trade and the colonies was established under the supervision of the Privy Council in 1696; colonial matters were hived off in 1768. Abolished in 1782, the board was re-established in 1786 and developed into an ordinary department (although its minister was still called "president"). It merged into a new Department of Trade and Industry in 1970 but was again separated in 1974 as the Department of Trade.

trade (or trades) union. An association of workers in a trade, or several related trades, organized to protect their interests. In the 18th century, at the start of the *industrial revolution, craftsmen began to organize themselves for the purpose of bargaining for better wages and working conditions. Legislation was introduced, forbidding such wage-bargaining "combinations", and fear of

revolutionary activity led to general *Combination Acts against them (1799, 1800). The acts were subsequently repealed (1824, 1825), and combination was permitted for bargaining wages and hours. Robert *Owen unsuccessfully promoted an all-embracing Grand National Consolidated Trades Union in 1833, and government fear of subversion by such an organization provoked the case of the *Tolpuddle martyrs (1834). Greater prosperity in the 1840s and 1850s allowed considerable development of the trade union movement, on a national scale: the Miners' Association of Great Britain and Ireland was founded in 1841, the Amalgamated Society of Engineers in 1851, and the Amalgamated Society of Carpenters and Joiners in 1862. Trade unions, however, were not regarded as legal bodies, and in 1868 the Trades Union Congress (TUC) was founded to coordinate action to secure legality. The Trades Union Act (1871) gave the unions legal status and enabled them to protect their funds by registering as *friendly societies. Peaceful picketing was permitted by the Conspiracy and Protection of Property Act (1875). The 1880s saw the development of the mass "new unionism" among unskilled workers, such as dockers, whose successful strike in London in 1889 greatly encouraged the movement. Its political activities were channelled into the emerging *Labour Party. Opposition to the *Taff Vale judgment (1901) led to the Trade Disputes Act (1906), which gave the unions protection from liability for losses caused by strikes; after the *Osborne judgment (1909) the Trade Union Act (1913) legalized the political levy. Cooperation between union leaders and government during World War I encouraged the development of machinery for employer–union negotiations. The TUC was reorganized under a general council, and *Bevin founded the influential Transport and General Workers Union (1921). The 1926 *general strike was a severe setback, resulting in losses in union membership. The retaliatory Trade Disputes and Trade Union Act (1927) made sympathetic strikes illegal and restricted the political levy; it was repealed in 1946. In the postwar period union membership has greatly increased, while the number of unions has declined as a result of amalgamation.

Trafalgar, battle of (21 Oct 1805). A naval battle of the Napoleonic War, a major British victory. The encounter, between a combined French and Spanish fleet of 33 ships of the line and seven frigates under Admirals Villeneuve and Gravina and a British fleet of 32 ships of the line and five frigates under *Nelson, in the Victory, took place off Cape Trafalgar, southern Spain. During the course of the fighting, 17 French and Spanish ships were captured and one sunk, and some 7000 casualties inflicted, without the loss of a single British vessel. British casualties numbered 450 killed and over 1200 wounded and included Nelson himself, mortally wounded by a sniper's bullet. Nelson's famous message—"England expects that every man will do his duty"—was signalled at Trafalgar.

trained bands (or **train-bands**). The units, each consisting of about a hundred men, into which the county levies of the 16th and early 17th centuries were divided. The standing royal order, that trained bands should be exercised annually, was rarely observed. Although the bands were chiefly citizens' forces, they were usually commanded by gentlemen with some military knowledge. See also militia.

Transjordan. A former British *mandate (1920-46), previously part of the Ottoman (Turkish) Empire. In 1946 it became an independent kingdom and in 1949 was renamed Jordan.

transportation. The deporting of convicts to a penal colony, a punishment used in England from the 17th century until 1868. From Charles II's time transportation to the American colonies was an alternative sentence to execution and was imposed, for example, on many of those who took part in *Monmouth's rebellion. During the 18th and early 19th centuries legislation provided for its

use (for a term of years or for life) to punish many, often petty, offences. From 1788, after the American Revolution, convicts were taken to Australia (see Botany Bay). Transportation to New South Wales ended in 1840, to Tasmania in 1853, and to Western Australia in 1868.

Transvaal. A province of South Africa. Settled by Boers from the *great trek after 1837, it was recognized as independent in 1852 (see Sand River Convention) and became the South African republic in 1857. In 1877 Natal annexed the Transvaal, which, however, regained virtual independence by the *Pretoria convention (1881). It was reconquered by Britain during the second *Boer War (1899-1902), became self-governing in 1907, and joined the Union of South Africa in 1910.

Treachery Act (1940). A statute that, during World War II, defined treachery as assisting, or conspiring or attempting to assist, the military operations of the enemy. It was punishable by death. The act expired in 1946. See also treason.

treason. Violation of the allegiance owed to the sovereign. Misprision of treason is failure to disclose knowledge of a committed treason. The first statutory definition of treason was in 1352, when five offences were declared treasonous: compassing or imagining the death of the king, his queen, or his heir; violating the queen, the king's eldest unmarried daughter, or the wife of his heir; levying war against the king within his realm or adhering to his enemies; forging his seal or his coins; and killing one of certain royal officials and judges while he is engaged in his duties. These high treasons contrasted with petty treason (subsequently abolished): the murder by an apprentice of his master, by a wife of her husband, or by an ecclesiastic of his superior (viewed as the betrayal of private allegiance). The scope of the treason law was temporarily enlarged in the 16th century to include refusal to take the oath of supremacy (1536) or affirming that the queen was a heretic (1571). Judicial decisions extended treason to include rioting against enclosure (1597) and the rioting of apprentices who pulled down brothels (1688). The Treasonable and Seditious Practices Act (1795) strengthened the law still further, but the Treason Felony Act (1848) converted into felonies punishable by life imprisonment attempts to depose the sovereign, to deprive him of his dominions, or to levy war against him.

The punishment for treason was, under the original act, hanging, drawing, and quartering; after 1795 it was beheading; and since 1870 it has been hanging (see capital punishment). Trials were at first by battle or by martial law before the constable of England, later before the lord high steward, then by act of *attainder, and from the 16th century increasingly by common law procedure. See also Treachery Act.

Treasury. The government department that manages the UK economy. The main medieval financial department was the *Exchequer, but during Elizabeth I's reign the nucleus of a new department, the Treasury, was formed under Lord Burghley. By 1660 the office had a permanent staff, and from 1714 lords commissioners of the Treasury were appointed, the first lord gradually assuming the role of *prime minister. After the abolition of the Exchequer (1833) the Treasury became a ministerial department under the chancellor of the exchequer, who is the second commissioner. In 1964 responsibility for economic planning was passed to the Department of Economic Affairs but after the department's dissolution in 1969 was restored to the Treasury.

Trevithick, Richard (1771-1833). Engineer who built the first steam-driven passenger-carrying carriage (1801) and the first railway locomotive (1804).

trial by battle. A form of trial introduced into England by the Normans. At first used in criminal cases, when the parties themselves fought, it was later extended to civil cases, when champions did battle. From about 1179 the *grand assize provided an alternative for the settlement of land disputes, but trial by battle was not abolished until 1819.

trial by ordeal. A method of determining an accused person's guilt or innocence when *oath-helpers were unavailable. Ordeal by fire, reserved for freemen, involved holding, or walking barefoot over, red-hot iron; if the resultant wound healed after three days innocence was assumed. Ordeal by water involved plunging the arm into hot water or being thrown into a river; absence of burns, or sinking, implied innocence. Trial by cursed morsel required the accused (always clergy) to eat food containing, e.g., a feather; choking showed guilt. The church was required to oversee trial by ordeal, which was abolished after the clergy were forbidden by the pope to participate (1215).

Triennial Act. 1. (1641) An act passed by the Long Parliament stipulating that not more than three years were to elapse between the dissolution of one parliament and the summoning of its successor and that parliament was to meet for at least 50 days. **2.** (1664) An act repealing that of 1641 and stipulating that parliament was to meet at least once every three years. However, no provision was made for its enforcement. **3.** (1694) An act providing for parliament to meet at least once every three years and to last for not more than three years.

Triers and Ejectors. Officers commissioned in 1654 by Cromwell to assess the fitness of ordinands (Triers) and eject unsatisfactory clergy from their benefices (Ejectors). The Triers included clergy and laymen; the Ejectors were all laymen. The measure was intended to control radical preaching and political disaffection.

Trimmer, the. See Halifax, George Savile, 1st marquess of.

Trinidad. An island in the Caribbean Sea, which together with *Tobago has been an independent state within the *Commonwealth since 1962. As a British colony it was valuable for its sugar plantations, long worked by slave labour.

Trinovantes. A British tribe occupying present-day Essex and south Suffolk. They submitted to Caesar in 54 BC to escape the aggression of *Cassivellaunus. Their capital was probably at Chelmsford (Caesaromagus).

triple alliances. Three alliances in British history: in 1668, between England, the Netherlands, and Sweden against France; in 1717, between Britain, France, and the Netherlands against Spain; and in 1788, between Britain, Prussia, and the Netherlands to maintain the existing state of international affairs.

Tristan da Cunha. An island in the South Atlantic, a dependency of St Helena. Britain annexed the island after stationing a defensive garrison there in 1816. The population was evacuated in 1961, when a volcano erupted, but was able to return in 1963.

Troyes, treaty of (21 May 1420). An agreement between England and France during the *Hundred Years' War. According to its terms the French king Charles VI betrothed his daughter Catherine to Henry V and made the English king his rightful heir in place of the dauphin.

Truck Act (1831). An act prohibiting the worst features of the truck system —payment of wages by goods, not money. Truck payments denied freedom of choice to employees and profited employers, who could calculate wages according to retail prices, while buying goods wholesale.

trust territory. The former mandated territories (see mandate) of the League of Nations, which were placed in the trusteeship of the UN in 1945. There are now no trust territories in the British Commonwealth.

Tudor, house of. The ruling dynasty of England from 1485 to 1603. The family originated in Penmynydd, Anglesey, and traced its ancestry to Ednyfed Fychan (d. 1246), steward of *Llywelyn ap Iorwerth, who was granted lands for his servies in several parts of Gwynedd and southwest Wales. In about 1429 Owain ap Maredudd (Owen Tudor; c. 1400-

1461) married *Catherine of Valois, the widow of Henry V. Their son Edmund Tudor was legitimized and created earl of Richmond by his half-brother Henry VI and married Margaret Beaufort, the great-great-granddaughter of Edward III; their son was Henry VII, the first Tudor monarch. The other four Tudor monarchs were Henry VIII (1509-47), Edward VI (1547-53), Mary I (1553-58), and Elizabeth I (1558-1603).

Tudor, Jasper, earl of Pembroke and duke of Bedford (?1431-1495). Second son of Owen Tudor (executed in 1461 after the battle of Mortimer's Cross) and of Catherine of Valois. Created earl in 1453, he fought for Henry VI in the Wars of the Roses and was attainted in 1468. He accompanied Warwick the kingmaker's invasion of England in 1470 but fled with his nephew, the future Henry VII, after the battle of *Tewkesbury (1471). He returned with Henry in 1485 and fought at *Bosworth (1485).

Tull, Jethro (1674-1741). Agriculturalist. Best known as the inventor of the wheeled seed drill (1701), Tull also devised a horse-drawn hoe as an aid to soil aeration. He published his "principles of tillage" in *Horse-Hoeing Husbandry* (1731, 1733). Although not all his innovations were practicable, Tull's work helped revolutionize agriculture (see agrarian revolution).

tunnage and poundage. Subsidies on each tun of imported wines and every pound of imported or exported merchandise other than the *staple commodities. They date from the reign of Edward III (1327-77), and from the reign (1413-22) of Henry V it became usual for the king to be granted tunnage and poundage for life by his first parliament. Charles I collected them, not without protest, in spite of the failure of his first parliament to grant them. They were legalized again in 1641, made perpetual in 1714-16, and abolished in 1787.

Turner, Joseph Mallord William (1775-1851). Landscape artist. Perhaps the greatest painter of his age, he reflected the Romantic concern with man and nature, while his experiments with light and colour foreshadow impressionism.

Turnham Green, battle of (13 Nov 1642). An encounter between royalist and parliamentary armies at the outset of the Civil War. Following *Edgehill, Charles I pursued the retreating parliamentary forces towards London and caught up with them at Turnham Green, on the outskirts of the capital. Neither side ventured hostilities and Charles retreated to Oxford, which became his capital for the remainder of the war.

turnpike (or tollgate). A gate across a highway preventing passage until a toll has been paid. Turnpikes were administered by turnpike trusts, which were authorized by private act of parliament to levy tolls for maintenance of the highway. The trusts laid down a network of soundly constructed roads throughout Britain, replacing the parochial maintenance system on many highways and substantially improving communications. The first English turnpike roads were authorized by an act of 1663; in Scotland they appeared after 1750. By the 1830s there were about a thousand trusts administering 8000 tollgates and 6%—35 200 km (22 000 mi)—of British highways. The trusts' engineers, outstandingly John *Macadam, constructed many new roads, which by the 1800s were being utilized by an efficient stagecoach system. However, railway expansion after 1830 led to the rapid decline of stagecoaches and turnpike revenue. Turnpikes were never popular locally; tolls were high, and until 1835 several restricted the types of vehicle that might use their roads, to the detriment of local traffic. After 1864 parliament abolished many turnpikes; others disappeared, leaving only two.

Tuvalu. *See* Gilbert and Ellice Islands Colony.

Tyburn. A hill in London, near present-day Marble Arch. Named after the Tyburn, a rivulet that flowed into the Thames from the north, Tyburn hill was notorious for being the main site of public executions until 1783, after which they took place at *Newgate.

Tyler, Wat (d. 1381). The leader of the Kentish rebels in the *peasants' revolt (1381). Tyler led the rebels on their march to London, where they occupied the Tower. He was killed by the mayor of London, Sir William Walworth, during negotiations with Richard II at Smithfield.

Tyndale, William (c. 1494-1536). Translator of the *Bible and a leading figure in the English Reformation. Tyndale began work on his translation of the New Testament in England, but ecclesiastical opposition forced a move to Germany, where the work was completed in 1525. Later (1525-29), he worked in Antwerp on parts of the Old Testament. Tyndale's translation became widely popular in England. A controversial figure, Tyndale continued to live on the Continent, where he was eventually seized by the church authorities in Flanders and executed.

Tynwald. The legislative assembly of the Isle of Man. Meeting annually, it is attended by the lieutenant governor (representing the sovereign), a council acting as the upper house, and the House of *Keys.

Tyrconnell, Richard Talbot, earl of (1630-91). Irish general. A personal friend of James II, he received the command of the Irish army in 1684 and on James' accession (1685) was created earl of Tyrconnell. In 1687 he was appointed lord deputy. After James' fall Tyrconnell held Ireland for him but was defeated by William III at the Boyne (1690). He died shortly after the final Jacobite defeat at Aughrim.

Tyrone's revolt. *See* O'Neill's revolt.

U

Uganda. A British protectorate from 1894 until 1962, when it became independent and a member of the Commonwealth. The first prime minister, Dr Milton Obote, was overthrown by Gen.

Idi Amin Dada in 1971 and Amin was in turn overthrown in 1979.

Ulster. A former province of north Ireland, in the 5th century AD the most powerful of the five ancient kingdoms (see also Connaught; Leinster; Meath; Munster). In the 6th century, after the rule of Niall, hegemony passed to the other kingdoms, although Ulster retained its independence until the 17th century, under the leadership of the O'Neills and O'Donnells.

Ulster Unionists. Those who seek to maintain the union of Northern Ireland with Britain. The political party was formed in the late 19th century to counter the *home rule movement, and rose to great strength in 1911-14. After the Government of Ireland Act (1920) the Unionists dominated the Northern Ireland parliament until its suspension in 1972.

undertaker. A person contracting to serve the crown in a particular way. Originally used in the 16th century to describe men who rented crown lands in Ireland, the term commonly refers to those supporters of James I, Charles I, and Charles II who undertook to try to influence parliamentary voting on the king's behalf.

Uniformity, Acts of. Parliamentary legislation aimed at securing the legal and doctrinal foundations of the Anglican church. Two Acts of Uniformity were passed during the reign of Edward VI. The first (1549) required that the moderately Protestant *Book of Common Prayer, drawn up by Archbishop *Cranmer, should be used in Anglican worship, but imposed only comparatively mild penalties on clergy failing to do so. The second act (1552), enforcing the use of a new more obviously Protestant prayer book, laid down more severe penalties for nonimplementation as well as fines for nonattendance at church. Both acts were repealed under Mary I (see Marian reaction). In 1559, as part of the Elizabethan religious settlement, a third Act of Uniformity reordered Anglican worship by the introduction of a new prayer book (slightly modified from

the 1552 version) and the imposition of weekly fines of 12 pence on absentees. Following the Restoration, a new Act of Uniformity was passed (1662) as part of the *Clarendon code. Church services were to be conducted according to a revised prayer book and liturgy, and some 2000 clergy who refused to comply were forced to resign their livings.

Unionists. Originally, supporters of the political union of Great Britain and Ireland, secured in 1800. The term was later applied to Liberal opponents of Irish *home rule who, led by Joseph *Chamberlain, broke (1886) with Gladstone over home rule. The Liberal Unionists allied themselves with the Conservatives, and the name Unionist came to be applied to both parties. In 1909 the official name of the Conservative Party became the Conservative and Unionist Party. See also Ulster Unionists.

Union Jack. The flag of the United Kingdom, officially called the Union flag. When first devised in 1606, following the union of the crowns of England and Scotland, the flag combined the crosses of St George and St Andrew. The cross of St Patrick was added in 1801, on the union of Great Britain and Ireland. Originally, and correctly, the name Union Jack applied only to the flag when used as a ship's jack—the flag flown at a vessel's bow—but it soon came to be applied generally to the flag.

Union of England and Scotland. The union of the crowns was effected by the succession (1603) of James VI of Scotland to the English throne as James I, and from 1608, following the decision in Calvin's case, all those born in Scotland after James' accession to the English throne were English citizens. From 1654 until 1660, under the Protectorate, England and Scotland were temporarily united, but the act establishing an "incorporating" union between England and Scotland was not passed until 1707. The act resulted from the increasing difficulties monarchs had experienced in reconciling the conflicting claims of the two British parliaments, culminating in a crisis over the failure (1701) of the Scottish parliament to accept the Hanoverian succession. Scotland lost its own parliament but was represented in the new parliament of Great Britain (in practice the former English parliament with the addition of Scottish members) by 45 MPs in the Commons and 16 peers. Scotland retained its legal system and established church and gained free trade with England.

Union of England and Wales. The union was achieved by a series of acts (1536-43). The act of annexation was passed in the last session of the Reformation parliament (1536) and formed part of Thomas Cromwell's policy of creating a national sovereign state at the time when Henry VIII was rejecting papal authority. The act dissolved the marcher lordships, divided Wales into shires (each of which was to be represented in parliament), added four new counties (Denbigh, Montgomery, Brecknock, and Radnor) to the six that already existed, and granted equal citizenship to the Welsh. Subsequent acts culminated in that of 1543, which introduced legal measures on the English model. The establishment of English law and administration led to a period of increased social and commercial prosperity, but the subsequent status of English rather than Welsh as the language of officialdom had an unfavourable effect on Welsh culture.

Union of Great Britain and Ireland. Achieved by legislation of the separate parliaments of Great Britain and Ireland, union was enacted on 1 Aug 1800, establishing the *United Kingdom on 1 Jan 1801. The *Irish rebellion of 1798 and French invasion threats convinced Pitt the younger that union was essential. He failed, however, in his aim of simultaneous *Catholic emancipation.

Unitarians. Religious believers recognizing Christ as God's messenger but not as divine. Unitarianism—seen as combining God, "reason", and scientific progress—became influential from the late 18th century, absorbing many nonconformist congregations and helping motivate a number of 19th-century social and political reforms.

United Empire Loyalists. American colonists loyal to the British crown who emigrated to Canada after the Declaration of Independence (1776) (*see* American Revolution). About 40 000 settled in Ontario and New Brunswick.

United Irishmen, Society of. An Irish secret society founded in 1791 in Belfast by Wolfe *Tone and other Protestant radicals. Inspired by the French Revolution, it desired to establish an independent Irish republic and, to this end, organized the unsuccessful *Irish rebellion of 1798.

United Kingdom. Great Britain (England, Scotland, Wales) and Northern Ireland. Originally created by the *Union of Great Britain and Ireland 1801, it took its present form in 1921 (*see* Irish Free State).

United Nations (UN). An organization, founded in 1945 in place of the *League of Nations, to foster international peace and cooperation in the resolution of the world's economic, social, cultural, and humanitarian problems. Britain was one of the 51 founder members.

Unlearned Parliament (Nov 1404). The parliament summoned at Coventry by Henry IV to raise taxes to relieve his threatened bankruptcy. Lawyers were excluded (hence its name) since, it was alleged, they would waste time on their own rather than the king's business.

Upper Britain. One of the two provinces (*compare* Lower Britain) into which Britain was divided by *Septimius Severus. Its capital was London and its boundary, a line between the Wash and the Mersey.

Uses, Statute of (1536). The act of parliament that sought to eliminate abuses in the application of uses. The use (deriving from the Latin *opus*, benefit) was the right of a person to profit from land held by another. The procedure facilitated the management of property but was widely abused by landowners seeking to evade feudal dues or to defraud creditors by making nominal transfers of land while retaining control of it. The statute laid down that the person having the use of an estate was its legal owner. The act aroused widespread discontent among land-owners.

Ushant, battle of. *See* Glorious First of June.

usury. The charging of interest on a loan of money, forbidden by medieval canon law and punishable in the ecclesiastical courts. Interest on loans, such as those made by Italian bankers to the crown in the late-13th and 14th centuries, was thus paid in other forms (e.g. annuities) until legally permitted in the 16th century. A series of 11 usury laws (1545-1850) fixed interest below a certain percentage (ranging from ten to five per cent) and usury came to mean the charging of interest above the permitted rate. The usury laws were repealed in 1854.

utilitarianism. An ethical theory propounded by Bentham and James *Mill and modified by J. S. *Mill. It asserted, in the words of J. S. Mill, that "actions are right in proportion as they tend to promote happiness, wrong as they tend to produce the reverse of happiness". The "utility" principle encouraged 19th-century administrative and social reforms.

Utrecht, treaties of (1713-14). Nine peace treaties negotiated among the European powers at the close of the War of the *Spanish Succession. The treaty between France and Great Britain was decisively in the latter's favour. France recognized the Hanoverian succession and ceded to Britain much of its North American territory, including Hudson Bay, Nova Scotia, and Newfoundland. In the partition of the Spanish empire, Britain received Gibraltar and Minorca.

Utrum Assize. A judicial proceeding, or the writ giving rise to it, that investigated whether (Latin word: *utrum*) land was held by a parish priest in *frankalmoign or was a lay fee. Dating from the constitutions of Clarendon (1164), it was taken only occasionally after a restrain-

ing act in 1571 but was not abolished until 1833.

V

V-1. A small jet-propelled pilotless aircraft, also called a flying (or buzz) bomb, used by the Germans to bombard London and surrounding targets from June 1944 to March 1945. Some 8000 V-1s (German *Vergeltungswaffe*, retaliation weapon) were launched (by rocket-assisted take-off) from sites in northern France and Holland. At first they caused considerable damage and loss of life (6184 people were killed), but later the RAF was able to shoot many of them down over the sea.

V-2 rocket. A German missile of World War II, carrying about 900 kg (2000 lb) of high explosive and having a range of over 320 km (200 mi). From Sept 1944 to March 1945, more than 1300 V-2s were launched against Britain. Belgium, too, was heavily bombarded.

vaccination. Inoculation with vaccine (originally a virus of cowpox) to produce immunity against a specific disease (originally smallpox). Vaccination was pioneered in 1796 by Edward Jenner (1749-1823), a country doctor, after he noticed that milkmaids infected with cowpox did not catch smallpox. After strong opposition from leaders of the medical profession was overcome free vaccination was introduced in 1840 and became compulsory for babies in 1853. Smallpox was quickly eradicated, and compulsory vaccination was brought to an end in 1946. Vaccination is now used to prevent such diseases as tuberculosis and poliomyelitis.

Valence, Aymer de, earl of Pembroke (c. 1265-1324). Soldier who fought in the *Anglo-Scottish wars. He was victorious at *Ruthven (1306) but was defeated at *Loudun Hill (1307). He briefly (1212) supported Thomas, earl of Lancaster, against Edward II, but subsequently became the king's lieutenant in Scotland.

Vanbrugh, Sir John (1664-1726). Dramatist and architect. Vanbrugh's success as a playwright (of Restoration comedies of manners) began with *The Relapse* (1696). As an architect, he worked in the baroque style, his designs including Castle Howard, Yorkshire (1701), and Blenheim Palace, Oxfordshire (1705).

Vancouver, George (1757-98). Navigator and explorer. Between 1792 and 1794 he explored and charted the Pacific coast from California to Alaska and circumnavigated the island named after him. His most northerly explorations proved that no continuous ice-free *northwest passage existed.

Van Dyck, Sir Anthony (1599-1641). Flemish painter. An assistant of, and influenced by, Rubens, Van Dyck was most successful during the period 1632-41, when he was in England as chief portrait painter to Charles I. His output was considerable and had a great influence on English art. His most perfect works are the equestrian portrait of Charles I and the group portrait of the Russell family.

Vane the elder, Sir Henry (1589-1655). Secretary of state (1640-41) on the eve of the Civil War. He served in a series of household posts in the 1620s and 1630s, becoming a privy councillor in 1630. He spoke for the king in the Short Parliament (1640) but as a member of the Long Parliament took part in the impeachment of Strafford. Dismissed from royal service, he supported the parliamentarians in the Civil War.

Vane the younger, Sir Henry (1613-62). Parliamentarian, son of Sir Henry *Vane the elder. A Puritan, he lived in Massachusetts (1635-37), of which he was governor (1636-37). After his return to England he became an MP and played a prominent role in the Long Parliament throughout the Civil War and Commonwealth periods. However, he opposed Cromwell's dissolution of the Rump (1653) and the army's subsequent domination of government. In 1659 he became an MP in Richard Cromwell's parliament, participating in the over-

throw of the Protectorate. He opposed the Restoration and in 1662, regarded as "too dangerous to let live", was convicted of treason and executed.

Vanuatu Republic. *See* New Hebrides.

vassal. A feudal tenant holding land from a lord in return for his sworn loyalty and service. The vassal had to do *homage and swear *fealty to his lord.

vavasor. A feudal tenant. Vavasors ranked immediately below the barons and their lands were called vavasories.

Verdun, battle of (Feb-July 1916). A battle of World War I. Gen. Falkenhayn, intending to force the French to defend a vital point and so "bleed them to death", chose Verdun, a major historic fortress on the Paris approaches. Empty of guns and troops, it was hard to reinforce and its loss, he believed, would be such a blow that the French would seek peace. Initial assaults had some success but Pétain held out, and British and Russian attacks prevented German reinforcements from moving to Verdun. French counterattacks regained most of the ground lost and by Aug 1917 only one German position remained. Falkenhayn had failed, but he had virtually destroyed the French army.

Vereeniging, peace of (31 May 1902). The peace that ended the second *Boer War. The British annexation of the Transvaal and Orange Free State was confirmed. English became the official language, Dutch being allowed in schools and law courts. Future self-government was promised and Britain granted £3 million to reconstruct Boer farms.

Vergil, Polydore (c. 1470-1555). Humanist, author of a notable history of England. Born in Italy, Vergil spent most of his life in England and became archdeacon of Wells in 1508. The chroniclers Hall and Holinshed were influenced by his *Anglicae historia libri XXVI*, the first parts of which appeared in 1534.

Verneuil, battle of (17 Aug 1424). A battle of the Hundred Years' War. A crushing English victory over combined French and Scottish forces, it marked the zenith of English power in France during the post-*Agincourt era of the war. The Scots were decimated and their leader, the 4th earl of *Douglas, was killed.

Vernon, Edward (1684-1757). Naval commander, who captured Porto Bello from the Spanish in 1739. In 1745 Vernon blockaded the French in their Channel ports in order to prevent them from reinforcing Charles Edward Stuart. He was cashiered in 1746 for writing anonymous pamphlets attacking the Admiralty.

Versailles, treaty of (1919). The treaty between the allied powers and Germany that ended World War I. It was aimed chiefly at ensuring that Germany would never again be a military power. In Europe, Germany ceded Alsace-Lorraine to France, parts of Prussia and Silesia to Poland (leading to the creation of the "Polish corridor"), and part of Schleswig to Denmark. All the German colonies were transferred to the *League of Nations as mandated territories. The German army was limited to 100 000 men and the navy to 6 battleships, 12 cruisers, and 12 destroyers. The allies were to occupy the Rhineland for up to 15 years, and Germany undertook not to fortify the left bank of the Rhine. Responsibility for causing the war was accepted by Germany, which agreed to pay *reparations for allied loss and damage.

Verulamium. One of the most important and best-preserved Roman towns in Britain, at St Albans in Hertfordshire. Much was demolished, soon after the Romans left, to provide building materials for St Albans abbey and other buildings, but extensive excavations (mainly 1930-34) have revealed most notably a theatre, three mosaic pavements, and a hypocaust. *See also* Alban, St.

vestiarian controversy. A 16th-century dispute over the wearing of ecclesiastical vestments. Puritan opposition to the *surplice, prescribed by the *Book of Common Prayer and confirmed in Archbishop Parker's *Advertisements* (1566),

led to some priests being deprived of their livings. Later in the century the controversy was absorbed into the general Puritan movement.

vicar. A priest of a parish of which the revenues are received by another. Before the Reformation the revenues, chiefly *tithes, of some parishes were appropriated by monasteries, which were obliged to appoint a vicar who would perform parochial duties in return for a portion of the tithes. After the dissolution of the monasteries the tithes of many such parishes were impropriated, or granted to laymen. A vicar has the same spiritual role in the Church of England as a rector, who, however, receives the parish revenues directly.

Victoria (1819-1901). Queen of the United Kingdom (1837-1901) and empress of India (1876-1901). Her reign, the longest of any British sovereign, coincided with the heyday of British overseas power, and Victoria became a symbol of the nation's solidarity and confidence. The only child of George III's fourth son, Edward, duke of Kent, and Princess Mary Louisa Victoria of Saxe-Coburg-Gotha. Victoria succeeded William IV, becoming the last sovereign of the house of *Hanover. Under five feet tall, but with royal dignity, she immediately showed her determination to rule by excluding her mother from any state influence. At first Victoria, while receiving advice from her uncle *Leopold, relied heavily upon the prime minister, Melbourne, a reliance that caused the constitutional *bedchamber crisis in 1839. In Feb 1840 she married her cousin *Albert, whose serious approach to life strengthened her own conscientiousness. He exerted considerable influence on Victoria, who, after his death (1861) tended to view all problems in the light of his likely opinion. They had nine children.

Constitutionally, Victoria's reign witnessed, in spite of her own aspirations, a limitation of the power of the monarchy in relation to ministers, defined by *Bagehot as "the right to be consulted, the right to encourage, the right to warn". Nevertheless, encouraged by Albert, Victoria long claimed special supervision of foreign affairs, leading to sharp disputes with Palmerston and John Russell (whom she privately called "those two dreadful old men").

After Albert's death she went into virtual, and unpopular, seclusion for ten years. For her last 30 years, however, she resumed public appearances (although always wearing mourning) and her popularity reached unprecedented heights, demonstrated in her *Golden Jubilee' (1887) and *Diamond Jubilee (1897). For much of this period politics were dominated by Gladstone, whom she came to dislike intensely, and Disraeli, who became her ideal prime minister. In her long widowhood, she travelled in Europe and supervised her family, which, through marriages, gradually extended to most of European royalty. She was greatly attached to her Scottish manservant, John Brown (1826–83), causing suggestions, periodically resuscitated, of a secret marriage. Victoria worked to the last months of her life, and her death was regarded as marking the end of a splendid era. She was succeeded by the prince of Wales, Edward VII.

Vienna, congress of (1 Oct 1814–9 June 1815). The congress of European powers held at Vienna following the French Revolutionary and Napoleonic Wars. Britain (represented by Wellington and Castlereagh), its control of the seas acknowledged, ensured its commercial and strategic security, retaining Malta, Heligoland, the Cape of Good Hope, Ceylon, Tobago, Santa Lucia, and Mauritius and receiving the protectorate of the Ionian Islands. Austria, Prussia, and Russia made large territorial gains. France, with the Bourbons restored, lost its post-1793 conquests but retained great-power status. The congress, at Britain's initiative, also condemned the slave trade and established regulations for the precedence of diplomatic representatives that are still in force. See also quadruple alliance (1815).

Vigo Bay, battle of (12 Oct 1702). A naval action during the War of the Spanish Succession. A Spanish treasure fleet was caught in Vigo Bay, off the northwest coast of Spain, by British and Dutch men-of-war under Admiral Sir George Rooke (1650–1709). Every Spanish ship was taken or sunk, and bullion worth £1 million was seized.

Vikings. Scandinavian sea warriors who raided much of northwest Europe between the 8th and 11th centuries. They penetrated most of the British Isles, Scotland and Ireland being settled mostly by Norwegians (Norsemen) and England by the Danes (see Danish invasions).

villa. The characteristic form of landed estate in the Roman empire. The villas in Britain were the estates of the aristocracy who had accepted Roman customs. Many have been excavated and mosaics, painted plaster, and other architectural features have been discovered.

villein. A medieval peasant. The word is derived from the Latin villanus, villager —the class of person most frequently mentioned in the *Domesday Book. Like the Anglo-Saxon *gebur or *geneat the villeins cultivated land in the village fields in return for labour services on the manorial farm. By the 13th century the villeins had become unfree peasants bound to their lords by rigid legal and economic ties. Economic and social changes, especially after the *black death, had greatly weakened the institution of villeinage by the 15th century.

Villiers, Barbara, countess of Castlemaine and duchess of Cleveland (1641–1709). A mistress of Charles II, by whom she had at least one child. She was married (1659) to Roger Palmer, who became earl of Castlemaine in 1661, but left him in 1662. She exerted considerable powers of patronage until 1670, when she began to lose the king's favour. Subsequent lovers included John Churchill (later 1st duke of Marlborough) and the playwright William Wycherley.

Vinegar Hill, battle of (21 June 1798). A battle in which General Lake, defending the property of Irish loyalists in Co. Wexford, defeated Catholic rebels during the Irish rebellion of 1798.

Virginia Company. *See* London Company.

Virgin Islands. A Caribbean island group, divided between Britain and the USA. The colony of the British Virgin Islands was first settled by the Dutch, being occupied by English planters in 1666.

Virgin Queen. *Elizabeth I. When pressed to marry she declared that she was already married to her realm and wore a ring in token.

viscount. A rank of the *peerage, below an earl and above a baron, originally a sheriff of a county and thus a deputy of a count or earl (Latin: *vicecomes*). The title was first used of a peer in 1440.

Vitoria, battle of (21 June 1813). An engagement fought in the Basque province towards the closing stages of the Peninsular War. The British army, under Wellington, numbered 79 000, and decisively defeated French forces of 66 000 at a cost of 5000 casualties; French casualties were 8000.

Vortigern (early 5th century). Romano-British king. According to Bede, Vortigern invited *Hengist and *Horsa to Britain to combat a threat from Pictish and Scottish invaders. Vortigern is not a personal name but a title meaning overlord. The extent of Vortigern's territory is unknown, but he probably controlled a large part of Britain.

Vote of No Addresses (Jan 1648). The decision of the *Long Parliament to break off all negotiations with Charles I. It was occasioned by news of the king's *Engagement with the Scots.

W

Wade, George (1673–1748). Commander in chief in Scotland from 1724 to 1740. He proved energetic in disarming the Highland clans and forming Highland companies to police the area.

His greatest achievement was the construction of about 400 km (250 mi) of *roads in the Highlands. He became a field marshal in 1743. Wade was commander in chief in England during the Jacobite invasion of 1745 but, failing to halt the southward march of Charles Edward Stuart, was replaced by the duke of Cumberland.

wager of law (or **compurgation**). The acceptance of the oaths of a varying number of people (compurgators) to establish fact in legal processes. Dating from Anglo-Saxon times, it was not used in criminal proceedings after the 14th century. It survived in civil cases, chiefly in actions of debt, until the 19th century, being abolished in 1833.

Waitangi, treaty of (6 Feb 1840). The treaty by which the Maori chiefs of New Zealand's North Island accepted British sovereignty in return for British protection. Britain's aim was to supervise traders, missionaries, and *Wakefield's settlements. On the basis of the treaty, Britain annexed New Zealand in May 1840.

Wakefield, battle of (30 Dec 1460). A battle of the Wars of the Roses, in which the Lancastrians besieged Richard, duke of York, in Sandal castle, near Wakefield. York was defeated and killed.

Wakefield, Edward Gibbon (1796–1862). Colonizer. Wakefield advocated controlled emigration of Britain's surplus population. In 1839 he helped establish the New Zealand Company to promote settlement (preceding the treaty of *Waitangi) and, in Canada, advised the governor general Lord Durham in the preparation of the *Durham Report.

Walcheren expedition (1809). An attempt by the British to send an army and fleet up the river Scheldt to seize Antwerp from the French during the Napoleonic War. The commander in chief, Lord Chatham, exhausted his troops' energies in laying siege to Flushing and, when Antwerp was strongly reinforced by the French, the expedition was called off. About a third of the force of 40 000 was temporarily left behind to garrison Walcheren, where they were decimated by malaria.

Wales, Statute of. *See* Rhuddlan, Statute of.

Wallace, Sir William (c. 1270-1305). Scottish national hero. Second son of a Scottish knight, Wallace emerged in 1297 as a leader of opposition to English rule (*see* Anglo-Scottish Wars). After defeating the English at *Stirling Bridge (1297), Wallace recaptured Berwick and invaded northern England. As a result of these exploits he was knighted and appointed guardian of Scotland in name of the king, John Balliol. Wallace was the only major Scottish leader of resistance to the English who was not a great landed magnate, and some probably resented the pre-eminence of a man of relatively humble origins; but he seems to have enjoyed considerable popular support. At *Falkirk in 1298 Wallace's army was decisively defeated by Edward I and support for him waned. He resigned his guardianship and the rest of his life is obscure, although he is known to have visited France, presumably to seek help. Wallace was eventually captured by the English and executed in London.

Waller, Sir William (c. 1597-1686). Parliamentary general in the Civil War. A member of the Long Parliament from 1640, he was made a colonel on the outbreak of hostilities. He acquired the nickname William the Conqueror after taking Portsmouth and other southeastern towns. Promoted to general, he captured Hereford but was then defeated at *Roundway Down (1643). Victories in early 1644 were followed by disaster at Copredy Bridge in June. After the formation of the New Model Army in Feb 1645 Waller resigned his commission (*see* Self-Denying Ordinance). Subsequently, as a leading Presbyterian in parliament, he came into conflict with the army and was imprisoned (1648-51). In 1659 he conspired against Richard Cromwell and in 1660 became a member of the convention parliament, which effected the Restoration.

Wallingford, treaty of. *See* Winchester, treaty of.

Walpole, Sir Robert, 1st earl of Orford (1676-1745). Statesman, regarded as the first prime minister. A Norfolk squire, he was an MP from 1701 to 1712 and from 1713 to 1742, when he was created earl of Orford. He became the Whig *junto's leader in the House of Commons, serving as war secretary (1708-10) and treasurer of the navy (1710-11). He was imprisoned by the Tories for alleged corruption (1712) but after the accession of George I was first lord of the treasury (1715-17) in the ministry dominated by James *Stanhope and Charles Spencer, 3rd earl of *Sunderland. He introduced the first *sinking fund (1717) but resigned after the dismissal of Charles *Townshend. He returned to office in 1720, as paymaster general and restored public confidence after the collapse of the *South Sea Company. In April 1721 Walpole again became first lord of the treasury and effectively prime minister. Strengthened by his firm response to *Atterbury's plot, he progressively secured the resignation of his rivals (*Carteret in 1724 and Townshend in 1730). After George II's accession he survived, with the backing of Queen Caroline, the attempt (1727) to replace him with Spencer Compton (earl of *Wilmington). During the 1730s, however, mounting opposition to his pro-French foreign policy, financial policies, and extensive use of *patronage undermined his influence in the House of Commons. In particular, the widespread opposition to his unsuccessful attempt to impose an excise tax on wine and tobacco (1733) strengthened the hand of the opposition—Tories, disgruntled ex-colleagues, and such rising talents as Pitt (the elder). Forced unwillingly to take the country into the War of *Jenkins' Ear with Spain (1739) he lost the support of the Commons and resigned in Feb 1742. He continued, however, until his death to influence George II. Walpole's outstanding collection of paintings was sold by his grandson to Catherine the Great of Russia and is now in the Hermitage museum in Leningrad.

Walsingham, Sir Francis (1532-90). Secretary of state (1573-90) to Elizabeth I. He built up an intelligence service that uncovered the *Ridolfi and *Babington plots and secured the conviction and execution of Mary Queen of Scots. A fervent Protestant, he constantly urged war with Spain but was overruled by Elizabeth and Burghley.

Walter, Hubert. *See* Hubert Walter.

Walter of Coutances (d. 1207). Archbishop of Rouen from 1184, having served in Henry II's Chancery. He became justiciar in 1191, after the fall of William *Longchamp, and was virtual ruler of England until Richard I's return in 1194. He was subsequently engaged in diplomatic activities abroad.

Wantage code. An important Anglo-Saxon legal document issued by King Aethelred II (d. 1016) at Wantage. The king gave official recognition to local customary laws, some of which played an important part in the development of the common law.

wapentake. An administrative subdivision of the northern and central English shires in which Danish influence predominated. Wapentakes, which corresponded to *hundreds in other English shires, were first formed in the 10th century. The word is derived from the Old Norse for weapon and take; taking or grasping weapons was probably a Viking way of signifying assent at meetings. The wapentakes were the units of tax assessment, and each wapentake was responsible for maintaining law and order in its own jurisdiction.

Warbeck, Perkin (?1474-1499). Imposter and pretender to the throne of Henry VII. While in Ireland (1491) he was persuaded to impersonate Richard, duke of York, who with his younger brother Edward V was presumed murdered in the Tower (1483). Margaret, duchess of Burgundy (Edward IV's sister), acknowledged him as her nephew and he was received by James IV of Scots as the duke of York. He invaded southwest

England (1498) but fled when faced with Henry's troops. He was caught and, following two attempts to escape from the Tower, was hanged.

Wardens of the Marches. Officials appointed on both sides of the Anglo-Scottish border, with responsibilities for local administration and defence. The offices emerged during the *Anglo-Scottish wars in the 14th century and disappeared with the union of the crowns in 1603.

Wardrobe. A department of the *royal household. In the 13th century, under Henry III and Edward I, it became a major financial institution. Used as a war treasury, it acted as paymaster to the major military expeditions commanded by the king. It subsequently declined in importance, being replaced by the *Chamber. Separate from the king's Wardrobe was the Great Wardrobe, for army clothing and military stores, peripatetic until 1361 and then at Baynard castle, and the Privy Wardrobe, for bows, arrows, pikes, and other weapons, in the Tower of London.

Wards, Court of. The court set up to control the *wardships that fell to the crown. It was formally created in 1540 by Thomas *Cromwell, although a Wards Office had existed for many years. The office of the surveyor of liveries was added to the court in 1542, which then became the Court of Wards and Liveries. It was abolished by the Long Parliament in 1645.

wardship and marriage. The rights of a lord respectively to administer the estates of a minor until he or she came of age (boys at 21, girls at 14) and to determine the marriage of the heir and of the deceased tenant's widow or daughter. Since the rights could be sold, they often led to ruthless profiteering and remained a lucrative source of income for the crown until abolished by the Long Parliament.

Warenne, John de, earl of Surrey and Sussex (or **Earl Warenne**) (?1231-1304). Warden of Scotland from 1296. He married (1247) Alice de Lusignan, half-sister of Henry III, whom he ultimately supported in the second Barons' War. He later gave distinguished service in the field during Edward I's Scottish invasion (1296). He took Dunbar castle but was routed at Stirling Bridge (1297); in 1298 he fought at Falkirk.

Warenne, John de, earl of Surrey and Sussex (or Earl Warenne) (1286–1347). Magnate, who vacillated between support for Edward II and the baronial opposition. He abandoned the lords *ordainers after the execution of the king's favourite Piers Gaveston (1312). In 1317 he helped Alice de Lacy, wife of the ordainers' leader Thomas, earl of Lancaster, to elope, and Lancaster seized most of Warenne's estates. He joined Edward in the final overthrow of Lancaster (1322) but sided with Queen Isabel and Roger de Mortimer in 1327, urging the king's abdication.

War of 1812. See Anglo-American War.

War Office. A former government department responsible for *army administration and operations. The War Office developed out of the Council of War, first recorded in 1620, and was formally established in 1785. The office of secretary at war, which had emerged during the reign of Charles II, declined after the creation in 1794 of that of the secretary of state for war (and, from 1801, the colonies). The secretary for war was relieved of responsibility for the colonies in 1854 (see Colonial Office), and in 1863 the office of secretary at war was abolished. In 1964 the War Office was abolished and its functions assumed by the newly created Ministry of *Defence.

warrants. Written authorizations of an action. They are issued especially in the administration of justice: hence their use for searching premises and arresting suspects. They are issued by an executive authority, whether the crown, an officer of state, or a justice of the peace, to a subordinate. A general warrant is a warrant for the arrest of persons suspected of an offence, none of whom is individually named. Their use rested on legislation of Charles II, which expired

in 1694. Their illegality was finally established in a series of cases brought by John *Wilkes, who was arrested in 1763 after the publication of an attack on the King's Speech in No. 45 of his journal, the North Briton.

Warwick, earls of. See Beauchamp.

Warwick the kingmaker. See Neville, Richard, earl of Warwick and Salisbury.

Washington, George (1732–99). General and first president of the USA (1789–97). A Virginian squire, he fought as colonel of the Virginian troops against the French and Indians (1754–58). Appointed at the outbreak of the *American Revolution (1775) to command the Continental Army, he remained commander in chief until Dec 1783. Chairman of the constitutional convention (1787), Washington was unanimously chosen as president of the new nation.

Washington conference (Nov 1921–Feb 1922). A conference, attended by nine powers, the USA, Britain, Japan, France, Italy, the Netherlands, Portugal, China, and Belgium, to discuss naval and Far Eastern affairs. Three agreements were negotiated. 1. (Dec 1921) The four-power treaty between the USA, Britain, Japan, and France ended the *Anglo-Japanese alliance (1902); the signatories agreed to respect the territorial status quo in the Pacific. 2. (Feb 1922) The Washington, or five-power, treaty between the USA, Britain, Japan, France, and Italy regulated the respective sizes of the signatories' fleets. 3. (Feb 1922) The nine-power agreement pledged respect for China's independence and territorial integrity.

watch and ward. Writs issued in 1233, 1242, and 1254, providing for the maintenance of the peace. They directed that guards be appointed for the protection of every community and that strangers unable to give good account of themselves be arrested. The measure was included in the Statute of *Winchester (1285).

Waterloo, battle of (18 June 1815). The battle, fought near Brussels, which marked the end of the *French

Revolutionary and Napoleonic Wars. Napoleon, exiled in Elba since April 1814, returned to France and reassumed power in March 1815. The allies (then negotiating the treaty of Paris at the congress of Vienna) prepared to invade France. Napoleon marched into Belgium against Wellington's combined army of British, Dutch, Belgian, and German forces and Marshal Blücher's Prussian army. The French defeated Blücher at Ligny (16 June), while Wellington withdrew his force of 68 000 from *Quatre-Bras to Waterloo. Napoleon attacked Wellington's position with 72 000 troops (18 June), putting in three waves of assaults between late morning and late afternoon. The delayed start to the attack allowed the Prussians time to reach the battlefield, where they eventually deployed 45 000 troops. Towards sunset, a last French attack failed. The French retreated, pursued by the Prussians, and left 25 000 dead and wounded and 9000 prisoners on the battlefield (Wellington's casualties were 15 000 and Blücher's 8000). Napoleon ultimately surrendered to the British (15 July) and was exiled to St Helena.

Watling Street. One of the major Roman roads. It runs northwest from London to Wroxeter. It was built in the first years of the invasion and later extended to Chester. In the 5th century it served as an important route for the Saxon invaders.

Wat's dyke. *See* Offa's dyke.

Watt, James (1736-1819). Inventor, whose improved steam engines made possible the industrial revolution. As mathematical-instrument-maker to Glasgow University, Watt began by overcoming the limitations of a model *Newcomen engine, to produce the first engine with separate condenser (1765). Further improvements included the centrifugal governor. Entering partnership with *Boulton in 1774, he developed his rotative engine, a universal power source, in 1781.

Wavell, Archibald Percival Wavell, 1st Earl (1883-1950). Soldier and administrator, who, as commander in chief,

Middle East (1939-41), conducted skilful campaigns against numerically superior Italian and German forces, notably during his conquest of Ethiopia (1941). He later served as commander in chief in India (1941), as supreme commander, southeast Asia (1942), and as commander in India and Burma (1942). From 1943 to 1947 he was viceroy of India.

Webb, Beatrice, Baroness Passfield (1858-1943). Social reformer and Labour theoretician. Beatrice (née Potter), daughter of a wealthy industrialist, married Sidney Webb in 1892. Together they wrote a number of works, including *Industrial Democracy* (1897). As a member of the Royal Commission on the Poor Laws (1905-09), Beatrice urged radical measures to prevent poverty and published a minority report on the welfare state.

Webb, Sidney, 1st Baron Passfield (1859-1947). Social reformer and Labour theoretician. Initially a civil servant, Webb joined the *Fabian Society in 1885. With his wife Beatrice Webb he wrote works such as *The History of Trade Unionism* (1894), and together they founded the London School of Economics and the *New Statesman.* Sidney also drafted the *Labour Party's home policy programme (1918) and campaigned for education reform. An MP from 1922, he was raised to the peerage in 1929.

Wedgwood, Josiah (1730-95). Potter. Wedgwood opened his own business at Burslem (Staffordshire) in 1759. He combined business enterprise with the ability to produce high-quality ware, and many of his designs, often of classical inspiration and beauty, are still in production. The sculptor John Flaxman was among his designers.

Wedmore (or Chippenham), treaty of (878). An agreement between *Alfred the Great and the Danish leader Guthrum after the latter's decisive defeat at Edington. Guthrum accepted Christianity and agreed to leave *Wessex. The treaty confirmed the preeminence of Wessex in England and led to the establishment of the Danes in East Anglia.

Welensky, Sir Roy (Roland) (1907–). Prime minister of the *Central African Federation (1956-63). After the Federation broke up, he tried briefly and unsuccessfully to promote his multiracial policies in Southern Rhodesia.

Wellesley, Richard Colley Wellesley, Marquess (1760-1842). Lord Mornington until 1799, he was the duke of Wellington's elder brother. As governor general of India (1797-1805) he embarked on a vast expansion of British-controlled territory and destroyed remaining French influence. By military campaigns, annexations, and alliances, he took control of Mysore, the Carnatic, Hyderabad, and Oudh, Foreign secretary (1809-12), he tried unsuccessfully to form an administration following *Perceval's assassination (1812). A strong supporter of Catholic emancipation, he was lord lieutenant of Ireland (1821-28, 1833-34).

Wellington, Arthur Wellesley, 1st duke of (1769-1852). Soldier and statesman. An Irish peer's son, Wellesley (created Viscount Wellington in 1809, duke in 1814) entered the army in 1787 and first saw action in Flanders (1794-95). Serving in India (1797-1804) under his brother Marquess *Wellesley, he won his first major victory at Assaye (1803) against* the Marathas. Resigning his military appointments, he sat as a Tory MP (1806-09) and served as chief secretary for Ireland (1807-09). Appointed in 1808 to command a British force in Portugal, he was superseded in the same year but reappointed in 1809. Wellington's ensuing campaigns in the *Peninsular War culminated in the invasion of southern France (1813). Following Napoleon's abdication (1814), he became British ambassador in Paris. After Napoleon's return from Elba, Wellington defeated him at *Waterloo (1815). Again in Paris as ambassador and commander of the British occupying forces (1815-18), he helped ensure the moderate treatment of France by the allies. Re-entering politics, Wellington

served in *Liverpool's cabinet (1819-27), but his rigidly conservative principles led him to refuse office in the liberal Tory administrations of *Canning and *Goderich. However, following his formidable sense of duty, he unwillingly accepted the premiership (Jan 1828-Nov 1830) and, with *Peel, carried Roman *Catholic emancipation (1829), against his personal inclinations. Acting prime minister from Nov to Dec 1834, he then served in Peel's cabinets (1834-35, 1841-46). By now regarded as an elder statesman, Wellington was appointed commander in chief (1842), holding the position until his death.

Wells, H(erbert) G(eorge) (1866-1946). Writer. Following the success of his science fiction, for example *The Time Machine* (1895), and realistic novels, for example *The History of Mr Polly* (1910), Wells turned to popular history and sociology. A *Fabian, he sought to influence the political and social outlook of his contempories. He wrote an *Outline of History* (1920) and, with his son G. P. Wells and Julian Huxley, *The Science of Life* (1929).

Wentworth, Peter (c. 1530-1596). MP and outstanding defender of parliamentary freedom during the reign of Elizabeth I. A Puritan, he defended parliament's right to discuss religious questions in 1571 and was subsequently imprisoned three times as a result of his outspokenness: in 1576, after attacking what he called "rumours and messages" —the attempts by the crown to influence parliamentary affairs through the speaker; in 1587, for challenging the queen's supremacy over the church; and from 1593 to 1596, for petitioning the queen to name her successor. His brother Paul Wentworth (1533-93) was also a prominent MP.

Wentworth, Thomas. *See* Strafford, 1st earl of.

wergild. In the Anglo-Saxon period, the price payable to the kin of a murdered man by his assassin or the assassin's kin. The amount varied according to the rank of the victim and the region in which the crime occurred. Wergild was also paid when the victim was disabled by the attacker. It was superseded by the Norman *murder fine.

Wesley, Charles (1707-88). Hymnwriter and evangelist. John *Wesley's younger brother and in common with him an Anglican priest, he organized the first Oxford Methodists (1729) and shared in John's subsequent evangelical work. He wrote over 6000 hymns.

Wesley, John (1703-91). Founder of *Methodism. An Anglican priest, Wesley was leader (1729-35) of a small group in Oxford, organized by his brother Charles *Wesley, the Methodists (originally a slighting description by outsiders of the group's serious-minded Christianity, but later transferred to Wesley's wider following). In 1738 Wesley experienced "conversion"—a conviction of personal salvation and call to preach. His evangelical enthusiasm, often causing hysteria among congregations, led to his exclusion from many Anglican pulpits. He began open-air preaching in Bristol in 1739 (following *Whitefield). Travelling 250 000 miles in the next 51 years, he preached 40 000 sermons, sometimes risking his life before hostile mobs. Wesley always regarded himself as an Anglican, despite having to organize the later Methodists into a potentially separate denomination. From 1784, however, he personally ordained clergy to work in America.

Wessex. The kingdom of the Gewisse or West Saxons, said to have been founded by Cerdic who conquered the region of the upper Thames basin (c. 514). During the 6th and 7th centuries Wessex expanded to the west and frequently fought its northern neighbour, *Mercia. Mercia, under Offa (reigned 757-96), dominated Wessex, but by 838 *Egbert of Wessex had made himself king of southern England. Alfred the Great (871-99) successfully mobilized Wessex against the Danish invaders (878). After capturing London in 886 he made a treaty with Guthrum for the partitioning of England. *Athelstan finally ousted the Danes and ruled all England by 926.

This unity was broken in 939, but was re-established by *Edred (954).

western rebellion (June-Aug 1549). Insurrections in Cornwall and Devon in opposition to the Reformation legislation under Edward VI. The rebellions began independently in each county, but both were precipitated by the imminent introduction of the new prayer book with a simplified liturgy. The rebels, who were almost exclusively peasants, succeeded in taking Plymouth and laying siege to Exeter but were then crushed with relative ease by government forces.

West Indies. The island groups extending in an arc across the Caribbean from Florida to Venezuela. Discovered by Columbus (1492), who believed he had found the west route to India, the Spanish were the first settlers. Spanish supremacy was challenged in the 1600s by the British, Dutch, and French, who established settlements amid incessant rivalry and fighting. Many African slaves were imported to work the sugarcane plantations, until the abolition of slavery in the 19th century. British possessions in the West Indies (*Antigua, *Barbados, *Dominica, *Grenada, *Jamaica, Montserrat, *St Kitts-Nevis-Anguilla, *St Lucia, *St Vincent, *Trinidad, and *Tobago) formed the British Caribbean (or West Indies) Federation from 1958 to 1962, when it was dissolved. The West Indies Associated States (Antigua, St Kitts-Nevis-Anguilla, Dominica, Grenada, St Lucia, and St Vincent), formed in 1967, were self-governing states in association with the UK; all save Antigua and St Kitts are now independent.

Westminster, Statute of (1931). The instrument by which the self-governing *dominions gained legislative independence from the UK. The Colonial Laws Validity Act (1865) gave the British government power to invalidate laws enacted by colonial assemblies and, accordingly, the ability, although it was never exercised, to involve the colonies in its own foreign policies. This act had become repugnant to the dominions, which, at the *imperial conference of

1926 were newly defined as "autonomous communities within the British Empire, equal in status and freely associated as members of the British Commonwealth of Nations". The Statute of Westminster gave parliamentary sanction to this statement, according legislative independence to the parliaments of Canada, Australia, New Zealand, the Union of South Africa, the Irish Free State, and Newfoundland.

Westminster abbey. The coronation church of the UK monarch. Largely because of its site, next to what emerged as the centre of government, Westminster abbey is one of the most important churches in the country, being the site of the coronation of the monarch since 1066 (Edward V and Edward VIII, who were not crowned, are the only exceptions). Originally a modest Saxon building, a much larger church in the Romanesque style was built in the reign of Edward the Confessor, being consecrated in 1065. In the late 13th century, under Henry III and Edward I, when it was once more almost totally rebuilt in the gothic style, the building took its present form. The only later addition of any importance was the beautiful chapel built to house the tomb of Henry VII and the two towers added to complete the west façade by Hawksmoor at the beginning of the 18th century. Apart from the exceptionally high quality of the architecture and decoration of the abbey, the building is notable for being the closest thing the nation possesses to a national mausoleum. In addition to the monarchs buried here, the abbey also contains a large number of tombs and memorials to eminent Englishmen. The abbey lost its monastic functions at the Reformation.

Westminster Assembly of Divines (1643-53). An assembly convened by the Long Parliament to reform the English church. It was attended by 121 divines, 30 lay assessors, and, following the *Solemn League and Covenant, five clerical and three lay commissioners from Scotland. Presbyterians formed the largest group, but Independents, Erastians, and Epis-copalians also attended. The assembly's most significant achievement was the Westminster Confession (1647), which remains the definitive statement of Presbyterian faith. It was never fully accepted in England, especially after the Independents rose to power in 1649.

Wharton, Philip Wharton, duke of (1698-1731). Son of Thomas Wharton and president of the *Hell-Fire Club, he was forced to sell his estates to pay his debts. He became a *Jacobite and a Roman Catholic and in 1729 was outlawed. He died in Catalonia.

Wharton, Thomas Wharton, 1st marquess of (1648-1715). An MP (1663-64, 1673-96), he wrote a doggerel "Lilli Burlero, Bullen-a-la" (1687) deriding Irish Catholics and supported the Glorious Revolution (1688-89). He was comptroller of the household (1689-1702), lord lieutenant of Ireland (1708-10), and leader of the Whig *junto. He was created earl of Wharton in 1706 and marquess in 1715.

Whigs. A political grouping that originated in the late 17th century and became the *Liberal Party in the second half of the 19th century. "Whig" was a pejorative name, of obscure origin, for the Scottish Presbyterian rebels of the Civil War period. It was first applied in English politics in 1679, to denote members of the *Country Party, which attempted to exclude the Roman Catholic duke of York (later James II) from the succession to the throne (see exclusion bills). Following the Glorious Revolution (1688-89), which had been effected largely by the Whigs, they formed the powerful *junto during the reigns of William III and Anne. In 1714 they ensured the Hanoverian succession and, as a result of the association of their rivals the *Tories with Jacobitism, formed a ruling oligarchy until the reign of George III. Family ties and *patronage, rather than policy, bound the rival groups of Whigs, who were supplanted after 1780 by the revived Toryism of Pitt the younger. The Whigs were subsequently associated with the new industrial interest, nonconformity, and reform.

They returned to power after 1830 and introduced significant reform legislation, notably the parliamentary *Reform Acts. Strengthened by the adherence of Peel's followers when the Tories split over the repeal of the *corn laws (1846), the Whigs under Gladstone evolved into the Liberal Party in about 1867.

Whitby, synod of (664). A general assembly of the English church held at Whitby, Northumbria, to resolve the differences between Celtic and Roman Christianity, notably over the date of Easter. *Colman and *Wilfrid were the respective spokesmen for the two parties. The powerful Northumbrian king Oswy was persuaded to support Roman usages, which were thus adopted by the Northumbrian church. Others followed his decision, leading to the unification of the English church under the Roman discipline. Colman's Celtic faction left Whitby isolated and embittered. *See also* Celtic church; church, pre-Reformation.

Whiteboys. One of many secret agrarian societies in Ireland in the 18th century. They terrorized the south, protesting against evictions, unjust rents, tithes, and other aspects of harsh landlordism.

Whitefield, George (1714-70). Evangelist. Whitefield, one of John *Wesley's early Oxford Methodists, became an Anglican priest in 1736. He began open-air preaching, with astonishing emotional effect, in 1739, to coalminers at Kingswood, Bristol, after being barred from local churches. His Calvinist beliefs later led to his breaking with Wesley. He became the countess of *Huntingdon's chaplain and a leader of her Connexion in 1748.

Whitehall. A street in Westminster, London, the buildings on and adjoining which form the administrative centre of the UK government. The site of a mansion built for Hubert de *Burgh in the 13th century, it became a residence of the archbishops of York, from one of whom—Cardinal Wolsey—it was acquired by Henry VIII, who named it Whitehall Palace. It was a royal residence until the 1690s, when, with the notable exception of the Banqueting Hall

by Inigo Jones, it was largely burned down. Most of the present-day buildings in the Whitehall area were built in the 19th century.

White Ship. A ship that sank near Barfleur on 25 Nov 1120 while on its way from Normandy to England. Among those drowned was Henry I's heir and only legitimate son, William. His death gave rise to the disputed succession after Henry's own death (1135) between Stephen and Matilda.

Whitgift, John (c. 1530-1604). Archbishop of Canterbury. Approving his opposition to Puritanism while professor of divinity at Cambridge (1567-69), Elizabeth I nominated Whitgift as archbishop in 1583. He opposed with equal severity papal and Puritan extremists, firmly upholding episcopal authority in the interests of uniformity.

Whittington, Richard (d. 1423). Lord mayor of London (1397-98, 1406-07, 1419-20). A mercer of great wealth, he supplied loans to three kings, Richard II, Henry IV, and Henry V, and was a generous benefactor. The legend of Dick Whittington and his cat probably dates from about 1605.

Wiglaf (d. 838). King of Mercia (827-38), who, after initial defeat (829), reasserted Mercian independence from the control of *Egbert of Wessex (830). During Wiglaf's reign Mercia remained the equal of Wessex in southern England, and the Mercians continued to rule London.

Wihtred (d. 725). King of Kent (c. 690-725), who maintained Kentish independence against Mercian expansion. His law code of 695, one of the earliest known in Britain, dealt primarily with ecclesiastical matters and granted considerable privileges to the church.

Wilberforce, William (1759-1833). Parliamentary leader of the movement to abolish the slave trade and *slavery. Wilberforce became an MP in 1780. Converted to *evangelicalism (1784-85), he joined other members of the *Clapham Sect in founding the Society for the Abolition of the Slave Trade

(1787). He introduced his first parliamentary resolution to abolish the trade in 1789, finally achieving abolition in 1807. From 1821 (although now strongly conservative in domestic politics) he campaigned to abolish slavery itself in British possessions. He retired from parliament in 1825 but lived to see abolition approved (1833).

Wilfrid, St (634-709). One of the greatest figures of the Anglo-Saxon church. He attacked, notably at the synod of *Whitby (664), Celtic practices in the church and advocated a closer relationship with the Roman church. Consecrated bishop of York in 665, he did not occupy his see until 669, living in the meantime in the monastery at Ripon. When Theodore, archbishop of Canterbury, divided the diocese into two (677) Wilfrid appealed to Rome. The pope ordered his restoration but Wilfrid never reoccupied the see and lived for many years in exile in Mercia. In 705 he returned to Northumbria, becoming bishop of Hexham. He is noted for introducing the Benedictine rule of monasticism to the kingdom. Feast day: 12 Oct.

Wilkes, John (1727-97). Outstanding champion of the rights of the individual. Born into a wealthy middle-class family, he entered fashionable society and became a member of the dissolute *Hell-Fire Club. An MP for the first time in 1757, he founded the political weekly, the *North Briton*, in 1762 and in the following year was arrested on a general *warrant for seditious libel. Discharged on the ground that his arrest infringed his privileges as an MP, he subsequently won damages against the 2nd earl of *Halifax for illegal arrest and the pronouncement that general warrants were illegal (1769). His enemies in parliament brought about his expulsion from the House, while he was in Paris, and he was outlawed (1764). Returning in 1768 he was elected MP for Middlesex, imprisoned as an outlaw, released, and then again expelled from parliament (1769). He was twice re-elected, but parliament, defying riots by his supporters, declared his election void. The

Society of the Supporters of the Bill of Rights was formed to further his cause and in 1774, once more re-elected, he was allowed to take his seat and remained an MP until 1790.

Wilkinson, John (1728-1808). Ironmaster. Wilkinson's invention (1774) of an accurate method of boring cannon made possible production of suitable cylinders for *Watt's engines. A passionate propagandist for iron, he built the first iron barge (1787) and was buried in an iron coffin.

William (I) the Conqueror (1028-87). The first Norman king of England (1066-87). Illegitimate son of Robert, duke of Normandy, he married his cousin *Matilda of Flanders in 1053. They had four children: Robert, William, Henry, and Adela. William succeeded his father as duke of Normandy in 1035 but was not able to exert full control over his territories until 1047. He visited Edward the Confessor of England in 1051, when he was almost certainly promised the English throne. In 1066, with the backing of the papacy, William claimed his right and landed an invasion force at Pevensey, Sussex. He defeated and killed his rival, King Harold, at *Hastings in October and then formally accepted the kingdom at Berkhamsted before being crowned in Westminster Abbey on Christmas Day. The Norman conquest was not, however, complete. William faced a number of English revolts during the years 1067 to 1071, which he effectively, if ruthlessly, crushed. Furthermore, the subjection of his new kingdom involved the introduction of Norman personnel and social organization (see feudalism), as well as administrative and legal practices. The effect of the conquest on English culture was considerable. William's reign witnessed reforms in the church under his trusted adviser *Lanfranc, who became archbishop of Canterbury in 1070, and, most notably, the compilation of the *Domesday Book (1086). William spent most of the last 15 years of his life in Normandy and died of an injury received while campaigning against Philip I of France.

He was buried in St Stephen's church at Caen.

William (I) the Lion (?1143-1214). King of Scots (1165-1214). Second son of Henry, the son of David I, William succeeded his brother, Malcolm IV, to the throne. Although at first on good terms with Henry II, William invaded England in 1174 and was captured at Alnwick. By the treaty of *Falaise he was forced to accept Henry as feudal superior of Scotland, but by the Quitclaim of *Canterbury (1189) Richard I surrendered this superiority in return for 10,000 marks. In 1209, by the treaty of *Norham, John of England exacted 15,000 marks and other concessions from William in return for peace. William married Ermengarde de Beaumont, who bore him one son, Alexander II, and three daughters. He also had six illegitimate children.

William II Rufus (c. 1060-1100). King of England (1087-1100). Called Rufus (red) because of his ruddy complexion, he was the second son of William the Conqueror and Matilda of Flanders. The support of Archbishop *Lanfranc was probably crucial in ensuring him the throne, which might otherwise have fallen to his brother Robert, duke of Normandy. Robert's greater popularity was attested to early in the reign when *Odo, bishop of Bayeux, Roger of Shrewsbury, and the bishop of Durham led a rebellion on his behalf, not wishing to see the Anglo-Norman territories of the Conqueror ruled separately. William, who had a high reputation as a soldier, successfully suppressed this rebellion and a second one in 1095. He regarded the church chiefly as a source of revenue, and his strained relations with Archbishop *Anselm ended in his seizure of Anselm's estates in 1097. He is described in the *Anglo-Saxon Chronicle* as being "hated by almost all his people", and his death, after being pierced by an arrow while hunting in the New Forest, might have been at the hand of an assassin—possibly in the employ of William's brother and successor Henry (I).

William III (1650-1702). King of England, Scotland, and Ireland (1689-1702) and stadholder of the Netherlands (1672-1702). Son of William II, prince of Orange, and Mary, daughter of Charles I of England, he married Mary, daughter of the future James II of England in 1677. In 1688, he was approached by seven disaffected English politicians, both Whigs and Tories, and invited to assist the overthrow of James. On 15 Nov he landed, at the head of an army, at Torbay and marched virtually unopposed to London. James fled and the *convention parliament offered William and Mary the crown (13 Feb) on condition of their acceptance of the *Declaration of Rights. On 21 April 1689 they were crowned. William was faced almost immediately with resistance in Scotland, which was short lived (see Killiecrankie, battle of), and Ireland, where James' Jacobite supporters were decisively defeated at the *Boyne (1690). For much of his reign William was preoccupied by war against France (King William's War), demonstrating his considerable diplomatic skills in negotiating a *grand alliance and leaving an army sufficiently strengthened to serve the genius of the duke of Marlborough. The king's popularity in Britain was undermined by the massacre of *Glencoe (1692), but he exercised a moderating influence on English politics and was a moving force behind the *Toleration Act (1689).

William IV (1765-1837). King of the United Kingdom (1830-37). George III's third son (he was known as the duke of Clarence from 1789 until his accession), he served at sea from 1779 until 1790. He lived with an actress, Dorothea Jordan, from 1790 until 1811 and they had ten children. The two daughters of his marriage (1818) to Princess Adelaide of Saxe-Meiningen, however, died in infancy; hence the crown passed to his niece Victoria. In the 1832 parliamentary reform crisis William ultimately ensured the passage of the government's proposals by agreeing (reluctantly) to create 50 new peers to defeat the opposition of the House of Lords. Later, in 1834, he was the last sovereign to try to choose his prime minister regardless of parliamentary support, replacing *Melbourne by *Peel.

William of Malmesbury (c. 1095-?1143). Librarian and precentor at Malmesbury abbey. In his historical writings, notably *Gesta regum Anglorum* (completed 1125) and *Historia novella* (which recounts English history to 1142), he attempted to explain, rather than merely record, facts.

William of Ockham (c. 1285-1349). Scholastic philosopher, who revived nominalism—the theory that the various objects designated by a single word (e.g. fish) have only that word in common. The maxim named after him—Ockham's razor—states that "entities are not to be multiplied beyond necessity".

William of St Calais (or of **Carilet**) (d. 1096). Norman bishop of Durham from 1080. An adviser to William I, he rebelled against his successor William Rufus in 1088. Pardoned in 1091, he returned from exile in Normandy and in 1093 began the building of Durham cathedral.

Williams, John (1582-1650). Archbishop of York from 1641. He held many ecclesiastical positions under James I but fell out of favour with Charles I after opposing the war with Spain. Convicted three times (1628, 1635, 1637) on various charges, he was imprisoned (1637-40). He was appointed archbishop of York as a compromise candidate acceptable to the Long Parliament because of his conflict with Archbishop Laud. After the outbreak of the Civil War (1642) he lived in retirement.

Willibrord, St (?658-739). Missionary to Friesland. A pupil of St Wilfrid at Ripon, he also spent 12 years in Ireland with St Egbert. In 690 he was sent by Egbert to convert the Frisians, being consecrated archbishop in 695. He continued his work in Friesland until his death at the age of 82.

Wilmington, Spencer Compton, earl of (?1673-1743). Nominal prime minister (Jan 1742-July 1743) in the administration dominated by Carteret. George II, on his accession in 1727, had envisaged Wilmington replacing *Walpole as prime minister, but abandoned the idea because of Wilmington's manifest incompetence and Queen Caroline's opposition.

Wilson, Harold, Baron (1916-). Prime minister (1964-70, 1974-76). An economist, and a civil servant in World War II, he became a Labour MP in 1945 and was president of the Board of Trade under *Attlee (1947-51), resigning in protest against social-service charges. He succeeded *Gaitskell as leader of the Labour Party and of the opposition in 1963 and became prime minister in Oct 1964. He retired from office and party leadership in April 1976 (to be succeeded by James Callaghan).

Winchester. The administrative centre of Hampshire. Originally a Roman town (named Venta Belgarum), Winchester first became a centre of political importance under the Saxons, when it became the capital of the kingdom of Wessex. Even after the unification of England it was still one of the main centres of government, being an important resting place for the king's court, and one of the main sites of the Treasury. A royal palace was maintained here throughout the middle ages, and in the 17th century there were plans, eventually abandoned, for Charles II to build a new palace. One of the most important figures in the history of Winchester is William of Wykeham, who, while bishop (1367-1404), largely rebuilt the old romanesque cathedral in the gothic style. The cathedral, one of the longest in Britain, was again partly rebuilt in the 16th century. It is notable above all for the high quality of the stone carving it contains. William of Wykeham also founded Winchester College, a school still in existence. Although once an important centre for the woollen industry, Winchester declined towards the end of the medieval period.

Winchester, rout of (14 Sept 1141). The defeat of Matilda's forces, which were besieging the royalist-held Wolvesey castle in Winchester, by a royalist relief force. Robert, earl of Gloucester, was taken prisoner and subsequently exchanged for King Stephen, who had been captured at *Lincoln.

Winchester, Statute of (1285). A collection of regulations for the maintenance of the peace, passed while Edward I was in Gascony. The measures incorporated included the Assize of *Arms and *watch and ward.

Winchester, treaty of (1153). The treaty, agreed at Winchester on 6 Nov and ratified at Westminster in Dec, that formally ended the civil war between King *Stephen and Matilda. It is sometimes called, incorrectly, the treaty of Wallingford. It stipulated that Stephen would retain the throne for his lifetime but would be succeeded by Matilda's son Henry of Anjou, who thus became King Henry II in 1154. Compensation was made to Stephen's surviving son William, earl of Surrey.

window tax. A tax on the number of windows in houses, first imposed in 1696 in place of the *hearth tax. It was greatly increased by Pitt the younger, who in 1782 introduced a graduated tax starting at one shilling per window up to ten and rising sharply on every window thereafter. Taxes on houses with less than seven windows were abolished in 1792, but in 1797, during the French Revolutionary War, the window tax was trebled. It proved unsatisfactory as windows were boarded and houses constructed in such a way as to avoid it. It was reduced in 1823 and replaced in 1851 by a duty on inhabited houses.

Windsor, duke of. See Edward VIII.

Windsor, house of. The royal family of the United Kingdom. The dynasty (and sovereign's family) took the name Windsor in 1917 because it was decided that the previous dynastic name *Saxe-Coburg, with its German associations, was inappropriate during World War I. George V thus became the first Windsor sovereign. His grand-daughter Elizabeth II declared (1952) that her successors as sovereigns would retain the name Windsor, rather than adopting her husband's name, Mountbatten. Her descendants in the male line, other than those ranking as royal highnesses, princes, or princesses, would be surnamed Mountbatten-Windsor.

Windsor castle. One of the principal residences of the UK monarch. There has been a castle at Windsor, on the Thames in Berkshire, since the Anglo-Saxon period. The first stone structure was built on the site shortly after the Norman conquest and the first keep, under Henry III, who also greatly extended and strengthened the walls after 1272. The present Round Tower was built for Edward III. St George's Chapel, one of the finest pieces of gothic architecture in England, was begun in the 15th century by Edward IV and finished under Henry VII. It is now a royal mausoleum and the chapel of the Order of the Garter. In the 17th century, when the castle was no longer required to withstand sieges, it was partly rebuilt in the baroque style, for Charles II, by John Webb (1611-72). The whole palace was again extensively remodelled at the beginning of the 19th century, for George IV, by Sir Jeffry Wyatville (1766-1840).

Windward Islands. A south Caribbean island group, in the West Indies. Discovered by Columbus, the islands alternated between French and English domination during the 18th century. Martinique became French, while *Grenada, *St Vincent, *St Lucia, and *Dominica formed a British colony. From 1967 each British island became a West Indies Associated State, responsible for its own internal affairs.

Wingate, Orde Charles (1903-44). Soldier, who achieved fame for his organization and leadership of the Chindit brigade of jungle fighters, which operated behind the Japanese lines (beyond the river Chindwin—hence their name) in Burma during World War II. Wingate served with the Sudan defence force (1928-33) and in Transjordan and

Palestine (1936-38). He was killed in a plane crash.

Winstanley, Gerrard (c. 1609-c. 1660). Leader of the *Diggers, whose colony he and William Everard established in 1649. After its dissolution Winstanley began pamphleteering for his communist ideals. *The Law of Freedom in a Platform* (1652), dedicated to Cromwell, condemned monarchs, landowners, and lawyers as enemies of the poor.

Wiseman, Nicholas, Cardinal (1802-65). The first archbishop of Westminster. Wiseman was created cardinal and archbishop in 1850, when the *Roman Catholic revival led the pope to establish a regular diocesan system in England.

Wishart, George (c. 1513-1546). Scottish Protestant. He fled to England in 1538 and visited Germany and Switzerland around 1540. Returning to Scotland in 1543, he became a close associate of John Knox and preached Calvinism. He was arrested in 1545, at the instigation of Cardinal *Beaton, and burned as a heretic. Knox attributed to Wishart the prophecy of Beaton's own death.

witan. The council of the Anglo-Saxon kings. It developed from Germanic assemblies summoned to witness royal grants of land. By the late 9th century the witan had become a formal gathering of the principal *ealdormen, *thegns, and bishops, summoned by the king to give him advice and to witness acts of royal administration, such as grants of charters and church benefices, new laws, and royal decisions on taxation, foreign policy, and defence. The witan played a valuable role in checking royal power and preventing autocracy. It also carried on the business of government during gaps in the succession.

Wolfe, James (1727-59). Soldier, whose victory over the French at Quebec (1759) ensured British control of Canada. Wolfe served on the Continent (1744-45), at Culloden, on the Rochefort expedition and during the siege of Louisburg (1758). In that year Wolfe was appointed to command in America, charged with driving the French from Quebec. Leading his troops via a secret path to the Heights of Abraham above the town, Wolfe stormed the stronghold, being mortally wounded in the hour of victory.

Wollstonecraft, Mary (1759-97). Feminist and writer. In 1795, deserted by Gilbert Imlay, the father of her 18-month-old daughter Fanny, she attempted suicide. On her recovery she went to live with William *Godwin, whom she married in 1797. She died later that year after the birth of their daughter Mary (who married Percy Bysshe Shelley in 1816). Her works include *Vindication of the Rights of Women* (1792). *See also* women's movement.

Wolseley, Garnet Wolseley, 1st Viscount (1833-1913). Military commander. He was closely involved in army reform, incurring thereby the enmity of Queen Victoria and the duke of Cambridge. Wolseley fought in the Crimean War and commanded in the Ashanti War (1873-74) and in the latter stages of the Zulu War (1879-80). His Egyptian campaign (1882) culminated in the victory of *Tel-el-Kebir, but his Nile expedition (1884-85) was too late to relieve *Gordon at Khartoum. Wolseley was commander in chief of the forces from 1895 to 1899.

Wolsey, Thomas, Cardinal (c. 1475-1530). Lord chancellor of England (1515-29). Son of an Ipswich butcher, he served Henry VII as chaplain and Henry VIII as almoner before becoming a privy councillor in 1511. He planned Henry's French campaign of 1512-13 and rapid promotion in church and state followed. He became archbishop of York in 1514, cardinal and lord chancellor in the following year, and papal legate *a latere* in 1518. He rounded off these achievements with a diplomatic triumph—the treaty of London (1518), a commitment to peace by the pope and the kings of France, Spain, and England. In 1521 he engineered an alliance against France with the emperor Charles V and England embarked on a war that hardly concerned it and that it could ill afford. Wolsey's demands for subsidy culminated in the *amicable grant of 1524, a forced loan that was violently resisted and almost brought the cardinal's fall. In 1527 he was charged with obtaining the pope's permission for the king's divorce from Catherine of Aragon. Unsuccessful, he was accused of treason and died on his way from York to face his fate in London. Wolsey's wealth and worldliness aggravated, on the eve of the Reformation, the church's ill repute, but he was a generous benefactor and is remembered as the founder of Cardinal College (later renamed Christ Church) at Oxford.

women's movement. The social and political movement towards changing the subordinate status of women. Mary *Wollstonecraft published the first feminist manifesto, *Vindication of the Rights of Women*, in 1792, and in the early 19th century the questioning of the social and sexual position of women was encouraged by radicalism and the early socialist movement. In 1882 the *Married Women's Property Act enabled women to own their own property but the continued control of men over women in the spheres of education, work, and politics led many women to believe that the key to change lay in the vote. Despite the political advocacy of their cause by, among others, J. S. Mill, the successive failure of a number of bills aiming to extend the *franchise to women (1886–1911) led to the emergence of the militant feminist movement (the suffragettes). The Women's Social and Political Union (WSPU), which was founded by Mrs Emmeline *Pankhurst in 1903, grew rapidly in wealth and numbers, and its members were repeatedly imprisoned for attacks on property, demonstrations, and refusal to pay taxes. Hunger strikes by feminist prisoners, and their forced feeding, led to the "Cat and Mouse" Act (1913), which allowed the temporary release of strikers whose health was endangered. The activities of the suffragettes came to an abrupt halt when World War I broke out, and the WSPU directed its activities to support for the war effort. In 1918 franchise was granted to women aged 30 and over, subject to educational and property qualifications, and in 1928 a bill granting full voting equality passed the House of Lords. Following the experience of World War II, and more specifically the radicalism of the 1960s, the feminist movement re-emerged as a social and political force. In 1969 the Women's Liberation Workshop was set up in London as a coordinating centre for local women's groups and in 1971 the first four basic demands of the movement (equal pay, equal educational and job opportunies, free contraception and abortion on demand, and 24-hour-nurseries) were put forward.

Wood's halfpence. A copper coinage minted in Ireland from 1723 to 1725 by an English ironmaster William Wood (1671–1730). He bought the patent to strike the coins from George I's mistress, the duchess of Kendal. The Irish parliament was not consulted, and uproar (including Swift's "Drapier's Letters") followed, forcing withdrawal of the coins.

Woodville. *See* Rivers, Anthony Woodville, 2nd Earl; Elizabeth Woodville.

Worcester, battle of (3 Sept 1651). A battle between an invading Scottish royalist force under Charles II and Commonwealth forces under Cromwell. The outcome was a decisive defeat for Charles and the Scots and, in Cromwell's phrase, a "crowning mercy" for the parliamentarians. The Scottish invasion was the final attempt to undo the parliamentary victory in the Civil War and prevented the royalists from raising another army for nearly a decade.

Worcester, 6th earl of. *See* Somerset, Edward.

Worcester, pact of (12 Dec 1264). An agreement forced upon the marcher lords, supporting Prince Edward during the second Barons' War, by the government of Simon de Montfort. The Montfortians gained Cheshire, Bristol, and other possessions in the west from Edward and the temporary banishment to Ireland of the marchers, while promising Edward's release from captivity.

Worcester, treaty of (March 1218). A peace treaty between Henry III, for whom the regent William Marshal, earl of Pembroke, negotiated, and *Llywelyn ap Iorwerth of Gwynedd. Llywelyn did homage to Henry, but the treaty confirmed the ascendancy he had established in Wales during the first *Barons' War.

Workers' Educational Association (WEA). An organization, founded in 1904 by Albert Mansbridge (1876–1952) and others, to help coordinate and expand existing voluntary adult education efforts. It arose from university extension lectures (begun in Cambridge in 1873) that pioneered extramural university courses. The WEA, using a system of tutorial classes to encourage active student involvement, aimed originally to provide for members of the trade unions, cooperative movement, and socialist societies, who were studying mainly politics, economics, and industrial history. Its scope and appeal have since widened enormously.

workhouse. *See* poor laws.

World War I (1914–18). The war, often called the Great War, between the *allied powers and the central powers (led by Germany and Austria-Hungary). The war was preceeded by decades of tension during which the great powers aligned themselves into two rival groups: the triple alliance of Germany and Austria-Hungary (1879) and Italy (1882) and the triple entente formed by a Franco-Russian agreement (1893) and the Anglo-French *entente cordiale (1904). The immediate cause of war was rivalry in the Balkans between Austria-Hungary and Russia, which came to a head following the assassination of Archduke Franz Ferdinand, heir to the Austro-Hungarian throne, by a Serbian nationalist at Sarajevo. Austria-Hungary declared war on Serbia; Russia leapt to Serbia's defence and Germany declared war on Russia and its ally France. Britain entered the war on 4 Aug 1914,

when Germany invaded neutral Belgium (*see* Belgian neutrality).

The German advance through the Low Countries, in pursuance of the Schlieffen plan, was halted at Mons (23 Aug) by the *British Expeditionary Force (BEF) under Sir John French. The allies counterattacked and, at the first battle of the *Marne (5–9 Sept), forced the Germans back beyond the river Aisne. The BEF stood firm at *Ypres (Oct–Nov), and the combatants on the western front, ranged on either side of a line from Ostend to Switzerland, were subjected thenceforward to futile trench warfare and appalling loss of life.

In Feb 1915, following the Turkish attack on Russia in the Caucasus, the allies launched the unsuccessful *Gallipoli campaign. Failing to break through the Dardanelles, they withdrew in Jan 1916. Meanwhile, Germany was gaining ground on the eastern front against Russia, and, after Poland, most of Lithuania, and Serbia submitted, the allies began (Oct 1915) the long-drawn-out Macedonian campaign. They failed to save Russia, which fell in March 1917, and the campaign continued, without advancing, until Sept 1918, when Bulgaria was at last conquered.

The allies engaged the Turks also in the *Mesopotamian campaign, which began on 6 Nov 1914, when an Indian force was landed at Abadan for the purpose of protecting oil installations. Advances were made in 1915 until Nov, when an attempt to take Baghdad, following disappointments in the Dardanelles, failed. The allies withdrew to Kut al-Amara, which was besieged by the Turks until submitting in April 1916. In 1917, however, Kut was recaptured in Feb and Baghdad fell in March, and the Turks were finally defeated by Allenby's campaign, aided by the Arab revolt, in Palestine: Jerusalem was taken in Dec, and Damascus and Aleppo fell in Sept 1918, following the allied victory at Megiddo.

The war at sea was fought chiefly between Britain and Germany. German cruisers defeated those of Cradock off Coronel in Nov 1914, but the British scored a victory off the Falkland Islands in Dec, which allowed the allies to proceed with the conquest of the German colonies in Africa and the Pacific. In Jan 1915 Beatty was victorious at *Dogger Bank, but the battle of *Jutland (May 1916) was inconclusive. Submarine attack posed the worst naval threat to Britain, which lost about 6000 vessels as a result of actions by German U-boats. The unrestricted submarine warfare was instrumental in bringing the USA into the war in April 1917 and was only countered by the subsequent introduction by Lloyd George of the *convoy system.

In the air, German Zeppelins, pioneering strategic bombing, attacked British cities from 1915. The Royal Flying Corps supplemented balloons in reconnaissance, and air combat occurred on both the western and eastern fronts. In 1918 the *Royal Air Force was formed by the amalgamation of the Royal Flying Corps and the Royal Naval Air Service and began to bomb German cities.

On the western front combat continued relentlessly: in 1915 at Neuve-Chapelle (March), Ypres (April-May), during which the Germans used poison gas for the first time, and Loos (Sept). A proposed German assault was thwarted at *Verdun (Feb-July 1916), but with disastrous French losses, and Haig, who had succeeded French, launched the battle of the *Somme, utilizing *tanks for the first time. In 1917 British attacks at Arras and the Scarpe were unsuccessful, while the French failed badly in Champagne. In Nov, however, with the USA now participating, Passchendaele was taken in the third battle of Ypres. Germany's offensive in 1918 was halted in the second battle of the Marne (July-Aug), and in Sept Haig broke the Hindenburg line. Meanwhile, in Italy, Austria-Hungary was finally defeated at Vittorio-Veneto, and on 11 Nov the armistice was signed. Some ten million combatants may have died in the war, of which the British Empire sustained some 1 089 900.

The Paris Peace Conference imposed peace treaties on the central powers:

Germany signed the treaty of *Versailles in June 1919 and Austria that of *Saint-Germain in Sept.

World War II (1939-45). The war between the *allied powers and the *Axis powers caused by the failure of the peace settlement after World War I and by the aggression of Germany under Adolf Hitler. Britain and France declared war on Germany on 3 Sept 1939, two days after Hitler's invasion of Poland and five months after his occupation of Czechoslovakia (see Munich agreement). In April 1940, having taken Finland in March, Germany invaded Denmark and Norway. Criticism of the British campaign in Scandinavia brought the resignation of Neville Chamberlain, whose place was taken by Winston Churchill as the Germans invaded Belgium. The *British Expeditionary Force (BEF), with the French First Army and the Belgian army, were isolated in the north, to be evacuated from *Dunkirk (29 May-4 June). Following the fall of France the German attack on England began—the battle of *Britain, in which the bombardment by the Luftwaffe was foiled by the RAF *Fighter Command under Dowding, backed by the employment of *radar.

The battle of the Atlantic began in Dec 1939 with an encounter between HMS *Exeter* and the German *Graf Spee* at the *River Plate in the South Atlantic. British naval strategy sought to secure supply routes, defend Britain's coasts, and facilitate the transfer of troops and their landing on foreign soil. Successes were scored with the naval air attack on Taranto (Nov 1940), at Cape *Matapan (March 1941), and with the sinking by the *Dorsetshire* of the German *Bismarck*, three days after the *Bismarck* sank the *Hood* (May 1941). The considerable threat posed by the German U-boats continued until the summer of 1943.

In Africa and the Middle East, Italy occupied British Somaliland in Aug 1940 and invaded Egypt but was repulsed by Wavell's troops, who retook Somaliland in May 1941. The advance of Rommel's Afrika Corps in 1941 was facilitated by the deployment of British troops to Iraq (occupied in April), Lebanon and Syria (taken in June), Iran (controlled by Aug) and, especially, Greece, which fell to Germany in April. Auchinleck replaced Wavell in July, attempted an offensive against Rommel, but was forced to withdraw to El Alamein (Jan 1942). In the decisive battle of *Alamein (Oct-Nov) the Eighth Army under Montgomery defeated Rommel, whom they then pursued along the north African coast. In Nov an Anglo-American force landed near Algiers. Advancing through Tunisia, it made contact with the Eighth Army in April 1943. The allies took Bizerta and Tunis, and on 13 May the Germans surrendered.

The Italian campaign began on 10 July 1943 with the landing in Sicily of Montgomery's Eighth Army and the US Fifth Army. After Mussolini's fall the allies crossed to the mainland (Sept) but did not break through German defences to Rome until 4 June 1944. Allied troops continued to move northwards until 2 May 1945, when Trieste fell and the Germans surrendered.

Meanwhile, on the western front, the allied invasion of Normandy under the supreme command of Eisenhower was launched on 6 June 1944 (see D-Day). The Americans took Cherbourg on 27 June and went on to invade Brittany, while the British under Montgomery captured Caen (9 July). The Canadians destroyed an encircled German army at Falaise (17 Aug). US and Free French troops moved north after landing in the south of France, and on 25 Aug the allies took Paris. They then advanced on the Ruhr. The British failed in the battle of *Arnhem (Sept) to penetrate German defences, and the German counterattack in the Ardennes pushed a salient, or bulge, in the allied lines. A US offensive early in 1945 allowed Montgomery, in command of the British Second and US Ninth Armies, to cross the Rhine (23 March). On 4 May he accepted the German surrender at Lüneburg Heath.

On the eastern front, the Axis powers invaded the Soviet Union in June 1941

and were not expelled until Aug 1944. Soviet troops invaded Germany in Oct, and on 2 May, two days before the German surrender on the western front, took Berlin. In July the allies met outside the ruined city, at the *Potsdam conference, and made plans for peace.

In Asia, following the Japanese attack on Pearl Harbor (7 Dec 1941), which brought the USA into the war, Japan invaded Malaya and captured Hong Kong, Manila, and Singapore, taking 90 000 British and Commonwealth prisoners. The USA halted the Japanese advance with a series of air and naval victories (1942-43) and in Oct 1944 defeated the Japanese fleet at Leyte Gulf. Burma was reconquered (Jan-May 1945) by Slim's Fourteenth ("Forgotten") Army, while the allies were also taking Manila, the Philippines, and Borneo. After the atomic bombing of Hiroshima and Nagasaki (see nuclear warfare) Japan surrendered (14 Aug).

Britain lost 92 673 civilian lives in the war and some 264 443 combatants.

Wren, Sir Christopher (1632-1723). One of the most accomplished and successful of English architects, Wren began his career as a mathematician and astronomer. He turned to architecture in 1663, when he designed the Sheldonian Theatre, Oxford, but did not do so fully until the Great Fire of London in 1666 gave him one of the greatest architectural opportunities in English history. For the rebuilding of the City, Wren designed most of the 51 new churches, as well as his masterpiece, St Paul's cathedral (1675). He also worked for the court, designing additions to *Hampton Court and Greenwich hospital (1696), and at Oxford (e.g. Sheldonian theatre, 1669) and Cambridge (e.g. the library of Trinity College, 1676). Wren was a crucial figure in the establishment of classicism as an acceptable architectural style in 17th-century England.

writ. A document, issued under the seal of the crown or a court, directing one or more persons to do or not to do a specified act. In Anglo-Saxon England, writs were brief vernacular notifications of the king's will. Their use was developed by the Normans, under whom three main kinds of prerogative writ emerged: *charters, letters patent, or overt (see patent rolls), and letters close (which were closed, not being for public examination). The judicial use of writs, largely a Norman innovation, was most commonly for the purpose of summoning a person to appear in court (an original writ), which was replaced by the writ of summons in 1832. See also prohibition, writ of; right, writ of.

Wulfstan, St (c. 1009-1095). Bishop of Worcester from 1062. Educated at Evesham and Peterborough, Wulfstan was the last of the Anglo-Saxon bishops. A supporter of William I, who allowed him to retain the bishopric, Wulfstan, although unlearned, was an excellent administrator and was also noted for his pastoral activities. He rebuilt Worcester cathedral and brought an end to the slave traffic at Bristol. Feast day: 19 Jan.

Wyatt's rebellion (Jan-Feb 1554). A revolt of some 3000 men of Kent, led by Sir Thomas Wyatt the younger, against Mary I's proposed marriage to Philip II of Spain. Intending to place Princess Elizabeth on the throne, the rebels entered London but were soon defeated. Wyatt and about a hundred others were executed.

Wycherley, William (1640-1716). Writer of Restoration comedies. *The Country Wife* (acted 1675) and *The Plain Dealer* (acted 1676) are masterpieces of the witty and sophisticated Restoration style.

Wycliffe (or Wyclif), John (c. 1330-1384). Church reformer, who inspired the *Lollards. Born in Yorkshire, he was educated at Oxford and became master of Balliol College in about 1360. In 1374 he was made rector of Lutterworth. In *De dominio divino* and *De dominio civil* (c. 1376) he argued that the church should not interfere in temporal affairs nor have temporal possessions. After the development of the great schism in the western church he attacked the claims to authority of the papacy and denied the doctrine of tran-

substantiation (see Eucharist). He is best remembered for supervising the translation of the *Bible into English.

Wykeham, William of (1324-1404). Bishop of *Winchester (1367-1404) and lord chancellor (1368-71, 1389-91) under Edward III and Richard II. He came into conflict with John of Gaunt and lost his office and see (1373) but was later pardoned by Richard. He founded New College, Oxford.

Y

Yalta conference (4-11 Feb 1945). A meeting towards the end of World War II at Yalta, in the Crimea, of Roosevelt, Churchill, and Stalin. Postwar settlements were discussed, notably German disarmament and *reparations, and the *Curzon line was recognized as Poland's frontier with the Soviet Union. By a secret agreement with Roosevelt, Stalin promised to declare war on Japan three months after the end of hostilities in Europe.

Yeomen of the Guard. The royal bodyguard employed on state occasions, also known as Beefeaters because of their magnificent physiques. They were founded by Henry VII for his coronation in 1485, being chosen for their skill as archers, and wear a scarlet uniform said to symbolize the dragon of *Cadwaladr ap Cadwallon. Numbering a hundred since 1669, they (and an English monarch) last appeared on the battlefield at *Dettingen (1743). They are now a purely ceremonial force that includes the Yeomen Warders of the Tower of London.

York. The administrative centre of Yorkshire and seat of the archbishop of York. A Roman city (named Eboracum) because of its strategic importance on the Ouse, York was until the 19th century the northern capital of England and a rival in importance to London. It was one of the most important bases for the Danes in England (see York, Kingdom of) and throughout the medieval and early modern period was an important trading centre. In the 19th century its national importance declined: it did not become one of the centres of the industrial revolution and was increasingly eclipsed by such towns as Manchester and Liverpool.

Between 1154 and 1470 its *minster was slowly erected, which, in a mixture of styles from early English to perpendicular, is one of the finest in England. There was also some development in the 18th century, including the building of the Assembly Rooms (1731-32), one of the best examples of the English Palladian style.

York, Henry Stuart, cardinal duke of (1725-1807). Jacobite pretender to the throne from 1788, as Henry IX. Younger son of James Francis Edward (titular James III), the old pretender, he was created a cardinal in 1747. He bequeathed the crown jewels, taken from England by James II, to the future George IV.

York, house of. A royal dynasty descended from Edmund de *Langley, fifth son of Edward III, who was created duke of York in 1385 by Richard II. His son *Edward of Norwich, 2nd duke of York, died at Agincourt (1415) and was succeeded by his nephew *Richard, 3rd duke of York, who also had a claim to the throne through his maternal great-grandfather Edmund *Mortimer, 3rd earl of March. In 1460, after the outbreak of the Wars of the *Roses, he was recognized as heir to Henry VI but was defeated and killed at Wakefield in the same year. His son Edward, earl of March, revived the Yorkist cause and was crowned Edward IV in 1461. After the brief rule of his son Edward V and brother Richard III the crown passed to Henry VII, the first *Tudor monarch, who married Edward IV's daughter Elizabeth. The last of the Yorkist dynasty, Edward, earl of Warwick, was impersonated by several pretenders to the throne of Henry VII and was executed in 1499.

York, Kingdom of. A Danish kingdom, approximating former *Deira, founded in 876. The Danes of York were defeated by Edward the Elder of Wessex at *Tettenhall (910). In 919 Irish Vikings (Norsemen) invaded York and established a kingdom recognized by Edward in 920. Led by Athelstan, the English conquered York (927), but the Norsemen returned to rule York in the years 940-44, 947, and 949-54. It was subsequently subjected to the rule of Wessex.

York, treaty of (Sept 1237). A treaty between Alexander II of Scots and Henry III of England, which established a border between their respective kingdoms along the river Tweed and the Cheviot Hills to Solway Firth. Alexander renounced his claim to Northumberland and Cumberland (in which he received lands to hold of Henry) and to Westmorland.

Yorktown, surrender at (19 Oct 1781). A British surrender, the conclusive military disaster of the *American Revolution. *Cornwallis, commanding in Virginia, established a base at Yorktown. Trapped by American and French troops under Washington, while French ships temporarily controlled the sea approaches, Cornwallis' force was compelled to surrender. Yorktown convinced most of British opinion that the war was unwinnable.

Young, Arthur (1741-1820). Writer on farming, whose work powerfully influenced agricultural improvement. In 1793 he helped found, and became secretary to, the Board of *Agriculture. Young's published accounts of his wide travels in Great Britain, Ireland, and France (notably *Travels in France*, 1792) provide invaluable information on late 18th-century economic and social conditions.

Young England. A movement, formed in the 1840s by Conservatives opposed to Peel. Its leading members were John Manners, later 7th duke of Rutland (1818-1906), and George Smythe, later 7th Viscount Strangford (1818-57). Disraeli also became a member, and his novel *Coningsby* (1844) depicts the movement's romantic and aristocratic ideals.

Young Ireland. An Irish nationalist movement, formed by young Protestant radicals in 1841 and led by the poet Thomas Davis (1814-45). Its advocacy, in the *Nation*, of the use of force if necessary to achieve abolition of the union with Britain provoked O'Connell's hostility. Young Ireland's rising in 1848, gaining little support, was a humiliating failure.

Young Men's Christian Association (YMCA). A Christian organization founded in 1844 for young men by George Williams (1821-1905), then a London draper's clerk. His purpose was to promote Christian living and to organize social and educational activities. The YMCA subsequently also provided hostel accommodation, and since 1971 its members have included women. *See also* Young Women's Christian Association.

Young Wales (Welsh: *Cymru Fydd*, Future Wales). A nationalist movement, both political and cultural, founded in 1886. Inspired by the earlier *Young Ireland organization, Young Wales sought Welsh home rule through the Liberal Party. It had ceased to exist by 1900, largely because separatism lacked support in Wales itself.

Young Women's Christian Association (YWCA). A Christian organization founded for women in 1855 by Emma Robarts and Mary Jane Kinnaird. They wished to promote Christian unity and interdenominational understanding through social and educational activities. Subsequently the organization offered hostel accommodation to members, which now include men.

Ypres, battles of. Three battles of World War I at or around Ypres, in Flanders. 1. (12 Oct-22 Nov 1914) A battle in which the Germans made three successive and ultimately unsuccessful attempts to break the allied front. The British lost more than 50 000 soldiers. 2. (22 April-25 May 1915) A battle in which the Germans, using poison gas for the first time, considerably reduced the Ypres salient. 3. (31 July-10 Nov 1917) A battle also known as the battle of Passchendaele. The aims of the British offensive were to break through the German trench lines to the German submarine bases in Belgium and to relieve pressure on the collapsing Russian army in the east. Neither of these objectives was achieved. For much of the three months' battle, successive attacks by Gough's Fifth Army and Plumer's Second Army foundered in terrain that had been turned into a swamp by intensive artillery bombardment, thus precluding the use of tanks. The limit of the British advance was five miles, at a cost of 250 000 casualties.

Z

Zambia. *See* Northern Rhodesia.

Zanzibar. An island off the East African coast. It was annexed by Britain in 1890 and regained its independence in 1963. In 1964 it joined *Tanganyika to form the republic of Tanzania.

Zimbabwe. *See* Southern Rhodesia.

Zinoviev letter (25 Oct 1924). A letter, allegedly from Grigori Zinoviev, chairman of Comintern (the Third International), inciting British Communists to sedition. Revealed in the British press just before the general election, the letter drew a protest from the Foreign Office to the Soviet Union but was almost certainly a forgery intended to discredit the Labour Party. It probably made little contribution to Labour's election defeat.

Zululand. A region of NE *Natal, South Africa, home of the Zulu nation. Britain defeated the Zulus, under Cetshwayo (d. 1884), in 1879 and occupied Zululand, which became a British protectorate in 1887 and part of Natal in 1897.

55 BC

Caesar's first invasion of Britain.

54 BC

Caesar's second invasion of Britain; Cassivellaunus agrees to pay tribute.

27 BC

Augustus becomes Roman emperor.

?42 AD

Death of Cunobelinus.

43

Roman conquest begins; Caractacus is defeated at the Medway.

61

The Romans invade Wales and massacre the Druids and women of Anglesey; Boudicca rebels.

83

Agricola defeats the Caledonians at Mons Graupius.

c. 127

Hadrian's wall is completed.

140

A Roman theatre is built at Verulamium.

142

The Antonine wall is completed.

166

The first church is built at Glastonbury.

180

The Romans are defeated in Caledonia and retire behind Hadrian's wall.

196

Clodius Albinus, governor of Britain, is proclaimed emperor and crosses to Gaul; the Picts overrun Hadrian's wall.

208

Britain is reorganized into two provinces; Hadrian's wall is rebuilt.

211

Death of Emperor Septimius Severus at York.

c. 286

Carausius proclaims himself emperor in Britain.

293

Allectus kills Carausius and becomes emperor in Britain.

The Roman Empire is divided into East and West.

296

Allectus is killed; Emperor Constantius orders the repair and rebuilding of Hadrian's wall and York.

304

Martyrdom of St Alban.

306

Death of Constantius at York.

Constantine the Great becomes Roman emperor (→337).

367

The Picts overrun Hadrian's wall.

369

The Picts are driven back; Hadrian's wall is repaired.

383

Magnus Maximus declares himself emperor in Britain; Hadrian's wall is overrun and not repaired.

410

The Roman legions are withdrawn after Alaric, king of the Goths, sacks Rome.

411–18

The Pelagian controversy rages.

c. 417

Roman troops probably return briefly to Britain.

449

First waves of Angle, Saxon, and Jute invasions; Hengist and Horsa land in Kent.

c. 450

St Patrick begins his Irish mission.

455

The Vandals, under Genseric, sack Rome.

476

Romulus Augustulus, the last Roman emperor, is deposed by the German king Odoacer.

477

Aelle and his Saxon followers land in Sussex.

491

Aelle completes the conquest of Sussex.

494

The Jutes complete the conquest of Kent.

496

Clovis I of the Franks becomes a Christian.

c. 514

Cerdic lands in Wessex.

c. 518

The British, probably led by Arthur, defeat the Saxons at Mount Badon.

c. 527

The Saxon kingdoms of Essex and Middlesex are established.

c. 530

Cerdic conquers the Isle of Wight.

c. 540

Benedict of Nursia founds the Benedictine monastic order at Monte Cassino, Italy.

c. 550

The Anglian kingdoms of East Anglia, Mercia, and Northumbria are founded; King Ida builds Bamburgh castle.

St David's mission to Wales.

560

The abbey at Bangor in Ireland is founded.

563

Columba founds the monastery at Iona.

577

The West Saxons advance to the river Severn and defeat the British at Deorham.

583

Defeat at Faddiley stops the West Saxon advance into Wales.

597

St Augustine lands in Kent, founds a Benedictine monastery at Canterbury, and converts King Aethelbert of Kent.

c. 607

The first St Paul's church is built in London.

615

The Angles reach the Irish Sea and massacre monks at Bangor.

620

Edwin, king of Northumbria, subdues the Isle of Man.

625

St Paulinus arrives in Northumbria.

c. 627

Sutton Hoo burial takes place.

635

St Aidan founds Lindisfarne monastery.

657

St Hild founds Whitby monastery.

c. 657

Caedmon begins writing poetry.

664

The synod of Whitby is held.

681

Benedict Biscop founds Jarrow monastery.

685

Battle of Nechtansmere; the Picts drive back the Northumbrians.

c. 685

Foundation of (Saxon) Winchester cathedral.

695

The law code of Wihtred is promulgated.

c. 715

Beowulf is composed.

718

Boniface begins his mission in Germany.

731

Bede completes his history of the English.

732

Charles Martel defeats the Arabs near Tours.

c. 735

Offa of Mercia introduces the silver penny.

744

Foundation of the abbey at Fulda.

751

Pepin the Short founds the Carolingian dynasty.

c. 760

The Book of Kells is composed.

779

Offa of Mercia defeats the West

Saxons at Benson and is regarded as overlord of all England.

c. 781

Alcuin is employed by Charlemagne.

c. 783

Offa's dyke is completed.

787

The first Danish raid takes place.

793

Danish raiders destroy Lindisfarne abbey.

795

The Danes sack Iona.

800

Charlemagne is crowned by the pope as the first emperor of the West.

802

Egbert becomes king of Wessex.

829

Egbert is recognized as overlord of England.

835

Egbert defeats the Danes and Britons in Cornwall.

839

Aethelwulf becomes king of Wessex.

c. 840

The Danes found Dublin and Limerick.

c. 850

Kenneth MacAlpin conquers the Picts and becomes the first king of Scotia.

866

Aethelred I becomes king of Wessex (→871).

870

The Danes conquer East Anglia.

871

Aethelred I dies fighting the Danes at Merton; Alfred the Great becomes king of Wessex (→899).

876

The Danish kingdom of York is established.

877

Wessex and the Danes partition Mercia; the Danes defeat and kill Constantine II of Scots.

878

Alfred the Great defeats Guthrum, and the Danelaw is established.

886

Alfred the Great recaptures London.

c. 891

The *Anglo-Saxon Chronicle* begins.

892

A new wave of Danish raids begins.

893

Alfred the Great originates the Royal Navy.

899

Edward the Elder becomes king of Wessex (→924).

910

The West Saxons defeat the Danes of York at Tettenhall and advance into East Anglia, the Midlands, and Essex.

916

Viking attacks on Ireland are renewed.

918

Edward the Elder annexes Mercia to Wessex.

c. 919

The princes in West Wales acknowledge the overlordship of Edward the Elder.

c. 920

The kings of Scotia, Strathclyde, and York acknowledge Edward the Elder as their overlord.

924-39 Reign of Athelstan, king of England.

927

Athelstan conquers Northumbria and receives the submission of the leading northern rulers.

937

Athelstan defeats the Scots, Danes, and Strathclyde at Brunanburh.

939-46 Reign of Edmund I, king of England.

c. 943

Hywel Dda issues a code of Welsh laws.

946-55 Reign of Edred, king of England.

954

Eric Bloodaxe, Norwegian king of York, is expelled; Northumbria comes conclusively under English control.

955-59 Reign of Edwy, king of England.

956

Edwy expels St Dunstan.

959-75 Reign of Edgar, king of England.

c. 960

St Dunstan becomes archbishop of Canterbury.

973

Edgar is crowned at Bath and receives the submission of the British kings.

975-78 Reign of Edward the Martyr, king of England.

978

Edward the Martyr is murdered at Corfe castle.

978-1016 Reign of Aethelred (II) the Unready, king of England.

980

Renewed Danish raids on the English coast.

991

The Danes defeat the English at Maldon.

c. 993

Aelfric writes Lives of the Saints.

994

Olaf Tryggvason of Norway and Sweyn I Forkbeard of Denmark besiege London.

998

The Danes raid on the Isle of Wight.

1002

Aethelred II orders the massacre of Danish settlers in England on St Brice's Day.

1003

Sweyn I Forkbeard again invades England.

1007

Aethelred II pays 30 000 pounds of silver (Danegeld) to the Danes.

1012

Aethelred II pays 48 000 pounds of silver (Danegeld)·to Sweyn I Forkbeard.

1013

Sweyn I Forkbeard forces Aethelred into exile in Normandy.

1014

Death of Sweyn I Forkbeard; Aethelred II is restored to the throne; Brian Boru of Ireland defeats the Vikings at Clontarf.

1016

Edmund II Ironside is chosen as king by the Londoners but is defeated by Cnut at Ashingdon.

1016-35 Reign of Cnut, king of England.

1017

Cnut divides England into four earldoms.

1018

Malcolm II of Scotia defeats the English at Carham and annexes Lothian.

1034-40 Reign of Duncan I, king of Scots.

1035-40 Reign of Harold I Harefoot, king of England.

1039

Gruffudd ap Llywelyn gains Gwynedd and Powys.

1040-42 Reign of Harthacnut, king of England.

1040-57 Reign of Macbeth, king of Scots.

1042-66 Reign of Edward the Confessor, king of England.

1052

Earl Godwine invades England and is restored to Wessex.

1054

The church splits between East and West.

1058-93 Reign of Malcolm III Canmore, king of Scots.

1059

Robert Guiscard establishes Norman rule in southern Italy.

1063

Earl Harold of Wessex and Tostig subdue Wales; Gruffudd ap Llywelyn is killed.

1064

Earl Harold pays homage to Duke William II of Normandy.

1065

Westminster abbey is consecrated.

1066 Reign of Harold II, king of England.

1066

Harold II defeats the Norwegian king Harald Hardraada and Tostig at Stamford Bridge; Duke William II of Normandy defeats Harold II at Hastings.

1066–87 Reign of William (I) the Conqueror, king of England.

1067

The first Welsh Marcher earldom (Hereford) is established.

1068

William I suppresses revolts in the southwest, the north, and the Midlands (→1075).

1070

Lanfranc becomes archbishop of Canterbury (→1089).

1071

William I defeats Hereward the Wake, ending the English resistance to him; the Welsh Marcher earldom of Chester is established.

1072

William I invades Scotland; Malcolm III of Scots pays homage to William at Abernethy.

1075

The Welsh Marcher earldom of Shrewsbury is established.

1077

Emperor Henry IV is absolved by Pope Gregory VII at Canossa.

1078

William I begins the Tower of London.

1079

(Norman) Winchester cathedral is begun.

1081

Gruffudd ap Cynan of Gwynedd and Rhys ap Tewdwr of Deheubarth defeat their rivals at Mynydd Carn.

1086

Important landholders pay homage to William I at the moot of Salisbury.

The Domesday survey is made.

1087–1100 Reign of William II Rufus, king of England.

1088

William II crushes a rebellion in favour of Robert II Curthose of Normandy.

1092

William II captures Carlisle and annexes Cumberland.

1093

Malcolm III Canmore dies fighting the English at Alnwick; Rhys ap Tewdwr dies fighting near Brecon.

1093–97 Reign of Donald III Bane, king of Scots.

1094

Cadwgan and Gruffudd ap Cynan of Gwynedd fight against the Normans (→1099).

1095

William II suppresses a baronial revolt.

1097–1107 Reign of Edgar, king of Scots.

1100–35 Reign of Henry I, king of England.

1100

Henry I marries Matilda, uniting the Norman and Saxon royal houses.

1101

Treaty of Alton confirms Henry I as king of England and Robert as duke of Normandy; Roger of Salisbury is made chancellor and institutes administrative reforms.

1106

Henry I defeats Robert at Tinchebrai and becomes duke of Normandy.

1107

Anselm, archbishop of Canterbury, and Henry I settle the investiture contest.

1107–24 Reign of Alexander I, king of Scots.

c. 1110

Earliest record of a miracle play—at Dunstable.

1114

Matilda, daughter of Henry I, marries Emperor Henry V.

c. 1115

Henry I establishes the menagerie at Woodstock.

1120

Henry I's son and heir is drowned when the White Ship sinks, and Matilda becomes Henry I's heiress.

1124-53 Reign of David I, king of Scots.

1127

The English barons recognize Matilda as heiress to the throne.

1128

Matilda marries Geoffrey of Anjou.

1132

Foundation of Fountains abbey.

1135-54 Reign of Stephen, king of England.

1138

Civil war begins; David I of Scots invades England and loses the battle of the Standard; Robert of Gloucester declares for Matilda and prepares for war.

1139

Matilda lands in England.

1141

Matilda and Robert of Gloucester defeat and capture Stephen at Lincoln; Matilda is routed at Winchester and Robert is captured; Stephen and Robert are exchanged.

1142

Matilda escapes the siege of Oxford by crossing the frozen Thames.

1145

Stephen is victorious at Faringdon.

1147

Henry Plantagenet campaigns unsuccessfully in England.

1148

Matilda leaves England.

1151

Henry Plantagenet succeeds his father as count of Anjou.

1152

Henry of Anjou marries Eleanor, heiress of Aquitaine.

1153-65 Reign of Malcolm IV, king of Scots.

1153

Henry of Anjou is recognized as Stephen's heir by the treaty of Winchester.

1154-89 Reign of Henry II, king of England.

1154

Nicholas Breakspear is elected Pope Adrian IV.

1155

The papal bull *Laudabiliter* empowers Henry II to conquer and rule Ireland.

Frederick Barbarossa is crowned holy Roman emperor.

1157

Owain ap Gruffudd of Gwynedd and Malcolm IV of Scots do homage to Henry II.

Henry awards special privileges to the Cologne merchants in London.

1160

Malcolm IV subdues Galloway.

1162

Thomas Becket becomes archbishop of Canterbury (→1170).

1164

Constitutions of Clarendon are issued.

1165-1214 Reign of William (I) the Lion, king of Scots.

1166

Assize of Clarendon is enacted.

Rory O'Connor drives Dermot MacMurrough of Leinster out of Ireland.

c. 1167

English scholars are expelled from Paris and settle at Oxford—the effective foundation of Oxford University.

1170

Richard de Clare (Strongbow) lands in Ireland and restores Dermot MacMurrough to his throne; an inquest of sheriffs is held; murder of Thomas Becket.

1171

Dermot MacMurrough dies, leaving Leinster to Richard de Clare (Strongbow); Henry II winters at Dublin and receives the submission of the Irish kings (→1172).

1173

Outbreak of the rebellion of Henry II's sons.

1174

Henry II defeats his rebellious sons, captures William the Lion of Scots at Alnwick, and compels him to do homage by the treaty of Falaise.

1175

Treaty of Windsor: Henry II recognizes Rory O'Connor as high king of Ireland.

1176

Assize of Northampton is enacted.

1177

John de Courcy begins the conquest of Ulster; Henry II's youngest son John is made titular lord of Ireland.

c. 1177

Belfast is founded when John de Courcy builds a castle there.

c. 1179

The grand assize is introduced.

1181

Assize of Arms is enacted.

1183

Henry, the Young King, dies.

1189

Henry II is defeated by his son Richard and Philip II Augustus of France.

1189-99 Reign of Richard I, Coeur de Lion, king of England.

1189

William Longchamp is appointed chancellor (→1191).

1190

The Jews are massacred in York.
Richard I joins the third crusade.

1191

William Longchamp falls from power.
Richard I defeats Saladin at Arsuf.

?1191

Henry Fitz Ailwin becomes the first mayor of London.

1192

Richard I is imprisoned in Germany and John tries to seize power.

1194

Richard I is ransomed and returns briefly to England.

1199

Richard is killed in France.

1199-1216 Reign of John, king of England.

1200

John makes peace with France and marries Isabel of Angoulême.

1202

Renewed Anglo-French conflict over English possessions in France.

1203

Arthur of Brittany is murdered, probably by his uncle John.

1204

John loses Normandy, Maine, Anjou, and Brittany to the French king (→1206).

1207

John grants a charter to Liverpool.
John refuses to accept Stephen Langton as archbishop of Canterbury.

1208

A papal interdict is imposed on England.

1209

William the Lion of Scots submits to John at Norham.
After riots in Oxford some students move to Cambridge—effectively founding Cambridge University.
The pope excommunicates John.

1212

John concludes the treaty of Lambeth with the count of Bologne.

1213

A council at St Albans demands liberties granted by Henry I.
John submits to the pope; war with France is renewed (→1214).

1214

John is defeated at Bouvines.

1214-49 Reign of Alexander II, king of Scots.

1215

The barons force John to accept Magna Carta; Hubert de Burgh becomes justiciar (→1232); the first Barons' War breaks out; Alexander II of Scots invades

England; Louis, dauphin of France, claims the English throne and invades England.

1216–72 Reign of Henry III, king of England.

1216

Magna Carta is reissued.

1217

Magna Carta is reissued; the Forest Charter is issued.

The English defeat the French at Lincoln and repel the French fleet near Sandwich; the treaty of Kingston-upon-Thames makes peace between France, the rebellious barons, and the royalists.

1218

Llywelyn ap Iorwerth of Gwynedd and the English sign the treaty of Worcester.

1220

The building of Salisbury cathedral begins.

1221

Alexander II marries Joan, daughter of King John.

1222

Hubert de Burgh quells an insurrection in Oxford in favour of Louis VIII of France.

1225

Magna Carta and the Forest Charter are reissued.

1227

Henry III declares himself of age and assumes full powers.

1232

Peter des Rivaux becomes treasurer; Hubert de Burgh is dismissed.

1233

Anger at Poitevin influence, notably that of Peter des Rivaux and Peter des Roches, provokes the Marshal rebellion.

1234

Henry III dismisses Peter des Rivaux and Peter des Roches.

1236

Henry III marries Eleanor of Provence, whose Savoyard relations are unpopular in England.

1238

Simon de Montfort marries Henry III's sister Eleanor.

1242

Henry III is defeated by France at the battle of Saintes.

1248

Henry III appoints Simon de Montfort lieutenant of Gascony.

1249–86 Reign of Alexander III, king of Scots.

1251

The Gascons rebel against Simon de Montfort.

1252

Simon de Montfort resigns.

1258

Henry III agrees to the Provisions of Oxford (limiting royal power).

Llywelyn ap Gruffudd defies Henry and styles himself prince of Wales.

1259

Provisions of Westminster are agreed.

The treaty of Paris between Henry III and Louis IX of France confirms the loss of England's Angevin domains.

1261

Henry III repudiates the Provisions of Oxford.

1264

The Provisions of Oxford are annulled by the mise of Amiens, and the second Barons' War breaks out; after the battle of Lewes Simon de Montfort becomes virtual ruler of England.

1265

Simon de Montfort summons a parliament of churchmen, barons, knights, and two representatives from each borough; Henry's son, Edward, defeats de Montfort at Newport and Kenilworth; Edward kills de Montfort at Evesham; the rebellious barons are defeated at Axholme.

1266

The dictum of Kenilworth is issued.

Norway cedes the Western Isles and the Isle of Man to Scotland by the treaty of Perth.

1267

The rebellious barons are defeated at Ely; the Statute of Marlborough institutes reforms.

Henry recognizes Llywelyn ap Gruffudd as prince of Wales by the treaty of Montgomery.

1271-1307 Reign of Edward I, king of England.

1271

Marco Polo goes to China.

1277

Edward I begins his conflict with Llywelyn ap Gruffudd of Wales (→1282).

1278

Statute of Gloucester is enacted.

Edward I has Jews and goldsmiths arrested and punished for coin clipping; many Jews are hanged.

1279

Statute of Mortmain is enacted.

1282

Llywelyn ap Gruffudd is killed.

1283

Statute of Acton Burnell is enacted.

Dafydd ap Gruffudd is captured and executed.

1284

Statute of Rhuddlan is enacted; Prince Edward is born at Caernarfon.

1285

Statutes of Winchester and Merchants are enacted; Kirkby's quest is undertaken.

1286-90 Reign of Margaret, queen of Scots.

1290

The statutes quia emptores and quo warranto are enacted.

Edward expels the Jews from England.

1291

Edward I arbitrates (→1292) between the competitors for the Scottish throne and chooses John Balliol.

1292-96 Reign of John Balliol, king of Scots.

1295

Edward I summons the Model Parliament; he suppresses a Welsh revolt.

1296

Edward I defeats the Scots at Dunbar, forcing John Balliol to give up the throne.

1297

William Wallace defeats the English at Stirling Bridge and ravages northern England.

1298

Edward I defeats William Wallace at Falkirk.

1299

Magna Carta is confirmed.

William Wallace withdraws to France.

1305

William Wallace is captured and executed.

1306

Robert the Bruce murders John Comyn at Dumfries.

1306-29 Reign of Robert I, king of Scots.

Robert I rebels against England and is defeated at Methven.

1307

Robert I defeats the English at Loudun Hill; death of Edward I on campaign.

1307-27 Reign of Edward II, king of England.

1308

Edward II marries Isabel of France; he sends Piers Gaveston to Ireland.

Edward seizes the Templars' property.

1309

Edward II recalls Piers Gaveston.

The papacy moves to Avignon (→1377).

1310

Edward II is forced to appoint the lords ordainers.

1311

The Ordinances limit royal power.

1312

Rebellious barons execute Piers Gaveston.

1314

Robert I defeats Edward II at Bannockburn.

1315

Thomas of Lancaster controls the administration of England.

Edward Bruce invades Ireland.

1316

Edward Bruce is crowned high king of Ireland.

1318

Edward II regains control of government; the Despensers come to the fore.

Edward Bruce is defeated in Ireland.

1319

The Scots defeat the English at Myton.

1320

The marcher lords protest against the Despensers' acquisitions and prepare to fight.

1321

The barons make Edward II banish the Despensers.

1322

The marcher lords submit to Edward II; he defeats Thomas of Lancaster at Boroughbridge and executes him; Edward repeals the Ordinances and recalls the Despensers.

1325

Queen Isabel goes to France.

1326

Queen Isabel and Roger de Mortimer invade England, execute the Despensers, and imprison Edward II.

1327

Edward II is deposed; Edward III (aged 14) succeeds but Isabel and Roger de Mortimer govern; Edward II is murdered.

The Scots invade England.

1327–77 Reign of Edward III, king of England.

1328

By the treaty of Edinburgh England recognizes Robert I as king of independent Scotland.

1329–71 Reign of David II, king of Scots.

1330

Edward III seizes power and executes Roger de Mortimer.

1332

Edward Balliol invades Scotland, wins at Dupplin Muir, and is crowned Edward I, king of Scots.

1333

The Scots expel Edward Balliol; Edward III defeats the Scots at Halidon Hill and takes Berwick.

1334

David II flees to France.

1337

The start of the Hundred Years' War with France.

1340

England wins a naval victory over France at Sluys.

1341

David II returns to Scotland.

1344

The Round Tower of Windsor castle is built.

1346

England defeats France at Crécy; England defeats a Scottish invasion at Neville's Cross and captures David II.

1347

England captures Calais.

1348

The Order of the Garter is founded; the black death reaches England.

1351

Statutes of Labourers and Provisors are enacted.

1352

Statute of Treasons is enacted.

1353

First Statute of Praemunire is enacted.

1354

Statute of Staples is enacted.

The Franco-Scottish alliance is renewed.

1355

The Hundred Years' War is renewed.

1356

Edward, the Black Prince, defeats the French at Poitiers and captures John II of France; Edward III attempts to terrorize Scotland.

1357
Edward III releases David II.

1360
The treaty of Brétigny is agreed.

1362
Edward III gives Aquitaine to Edward, the Black Prince.

c. 1362
The first version of William Langland's *Piers Plowman* is written.

1365
Second Statute of Praemunire is enacted.

1366
Statutes of Kilkenny are enacted.

1367
Edward, the Black Prince, defeats Henry of Castile at Najera.

1368
Charles V of France aids the Aquitaine rebels against Edward, the Black Prince.

1370
Edward, the Black Prince, orders the massacre at Limoges.

1371-90 Reign of Robert II, the first Stuart king of Scots.

1376
The Good Parliament attacks the royal administration; death of Edward, the Black Prince.

1377-99 Reign of Richard II, king of England.

1378
The Hawley-Shakell case is tried.
The great schism divides the church (→1417).

1381
The Peasants' Revolt breaks out.
Wycliffe publishes the heretical *Confessio*.

1383
The Norwich crusade is launched.

1386
Parliament impeaches the chancellor Michael de la Pole, while John of Gaunt is absent in Spain.

1387
The English defeat a Franco-Castilian fleet off Margate; the lords appellant defeat Richard II's army at Radcot Bridge.

1388
The Merciless Parliament impeaches the king's friends.
The Scots defeat the English at Otterburn.

1389
John of Gaunt returns from Spain.

1390-1406 Reign of Robert III, king of Scots.

1390
Second Statute of Provisors is enacted.

c. 1390
Chaucer completes *The Canterbury Tales.*

1393
Third Statute of Praemunire is enacted.

1394
Richard II leads a successful expedition to Ireland (→1395); the Irish lords do homage.

1396
Treaty of Paris between England and France; Richard II marries Isabel of France.

1397
Haxey's case is tried; death of Thomas of Woodstock; the children of John of Gaunt and Catherine Swinford are legitimized; Richard II destroys the lords appellant.

1398
Richard II banishes Henry Bolingbroke.

1399
Death of John of Gaunt; Richard II seizes Henry Bolingbroke's inheritance; Bolingbroke deposes Richard II to become king.

1399-1414 Reign of Henry IV, king of England.

1400
Richard II dies (probably murdered); Owain Glyndŵr begins a war of independence in Wales; a conspiracy of four earls is suppressed.

1401

Statute *de heretico comburendo* is enacted; the first Lollard martyr is burned at Smithfield.

1402

Sir Henry Percy repels the Scottish raiders at Homildon Hill; Owain Glyndŵr defeats the English at Pilleth.

1403

The Percys revolt; Henry IV is victorious at Shrewsbury, where Sir Henry Percy is killed.

1404

The Unlearned Parliament meets.

1405

French forces land in Wales to support Owain Glyndŵr; Henry IV crushes Scrope's rebellion.

1406–37 Reign of James I, king of Scots.

1406

The duke of Albany becomes guardian of Scotland (→1420).

1408

Henry IV's victory and Northumberland's death at Bramham Moor end the revolt of the Percys.

1409

The English take Harlech; Owain Glyndŵr disappears.

1411

Foundation of the Guildhall in London.

1413–22 Reign of Henry V, king of England.

1414

The Lollard rising is suppressed.

Henry V negotiates an alliance with Burgundy.

1415

The leaders of the Cambridge plot are executed.

Henry V renews war against France, takes Harfleur, and wins at Agincourt.

1416

Emperor Sigismund visits England and makes an alliance with Henry V.

1418

The English capture Falaise.

1419

The English capture Rouen; peace negotiations between England, France, and Burgundy take place.

1420

By the treaty of Troyes Henry V becomes heir to the French throne.

c. 1420

The Paston letters begin.

1422–61 Reign of Henry VI, king of England.

1422

Humphrey, duke of Gloucester, and John of Lancaster become protectors for the infant Henry VI.

1424

Henry Beaufort becomes chancellor.

A Franco-Scottish force is defeated at Verneuil.

1429

Joan of Arc and the dauphin relieve Orléans and enter Reims, where the dauphin is crowned Charles VII; the French defeat the English at Patay.

1431

Joan of Arc is burned at Rouen.

1435

France and Burgundy ally.

1437–60 Reign of James II, king of Scots.

1445

Henry VI marries Margaret of Anjou.

1447

Humphrey, duke of Gloucester, dies.

1449

The French take Rouen.

1450

William de la Pole is murdered at sea; political conflict between Edmund Beaufort and Richard, duke of York, begins; Cade's rebellion is suppressed.

The French win at Formigny and expel the English from Normandy.

1452

Richard, duke of York, marches on London.

1453

The Hundred Years' War is effectively ended when France defeats England at Castillon.

Constantinople falls to the Turks; Gutenberg produces the first printed Bible.

1454
Henry VI is temporarily insane and Richard, duke of York, becomes protector.

1455
The Wars of the Roses begin; at the first battle of St Albans the Yorkists defeat the Lancastrians, and Edmund Beaufort is killed.

1459
The Yorkists are victorious at Blore Heath but are routed at Ludford Bridge.

1460
Warwick defeats and captures Henry VI at Northampton; Queen Margaret defeats and kills York at Wakefield.

1460-88 Reign of James III, king of Scots.

1461
Edward, duke of York, defeats the Lancastrians at Mortimer's Cross and proclaims himself Edward IV; Queen Margaret defeats Warwick at the second battle of St Albans and rescues Henry VI; Edward IV wins at Towton; Henry and Margaret flee to Scotland and Edward IV is crowned king; the Scots take Berwick.

1461-83 Reign of Edward IV, king of England.

1464
The Yorkists defeat the Lancastrians at Hedgeley Moor and Hexham.

1465
Henry VI is captured and imprisoned in the Tower of London.

1467
Edward IV and Warwick quarrel.

1469
Warwick and George, duke of Clarence, plot against Edward IV, who is briefly imprisoned.

1470
Edward IV defeats the Lancastrian rising at "Lose-Coat" field; Warwick and George, duke of Clarence, flee to France; Warwick is reconciled with the Lancastrians; Warwick lands in England and restores Henry VI; Edward flees to Flanders.

1471
Edward IV lands in England and defeats and kills Warwick at Barnet; after his victory at Tewkesbury Edward murders Henry VI and Prince Edward; the Council in the Marches is established.

?1474
William Caxton produces (in Bruges) the first printed book in English.

1475
Edward IV invades France but is bought off by the treaty of Picquigny.

1476
William Caxton begins printing at Westminster.

1478
The duke of Clarence is executed.

1479
Aragon and Castile are united under Ferdinand and Isabella.

1482
By the treaty of Fotheringhay the duke of Albany agrees to dethrone his brother James III of Scots; the English take Berwick.

1483 Reign of Edward V, king of England.

1483
Richard of Gloucester imprisons Edward V and his brother in the Tower, where they are probably murdered.

1483-85 Reign of Richard III, king of England.

1484
James III of Scots suppresses Albany's rebellion, with the help of Richard III.
Richard III bans benevolences.

1485
Henry Tudor defeats and kills Richard III at Bosworth.

1485-1509 Reign of Henry VII, king of England.

1485
Henry VII forms the Yeomen of the Guard.

1486
Henry VII marries Elizabeth of York;

Morton becomes archbishop of Canterbury (→1500).

1487

The statute later called *Pro Camera Stellata* extends the judicial powers of the council; Lambert Simnel's rebellion is crushed at Stoke.

1488

James III of Scots is defeated and murdered at Sauchieburn by rebels.

1488-1513 Reign of James IV, king of Scots.

1489

The treaty of Medina del Campo is negotiated with Spain.

1491

Perkin Warbeck claims the throne.

1492

Margaret of Burgundy and the French and Scottish kings recognize Perkin Warbeck as Richard IV.

The treaty of Etaples concludes war with France.

Christopher Columbus discovers America.

1494

Poynings' Law is enacted.

Bishop Elphinstone founds King's College in Aberdeen.

Charles VIII of France invades Italy.

1495

James IV of Scots gives Perkin Warbeck a state welcome in Stirling; Warbeck unsuccessfully invades Kent.

1496

Intercursus magnus is agreed.

Henry VII licenses the Cabots to explore the New World; weights and measures are standardized in England.

1497

Perkin Warbeck is captured by Henry VII.

Truce of Ayton is made between England and Scotland.

The Cabots reach Nova Scotia.

1499

Erasmus pays his first visit to England.

c. 1500

The present Holyroodhouse is started.

1501

Prince Arthur and Catherine of Aragon marry in London.

1502

Death of Prince Arthur.

1503

Betrothal of Prince Henry to Catherine of Aragon; James IV of Scots marries Henry VII's daughter Margaret Tudor.

William Dunbar writes *The Thrissil and the Rois*; the Paston letters end.

1506

Edmund de la Pole is imprisoned; intercursus malus is agreed.

1509-47 Reign of Henry VIII, king of England.

1509

Henry VIII marries Catherine of Aragon.

c. 1509

Colet founds St Paul's school.

1510

Parliament meets (Jan-Feb).

Empson and Dudley, Henry VII's hated tax collectors, are executed.

1511

Parliament meets (→1513); Thomas Wolsey becomes a privy councillor.

England joins the Holy League against France.

Encomium Moriae (The Praise of Folly) by Erasmus is published.

1512

Laws are passed enforcing archery practice under the supervision of JPs.

Henry VIII attacks France.

1513

Henry VIII defeats France at the battle of the Spurs; James IV of Scots invades England and is defeated and killed at Flodden.

1513-42 Reign of James V, king of Scots.

1514

Parliament meets (→1515); Margaret Tudor marries Archibald Douglas.

Thomas Wolsey becomes archbishop of York. Henry VIII makes peace with France and his sister Mary marries Louis XII.

Wolsey starts Hampton Court palace.

1515

Thomas Wolsey is made lord chancellor (→1529) and a cardinal; the duke of Albany becomes regent of Scotland; Mary Tudor secretly marries Charles Brandon, duke of Suffolk.

Francis I becomes king of France (→1547).

1516

Birth of Princess Mary, the only child of Henry VIII and Catherine of Aragon to survive.

Thomas More's *Utopia* is published.

1517

Thomas Wolsey appoints a commission to inquire into land enlosures; "Evil May Day" riots in London against alien merchants.

Martin Luther's 95 theses attack indulgences.

1518

Thomas Wolsey is made papal legate *a latere.*

Thomas Linacre founds the Royal College of Physicians.

1519

Charles V becomes holy Roman emperor; Ferdinand Magellan begins to circumnavigate the world.

1520

Henry VIII and Francis I of France meet at the field of the cloth of gold.

1522

Emperor Charles V visits Henry VIII at Windsor; they agree to invade France.

1523

Parliament meets (April–Aug).

1524

Albany leaves Scotland.

The amicable grant is demanded.

1525

The Council of the North is revived.

France is defeated at Pavia by imperial troops.

1526

The royal household is reformed.

Holbein visits England.

1527

Henry VIII's attempts to divorce Catherine of Aragon fail.

Imperial troops sack Rome and confine the pope.

1529

The Reformation parliament meets (→1536); Cardinal Wolsey falls from power; Sir Thomas More becomes lord chancellor (→1532).

1531

Thomas Cromwell becomes a privy councillor.

An act against vagabondage is passed.

Elyot's *Boke Named the Governour* is published.

1532

The submission of the clergy; Sir Thomas More abandons the chancellorship; payment of annates is suspended.

1533

Henry VIII secretly marries Anne Boleyn; Cranmer is made archbishop of Canterbury (→1556); Cranmer grants Henry's divorce; Act in Restraint of Appeals is passed; birth of Princess Elizabeth.

1534

First Act of Succession and the Act of Supremacy are passed; Statute of Treasons is extended; Elizabeth Barton (the Maid of Kent) is executed.

Geraldine (Fitzgeralds') revolt breaks out (→1536).

Ignatius Loyola founds the Society of Jesus (Jesuits).

1535

Fisher and More are executed.

The general visitation of the monasteries takes place.

1536

Parliament meets (June–July); death of Catherine of Aragon; Anne Boleyn is executed; Henry VIII marries Jane Seymour; death of the duke of Richmond; Act of Succession is passed; Wales is annexed to England.

The ten articles and the reforming Injunctions are issued; the smaller monasteries are suppressed; the Pilgrimage of Grace begins (→1537).

John Calvin publishes Institutes of the Christian Religion.

1537

Birth of Prince Edward; death of Jane Seymour. The *Institution of a Christian Man* (the "Bishops' Book") is issued.

1538

James V of Scots marries Mary of Guise.

Becket's shrine at Canterbury is destroyed; Henry VIII is excommunicated.

1539

Parliament meets (→1540).

The six articles are issued; Matthew's Bible is placed in the churches; the remaining larger monasteries are suppressed (→1540).

1540

Henry VIII marries and divorces Anne of Cleves; Thomas Cromwell is executed; Henry marries Catherine Howard; Henry assumes the titles of king of and head of the church in Ireland.

The Company of Barber-Surgeons is founded.

1541

Parliament meets (→1544).

1542

Catherine Howard is executed.

The English defeat the Scots at Solway Moss.

1542-67 Reign of Mary Queen of Scots.

1543

Henry marries Catherine Parr; Act for the Government of Wales is passed.

Copernicus publishes his theory of a heliocentric solar system.

1544

Third Act of Succession is passed.

The English, at war with France (→1546), capture Boulogne.

1545

Parliament meets twice (Jan, Nov→Jan 1547).

The French burn Brighton.

The council of Trent meets (→1563) to promote the Counter-Reformation.

1546

Anne Askew and George Wishart are executed; Cardinal Beaton is murdered.

England and France make peace.

1547-53 Reign of Edward VI, king of England.

1547

Parliament meets (→1552); the protectorate of Somerset begins (→1550).

The Scots are defeated at Pinkie.

1549

The protector Somerset is imprisoned by Warwick (later Northumberland).

Kett's rebellion is suppressed.

The first Book of Common Prayer is issued.

The English withdraw from Scotland; Anglo-French war (→1550).

1550

Somerset is released.

A new Ordinal is issued.

1551

Somerset is finally overthrown.

1552

Somerset is executed.

The second Book of Common Prayer is issued.

1553

Parliament meets (March); Edward VI makes Lady Jane Grey his heir; on his death she is proclaimed queen, but Mary secures the succession.

The 42 articles are issued.

1553-58 Reign of Mary I, queen of England.

1553

Parliament meets (Oct-Dec); Northumberland is executed.

The reversal of the Reformation begins.

1554

Parliament meets twice (April-May, Nov→Jan 1555); Wyatt's rebellion is suppressed; Lady Jane Grey is executed; Mary I marries Philip II of Spain; Princess Elizabeth is imprisoned in the Tower, then at Woodstock.

1555

Parliament meets (Oct-Nov); Ridley and Latimer are executed.

The Muscovy Company is founded.

1556

Cranmer is executed.

Philip II becomes king of Spain (→1598).

1557
The Anglo-French war begins
(→1559).

1558
Parliament meets (Jan–Nov).
England loses Calais.

1558–1603 Reign of Elizabeth I, queen of England.

1558
Cecil becomes secretary of state
(→1572).
Mary Queen of Scots marries Francis,
dauphin of France.

1559
Parliament meets (Jan–May).
Protestantism is re-established;
Matthew Parker becomes archbishop of
Canterbury (→1575).
John Knox returns to Scotland;
Scottish reformers destroy the abbey
church of Scone.
Peace is made with France at Cateau-
Cambrésis; war breaks out in Scotland
between the queen regent and France
against the reformers and England
(→1560).
Francis II becomes king of France
(→1560).

1560
Death of Lady Dudley (Amy Robsart).
The treaty of Edinburgh ends the war
in Scotland, and a reformed Calvinist
church is approved.

1561
Mary Queen of Scots returns to
Scotland.

1562
England makes the treaty of Richmond with the French Protestants and
sends a force to Normandy; the English
are besieged in Le Havre (→1563).
Hawkins sells West African slaves in
the West Indies.
The French Wars of Religion begin
(→1598).

1563
Parliament meets (→1567).
Legislation against enclosures and the
Statute of Apprentices are passed.
The 39 articles are issued.

The treaty of Troyes confirms French
possession of Calais.

1565
Mary Queen of Scots marries Darnley; Moray's rebellion in Scotland is
suppressed.

1566
Tobacco is probably introduced to
England.
Rizzio is murdered.

1567
Darnley is murdered, and Mary Queen
of Scots marries Bothwell; Mary is
defeated at Carberry Hill, is imprisoned
at Loch Leven, and abdicates; Moray
becomes regent for the infant James VI.

1567–1625 Reign of James VI, king of Scots.

1567
The Revolt of the Netherlands begins.

1568
Mary escapes and flees to England,
where she is imprisoned by Elizabeth;
attempts are made to colonize Ireland
with Protestants (→1575).
The Spanish attack Hawkins at San
Juan de Ulloa; the English seize Spanish
treasure; an English college is founded
by William Allen at Douai.

1569
The northern rebellion breaks out
(→1570).

1570
The pope excommunicates Elizabeth
I; Moray is assassinated and Lennox
becomes regent of Scotland.

1571
Parliament meets (April–May); the
Ridolfi plot is suppressed.
Death of Lennox; Mar becomes regent
of Scotland.
Publication of the Puritan *Admon-*
ition to Parliament; the first anti-
Catholic penal law is passed.

1572
Parliament meets (→1583); Cecil
becomes lord treasurer (→1598).
Mar dies; Morton becomes regent of
Scotland; the duke of Norfolk is
executed.
Negotiations for the marriage of

Elizabeth I and the duke of Alençon take place; Drake attacks Nombre de Dios.

The Society of Antiquaries is founded.

1575

Grindal becomes archbishop of Canterbury (→1577).

1576

Frobisher voyages overseas (→1578).

1577

Grindal is suspended from office.

1578

Elizabeth renews marriage negotiations with Anjou (formerly Alençon).

1579

The Desmond revolt breaks out (→1583).

The Eastland Company is founded.

Spenser's *Shepheardes Calender* is published.

1580

Drake circumnavigates the world; the Levant Company is founded.

A Jesuit mission is sent to England.

The Spanish land at Smerwick (Ireland).

1581

Morton is executed.

Edmund Campion is executed.

1582

James VI of Scots is seized in the Ruthven raid.

1583

The Throckmorton plot is revealed; the Desmond revolt is suppressed.

The Ruthven raiders are defeated.

Whitgift becomes archbishop of Canterbury (→1604).

1584

Parliament meets (→1585); the signatories of the Bond of Association pledge themselves to protect Elizabeth I from assassination.

1585

Leicester leads an expedition to the Netherlands; Spain seizes English ships and prepares to invade England; Drake raids Spanish possessions in the New World.

1586

Parliament meets (→1587); the Babington plot is discovered.

Death of Sidney at Zutphen; Kyd's *Spanish Tragedy*, Marlowe's *Tamburlaine*, and Camden's *Britannia* are written.

1587

Execution of Mary Queen of Scots; the Marprelate tracts are published (→1589).

Leicester is recalled from the Netherlands; Drake attacks Cádiz.

1588

Parliament meets (→1589).

The Spanish armada is defeated.

Marlow's *Doctor Faustus* is published.

1589

The English aid Henry IV of France (→1594).

Publication of Hakluyt's *Voyages and Discoveries.*

Henry IV becomes king of France (→1610).

1590

The first part of Spenser's *Faerie Queene* is published; Trinity College is founded in Dublin.

1591

Death of Grenville on the *Revenge.*

1592

Shakespeare's great plays are produced (→1616).

1593

Parliament meets (Feb-April); the 1563 statute against enclosures is repealed.

Conventicle Act is passed.

1595

O'Neill's revolt starts in Ulster.

Ben Jonson's *Volpone* is written.

1596

Robert Cecil becomes secretary of state.

Howard and Essex sack Cádiz.

1597

Parliament meets (→1598).

1598

Death of Burghley (formerly Cecil); legislation is enacted against enclosures; O'Neill is victorious at Yellow Ford.

France abandons the English alliance; an Anglo-Dutch alliance is formed against Spain.

The French Protestants obtain toleration by the edict of Nantes.

1599

Essex returns against instructions from Ireland and is imprisoned.

1600

Essex is set free.

The East India Company is incorporated.

An Anglo-Dutch force is victorious against Spain at Nieuport.

1601

Parliament meets (Oct–Dec); Essex rebels and is executed; the Commons debate monopolies; the Poor Law Act is passed.

An Anglo-Dutch force defends Ostend; Spanish troops land at Kinsale.

1603

The O'Neill revolt is suppressed; Elizabeth I is succeeded by James VI of Scots.

1603–25 Reign of James I, king of England.

1603

The bye and main plots are discovered; Raleigh is imprisoned.

The millenary petition is presented.

1604

Parliament meets (→1611); the Apology of the Commons outlines their privileges.

The Hampton Court conference takes place.

Peace is made with Spain.

1605

The gunpowder plot is discovered.

Bacon's *Advancement of Learning* is published.

1606

Bate's case is tried.

1607

The flight of the earls is followed by the plantation of Ulster; Virginia is colonized.

1610

The Great Contract is proposed;

Arabella Stuart is married and imprisoned.

1611

Robert Carr is made Viscount Rochester.

The Authorized Version of the Bible is published.

The Bermudas are settled.

1612

Death of Lord Salisbury (formerly Cecil); death of Henry, prince of Wales.

1613

Princess Elizabeth marries the Elector Palatine; divorce of Lady Essex and her subsequent marriage to Somerset (formerly Rochester); Overbury is murdered.

1614

The Addled Parliament meets (April–June); George Villiers arrives at court.

1615

The Overbury scandal breaks.

1616

Somerset is imprisoned; James I dismisses Coke.

Death of Shakespeare.

1617

A Spanish marriage is proposed for the prince of Wales; George Villiers is made earl of Buckingham.

The transportation of criminals begins.

Raleigh leaves for Eldorado.

1618

Raleigh is executed.

The Five Articles of Perth are issued.

The Thrity Years' War begins (→1648).

1619

Buckingham is made lord high admiral.

An Anglo-Dutch trading agreement is signed.

The banqueting hall is built in Whitehall (→1622).

1620

The pilgrim fathers set sail; Scottish settlement is begun in Nova Scotia.

1621

Parliament meets (→1622); the Commons issue a Protestation against James

I's violation of their privileges; Bacon is impeached.

1622

The Virginia settlers are massacred.

1623

The prince of Wales and Buckingham visit Spain; English settlers are massacred at Amboina.

Death of Willian Byrd.

Frederick V, Elector Palatine, is ousted.

1624

Parliament meets (→1625).

Statute of Monopolies limits their issue.

Cardinal de Richelieu becomes chief minister to Louis XIII of France (→1642).

1625-49 Reign of Charles I.

1625

Parliament meets (May-Aug); by the Act of Revocation Charles I appropriates crown and church lands alienated since 1542; he marries Henrietta Maria.

Buckingham organizes an expedition against Cádiz; Virginia, New England, and Bermuda are placed under royal control; Barbados is annexed.

Death of Orlando Gibbons.

1626

Parliament meets (Feb-June); parliament refuses to grant subsidies, impeaches Buckingham, and is dissolved by Charles; Charles collects a forced loan.

1627

The five knights are tried.

England is at war with France; an expedition is sent to La Rochelle.

1628

Parliament meets (→1629); Buckingham is assassinated; the Petition of Right is issued.

Harvey publishes his discovery of the circulation of the blood.

1629

Charles dissolves parliament and rules without it (→1640).

Peace is made with France.

1630

Peace is made with Spain.

1632

Wentworth arrives in Ireland; Baltimore is granted a patent for the colony of Maryland.

Van Dyck settles in England.

1633

Laud becomes archbishop of Canterbury (→1645).

Donne's poems are published.

1634

Ship money is raised; Prynne is imprisoned.

1637

The Scottish riot against the new prayer book.

1638

The judges find Hampden guilty.

The National Covenant is drawn up; the Book of Sports (1617), listing sports permissible on Sundays, is reissued.

1639

The first Bishops' War ends with the treaty of Berwick.

1640

The Short Parliament meets (April-May); The second Bishops' War ends with the treaty of Ripon; the Long Parliament meets (→1653). The Root and Branch petition is drawn up; Strafford is impeached.

1641

Strafford is executed; the Triennial Act is passed; star chamber is abolished; ship money is declared illegal; the Grand Remonstrance is issued.

The Irish rebellion breaks out.

1642

Charles I attempts to arrest the five members; he leaves Whitehall, is refused entry to Hull, and raises his standard at Nottingham: the Civil War starts (→1649); after the battle of Edgehill the royalists take Oxford but withdraw at Turnham Green; parliament issues nineteen propositions to Charles.

The theatres are closed by ordinance.

1643

The battles of Adwalton Moor, Roundway Down, and Newbury are fought; the Scots and parliament sign the Solemn League and Covenant.

The Westminster Assembly meets (→1653); George Fox is converted.

Louis XIV becomes king of France (→1715).

1644
The battles of Marston Moor, Lostwithiel, and Newbury are fought.

1645
The abortive Uxbridge negotiations are held; the Self-Denying Ordinance is issued; the New Model Army is established; the battles of Naseby, Langport, and Philiphaugh are fought; Laud is executed; use of the prayer book is forbidden.

1646
Charles surrenders to the Scots; the royalists surrender Oxford; Charles receives the propositions of Newcastle.

1647
The Scots hand Charles I over to the English; the army draws up the Heads of the Proposals and the Levellers present the Agreement of the People; Charles escapes but is imprisoned at Carisbrooke castle; he makes the Engagement with the Scots.

1648
Parliament passes the Vote of No Adresses; Civil War resumes; the Scots are defeated at Preston; parliament proposes the Newport treaty; Pride purges parliament, leaving the Rump.

The peace of Westphalia ends the Thirty Years' War.

1649
The trial and execution of Charles I; the monarchy and House of Lords are abolished; the Commonwealth is declared.

The Scottish estates proclaim Charles II as king; Cromwell orders the massacres of Drogheda and Wexford.

1650
Cromwell defeats the Scots at Dunbar.

Adultery is made a capital offence and swearing is to be punished by fines.

1651
Charles II is crowned at Scone; he invades England, is defeated at Worcester, and escapes to France.

The Navigation Act is passed.

Hobbes' *Leviathan* is published.

1652
The Act of Settlement (Ireland) is passed.

The first Dutch War begins (→1654).

1653
Cromwell dismisses the Rump of the Long Parliament; Barebones Parliament meets; the Instrument of Government is drawn up; Cromwell becomes lord protector (→1658).

Walton's *The Compleat Angler* is published.

1653
Royalists rise in Scotland (→1654).

1654
The first Protectorate parliament meets (→1655).

Peace is made with the Dutch.

1655
Penruddock's rising is suppressed; rule by the major generals is instituted.

Jamaica is captured.

1656
The second Protectorate parliament meets (→1658).

War against Spain begins (→1659).

1657
Parliament issues the Humble Petition and Advice.

1658
Death of Oliver Cromwell; Richard Cromwell becomes lord protector (→1659).

The Spanish are defeated in the battle of the Dunes; England takes Dunkirk.

Milton begins *Paradise Lost.*

1659
The third Protectorate parliament meets (Jan-April); the Rump Parliament is recalled; the Commonwealth is re-established.

The treaty of the Pyrenees secures peace with Spain.

1660
Monck restores the Long Parliament; Charles II issues the Declaration of Breda and is restored.

1660-85 Reign of Charles II.

1660

The convention parliament meets (April-Dec); Clarendon becomes lord chancellor (→1667); Act of Indemnity and Oblivion and the Navigation Act are passed; the marriage of the duke of York (later James II) to Anne Hyde is revealed.

Pepys begins his diary (→1669).

1661

The cavalier parliament meets (→1679); the Clarendon code is enacted (→1665).

1662

Charles II marries Catherine of Braganza.

Dunkirk is sold to France.

The Royal Society is incorporated; Boyle's law is published.

1663

The King's Company settles at the Theatre Royal, Drury Lane.

1665

The great plague rages (→1666).

The second Dutch War begins (→1667).

1666

The Fire of London burns; the Pentland rising of covenanters is suppressed in Scotland.

1667

The Dutch raid the Thames; the treaty of Breda is signed.

Clarendon falls from power.

c. 1667

The cabal is in power (→c. 1674).

1668

The triple alliance is formed against France.

1670

Conventicle Act is passed.

The treaty of Dover is signed with France.

Hudson's Bay Company is incorporated.

1672

Charles II issues the Declaration of Indulgence.

The third Dutch War begins (→1674).

1673

The Test Act is passed; the duke of York resigns from the Admiralty and marries Mary of Modena; Danby becomes lord treasurer.

1674

The treaty of Westminster ends the Dutch War.

1675

Wren's St Paul's cathedral is started.

1677

Shaftesbury is imprisoned; Princess Mary marries William of Orange.

1678

The popish plot is proclaimed.

Bunyan's *The Pilgrim's Progress* is published.

1679

Parliament meets (March-July); Danby falls from power; the Habeas Corpus Act is passed; the Country Party attempts to exclude the duke of York from the throne (→1681).

The Covenanters are defeated at Bothwell Bridge; they murder Archbishop Sharp.

1680

Parliament meets (→1681).

1681

Parliament meets (March); Charles rules without parliament (→1685).

Execution of Oliver Plunket.

1682

Shaftesbury flees to the Netherlands.

1683

The Rye House plot is discovered.

The Turks besiege Vienna.

1685-88 Reign of James II.

1685

Parliament meets (→1687); Monmouth rebels; he and Argyll are executed; the Bloody Assizes are held; parliament is prorogued.

The edict of Nantes (1598) is revoked.

1686

Godden versus Hales is heard.

1687

James II dissolves parliament.

James issues his first Declaration of Indulgence.

Newton's *Principia* is completed.

1688

James II issues his second Declaration of Indulgence; the seven bishops are imprisoned; birth of James' son; William of Orange lands in England and James flees abroad.

1689 .

William and Mary accept the Declaration of Rights.

Peter the Great becomes tsar of Russia (→1725).

1689-1702 Reign of William III and Mary II.

Parliament meets (→1690); the Bill of Rights and Toleration Act are passed; Danby becomes lord president of the council.

Scottish royalists are defeated at Killiecrankie; James II besieges Londonderry.

The grand alliance is formed against France.

1690

The Irish Jacobites are defeated at the Boyne.

Locke's *An Essay concerning Human Understanding* is published.

1691

The treaty of Limerick ends the Irish war.

1692

Marlborough is imprisoned; the MacDonalds are massacred at Glencoe.

The national debt originates.

1694

Death of Mary II; Triennial Act is passed.

The Bank of England is founded.

1695

The Bank of Scotland is founded; the Company of Scotland is established to colonize the Darién coast of Panama.

Death of Purcell.

1696

A plot to assassinate William III is revealed.

1697

The treaty of Ryswick ends the War of the Grand Alliance.

1698

The Society for Promoting Christian Knowledge is founded.

Savery invents the first steam engine.

1699

The Darién colony is evacuated.

The 3rd earl of Shaftesbury's "Inquiry concerning Virtue or Merit" is published.

1700

Death of Dryden.

1701

Act of Settlement provides for the Hanoverian succession; death of James II; Louis XIV of France recognizes the old pretender as king.

The Society for the Propagation of the Gospel is founded.

1702-14 Reign of Queen Anne.

1702

Parliament meets (→1705); Godolphin becomes lord treasurer (→1710).

The War of the Spanish Succession begins; death of Admiral Benbow.

Clarendon's *History of the Great Rebellion* is published (→1704).

1703

The Methuen treaty with Portugal is concluded.

1704

Marlborough wins at Blenheim; Gibraltar is captured.

Newton's *Opticks* is published.

1705

Joseph I becomes Holy Roman Emperor (→1711).

1706

Marlborough wins at Ramillies; Ostend is captured.

1707

Act of Union with Scotland is passed.

1708

Parliament meets (→1710); last royal veto of legislation (a bill to reorganize the Scottish militia).

Sardinia and Minorca are captured; Marlborough wins at Oudenarde; Lille is captured.

1709

Sacheverell is impeached.

Marlborough wins at Malplaquet; the first barrier treaty is agreed.

Steele starts the *Tatler*; Darby invents an iron-smelting process.

1710

Parliament meets (→1713); Godolphin is dismissed.

1711

Marlborough is dismissed; Oxford (formerly Harley) is made lord treasurer; Act of Occasional Conformity is passed.

The South Sea Company is incorporated.

Addison and Steele start the *Spectator*; Newcomen develops a steam pump.

Charles VI becomes holy Roman emperor (→1740).

1712

Marlborough leaves England; the last execution for witchcraft in England occurs.

John Arbuthnot's *John Bull* is published; Handel settles in England.

1713

The treaties of Utrecht (→1714) end the War of the Spanish Succession.

Bishop Berkeley's *Dialogues between Hylas and Philonous* is published.

1714

Schism Act is passed; Oxford is dismissed.

Death of Electress Sophia.

1714-27 Reign of George I.

1715

Parliament meets (→1722); four Tory ministers are impeached; the Jacobites revolt.

1716

Septennial Act is passed.

1717

George I dismisses Townshend and Walpole resigns; the Whigs split.

The first sinking fund is introduced.

The triple alliance is formed against Spain.

1718

The quadruple alliance is formed; Byng destroys a Spanish fleet off Cape Passaro.

1719

Occasional Conformity and Schism Acts are repealed; peerage bill is defeated; a Jacobite invasion fails.

Defoe's *Robinson Crusoe* is published.

1720

South Sea bubble "bursts"; Townshend returns to office.

1721

Death of Stanhope; Walpole returns to office.

1722

Parliament meets (→1727); death of Sunderland; Walpole is prime minister (→1742).

Atterbury's plot is foiled.

The patent for Wood's halfpence is granted.

1724

Walpole ousts Carteret.

Defoe's *Tour through Great Britain* is published (→1726).

1726

Riots occur against turnpikes; famine in Ireland (→1729).

Swift's *Gulliver's Travels* is published.

1727-60 Reign of George II.

1727

Death of Isaac Newton.

1728

Parliament meets (→1734).

The Irish Catholics are deprived of the vote.

Pope's *Dunciad* and Chambers' *Universal Dictionary* are published; John Gay's *The Beggar's Opera* is produced.

1729

Charles Wesley founds the Oxford Methodists.

1730

Walpole ousts Townshend.

The Serpentine is laid out in Hyde Park, London (→1733).

1731

Capt. Jenkins loses his ear.

Tull's *Horse-Hoeing Husbandry* is published (→1733).

1732

A charter for the founding of Georgia is granted.

1733
John Kay invents the flying shuttle.

1734
Death of Rob Roy.

1735
Parliament meets (→1741).

1736
The Porteous riots occur.
Witchcraft is abolished as a crime.

1737
Construction of the Radcliffe Camera at Oxford (→1749).

1738
Bolingbroke writes *The Patriot King*.

1739
The War of Jenkins' Ear against Spain begins; the Black Watch, the 42nd regiment, is formed.
A charter for Coram's Foundling Hospital is granted.
John Wesley begins open-air preaching.
The Philosophical Society is founded.

1740
Famine in Ireland (→1741).
The War of the Austrian Succession begins (→1748).
Arne composes *Rule Britannia*.
Maria Theresa succeeds to the Habsburg possessions (→1780); Frederick the Great becomes king of Prussia (→1786).

1741
Parliament meets (→1747).

1742
Walpole resigns; Wilmington becomes prime minister (→1743).
Handel's *Messiah* is performed in Dublin.

1743
Pelham becomes prime minister (→1754).
The battle of Dettingen is fought.

1744
The broad-bottom administration is formed.

1745
The last Jacobite rebellion breaks out (→1746); the Jacobites are victorious at Prestonpans.
The battle of Fontenoy is fought.

Hogarth's *Marriage à la Mode* is published.

1746
Pitt the elder becomes paymaster general; the Jacobites are defeated at Culloden.
The French take Madras.

1747
Parliament meets (→1754).

1748
Peace is made at Aix-la-Chapelle.
Hume's *An Enquiry concerning Human Understanding* is published.

1749
Henry Fielding's *Tom Jones* is published.

1751
Death of Frederick, prince of Wales.
Clive captures Arcot.

1752
The Gregorian calendar is introduced.

1753
Hardwicke's Marriage Act is passed.

1754
Parliament meets (→1761); death of Henry Pelham; Pelham's brother Newcastle becomes prime minister (→1756).

1755
Pitt the elder is dismissed.
The French are expelled from Nova Scotia.
Dr Johnson's *Dictionary* is published.

1756
Pitt the elder forms his ministry.
The Seven Years' War starts; British soldiers are confined in the black hole of Calcutta.

1757
The Pitt-Newcastle ministry is formed; Militia Act is passed.
Calcutta is recaptured; Clive wins at Plassey.

1758
Blackstone's *Commentaries on the Laws of England* are delivered at Oxford; the comet whose reappearance Edmund Halley forecast returns.

1759

The battles of Quiberon Bay and Minden are fought; Wolfe wins on the Heights of Abraham.

Wedgwood opens the Burslem pottery.

1760-1820 Reign of George III.

1760

The conquest of Canada is completed.

The Carron ironworks starts production.

1761

Parliament meets (→1768); Pitt the elder falls from power. Pondicherry is captured.

The Bridgewater canal is opened.

1762

Newcastle resigns; Bute becomes prime minister (→1763).

Boulton starts the Soho foundry.

John Wilkes founds the *North Briton*.

1763

Bute resigns; Grenville becomes prime minister (→1765); John Wilkes is arrested after issue no. 45 of the *North Briton*.

The treaty of Paris ends the Seven Years' War.

Boswell meets Dr Johnson.

1764

Wilkes is expelled from the Commons and outlawed.

1765

Stamp Act is passed; Rockingham becomes prime minister (→1766).

Hargreaves invents the spinning jenny.

1766

Grafton becomes nominal prime minister (→1770); Pitt the elder becomes lord privy seal (→1768); Declaratory Act is passed.

Oliver Goldsmith's *Vicar of Wakefield* is published.

1767

The Townshend duties are imposed on America; the Junius letters are published (→1772).

Tristram Shandy is completed by the Rev. Laurence Sterne.

1768

Parliament meets (→1774); Wilkes wins the Middlesex seat at the general election; disturbances occur at St George's Fields.

The Royal Academy of Arts is founded; the Adam brothers design the Adelphi.

1769

Wilkes is expelled from the Commons for the second time.

Capt. Cook lands on Tahiti.

Watt's steam engine and Arkwright's waterframe are patented; Wedgwood opens the Etruria works.

1770

Grafton resigns and Lord North becomes prime minister (→1782); the Townshend duties are withdrawn (except on tea).

The Boston massacre takes place.

Burke publishes *Thoughts on the Cause of the Present Discontents*.

1772

Royal Marriages Act is passed.

Warren Hastings becomes the first governor general of Bengal (→1785).

1773

Regulating Act is passed.

The Boston tea party occurs; Capt. Cook reaches the Antarctic.

1774

Parliament meets (→1780); Wilkes is re-elected by Middlesex in the general election; Intolerable Act is passed.

Priestley isolates oxygen.

1775

The American Revolution starts at Lexington and Concord; the battle of Bunker Hill is fought; Washington is appointed commander in chief of American forces.

1776

The American Declaration of Independence is made; Howe evacuates Boston.

Adam Smith's *The Wealth of Nations* and Bentham's *Fragment on Government* are published.

1777

The British surrender at Saratoga.

John Howard's *State of the Prisons* is published.

1778

Death of Pitt the elder.

France joins America against Britain.

1779

Capt. Cook is killed in Hawaii.

Crompton produces his "mule"; the first iron bridge is completed at Coalbrookdale.

1780

Parliament meets (→1784); Dunning's resolutions are made.

The Gordon riots occur; Raikes begins the Sunday school movement; the first Epsom Derby is held.

1781

The British surrender at Yorktown; battles of Dogger Bank and Porto Novo are fought.

Watt patents his adaptation of the steam engine for rotary motion.

1782

North resigns; Rockingham forms a ministry; Rockingham dies; Shelburne becomes prime minister (→1783); Crewe's and Clerk's Acts are passed; Grattan obtains legislative independence for the Irish parliament.

The battle of the Saints is fought.

1783

The Fox-North administration is formed; the India bill is rejected; Pitt the younger becomes prime minister (→1801).

The treaty of Paris ends the American Revolution.

The Bank of Ireland is founded.

1784

Parliament meets (→1790); India Act is passed.

Cort's puddling process is invented.

1785

The first issue of *The Daily Universal Register* (*The Times* from 1788) appears.

1786

Pitt the younger's sinking fund is created.

1787

Free Town (Sierra Leone) is founded.

Edmund Cartwright patents his invention of the power loom.

1788

The Impeachment of Warren Hastings begins (→1795); George III's insanity causes the regency crisis (→1789).

The triple alliance is made.

Gibbon completes *Decline and Fall*.

1789

Blake's *Songs of Innocence* are published.

The French Revolution breaks out (→1799); *George Washington becomes the first US president* (→1797).

1790

Parliament meets (→1796).

Burke's *Reflections on the French Revolution* are published.

1791

Constitutional Act creates Upper and Lower Canada.

1792

The Corresponding Society is founded.

Tom Paine's *Rights of Man* is completed; death of Joshua Reynolds.

The French Revolutionary War breaks out.

1793

Sedition trials are held.

The Board of Agriculture is established.

Britain enters the war against France; the British attack the French in Flanders, Toulon, and the French West Indies.

1794

The Glorious First of June is fought.

1795

Warren Hastings is acquitted; Seditious Meetings and Treasonable Practices Acts are passed.

The Speenhamland system is introduced.

Wolf Tone leaves Ireland; the British retreat from the Netherlands.

1796

Parliament meets (→1802).

Jenner's method of cowpox vaccination is tested; death of Robert Burns.

1797

The Nore and Spithead mutinies occur.

The Bank of England suspends cash payments.

The battles of Cape St Vincent and Camperdown are fought; Richard Wellesley is made governor general of India.

1798

The Irish rebellion is crushed.

Nelson wins at Aboukir Bay.

Malthus publishes his *Essay on the Principle of Population*; Wordsworth and Coleridge publish *Lyrical Ballads*.

1799

The first Combination Act is passed; the Corresponding Society is suppressed.

Income tax is levied; Robert Owen becomes manager at New Lanark.

Acre is besieged.

Napoleon comes to power in France.

1800

The second Combination and the Census Acts and the Act of Union with Ireland (effective 1801) are passed.

The league of armed neutrality is formed; Britain takes Malta.

1801

Pitt the younger resigns; Addington becomes prime minister (→1804); the battle of Copenhagen is fought.

Thomas Jefferson becomes US president (→1809).

1802

Parliament meets (→1806).

The treaty of Amiens ends the French Revolutionary War.

West India Docks are completed in London; the Royal Military College is opened; the *Edinburgh Review* is launched; Cobbet founds the *Political Register*.

1803

Robert Emmet's rising in Ireland is crushed.

The Caledonian canal is started.

The Napoleonic War begins.

1804

Addington resigns and Pitt the younger again becomes prime minister (→1806).

1805

Dundas is impeached.

Grand Junction canal is completed.

Nelson wins and dies at Trafalgar; a triple alliance is formed against France.

1806

Parliament meets (→1807); death of Pitt the younger; the Ministry of All the Talents is formed (→1807); death of Fox.

East India Docks are completed in London; Trevithick's railway is completed at Coalbrookdale.

Britain takes the Cape of Good Hope.

The Holy Roman Empire falls.

1807

Parliament meets (→1812); the slave trade is abolished;

Portland becomes prime minister (→1809).

Lamb's *Tales from Shakespeare* is published.

1808

The Peninsular War begins (→1814).

1809

Spencer Perceval becomes prime minister (→1812); Castlereagh and Canning fight a duel.

The battles of Coruña and Talavera are fought; Walcheren is evacuated.

Bentham writes the *Parliamentary Reform Catechism*; the *Quarterly Review* is launched.

Metternich becomes Austrian foreign minister (→1848).

1810

George III becomes insane.

Ricardo's *The High Price of Bullion* is published.

1811

The Prince of Wales becomes regent; Hansard begins publishing parliamentary reports.

Organized Luddism begins.

Macadam outlines his new road-building methods.

Jane Austen's major novels are published (→1818).

1812

Parliament meets (→1818); Spencer Perceval is assassinated;

Liverpool forms a ministry (→1827).

The battle of Salamanca is fought; the Anglo-American War begins (→1814).

Napoleon marches on Moscow.

1813

The battles of Vitoria and the Nations are fought.

Nash's Regent Street is constructed (→1820).

1814

Gas lighting is installed in St Margaret's parish, Westminster.

Wellington takes Toulouse; the treaty of Ghent ends the Anglo-American War.

Sir Walter Scott's *Waverley* is published.

Napoleon is exiled to Elba.

1815

A corn law is passed.

Napoleon is finally defeated at the battle of Waterloo; the congress of Vienna begins.

Davy's safety lamp comes into use.

Napoleon is exiled to St Helena.

1816

Riots occur at Spa Fields; habeas corpus is suspended.

1817

The Blanketeers march; gold sovereigns are issued; Ricardo's *Principles of Political Economy and Taxation* is published.

1819

Parliament meets (→1820); Factory Act is passed; the Peterloo massacre occurs.

The East India Company buys Singapore.

1820-30 Reign of George IV.

1820

Parliament meets (→1826); the Six Acts are passed; the Cato Street conspiracy is discovered.

James Mill's *Essay on Government* is published.

1821

George IV excludes Queen Caroline from the coronation.

Death of Napoleon.

1822

Castlereagh commits suicide; Canning becomes foreign secretary and Peel becomes home secretary (→1827).

The War of Greek Independence begins (→1830).

1823

Huskisson joins the cabinet; Peel starts to reform the criminal law and prisons; O'Connell forms the Catholic Association.

1824

The Combination Acts are repealed.

The *Westminster Review* is launched; death of Byron.

1825

The Stockton and Darlington railway is opened; Telford's Menai Bridge is completed.

1826

Parliament meets (→1830).

Joint-stock banks are allowed outside London.

1827

Death of Lord Liverpool; Canning and then Goderich become prime minister.

The battle of Navarino is fought.

1828

Wellington becomes prime minister (→1830); the Corn Laws are amended; Test and Corporation Acts are repealed; O'Connell wins the Clare by-election.

The University of London is opened; Thomas Arnold becomes headmaster of Rugby.

1829

Catholic emancipation is carried; the Metropolitan Police is formed; the Birmingham Political Union is founded.

Stephenson's engine *The Rocket* succeeds at the Rainhill trials.

1830-37 Reign of William IV.

1830

Parliament meets (→1831); Wellington's ministry falls and is succeeded by Grey's (→1834).

The Liverpool and Manchester railway is opened. Cobbett's *Rural Rides* and Lyell's *Principles of Geology* are published (→1833).

The July Revolution brings Louis Philippe to the French throne (→1848).

1831

Parliament meets (→1832); riots take place after the Lords reject the reform bill.

The Law Society is incorporated; a cholera epidemic occurs (→1832).

Faraday starts his research on electricity; Darwin's voyages on *The Beagle* (→1836).

1832

The first Reform Act and the Tithe Act are passed.

1833

Parliament meets (→1834); Factory and Bank Charter Acts are passed; slavery is abolished.

The Oxford movement is launched.

1834

Melbourne becomes prime minister but then resigns; Peel becomes prime minister (→1835); Poor Law Amendment Act is passed; the Tamworth Manifesto is announced; the Houses of Parliament are burned down.

The Grand National Consolidated Trades Union is founded; the Tolpuddle martyrs are transported.

Britain, France, Portugal, and Spain negotiate the quadruple alliance.

Dickens publishes *Sketches by Boz.*

1835

Parliament meets (→1837); Peel is succeeded as prime minister by Melbourne (→1841); Municipal Reform Act is passed.

1836

Act for the registration of births, marriages, and deaths is passed.

The London Working Men's Association is founded.

1837-1901 Reign of Victoria.

1837

Parliament meets (→1841); Papineau and Mackenzie lead revolts in Canada.

1838

The People's Charter is issued; the Anti-Corn-Law League is founded.

The Durham report is issued; the first Afghan War breaks out (→1842).

The Public Record Office is established.

1839

The bedchamber crisis occurs; the first Chartist petition is drawn up; the Newport rising erupts.

The Opium War (→1842) breaks out.

c. 1839

W. H. Fox Talbot's first photographs are produced.

1840

Victoria marries Prince Albert.

The penny post is introduced.

The treaty of Waitangi is agreed.

1841

Parliament meets (→1847); Melbourne is succeeded as prime minister by Peel (→1846).

1842

The second Chartist petition is rejected; the Mines Act is passed; Chadwick reports on sanitary conditions; Disraeli joins Young England; the Rebecca riots occur (→1844).

The treaty of Nanking ends the Opium War.

The *Nation* is founded.

1843

The disruption in the Church of Scotland occurs.

J. P. Joule announces his first law of thermodynamics.

1844

Bank Charter and Factory Acts are passed.

The Rochdale Pioneers society is founded.

The first telegraph line in England is laid.

1845

The Maynooth grant causes controversy.

The Irish famine starts.

The first Sikh War breaks out (→1846).

Disraeli's *Sybil* is published.

1846

The corn laws are repealed; Peel's ministry falls and the Conservatives split; Russell becomes prime minister (→1852).

1847

Parliament meets (→1852); Ten Hour Act is passed.

Dickens' *Dombey and Son,* Charlotte

Brontë's *Jane Eyre*, and William Thackeray's *Vanity Fair* are published.

Marx and Engels publish The Communist Manifesto.

1848

The third Chartist petition is drawn up.

A cholera epidemic occurs (→1849); Public Health Act is passed.

Dalhousie arrives in India; the second Sikh War breaks out (→1849).

Macaulay's *History of England* (vols 1–2) are published.

Revolutions occur in France, Germany, Italy, and Austria.

1849

The conquest of the Punjab is completed.

1850

The first Public Libraries Act is passed.

Palmerston defends Don Pacifico.

Tennyson succeeds Wordsworth as poet laureate (→1892); *The Germ* publicizes pre-Raphaelite ideas.

1851

Palmerston is dismissed from the Foreign Office.

The Great Exhibition is held; the Royal School of Mines is founded; the Amalgamated Society of Engineers is founded.

Death of Joseph Turner.

Louis Napoleon seizes absolute power in France.

1852

Parliament meets (→1857); Russell is succeeded as prime minister by Derby, who is replaced by Aberdeen (→1855).

The Sand River convention is agreed.

Napoleon III becomes emperor (→1870); Count of Cavour becomes premier of Piedmont-Sardinia (→1859).

1853

The Northcote–Trevelyan report on the civil service is issued.

1854

The Crimean War breaks out (→1856); the battles of the Alma, Balaclava, and Inkerman are fought; Florence Nightingale arrives at Scutari; the Bloemfontein convention is agreed.

The Working Men's College and the British Medical Association are founded.

1855

Aberdeen is succeeded as prime minister by Palmerston (→1858); the Civil Service Commission is established.

Sebastopol is captured.

Publication of *The Daily Telegraph* starts; Bessemer's steelmaking process is patented.

1856

The Department of Education is set up.

The treaty of Paris ends the Crimean War; the *Arrow* War breaks out (→1860).

Ellen Terry appears on the stage for the first time.

1857

Parliament meets (→1859).

The Indian Mutiny breaks out (→1858).

Anthony Trollope's *Barchester Towers* is published.

1858

Palmerston is succeeded as prime minister by Derby (→1859); Rothschild becomes the first Jewish MP. The crown takes over the government of India; the Fenian Society is founded.

1859

Parliament meets (→1865); Derby is succeeded as prime minister by Palmerston (→1865). John Stuart Mill's *On Liberty*, Darwin's *Origin of Species*, and George Eliot's *Adam Bede* are published.

1860

Giuseppe Garribaldi conquers Sicily and Naples; Abraham Lincoln becomes US president (→1865).

1861

Death of Prince Albert.

Victor Emmanuel II becomes first king of a united Italy (→1878); the American Civil War breaks out (→1865).

1862

The *Alabama* is launched on Merseyside.

Bismarck becomes Prussian premier (→1871).

1863
The prince of Wales marries Alexandra of Denmark.

1864
The Albert Memorial is built.

1865
Death of Palmerston; Russell becomes prime minister (→1866).
Abraham Lincoln is assassinated; slavery is abolished in the USA.

c. 1865
Diamonds are discovered in south Africa.

1866
Parliament meets (→1868); the reform bill is defeated; Russell is replaced as prime minister by Derby (→1868).
The Atlantic cable is laid.

1867
The second Reform Act and British North America Act are passed; the National Union of Conservative and Constitutional Associations is started; the Fenian rising takes place.
The first bicycle is produced.
The Dual Monarchy of Austria-Hungary is created.

1868
Parliament meets (→1874); Derby is succeeded as prime minister by Disraeli, who is succeeded by Gladstone (→1874).
Flogging in the peacetime army is abolished; transportation of criminals is ended.
The Trades Union Congress is founded.
Browning's *The Ring and the Book* is published (→1869).

1869
Imprisonment for debt is abolished.
Bedford College for women is incorporated.
The *Cutty Sark* is launched.
The Anglican church in Ireland is disestablished and disendowed.

1870
Forster's Education Act and Gladstone's first Irish Land Act are passed; Cardwell's army reforms begin; the Home Government (later Home Rule) Association is formed.

The first Dr Barnardo's home is opened.
Death of Charles Dickens.
The Franco-Prussian War begins (→1871).

1871
Trades Union Act is passed.
Bank holidays are introduced.
Stanley meets Dr Livingstone at Ujiji.
William I of Prussia becomes the first German emperor (→1888), and Bismarck the first German chancellor (→1890).

1872
Ballot, Licensing, and Coal Mines Acts are passed; the Tichborne case is tried (→1874).
Britain pays compensation for damage caused by the *Alabama*.

1873
Judicature Act is passed.
The Ashanti War breaks out (→1874).

1874
Parliament meets (→1880); Disraeli becomes prime minister (→1880).

1875
Public Health and Artisans' Dwellings Acts are passed.
Suez Canal shares are purchased.

1876
Victoria becomes empress of India; Gladstone's *The Bulgarian Horrors* are published.
The Plimsoll line is introduced.
An Anglo-French condominium over Egypt is established.

1877
The Transvaal is annexed by Natal.
The Russo-Turkish War begins (→1878).

1878
The Salvation Army is named.
The congress of Berlin meets; the second Afghan War (→1880) and Zulu War begin.
Gilbert and Sullivan's *HMS Pinafore* is produced; Swan demonstrates the electric light bulb.

1879
Gladstone's Midlothian campaign

takes place; the Irish Land League is formed.

1880

Parliament meets (→1885); Gladstone becomes prime minister (→1885); the Democratic (later Social Democratic) Federation is formed; Bradlaugh case begins (→1886); boycotting is started in Ireland.

George Newnes starts *Tit Bits*.

1881

Death of Disraeli; Gladstone's second Irish Land Act.

The first Boer War (→1881) and the Mahdi's rebellion begin.

1882

The Kilmainham treaty is followed by the Phoenix Park murders in Dublin; the Married Women's Property Act is passed.

The Pretoria convention ends the first Boer War; the British occupy Egypt.

The triple alliance is formed between Italy, Austria, and Germany.

1883

Corrupt and Illegal Practices Act is passed.

Stevenson's *Treasure Island* is published.

1884

The third Reform Act is passed.

The Fabian Society is formed.

1885

Gladstone is succeeded as prime minister by Salisbury (→1886); Chamberlain presents an "unauthorized programme"; the age of consent is raised to 16.

Death of Gordon at Khartoum.

1886

Parliament meets twice (Jan–June, Aug→June 1892); Salisbury is succeeded as prime minister by Gladstone; the home rule bill is defeated and Gladstone resigns; Salisbury becomes prime minister (→1892); Burma is annexed.

The Rover safety bicycle is launched.

Hardy's *The Mayor of Casterbridge* is published.

1887

Queen Victoria's Golden Jubilee; Bloody Sunday occurs in Trafalgar Square; the first colonial conference is held.

1888

Local Government Act is passed.

Dunlop's pneumatic tyre is patented.

Jack the Ripper murders six women in London.

William II becomes German emperor (→1918).

1889

The London dock strike called.

The British South Africa Company is chartered.

1890

Parnell resigns.

Bismarck is dismissed.

1891

Elementary school fees are abolished; the Liberals adopt the Newcastle programme.

1892

Parliament meets (→1895); Salisbury is succeeded as prime minister by Gladstone (→1894).

1893

The second home rule bill is defeated; the Independent Labour Party is formed. The Matabele rise (→1894).

1894

Gladstone is succeeded as prime minister by Rosebery (→1895). Harcourt's death duties are introduced; the Manchester ship canal is opened.

1895

Parliament meets (→1900); Rosebery is succeeded as prime minister by Salisbury (→1902).

The Jameson raid is made (→1896).

Westminster cathedral is begun; the National Trust is formed; Oscar Wilde is tried.

1896

The *Daily Mail* is launched.

The Kruger telegram is sent; the Matabele rise.

1897

Victoria's Diamond Jubilee.

1898

Death of Gladstone. The battle of Omdurman is fought; the Fashoda crisis occurs (→1899).

1899
The second Boer War breaks out.

1900
The Khaki election is held; the Labour Party is formed.

The Central London Railway is opened; the *Daily Express* is launched.

Ladysmith and Mafeking are relieved; the Ashanti rebel.

Elgar's *The Dream of Gerontius* is performed.

The Boxer rising occurs in China.

1901-10 Reign of Edward VII.

1901
Parliament meets (→1906); the Taff Vale judgment is made.

Concentration camps are established in South Africa; Australia becomes a dominion.

Theodore Roosevelt becomes US president (→1909); the first Nobel prizes are awarded.

1902
Salisbury is succeeded as prime minister by Balfour (→1905); Balfour's Education Act is passed.

The peace of Vereeniging ends the second Boer War; the Anglo-Japanese alliance is formed.

1903
Chamberlain resigns to campaign for tariff reform.

The Women's Social and Political Union is founded by Emmeline Pankhurst.

1904
The Committee of Imperial Defence is set up.

The Workers' Educational Association is founded.

The Anglo-French entente cordiale is formed.

The Russo-Japanese War begins (→1905).

1905
Balfour is succeeded as prime minister by Campbell-Bannerman (→1908).

The first motor buses are put into service in London; the Piccadilly and Bakerloo tubes are opened.

1906
Parliament meets (→1910); Trade Disputes Act is passed.

The *Dreadnought* is completed; the Algeciras conference is held.

1907
Territorial and Reserve Forces Act is passed.

The Anglo-Russian entente is formed.

1908
Death of Campbell-Bannerman; Asquith becomes prime minister (→1915).

The Borstal system is started.

1909
The Lords reject Lloyd George's budget; old age pensions are introduced; the Osborne case is heard.

1910-36 Reign of George V.

1910
Parliament meets (Feb-Nov); two general elections are held; Carson becomes leader of the Ulster Unionists.

The Union of South Africa is established.

1911
Parliament meets (→1918); Parliament and National Insurance Acts are passed.

The Agadir crisis erupts.

1912
The Marconi affair is divulged; Haldane visits Berlin; the Ulster Volunteer Force is formed.

Scott reaches the south pole.

The Balkan Wars break out (→1913).

1913
Trade Union Act and Cat and Mouse Act (to release hunger-striking imprisoned suffragettes) are passed; the Irish Volunteers are formed.

Woodrow Wilson becomes US president (→1921).

1914
Irish Home Rule Act is passed; the Curragh mutiny occurs.

World War I breaks out (→1918); the British Expeditionary Force lands in France; the battles of Mons, the Marne, and Ypres are fought; Kitchener's "new army" of volunteers is formed.

1915

The Liberal government is replaced by a coalition; Churchill resigns from the cabinet.

The Gallipoli expedition is launched; the second battle of Ypres and battles of Loos and Neuve-Chapelle are fought; a German U-boat sinks the *Lusitania*; Zeppelin raids on British cities start.

1916

Asquith is replaced as prime minister by Lloyd George (→1922); the Easter rising occurs in Ireland.

The evacuation from Gallipoli is completed; the battles of the Somme and Jutland are fought; conscription begins; Kitchener is drowned.

1917

The USA enters the war; the Imperial War Cabinet meets; battles of Vimy Ridge and Passchendaele are fought; the convoy system is introduced; the Balfour declaration is made; Jerusalem is captured.

The Russian Revolution occurs.

1918

The RAF is formed; the second battle of the Marne is fought; Damascus and Aleppo are captured; World War I ends with the fall of the German empire.

The coupon election is held; Henderson reorganizes the Labour Party; Representation of the People and Fisher's Education Acts are passed; Sinn Féin MPs declare themselves the Irish Dáil; the Montagu-Chelmsford report is issued.

Rationing is introduced.

Marie Stopes publishes *Married Love*.

1919

Parliament meets (→1922); Lady Astor becomes the first woman to sit as an MP; Government of India Act is passed; the Irish Republican Army is formed.

Keyne's *Economic Consequences of the Peace* is published; the gold standard is suspended.

The treaty of Versailles is signed; Indians are massacred at Amritsar.

1920

The Black and Tans are sent to Ireland; Government of Ireland Act.

The Communist Party of Great Britain is formed; Welwyn Garden City is started.

The Anglican church in Wales is disestablished.

The League of Nations is founded.

1921

The Irish Free State is created; the Washington conference is held (→1922).

1922

Parliament meets (→1923); Lloyd George is succeeded as prime minister by Bonar Law (→1923); the Labour Party forms the official opposition.

James Joyce's *Ulysses* is published; the "baby" Austin car is on sale.

Benito Mussolini becomes Italian prime minister (→1943); Joseph Stalin becomes Soviet leader (→1953).

1923

Bonar Law retires; Baldwin becomes prime minister (→1924); self-government is granted to Southern Rhodesia.

Shaw's *St Joan* is produced.

1924

Parliament meets (Jan-Oct, Dec→1929); MacDonald forms the first Labour government; Zinoviev's letter is issued; Baldwin becomes prime minister (→1929).

Death of V. I. Lenin.

1925

The gold bullion standard is adopted.

1926

The Samuel report on coalmining is issued; the general strike occurs.

1927

The Trade Disputes Act is passed.

The British Broadcasting Corporation is formed.

1928

Women over 21 are given the vote.

The Commons reject the revised prayer book.

1929

Parliament meets (→1931); MacDonald succeeds Baldwin as prime minister

(→1935); Beaverbrook launches his "Empire Free Trade" campaign.

The great depression begins.

Herbert Hoover becomes US president (→1933).

1930
The Coal Mines Act is passed; the Simon commission reports on India.

1931
Parliament meets (→1935); the national government is formed.

The Invergordon mutiny occurs; Britain comes off the gold standard.

The Statute of Westminster defines dominion status.

1932
Mosley founds the British Union of Fascists.

1933
The Oxford Union resolves "this House will not fight for King and Country".

The London Transport Board is set up.

Adolf Hitler becomes German chancellor (→1945); F. D. Roosevelt becomes US president (→1945).

1935
Parliament meets (→1945); George V's Silver Jubilee; MacDonald is succeeded as prime minister by Baldwin (→1937).

The Hoare-Laval pact is proposed; Government of India Act is passed.

T. S. Eliot's Murder in the Cathedral is produced.

Italy invades Ethiopia.

1936 Reign of Edward VIII.

1936
Abdication of Edward VIII.

The Spanish Civil War begins (→1939); the Berlin-Rome Axis is formed.

1936-52 Reign of George VI.

1937
Baldwin is succeeded as prime minister by Chamberlain (→1940).

1938
The Munich agreement is made; air-raid precautions are introduced.

Austria is annexed by Germany.

1939
World War II begins; conscription is introduced.

The British Overseas Airways Corporation (BOAC) is formed.

Francisco Franco becomes Spanish dictator (→1975).

1940
Chamberlain is succeeded as prime minister by Churchill (→1945). Dunkirk is evacuated; the battle of Britain is fought; the British launch an offensive in North Africa; rationing is introduced.

1941
Lend-lease begins; the Atlantic Charter is announced; an Anglo-Soviet treaty is agreed; the *Bismarck*, and then the *Prince of Wales* and the *Repulse*, are sunk.

1942
·The Beveridge report is issued.

Rangoon and Singapore fall; the British withdraw from Crete and win at Alamein; Churchill and Stalin meet in Moscow; Cripps goes to India.

1943
Sicily is invaded; the Tehran conference is held.

1944
Butler's Education Act is passed.

Normandy is invaded; Paris and Brussels are liberated; the Arnhem operation fails.

1945
Parliament meets (→1950); Attlee becomes prime minister (→1951); Family Allowances Act is passed; Yalta and Potsdam conferences are held; Dresden is destroyed; Germany and then Japan surrender.

Charles de Gaulle becomes French provisional president (→1946); Harry S. Truman becomes US president (→1953); Tito becomes Yugoslav prime minister (→1953).

1946
National Insurance and National Health Service Acts are passed; the Bank of England and coal industry are nationalized.

The UN is founded.

1947
A fuel crisis and the severest winter since 1894 provoke austerity measures.

The British withdraw from Greece; India becomes independent and is partitioned.

1948
Railways, canals, and road transport are nationalized.

The Berlin airlift (→1949) and the Marshall plan (→1951) begin; Britain ends the Palestine mandate; Ceylon and Burma gain independence.

Gandhi is assassinated.

1949
Parliament and Iron and Steel Acts are passed.

The pound is devalued.

NATO if formed; the Republic of Ireland becomes fully independent.

Orwell's 1984 is published.

1950
Parliament meets (→1951).

The Korean War breaks out (→1953).

1951
Parliament meets (→1955); Churchill becomes prime minister (→1955).

The Festival of Britain is held.

1952 Reign of Elizabeth II begins.

The Mau Mau rebellion in Kenya starts.

The British atomic bomb is tested.

1953
Edmund Hilary and Tenzing Norgay conquer Mount Everest.

Iron and steel and road transport are denationalized.

The Central African Federation is established.

Tito becomes Yugoslav president; Dwight D. Eisenhower becomes US president (→1961).

1954
Dylan Thomas' *Under Milk Wood* is published posthumously.

The South-East Asia Treaty Organization (SEATO) is formed.

1955
Parliament meets (→1959); Churchill is succeeded as prime minister by Eden (→1957).

A state of emergency is declared in Cyprus.

1956
An Anglo-French force attacks Egypt after Egypt nationalizes the Suez Canal Company.

John Osborne's *Look Back in Anger* is produced in London.

1957
Eden is succeeded as prime minister by Macmillan (→1963).

Wolfenden reports on homosexual offences and prostitution.

The Gold Coast becomes the independent state of Ghana.

1958
Life Peerages Act is passed; riots occur in Notting Hill, London.

The West Indies Federation is formed.

Khrushchev becomes Soviet premier (→1964); the EEC is formed.

1959
Parliament meets (→1964).

Oil is discovered in the North Sea.

The European Free Trade Association (EFTA) is formed.

De Gaulle becomes French president (→1969); the Vietnam War begins (→1975).

1960
Macmillan makes his "wind of change" speech in Africa; Cyprus and Nigeria become independent.

1961
South Africa leaves the Commonwealth; Sierra Leone and Tanganyika become independent.

J. F. Kennedy becomes US president (→1963).

1962
The National Economic Development Council (NEDC) is formed; Commonwealth immigration is controlled.

Uganda becomes independent; the West Indies Federation breaks up.

1963
Macmillan is succeeded as prime minister by Douglas-Home (→1964); Beeching reports on the railways; the Profumo affair breaks.

The nuclear test-ban treaty is signed; Gen. de Gaulle vetoes British entry to the EEC; the Central African Federation is dissolved; Kenya becomes independent; Zanzibar becomes independent; the Malaysian Federation is formed.

Assassination of John F. Kennedy; Lyndon B. Johnson becomes US president (→1969).

1964

Parliament meets (→1966); Wilson becomes prime minister (→1970).

Northern Rhodesia becomes independent as Zambia.

Kosygin and Brezhnev become Soviet leaders.

1965

Southern Rhodesia makes a unilateral declaration of independence (UDI).

1966

Parliament meets (→1970).

1967

The pound is devalued.

Gen de Gaulle again vetoes Britain's entry into the EEC.

1968

The Commonwealth Immigration Act is passed.

1969

Prince Charles is invested as prince of Wales at Caernarfon; Ulster troubles begin.

The Open University is chartered.

Richard M. Nixon becomes US president (→1974).

1970

Parliament meets (→1974); Heath succeeds Wilson as prime minister (→1974).

The Gambia becomes independent.

1971

The Industrial Relations Act is passed.

Decimal currency is introduced.

East Pakistan secedes from Pakistan to form Bangladesh.

1972

The Northern Irish Parliament is suspended and direct rule from Westminster is established; a state of emergency is declared in response to a miners strike.

1973

Britain joins the EEC; an energy crisis

leads to a state of emergency and a three-day working week (→1974); Value Added Tax is introduced.

1974

Parliament meets (Mar→Sept, Oct→1979); Wilson becomes prime minister (→1976). The Industrial Relations Act is repealed. Ulster power-sharing executive collapses; the IRA conduct a bombing campaign in England.

Gerald R. Ford becomes US president (→1977).

1975

British membership of the EEC is confirmed in a referendum; the Sex Discrimination Act is passed.

First oil from the North Sea comes ashore.

1976

Callaghan succeeds Wilson as prime minister (→1979); the Race Relations Act is passed.

Concorde makes its first passenger flight; the British National Oil Corporation is established.

1977

The aircraft and shipbuilding industries are nationalized; Liberal MPs support the Labour government (→1978).

Jimmy Carter becomes US president (→1981).

1978

Karol Wojtyła becomes pope as John Paul II (→   ).

1979

Parliament meets (→1983); Thatcher becomes prime minister (→   ).

Scottish and Welsh referendums reject devolution; Airey Neave and Earl Mountbatten are assassinated by Irish terrorists.

Islamic Revolution in Iran brings the Ayatollah Khomeni to power.

1980

Southern Rhodesia becomes independent as Zimbabwe.

THE KINGS AND QUEENS OF WESSEX, ENGLAND, GREAT BRITAIN AND THE UNITED KINGDOM

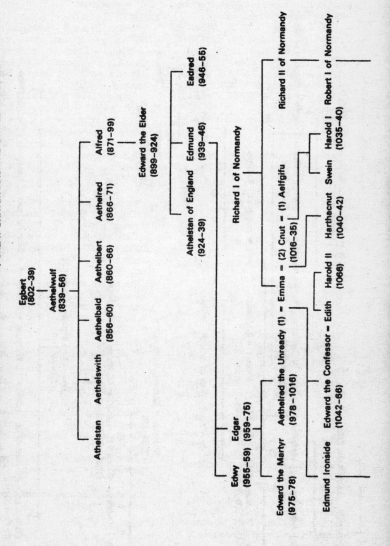

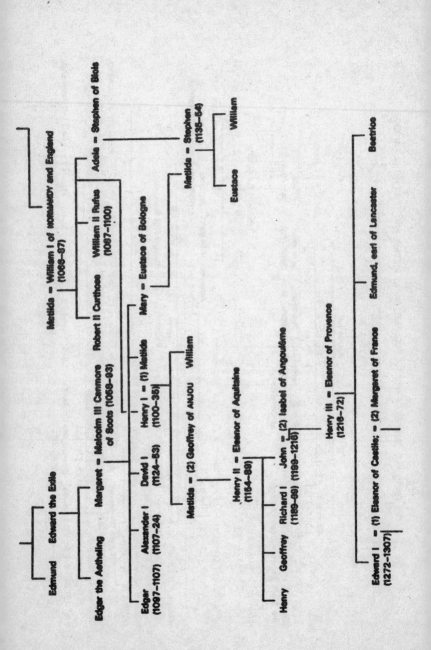

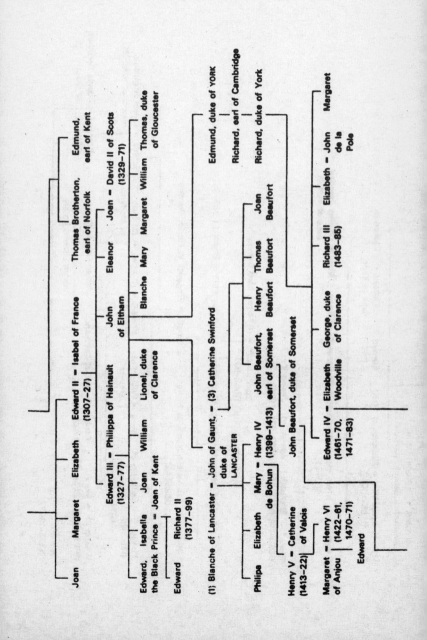

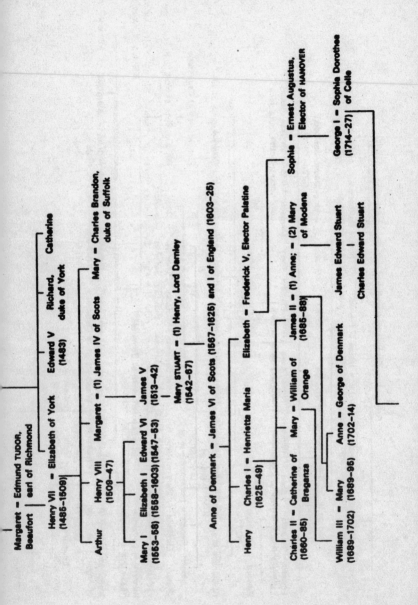

Margaret = Edmund TUDOR,
Beaufort | earl of Richmond

Henry VII = Elizabeth of York
(1485–1509)|

Arthur   Henry VIII   Margaret = (1) James IV of Scots   Mary = Charles Brandon,
           (1509–47)   duke of Suffolk

Mary I Elizabeth I Edward VI   James V
(1553–58) (1558–1603) (1547–53)   (1513–42)|

                                   Mary STUART = (1) Henry, Lord Darnley
                                   (1542–67)|

Anne of Denmark = James VI of Scots (1567–1625) and I of England (1603–25)

Henry   Charles I = Henrietta Maria   Elizabeth = Frederick V, Elector Palatine
          (1625–49)|

Charles II = Catherine of   Mary = William of   James II = (1) Anne; = (2) Mary   Sophie = Ernest Augustus,
(1660–85)   Braganza   Orange   (1685–88)   of Modena   Elector of HANOVER

William III = Mary   Anne = George of Denmark   James Edward Stuart   George I = Sophie Dorothee
(1689–1702) (1689–95) (1702–14)   (1714–27)   of Celle

                                                                              Charles Edward Stuart

x

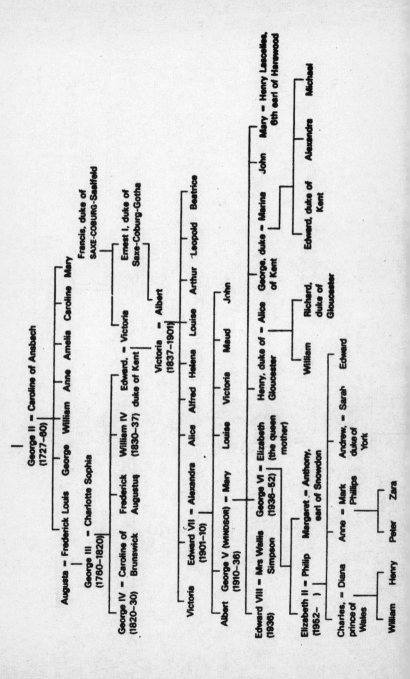